# AUSTRALIAN FAMILY ROAD TRIP

Daniel Beauglehole

 A catalogue record for this book is available from the National Library of Australia

Copyright © 2021 Daniel Beauglehole

All rights reserved. No part of this publication may be reproduced, stored in a retrieval system, or transmitted in any form or by any means, electronic, mechanical, photocopying, recording or otherwise without prior permission of the author.

**Publisher:**
ASPG (Australian Self Publishing Group)
P.O. Box 159, Calwell, ACT Australia 2905
Email: publishaspg@gmail.com
http://www.inspiringpublishers.com

National Library of Australia Cataloguing-in-Publication entry

Author: Beauglehole, Daniel

Title: **Australian Family Road Trip**/*Daniel Beauglehole*

*Cover picture by* Sam Beauglehole

ISBN: 978-1-922618-86-3 (pbk)

# Introduction

Hello, I am Cassie... let me introduce you to my parents.

My Dad's name is Daniel Fred Bontel, he has mild autism and was born on January the sixteenth, 1970. Dad has dark brown hair which is always neatly combed and styled, he has bright blue eyes and rosy cheeks with a moustache below his straight nose.

He has a smiling mouth and red lips that cover gleaming white teeth. His strong chin sits on an elegant neck, he has broad shoulders and chest, his lily-white skin covers a lean stomach and ramrod straight back.

Long arms are ended with elegant hands and fingernails. He has strong, shapely legs and sings with an 'eighties' popstar voice. He wears a bowler hat, and he favours clothes made of silk. He has a 'Seiko' watch which he wears on his right wrist.

His favourite outfit is a green tee shirt, green pants and green socks. He is five feet eight inches tall. He wears dark black sunglasses which he has worn all during his music career, and he has a powerful singing voice which has been compared by fans and music critics alike, to Rick Astley!

My Mum's name is Mikayla Natalie Bontel (nee Macdonald), she has mild autism also and was born on February the sixteenth, 1970. She has long coal black hair which brushes her shoulders. Mum has emerald green eyes and rosy cheeks, with a button nose.

Her mouth is shaped in a cupid's bow, with shining teeth and ruby lips. Her neck is swan-like, leading down to rounded shoulders of creamy coloured skin. She has a good figure, with a strong back and shapely arms and legs.

She likes to wear a Panama hat and her clothes are made of satin, she has a ring on her right middle finger and a 'Michel Herbelin' watch on her right wrist. Her favourite colour is yellow and she wears a shirt and pants in that colour.

She is five feet eight inches tall and in her right ear she wears a diamond pearl earring, that she has worn since she was seventeen years old. Her powerful singing style has been compared to Madonna by her fans and music magazines.

Now I will tell you about myself!

I am Cassie Annabelle Bontel I am sixteen years, two months and three days old. I was born on April the twenty-first, 1995. I live at twenty-three Henry St, Melbourne in Victoria, Australia.

I have mild autism, an autism spectrum condition. I have long, charcoal black hair, which reaches past my shoulders. My sky-blue eyes and rosy cheeks compliment my button nose. I have a smiling mouth that shows straight teeth and crimson lips.

My strong chin is located right on top of my gracious neck which continues on to my broad shoulders of ivory coloured skin. My strong arms end in hands that have long fingers finished with long fingernails.

I like to wear a Fedora hat and my clothes are always made of cotton. I don't wear any jewellery, apart from a 'Citizen' watch that I have on my right wrist. I have a blue head-band to match my favourite outfit of a blue t-shirt and pants.

I am five feet nine inches tall and my vocal sound has been compared to the voice of Nikki Webster.

We are going to take a trip around Australia...this will mean lots of changes to my routine!

I am nervous, because there will be many new places to visit, many new people to meet and interact with, new environments to explore... and all the sensory issues that may arise!

I've never travelled interstate before! Mum, Dad and I have been to places in Victoria, the state that I was born and raised in, but we have never travelled interstate as a family together. I have always resisted, every time Mum and Dad planned to go somewhere like South Australia, or New South Wales.

Although I am nervous, at the same time I am excited... because I am keen to learn new things about Australia's history and see Australian cities and landmarks along the way. Mum and Dad are going to help me throughout this road trip, we will navigate this journey of a lifetime as a family and help each other with the challenges!

It may be tough, but I guarantee we can do it. We can do it!

Because I am a visual learner, Mum and Dad showed me a map of our schedule, to let me understand what's happening next. The day before we are due to leave, Mum shows me the plans.

"This is what's going to happen, Cassie."

"Here are the plans for our road trip around Australia!"

"We will pack everything up tonight and be ready to leave in the morning!"

"We are going to start in Melbourne, we will visit places like Emerald, Moe, Traralgon, Bairnsdale, Echuca, Shepparton, Wangaratta, Wodonga and that is just Victoria!"

"We may stay in motels sometimes, we plan to change drivers every two hours or so, that way we won't get too fatigued... we will all be able to stretch our legs at changeover times."

"After Victoria, we plan to go the Australian Capital Territory, then New South Wales, followed by Queensland, Northern Territory, Western Australia, South Australia and Tasmania, finally returning to Victoria!"

"We can try out some fun activities in all those places... do you understand Cassie?" Mum asked

"Yes, Mum... I understand." I reply

"Also, I want you to be on your best behaviour... if you get upset or angry try and use your words... so that we can work out what has upset you... that way we can help you."

"We are always here for you... if you have any questions along the way, don't be afraid to ask us." Mum smiled

"You can ask us anything especially on this road trip...we'll do our best to answer." said Mum, I nodded

Next it was preparation time, everyone had to make a list of what they would need to take... on our 'Aussie Family Trip'!

## Cassie's road trip list!

- DVD player and DVD's, comedy movies, animal documentaries, Australian history.
- Toy cars and stress balls
- Game Boy, GB Colour, GB Advance, DS, charger and games
- Magazines-That's Life and Take 5
- Batteries
- Music CD's and headphones, plus noise-reduction ones, music CD's, Aqua, Kylie, Katy Perry, Quirky Service, Nikki Webster
- Pens and pencils

- Australian history books, sports books, Mikayla's jokes
- iPad and iPod
- Laptop
- Guitar

Next, or should I say 'Most Important' on my list... is my super '**survival bag**'!

This is what I use whenever I go out! It's full of necessities that I always carry to help me feel calm and safe. Especially, when the places I go to are likely to be noisy and crowded or smelly too!

These are the little things that help me when I get overwhelmed from 'sensory' overload, this bag is really great and the best item I own! Here are the items that I have in my 'survival' bag that have helped me since I was three years old, they have been added to or changed as I have grown older... hopefully they can help me again... on this road trip!

## ■ Noise-Reduction Headphones/MP3 Player

This is the best item I have ever had... honestly, it's a lifesaver! When I wear them, it helps me to cope with loud noises in public places... so I can focus on what I am doing. I'll take them off to hear something that Mum and Dad have to say to me when we are in a quiet place. I also have an MP3 player that I got when I was thirteen, it has many of my favourite pop artists/bands including Nikki Webster and Quirky Service, I also listen to soothing classical music and Eurodance beats.

## ■ My Dolphin Soft Toy

I have had this dolphin soft toy since I was five years old, it is one of my comforting tools, I get very distressed and upset if I misplace it. I still keep it today, I stroke the plush fabric with my fingers to feel the soft sensation, it helps to calm me. It's my ultimate comfort item, I would not go anywhere without it! I know what you're thinking... you're sixteen! DO you really need to carry it everywhere? I DO carry it everywhere and it's FINE by me!

## ■ Weighted Lap Blanket

I always have the weighted lap blanket with me in case I get nervous on public transport. Besides calming me down at home when I meltdown it also helps me if I'm on public transport for more than a couple of hours. It gives me a positive feeling of comfort and relaxation. It's a no-brainer idea... it's a great tool for me to use!

## ■ Notebook, Wallet, Essential Items and Bag

I use my notebook to write down ideas for my music projects... to compose songs... I also draw little pictures in it as well as my sketchbook... which relaxes me. My wallet is a cute 'Minnie Mouse' wallet from Disney... it contains coins, Mum and Dads' emergency numbers and my autism card.

When I get nervous or shy, I find it difficult to talk to anyone, which could cause a meltdown. When this happens, I get out my card which says... 'My name is Cassie and I have mild autism, I am shy, I find it hard to talk to new people, especially in unfamiliar environments. Please call my Mum or Dad on the following numbers'.

This lets other people know that I need help, or I can call my Mum or Dad when things get too much. I have used it twice... hopefully I don't need to use it for a long time.

I have an emergency kit which has band-aids... in case I cut myself, pens, pencils, Advil and other bits and pieces. It's very helpful and I wouldn't go anywhere without that kit.

## ▪ Books

I've always been a bit of a bookworm, I got that from Dad. He is good with English, English Literature and languages, so I usually pack a few books wherever I go. Most of the time, I take two fantasy novels, a pop music book and a best-selling novel. I love to get lost in a book when I read them. For this road trip I'm taking the 'Twilight' series by Stephanie Meyer, an autistic daughter of Mum's friend, gave them to me on my fourteenth birthday, I still love reading them today. They are brilliant, fantastic and very thrilling.

## ▪ Food and Drink

For food I have various chocolate bars, little packets of Doritos and Twisties. On days when I don't want to eat anything due to my food sensitivities, or when my acceptable foods have run out, these foods are my staple items.

They are my favourite 'junk' foods, I know I'm supposed to eat them in moderation, but these foods are the only foods I take with me. Don't listen to me for dietary advice and don't ask me for any either!

I also have a bottle of Mount Franklin water, in case the weather gets hot, it's the only brand of water I will drink! Some brands from the supermarket are disgusting 'Eeeuuw'... others are too expensive... Mt Franklin is the only water I like... it's refreshing and cool every time I drink it! This 'survival' bag is the best idea Mum and Dad ever had! I will use it if things get overwhelming. It's a winner

## ▪ Mikayla's road trip list

Movie DVDs... no horror movies!
Iphone
First aid kit... including insect repellent!
Camera
Music CD's
Laptop

## ▪ List for everyone

Medication
Toiletries/Hankies
Clothes
Bottles of water
Spending money
Snacks

## ▪ Daniel's road trip list

Iphone
Camera
Music CD's
Laptop
iPad
Guitar

## *Chapter One*
# Monkeys-Model Trains-Machinery

The next morning bright and early, we put our suitcases into the back of the vehicle and climb into our silver Holden Colorado four-wheel drive. Dad is taking the first two hours shift, he and Mum have agreed to share the driving during our Australian road trip, to avoid fatigue which is a good idea! Mum and Dad also thought another good idea sometime on this road trip, would be to teach me how to drive! I feel nervous about 'that' idea… but a little excited as well! We agree that I can have my first practice on a quiet back road with little traffic, where I can take it as slowly as I need to. It is something to look forward to later in the trip, with both excitement and trepidation. It may take some time but our road trip should give us the perfect opportunities for practice along the way, once we get into the outback.

"What would you like to do first Cassie?" asked Dad

"I would like to see and feed the animals at the Melbourne Zoo!" I replied, excitedly

Dad smiled at my excitement as we took the short drive to the zoo.

"Hello, can I help you?" asked the Zoo operator

"We would like to see and feed the animals please." Dad replied

"That will be fifteen dollars please." said the zoo park operator

There were elephants, penguins, monkeys, tigers and lions, we walked up to the tiger's enclosure. They looked relaxed lying on the grass, I put on my noise-reduction headphones just in case the tigers growled and frightened me. We went up to the monkey enclosure, they were funny, we all laughed at their antics.

Next, we went to see the penguins who were waddling around the pool and diving into the water. Then we went to see the elephants, I laughed when an elephant tickled my hand with his trunk.

"Hee, hee, that tickles!" I giggled

It made Mum and Dad laugh too, a second elephant scooped up a handful of water and squirted it at Mum.

"Glug! Glug!" spluttered Mum

Dad and I laughed at her, Mum saw the funny side and laughed as well! Just then another elephant scooped up water and squirted me right in the face!

"Wah! I shrieked

Mum and Dad laughed at me, I laughed too, it didn't end there though, Dad copped a 'trunkful' just as he threw back his head to laugh!

"What the…" spluttered Dad, trying to catch his breath

Mum and I sniggered.

"Looks like we all got a good soaking there." said Mum, ruefully

"We sure did, those elephants were cheeky today!"

"They definitely were, how mischievous!" agreed Dad
A zookeeper came up to us with three towels.
"Are you all right?"
"You look wet." he added
"We're fine thanks, it's all in good fun." Mum smiled
"Here dry yourselves off with these." the zookeeper nodded
"Thank you." I said, grabbing a towel to wipe off my face
Mum, Dad and I, dried ourselves, it had been an embarrassing moment; but we laughed it off.
We decided to go and see the koalas.
"Hey, you're that 'famous' family... aren't you?" said the keeper, looking closely at our faces
"We might be... why do you ask?" said Mum
"I've heard about your music career and your celebrity life."
"I've got a koala that I would like you to meet."
"You may hold him if you wish."
"Would you like to meet him?" asked the keeper
"Yes, we would!" we all said in unison
The keeper came out holding a koala.
"His name is George." said the keeper
He gave him to Dad to hold.
"My gosh!"
"He's so furry."
He's a handsome fellow!" Dad said, admiringly
Then it was Mum's turn.
"Aw."
"He is so cute."
"His coat is so soft."
"His nose is shiny too."
Then it was my turn, I was reluctant to hold George at first.
"Don't be shy Cassie, George is so friendly." said Mum, encouragingly
The keeper gently placed George into my arms.
"He's so handsome, and his ears are soft." I said
"Would you like to have your photo taken with George?" asked the keeper
"Yes please, we'd love to!" said Mum and Dad, together
"I will wear my black sunglasses...I'm not being a superstar... I just want to protect my eyes from the flash!" I laughed

I got out my black sunglasses and put them on. We then had our photos taken with George it was one experience that I will remember for a long time. To finish our trip to the zoo, we went to see the lions. I was nervous when I saw them and shook, I became emotional at the sight of them. Mum and Dad told me to take some deep breaths, which I did and it calmed me down.
"Cassie, let me tell you something."
"The lions are in their cages as you see here."
"They are behind their fences you are safe they can't get to you."
"The lions eat meat for nourishment and they swim in a pool to cool them on hot days."
"The males have manes around their head and necks, so you can recognise that feature."

"The male lion is referred to as the 'King of the Jungle', they fight to keep their lionesses by beating other lions for their pride, (which is the name of a lion's family)." Dad told me

Now that is Dad at his teaching best!

As we left the zoo the monkeys decided to give us something...they threw rotten fruit at us!

"Yuck!" shrieked Mum

"Eeuuw!" I yelled

"Urgh!" moaned Dad, as some 'squishy' fruit landed in his hair

There was 'squishy fruit everywhere, all over our clothes and hair! I was embarrassed, some children were laughing at our predicament, but I wasn't sure I could see the funny side just yet!

"Oh dear!"

"It looks like the monkeys got you!"

"They do that sometimes they have a mischievous sense of fun."

"I'm very sorry about that! said the zookeeper, shaking his head

"That's all right, I guess we will have to make a pit stop to freshen up before lunch!" said Mum, wiping fruit out of her eyes

We were given wet towels by the zookeeper to clean off the fruit from our hands and faces, before finding some facilities to spruce up again.

Once we were presentable it was time for lunch... we decided on KFC! We went inside, it wasn't too noisy, bright or crowded for me, so we walked up to the counter.

## Dad ordered
- **Tower burger**
- **Large chips**
- **Can of orange lemonade**

## Mum ordered
- **Original BBQ bacon and cheese burger**
- **Large chips**
- **Can of raspberry lemonade**

## My order was
- **Original fillet burger**
- **Large chips**
- **Can of lemonade**

"Eat-in or takeaway?" asked the cashier

"Takeaway." said Mum

"That will be thirty-two dollars and ninety-five cents please." the cashier said

"Everybody got their seatbelts on?" asked Dad

"Yes." said Mum and I, together

"Wagons Ho!"

"Let's get this road trip rolling! said Dad, with a big grin

Mum turned in her seat.

"It's time for Australian Trivia Book Number One … are you ready?"

Yes… I'm ready." I replied, with a mouthful of fillet burger

"Which antique steam train has been running between Belgrave and Gembrook since 1900?" Mum questioned

"Puffing Billy."

"You can also race alongside it to beat it to the finish line." I added

"When did the Emerald Post Office open?" Mum continued

"December the twenty-second, 1899." I replied

"Which Australian TV series screened in 1976, involved a fictional local policeman solving crimes in Emerald?" asked Mum

"Solo One." I replied

An hour or so later we arrived in Emerald, Dad whipped out his mobile phone to check out what's happening in Emerald.

"We could try the Emerald Lake Model Railway, walk through Cardinia Reservoir Park or go to Emerald Lake Park."

"Which one would you like to do?" he asked

"Let's go to the Emerald Lake Model Railway!" I said

"Okay, Emerald Lake Model Railway it is then." said Dad

When we arrived, we were given a lovely welcome.

"Hello, Sir, Madam and Miss, how may I help you?" asked the receptionist

"We would like to see the model railway, there are three of us as a family." Mum told the lady

"That will be twenty-five dollars please." said the receptionist

Dad paid the entrance fee. We were amazed by the model trains I was so excited there were so many trains to see. *'Mia, my cousin would love this.'* I thought

"Look Cassie." called Dad

"That's the 'Orient Express'… in 1883 it began service from Paris to Istanbul."

"It crossed six countries over ten different railroads… it was most famous for its five-course French meals… its passengers included diplomats, royalty and government couriers!"

"Wow!"

"That is one first class train!" I said, very impressed

"Look Cassie that's the 'Flying Scotsman'." said Mum

"In 1928 it became the first non-stop train from King's Cross in London to Edinburgh in Scotland!"

"It was a luxury express train full of amenities, featuring a hairdressing salon, a Louis the XVI style restaurant and bar, and for a short time it even had a cinema coach."

"Amazing!"

"That's one train you would like to ride on." I said

"Look Cassie there is the" 'Super Chief'." said Dad

"In 1936 it was originally operated by the Santa Fe Railroad… it ran from Chicago to Los Angeles… it was considered to be one of the best long-distance trains in the US."

"It was also renowned for its gourmet food and Hollywood clientele."

"The Flying Scotsman would have to be my favourite train!" I exclaimed

"The Amtrak currently operates a long-distance train over the same route." said Dad

After an hour looking at all the model trains we left.

"Mia would've loved that place!"

"She loves trains so much...she would be so excited to see all those trains."

"You are right about that Cassie."

"Mia would be very excited...it's train heaven to someone with a train obsession like Mia...absolute paradise." said Mum

"I remember the last time I was in Emerald."

"What do you remember about Emerald, Cassie?" said Dad, surprised

"It was May the sixteenth, 2003 and I was eight years old."

"You brought me here for a week's holiday."

"I played in the park and I saw a train in a museum."

"It was a happy time... and now here I am again today... having visited the new train model museum... learning even more about trains!" I smiled

"We had a good time in Emerald back then and we are enjoying it just as much today." said Mum, happily

"Let's walk through Cardinia Reservoir Park, I would like that." I said

"Yes, why not?"

"It'll be good for us." Dad agreed

As we drove to the park, Dad proceeded to tell one of his really bad 'Dad' jokes.

"Dad, you've told me that ten times before... ever since I was two years old... and it's still bad!" I said, cringing

"It may be an oldie... but it's a goodie!"

"The old ones are the best!"

"That one's a classic!" said Dad, laughing heartily at his own 'bad' joke

"It's definitely a classic one, dear." said Mum, 'egging' him on

I groaned..._you are both so embarrassing_... I mumbled under my breath... my head in my hands. Mum and Dad can be 'so' embarrassing sometimes, especially when Dad tells bad, cheesy jokes then Mum follows up with the punchline!

They make me cringe... especially when it happens in front of my friends or classmates... but I still love them regardless... I know it's all 'meant' in good fun.

We parked the car and prepared to walk through the gardens. Along the way, I stopped to smell the flowers and Mum and Dad collected some leaves. After a lovely walk of nearly an hour, we got back to the car and on the road again.

"Our road trip started off with a comedy moment with those cheeky monkeys." said Mum, smiling

"Yes, it did Mum."

"They were even funnier than Dad's jokes!" I said, laughing

"Waddya mean!" said Dad, in an offended tone of voice

"Cut down in my comedic prime by my own daughter." he said, pretending to be mortally wounded

We all burst out laughing at that!

I took out my iPod, put in my earplugs and listened to my favourite music, Katy Perry was playing, I watched the scenery out the window as we drove along. An hour and fifteen minutes later we arrived in Moe, Mum looked in her driving guide book for some activities to do.

"We could go to Old Gippstown, discover Walhalla, or walk the Yallourn Rail Trail."

"Which one shall we do?" she asked us

"Let's go to Old Gippstown and see the machinery collection." I said

We arrived at Old Gippstown and went inside the town… it was like stepping back in time. We were amazed by the variety of old buildings, there was a large collection of horse-drawn carriages too. Every time I found something new, I learnt as much as I could about it.

After we had finished looking around Old Gippstown Heritage Park, we drove to Traralgon twenty-six minutes down the road.

"Here we are in Traralgon, let's book a room overnight, and 'chill out' after our first big day." said Dad

We found the Motel Traralgon and were given room Number Six for our stay. We took our suitcases up to our room, and unpacked just the things we would need for an overnight stop. After our first big day, I was ready for some downtime.

"That was a big day… I need to chill out." I said

"We do too!"

"We're going to watch some TV… what are you going to do Cassie?" asked Mum

"I'm going to play on my laptop for an hour or two."

"We'll go out and have dinner then… so be ready when we call you." said Dad

"Yes, I'll be ready." I replied

Later Dad said…

"What do you want for tea?"

"We are feeling too tired to dine out somewhere tonight." said Dad

"Subway!" I called out

We drove to Breed Street in Traralgon, where Subway was located… there were a couple of people in line before us… I used to dislike waiting in lines in takeaway shops… but I have learnt to wait patiently until the other people in front of me have done buying their lunch or dinner.

I patiently waited until they collected their dinners. Next it was our turn we ordered our usual favourites. We drove back to the inn to have our tea.

After we finished eating, Dad made a phone call on his mobile phone to his Mum… Maria Bontel.

'Hi Mum.' he said

'Yes, we are in Traralgon.'

'Yes, we have started our journey well, Mum.'

"Thanks Mum, we just had tea, tomorrow we are making our way to Bairnsdale." Dad continued

'Bye, Mum, we'll be sure to take some photos!' said Dad

Mum then made a phone call on her mobile to her Mum… Belinda Macdonald.

"Hi Mum we're having a great time." Mum said over the phone

"Our road trip is off to a good start, at the Melbourne Zoo we got to hold a koala named George."

"His fur was so soft and cuddly Mum."

"While we were there Daniel, Cassie and I, got squirted by three elephants, we got quite a soaking!" Mum laughed

"Yes, Mum they were very cheeky."

"As we left the zoo the monkeys were even cheekier!"

"They threw rotting fruit at us… it was embarrassing." Mum giggled

"Yes, we did have a great time at the Melbourne Zoo… even with the monkeys!" Mum laughed out loud

"We're going to watch a movie now… I think we've decided to watch the 'The Nutty Professor'… so I will say bye now Mum." Mum ended her phone call

"Our Mums are right behind us every step of the way!" said Dad, cheerily

"Yes, they are!"

"Mum supports what I do and she says quality time with family is important!" Mum said, firmly

"The same goes for my Mum too!" Dad said, proudly

"Mum always encourages us to spend time with our loved ones and that's what matters, even on a road trip!" Dad exclaimed

"Right, let's put 'The Nutty Professor' on." said Mum

"Cassie, do you want to watch the movie with us?" asked Dad

"Yes please, I would like to."

I paused what I was doing on my laptop and went to watch the movie. We all laughed at the funny bits, especially when Sherman Klump, (played by Eddie Murphy), knocked Jason out, (played by John Ales), when he tried to stop him from going to the Alumni Ball! Ninety-five minutes later, it was bedtime.

"I hope you don't snore, Mum!"

"You might keep me awake... as well as Dad." I said

"I'll try not to." said Mum

We all woke up at seven-thirty the next morning, we had our breakfast, showered and dressed, and went for a drive around Traralgon. At nine-thirty we went to the Traralgon Railway Reservoir Conservation Reserve.

"It says in the 1930's, there was once a nine-hole golf course and in the north eastern corner there used to be a rubbish tip, but they were both closed in 1939."

Inside the conservation reserve there were different areas, including a lake in the middle and various birds and vegetation.

"There's a blue bird over there!" I pointed

Dad got out his binoculars and looked for it.

"You're right Cassie!"

"There is a blue bird... your favourite colour!" Dad smiled

"Yes, it is Dad." I agreed

"There's a yellow bird over here, it's yellow like my shirt!" said Mum, getting out her binoculars and looking through the lenses

"Hey, I can see a green bird up there!"

"It's the same colour as an emerald!" says Dad, looking through his binoculars.

"You're right darling."

"It is like the colour of an emerald." Mum agreed

We took out our cameras and snapped a few photos, they're going to look good to show our family!

In the nature reserve we saw some ducks, I let a couple of tiny ducklings walk on my hand, but I wouldn't let the mother duck because I was afraid, she might bite me! Mum and Dad assured me that the ducks are harmless, so I let the mother duck closer to me.

"These ducks are so cute." I said

"They sure are if we had some bread with us... we might be able to feed a few of them." said Mum

"Well, I've got some... so we can!" said Dad

He gave us all a handful, and we proceeded to feed the ducks.

"Here ducks, come and get your bread!"

"We've got plenty for you, so come and eat it all up." I cried out to them

The ducks needed no second invitation, they were very keen to get to the bread!

"Hey!"

"Hey guys!

"Don't be greedy!"
"There's plenty to share round."
"I know you all love it." I said
"We all enjoy feeding the ducks don't we." said Mum
"Yes, we do!" Dad said, with a grin
"Ducks are fun birds to interact with, they will follow you around like you're their mother then try to nibble your feet... but I enjoy being around them." I reflected

When we saw the swamp hens, I got nervous and backed away a little. I've never encountered a hen of this type and it looked scary to me at first glance.

"It's all right Cassie, the swamp hens won't hurt you." said Mum, reassuringly

I settled down to admire the swamp hens, they weren't so bad after all, once you learn about them.

"They're so colourful and they're not so scary after all." I agreed

We finished off our visit by visiting the swans.

"This place is tranquil and the birds are beautiful, their birdsong is music to my ears." said Mum

After lunch, Mum made a phone call to Jessica Smith her best friend, she put it on speakerphone.

'Hello Mikayla.' said Jessica
"Hi Jessica."
"We're staying in Traralgon, this morning we saw some birds in the Traralgon Conservation Reserve." said Mum
'Those birds must've been a pretty sight to see.' Jessica replied
"Oh yes they were Jessica." Mum agreed
'Remember when we were both sixteen years old fishing in the Yarra River with our Dads?'
'It was only our third time fishing we fished for three hours from one to four.'
'You caught a Murray Cod, you were delighted... I was also delighted when I caught a Macquarie Perch!'
'In total we caught four fish... two each!'
'Whilst we were there our Dads' taught us about the Murray River... how to appreciate its beauty.'
'We cooked the fish we caught for our tea and they were delicious!' said Jessica
"I did enjoy fishing, and that day was the best fishing day I've ever had!"
"Cassie dislikes fishing." said Mum
"No, I don't!"
"I'm afraid the fish might bite me!" I said
'I'm sure they won't Cassie.' said Jessica
"Well okay then... I will have a go at fishing... at some point on this road trip."
"Who knows... I might even catch one!" I laughed, at the thought of that
'Good on you Cassie!'
'If you do catch one, send me a photo of it.' said Jessica, laughing down the phone too
"Will do, Jessica." I replied
"My Dad is on holiday with his mates, for a men's month away." said Mum, to Jessica
"At the time, I thought." *'What are they up to without the womenfolk!'* Mum added
'I would've thought the same thing myself.'
'I don't blame you.' added Jessica
"Anyway... I wonder what he's doing there." mused Mum
'Well, why don't you ask all about it when you skype your Mum tomorrow?' said Jessica
"Great idea." Mum said

'I'd better go now... my mother Josephine is visiting me for a 'cuppa'... she is going to show me her new coat that she bought yesterday... from 'Keep Warm, Dress Warm'... the winter clothing shop.' said Jessica

"That will be sure to keep her warm all winter!" said Mum

'It sure will... bye Mikayla.' Jessica signed off

"Bye Jessica." said Mum, doing the same

After Mum finished her phone call, we got changed into our bathers, I got my bucket and spade, Mum and Dad collected their books and we drove to the nearest beach. That was ninety-mile beach at Woodside... it was sixty-eight kilometres from Traralgon and took us about an hour to get there. When we arrived Mum and Dad set up their beach chairs and settled down to read, I walked down the beach to collect some seashells.

"Don't go too far, Cassie."

"You can have a paddle in the water if you want to... but stay at a distance where we can see you."

"We don't want you to get lost." Mum worried

"Okay, Mum."

"I'll be fine." I sighed, to myself

I'm only sixteen years, two months and four days old! I'm not a little child anymore for goodness sake. I sighed again. I wish Mum and Dad would let me have a bit more independence. What is a girl supposed to do to prove she is growing into a young woman? They still talk to me like I'm eight years old or something... I muttered to myself as I 'stomped' up the beach searching for shells.

I needed to get that out of my system, I still get embarrassed when Mum and Dad tell me all that at my age. I think it is time that I tell them I need a bit more independence... I also have to listen to what they say... I just hope in the end the outcome will be positive and preferably accomplished without too many arguments. All I have to do now is to find the right time to tell them all of that!

Whenever I go somewhere on my own such as the general store... or whenever I am with the family... I have to let Mum and Dad know in case I get lost! I can be independent doing most things and hopefully I will do more... but Mum and Dad feel the need to protect me and keep me safe... especially from the 'paparazzi'... but I always know where Mum and Dad are...once I've done whatever I need to... I always walk back to them safe and sound!

I know Melbourne like the back of my hand because I was born there... I'm a Melbourne born and bred celeb girl you see!

I collected several seashells, including a few pink ones, I studied them one at a time, for several minutes. They look so pretty and delicate they are shiny like my birthstone... Diamond! I might take some home with me and keep them in my crystal jewels collection.

I put the seashells in my bucket and walked back to where Mum and Dad were sitting.

"Mum, Dad, look at the seashells I've collected." I said, showing them

"They look very pretty Cassie... and shiny too."

"Almost as shiny as your long black hair." said Dad

"Why don't you take them with you and add them to your collection."

"They would look great." said Mum

"I will." I replied

"When Dad and I were young, we sometimes went to the beach, not only to collect seashells, but to play in the water and to build sandcastles in the sand, I still remember those days."

"When Dad and I were sixteen years old, we walked down to the beach during one of our evening walks, we stood near the water's edge holding hands and watching the sunset."

I said to him...
"This is so romantic, it's one of the best walks I've ever been on."
Dad said...
"It is romantic, you're my darling Valentine and this sunset signifies our love for each other." Mum said, with a dreamy look on her face
"Even though I'm not interested in that romance stuff, it's a pretty good story to hear." I told Mum
I put the seashells in a plastic bag, then I started making a sandcastle using my bucket and spade, I did most of the building, then Mum helped me to decorate it with the shells.
"It looks great Mum we did a good job!" I smiled
"Yes, we did." said Mum, standing back to admire her handiwork
I filled up my bucket with water... but instead of filling the moat with it... I threw it all over Mum!
"Aah!"
"What was that for?" spluttered Mum
"Ha Ha!"
"I got you Mum!"
"You are drenched!" I laughed, pointing at her
Dad laughed as well.
"You got me good Cassie!" Mum said, in a tone that meant... I'm going to get you back for that later
"That's a great sandcastle, all it needs is some water to fill up the moat and it will be finished." said Dad, admiringly
I filled up the bucket again... but this time Dad copped it... just as he sat down to admire my sandcastle.
"Glug!"
"What was that?" spluttered Dad
"Hee Hee!"
"I got you Dad!" I laughed, pointing at his dripping face
Mum's turn to laugh now.
"You did get me... you really did!" said Dad, with an expression on his face that says payback will happen, as he pointed his finger towards me and wagged it accusingly...

# Chapter Two
## Meeting Lucy, AFL & Mini Golf

I filled up the bucket for a third time and gently poured it into the moat of my castle. My sandcastle is complete, and it looks great! Some kids are playing further along the beach, and a little girl wanders over to look at my sandcastle, I run away and hide behind Mum's beach chair.

"It's okay, Cassie."
"The little girl has just come over to admire your sandcastle." Mum said
"I'm not so sure about that... what if she stands on my sandcastle?"
"She might ruin it all." I said, nervously
"I'm sure she won't stand on it." Mum said
"Can you use your anxiety techniques to help you?" asked Dad
The little girl approached and smiled shyly at me.
"Can you please show me how to make a sandcastle like that?" she said, quietly
"Of course, I can."
"I can show you how to do it." I said
"What is your name?" I asked the little girl
"My name is Lucy"
"Lucy?"
"That's a nice name."
"My name is Cassie."
"We can have lots of fun building a sandcastle together." I told her

Lucy smiled happily. We had lots of fun building a sandcastle together, we added decorations to it and chatted to each other about our favourite things... like sisters do.

Mum and Dad watched, proud that I have had a breakthrough and made a new friend. After a while, the sun got a bit hotter in the late afternoon.

"Mum, can we have an ice-cream from the ice cream van over there?"
"Yes, we can."
"Let's all get an ice-cream each." said Dad
"I'll just ask my Mum and Dad." said Lucy
"My favourite is chocolate." said Mum
"I like butterscotch the best." said Dad
"What about you, Lucy?" I asked
"I like strawberry... I like banana... I like bubble-gum..." said Lucy, counting them off on her fingers.
We all laughed together and Dad said...

"I think we had better get you a rainbow coloured ice-cream if you want all those flavours!"

"I think I will stick with one… I'll have my favourite flavour… Vanilla." I said

Before we go to get the ice-creams, Mum says…

"It will be a good idea for Lucy to ask her Mum and Dad for permission first, so they know where she is for safety reasons."

Lucy ran over to her family and soon was back with a happy smile on her face

"It's okay!"

"I'm allowed to go." said Lucy, happily

We are very lucky that an ice cream van has driven out here to the beach, because it's half an hour's drive back to the little township of Woodside. We all set off across the beach to the spot where the van has parked. When we get there, the queue is quite long as everybody has the same idea on a hot sunny afternoon. Finally, we get up to the van and order our ice-creams. As we walk back up the beach, we are licking our ice-creams as fast as we can, so they don't melt everywhere and become puddles on the sand.

We gathered up our beach gear and waved goodbye to Lucy, who was going back to her family. We packed our things into the back of our vehicle and jumped in, we were all feeling tired, salty, sandy and gritty! Now for a lovely hot shower back at the hotel!

"Since I've been in the sand for most of the day, I'm having the first shower tonight!" I bagged

"You might as well Cassie… but please don't use all the hot water when we get back… Mum and I will need some as well!" reminded Dad

"OK Dad." I replied

It was a sandy, itchy trip back to the hotel in Traralgon, where I dashed in to the shower room.

Whilst I was showering, Mum had a look through the in-house menu.

*'I'm so hungry after our day at the beach, this looks appetising'* Mum thought

*'I think I'll choose spaghetti bolognaise'*

"I would really love a good rump steak."

"You know how much I love steak!" said Dad, licking his lips

"You sure do…you love your steak." said Mum

I finished my shower and came out of the bathroom.

"It's your turn to choose Cassie, pick anything you want." said Dad

I picked up the menu and studied it very carefully. I dislike fruit and vegetables very much, but Mum says they are good for you… if you want to keep a healthy body!

*'Yeah, that's what Mum says, anyway!'* I thought, suspiciously. Soup is another food I dislike… because most soups are full of vegetables! Erk! I only like roast chicken with chips… I also dislike fish because they're slimy and full of bones!

*'Maybe I can have roast chicken and some chips to go with it.'* I muse

'It's going to be a very long road trip before I get used to eating fruit and vegetables!!" I say out loud

Mum and Dad grinned at each other, they know my likes and dislikes by now.

They have a very long list to keep check of!

They use the list as a guide for my carers and people in my support network.

Mum said…

"Have you chosen yet Cassie?"

"I want to ring our order through."

"Yes, Mum." I said

"Chicken and chips!" We all said together… and burst out laughing

"You know me very well... I always go for my favourite meal." I grinned ruefully

Mum put the order through and soon the evening meal arrived. After dinner, Mum and Dad want to discuss something with me. They sit down on their bed and I sit down on mine facing them with my hands on my knees.

Dad said...

"Mum and I, are so proud of your progress this afternoon with Lucy."

"You got over your fear and had a lovely time playing with a new friend today." smiled Mum

"I was so happy to see you interacting with Lucy, and she had a good time too."

"Dad and I want to reward you with a little gift for your perseverance."

"What would you like Cassie?" asked Dad

I thought about it for several minutes and said,

"I have decided to try something... I have never done before."

"What's that Cassie?" asked Mum, with a note of surprise

"I've decided to try horse-riding."

Mum was delighted to hear that I was keen to try something new and so was Dad.

"Good choice Cassie!" Mum said

"I know you love horses." added Dad

"Do you remember when you took me to see the horses at a couple of festivals and shows, and even at a horse-riding club?"

"I would rather watch the horses canter and gallop about than to get on one... because I feared I would fall off and get trampled!" I said

"We will help you."

"Dad and I have been horse-riding years ago... if there are horse-riding trails nearby, we'll get a guide to take us... then you should be okay." said Mum, reassuringly

I was relieved, I was feeling a little more confident about riding a horse for the first time. I wonder if I will get a brown horse or a white horse... they are all beautiful no matter what colour. If I take a carrot with me, I may be allowed to feed them. I know with some encouragement I can do it.

Then Dad asks me...

"Cassie, how do you feel about the afternoon we just had?"

"I feel happy and great about this afternoon!"

"I had the best afternoon I've had in about two years."

"I enjoyed the day at the beach, especially when I threw the water all over you both!" I grinned

"Then building that great sandcastle... the best I've ever built and decorated!"

"When Lucy came over... I had an anxiety attack and hid behind the beach chair.... I thought *'She's so scary like a shark, don't let her near me!'*... then I used my anxiety techniques like you told me to, then I felt better and a lot calmer."

"When Lucy asked me to show her how to build a sandcastle like mine... I agreed and we both had lots of fun building and talking like sisters."

"Lucy enjoyed having an ice-cream and so did we... I had a wonderful afternoon... I would like to play with another friend and help them." I said

"I'm glad you had a lovely time."

"Your Mum and I did too."

"Well done for making a breakthrough... we're so proud of you." said Dad

"Thanks Mum and Dad... I am proud of myself too!"

"I am starting to make breakthroughs even though it's only the beginning of our road trip... hopefully I can make some more!" I beamed

"That's the way Cassie, my darling girl." said Mum

"Let's have a look at the television and see how Collingwood is doing shall we?"

We switched on, it was at the twelfth minute mark in the first quarter, Sydney were winning 3.0.18 to 2.1.13 a margin of five points. Jarred McVeigh kicked the goal, a close one this is.

Can Collingwood win this match for Mum at ANZ stadium in Sydney?

Mum barracks for Collingwood Magpies she's only seen one premiership in 1990 against Essendon when she was twenty years old, that was a few months after she and Dad got married.

She was so delighted back then she had a celebratory party! She did the same when Collingwood won the 2010 premiership a week after the Grand Final draw. She was born to be a Collingwood fan...she is a member!

Mum was getting excited.

"Ooh it's a close one already... it's only the first quarter but this is great AFL viewing!" she exclaimed

I was excited too.

"It sure is Mum!"

"ANZ Stadium is a good place for the Sydney Swans to play... let's hope Collingwood can do it for you Mum!"

Even Dad was excited.

"It is definitely a close game."

"It's good, this!"

"'carn the Pies!" shouts Mum

Dad and I shouted,

"'carn the Maggies!"

It was close throughout the second quarter too... barracking for Collingwood and cheering well done you beauty... whenever Collingwood kicked a goal. It's is a great game... but when the third quarter started, we were so tired from our afternoon on the beach... we could barely keep our eyes open.

Dad and I collapsed onto our beds still wearing our clothes and Mum turned off the TV thinking *'Daniel and Cassie must be exhausted they have had a big day and so have I... I'm exhausted too... I might as well get some much- needed sleep... there's going to be another big day ahead for the three of us tomorrow'*... then she too fell asleep... still wearing her clothes, soon everyone was sleeping soundly and some of us... (no names mentioned) ... were snoring too.

We woke up at seven-thirty... I looked down and instead of my pyjamas I was still wearing my clothes. I was shocked. Crikey! I didn't even have time to put on my pyjamas!

Mum and Dad looked down too. Uh, oh! Dad was surprised.

"Oh, it's too late to put on my pyjamas now!"

Mum was bewildered.

"Oh, my dear, how did that happen!?"

"We were watching the game last night and we couldn't keep our eyes open for a moment longer... so we collapsed on our beds with our clothes on!" I said, laughing

"I remember I managed to turn the TV off... then I must have fallen asleep beside your Dad and we have all missed the final scores now." said Mum, with a crestfallen look

"Let's see if we can find out the results."

"I'll turn on the radio." said Dad

He turned the radio on but no sound came out of it. Dad was puzzled.

"Hmm... I don't know why that's happening."

"It worked yesterday!"

He tried it again still no sound came out of it. What could the problem be?

"Try it again, Dad."

"If it doesn't work this time, we'll try the television." I said

Dad tried a few stations, but there was no sound from any of them. He inspected the radio to see what the problem was.

"What's wrong with it dear?" asked Mum

Dad turned the radio over and opened the battery section.

"The batteries must be flat." said Dad

"Shan't get the AFL result that way." Dad said, shrugging his shoulders

"Let's try the TV."

I turned on the TV but when the screen came on it was just static.

"For goodness sake, now the TV's on the blink!"

"We can't get the AFL results that way either." I sighed, mournfully

"We will report this to the hotel reception and hopefully they will fix it in time for the next guests that stay." said Mum, grumpily

"Well, after we pack up our stuff and put it in the car, we'll drive to the newsagency to buy a paper and check the results." said Dad

"I hope so Dad!" I said

"Well we'd better order our breakfast from room service, then pack up our stuff and head to the newsagency." said Mum

"All right." said Dad and I, together

After breakfast we put on fresh clothes, then reported the flat radio and broken TV to reception, before packing the car to leave.

"If there are no papers left... we'll have to use one of our iPhones."

"I hope we find out last night's result soon!" said Dad

Mum was anxious to find out how her team had done.

"Yes, I hope so too!"

We drove to the newsagency hoping to find a newspaper.

Can we find last night's AFL results?

When we arrived, it was closed! Dad put his hand on is head and said...

"Oh, of course!"

"We forgot the newsagency won't be open on a Sunday!"

"Sorry... Mum and I forgot as well." I said, with an embarrassed grin

"Looks like we might have to use our iPhones." said Mum

Dad and I agree, as we walk back to the car. Mum took her iPhone out first she turned it on and accessed Google. Mum typed AFL into the search engine and clicked on the top link entering the AFL website. She couldn't see the results properly so she tapped on one and crossed her fingers hoping it was the Sydney Vs Collingwood match from last night. When the next screen loaded up, a big smile played over Mum's face.

She likes what she sees.

The score was 14.9.93 Sydney to 13.21.99 Collingwood. Collingwood has won by a goal!

Mum got excited.

"You little beauty!" she said, jumping up in the air and doing a fist pump
A couple looked at her weirdly but she didn't mind that all.
"Did Collingwood win?" asked Dad, guessing the answer
"Yes, they did."
"Just by six points!" said Mum
"I knew they would win it!" I said
"Yes, they did well to get that win!" said Dad
"I'm glad we finally got the results, I'm so happy that Collingwood won let's continue on our road trip!" said Mum happily, as we got back in and 'buckled up'
"It's time for Australian Trivia number Two!"
"I'm always ready!" I said
"Which Australian cricketer who played for the Victoria Bushrangers since 1999 as well as the Australian National cricket team since 2005 was born in Bairnsdale?" asked Mum
"Cameron White."
"He became Victoria's youngest ever captain at age twenty in the 2003-04 cricket season." I responded
"Bairnsdale's Water Tower… currently an icon of Bairnsdale's skyline has been out of commission since which decade?" asked Mum next
"The 1980s."
"It cost six thousand, one hundred and thirty-two pounds, to build the whole tower." I said
"A man named Frederick Jones, an early squatter in the Bairnsdale shire, previously worked for some time as a 'what' in Castlereagh Street, Sydney?" Mum asked
"He previously worked as a school teacher." I replied
We arrive in Bairnsdale, one hour and twenty-six minutes later. Dad checked his mobile to see what attractions were available.
"We could go to 'Bairnsdale Bazaar'… the 'Historical Museum and Resource Centre'… or the East Gippsland all abilities playground situated in Main Street Bairnsdale."
"Some of the activities we could do at Bairnsdale Fun Park are archery, mini golf, swimming and go-karting, and of course we can go shopping!"
"What would you like to do first?"
"I choose Bairnsdale Bazaar." I said
There were all sorts of antiques everywhere from precious vases, to wooden furniture. We walked around the shop, amazed by the antiques. Dad looked at antique clocks, Mum looked at antique figurines and I looked at antique furniture. I did not touch, (because I've learnt not to), but I admired the beauty of all the different pieces.
"These antique clocks are precious masterpieces."
"My grandad used to own one, I enjoyed looking at it when I used to visit him."
"He gave it to me for my twenty-first birthday… it's not working at the moment… it needs cleaning and putting back together." said Dad
"Jessica owns two she's been looking after them very carefully."
"She may, or may not plan to sell them… she loves her job as an antique dealer." Mum added
"The antique furniture is fascinating they remind me of your Nan's house." I said
Next, Mum looked at the dolls Dad looked at the glassware and I looked at the pottery.
"I used to own a few dolls like that… besides my 'barbies'." said Mum, admiring the old-fashioned dollies
"I sometimes played with them for hours…gosh I enjoyed them." said Mum

"That glassware would look great in any home."
"It's crafted so beautifully."
"You have to be careful not to break them." Dad said, admiring the glassware
"This pottery looks amazing!"
"I would consider giving it a go... you know how much I love getting messy." I said, with a grin

After an hour's browsing, we decided to buy something. Dad bought a couple of classic videos, (seventies and eighties), which he watched years ago...Mum bought a doll which was similar to one that she owned as a child... I bought a few classic novels. Together our items cost forty dollars, we gave the right amount of money and left the shop... by that time it was almost eleven-thirty.

"What would you like to do next?" asked Mum

"I choose Mini Golf." I said

We drove to the Fun Park. As we were getting ready to play our mini golf game, there was plenty of 'banter' going on between us!

Dad said...

"I have played some mini golf on the odd occasion... I'm sure I can out hit the two of you!"

Not to be outdone, Mum piped up with...

"I've played more mini-golf than you two combined...I'm a many time Australian and World Champion... so try and beat me but I bet you won't... because I'm too good at it!"

I didn't want Mum and Dad to outdo me, so I said...

"I've played mini-golf for many years... I'm thinking that I can outsmart the two of you...if you think the two of you combined can beat me... there is no chance at all!"

The Mini Golf Park owner had been listening to all of this 'bragging' with amusement. When we went to select our equipment, he said...

"You three are hilarious!"

"We're a bit competitive." Mum had to admit, ruefully

"Good luck with that!"

"Let me know who wins this one!"

"I can't wait to hear!" said the owner, with a big grin on his face

At the fifth hole which was a straight putt it was a good opportunity for me to get a hole in one. I went up, placed my blue golf ball on the tee, stood to the left side of it and placed my club next to it with the head facing the right side of the ball. I've hit a hole in one a few times on similar mini-golf courses, so can I do it again on the Bairnsdale course?

Here I go!

I hit the ball a bit hard... it whizzed straight across the hole... bounced off the front wall and teetered near the hole edge for a few seconds. Oh, it's nearly in! Will it go in? The ball dropped into the hole after what felt like a lifetime...excitement is spreading all over me!

A big grin spreads all over my face!

"YES!"

"A hole in one for me!"

"Oh, YES!" I said, fist pumping twice into the sky

Dad was happy for me.

"Good job, Cassie!"

"That was a cliff hanger... but it went in!" shouted Dad, excitedly

"Well done, sweetie!"

"That was your fifth hole-in-one!"
"Very good shot." Mum congratulated me
"You'll be able to earn a' hole-in-one' certificate when we finish our game."
"You can put it with the three others that you won years ago." says Dad, smiling
"That's awesome, I'm still good at it." I grinned
Mum had her shot next...her shot was similar to mine... but it went in the hole easily.
"Oh, yeah!"
"A hole-in-one for me as well!"
"Woohoo!"
I was happy for Mum.
"You did well, Mum!"
"You will earn a 'hole-in-one' certificate as well."
"Well done, dear." Dad added
"That was similar to Cassie's shot... I couldn't tell the difference if I tried."
"Thanks."
"It's my first one in about twelve years!"
"Daniel... Cassie and I will bet you can't do the same!" said Mum, winking at Dad
"Five dollars each."
"You're on!" said Dad, shaking Mum's hand as well as mine
He lined up to take his shot. Can he do it and win the bet?
I hope he doesn't... but he reckons he can! Let's find out. Dad lines up to take his shot. He lines his club up next to the ball on the right side and hits the ball. It hits the walls in a zig-zag style and the ball rolls closer to the hole and then.... it just plops in the hole!
"Wow!"
"I did it!" says Dad, in a shocked voice
"You have won the bet Dad!"
"Well done!"
"Coincidence or what?"
"Here's my five dollars."
I handed Dad a five dollar note.
"I don't know how you did it dear, but 'WOW' that was great!"
"Here's a fiver from me." said Mum, handing Dad his winnings
"Looks like I will be earning a 'hole-in-one' certificate as well!"
"Goodness me!" said Dad, still stunned by his performance
"That has never happened to us in our mini-golf career before!"
"This is a lucky game so far! Mum said
"Now, we'll let the competition continue and see who wins!" Dad added
The mini-golf competition between Mum, Dad and I, is certainly heating up I can tell you it's a close one. At the eleventh hole, I hid Dad's golf ball and when he went to make his shot there was no golf ball!
"Ok, what's going on here?"
"Did either of you pinch my golf ball?" asked Dad, suspiciously
"No Dad."
"I haven't got it." I said, innocently
"No, dear."

"I haven't got it either." said Mum, trying not to laugh

"Yeah, right!"

"I'm sure one of you has it!"

Did anyone else pinch my golf ball?" asked Dad

No one else said anything, they shrugged their shoulders and some of them 'smirked' at the 'crazy' golfer

"I'll find out who did it soon enough." said Dad, grimly

Mum gave Dad a spare golf ball and he hit it near the hole, then I got out the golf ball I pinched and sneakily put it in the hole.

"Hey!"

"What's this?" Dad squeaks

He then realises I had it the entire time.

"Ah, ha!"

"Cassie did you put my original golf ball in this hole?" asked Dad

"Umm...maybe." I said, sheepishly

"I thought it was you!"

"You, cheeky rascal!"

"I'll get you back somehow." threatened Dad

I just laughed I love a good prank!

At one point, I got frustrated because I missed some easy shots, Mum and Dad took me aside for a bit of advice.

"Cassie don't let the course get the better of you."

"Work out how to beat them... like you're working out a puzzle."

"The obstacles on the courses are the puzzle pieces." said Dad

"The golf club is your hand putting the puzzle pieces together... every time you hit the ball around the obstacles a puzzle piece is put in place... when you 'putt' the ball into the hole the puzzle is complete and job done!" Mum added

"Thanks for the advice."

"I will continue my game and not let the obstacles get the better of me." I said

"That's the way Cassie."

"Don't give up." Dad encouraged

I concentrated on my game and I ended up being the overall winner with a score of thirty-seven.

"We have played mini-golf for many years, but today you were just too good for us Cassie."

"Well done!" said Mum

"Thanks Mum and Dad." I said

Dad came second with a score of thirty-nine and Mum scored forty-two.

We walked up to the counter and told our scores to the owner, Mike.

"I'm pleased to hear you all had a good game."

"Do you know what?" said Mike

"What?" we all said, keen to know what Mike was going to say next

"Well..." he said, sounding excited

"Not only are you the highest scorers for the Bairnsdale section... you are also the highest scoring family for the international section!"

"Oh Wow!" said Mum

"Yippee!"

"A double victory!" I said, fist pumping the air
"That's a great result!" said Dad, looking stunned
Everybody clapped, they were pleased for us. Mike was pleased as well!
"The previous highest scoring family were the Baker Family from the USA with one hundred and twenty-three…you have set a new record with one hundred and eighteen!"
"Congratulations!"
"You will receive a special trophy with your names engraved on it."
"Please let me know your names for the engraving."
"I am Daniel Bontel and this is my wife Makayla." said Dad
"I am their daughter, Cassie Bontel." I said happily
This was a 'cool' moment we will celebrate it with family and friends when we return from our trip.
"I wish you the best on the rest of your trip." said Mike, smiling at us
"Thanks Mike." I said
"It's great winning these trophies."
"Yes, it is Cassie!"
"We've never beaten a mini-golf record before! Mum laughed
"Great work girls, apart from pinching my golf ball Cassie!" Dad winked at me
"Thanks Dad."
"Thanks Daniel." Mum smiled
We drove to the Bairnsdale Colonial Motor Inn and booked a room for the night.

## *Chapter Three*
# Falls Creek fun in the Snow

Bright and early the next morning after breakfast we made plans to discuss where to go next.
"How about we take a side trip through some national parks?"
"Alpine National Park and Snowy River National Park, might be good places to visit?" Mum pondered
Dad was happy with that idea.
"Yes, and whilst we are doing that, we can also see Bright, Falls Creek and Mt Buffalo too...the skiing is great there!" he added
I agreed, but I was bit nervous.
I like the idea of the places... but... about the skiing bit." I said
"Hmm."
"Can you tell us what you are nervous about?" asked Dad
"I've never skied before in my life!"
"I don't know about doing it."
"I might hurt myself... or get tangled up in the skis... or slam into a tree... or get frostbite!"
"Can you help me learn how to ski?" I asked, tentatively
"Yes, of course we can Cassie."
"Good explanation of all your worries Cassie thank you for telling us."
"You will get to see the snow at Falls Creek or Mount Buffalo." said Mum
I was very excited about that.
"Oh great!"
"I've never seen snow before!"
"I've only seen it on TV, this is a great opportunity for me to experience it firsthand."
"I will love it!" I said, bouncing up and down in my seat with excitement
"That's for sure sweetie."
"Mum and I love the snow!" said Dad, with a big grin on his face
As we got closer to Falls Creek, Mum who is currently driving pulled over on the side of the road to check her information about the area.
"Falls Creek is an alpine ski resort with 4,500 accommodation beds... a large number of restaurants... bars... nightclubs and... some privately-owned apartments that can be hired."
"It has a summer base to explore the national park."
"We can ski on Mount McKay... which is near the resort."
"Mt Buffalo is a national park as well a plateau."
"It's one of Australia's oldest national parks."

"There is quite a view from the north at 'The Horn'… we need to access the walking track to get there… where we can see a three-hundred and sixty-degree view from the top."

"People can enjoy cross-country skiing during the winter season… there are lessons available for beginners and experienced skiers."

"We can also stay at Bright which is near Mt Buffalo…with flora, fauna, vegetation and fungi… but there's not much snow there."

"All right Cassie, where do you want to learn to ski?" asked Mum

"I choose Falls Creek."

"It has more snow than Mt Buffalo it covers the mountains there!" I said

"Right then let's go to Falls Creek!"

"We'll have fun together." Mum said, and started the vehicle

"Yes please, there's plenty of snow for skiing there." I replied

When we arrived at Falls Creek it was well worth it… with snow all around everywhere I looked… I was excited and ecstatic. I had never seen snow before… everything looked so different and so amazing!

"Wow!"

"There is snow all over!"

"This is wonderful!" I said, excitedly

Mum and Dad were happy to see snow again.

"We haven't been in the show for about sixteen years… it's great to see it again!" said Dad

"I'm glad to see snow again, I'm glad you are enjoying it too Cassie." Mum said

"Yes, I am Mum!"

Dad looked around.

"We need to find somewhere for lunch… I'll take a look on my iPhone and see what's available."

He found three different places and showed me the list.

"Choose which one you want Cassie." Dad said

I chose the 'Last Hoot-Café Bar and Pizzeria'.

"There's plenty of pizza at the pizzeria and the café seems good as well as the bar."

"It might be noisy… so don't forget your headphones Cassie!" Dad informed me

"Let's get into our winter gear to keep warm and avoid catching a cold!" Mum said

Dad and I agreed.

We put on our winter gear, (in our favourite colours, of course), then made our way to 'Last Hoot'. It was not easy walking through the snow, at one point we fell over. Oops! We picked ourselves up and continued on. We eventually made it to 'Last Hoot', it was noisy inside with many people…I put on my headphones and we made our way to the table we had booked.

We looked over the menu. It was mostly pizzas, some of them had vegetables on them and one had egg in a form I do not like… *'Yuck, they're not getting me with that one… I don't think so…* I thought. I liked the look of the meat lovers, (my favourite pizza), as well as the herbs pizza. I also looked at the pasta menu. I love the look of the Spaghetti Saltati…I am not sure of the sauce that they use with that recipe… *'If the sauce is a flavour or texture I dislike, I'm not eating it … I hope it's one I like'* I think to myself. The desserts look pretty tempting, but I better get the main meal sorted out first!

"Have you decided yet, Cassie?" asked Dad

"I've decided on 'Spaghetti Saltati'…I'm not sure about the sauce they use."

"It could be cheese or something else…if you give it a try Mum and I will be happy with that." said Dad

I gave it some thought.

"Okay, I will give it a try."

"Good girl Cassie." said Mum, hopefully

The waiter put down our meals... Mum had chosen Fettucine Carbonara and Dad had the Mediterranean Salad... I asked the waiter what the sauce is on the Spaghetti Saltati which is the house speciality!

"That is cheese signorina." said the waiter

I picked up my fork and looked at it nervously... I couldn't bring myself to eat... it was staring at me like it was going to scare me... *'That cheese sauce looks a different colour to ones that I have see before... it looks like it has gone off...Eeuuw'*. I thought, suspiciously

Mum and Dad notice my trepidation and try their best to support me.

"Come on sweetie you can do this."

"That pasta will taste good when you eat it." said Mum

"You and your Mum love pasta...give it a try." said Dad, coaxingly

I slowly brought my fork to the spaghetti, twirled a mouthful on the fork and put it in my mouth. Mum and Dad watched me, concerned that I might not like it and would refuse to eat.

In the past, either at home or in an eating establishment if I am given a meal which I dislike, (due to sensory issues of texture, smell, flavour or taste), I would refuse to eat it... throw it across the room and have a meltdown!

Now, I just say 'No thanks'... then I would order another meal that I can eat. Sometimes, Mum and Dad would make a compromise, in order to get me to eat a meal. Sometimes it works, sometimes it doesn't. I'm going to try this unusual spaghetti. Here I go!

I chewed the spaghetti and swallowed it! Mum and Dad held their breath, hoping that I would like it. Are they right?

I turned to Mum and Dad and gave them a smile and the 'thumbs up'!

"This pasta is great!"

"I love it!" I said

Mum was 'SO' happy!

"Well done Cassie, I knew you could do it!"

Dad was also happy!

"You did a good job Cassie, well done!"

I was proud of myself and happy too... that I tried a new food.

"Yes, I did!"

"That cheese sauce didn't bother me, I enjoyed it, I would eat it again!"

At the end of the meal the waiter came and asked

"How were your meals?"

"Mine was delicious, I felt like I was in the Mediterranean eating it." said Dad, smiling

"Mine was delicious too just like one my Mum would make." Mum said

"Mine was the best in this place!"

"I was hesitant to try but with Mum and Dad's support and encouragement I enjoyed it!"

"I would eat it again." I said, very pleased with myself

"I'm very glad you did."

"Would you like to order some dessert?" asked the waiter

Mum, Dad and I, looked at each other and whispered together, then Mum said to the waiter...

"No thank you... we're as full as we can be!"

"We couldn't fit it in if we tried to!"

We left 'Last Hoot' and took a leisurely stroll to the Alpine Resort to let our food settle. When we finally arrived at the resort, we took a look inside at the skiing lessons on offer. Mum and Dad chose a veteran lesson for themselves and booked a first-time lesson for me. I hope I do well.

"How many in your family?" asked the resort receptionist

"Two adults and one child." said Dad

"That will be sixty dollars please."

"You can get your ski gear and change in the rooms next door." said the receptionist

"Thank you." said Mum

"Don't forget your lesson starts in fifteen minutes... so please be on time." she concluded

"We will." I said

After we had changed into our ski gear and picked up our ski equipment, we made our way to the ski lesson area where our instructor was waiting. I was a bit shy about meeting her, I hope she can help me to learn to ski... I also hope she has worked with special needs kids before! Wish me luck!

"Hello, you must be the Bontel Family."

"I'm Shelia, I will be your instructor for this lesson."

Dad shook Shelia's hand.

"I'm Daniel Bontel."

"I have skied here before... years ago... I really enjoyed it!"

"I'm keen to ski again."

Mum does the same.

"I'm Mikayla Bontel."

"I've skied here before as well... at Mount Buller with Daniel."

"I loved it and I'm ready to ski again."

I was a bit shy and nervous... I am too scared to say hello to Shelia or shake her hand. She looks nice, but a bit scary.

"It's okay Cassie."

"Shelia will help you to learn how to ski."

"Don't be shy." said Mum, in a soothing voice that she always uses when I get shy or nervous... which helps to calm me down

I quietly said...

"I'm Cassie Bontel."

"I've never been to Falls Creek before, I would love to learn how to ski it's my first time." I shook Sheila's hand

"It's all right to be shy... but we won't let it stop us from having a fun time, will we?" asked Shelia

I nodded to let Sheila know I understood.

"Cassie can be shy when she is around new people, new environments, or even familiar environments if there are unfamiliar people in them."

"She can be sensitive... so please be understanding." said Mum, explaining to Sheila

"Don't worry I've worked with people of all abilities... I'll do my best to make sure that Cassie enjoys her lesson." said Shelia, smiling

"May we have a word with you Shelia?" Dad asked

"Of course." Sheila replied

"Cassie, you wait here while we talk to Shelia."

"Do you mind?" asked Mum

"Not at all Mum."

"I'll be fine waiting here." I said

Mum and Dad walked to the side to talk to Shelia, while I waited. I listened to them but I couldn't make out what they were saying. I imagine it would be something along the lines of...

(Dad)...Shelia, just to let you know Cassie our daughter has mild autism... she can talk very well and has an IQ of one hundred and ninety-seven... which makes her a genius. She is very nervous about skiing so please make her feel confident by teaching her a few basic skills... encourage her to try again if she falls. Cassie has anxiety so if she suffers an attack tell to her use her anxiety techniques which we have taught her.

(Mum)...Cassie is shy and may hide or not look you in the eyes when she feels like that... she's improving all the time but just in case... get down to her level... encourage her in a gentle soothing voice to look at you in the eyes... then tell her that you will help her throughout the lesson.

Offer her praise when she does well... if she gets upset or anxious and needs a break please let her... when the break is over take up the lesson from where you left off. It's her first time here... so you can point out the mountain runs for all the different levels of skiers... where the beginner slopes are... what obstacles the expert skiers have to navigate on their more complicated ski runs etc.

"Right then, we have a skiing lesson to get to!" said Sheila, smiling

"Are you ready Cassie?" she asked me

"Yes, I am Shelia." I replied

"I will be the ski instructor for your first lesson... we'll go to the nursery slopes where first-time skiers learn the basics." said Shelia, explaining

That's good."

"I hope I can do this."

"I will try my very best!" I said

"That's the spirit Cassie!" said Sheila

"Daniel, Mikayla, your ski instructor for the refresher lesson will be Barry."

"Barry, can you take Daniel and Mikayla for their lesson on the more advanced slopes please?" Sheila added

"Will do, Shelia." Barry grinned

"Barry has taken this class for many years, refreshing veteran skiers on their skills, he's very good at it!" said Mum

"Good luck with Shelia, Cassie."

We'll see you after our lesson." said Dad, cheerfully

"Thanks Dad."

"Good luck to you and Mum." I replied

"Ok Cassie, we're going to the nursery slopes just over there... the starting point for all first-time skiers... young and old."

"I will teach you all the basics like how to 'clip in' to your skis, how to stand upright, how to use your ski poles, 'how to walk' in skis, how to glide safely and how to stop!" Shelia promised

"It will take lots of practice to master all those new skills, after a week or two you will become familiar with the feeling of being on skis, just like walking in your trainers!" Sheila laughed and I smiled

"Come on Cassie, let's have some fun... oh and don't worry if you fall over in the snow... everybody does when they are learning... it's all part of the fun!" Sheila laughed again and this time I did too

"I can't wait!" I said, excitedly

"Good, let's start!"

"We are dressed appropriately for skiing and we have our equipment ready, poles, skis, snow goggles."

"Let's start by putting our booted feet into the ski slots on our skis... one by one." Shelia said

I clipped my feet into the slots... Whoa! Now I feel like I have feet that are longer than my body. Shelia shows me how to balance on the ski poles on either side of my body.

"Good now put your poles and place them by your side a few inches from the snow like this." Sheila demonstrates

I didn't know what height to adjust the poles to until Shelia showed me how.

"Good job Cassie."

"Now the next basic move you need to learn is how to walk."

"I already know how to walk Sheila... you just put one foot in front of the other like this!"

I took a big step forward but skis are very long and the front of one ski got tangled up with the front of the other ski and I fell in an awkward heap in the snow!

Sheila made her way to me swiftly and bent down to assist me.

"Are you all right Cassie?" Sheila asked, in a concerned voice

"Yes, I'm just tangled up and covered in snow!" I muttered

"Why did that happen?" I said in amazement

"Well, you can't walk the way you usually do in shoes... when you are wearing skis Cassie."

"That's why you have to 'learn' to walk in skis as I was just going to show you before you took off." Sheila said

"Oh." I said, sheepishly

"Then how do you walk in skis." I asked

"Let me help you up on your feet again and then I will demonstrate for you." said Sheila giving me a grin

Once I was standing up and reasonably stable... Sheila began the demonstration. I could see that there was going to be a lot more to this 'learning how to ski'... than I realised!

"When walking on skis you must think like a crab!" said Sheila, which gave me a fit of the giggles and I nearly over balanced and fell again.

It was even funnier when Sheila did the walk steps!

You had to lift up a leg with ski attached and step sideways... then lift up the other leg and step sideways to bring your legs together again... and so on... just like a crab scuttling sideways.

Except there is no scuttling with skis on... it was hard... slow... painstaking work with every step... just to move a few feet!

What a workout! When I had mastered how to walk sideways in both directions, we took a short break. I already feel like I have run a marathon and we haven't even started skiing yet!

Next move I need to learn is how to do a short glide on my skis. The nursery slopes are quite gradual and mostly level so that we don't pick up too much speed and get out of control.

Sheila demonstrates how to push off in the snow with the ski poles and glide along the snow for a short distance... she tells me that before I practice this move I need to learn how to slow my forward momentum and bring myself to a stop... or else I will just keep skimming along the snowy surface... which could become a problem as I don't know how to ski yet!

The stopping process looks a little tricky! I think this move is going to take a lot of practice to get it right!

As you are gliding along in a straight line with both skis parallel, you need to begin to angle the front points of the skis in to meet each other, in and out, to slow your forward motion, this should arrest your momentum and bring you to a stop. Sounds easy doesn't it? Well I am here to tell you that it isn't!

If you bring the points of the skis together too quickly or sharply… you will stop all right!

Or rather your feet will stop… but the rest of your body will go sailing over the top of your skis…where you will end up in the snow in a tangled heap again! Which is what I did on several occasions… until I learned how to do the manoeuvre very slowly to gently roll to a stop.

Sheila says we are now ready to put it all together.

"Right Cassie… we are going to crab walk up to that first little slope… then we are going to glide slowly down and make a safe stop at the bottom… that will be enough practice for this lesson… or you will be too sore to ski again tomorrow!"

"Do you think you are ready for your first little ski run?"

"Oh yes please Sheila… I can't wait to try out everything you have been teaching me it will be so exciting!"

"Good Cassie, remember everything I have told you and take it slow and steady… I shall be right beside you."

"If you feel out of control or anxious… you can always fall over or sit down in the snow… it may not look very elegant… but it is better to do that and build up your confidence than to rush things…then you can get up and start again when you feel ready."

"All right Sheila, let's do this!"

Sheila and I, began our slow crabwalk up the gentle slope no wonder skiing keeps people fit! It seemed to take ages for us to reach the taking off point, but finally we got there. We had a little breather, adjusted all our equipment and prepared to push off.

I looked down at what had seemed a gentle slope from the bottom and thought…

*'Oh dear… it feels high from up here… it looks such a long way down! I can't do this! I just can't do it!*

It felt overwhelming… I was having an anxiety attack.

"I can't do this!"

"I just can't!" I said, in a frightened voice

"It's okay Cassie, I'm here to help you."

"Use your anxiety techniques that your Mum and Dad taught you."

"They can help you to feel calm and get through this attack." Shelia said

After I used my anxiety techniques, I felt calmer.

"Cassie do you feel better now?" asked Shelia

"I do feel better now… thanks Shelia." I said

"That's good… I'm glad your Mum and Dad suggested your anxiety techniques to me."

"Are you feeling more confident about skiing now?" asked Shelia.

"I feel a little more confident… I am ready to try again." I said

"Then let's do it together Cassie." Shelia replied

On a more advanced run nearby, Shelia and I could see Mum and Dad skiing down the mountain side in style, they were enjoying themselves.

Mum was feeling the adrenaline rush!

"Wahoo…you little ripper…this is so awesome!" Mum shrieked, laughing

Mum is acting like a teenager!

I laughed at her antics Mum can be so hilarious when she says things like that. Shelia was laughing too. Not to be out done here comes Dad.

"Yahoo…you little beauty…it's a blast!" Dad shouts, excitedly

Dad is laughing so much it makes me laugh as well, which starts off Sheila again.

"Your Mum and Dad are so funny… they are really enjoying themselves!" Shelia grinned

"They sure are... they are often wacky and funny."

"They have 'dabbled' as comedians at one point in their careers during the early nineties." I told her, laughing

"Cassie!"

"Shelia!"

"We'll meet you at the bottom... come and join us!" Dad yelled as he raced down

"Ready, Cassie?" asks Shelia

'Ready, Shelia." I replied

We both pushed off and began to gently glide down the slope, using our poles in the snow.

"This is such fun!" I laughed

"You are doing very well for a first attempt." Sheila encouraged

As we went further the skis began to pick up a little speed and I could feel the wind moving over my face. Sheila called across to me

"Now remember Cassie you will need to begin your slowing down and stopping procedures well before we get to the bottom...give yourself time to slow down and brake to a stop!" Sheila reminded me

I looked and was surprised to see how far we had already covered I had been having so much fun I didn't even realise that we were almost down! I saw Sheila slowing down and copied her moves, I didn't want to crash and end up in a heap at Mum and Dad's feet!

I began to angle my ski tips in and out to slow everything down, Sheila pulled up neatly in front of Mum and Dad and I 'wobbled' to a stop behind her.

"That was awesome! I yelled

They all laughed at my excitement.

"I knew you would love it Cassie...well done!" said Dad happily

"We're so proud of you!" said Mum, with a big smile on her face

"I did it... my first ski!"

"That's right a very good first attempt!" Sheila congratulated me

We can try some more in tomorrow's lesson." Shelia said

"Yes, please!" we chorused together

"Right... now you need to go and change out of your skiing gear... return the equipment and have some nice hot showers to ease your aching muscles... we don't want you to stiffen up!" smiled Sheila

"See you tomorrow Cassie... we have lots to learn."

"Bye Sheila." I said, as we turned to go

...but Mum, Dad and I, have all made the same move with disastrous results... our skis become entangled and we all fall in a heap in the snow!

"UGH

"OOF!

"SPLAT!

"Oh dear... are you all right you three?" said Shelia, trying not to giggle

"It's possibly just as well that you have several weeks to practice your skiing moves this ski season." Shelia grinned "Mmmn." said Dad ruefully, rubbing his shins

"Every time we fall... we will just get back up again!" I said, laughing out loud

"We will practice until we get it right!" Mum added

"That's the spirit Bontel Family!" said Shelia, as she helped us to our feet one by one

"Cassie, how was your first skiing lesson?" asked Dad

"I loved it...I felt the wind rush over my face as I skied down the slope...it was a blast!"

"I'd love to try it again... thanks Shelia for teaching me and helping me through when I got anxious."

"You're a very good skiing teacher I appreciate it." I said

"Thanks Cassie... I enjoyed teaching you...I'm proud of you and so are Mum and Dad." said Shelia

"Yes, we are proud of you for trying a new activity Cassie... and Shelia thank you for teaching Cassie today." said Mum

"My pleasure... I guess you're staying in Falls Creek?" asked Shelia.

"Yes, we are taking a family road trip around Australia!" said Dad

"That's great... I wish I could do one with my family." said Shelia, enviously

"Thanks Barry... for giving Mikayla and I a refresher lesson."

"We had a fun time and enjoyed ourselves." Dad added

"No problems... Mr and Mrs Bontel." said Barry

After we said goodbye to Shelia and Barry, we returned the skiing gear we hired, got changed back into our winter clothes and drove to the Falls Creek Alpine Resort to book an apartment.

"Hello... we're here to book an apartment for three." said Dad

"I see... names please." said the receptionist

"Daniel Bontel."

"Mikayla Bontel."

"Cassie Bontel."

The receptionist looked puzzled... she had never heard our surname before. Looks like we will have to help her out.

"Could you spell that surname for me please." said the receptionist

"B-O-N-T-E-L... Bontel." Dad spelled out our name

"Thank you."

"I'll just see if there are any apartments available."

The receptionist smiled happily.

"You are in luck, there is just one vacant three bedroomed apartment."

"You'll have plenty of room to move."

"You can view the Falls express chairlift from your outdoor terrace or sample the apartment hot tub."

"Use this key to access your apartment... you'll find everything as described in the brochure."

"I hope you enjoy your stay Bontel Family."

"Thank you... we will." said Mum

When we got to our room, there was a queen-sized bed in one room, twin beds in another room and kitchenette features, it looks like a great apartment to stay in.

"Wow!... It looks a wonderful apartment."

"There are comfy beds to sleep on."

I tried the queen-sized bed.

"We can do all our cooking with the kitchenette features, that's pretty good." Dad was impressed

"We can watch movies on demand as well... great!" said Mum

"Look at the balcony?"

"We have spectacular views from here!" I said

"This is a great place... it's one of the best resorts we've stayed in... what more could you want?" said Mum, happily

"Let's make the most of the facilities... let's unpack then hire a movie to watch." Dad decided

After we unpacked, Mum chose a movie.

"This is one of my favourite movies of all time, it stars Pierce Brosnan and it's from 1995."

I read the title… 'Goldeneye'

"It was Pierce's first role as James Bond… it is set in the times of the dissolution of the Soviet Union during the cold war." I said

"Let's watch it… shall we?" said Mum

"Yes, I love a thriller!" Dad added

"There will be weapons, thrills and explosions, can you cope with that Cassie?" said Mum

"I'm sure I can… I'm getting used to those kinds of effects in films." I said

"If you get overwhelmed let us know… and we can stop the film." Dad said

"Ok Dad." I nodded

After we had finished watching the movie, I found two newspapers that the hotel had provided. I quietly switched some of the pages out of one and put them in the other and vice-versa. A short while later, Mum and Dad decided to check the papers for updates about the snowfalls for skiing conditions. They were very puzzled when they discovered some of the pages didn't match.

"Hey, something is wrong with this newspaper!" said Mum, in a puzzled voice

"I don't know what paper I'm reading." said Dad, looking confused

They both collaborated over their newspapers and found that the issues had been mixed up.

"Well I think we know how this might have happened." said Mum, suspiciously

"Yes, I'm sure we know someone who could be responsible for this." Dad added

"It also sounds like that someone is nearby!" stated Dad

Mum and Dad could hear me giggling in my room.

"Cassie, can you come out here please." said Mum, with her arms folded

"Yes?" I giggled

"Was it you that swapped the pages of these two newspapers around?" asked Mum, raising her left eyebrow

I just laughed.

"Come on own up… did you do all this?" asked Mum, pointing to the muddled-up newspapers

"You must have mixed them up Mum when you were reading." I said, trying to keep a straight face

"It wasn't me!" said Mum, huffily

"Maybe it was Dad." I said, with an air of innocence

"No, it was not me!" said Dad, crankily

I burst out laughing …

"Oh, all right it was me… it was funny!"

"Very funny Cassie…we shall get you back!" said Mum, too quietly for my liking

"Better watch out Cassie." said Dad, winking at me

We decided not to go to the restaurant and used the kitchenette features instead…we prepared the food we got from the Falls Creek shop. When we had finished our meal, we sat out on the balcony watching the evening sky.

"What do you think of the resort Cassie?" asked Mum

"It is like a paradise in the snow."

"You can see white snow from our rooms, there are skiers and snowboarders, amazing views and the beds are soft and comfortable!"

"I've never been in a resort before… but it has to be the best I've ever seen!" I said, happily

"We thought the same."
"Dad and I, have stayed in resorts in Europe, Asia, and Australia."
"This is one is lovely right here in Falls Creek!"
"We learned to ski in Falls Creek. when we were thirteen years old."
"Every year before you were born, we skied here or at Mt Buller, we fell many times but eventually we got the hang of it, fun wintery times we had... didn't we dear?" said Mum, looking over at Dad
"We sure did, darling!"
"We skied for hours every day."
"Not only did we ski... but we made snowmen... threw snowballs at each other and tried snowboarding too."
"One year, when we were seventeen, we had just finished skiing and our parents were inside a nearby cabin drinking hot chocolate...when Mum had an idea."
"We crept up to the cabin, opened the door halfway and threw some snowballs in...they got quite a surprise...we ran off laughing before they could see who it was!"
"Oh, did you two get into trouble?" I asked, hoping Dad was going to 'dish the dirt' on their punishments
"Nope!"
"We got away with it."
"They didn't find out who had done it until our Australia Day concert in 1993!"
"They got quite a surprise when we revealed we were the ones that threw the snowballs at them." said Mum, chuckling
"You were sneaky to pull that one off." I said, admiringly
"It was one of our better pranks!"
"Anyway, this night sky and the lights near the snow, make this evening snow scene look like a snowy wonderland!"
"What do you think, Cassie?" asked Dad
"It looks like a midnight snow party from what I can see."
"There are some skiers trying some last-minute skiing before they turn in... they are having as much fun as we did on the slopes." I replied
"They definitely are having the time of their lives in the snow!"
"Why don't we get another drink before we watch the next movie?"
"Might as well."
Mum and Dad went to get the drinks... unknown to me they had placed a rubber spider under my can.
*'Imagine the look on Cassie's face when she sees this'*...thought Mum, sniggering
*'It will be priceless'*... thought Dad, as he grinned
They went to the balcony and placed the soft drinks on the table then went back to the kitchen to get some munchies. I picked up my soft drink can and felt something squishy underneath, I looked and what I saw made me jump up in fright!
"AAGH"
"It's a SPIDER!" I shrieked
I backed away to the railing, I encouraged myself to look closer and it hadn't moved, I reached out and it still didn't move...something funny was going on here...I gingerly put out a finger and touched it very gingerly...it was RUBBER...I took it off the can and I realised I have been tricked...I hear laughing inside the resort room!
"Mum!"

"Dad!"

"Come out right now!" I said, with 'my' arms folded across my chest and a big frown across my face

Mum and Dad came out of the bathroom grinning.

"OK, what have you got to say for yourselves!" I said, like a very cranky school teacher

Mum and Dad tried to keep straight faces but they completely lost it, collapsing on the couch laughing till they were crying!

Mum and Dad eventually pulled themselves together.

"All right we put the spider under your soft drink, to get you back for the bucket of water prank at Traralgon!"

"It was good though!"

"You should've seen your face." said Mum

"It was priceless!"

"So funny that we nearly died from laughing." added Dad, grinning

"I admit you got me." I said, grudgingly

We decided it was time to watch the next movie before anything else happened!

This movie is called 'Australia', it stars Hugh Jackman and Nicole Kidman, it is a fair dinkum Aussie movie. Mum, Dad and I, enjoy it every time we watch it! After the movie had finished, we decided to get some shut-eye.

Over the next two weeks, we played in the snow, built snowmen and threw snowballs at each other, as well as skiing. What a wintery blast we had I will always love to spend time in the snow after this first introduction to it.

A few days later, Mum gave me a reward for my efforts at skiing. It was a bag of 'Clinkers'... it's one of my favourites!

"Don't forget to share them with us." reminded Mum

"Ok Mum, I will."

A couple of weeks later... the day before we left for Echuca, Mum skyped Belinda hoping to find out what her Dad was doing on his men's holiday.

If I know Belinda, she will probably not give anything away... but also knowing Mum she will definitely try her best to find out!

'Hi, Mum. How are you doing? I'm fine thanks, darling. How are you? I'm doing very well thanks Mum.'

I couldn't resist butting in and being a bit cheeky!

'Hello, Belinda Bonkers. Very funny Cassie! Mikayla, I hope you haven't been giving Cassie cheeky ideas, I know what you're like! Who, me Mum?'

Dad and I struggled not to laugh.

'You'll receive a clip under the ear if you do! Nice try Mum, but I'm way too old for that. Oh... ARE you... young lady! We shall see about that.'

Dad and I love it when Mum is in trouble with Belinda, it's a 'hoot' and it keeps the heat off us for a change!

'We've been in Falls Creek having a fun time. What a lovely place despite the cold. Are you keeping rugged up? Yes, Mum, we rugged up when we got here. What have you been doing? We all had skiing lessons. It was Cassie's first attempt at skiing. Shelia her instructor, helped her throughout the whole process.' Good job Cassie, I'm so proud of you for trying a new activity. I'm proud of myself too for giving skiing a go. I had a blast! That's great Cassie! Anyway Mum, how's Dad doing on his men's month away? I don't know what he's up to. I'm not telling you anything! You're keeping a secret from me? I don't think so

Mum, it's not going to work you know, I always find out in the end! Nope! I'm not telling. Come on, Mum. I know Dad's up to something, tell me what he's up to, reveal the secret to me. Nice wheedling Mikayla, but my lips are sealed!'

Dad and I were 'corpsing' in the background, clutching our bellies which were sore from laughing.

'Is that Daniel and Cassie I hear laughing? Yes, they think this is funny!'

Mum was not impressed with Belinda, and she was even less impressed with us for laughing at the situation, when she was deadly serious about finding out where the men's secret camp was located! Too bad, she was going to have to admit defeat this time because Belinda wasn't budging!

'Mikayla, I've never forgotten the time that you, Daniel, Olivia and Rebecca left Maria, Jim, Dad and I, in Alice Springs! We flew to Darwin, then we drove hire cars to Alice Springs, spent a week there, then a day before we were meant to leave you crept out of there with your hire cars, drove to Darwin airport and flew all the way back to Melbourne, without a word! What a sneaky trick you played on us back then! Luckily, we had our own hire cars and drove back to Darwin, before we flew back to Melbourne. Of course, by that time you four were all back in your houses… we didn't find out what had really happened until your twentieth wedding anniversary! You were very sneaky back then! We got the idea when we appeared on 'Family Game' in 1992. We planned it all when we won the five thousand dollars gold and the trip to Alice Springs! Our friends thought it was a hilarious gag back then. We never let you, Dad, Maria and Jim live it down!'

Every now and then on special family occasions Mum brings it up… much to our delight.

'Changing the subject Mikayla, there's a family member that hasn't been seen for about twenty-two years. Are they male or female?'

Dad and I stopped laughing and listened in.

'I will give you little clues as we go along. Here's your first clue. He's a man, but I'm not going to tell you anymore at the moment. Oh, come on, Mum! That's not enough for me. Tell me more. That is your clue for today. Before you say it Mikayla… NO… we are not going to skype every day either!'

"Blah, blah, blah, I'll find out no matter how long it takes." muttered Mum, under her breath

'Tune in to for your next clue in a week.'

'We are leaving for Echuca tomorrow.

Bye, Mum.'

# *Chapter Four*
## Camping memories at Echuca

We left Falls Creek for Echuca at seven-thirty in the morning, it will be hotter than Falls Creek, but I will be fine. When we arrived there at around eleven-thirty, Mum and Dad decided we would stay at the Echuca Holiday Park to take a break from staying in hotels all the time. As we arrived, I felt a sense of dread it triggered a frightening memory from my past. I managed to stay calm as I helped Mum and Dad set up the tents and put the sleeping bags and gear in them. It was hard work, but we managed to get it all done. We had lunch from a nearby eatery and sat down on our camping chairs near the tents. We read our books for about an hour, before I looked around the holiday park. Even though it was not quite a camping ground I felt the sense of dread again. I looked down and tears were tracking my face. Mum and Dad noticed and came over to see what was wrong.

"What's wrong, Cassie?" asked Dad, in a worried voice

"Can you tell us what has made you upset, Cassie?" asked Mum

I just couldn't find the words at that moment... I sobbed a little.

Mum and Dad always let me take the time to process the environment and rub gently on my hands. It's the only touch I can tolerate and soothes me when I get upset, it helps me a lot. I eventually calmed after a few minutes had passed by.

"Are you all right now, Cassie?" Mum asked

"Yes, I'm all right." I sniffed

"Can you tell us why you got upset?"

"You can tell us anything." said Dad

"Let's sit down on that log over there, then I'll tell you." I replied

We went over to the log and sat down, I opened up to Mum and Dad about the memory from my past.

"Mum, Dad, the reason I got so upset is that this holiday park reminded me of a camping memory, from June 1999 in Glenelg, Victoria." I said

"Hmm."

"Can you remember what happened in Glenelg in 1999?" asked Mum, surprised

"I was four years old back then."

"We were at the Glenelg camping ground... Mum you were cooking lunch and Dad you were hanging out the washing... I was playing with my toy cars in the tent."

"I left the tent whilst you were both busy and wandered off into the bushland."

"I was still non-verbal at the time... it was just before I became fully verbal later that year."

"It was sometime later that you both discovered I was no longer in the tent!"

"You were searching for me with the other campers for about two hours… a news crew helicopter was also searching from the air."

"You were concerned that I may not my find my way back to the site, where we were staying."

"It was another three hours before I found my own way back thanks to my genius memory." "I made my own way back to camp by retracing the steps I had taken in my mind… I was dirty and wet."

"You were both so relieved that I had found my way back."

"I remember Mum… you scooped me up in your arms tears streaming from your eyes… saying… my darling cutie, I missed you so much… where have you been?… I'm glad you came back… please don't wander off from us again."

"I remember you hugged me tight… even though I disliked being touched."

"Dad, you said… Cassie… we're so glad you are safe… we thought we'd never see you again…you gave us such a fright… we're glad to have you back again."

"We packed up our camp and drove all the way home."

"I remember rocking myself back and forth sobbing… while you and Dad were shaken but relieved that I was safe and sound."

"We were featured on several news channels as well as several radio stations."

"Our family and friends were shocked to hear about it… but relieved that I was still alive and well."

"Since then I have had a fear of camping… I don't even like going into camping stores."

"That's what I remember about camping in June 1999." I told Mum and Dad

"That was a frightful event for all of us…one that we will never forget!"

"Well done for opening up to us about that, Cassie."

"You were very courageous for doing that."

"Dad and I are so proud of you for telling us what you remembered." said Mum

"This time, we're going to make camping a bit easier for you… help you to overcome your fears."

"Let's put that memory behind us… move forward… and create some new memories."

"Whilst we are camping this time… we might have marshmallows around the campfire… go fishing or swimming in the river… or maybe for a bush walk." said Dad

"Cassie, we can also try some horse riding as we will be camping here for a few days."

"The weather looks a bit grey… but hopefully the rain will stay away."

"Why don't we have a swim before we prepare the dinner?" asked Dad

"Yes, let's do that!" agreed Mum

"It will be good for all of us together… to have fun swimming." I agreed

We got changed into our bathers and I walked down to the river. I checked to see if there were any logs or sticks and then entered the water. It was cold at first, but as I moved around in the water, I got used to it. Mum and Dad arrived a few minutes later, Dad was carrying a newspaper and folding chair to sit on.

"What are you two waiting for?"

"The water's lovely!" I said

"Erm… I can't swim in the water because… I've broken my arm!" said Mum, very unconvincingly, setting up her folding chair and sitting down on it

"I can't swim either… because I have a cold." said Dad, also sitting down

"Don't be wusses, you two!"

"Come on in."

"The water's warm."

"I'm enjoying it!" I said

"Well... ok."
"I will." Mum said, jumping in beside me... to find out it wasn't warm at all
"ARRGH! (Bleep!)"
"That water is NOT warm!" she said, shivering
"It was freezing cold the whole time Mum."
"Got you!" I said, laughing and pointing at her
"You tricked me, Cassie."
"I'll get you back... you wait and see." Mum said, pointing a finger at me
"Not if I get you first." I said, laughing

Mum started to climb her way back to the top, shivering all the way and sat down in her chair, still shaking. Dad sniggered, he found it all very funny. Mum did her famous 'glare stare' at him and Dad kept his mouth shut and hid behind his newspaper quickly. It was hilarious tricking Mum. I swam for another twenty minutes before Dad joined me.

"How's the swimming going Cassie?" asked Dad
"I'm loving every minute of it, Dad."
"I've never swum in a river before... but I love it!" I added
"I do too!"
"Mikayla, are you joining us?" asked Dad
"Ok, I will."
This time she had no problems with the water.
"The water is cold... but I'll get used to it."
After half an hour, we got out and dried ourselves off. What a swim, I'm starting to enjoy camping!
"I need a shower after all that swimming... do you want a shower you two?" asked Mum
"Um... no thanks, dear."
"I'd rather stay dirty." Dad said
"Me too, Mum!"
I love getting dirty." I said, winking at Dad
"Ok, it's your choice."
"I'm off to have a hot shower... it will help to warm me up!" said Mum
"We recommend the hot tap!"
"You just have to adjust it to the right temperature and you should be fine." Dad said, winking
"Thanks very much for that!"
Mum went off to the showers to warm herself up. Dad and I sniggered.

We are setting up a trick to play on Mum. We alerted the other campers to what was happening, they agreed not to tell Mum. Mum closed the door to the shower and turned on what she thought was the hot tap... no one has told her that there is only cold running water at this campsite!

"Three, Two, One..." said Dad and I together
"Arrgh! (bleep)!" shrieked Mum
Dad and I collapsed on the ground laughing hysterically... the other campers were laughing too... they found it hilarious!

"Good trick you two." said one camper
"Sure was." I said, grinning
Mum put her head around the shower door.
"Just you wait!" said Mum, putting her head around the shower door

Dad and I, tried not to laugh again. We kept our mouths shut to avoid being detected.

At six o'clock we set up the campfire, we stacked up the wood, then used the matches to light the fire.

"All we need now is marshmallows and a forked stick each, to put them on to cook." said Dad

We found some forked sticks and placed marshmallows on the tips. Then we pulled our camping chairs around the fire and began to toast our marshmallows.

"I'm enjoying camping so far."

"Echuca is a great place to camp…you are helping me to appreciate it…thanks." I said

"That's good, Cassie."

"It's nice of you to thank Dad and I."

"It takes courage to talk about your fears." said Mum

"I did use courage today to open up to you both…thanks Mum." I said

"You're becoming a brave girl… we're proud of you."

"It makes us happy that you can enjoy a family activity together like this." said Dad

"We have a story or two to tell you about camping."

"I'll start us off." said Mum

"In 1993, Dad, Olivia, Rebecca and I, went camping at Lower Glenelg National Park… nearly four and a half hours from Melbourne."

"We took out our tents… set them up on a big site and stayed there for a week."

"On the second day Dad and I went swimming in the Glenelg River… while Olivia and Rebecca went kayaking."

"Later, we went on a walk, where Olivia spotted a kangaroo bouncing past us."

"It stopped for a moment, to look at us and I took a photo of it."

"The kangaroo had a joey in her pouch…it was so cute."

"Dad spotted a koala up a tall tree chewing on some gum leaves… we couldn't resist taking a photo of him for our camping album."

"We had a campfire and cooked marshmallows… just as we are doing now…then we told funny stories."

"On the third day Dad and I did the kayaking… while Olivia and Rebecca went swimming in the morning."

"We drove into town to get our lunch at a fish and chip shop."

"We had tried fishing for our lunch but we didn't catch much… we had fun regardless."

"On the fifth night Olivia was snoring so loudly, that Dad, Rebecca and I, carried her tent to the Glenelg riverside, tied the tent up to a low branch and left it there overnight."

"The next day Olivia found out what we did…we watched as she stepped out of the tent and straight into the water!"

"We were all rolling around the ground, laughing hysterically, we high-fived each other, it was a good trick!" said Mum

"Good story, Mum."

"You had a good time at Glenelg!"

"I've a got a camp story too it was in 1990." Dad added

"Mum, Olivia, Rebecca and I, went camping at a Melbourne camping ground."

"It was raining when we arrived there, Mikayla, Olivia and Rebecca got soaked while driving…but I didn't."

"I was listening to Rick Astley on the radio…feeling smug all the way."

"When I got there, Mum, Olivia and Rebecca chased me around the campground for ten minutes, eventually tackling me to the ground and holding me in a headlock, leglock and wristlock!"

"We've got you now Daniel." Mikayla said

"Torture!" I cried
"That's not fair!"
"They wouldn't let go of me until I agreed to fix their car which was leaking!"
"On the second night we drove into town to a local hotel bar to attend a comedy night."
"We had plenty of laughs, then when a comedy group that was expected didn't turn up, we filled in for them."
"We told a few story jokes and I finished off the act, by putting a cream-pie in Olivia's face!"
"Another day, we went shopping for some mementos in town."
"I bought a nice necklace for Mum and she bought a statue for Olivia, although it was a bit heavy."
"Olivia bought a box of fragrance soaps for Rebecca, and she bought a couple of cricket books for me."
"We had fun shopping together, and in the evening, we had dinner at our favourite Italian restaurant."
"Later, Olivia and I, got our guitars and sang a few covers of pop songs around the campfire, it was good times and fun together, back then!" said Dad, reminiscing
"That was a very good story, Dad."
"Cassie, would you like to have Olivia and Rebecca come camping with us next time?" asked Dad
"I'll think about that and get back to you with an answer."
We continued cooking marshmallows and Mum made a phone call to Caroline Williams.

Caroline Williams has known Mum for many years, her husband Andrew gets along well with Dad, and their daughter Jenna, became my first official friend. We met earlier in the year at the Melbourne Special Centre for autistic girls or (MSC). They have been staying in Shepparton, about an hour from where we are. They were getting ready to watch a movie when Caroline received the call from Mum.

"Hello, Caroline."
"Guess where we are?" says Mum, down the phone
"That's right... we are in Echuca!"
"We're camping at the moment and so far, so good!" Mum added
"How is your week's holiday in Shepparton going?" I heard Mum ask Caroline
"We shall be in Echuca for about a week too!" she added
"We're planning to go horse riding at the Billabong Ranch Adventure Park in a couple of days, time."
"It will be Cassie's first time, horse-riding." said Mum
"I know that you and Andrew have loved horse riding for years, and it's Jenna's thing too!" said Mum, smiling down the phone
Mum switched her phone to speaker phone so that we could all listen to the conversation.
"She would like to work with horses one day." Caroline said
"She would also like to work with 'special needs' people and horses as well." she added
"Would you like to come horse-riding with us later in the week?" asked Mum
"We would love to!" Caroline said happily
"We'll get our gear and meet you there." she added
"Great!"
"See you in a couple of days."
"We'll have lots of fun." said Mum, happily
It was an hour later that we went back to our tents to get some sleep.
"Night, Cassie." said Dad
"Night, Dad." I replied

"Night Mum." I said

"Night sweetie... Love you." replied Mum

"Love you too, Mum."

I got changed into my blue pyjamas and settled into my sleeping bag, it's made from a combination of cotton and silk, which I am comfortable with...I tolerate cotton fairly well. It feels so warm and snug like my bed at home. I stare up at the ceiling of my tent for a few minutes... *'Even though it's only the first day... camping is fun so far... sleeping under the stars seems good...marshmallows on a campfire... swimming in the river... walking through the bush... what more could you want?'* I thought

Then I drifted off to sleep dreaming of riding a horse in the wind along the beach. It's one of my favourite dreams...I still remember it today.

When we woke up the next morning, we decided to go for an early morning swim before we had breakfast. We planned to do some shopping later, but when we looked up the shops in the local area on our phones, we found there weren't many big stores just a pet store and a clothing shop.

"Looks like we need to go to Shepparton to do our shopping."

"They have some good stores there." said Mum

"Shepparton it is then Mum!" I said

"Don't forget to take your wallet with you...you will need that for shopping!" laughed Dad

It took us an hour to reach Shepparton, it's amazing, a big city, though not as big as Melbourne of course.

"I'll look up the shops to see where they are located." said Mum

"I've found several interesting ones."

"We can go shopping for a couple of hours."

"I would like to buy a music CD... a pop music CD." I said

"I'm sure we can do that."

"We'll find a good music store and you can choose something there." said Dad

"Cassie, there's a JB Hi-Fi store."

"You can choose your music CD there." Mum added

"There's also a Collins bookstore."

"I do love a good read, particularly the 'Jo Nesbo' books." said Dad

"You do love your mystery books, dear."

"I like a nice romance book, or a story joke book!" said Mum

"You sure love your romance and humour."

"A bit of spice in the bedroom eh?" said Dad, winking at Mum

"I'll be in another room la-la-la-ing, with my hands over my ears, so that I hear NOTHING!" I said, giving Dad the look!

"Er... right... let's go shopping." said Dad, getting a little flustered

"I'm with you dear." followed Mum, looking slightly pinker than before

We started at JB Hi-Fi, there were so many genres and artists to choose from. I looked up the pop section and there was 'Quirky Service', (a family band that Mum and Dad were in from 1985-1994).

Currently, my three aunts, Kate, Nicole and Amelia, plus my uncle Adam, make up the line-up in the band. Kate has mild autism Nicole has high functioning autism and Amelia has Asperger's. Adam, who is married to Kate, has mild autism, they have two autistic children a daughter and a son, Eve and John, who both have savant syndrome.

Their thirteenth album was named 'Blizzard Blast', the cover featured Kate, Nicole, Amelia and Adam in their coloured gear, skiing at Mount Buffalo. They were having a fun time holidaying in Mount Buffalo, when their album was released in May 2011. Currently, they are touring North America, Europe, Australia and New Zealand to promote 'Blizzard Blast'.

We may not see them during our road trip, but who knows? We may be 'special guests' at one of their concerts if we are lucky!

## Disc One:

| Song Title/Track | Lead Vocals | Genre | Composer/s |
|---|---|---|---|
| Blizzard Blast | Kate White | Eurodance | K.White. A.Hunter. N.White. A. Hunter |
| Mountain High | Kate White | Eurodance | K.White. A.Hunter. N.White. A.Hunter |
| Ice World | Kate White and Adam Hunter | Bubblegum Dance/ Eurodance | K.White. A.Hunter N.White. A.Hunter |
| Snowy Night | Kate White | Dance | K.White. A.Hunter N.White. A.Hunter |
| Blissful Winter | Nicole White | Dance | K.White. A. Hunter N.White. A. Hunter |
| Snow Love | Amelia Hunter | Dance-Pop | K.White. A. Hunter N. White. A.Hunter |
| Ice Skate Blitz | Kate White Adam Hunter | Bubblegum Dance/ Eurodance | K.White. A. Hunter N. White. A.Hunter |
| Yeti | Kate White Adam Hunter | Bubblegum Dance/ Eurodance | K.White. A. Hunter N. White. A.Hunter |
| Snow Girl | Kate White | Dance-Pop/ Europop | K.White. A.Hunter N.White. A.Hunter |
| Angel of the Snow | Kate White | Eurodance | K.White. A.Hunter N.White. A.Hunter |
| Hailstone | Adam White | Europop | K.White. A.Hunter N.White. A.Hunter |
| Fireplace | Adam White | Eurodance | K.White. A.Hunter N.White. A.Hunter |

## Disc Two:

| Song Title/Track | Lead Vocals | Genre | Original Artist |
|---|---|---|---|
| 1. Koko Soko | Kate White Amelia Hunter | Bubblegum Dance | Smile.dk (Sweden) |
| 2. Hummingbird | Kate White Amelia Hunter | Bubblegum Dance | Smile.dk (Sweden) |
| 3. Tomoe | Kate White Amelia Hunter | Bubblegum Dance | Smile.dk (Sweden) |
| 4. Summer Party | Kate White Amelia Hunter | Bubblegum Dance/Eurodance | Smile.dk (Sweden) |
| 5. It's in Your Melody | Kate White Amelia Hunter | Bubblegum Dance | Smile.dk (Sweden) |
| 6. Doki, Doki | Kate White Nicole White | Bubblegum Dance | Smile.dk (Sweden) |
| 7. Dragonfly | KateWhite Adam Hunter Nicole White Amelia Hunter | Pop, Bubblegum Dance | Cherona (Germany) |
| 8. Live Your Dream | Kate White. Adam Hunter, Nicole White Amelia Hunter | Pop, Bubblegum Dance | Befour (Germany) |
| 9. Discotheque | Kate White, Adam Hunter, Nicole White Amelia Hunter | Pop, Bubblegum Dance | Cherona (Germany) |
| 10. Hurry Up (SOS) | Kate White, Adam Hunter, Nicole White Amelia Hunter | Pop, Bubblegum Dance | Cherona (Germany) |
| 11. You're My Best Friend | Kate White | Bubblegum Dance | Melanie |
| 12. Lucky Number | Kate White, Nicole White and Amelia Hunter | Bubblegum Dance | Three (Sweden) |

Mum and Dad were looking for music CD's they wanted to buy. Dad's favourite artists include Rick Astley, The Wolverines, John Farnham, Elton John, John Williamson, Roy Orbison and A-ha. He found a recently released Wolverines Album called 'Good Ol' Boys' from their earlier days, it was a good find!

'Great!... the Wolverines Good Ol' Boys...this could be good... Dad is a big fan too he might like to hear this one! If there's another copy, I might grab one for him too!' Dad thought

Mum was looking for a great music CD as well. She loves Madonna, Whitney Houston, Fleetwood Mac, Kate Ceberano, The Go-Go's, The Cockroaches and Kylie Minogue! She was surprised to find 'Aphrodite'... Kylie's eleventh studio album, which was released in 2010.

'Wow!... Kylie's at it again with the shades of blue... what a nice dress that is.... she is one pop diva... so pretty with that blond hair! I'll definitely enjoy this when I get it and Cassie might like it as well.' Mikayla thought

I was looking for another music CD and guess what I saw? A 'Shyness' CD! Shyness was Quirky Service's original band name, from 1982-1984. The cover art featured Mum, Dad, Olivia and Rebecca in four squares playing their instruments. Shyness was descriptive of Mum, Dad, Olivia and Rebecca's personalities at the time.

They still managed to perform gigs including birthday parties and at local clubs, when they became 'Quirky Service' in January 1985 they made worldwide music history and sold approximately one hundred and ninety-five million records. They have currently sold one hundred and seventy-four million records since reforming in 1998.

We met up near the counter to show our purchases to each other.

"Cassie, what music CD have you chosen?" asked Mum

"I chose 'Quirky Service's 'Blizzard Blast'... it's a very wintery album." I said

"Very good choice, Cassie!" said Mum, laughing

"I chose the Wolverines 'Good ol' Boys', it's a rock/country album."

"My Dad would love it too!" said Dad

"I have decided on Kylie Minogue's 'Aphrodite'!"

"I'm looking forward to listening to it." Mum said

"You might enjoy it as well, Cassie." she added

"I definitely would Mum!"

"I have found a rare music CD."

"It may be a remastered copy or newly re-released." I said, holding up the Shyness CD

Mum and Dad were surprised and amazed that I had found a rare Shyness CD from 1983!

I was surprised too, when I found it!

"Cassie!"

"That's a Shyness CD!"

"How lucky was that!"

"You were so lucky to find one of those still around!" said Dad, excitedly

"That's me, Dad, Olivia and Rebecca on that album!"

"We were thirteen years old when that album was released in 1983!" said Mum, as excited as Dad

"That's so great!"

"That's the rarest find I will ever make!" I said, laughing happily

"Let's go and buy our CD's."

"We can listen to them when we leave Echuca." Dad said, grinning

We walked up to the counter and I gave the Shyness CD that I had found, to the cashier.

"Wow!"

"You were very fortunate to find that CD!"

"It contains eight songs plus four extra ones that were recorded in 1982, but didn't make the final cut onto the original album."

"It was released in 1983 in Australia only... it reached number forty on the Australian Album Charts and the single 'Shy' reached number twenty-nine... on the Australian Singles Charts."

"It was re-released earlier this year by popular demand... it will be released worldwide in three weeks' time." said the cashier

"This is so great...our family and friends will be amazed when we show them this rare CD!" I said

1. Shy* (D.Bontel. M.Macdonald. O.Bontel. R.Macdonald)
2. Friends (D.Bontel. M.Macdonald. O.Bontel. R.Macdonald)
3. Family (D.Bontel. M.Macdonald. O.Bontel. R.Macdonald)
4. Beach (O.Bontel)
5. Star* (D.Bontel)
6. Blue Sky (D.Bontel)
7. Sun (D.Bontel)

8. Paradise *(M.Macdonald)
9. Love (D.Bontel. M.Macdonald)
10. Winter Snow (M.Macdonald. R.Macdonald)
11. Saturday* (D.Bontel. M.Macdonald. O.Bontel. R.Macdonald)
12. Night City (D.Bontel. M.Macdonald. O.Bontel. R.Macdonald)

The cover art features Mum, Dad, Olivia and Rebecca playing their instruments on a background of blue sky with a yellow sun shining overhead... I think it's well designed and photographed. It's a great cover... the original cover in 1983 had a different background... featuring a night sky with stars and moons.

After we paid for our CD's, we drove around looking for somewhere to have dinner. There was a Thai restaurant, a Chinese restaurant, and a restaurant called 'The Teller Collective'. We decided to dine at the Chinese restaurant... but I've never been inside one before...I dread the thought of trying the 'strange' food. I decide to give the Chinese food a try...I will need to try foreign cuisine if I want to travel to other countries around the world!

We got changed to go out for our evening meal. Mum and I were in coloured dresses of yellow and blue... Dad was wearing his green suit.

When we arrived at the Chinese restaurant, I put my headphones on just in case of any loud noises. We were shown to the table that we had booked and were given our menus.

The menus were written in English and Chinese... I looked at the menu... some of the dishes from the Chef's suggestions... to soups... noodles... seafood... also Malaysian and Thai dishes... are full of vegetables and nuts!

*'Yuck!... I might have trouble eating those dishes... they are full of vegetables and nuts... I might try one of the Australian dishes... but most of them seem like children's meals.... I have no choice but to try one of the other dishes'* I thought, concerned

"Cassie, what would you like to choose?" asked Mum

"I'll choose San Choi Bow, from the Chef's Suggestions." I said

"Good choice, Cassie."

"That 'Duck with Pineapple' looks good!"

"I think I'll try it." said Mum

"I'll try the fillet steak with plum sauce."

"It looks like a pretty tasty combo." Dad licked his lips

When our meals arrived, Mum and Dad started to eat. I was reluctant to eat mine... because of the vegetables and nuts that I saw.

"Cassie?"

"What's wrong?" queried Mum

"There are vegetables and chestnuts in that San Choi Bow."

"I'm not sure if I can eat it."

"It looks awful to me." I said, nervously

"You'll enjoy it once you try it." said Dad, encouragingly

"You can try some, Cassie... it's fine if you can't manage to eat all of it."

I was a little bit reluctant, but I decided to give the San Choi Bow a go! I decided to start eating the nuts and the chicken, which are the main ingredients. The chicken was tasty and the nuts were very good after all. Mum and Dad could see that I was starting to enjoy the meal.

Next, I tried the vegetables... slowly I put my fork towards one and ate it. It was delicious... so delicious... that I ate all the vegetables on the plate! I can't believe I've done it! I've have eaten all my vegetables...it's been such a long time.

A battle every day... for many years...has now ended in the Chinese restaurant! I love these vegetables! I will eat more of them every day and I will become healthier and give myself more energy and strength.

"Well done, Cassie!"

"You have done it!"

"How were the vegetables?" asks Mum

"They were pretty tasty after all... I loved them!" I said

"We're so proud of you of darling for trying something new!"

"Those vegetables will bring you good health." said Mum

"Thanks for encouraging me to eat them."

"Well done, darling." said Dad

"Thanks, Dad." I grinned, happily

"Cassie, for being adventurous with your food we will let you choose the next activity."

"An experience perhaps?" Mum mused

"Or maybe a visit to a festival?" Dad added

They both sounded like great choices but eventually I decided. It's going to be an awesome activity!

"Mum, Dad... I have decided the activity that I want to experience...I choose the Sydney Harbour Bridge Climb!" I said, excitedly

"Wow!"

"That's a great choice, Cassie."

"Are you sure?" asked Mum

"I'm sure."

"I know it's a long way to reach the top, and it's very high." I said, a little nervously

"We can help you through that, Cassie."

"There would also be guides there helping you too." said Dad

"You don't have to make a decision today... you can think it over." Mum said, reassuringly

A couple of days later, the sun was shining through my tent like it does through my bedroom window most days. It felt so good to feel the sun, I rolled out of my sleeping bag, quickly got dressed, and strolled over to Mum and Dad's tent where they were already up and making preparations for breakfast.

"Morning, Cassie."

"How did you sleep?" asked Mum

"I slept really well, thanks."

"How about you two?" I asked

"Mostly well, thank you."

"Apart from your Mum 'snoring' for some of the night!" said Dad, gesturing to Mum

"I do not snore!"

"It's Dad that usually does." said Mum, cheekily

"I don't!"

"I heard you loud and clear!" stated Dad

"I heard it loud and clear too!"

"You snore like an elephant!" I said, grinning

"Oh!"

"Do I?!"
"I definitely do not!"
"How many times do I have to tell you that?" said Mum, indignantly
"I'll consider getting out a tape recorder... to record 'someone not snoring'... next time I hear it!"
"I'll have it ready to record the proof!" said Dad, adamantly
"Yeah, right."
"That won't be happening."
"Nice try." said Mum, laughing off Dad's idea
"Let's get some breakfast."
"We're going horse-riding today!"
"We need to keep our strength up for the ride." said Dad, winking at me
"I second that Dad... lead me to the food!" I said, winking back at him whilst Mum rolled her eyes at us both

# Chapter Five
# Horse Riding

"Are you excited about the horse-riding tour Cassie?" asked Mum
"Yes, I am!"
"I can't wait for it!"
"I'm so excited... not only to see the horses but to ride on one for the first time!" I exclaimed
"That's very good, darling."
"We can ride with you... Jenna, Caroline and Andrew as well."
"Won't it be fun riding with our friends?" said Dad
"Yes, so much fun!"
"We will be able to catch up with them and talk to each other, as we ride along." I said, joyfully
After we had our breakfast, we drove to Billabong Ranch Adventure Park, where we are to meet the horses and the tour operators. When we got there, we saw the owner tending to the horses in a field next to the ranch. Jenna, Caroline and Andrew were there, waiting for us. We all hugged each other.
"Hello, we never expected to be doing this today, when you called the other day!" said Caroline, smiling
"It was a surprise finding out you were in the same area!"
"We are going to have such fun riding together!" said Mum, excitedly
"It's the first time we will try it together as a family."
"It's good for us to get together, the first time since Cassie and Jenna met in February." Andrew commented
"The horses build trust with us as we build trust with them." stated Jenna
"Cassie, don't worry if you are feeling nervous about the horses."
"The owner will help you to feel safe and confident." she added
"I sure hope so, Jenna." I replied, warily
We walked up the paddock to meet the owner and her horses.
"Hello."
"My name is Jeanette Sanders, the current owner of the Billabong Ranch Adventure Park."
"Hi, Jeanette."
"I'm Daniel Bontel." said Dad, shaking the owner's hand
"I'm Mikayla Bontel." said Mum, also shaking the owner's hand
"I'm Cassie Bontel." I replied
"Are you here for the horse-riding tour?" she asked
"We are indeed!"
"I know Caroline, Andrew and Jenna... I have met them several times." Jeanette added

"Nice horses... we see you have been looking after them." said Mum

"Thank you."

"These are some of the horses that Billabong Ranch Adventure Park uses... they are very well-behaved." said Jeanette

"Cassie, I hope you will enjoy riding for the first time."

"Cassie is a 'honeybun'... she even has a blue headband to match her outfit." said Mum, fondly

"Mum!"

"How embarrassing!"

"Not in front of Jeanette and Jenna too!" I said, cringing and face-palming myself I went red with embarrassment

Dad tried not to laugh, so did the owner... and I'm pretty sure the horses nearby were laughing! Caroline, Andrew and Jenna thought it was very amusing too!

"Sorry sweetie!" said Mum

"Your Mum is funny." said Jeanette, smiling

"She embarrasses me in public... especially when my mates are around." I muttered

"That's what Mums' and Dads' do!" replied Jeanette, laughing

"My two kids say the same thing about me!"

"I have loved horses since I was three years old." I said

"Have you?"

"I love watching them in their paddocks."

"For many years I preferred to watch, rather than ride."

"When someone asked me if I would like to go for a ride on one I would refuse."

"I was frightened of falling off... or feared that I might get trampled."

"Now that I am older, I have talked with Mum and Dad about feeling confident enough to try riding." I explained to Jeanette

"That's wonderful." she replied

"What lovely horses you've got."

"Do they all have names?" I asked

"Yes, they do."

"I have seven horses, there is Star, Moon, Sun, Cloud, Sky, Darkness and Storm." said Jeanette

"Could I feed one of them a carrot... if that's okay with you?" I asked

"Yes, of course you can."

"I'll bring Sun over to meet you." said Jeanette

Sun is coloured a golden brown with a long silver mane. He's so cute, with those eyes of his. I got out a carrot, broke it into big chunks and put it on the flat of my palm, as Jeanette had shown me. I keep my palm as flat as possible as Sun 'snuffled' up the carrot chunks and chewed them. His nose was soft and velvety and his whiskers tickle my hand.

"Who's a handsome horse then?" I said

Then I did a funny thing... I gently put my hands on either side of his head and kissed him on his 'velvety' nose! Mum and Dad laughed and so did Jeanette. I laughed as well and Caroline, Andrew and Jenna laughed too!

"You are so funny Cassie."

"Kissing a horse!"

"Hilarious." said Mum, laughing

She had managed to capture that funny moment with her camera!
"Cassie, I've never in my life seen you kissing a horse before!"
"It was very unexpected." said Dad, smiling
"I agree." laughed Jeanette
"I've done many weird things in sixteen years... but that seemed quite natural to me."
"I must say I quite enjoyed it." I laughed
"Whatever next?" laughed Jenna
"Cassie and Jenna are always laughing together!" smiled Caroline
"What funny thing will Cassie do next?" Andrew asked
We had just composed ourselves when something loud happened. Sun let go a big one!
The smell was overpowering...it was almost like a 'stink bomb' going off!
"Oh, phwoar!"
"That's so gross!" I gagged
"Whatever has he been eating!" said Mum, gasping for fresh air
"It's worse than a rubbish tip!" said Dad, grimacing
"Strewth!"
"It's more like a compost bin in the middle of summer!" said Andrew, covering his nose
"EEW!"
"That smells worse than rotting fruit." said Caroline, taking big gulps of fresh air
"Eurgh!"
"My room never smells that bad... like a smelly stink bomb has gone off!" said Jenna, disgustedly
Mum, Dad, Caroline, Andrew, Jenna and I, had to use our hands to cover our noses, or we would be overwhelmed by the smell. We race over to the ranch to get away from it and breathe clean fresh air again.
"Sorry about that... Sun can be a little cheeky sometimes." said Jeanette smiling
"What a way to start our horse-riding trail ride, we haven't even got on yet!" said Dad, grinning
"Sun, Moon, Star and Cloud, are ready to go!" Jeanette announced
"So are we."
"Jeanette, can we talk to you for a few minutes?" asked Mum
"Sure." Jeanette replied
"Cassie, we're going to talk to Jeanette for a few minutes."
"Look around, but don't touch anything... ok?" Dad said
"I won't Dad." I replied
"Jenna, can you go with Cassie?"
"You can choose your snacks with her."
"Yes, Mum."
"I'll go with Cassie." Jenna said
"There are several snack foods here."
"You can buy some with your pocket money." Jeanette smiled
"Thanks, Jeanette." I replied
Mum, Dad and Jeanette, went to the field to talk... while Jenna and I are thinking about which snacks to buy.
"Our daughter, Cassie has a condition called mild autism and she also has anxiety."
"She's never ridden a horse before."
"Can you please teach her the basics... so that she can gain confidence?"

"If she becomes anxious… get her to use her anxiety techniques… she will tell you when she needs a break."

"Let her have five or ten minutes, then she will feel calmer and be ready to continue the ride." Mikayla gave instructions to Jeanette

"Cassie loves nature… so if you can teach her about Echuca's flora and fauna as we go along… it will help to keep her interest and give her information as we ride."

"Hopefully, Cassie will enjoy herself and will want to ride again after today's trail ride." Daniel added

"I've taken special-needs children on rides before and I'm sure that Cassie will enjoy herself… especially as she has her friend Jenna along to share the experience with." smiled Jeanette

I couldn't make out what they were saying, except, "tism."

"Cassie, are you all right?" asked Jenna

"I'm all right, thanks, Jenna."

"Just a bit suspicious about "tism" that's all." I said

"I'm fine with that."

"I'm sure you will be all right."

"I had that talk a year before… I always understood why I'm different…I accepted it as a gift."

"If Daniel and Mikayla ask you questions about it…take your time and do your best to answer them…ask them questions if you're unsure." said Jenna

"Thanks for that advice, Jenna."

"I will think about it later." I replied

"Whenever you're ready."

"Let's go choose those snacks!" said Jenna, smiling

I was unsure about when 'the talk' will happen… but I didn't want to have it just yet… Jenna and I have got snacks to choose! After that, we went outside to where Mum, Dad, Caroline, Andrew and Jeanette were waiting for us.

"Are you ready to ride, Cassie?" asked Jeanette

"Yes, I am, Jeanette."

"I'm ready to ride!" I said

"Good."

"You can choose to do the bush and creek trail ride worth seventy dollars… the Goulburn river ride worth one hundred and twenty dollars…or the Goulburn Murray and river ride worth one hundred and ninety dollars… there is also the Winery ride worth two hundred and thirty dollars."

"We choose the Goulburn River ride, please." said Mum

We paid the money and put on the safety riding helmets provided to us. We are wearing fully enclosed shoes, long pants and shirts, so we are prepared for our long trek. Mum was riding Star, my mount was Moon, Dad was seated on Cloud, Jeanette had Sun as her horse, Caroline was on Storm, Sky was Andrew's mount and Jenna's ride was Darkness.

Jeanette taught me the basic skills before we left, such as how to hold the reins, where to put my feet in the stirrups and some simple commands, the horses we were riding were all very experienced riding horses, used to having all kinds of people on them from non-riders to experienced hands. We were now ready to get started, I looked up at the sky, grey clouds were hovering above. We may not get good weather all the way, but I hope it holds up!

"Excuse me, Jeanette."

"There are grey clouds in the sky… if it rains… what will we do?" I asked, nervously

"We will keep going and keep our horses steady, they are very used to all kinds of weather." said Jeanette
"I have some plastic ponchos we can use if we do encounter rain." she added
I was relieved to hear that as we started off.
"Cassie, have you been to Echuca before?" asked Jeanette
"This is my first time in Echuca, Jeanette."
"I'm enjoying it so far... we are camping here for a few days." I said
"Do you like camping?" Jeanette asked
"I love it!"
"I originally became upset because it reminded me of a horrible memory, but I opened up to Mum and Dad about it...it's making camping much easier for me this time." I said
"That's brave of you, Cassie." Jeanette replied
"Cassie's opening up more to us since we started our road trip."
"Becoming braver over the past several months." said Mum, proudly
"Cassie's an inspiration to both of us... and our families too." Dad added
"Jenna... I hear you are four times Australian horse-riding champion... two times world champion... and have won many ribbons."
"What's the secret to your success?" asked Jeanette
"The secret to my success with horse riding... is confidence, patience and persistence."
"They are the three main keys to a successful horse-riding championship." said Jenna
"I hope you will continue to win many more championships and work with horses and special needs children one day." Jeanette, smiled
"I have been destined for that path since I started riding, at the age of seven." said Jenna
"She was born to ride since we took her to a horse-riding show in Melbourne, she tried the basics... then soon enough she was hooked!"
"We were so proud of her winning her first horse riding championship in Australia, and then winning the two World Championships in New York in 2009 and London in 2010." said Caroline, smiling proudly
"Caroline and I, took part in horse riding championships ourselves years ago, we won three Australian titles, two world titles and many ribbons between us."
"It's in the blood...our parents were horse riding champions in their day as well... they have two Australian titles between them."
"We are an equestrian family and proud of our heritage." beamed Andrew
"You must be the best riders that I know!" said Jeanette, laughing
"We always knew they were good!" said Mum, laughing too
One Hour later...
"Daniel and Mikayla, how long have you been riding?" asked Jeanette
"We have been riding since we were both six years old."
"Mikayla rides more often than I do... she loves it."
"Mikayla and I used to help out a bit with a special-needs kids ride, in the 90's."
"One horse I remember riding was called Maxine T."
"She was a beauty of a horse!" said Dad
"I remember riding one horse named Lewis Harry."
"He was a handsome horse I would feed him carrots."
"The kids loved riding on both those horses and a few others... with help, encouragement and support from Daniel and myself."

"Seeing the smiles on their faces made it worthwhile and made us smile too." said Mum

"Horses are wonderful animals."

"They make you smile when you see them, they are such lovely animals." said Jeanette

"Yes, they are, with their smooth manes and their beautiful eyes."

"I might try a horse club one day." I said

"You'll be able to help with the horses, like your Mum and Dad did years ago." said Jeanette

"I might be able to help out special kids like me with their riding."

"With gentle encouragement and support, they can feel confident about learning to ride a horse."

"We sometimes go to my Aunt Petra's house, where she has plenty of room for her two horses, Nuala and Edwina."

"I ride them every time I go there… I not only enjoy it… but I also get lots of practice for my horse-riding championships… and build up my confidence too!" said Jenna

"That is good practice for you."

"Keep it up for the next championship!" said Jeanette

"I will."

"I will practice good and hard!" said Jenna, with a smile

Sometime later, the rain poured down. Jeanette handed out the plastic ponchos, which did a good job of keeping us fairly dry underneath, of course our hands got wet holding the reins. We managed to keep our horses and ourselves steady on the track.

"Cassie, what do you think of Moon?" asked Jeanette

"She is very pretty… just like Mum!" I said

"She certainly is, with that blonde mane of hers."

"She's a popular horse for visitors and tourists to ride on." said Jeanette

"Star, Sun and Cloud are popular with children, aren't they?" asked Mum

"Yes, they love the children."

"We usually get first-timers to ride them, they enjoy it very much." said Jeanette

"This is such a good ride, the part we're riding through at the moment would make a fabulous backdrop for a music video." I said

"It sure would Cassie." Dad agreed

"Do you have Melbourne Cup sweepstake draws at your house?" asked Jeanette

"We do…we have had them ever since Daniel and I were about twelve."

"In 1993, we appeared at the Melbourne Cup in Flemington as VIP guests alongside our twin sisters."

"I was wearing a yellow dress with a diamond necklace and a yellow sapphire ring."

"Daniel was wearing a shiny green suit with a diamond tie pin on his tie."

"We both participated in fashions on the field that year, I won the 'Ladies Best Dressed' award and Daniel won the 'Men's award."

"We sang the national anthem… then to put the icing on the cake… Daniel tipped the winner… Vintage Crop!"

"We celebrated back at the family mansion, where Daniel and I and our twin sisters used to live." said Mum

"You must have had one of the best days of your lives!" said Jeanette

"Yes, it was a special day!"

"Since Cassie was ten years old, we have had Melbourne Cup draws with family and friends."

"One of us usually wins…on some years there have been two of us that have won."

"We sometimes watch the Melbourne Cup and have a celebration after the race." said Dad

"We also bet on the Melbourne Cup each year Caroline was the only winner out of our family in 1991." said Andrew

"She picked 'Let's Elope as her runner in the cup!"

"We had quite a party back then!" said Andrew, remembering

"I've been in the family and friends Melbourne Cup sweep draw since I was ten."

"I won in 2009 when I was fourteen, I collected two hundred dollars for my win!" Jenna said

After two hours riding, we reached the halfway point of our ride… it was time to break for lunch.

"How is everyone feeling." Jeanette asked, looking around at us all

"It was good to be on a horse again." said Mum, smiling happily

"It was awesome, I enjoyed riding on a horse once again too!" Dad said, grinning

"Cassie, did you enjoy your ride?" asked Jeanette

"It was really great!" I said

"I'm glad you enjoyed it."

"Well done for giving it a go!"

Jeanette turned to Caroline, Andrew and Jenna to see how they were feeling.

"No complaints from me!" Caroline smiled and the others nodded in agreement

We took our time on our lunch break stop to stretch our legs thoroughly, we also watered the horses and let them graze lightly, whilst we relaxed over lunch. When our leisurely lunch was finished, we re-saddled the horses and mounted for the return trip. We circled back and began the journey home to Billabong Ranch.

When we arrived back at the ranch, there were many large water puddles on the ground, from the heavy rainfalls during the day. Tired and ready for a nice hot bath, Mum, Dad and I prepared to dismount, unfortunately our legs were like rubber at the end of a hard day's ride. Combine that with slippery, muddy, wet ground… a recipe for disaster! As our feet touched the ground and we buckled at the knees, we slipped and landed in the mud!

We crumpled right in front of a group of European tourists, who thought it was all hilarious! How embarrassing was that? Mum, Dad and I were blushing crimson. Caroline, Andrew and Jenna laughed out loud. I noticed that one of the French tourists and his wife were filming it all on their video camera! They are probably going to show it to their families back home! When I looked up at Caroline, Andrew and Jenna… they had also taken their iPhones out and were busy 'snapping' too!

"Jenna… I hope you're not uploading those photos to our classmates on Facebook, Twitter or Instagram pages, are you?" I frowned

"I already did, Cassie!"

"You'll be more famous than ever now!"

"Ha-ha!" laughed Jenna

"Oh crap!"

"How embarrassing!" I groaned

"Oops!" said Mum

"Well that was a blunder!" said Dad

Every time we tried to get up, we kept slipping over… making everyone laugh even louder.

Eventually, we crawled out… wet… muddy… and red-faced as well.

"If a movie was being made called 'How to Make a Fool of Yourself' starring Cassie Bontel…this would be it!" I groaned

"So funny, though!" said Jeanette, laughing
"Yes... it was."
"Do you have a shower in the ranch, so we can get clean?" I asked
"Fortunately, I do!"
"Do you have clean clothes with you?" said Jeanette
"Fortunately, we do!"
"We always come prepared for times like these!" said Mum, grimacing
We showered and changed into our fresh clothes.
"Thanks Jeanette, for teaching me how to ride a horse."
"I enjoyed the ride very much and I feel much more confident." I told her
"That's great Cassie!" said Jeanette
"Another new activity undertaken... well done Cassie!" said Mum
"Thanks Mum and Dad, for helping me."
"How nice of you to say that, Cassie." Mum replied
"You are doing really well Cassie." said Dad
"Would you go for a horse ride again Cassie... if you had the chance?" Jeanette asked
"Yes, I would...I would love to do it again." I said
Before we left, Jenna showed me the photos she had taken of us in the mud. One comment said...
"Cassie is so hilarious, even when she is muddy!"
Another one...
"Cassie the mud princess!"
Another...
"Who's the next mud girl, Cousin Cassie!"
"I apologise for uploading the photos, I thought it might be funny and our classmates did too." said Jenna
"That's all right, Jenna."
"We can laugh about it now and later, when I finish the road trip." I said, screwing up my face
"It will probably go viral and I'll receive more than ten thousand views!"
"Who knows, you Mikayla and Daniel might appear on a TV show talking about it." said Jenna
"Maybe, Jenna, maybe."
"The horse-riding was fun, though."
"We had a good time!" I said
We said our goodbyes to Jenna, Caroline and Andrew, they returned to Shepparton and we drove back to our campsite.
"Cassie, well done for giving horse riding a go, you lasted out for four hours on a horse...that's pretty amazing!" Mum said
"We are proud of you... good job!" Dad said
We had a hearty dinner of sausages and mash. I didn't want the mash... but I ate the sausages they were good... especially as they were honey beef flavoured. We had marshmallows at the campfire like the night before and chatted about the amazing day we had.
"Cassie you started things off by kissing Sun!" said Mum, laughing
"You've done some strange, funny and weird things... this one was funny to see!" she added
"I suppose it was funny...but I didn't mind it at all." I said, thoughtfully
"Then after four hours in the saddle not surprisingly, we fell over when we got off and slipped up in the mud!"

"It was embarrassing at first, but we can laugh about it now." said Dad
"It's turning out to be the funniest camping trip I've ever been on!"
"I'm loving every minute of it." I said
"We're so glad you are, Cassie."
"We are having plenty of laughs as well and our bond as a family has definitely grown stronger since we started this road trip." Mum added
"We are inspired by our 'life lesson' family quote: 'Family is like music... some high notes... some low notes...still when put together... they make a beautiful song." Dad said
"I love that quote hanging in our lounge room at home, it inspires me." I said, happily
"For future generations too." Mum added
"Let's enjoy some marshmallows."
"Cassie, would you like to go for a walk tomorrow?" Dad asked
"I would love to."
"We might see a koala or a kangaroo if we're lucky."
"As we haven't started our tour yet, do you have any ideas about it?" Dad asked
"I've written down some possible cities and venues for us to perform in, I've also added a few charity events that we could do as well." I replied
Mum and Dad looked at the 'Bontel Family Tour' list I've written and they like my ideas.
"That's a good list Cassie, well planned!"
"We can do this...we just need to choose a starting point." said Dad
"I suggest Sydney." Mum interjected
"That's perfect!"
"We'll start our tour from there then." I agreed
"Let's eat these marshmallows!"
"They may be sticky... but oh so delicious!"
The next day in the middle of the morning Mum said.
"What can we do this afternoon?"
"Why don't we go kayaking on the Murray River?"
"It will be fun for us all." said Dad
A few hours later, after we had prepared our equipment, put on our lifejackets and picked up the kayak... we carried it to the riverbank. When we reached a point where we could put the kayak safely into the river... we climbed in... picked up our paddles and started to stroke through the water.
"Isn't it nice, Cassie?"
"Paddling in a kayak on the wide Murray river." said Mum
"It is nice."
"To tell the truth though I have never kayaked before." I remarked
"Why not, Cassie?" asked Dad
"I've never kayaked before because I feared I may fall out and drown... or not rise back to the surface!" I said
"That won't happen, Cassie."
"You've got your life jacket on and you are safe with us."
"The life jacket will keep you afloat." said Mum
We paddled for another half-hour, I could see trees on one side and camping grounds on the other. Despite being cold, the sun somehow managed to shine through the white clouds, it is a wonderful day so far and I'm having fun kayaking along the Murray River with Mum and Dad.

"Cassie, are you enjoying Echuca?" asks Dad

"I am!"

"It's a great place to be camping."

"We have had lots of fun."

"Horse riding was the best thing of all!" I said, enthusiastically

"Echuca is good too... getting back to nature and appreciating our beautiful landscapes." added Mum

"I love the fresh air of the countryside." Dad said

We were heading towards the riverbank getting ready to make land... when a speedboat roared by creating a wave. I only got time to glimpse the boat... before the wave sent us tumbling out of the kayak and into the water.

Splosh! Oh, dear.

Mikayla rose to the surface first and spat out some water.

"Pfft! What the flamin' heck was that?" said Mikayla, in a shocked voice

Daniel surfaced next, spitting out water as he broke the surface.

"Blah! I don't have a clue what happened just now!"

"It happened too fast to see anything!" Daniel said with a grimace

I popped up beside Mum and Dad.

"Ugh! the speedboat that 'swamped' us and caused us all fall out of the kayak... was a Polycraft 5.99 Frontier Centre Console." I said

"How do you know that, Cassie?" said Mum, amazed

"It was white and had a black stripe on the right side, it also had the word Polycraft on the same side." I said

"You were lucky to see and remember the details so well!"

"That's impressive!" said Dad, admiringly

"Well done, Cassie."

"Look at us... we are all soaking wet!"

"What a mess!"

"I think that's enough kayaking." Mum added

"Let's get out and carry our kayak back to our camp... we can leave it to dry near the tents." I said

"Good idea, Cassie."

"I think it's time to pack up our stuff and leave for the next destination tomorrow." said Dad

"I agree." Mum nodded

"Me too." I said

Mum, Dad and I, picked up the kayak and carried it all the way back to camp. Mum was at the front... Dad at the back and I was in the middle... it was a wet and uncomfortable walk... we were glad when we reached our tents!

We placed the wet kayak by the right side of the tent and left it to dry out... then we started drying ourselves off with towels. We got changed into warm, dry clothes and decided to go for a walk to warm us up before we prepared our dinner.

Having decided to leave for our next destination tomorrow... we needed to pack up everything we could tonight... just leaving our tents to be taken down and our bedding to be put in the car in the morning.

We had plenty of excitement in Echuca... as well as a couple of embarrassing moments!

I had a fun time though... and so did Mum and Dad!

# Chapter Six
# 'Margaret' and Rebecca

As we were driving the next day... something landed with a thud on our car roof.

"What was that?" Mum said

"It sounded like something fell on the roof." Dad replied

"It could be a small creature... it might possibly be injured and need help in some way." I said

We got out of our car to see what had made the noise. It gave us a bit of a fright with a loud thud! We looked on top of the roof and saw an injured magpie. I wonder what could be wrong with it?

"It's an injured magpie!"

"I wonder where it fell from?" said Dad.

"It may have been flying along and hit something." I replied

"The magpie's wing could be injured."

"We can't leave it here."

"We'll have to take it to the nearest vet... or wildlife centre... and get it treated." said Mum

"I'll get it down from the roof and sit it next to me in the car." I said

"Okay Cassie, be careful." Dad said

I carefully climbed on top of the car... gently lifted the stunned magpie... then slowly climbed down to the ground showing the magpie to Mum and Dad.

Mum and Dad looked at the magpie to see where it was injured.

"Yep, just what I thought!"

"The left wing is injured, looks like it needs vet treatment." said Mum

"Let's get in the car and drive to the nearest available vet." Dad said

He looked it up and found the nearest vet was in Shepparton. We drove to Shepparton and found our way to the vet clinic. However, when we arrived, we found the doors were shut with a note attached to them that read... 'The Shepparton Vet Clinic is closed due to relocation. Thank you for your patience and cooperation.'

"Blast!"

"The Shepparton Vet Clinic is being relocated."

"We might have to go to the Wangaratta clinic to get this magpie some help!" said Dad

"Luckily, we have our first-aid kit and some extra first aid supplies, that I can use for a small bird like this magpie."

"Cassie, can you get me the small bandages and some clean icy pop sticks from the first-aid kit?" Mum asked

"I'm on to it Mum!" I replied

I went to the back of the car, found the first-aid kit with the necessary supplies and took them back to Mum and Dad.

"Good."

"Cassie watch carefully and I will teach you how to splint the magpie's wing."

"Start by strapping the wing carefully using the popsicle sticks to keep the broken wing stable on both sides, then wrap the bandage around them firmly to keep it all in place."

"This will keep the magpie from moving it too much and avoid further injury to itself." Dad instructed

I did as Dad instructed gently and slowly, so as to not hurt the magpie even further.

"Good job, Cassie."

"Now you check the magpie over to make sure there aren't any other injuries or conditions before we move." Mum added

I checked over the magpie carefully and gently like I've seen on 'Bondi Vet'. There doesn't seem to be any other problems with the magpie. It's all good.

"I can see nothing else wrong with the magpie, apart from the broken wing." I said.

"Great."

"All we need now is a container to place the magpie in to get over the shock, a warm, dark, place."

"The magpie will not be likely to escape it can rest and recover." said Dad

"Also, we need either a perch or a branch for the magpie to sit comfortably on."

"Where will we find either of those!" said Mum.

"We might find a small one at the Wangaratta Pet and Hobby Store." I suggested

"Well, let's go!" Dad added

To our dismay when we got to the Wangaratta Vet Clinic it was closed as well! A large notice said

'The Wangaratta Vet Clinic is closed due to repairs. Thank you for your patience'.

"For goodness sake!"

"The Wangaratta Vet Clinic is closed for repairs!"

"Oh dear." I said, sighing

"We'll have to try the Wangaratta Pet and Hobby Store and see if they have any perches for this magpie." I said, feeling frustrated

"Yes, let's try that!" said Mum

We drove over to the Wangaratta Pet and Hobby Store.

"Could we give the magpie a name?" I asked

"Sure."

"What you do think would be a good name?" asked Dad

"Margaret the Magpie." I said

"That's a very nice name, Cassie."

"You named it after my grandmother." said Mum, smiling

We walked into the pet and hobby store.

"Hello!"

"Can I help you with anything?" asked the owner

"We would like a perch for an injured magpie that landed on our car roof." said Dad

"That's why we came here." Mum added

"I have several types for pet birds."

"Come this way." said the owner

There were perches for pet parrots, ones for budgerigars, and ones for cockatoos. We chose a nice perch for Margaret.

"Good choice, young lady." said the owner

We walked up to the counter and paid ten dollars for the perch we also purchased a container for twelve dollars. Then we went back to the car, placed Margaret on the perch inside the bird cage, and covered the cage with a cloth to keep it dim inside.

"Now we have to take Margaret to find another vet, if that's closed, we are going to have to decide what to do with her!" said Dad

I found a vet clinic in Wodonga on my phone.

"There is a Family Vet Centre in Wodonga." I said

"Well then, let's try that one." said Mum

When we arrived in Wodonga, we drove to the Family Vet Centre. We parked our car in the parking area and walked into the reception.

"Can I help you?" asked the receptionist

"We found an injured magpie a couple of hours ago and we wonder if the vet can help us?" Dad told the receptionist

"I see."

"Name please?" asks the receptionist

"Daniel Bontel." Dad said

"Mikayla Bontel." replied Mum

"Cassie Bontel." I said

"I thought I recognised you, I've been listening to your music, it adds a positive atmosphere to the centre." the receptionist smiled

"We use some of our songs to relax our clients at our massage therapy centre that we run in Melbourne." said Mum

"Please take a seat."

"The vet will see you very soon." she added

We sat down on the seats in the waiting room, there were a few other pets and their owners waiting too. I saw a 'posh' lady with her poodle, she was waiting to get her poodle's nails clipped. There was also a man whose budgerigar was poorly and off his food. A young boy and his Mum had bought in his pet parrot …for some reason his parrot had stopped talking…they hope the vet will get him talking again. I spoke to Margaret soothingly and said…

"It will be all right Margaret…the vet will help you to get well."

"Hopefully, the vet will release you back into the trees then Margaret."

"You've been a good patient since we found you." Dad added

"You will be in good hands." said Mum in a calming voice

Eight minutes later the receptionist said

"The vet will see Margaret now."

We walked into the vet's office with Margaret, where the vet introduced himself.

"I'm Dr John Parr, the vet here at Wodonga Family Vet Centre."

"You can call me Dr John." he added

"Nice to meet you Dr John."

"I'm Daniel Bontel." said Dad

"I'm Mikayla Bontel." said Mum

"I'm Cassie Bontel." I said

We all shook his hands, he seemed like a nice man and we hoped he could be helpful in treating Margaret.

"I hear you have an injured magpie."

"Would you like to show her to me?" asked Dr John

I uncovered the birdcage and took Margaret out, gently placing her on the examination table.

"We named her Margaret, after my grandmother who came from Scotland."

"Hmm... she has a broken wing... but that seems to be her only injury...it will take some time for that break to mend itself...but with rest and care she should make a full recovery."

"She fell onto our car roof when we were leaving Echuca, we've been caring for her, Mum and Dad taught me how to look after Margaret."

"Well you did very well, caring for her."

"I know a lady in Wodonga who cares for injured birds like Margaret."

"I'm sure she would love to help her." said Dr John

"We are staying in Wodonga overnight, so we can take Margaret to the lady for you." Dad said

"That would be lovely, come back tomorrow at midday."

"Hopefully, I will be a bit less busy then." Dr John smiled

"We'll be here to pick Margaret up at twelve noon then tomorrow."

"Thanks, Dr John." said Mum, gratefully

"See you then." Dr John smiled at us

We left Margaret in Dr John's capable hands, then drove to our hotel. I decided to go to the bathroom to wash my hands with hot water and soap after handling the magpie. Mum went to get out the Tim-Tam packet... only to find there aren't any left!

"Hey!"

"There's no Tim-tams left!"

"There were three left before... who ate them all?" asks Mum, suspiciously

She looked at Daniel.

"Wasn't me!" he said, shrugging his shoulders

"I didn't eat them." Dad said

"Well if it wasn't you dear, there's only one other person who could have eaten them!" says Mum, turning to look at me

I let out a giggle.

"Cassie!"

"I knew it was you all along!"

"Come out here!"

"No way!"

"No chance of that happening Mum!" I said, laughing

"Just you wait Cassie." said Mum darkly

"Cassie can be cheeky...she always is." said Dad

"Yes, she is...she is trouble... always trouble... but we love her all the same." said Mum, with a sigh

The next day, Mum, Dad and I, drove to the Wodonga Family Vet Centre to pick up Margaret. She's been in the good hands of Dr John, but she will be happy to see us again. We walked into the Vet Centre where the receptionist recognised us.

"You have come for Margaret, she's ready to be picked up Dr John is waiting to hand her over to you." she smiled

"Thank you." Dad said
We walked into Dr John's office where he was waiting for us.
"Margaret is ready, she will be happy to see you again." smiled Dr John
"How is she?" asked Mum
"She is fine, it will take a little while for her wing to heal, before she can make a full recovery."
"I'll get her for you."
Dr John carried Margaret over to us, she seems pleased to see us.
"Hello, Margaret."
"Good to see you again."
"We're going to take you to a nice lady who cares for small injured birds just like you."
"Isn't that great?" I said, stroking her head
"I'll give the lady's name and address to you." said Dr John
He handed it over to us, 'Valerie Kingston, 'Caring Bird', 11 Curtin Street.
"She sounds like a nice caring lady, who loves birds." said Mum
"It sounds like a great business too, doing something wonderful for the community." Dad said
"Margaret will be well looked after, it's Valerie's turn to take care of Margaret now." I said
"I hope Margaret does well with Valerie."
"You three have done well with her so far, I'm sure Valerie will keep up the good work she is a very experienced bird carer."
"Goodbye, Bontel family." Dr John waved, cheerily
"Bye, Dr John, and thanks for looking after Margaret." Dad replied
"My pleasure."
We drove to 11 Curtin St, where Valerie Kingston lived, walked up to her door and knocked on it.
"Margaret, you will be well looked after by Valerie, you will be safe with her and she will help you to get back into the flying spirit." I soothed
Valerie answered the door, saying...
"Hello, welcome to 'Caring Bird', where all small birds who are injured or sick receive tender loving care from me." Valerie added, smiling
"Hello Valerie, we're the Bontel Family and we've got a magpie for you take care of."
"Her name is Margaret." said Mum
I handed Margaret over to Valerie.
"She's lovely." said Valerie
"She is, we've been looking after her since she injured her wing near Echuca, we left her with Dr John yesterday, he suggested handing her over to you, for some TLC before you release her." I explained
"Well, sounds like you three have done a great job of looking after her so far, I admire you for that!"
"I'll be happy to look after her, until her wing has healed enough to fly again." said Valerie
"I'm normally busy with all these birds... but would you like a cup of tea?" asked Valerie
"Thanks for the offer, but no thank you."
"We are taking a road trip around Australia we need to get back on the road!" said Mum
"That's great, I wish you the best of luck for your trip." said Valerie, smiling at us
"Thank you, Valerie." I replied
We were walking back to our car when we heard a voice call out to us.
"I'll go and see who it is."
"I will call you two later." said Mum mysteriously, as off she went

I knew whose voice that was... very well! It was the voice of Rebecca Macdonald, (Mum's twin sister)!

They like to play their famous trick, it involves them wearing the same coloured clothes, (either pink or yellow), then one will chat to a visitor, while the other stays around the back doing something out of the way.

One will talk to the visitor for an hour or two, (pretending to be her twin), occasionally the other twin will creep around making sure not to be seen. Eventually, they both reveal themselves to the unsuspecting visitor who does a double-take after realising they have been the victim of the 'substitution' trick, causing Mum and Rebecca to roll around the floor with laughter!

It's their favourite trick... they play it on everyone... including Belinda and Darren... their friends... every family member they can...even their grandparents! It always makes me laugh no matter how many times I see it happen. Dad still gets fooled today... he nearly married Rebecca because of that trick!!!

I'm the only one who can tell them apart, (including their voices), I never get fooled!

This is what's going to happen!

Mum goes off to see that familiar voice... and Rebecca (who is that familiar voice) wearing a yellow shirt and pants... instead of her usual pink shirt and pants... will call us over to the house she is renting.

Thinking that Mum has rented the house for us... Dad will go inside with me and sit down in the lounge room... then Rebecca, (pretending to be Mum),will offer us tea and biscuits and make conversation with Dad for a couple of hours.

Mum will occasionally sneak by to peep, avoiding being seen by Dad. At the end of the prank Mum will reveal herself...Dad will do a double-take before realising he's been tricked once again...at which point Mum, Rebecca and I, will laugh like mad!

If at any time during the two hours Dad asks...

"Who was that?" I will tell him a 'made-up' person is doing something, to ward off suspicions.

This is going to be one great trick! Ha, ha, ha! I will say 'Mum' to Rebecca... until Mum reveals herself at the end of the trick! This is going to be so funny! Dad and I, walk into the house that 'Mikayla' has rented and sit down on the chairs.

The house is so beautiful, I see plenty of flower pictures on the walls, some of them inspired by the sixties ...the flower-power era.

"Would you two like some iced-biscuits that I made earlier?" asks Rebecca

"Yes please, dear."

"I would love some." says Dad

"Yes, Mum."

"I'd love some." I say

"Would you two like some tea?" said Rebecca

"Yes, please." I answer

"Daniel, would you like green tea?" Rebecca asks

"Yes, thanks." says Dad

"Cassie?"

"Yes, thank you."

"Coming right up." replies Rebecca

Rebecca goes into the kitchen where she gets the iced biscuits and green tea that Mum has been getting ready for her to take in. She comes into the lounge room with the biscuits and three teas on a tray and places them on the coffee table. We all get a biscuit each and a cup of tea, then we talk as a family together, I start recording the conversation with my video camera which I have kept out of sight of Dad.

This is what I recorded...
Rebecca says... "How are you, Daniel?"
Dad replies... "I'm fine thanks, dear."
Rebecca says... "How are you going, Cassie?"
I say... "I'm great, Mum."
Rebecca says... "Isn't Wodonga a great place?"
Dad replies... Yes, we can plan to stay for a day or two, have a look around, maybe eat at Hollywood's Pizza Bar!"
Rebecca says... "That seems like a nice place to eat, I do love my pizzas!"
I say... "Me too!"
Rebecca says... "What else shall we do in Wodonga?"
Dad replies... "We could visit the Botanical Gardens or the War Memorial whilst we are here."
Rebecca replies... "It sounds like we are going to have a busy time."
Rebecca says... "What do you think of the house I rented for us?"
Dad replies... "It has a sixties feel to it."
I add... "It feels like we are back in the flower power era!"
Rebecca replies... "It feels like I'm back in the flower power age too!"
"Do you like the painting of the koala?"
Dad replies... "Yes, I do, it's very well painted."
I say... "It's very Australian, with that koala in a tree!"
Mum says... "The woman who painted it, is a local artist, she mostly does Australian themes."
Dad said... "Wodonga has a good community feel to it, the people here help each other out, they have 'Meals on Wheels' delivery here, it's a good not-for-profit organization."
I reply... "I did 'Meals on Wheels' in Year nine at Melbourne High School and I loved it, I did it with an aide, I would love to do it again sometime soon."
Mum added... "I've been doing 'Meals on Wheels' since 1993, I love helping the elderly and people who cannot cook for themselves."
"For some people it is their only contact with the outside world."
"I chat for a few minutes it makes me feel happy and I appreciate helping my community."
"My grandmother is one of the recipients, I feel lucky to do volunteering work like this."
Dad said... "That green tea is very refreshing, I don't mind having another one."
I said... "Me too, these iced biscuits are delicious, I wouldn't mind having a couple of those too!"
Rebecca said... "I'll get them for both of you."
Rebecca went to the kitchen where she met Mum.
"This trick is going well isn't it?" says Mum, whispering
"It's going extremely well!"
"We should be able to get another hour out of this, before you reveal yourself!" said Rebecca, grinning
"Daniel will be fooled once again!" grinned Mum back at her
"You put the iced biscuits and green tea on the tray, and I'll carry on impersonating you!"
"This is such fun." giggled Rebecca
They both giggled together, shushed each other, then giggled again.
Rebecca returned with the tray of iced biscuits and green tea... the conversation continued.
Rebecca said... "Shall we visit Sydney on our road trip?"

Dad replied… "Yes definitely, your big sister Betty is there, we will want to see the new house she has moved to with Glenn and Jacinta!"

I added… "It's not far from here, we could visit them."

Rebecca said… "I'm sure we would have a great time."

Dad replied… "Of course, we would!" looking a little strangely at Rebecca

"I hear there's a fabulous chocolate shop in Beechworth, we might go and find it while we're there!"

Rebecca quickly added… "That would be a great shop to go to, I do love my chocolate, I have a very sweet tooth!"

I jumped in quickly

with… "I do too!"

"White chocolate is my favourite I love Cadbury's chocolate!"

Rebecca replied… "It's my favourite too!"

Dad said… "I like white chocolate occasionally, but mostly I prefer Cadbury's original milk chocolate."

Rebecca says… "There is some sort of tour at Albury/Wodonga, I think a half-day tour with Chelbec Tours and Charter… it's one of the options."

Dad replies… "Sounds promising, we may consider it."

I say… "That sounds historical, I might enjoy that."

Rebecca replies… "It's an historical region in Albury/Wodonga."

Dad adds… "It sure is, Victoria is a lovely state to be born in and grow up."

"I always enjoy looking up Australian history… all about each state… as well as other things… like quiz shows."

"I'll learn more about them, as we visit the other states of Australia!"

Mum added… "Victoria is such a great place to be, it's got history, good food, big buildings and a couple of gems to find!"

"I hope we find wonderful things in all the states."

Dad said… "I'm sure we will!"

"Cassie you can help me find each state's treasures!"

I replied… "Sure thing Dad!"

"I love helping our family out."

Another hour has passed and it is time for Mum to reveal herself! Dad is going to be shocked and red-faced when he finds out that he's been talking to Rebecca the entire time instead of Mum!

This is going to be hilarious I've got my iPhone ready to take a picture of it! Mum comes into the lounge room, just as Dad is drinking his cup of tea.

"Hello, darling. Why don't you come and join …" he starts before he does a double-take and spits out his tea!

Dad realises he has been tricked once again by Mum and Rebecca! Rebecca, Mum and I, are holding our breath, I stopped recording the conversation.

"Have I had too much green tea to drink… or am I seeing double?" asks Dad, his face turning bright red when he remembers calling Aunt Rebecca 'dear'!

Mum, Rebecca and I lose it, we are laughing hysterically! We are laughing so much that tears are running down our cheeks. We 'nailed' that 'switcheroo' brilliantly! OMG! Dad's face is a picture!

Dad is muttering under his breath

"I've been tricked again."

"I've been tricked again."

"Tricked by, (bleeping) Mikayla and Rebecca again!"

"I picked the wrong day to drink tea... I might need a few VB's after this, to live it down!"

"Why do I always fall for that trick!"

"I should know by now those twins are 'loopy' they sure had a big bowl of 'Fruit Loops' today!"

"C'mon Dad, you always see the funny side eventually." I cajole

"Mmmn." said Dad, not sounding very convinced

Rebecca sidled over to Dad and put her arm around his shoulder.

"Oh, but 'dear' you can't be cross with me, can you?" she said, looking up at Dad and fluttering her eyelashes, which made Dad crack up and Mum hold her belly because it was hurting so much from laughing!

"OK, OK, I know when I'm beaten!" said Dad, chuckling out loud

"It's funny!" laughs Dad

"Oh Daniel, your face!" said Mum, pointing at Dad's embarrassed look

"Don't you start!" said Dad, who can't help laughing at Mum

"Daniel, you are so funny!" gasps Rebecca, in between laughing and pointing

"You two always get me!" Dad points his finger accusingly, at Mum and Rebecca

"They always get you all right Dad!" I say, pointing at Dad and laughing as well

"Something tells me that they get a lot of help from you as well, these days Cassie!" he said, laughing and pointing right back at me

"Who me, Dad?"

"Don't know what you mean." I reply with a grin

"Because you are cheeky like the two of us, that's why!" laughed Mum

"We've played that trick on many people over the years, since we were little girls, including our family and friends, but Daniel is 'always' our favourite target!" smiled Rebecca

"Dad is easily fooled by you two when you wear the same coloured clothes, it doesn't matter where it takes place!" I said

"Yes, he is!" said Rebecca, with a smirk

She took a sideways look at Mum and she was grinning as well. It is clear to everyone that these two have not lost their enthusiasm for playing tricks!

Rebecca went to get changed back into her pink shirt and pants, she came back carrying a tray with more iced biscuits, but this time she had cans of lemonade instead of tea to drink.

"The lady who owns this house kindly stocked her fridge with lemonade for me when I agreed to rent her house." said Rebecca

"I'm renting the house from a woman who is a fan of my 'Rebecca' talk show."

"Whenever I take time off and someone fills in for me, I usually fly or drive back to Melbourne, where 'Rebecca' is filmed."

"I enjoy my work very much." she added

"Daniel, Cassie and I, watch your show regularly, we love it!" said Mum

"Thanks, it's a smash in the ratings!"

"Cassie, would you like to appear on my show?" asked Rebecca

"Oh, yes please."

"I would love to appear on 'Rebecca'." I said

"I can arrange that, Mikayla and Daniel can drive you there, then you can appear as a special guest." said Rebecca

"That would be great Rebecca!" I replied

"Daniel and Mikayla, I know you two have been married for twenty-one years now, but do you remember back in 1990 Daniel, when you nearly married me?!" said Rebecca

"OH HO!" I gasped, looking at Mum and Dad to see if that could be true!

"I'll tell you what happened… three weeks before Daniel got married to Mikayla he was at Dina's Diner with Mikayla."

"They were having a good time like young couples do, pop music was playing at Dina's Diner, which created a lovely atmosphere."

"Before dessert was ordered, Mikayla went to the bathroom and I came back out and sat in her place at the table, we ordered dessert, Daniel's was ice-cream sundae banana flavour with cherry on top, and mine was cheesecake with extra cream, they were delicious!"

"This is where the fun began, Mikayla came out of the room, (she and I were both wearing identical yellow outfits), Daniel was drinking his banana milkshake which ended up all over him, when he saw Mikayla wearing the same clothes!"

"Mikayla and I laughed, so did the whole restaurant who had been informed of the trick earlier in the evening, before Daniel came!" Rebecca grinned

We all laughed at that funny memory including Dad.

"Yes, I was red-faced when I realised it wasn't your Mother at the table after all!"

"A similar trick happened years ago, when Mikayla, Rebecca and I, were eighteen years old."

"This time I thought I was talking to Rebecca, when I was actually talking to Mikayla!"

"It happened at a party at our 'Quirky Service' headquarters in 1988, everyone was in on the act, including our families!" said Daniel

"It was one of the best we've ever done!" said Mum, sounding very pleased with herself

"Mikayla, I still remember the time you ran my pink pants up a flagpole on the world tour in 1989!" Rebecca remembered

"It was very embarrassing!"

"Yes, it was!"

"You had to climb up all the way to the top to get them back, while I filmed it all with my video camera!" said Mum, triumphantly

Dad and I giggled thinking about that!

"Well anyway, how are you three doing on your road trip?"

"I would love to hear what you have done so far." Rebecca said

"We spent some time at a beach, where Cassie made a new friend called Lucy, although she was shy at first, they soon had a wonderful time building sandcastles and chatting to each other." said Dad

"That's good for Cassie, she must've had a lovely time playing with Lucy." said Rebecca

"Cassie did… we also had ice-cream and Lucy made us laugh by telling us all the ice-cream flavours that she wanted… by counting on her fingers." Mum laughed

"How good for you Cassie making a new friend, I'm very happy to hear that." Rebecca smiled

"We went camping in Echuca, we went horse-riding with Caroline, Andrew and Jenna, we had great fun riding on a horse trail ride."

"We experienced quite a bit of rain on the ride, but we managed to reach the destination and back."

"It was Cassie's first time on a horse and we all helped her overcome her fear of riding."

"For many years, she would rather watch than get on one, but this ride changed all that!"

"Her horse was a mare, called Moon." said Dad

"What a lovely name for a mare, what was she like?" asked Rebecca

"She was beautiful like Mum." I said

"Ooo Mikayla."

"You are beautiful like a mare." said Rebecca, in a sing-song voice

"I certainly am!" said Mum, prancing around like a pony

"Instead of a silvery mane like Moon, mine is a black waterfall!" she said, flinging her hair over her shoulder like a model

We all laughed at Mum parading around like a champion show pony!

I told Aunt Rebecca all about Margaret.

"When we were leaving Echuca, a small creature landed on our car roof, it turned out to be a magpie that had an injured wing."

"Mum and Dad, showed me how to take care of it, we tried a couple of vets, then we found one in Wodonga and left it there overnight." I explained

"You did a good job caring for that magpie, one of our relatives in Sydney is a vet, she cares for all creatures great and small!" said Rebecca

"We also gave the magpie a name... Margaret...which is also our grandmother's name." said Mum

"That's right!" Rebecca smiled

"We picked her up from Dr John the next day and took her to a lady named Valerie."

"Valerie was in charge of a refuge caring for small and injured birds like magpies."

"We left her in the capable care of Valerie's hands."

"Margaret was very lucky that you found her and took her to Valerie's bird refuge, that was a very kind and caring thing to do." said Rebecca

"I learnt new skills as well, caring for a small bird." I said

"Yesterday, I watched you three falling over in the mud after your horse riding at the ranch!"

"It was so funny, when I resume my hosting on 'Rebecca, I'll show that clip to the audience and viewers!" laughs Rebecca

"Well thanks for the warning! said Dad

"It was embarrassing at first, but we can laugh about it now, we shan't forget it in a hurry!" he added

"Daniel, Cassie and I, are trying to find out what Dad is up to on his Dad's month holiday, but Mum won't tell me where he is going, no matter how much I ask her!" said Mum, sulkily

"Mum can be sneaky not telling us where Dad is, I hope you have luck finding him." said Rebecca

"I hope so too!" said Mum in a determined voice

"Good luck with that!"

"If you do find them, and what they are up to, record it and send it to my iPhone so I can show it on 'Rebecca'!"

"Don't forget to play a trick on them while you're at it, too!" giggled Rebecca naughtily

"I will!"

Daniel and Cassie will help me out, won't you? asked Mum, turning to look at us

"Yes, we will, Mum." I said

"We certainly can, dear." said Dad, glad not to be the one on the receiving end of the twins pranks this time!

"Also, we are looking for a family member whom we haven't seen for about twenty years." says Mum.

"Oh, that's very inspiring."

"Do you have any clues?" asked Rebecca

"I've only got one so far."

"He is a man!"

"Mum won't let me skype every day to get more clues either!"

I'm determined to find him, no matter how long it takes!"

"That will wipe the smile off Mum's face if I find him!" said Mum, gleefully

"Well I wish you the very best of luck with that!"

"When you find him, ring me and tell me all the good news." said Rebecca

"We sure will Rebecca."

"Thanks for letting us spend the afternoon with you, even though you two played that trick on me again!" said Dad, ruefully

"I enjoyed seeing you all… when I get time, I will bake something for you all… a cake… but I'm not telling you what flavour…that will be a surprise!" she added

"We can't wait to see what it is."

"We'll see you when we finish our road trip." I said

"Good luck, see you then!" Rebecca said

"Rebecca, can you please look up red-faced with embarrassment in the Australian dictionary for me, please?" said Dad, laughing

"I sure can!"

We all laughed… Dad will play a prank on Rebecca to get her back sometime.

He is bound to get Mum back as well!

I can't wait!!!

## Chapter Seven
# Beechworth and Wodonga

We left at ten the next morning for Beechworth. During the mid-1850's, it was 'gold rush' days in Victoria, it caused major growth as people from all over the world came to join in the rush for gold! Over sixty-one million ounces...one million kilograms of gold... was mined. There was a lot of money made... Australia was very rich back then with fortunes made and lost on the goldfields.

The 'Beechworth Sweet Company' seems like a great shop to explore so we go inside to find that it is chocolate heaven... for Mum and I!

"There is every type of chocolate and lolly you could think of... where do I begin?" said Mum

"There is every kind you could ever want!" I shout, excitedly

"The temptation is too great for me... I shall have to give in!" said Dad

Truthfully, I don't think he put up much of a fight!

Mum bought a jar full of banana split toffees... Dad bought a jar full of chocolate fudge...I bought a box full of white chocolate... we also bought a few extras! All our items added up to fifty dollars.

"Where shall we go next?" asked Dad

"Let's go to 'Beechworth Honey'." I said

"Although... I dislike bees." I said, nervously

"Why do you dislike bees darling?" asked Dad

"I have a fear of bees!"

"They sting and make me scream!" I said, nervously

"It will be all right, Cassie."

"Bees might seem a bit scary... but they are one of nature's many wonderful creatures." said Mum

"They provide honey...a true 'wonder' food."

"You will be safe with us." Dad added

"You're right... I can do this." I said

I dislike bees! Their sting hurts like 'billyo'... it makes me scream and cry out in pain! When I was ten years old in 2005, I was stung by a bee... it was a painful experience one I would rather forget...except with my memory I can't!

I was in my backyard when it happened... that's why I only go into the backyard when there are no insects around and I wear gloves every time. I should be fine at Beechworth Honey... I tell myself. I can do it...I give myself a 'pep' talk!

We drive to Beechworth Honey... to see how the honey is made. We paid twenty dollars for the experience and had to put on special beekeeper protection suits, so we wouldn't get stung.

"Will the bees sting us?" I ask nervously

"Don't worry, the bees won't sting you."
"The special protection beekeeper suits will help to protect you from the bees."
"Your Mum and Dad will be there too." said the beekeeper, reassuringly

We actually had a good time on the honey tour... I didn't even have to worry about the bees stinging me... we all enjoyed the experience.

"Cassie, you did very well coping with the bees."
"Very well done." said Dad proudly
"Yes, I coped Dad!"
"I won't be so scared of bees now." I said
"That is another good experience we have shared together."

Thirty-five minutes later Dad said...

"Now that we are back in Wodonga again... let's see what other activities we can do here."

Let's see, we could go to the army museum at Bandiana or Gateway Island Gallery and Studio, (GIGS), for short... what would you like to do?" he asked

"I would like to go to the Gateway Island Gallery and Studio."
"It sounds very creative." I said

We drove to GIGS and went inside, there were many different types of artworks, high quality contemporary works of over fifty regional artists. They were very creative, most of the artworks represented Australian themes. Everything looked so amazing!

Mum had a look at the jewellery, pottery and some drawings. Dad focused on paintings and sculptures... I was interested in the ceramics section.

Later, we decided to visit the Army Museum at Bandiana, which was only fifteen minutes away, where we viewed guns, tanks, vehicles, motorcycles, uniforms and medals.

After a while, we took a drive around Wodonga looking at the sights, and then finally on to the Border Gateway Motel where we intended to stay.

The motel featured an outdoor pool, a golf course and free Wi-Fi, it had great facilities including a playground, a barbeque/picnic area and a library. We were given room twelve, we went inside to find a flat-screen TV and all the usual features. This is another motel where we all sleep together in the same room, as in the previous motel we stayed at.

Mum and Dad watched TV for a few hours, whilst I played 'Angry Birds' on my iPad, I also listened to a couple of pop music videos. Later, we decided to have some 'Canadian Rooster' for tea, we drove to the store and ordered our favourites meals.

When our orders came out, we checked to see if everything was there. I saw a fish burger instead of a classic crispy burger in mine, I decided to tell the worker in a calm voice... it has to be done!

"Excuse me, but I think you got the order wrong."
"There's a fish burger in mine, instead of a classic crispy burger." I said
"Whoops, sorry."
"I got a bit confused there."
"I'll sort the orders out for you... so you receive the food you have asked for." replied the girl
"That's all right, it must've been a busy day for you." I said
"It sure has been!" she smiled gratefully, happy that I wasn't cross with her for making a mistake

Sometimes, when I'm at a restaurant or a take-away place, the food I order must be exactly the way I want, otherwise I get cranky! I can cross my arms and fume, and even the occasional swear word comes out!

No matter that each time, Mum and Dad try to calm me down, I just can't stop myself and listen to them. I only calm down when my food arrives in the exact way that I ordered it. Over time, with Mum, Dad and my social skill worker's help, I have learnt to be calm and tell the server that I didn't receive the food I ordered, and make it known in a positive voice... as I did today... and it worked! We enjoyed our dinner despite the mix-up... it was the best I have tasted!

After that, Mum made a phone call to our neighbour Abby, who is looking after our house whilst we are away on our road trip.

"Hi, Abby." said Mum, on the telephone

"Are the plants watered, fish fed, and the garden tended to?"

"Thanks Abby, keep up the great work!"

"Bye, Abby." Mum rang off

"All is well at home Abby is doing a great job caring for our place whilst we are away." said Mum, happily

"Let's watch 'Bridget Jones' Dairy'."

We found our favourite 'munchies', put the movie on and started watching, it is one of Mums' favourite movies, it's very funny, especially Renee Zellweger in the title role!

After the movie Dad said...

"Well, we'd better get some sleep."

"There's plenty for us to do tomorrow."

The Chelbec Tours seem like a good thing to try as a family, we decide to go on a half day tour, starting at one in the afternoon. The tour we have chosen covers, Albury-Wodonga and surrounding districts.

What a surprise! Who should walk in to Chelbec Tours office...but... Zoe Jones...Dads' best friend! Accompanied by Peter her husband, and their three children, Nina, Ivy and George. George is the eldest, followed by Nina, Ivy is the youngest of the Jones' children.

"Hello, Zoe."

"Hello Peter."

"We never expected to bump into you two here!"

"Or George, Nina and Ivy!" exclaimed Dad

"Hello, Daniel, Mikayla and Cassie!"

"We never expected to see you either!"

"We are staying in Albury-Wodonga and decided to do the half day tour to show George, Nina and Ivy a couple of our relatives who lived here." Zoe said

"A couple of our relatives were born here too, so we decided to bring Cassie as well!" said Mum with a smile

"Cassie, we haven't seen you in a long time, how are you doing?" asked Nina

"I'm doing very well thanks Nina." I smiled

"We're having fun in Wodonga so far, how about you Cassie?" asked George

"I'm having fun too, George!"

"Have you been to Wodonga before, Cassie?" asked Ivy

"No, it's my first time here."

"We're going to have fun on this tour, maybe we can have tea with you later tonight? said Nina hopefully

"Maybe, I'll ask Mum and Dad after the tour." I said with a wink

We paid one hundred and twenty dollars for our tour...it was forty dollars per person. First of all, we looked at the Hume Dam, which was formerly called the Hume Weir, it is a major dam across the Murray River, in the Riverina region of New South Wales.

It was just breathtaking and the water was clear and sparkly blue. Then we admired the view from the Kurrajong Gap Lookout, I was nervous when we got onto the platform, I had an anxiety attack and thought I was going to pass out!

Luckily, Mum and Dad told me use my strategies involving deep breathing, which calmed me down and I was able to enjoy the view. It was an amazing and lovely sight!

Next on our tour was the rural locality of Bonegilla, we looked at the 'Tribute Wall' which is Block Nineteen's way of honouring the many migrants who came through the Bonegilla migrant centre.

The wall is about migrants and their families, it was great to hear the stories and Mum, Dad and I, learnt about the migrant's life when they arrived in Australia in those times.

Mum's grandad Percy Macdonald, was born in Edinburgh Scotland in 1925, and came to Australia in 1927 when he was two years old. He spent some time in Wodonga during World War II, working as the owner of the Kurrajong Heights Hotel from 1943 until 1975.

During that time, he had two children… a son born in 1948, Darren… (Mums' Dad), and a daughter Janet, born in 1950 in Bendigo… they moved back to Wodonga to raise them both. He was a well-known barman with the locals and his wife Wendy was born in Bendigo in 1929. She helped her husband Darren whenever she could, whilst raising their two children through tough times, mainly the decline of tourism in later years, then the Kurrajong Hotel burnt down in 1975, so Percy and Wendy retired and spent the last years of their lives in Bendigo, before Percy passed away peacefully in 1996 aged seventy, and Wendy passed away two years later aged seventy-two.

Both contributed to Wodonga's tourism and society, Percy receiving the Member of the Order of Australia in 1993, for his contribution to tourism. He was a distinguished man, Mum talks about him sometimes, with Dad and I.

"Your great-grandfather was a notable Australian man, Cassie."

"He contributed to tourism despite the decline in the 1950's and the 1960's, he was well known and liked in Wodonga."

"Your great-grandad left his OAM medal to Dad… who will leave it to me."

"He will never be forgotten in our family." said Mum

"We can still talk about him… his memory is alive in our minds." I said

"I'm glad you can celebrate and commemorate the contributions of the migrants who came to this land… including your own ancestors." said the tour guide

Zoe's grandmother… Edith Jones, was involved in the cooking industry and Peter's grandad, Harold Jones… born in 1922 was a former AFL footballer who played for Richmond and was part of the 1943 Premiership Team!

In that match he kicked six goals to help Richmond win their fifth Premiership and he was the best on ground! He played from 1940 to 1957 and became an AFL commentator from 1958 to 1987 for twenty-nine years, he received an OAM for services to football in 1989.

In 1943 his son Bob, (Peters' Dad), was born… he would go on to play for Richmond during 1959 to 1969 for eleven seasons, before retiring when his wife Mable, gave birth to Peter in that last year.

"Peter… Harold was such a legendary footballer and a great commentator too."

"Well-known in football circles and one big Richmond Legend!" I said

"Thanks Cassie!"

"My Dad followed in his footsteps and won two premierships in 1963 and 1969, he was man of the match in the 1963 premiership as well!"

"I chose a popstar career in the 1980's, but I'm considering working with the Richmond Football Club... being a member like Daniel... I will probably help the Richmond Coaching Staff... maybe even coach one day!"

"My Dad doesn't mind if I choose to work for the Richmond Football Club... he worked there for a few years in between raising my two sisters and I."

"Daniel is a die-hard Richmond supporter like Zoe, Helen, George, Ivy and I!"

"It's fine whether he chooses to work with Richmond or not... he was born to be a Richmond fan like us!" said Peter

"He definitely was!"

"My grandad Jim also barracks for Richmond... but he didn't have time for a football career."

"Instead he was a popstar in the sixties pop band called 'The Fruits'!"

"They disbanded a year before Mum and Dad were born, they didn't meet again until 1975 at a special school in Melbourne." I said

"Your grandparents are Australian pop stars of the sixties!"

"They have inspired your parents... and hopefully you one day!" added Peter

"They definitely have... I've formed a pop band with Mum and Dad... but I will talk to you about it tonight at the restaurant." I said, giving Peter a wink

The last stop on our tour is historic Yackandandah, a small tourist town in northeast Victoria, near Beechworth which we visited earlier in the day. The Yackandandah railway line once linked Yackandandah to Beechworth, it was opened in 1891 the last train ran on the line in July 1954.

Although it was torn up after that, you can still see many sections of the original railway route on the roadway between Beechworth and Yackandandah.

"The route was steep, so the guard would need to apply the hand-brakes to the carriages and wagons." I said

"That's right young lady... you are one 'clever cookie'." said the tour guide, grinning

"I love Australia and its history... I am learning more at every destination we are visiting and staying at." I said, grinning back

We arrive back in Wodonga and go shopping for our evening dinner engagement with the Jones family. We need some fancy clothes and make-up, even though I'm not really that interested in make-up... at the moment.

We made our way to the Wodonga Plaza Shopping Centre to choose our outfits. I decided to try a blue dress in a different type of material than cotton, which is the fabric I have usually preferred for my clothes, for many years.

I have refused to try any other types of fabric, or any colours other than blue... if Mum and Dad tried to encourage me to branch out.

This time I chose a light blue lace dress by Calvin Klein!

"Good choice Miss."

"This would suit you for a date, or dinner in a restaurant." The shop assistant said

"It most certainly will!" I said, very pleased with myself

"I will stand out from the crowd wearing this dress!" I beamed

I did a little twirl and giggled... 'Ooh, Cassie. You're looking pretty as a picture... that light blue dress suits you and your long black hair...you will be the talk of the town... all you need is a few accessories...then you will be sensational.' I dreamed

I came out of the changing rooms and said to Mum...

"This dress suits me well Mum... the lace is very soft too."
"It certainly does Cassie... well done for trying a new fabric too!"
"I have chosen a yellow dress... when I finish putting it on... I'm sure you'll love it Cassie!"
"I'm sure I will and so will Dad." I grinned
"He's selected a green suit and is trying it on at the moment."
"When he comes out with it... I'll let you know so you can see it." I said
"Ok Cassie."
"Wish me luck trying this one."
"I think it will make me look like 1988!" said Mum, reminiscing
"You're thinking about your heydays Mum, aren't you?" I asked, giggling
"Yes, I am!"
"It was a beautiful year." said Mum, grinning

Mum went into the changing rooms to try on the dress... whilst she's doing that...Dad comes out wearing a green 'Armani' suit and boy... does he look handsome!

"Oh, WOW Dad!"
"You look very handsome in that 'Armani' suit!"
"You'll be a 'hit' in that!" I said, admiringly
"Thanks, Cassie."
"Who doesn't love Armani?"
"It fits me like a glove!" Dad says, preening like a peacock in front of the mirror
"Mum's busy trying on a beautiful yellow dress at the moment, you'll be amazed when you see her." I said
"Well I'm ready for when she does... your Mum always looks pretty." Dad smiled
"Mum... how's it going in there?" I asked.
"Fine sweetie... I'm just about finished." Mum replied
When Mum stepped out of the changing cubicle, she looked very beautiful in the yellow dress.
"You look beautiful just like 1988!" smiled Dad
"Thank you darling it's like 1988 again!" Mum smiled back at him
"Mum that dress looks lovely on you... I always thought it would." I smiled
"Thank you, sweetie... we'll be a hit at the restaurant tonight!"
"Let's pay for our purchases." said Mum decisively
"Now, for our accessories!" said Mum
"Right!" said Dad and I, together
"We paid for our fashionable clothes...next stop...the accessory store!

Mum was a lady on a mission as she strode off looking for the perfect accessory to go with her new dress! Mum and I, settled on a bangle each, Dad decided on a men's ring, we paid for them and regrouped.

"The last part of our shopping spree involves a visit to the salon."
"We'll get our nails done we can do the rest of our make-up at the hotel."
"Are you ready you two?" asked Mum
"Yes, we are ready." said Dad and I

We went to a salon... as soon as I saw the name' SALON,' it was my autistic girls' nightmare! I need to speak up about this... it's time to do it...otherwise how can I go on a date in the future... if I have issues with make-up and perfume!

"Mum, before we go in, can I talk to you for a few minutes?" I asked
"Sure, Cassie." Mum said

We found a seating area close by and sat down, I started to talk to Mum and Dad about the issues I've had with make-up and perfume.

"Mum, for many years I've never been interested in make-up or perfume like other girls are."

"Certain perfumes overwhelm me… some even make me throw up!"

"Like when Zoe, Peter, Ivy, George and Nina came over in 2010 for tea!"

"Dad, you cleaned up the mess… I apologised to everyone for ruining the night… everyone was fine and accepted my apology."

"Mum that perfume you wore was not one of the ones you have created… it was a well-known brand perfume."

"The perfumes, like 'White Chocolate,' and 'Red Rose', are fine… I would love to wear them and smell like those scents."

"Thanks for speaking up to us about these issues."

"Remember, if perfumes make you ill… there is no need to wear them."

"Lots of people are allergic to different things… and perfume ingredients can have some of those in them." Dad said, explaining

"The same goes for make-up… but you can get ones these days without perfume added… so you can try those types if you want to… or just go natural!" Mum said, helpfully

"I'm ready to give make-up a try." I said

"You are starting to speak out about your issues to us… which is good!"

"It means that you are becoming confident." Dad smiled

"I sure am Dad."

"I guess I am growing up!"

"I'll teach you how to apply your make-up if you want me to…soon you'll be ready for whatever social occasion comes your way." said Mum, encouragingly

"Thanks Mum." I said, smiling

We went into the beauty salon, where the owner greeted us warmly.

"Welcome to the Wodonga Beauty Room Salon!"

"I'm Stella Lafont."

"Oo la la, is that Rick Astley?" said Stella with a French accent, looking as though she was going to swoon all over Dad

"Uh… No…Stella."

"I'm Daniel Bontel."

"Rick Astley doesn't have a moustache."

"I know I look similar to him and have a voice like his as well." said Dad, starting to turn pink

Mum and I giggled. Dad often gets mistaken for Rick Astley the English pop singer. Mum and I think it's hilarious! Dad finds it embarrassing but what can he do…he is Rick Astley's doppelganger!!!

"Sorry about that, Daniel."

"What treatments would you like?" asked Stella

"Our daughter Cassie is here to get her nails done." Mum said

"Ah, Mademoiselle wants a manicure and pedicure." Stella replied

"My husband Daniel, is here to get his treatment…but don't cut his hair or his moustache!"

"I would like the same treatments as Cassie, please." said Mum

"You three are going to look so fabulous when you are finished!" exclaimed Stella

"Ladies, please sit over here on these chairs."

"Helen and I will do your manicure and pedicure."

"Daniel, you sit in this chair here... my assistant Eva will tend to you." Stella motioned

I chose to have my fingernails and toenails painted blue, Mum chose to have hers painted yellow, and Dad...well, I don't know what he's getting done...but I can't wait to see!

Time passed and the treatments were finished, Mum and I looked pretty with our coloured nails, Dad retained his Rick Astley hairstyle and moustache but his skin looks smoother and younger like Mum.

"Wow Dad!"

"You and Mum look years younger after your treatments." I said

Mum and Dad spluttered with laughter.

"They certainly do mademoiselle Cassie!" smiled Stella

"We look like our younger selves, maybe fifteen years younger I reckon!" said Dad, admiringly in the mirrors

"We look like a royal popstar family!" said Mum, grinning

"I hope you enjoyed the 'Stella' treatment, Bontel Family?" Stella waved her hands in the air

"Yes, we did Stella, 'cest magnifique'!" I said, grinning

"Ah, mademoiselle speaks French." said Stella, nodding her approval

"Where are you planning to go tonight?"

"We're going to a pizza parlour with our friends." said Mum

"Oh, la, la!"

"Have fun tonight." laughed Stella

We are just about to leave the shopping centre when an elderly woman approaches us.

"Can you help me?"

"Of course, what do you need help with?" Mum replied

"I have just been shopping, I've three bags of heavy shopping that I can't lift."

"Can you help me put them in my car?" she asked

"No problem, everybody 'grab' a bag each." Dad said

We put the shopping bags in the lady's car, which I noticed was a Holden from the 1970's.

"Thank you for helping me."

"It's our pleasure." we said

Back at our hotel, Mum teaches me how to use basic make-up, like applying a lipstick without making a mess, also a little blusher.

"If you learn how to apply your makeup deftly, you'll look lovely when you go out on a 'special' date in the future." Mum said, smiling at me

I applied the lipstick for a start, slowly and carefully, not to go outside the area of my lips and then I had beautiful lips like Mum.

"Good job, Cassie."

"That's a great start!"

Mum showed me how and where, to apply the blusher on my face. She showed me that less is more... not to be too heavy handed with my make-up... or I would end up looking like a clown!

Before we went out for the evening, Mum skyped Belinda to get another clue about her family member, Belinda might not give any more clues after that. Mum thinks differently...does she listen to Belinda? I don't think so!

'Hi Mum. Hello, Mikayla. How's the road trip going? Are you having a good time so far? We ARE having a good time Mum! We went on the 'Chelbec Tour' in the Albury-Wodonga region, we learnt about my great-grandad, alias your father-in-law moving to Australia from Edinburgh when he was two.'

We learned about the effects of World War II in Australia...Daniel, Olivia, Rebecca and I, have been marching in the Anzac Day Parade wearing our great-grandads' and grandads' war medals with pride since they passed away.

'Maybe Cassie might do the same one day, if she chooses too.'

'I certainly will honour my great-great-grandads' and great-grandads', like Mum, Dad, Olivia and Rebecca. It will fill me with pride to honour their sacrifices and keep our family traditions alive. Well said Cassie!' Belinda beamed at me

'Mum, would you give me another clue to my long-lost family member?' pleaded Mum

'Nope! I said before, my lips are sealed on that one! Come on Mum, give me that second clue! All right. He is one hundred and seventy-six centimetres tall. That's all you're getting today!' said Belinda, grinning

'Oh, Mum! Give me one more clue please Mum. Just one more should do. Nope! That's it for today! Can we skype every day? NO, we cannot!

Blah! Blah! Blah!' said Mum grumpily, as Belinda thwarted her plans for more clues

Dad and I giggled. It is always funny when Mum gets cranky! At least Dad and I think it's funny anyway... not so sure about Mum though!

'Very funny dear. said Belinda, talking to Mum like she is a naughty little school girl again instead of an adult. You're always being cheeky to me when we skype.' said Belinda, wagging her finger at Mum

'Daniel, Cassie and I, are going out for tea with Zoe, Peter, Ivy, George and Nina at a pizza place. It seems like a nice place to eat...you how much I love pizzas! You do, I know your favourite flavour is ham and pineapple!

I'm off to the RSL to bowl with my team, we're playing against Ballarat. You are doing well as an RSL player, perhaps you could compete against me... Mother and daughter... one day! Well if you do that, you've no chance of beating me! I'll recruit Daniel, Olivia and Rebecca, we'll make a powerhouse lawn bowls team! It's game on then! I have to get ready now.'

'Don't get any cheeky ideas Mikayla! Bye, Mum.'

Dad and I laughed.

"Any luck with the clues so far on our long-lost family member Mum?" I asked

"Well, the second clue was that he is one hundred and seventy-six centimetres tall."

"Mum can be so sneaky sometimes."

"I'm determined to find that long-lost family member, no matter how long it takes!" said Mum, with a steely look on her face

"We will help you it will be a joyful reunion with plenty of catching up to do!" I said

"For the Dads' weekend, all we need is someone who is related to let slip the location... then we can set up a prank!" said Mum, in an excited voice

We all laughed together. This family sure likes playing pranks on each other, but they can have a habit of back-firing sometimes! Let's hope not!

"Cassie do you remember when you were five years old and we were visiting the Old Melbourne Gaol, on a tour with fifteen or so other people." Mum asked

"I had to carry you around everywhere because you disliked the other people and wouldn't speak to anyone when they talked to you."

"The tour was proceeding fairly well, until the second part of the tour where I had put you down to walk, as you were getting too heavy to carry all the way round...then you wandered off."

"When I noticed you weren't with the group any longer Dad and I realised that you must have made your escape whilst we were looking in the cells."

"We all started looking for you... the people in the tour, the guide, Dad and I... searching everywhere!"

"Somebody spotted a dropped white 'Freddo Frog' wrapper and we eventually found you in Ned Kelly's cell!"

"You were examining a tile that was loose!"

"You were happy to see us, although you wouldn't let us touch you."

"We had to bribe you with another Freddo Frog!"

"We decided to leave as we couldn't risk you wandering off again... it was such a big place."

"As we were leaving, the wind made a ghostly sound which upset you."

"You didn't calm down until we arrived back home." Mum added

"That Old Melbourne Gaol was the most frightening tour I've ever been on!"

"I refuse to set foot in that place again!"

"It scared me like a haunted house." I remembered

"I don't want to go there again thank you!"

"Neither do we!"

"It gave us the creeps!" said Mum and Dad together, laughing

We finished our preparations and got ready for our evening out.

We arrived at Wodonga Pizza Place, where the Jones family met us at the table that we had booked... they were amazed when they saw us!

"Wow, you look fabulous tonight!"

"Where have you three been!" asked Zoe, looking very impressed with our appearances

"We went to the Wodonga Beauty Room Salon."

"Stella Lafont and her staff treated us to a small make-over session!" said Dad, with a grin

"Goodness you three look stunning! Peter said, with his mouth open

"It's going to be a good night for us!" said Mum, winking

"Cassie, you look lovely!" said Ivy, gasping

"You look hot Cassie!"

"You will be a hit with the boys around Australia!" said George, admiringly

"Thanks George, but I'm not interested in having a boyfriend just yet!" I grinned back at him

"Cassie you look so pretty." said Nina, smiling at me

"Thank you, Nina."

"Now that we're all together let's order." said Mum

I've decided to choose the tropical pizza...although I'm not sure about the fruit that's on there... pineapple...I've decided to give it a go...I can order my usual 'Meat-lovers'... if I don't like it!

We ordered our pizzas and sat at the table with Nina, Ivy, George and I on one side, Mum, Dad, Zoe and Peter on the other. This gives me the chance to chat with Nina, Ivy and George.

"Cassie, the road trip around Australia you are taking with your family, is great!"

"How long are you travelling for?" asked Ivy

"Mmmn...probably a year...we are having lots of fun." I said

"We've heard your Dad was tricked again by your Aunt Rebecca and Mum, a couple of days ago."

"We all watched the clip, it was so funny, also the photos that were taken as well!" George laughed

"It was hilarious!"

"I took part by referring to Rebecca as Mum, I recorded the whole conversation with my video camera, when Dad spat out his tea in shock when Mum revealed herself, I stopped recording because I was laughing too much to carry on!"

"Dad was red in the face with embarrassment!" I grinned, mischievously

"You're quite the prankster, and so is your Mum and Aunt Rebecca!"

"The last time you visited us, you sent cheeky messages to each of us under an anonymous name, so we didn't know who sent them to us!"

"Then later we caught you giggling about it, so we worked it out… you're very cheeky! said Nina, pointing her finger at me

"I definitely am."

"Hey, I got a new watch in April that I would you like to show you."

"It's a very shiny silver one, from a well-known Japanese maker!" I said

I showed Nina, Ivy and George the watch I was wearing on my right wrist.

"Wow, what a nice silver watch, where did you get it?" asked Ivy, admiringly

"I got it for my sixteenth birthday, from Mum and Dad."

"It has become my favourite accessory I wear it all the time." I replied

"That's a nice present, what make is it?" asked George

"It's a Citizen, they have been made in Tokyo since 1924, originally as a pocket watch!"

"That's great, you must love wearing it."

"I've got a Seiko." said Nina

"Mine's a Versace!" said Ivy

"I have a Brequet." added George

They showed me their shiny, luxury watches from Italy, Switzerland and Japan.

"They are great watches…we all look very stylish tonight!"

We all laughed together.

"Nina and I both started working at an IGA store earlier this year, in Melbourne." said Ivy

"That's good you love to shop there, don't you?" I asked

"Yes, we do!"

"Before Nina started working, she and I used to go there once a week for our shopping." Ivy replied

"Nina completed her work experience there, when she was in year nine in 2006, I worked mine there too in 2010!"

"Nina enjoyed her time there so much, that she worked there again in year ten."

"We prepared ourselves by shopping independently for two years, twice a month."

"That's how we got our jobs there!" said Ivy, happily

"You probably have seen us there, when you have all been doing your grocery shopping at different times."

"I remember seeing you wearing your headphones to block out the loud noises, we still managed to have a chat together." smiled Ivy

"You're doing a good job at IGA!" I said

"Thanks, Cassie!" said Ivy

Our pizzas arrive, boy do they look good and smell even better! I look at my tropical, Hawaiian pizza, there are pineapple slices on it, I pick up a slice but I'm too afraid to eat it!

"You can do it Cassie!"

"Tropical pizzas are good!" said Nina

"It's my favourite pizza, the pineapple adds the juicy flavour to it!" said George

"We all love our pizzas!" says Zoe

"Pineapples are a great fruit for you Cassie!"

"Pineapples help me feel good and healthy!" said Peter, showing off his muscles which made everyone laugh

"Can you try the tropical pizza Cassie?" asked Mum

"I can and I will." I said firmly, convincing myself

I took a bite out of the tropical pizza I felt the juiciness of the pineapple in my mouth and the soft cheesy taste of the melted cheese. It was... quite delicious...I think I love the taste of pineapple...I might have to try other fruits if they all taste as good as this one!

"Well done, Cassie."

"I knew you could do it!" said Mum

"Thanks Mum, I think I might try other fruits now that I have broken the barrier!"

"That's good Cassie, you've made progress!" Dad smiled

"I have!"

"Let's all enjoy our pizzas, let's get into them!" I said happily, munching away

Later in the evening, we said goodbye to the Jones' family after leaving Wodonga Pizza Place.

"Goodbye, we've had such a lovely time together finding out some of our family history." said Zoe.

"We sure did!" said Mum

"Cassie, we've had so much fun spending time with you." Nina added

"Me too!" I replied, as we waved goodbye

The next day we returned to Wodonga's Gateway Island Gallery and Studio again, but this time there was an art class happening, luckily for us there were three spots left!

"Are you the Bontel family? asked Hilary, the art teacher

"Yes, we are." said Dad

"I'm pleased to have you in my art class, I'm looking forward to seeing your paintings!" Hilary smiled

"You will be amazed... I can promise that!" I said, cheekily

"Ok everyone, welcome to art class, today our painting theme is Australia!"

"Using the paints and brushes provided, paint your favourite Australian things."

"I can't wait to see your artistic creations!"

"Have you all got your art smocks on?"

"Painting can be a messy business!" Hilary laughed

"Yes!" we all laughed together

"Great, paint away, show me what you can do!"

Mum painted a lamington! Dad painted the Sydney Harbour Bridge because it's his favourite landmark. I painted the city of Melbourne because it's my hometown, as well as a butterfly, a diamond, (my birthstone), and the sun!

Mum looked smug. She looked very pleased with her painting. I was smug too...I couldn't resist painting a line down her face, Mum retaliated by painting a line on my forehead. The whole class burst out laughing!

"All right, what's going on here you two!" said Hilary

"Nothing." said Mum and I, trying to look innocent.

"Nothing?"

"Nice try... whose idea was this?" Hilary said, pointing to our painted faces

"It was hers." said Mum and I, pointing fingers at each other with sheepish looks on our faces

The whole class erupted into laughter.
"Come on... tell me who did this?" said Hilary
"Hilary... I know who it was... I saw the whole thing." Dad said, 'dropping' us in it
"It was Cassie and Mikayla!" said Dad, pointing to Mum and I
"Thank you, Daniel."
"They had 'Fruit Loops' for breakfast this morning!" said Dad, grinning slyly
"Did they now... hmm... Mikayla...Cassie... I shall be keeping an eye on you two to make sure you don't get up to any more mischief." said Hilary, sternly
"Yes, Hilary." said Mum and I together, like naughty school children
An hour later, when the art class had ended there was a 'real' face painting event scheduled.
"It might be fun to take part." mused Mum
"It could be fun." agreed Dad
"Cassie, would you like to have your face painted properly?" asked Mum
"Yes, I would love to." I replied

Mum and I washed our faces clean, to prepare for the face painting to begin. Mum chose to be painted as a fairy, I chose a butterfly design, Dad thought 'WE' were funny, even though his face was painted to resemble a tiger!

You two crazy girls are hilarious...you look like little girls." said Dad, laughing
"We're not crazy Daniel!" said Mum, giggling
"I think you are!"
"I can't wait to see what Olivia and Rebecca think!"
"I'm sure they will enjoy our face painting choices and get a laugh!"
"Just let me get my iPhone out."
"Cassie, get your sunglasses out." said Dad

I put on my black sunglasses and Dad took a photo! It was hilarious! He then took a 'selfie' (when you take a photo of yourself using your mobile or iPhone), I didn't know what that word meant, until Mum explained it to me yesterday! The art class had been fun and the face painting was creative magic!

My artistic work shows that I'm creative, I create my pictures as a way to express myself, I'm opening up and speaking more, I'm also coming out of my shell of shyness gradually. If Mum asks me to illustrate her next children's book, I would love to take that opportunity, as Dad has been illustrating them since 1995.

The younger me would have been terrified at the face painting event... I would have flatly refused to do it... but I enjoyed this face painting so much that I would like to have my face painted as a fairy next time!

"I've decided I want to visit Canberra, our nation's capital!" I said
"That's a great place to visit next, Cassie!"
"Dad and I have been there a few times, we really enjoyed it." said Mum
"It will be fun to visit Parliament House, where all our politicians go to speak in the House of Representatives, where they discuss issues that we Australians currently face, and where they vote on important bills!" I said, excitedly

The next morning, bright and early, we left Wodonga to travel to the Australian Capital Territory. This part of the road trip will take us about three and a half hours drive until we reach Canberra. Dad has decided to take the first couple of hours driving this morning, as we hit the road once again.

# Chapter Eight
## 'Canberra' and other problems!

"Here we are."
"This is our nation's capital... Canberra!"
"Isn't this a grand city?" said Mum
"It sure is grand!"
"I can see Parliament House from here."
"I see Lake Burly Griffin."
"It's a lovely sight to see." Dad agreed

As we were driving past Parliament House, a man wearing a smart business suit with a political badge that said Australian Labour Party, Member of Parliament, waved us over to stop.

"How can we help." asked Mum
"I've lost my briefcase full of personal papers for a meeting that I'm about to have with my fellow ALP members in fifteen minutes time!"
"If I don't have my briefcase, I could get in trouble with the Prime Minister."
"We can help you look for it, to get you to your meeting on time." said Mum
"We wouldn't want you to get into trouble with the Prime Minister!" said Dad
"Where do you think you lost your briefcase." I asked
"I think I lost it somewhere near Parliament house."
"If you can help me find it, to get me to my meeting on time, that would be great!"
"We'll find that briefcase in no time." I said, confidently

Mum, Dad and I, have to help find the briefcase! There is only fifteen minutes to the meeting so there is no time to lose! We started looking in the hedges, there are two rows of fifteen hedges, how the heck are we going to find the briefcase in this lot?

"The briefcase is not in this hedge!" I said, shrugging my shoulders
"It's not in this one either." said Mum
"It's definitely not in this hedge. said Dad
"I've had no luck either finding it so far...I only have twelve minutes left... otherwise it will be big trouble for me."
"I am Darryl Samson."
"I am one of the Labour MP's, I work with the Prime Minister on some important issues." said Darryl, with a worried look on his face

We searched a few more hedges. I was looking under the bottom of another hedge and turned to speak to a man beside me.

"You haven't seen a briefcase full of papers anywhere, mate, have you?" I said

Then I looked up properly to see that I had been talking to a large 'STOP' sign!

What was I doing talking to a stop sign! I felt a bit silly about this. I hope the passing motorists didn't see me. Oh well, accidents happen, I shrugged and kept looking, we were running out of time!

"Exactly what does the briefcase look like, Mr. Samson?" I enquired

"It's a brown attaché, with an ALP badge and an ALP MP badge on it."

"Ah... aha I've found it!" I said, excitedly

"Yes, that's my briefcase!"

"Thank you for helping me find it!"

"I'm so grateful and relieved." Darryl said

"Thanks Mr Samson... we're glad we could help you out." Dad said

Darryl checked his watch he had a concerned look on his face.

"Oh dear, there's only eight minutes left... my car's too far away, I will not get to my meeting in time."

"Well, our car is nearby, we can get you there in time for your meeting, come with us." said Mum

We ran to our car, jumped in and Mum sped off to Parliament House.

"I hope we get there in time." Darryl said

"We'll be on time... I promise you." said Mum

"Mr. Samson, just between you, me and Dad... Mum drives like a speed demon!" I whispered to him

"Oh, does she?" said Minister Samson in a fake 'serious' tone

Dad chuckled.

"I heard that young, lady!" said Mum, chuckling too

"What is the Prime Minister like?" I asked

"She's good... humorous and a hard worker."

Since she became Prime Minister just about a week ago, the Labour MPs have been working hard to help her change Australia for the better." said the minister

"That's very good... keep up the good work and hopefully... Australia will have many positive outcomes in the future." said Dad, encouragingly

Thank you... I hope so too!" replied Darryl

With three minutes to spare we arrived at Parliament House... Darryl grabbed his briefcase... got out of the car and raced towards the entrance... hurrying inside.

"Well, we all did a really good job, helping Darryl find his briefcase... especially you, Cassie!"

"You used your eagle eyes to find it under the hedge, well done!" Dad beamed

"Phew!"

"I thought we would never find it and get Darryl to Parliament House on time... but we did!" I grinned happily

"It's rewarding to help someone out."

"Why don't we find somewhere nice to eat our lunch now?"

"I think I know a couple of places." said Mum

We were just about to leave, when a lady with red hair and glasses, wearing a white shirt with a PM badge on it and black pants, came over to our car and knocked on the window. I knew who that politician was... I could tell by her badge that she is the Prime Minister of Australia!

We stepped out of the car, to meet this professional looking lady, her name is Sophie Lewis, the leader of the Australian Labour Party since June the twenty-fourth, 2010... but we most often refer to her as... Prime Minister!

"Hello, I'm honoured to meet you." said the Prime Minister, shaking our hands

"It's an honour to meet you... Prime Minister." I said, shaking her hand

Mum and Dad shook hands with her too they are excited to see her as much as I am!

I notice that her accent is Welsh I know that she comes from Wales... she is our first female Prime Minister... I like the idea of a woman in the top job!

"I heard you helped one of my MP's find his lost briefcase earlier."

"That was very nice of you to help him out."

"You helped him to avoid getting into trouble... saved his job!" the Prime Minister said

"It was a pleasure Prime Minister."

"We were happy to lend a hand." Mum replied

"How are you enjoying being the Prime Minister?" asked Dad

"I'm really enjoying the challenge." she replied

"We are travelling around Australia on a road trip." I blurted out, excitedly

"Oh, goodness me!"

"That must be fantastic!" the Prime Minister laughed

"Yes, we love travelling... now Cassie is enjoying travelling with us." said Mum

"I'm sure she is."

"Congratulations Daniel and Mikayla, on receiving your OAM medals earlier this year."

The Prime Minister, shook Mum and Dads' hands.

"Thank you, Prime Minister."

"Along with our sisters, Olivia and Rebecca, we were joint recipients for services to music, TV and disability."

"We're changing the way Australia thinks about disability... hopefully there will be positive outcomes for everyone!"

"We're taking one step at a time." said Dad

"We travelled to Canberra to receive our special medals... it was well worth the effort!"

"Cassie couldn't be there due to her fear of flying... but she was so proud of us when we told her the news and very excited!" said Mum

"I certainly was!"

"Mum, Dad, Aunt Olivia and Aunt Rebecca are awesome at what they are doing!"

"One day, I would like to receive an Order of Australia medal for services... just like them."

"If I work really hard it could happen!" I said

"I am sure you will do a good job in contributing to changing Australia for the better, Cassie."

"I must get back to my parliamentary work now and leave you to continue with your road trip."

"Good luck with your upcoming music concert... I have heard that there is going to be one in Sydney soon... so I'm sure you'll want to make preparations for that." the Prime Minister said

"Prime Minister, will you be able to come to our Sydney concert... if you have time?" I asked, eagerly

"I would love to... but I would have to consult my work diary and see what functions I have on at that time, first." the Prime Minister said, as she smiled at me

"We hope we will see you there, Prime Minister."

"Good day." Dad added

We waved goodbye to the Prime Minister and drove off.

"Well... what about that?"

"We retrieved an MP's brief case, met the Prime Minister and spoke to her... after only a few minutes of arriving in Canberra!"

"What a whirlwind it's turning out to be here... but a very good time!" Mum said

'What do you make of the day so far Cassie?" asked Dad

'It's awesome!"

"I can't wait to see what the rest of Canberra looks like!" I replied

"We can't wait either, Cassie."

"We might have a picnic lunch at Lake Burley Griffin."

"Would you like that?" asked Mum

"Yes, please!"

"That would be a great place to see... I can take some cool pictures." I added

We took sandwiches, drinks and sweets, to Lake Burley Griffin and what a view! This is cool! The water is crystal clear. There are a few spots to have our picnic, so Mum, Dad and I, select one, sit down on our picnic rug and lay out the picnic.

"Wow!"

"This is the most amazing view I've seen so far!"

"Awesome!" I said, happily

"I can see the bridge from where we're sitting... it could be interesting to drive on." said Mum

"Over there, several metres away from the bridge the Captain Cook Memorial Jet sprays water."

"We might get to see it today, if we are lucky." Dad commented

Several minutes late, as if on cue, the jet passed by and sprayed water three metres into the air...how cool is that!

"Whoa!"

"This is wicked!" I said, excitedly

"That is amazing!" said Mum

"It's wonderful." Dad grinned

"That is one awesome water spray!" I gasped

"I'll take a photo of it on my iPhone and upload it to my Facebook page." Mum added

I hope our friends and family enjoy seeing the photo that Mum took, she's the photographer in our family... I've been taking several photos on my iPhone too. I took a photo just as the spray started to come down and uploaded it on my iPhone, hoping my friends would enjoy seeing it.

"Well, what do you think of that Cassie?" asks Dad, grinning at me

"It was wicked!"

"It was great!"

"I would like to see that again sometime." I said laughing

"I'm sure we will, Cassie." Dad replied

"Let's drive back to our hotel and wind down, after our exciting day so far!" said Mum

We stopped off at a newsagent to buy a newspaper, Dad checked to see what footy teams would be playing, it turned out to be Carlton playing against Richmond at the MCG.

"That is going to be a good match on Saturday!"

"I bet Richmond are going to wallop Carlton by sixty points!" said Dad, cheekily

"Oh... I doubt that Dad!"

"Carlton will be the ones being thrashed by Richmond... by about sixty-five points... I reckon." I laughed

Mum laughed as well

"Oh, you two have a good rivalry going on there... it's hilarious when you two get started over your footy teams!" laughed Mum

"We'll see who laughs the longest, Dad!" I said, pointing my finger at him

Afterwards, we ordered room service, then I went for a bath.

"Ahh...that feels so lovely." I murmured, as I relaxed down into the water

A bath always helps me feel relaxed and calm, especially after a tough day. I turn on the jets and it bubbles all around me, I giggled and sank deeper into the soothing liquid.

"Ahh, yes, that's so good."

The radio was playing nearby, I could hear soft pop music.

Mum and Dad were watching 'Antiques Roadshow'... one of their favourite shows... they could hear me singing in the bathroom.

I could hear Mum's iPhone ringing, then I heard her say...

"Hello, Kate."

"How are you?"

"Yes, we are having a great time in Canberra."

"Yes, that is Cassie you can hear singing in the background, she is in the spa bath relaxing

"Sorry Kate, Cassie can't use the phone whilst she is in the bath."

"I will get her to call you back later when she has finished." Mum concluded

Mum came to the bathroom door and knocked on it.

"Cassie, your Aunt Kate just called... when you have done with your spa bath can you call her back... as she would like to talk with you." Mum said, through the bathroom door

"Okay Mum, I'll do that as soon as I get out."

"This spa bath is so relaxing and soothing to me... I certainly needed one." I replied

"I'll leave you to your singing practice... don't overdo it." she said, in her 'Mumsy" voice

"I won't Mum." I replied, smiling to myself

When the bubbles settled down and the water became colder, I dried my hair and all over my body and put on my blue cotton dressing gown, it feels snug and keeps me warm. I sat down on my bed, looked on my iPhone for Kate's number and rang her up.

The conversation between her and I went like this:

"Hello, Aunt Kate... how are you?"

'I'm well thank you... I heard you singing in the bath on my phone call to Mum.'

"Yes, it's a soothing and relaxing place to practise after a hard day."

'You know what?'

'I relaxed in a jacuzzi spa and your Uncle Adam served me drinks whilst I was in there.'

"Pardon?" I said, giggling

'I'm living the life of luxury currently relaxing on my towel... your Aunt Nicole is serving me food and your Aunt Amelia has given me a book to read whilst I'm relaxing... but I can't read my book in the spa.'

"You 'ARE' living the life of luxury." I laughed

Mum chimes in...

"Kate, I hope you're not giving Cassie any of your cheeky ideas."

'Who me?' said Kate, in an innocent voice down the phone, which made me laugh harder

Adam's voice wafted over the phone line

'Kate, here's the Fanta drink you ordered.'

'Thank you, my dear sir.' I heard her reply

Then Nicole's voice drifted over the line.

'Kate, here are your white chocolate 'Tim-Tams' that you asked for.'

'Thank you, my dear Madam.'

'Cassie... we're enjoying the Bontel Family CD...you could be a powerhouse band one day.'

"We'll see Kate... we are taking it one step at a time!"

'I'd better finish up now...we have to fly to the next destination on our 'Blizzard Blast' tour... we'll see you when we finish the tour.'

'Bye, Cassie.'

"Bye, Aunt Kate."

"I'll see you then."

"Cassie, your Aunt Kate can be a bit cheeky sometimes." said Mum, with a smile

I grinned to myself when I heard Mum say that, because no one is cheekier than Mum!

The next morning after we had breakfasted, we went for a stroll. Today feels like a good day for a walk through the Australian National Botanical Gardens. Mum and Dad thought so too, as they love walking through botanical gardens and admiring the flowers, just like they did during their 'dating' days. I have been to the Melbourne Botanical Gardens many times, Mum and Dad always taught me to appreciate and respect nature wherever we go.

We were enchanted by the many flowers as we walked around, there were plenty of types of plants like Brachyscome segmentosa and Eucalyptus socialis. There were plenty of things to look at and to learn about, with beautiful colours, shapes, and sizes of every kind, wherever we looked during our walk.

"That is awesome!"

"There are so many flowers and plants to see!"

"I'm sure to have fun learning as many as I can." I said

"I'm sure you will!"

"Take the time to learn all about them... if you have any questions just ask us... or any of the National Botanical Gardens staff." Mum said

"Yes, Mum." I replied

A particular plant which amazed me had colours of white, yellow and green, there were daisies on it.

"Is it a Brachyscome segmentosa?"

"It looks fascinating." I said

"Yes, it is young lady... good pronunciation too." said one of the ground keepers

"It is also known as the Lord Howe Island Daisy and it is commonly found on Lord Howe Island in the Tasman Sea."

"Wow, I didn't know that!" I said, amazed

"We didn't either." said Mum and Dad

We continued walking through the Botanical Gardens, where we saw the Eucalyptus socialis.

"That's so beautiful a koala would love to live there." I mentioned

"That's one amazing Eucalyptus tree, indeed."

"I wouldn't mind getting a photo of that." said Mum

"That's nature at its best right there, it stands out above the rest!" said Dad

After Mum took the photograph, we continued walking.

"I remember the times I went to the park... I would have a sketchpad in one hand and a pen in the other."

"I would sit down under a tree and I would draw nature that I saw... such as trees and rivers."

"The sketching would calm me as long as it was quiet and peaceful... with no kids to scare me... then I would add colour to my drawings."

"I would occasionally hear the birds singing which would make me smile."

"That's what the National Botanical Gardens reminds me of." I said, peacefully

"It reminds us of similar times too... Mum would draw in her sketchbook...I would provide flowers for her drawings."

"One time when we were sixteen, she drew a sky with a love heart with the letters D and M in it."

"Then I appeared with a rose in my hand, to add to her drawing... she thought it was lovely...we shared our first kiss in that special moment." remembered Dad

"That was a beautiful moment you two had back then."

"I might even sketch a flower or plant when we finish here." I said

"I can't wait to see what you draw."

"When you are finished... show it to us." Mum smiled

"I will Mum." I replied

We had a great time at the National Botanical Gardens, taking photos, learning about some of the plants and flowers that we had never heard of before. I asked a few more questions, and so did Mum and Dad.

Just before we went to the Hotel Realm restaurant, Dad checked the result of the Carlton and Richmond match. He was not a happy camper!

The smile had been wiped from his face, because Carlton have given Richmond a walloping, 28.16 (184) to 12.9 (81), to the tune of one hundred and three points!

"Oh, dear, lord!"

"Richmond have been thumped by a huge margin...one hundred and three points!"

"We didn't play well today and Carlton were just too good."

"I bet Damien Hardwick, was fuming and gave his boys a blast!"

"Still, you can't win all the time." Dad said, philosophically

Mum and I giggled quietly it was funny whenever Carlton defeated Richmond in our house.

"You two think that's funny, do you?" said Dad, in a niggled voice

"Nice try... but I can still hear you giggling!" said Dad, grumpily

"Sorry Dad but it looks like Richmond got the blues." I laughed out loud this time

"Ha ha... very funny Cassie!"

"Carlton won't get away with it next time when they meet Richmond! said Dad, emphatically

"Sorry, dear."

"Today is not Richmond's day... is it?" said Mum, laughing

"Don't you start Mikayla!"

"Richmond will beat Carlton next time." said Dad, laughing at Mum

Dad started to receive texts from Rebecca... she had been at the game... she was delighted with Carlton's win... *'Oh, now Rebecca is into the act as well, better see what she has to say'* thought Dad, as he groaned.

He opened the text message and read...

'Ha ha Daniel, Richmond aimed to maul the Blues, but it looks like Richmond got mauled instead. Richmond tried to get through the AFL maze, but Carlton pipped them at every turn and got them lost. Goodness me! Richmond boys tried to talk to some Carlton girls... but got laughed at!'

Rebecca loves to score a few points against her brother-in-law and make poor Dad squirm when she can... Mum being her twin...thinks it's funny too! I must admit... so do I...sometimes!

Mum and I 'cracked up'! Rebecca's cheeky quips are so funny, especially when she shares them on her 'Rebecca' show in the segment called 'Funny AFL Quips'.

"Well done to the Carlton boys, Brett Ratten will be happy with that effort." I said

"Yes, he would, it was a good game for Rebecca to watch." Mum agreed

"My Mum would be proud of that Carlton win too!"

"Being a die-hard Carlton fan just like you and Rebecca."

"Well, it was a one-sided game... but I suppose it's good to see Carlton get a win." said Dad, grudgingly

"Let's get some tea before we go to the concert tonight... I'll just check the time."

It was six-thirty in the evening, we had one hour till the concert started.

"Looks like it will have to be a quick takeaway meal."

"Who's up for KFC?" Dad said

"I am, Dad!"

"I'm always up for it!" I said, enthusiastically

"I'm up for it as well, dear." replied Mum

We quickly had our tea, then went to our hotel rooms to get changed. Once we were all dressed... we went to Llewellyn Hall... to see a performance of the Canberra Symphony Orchestra!

"This is so exciting!"

"It's going to be a fantastic night for the three of us!" I said, happily

"It certainly will be!"

"The Llewellyn Hall is marvellous... it looks like a great place for an orchestra to perform in."

"We will have a great time tonight!" Dad smiled at me

The conductor walked onstage and spoke to the audience.

"Hello and welcome to tonight's Llewellyn Hall performance by the Canberra Symphony Orchestra."

"This will be a special performance from our capitals' premier orchestra!"

"Please sit back, relax and enjoy this musical feast."

The audience clapped loudly as the performance began.

The next morning when we were packed and ready to leave for Sydney...Mum had decided to take the first leg of the journey... so she put the key into the ignition and turned...but nothing happened.

"The car normally starts with no trouble." said Mum, puzzled

"Try it again dear." said Dad, hopefully

Mum turned the key again but the car would not start. We can't go anywhere if the car won't go!

"This car will not '*bleepin*' start!"

"I don't know what's wrong with it!" said Mum, in a very aggravated tone

"Language dear!"

"Please don't say things like that...especially in front of Cassie."

"Swearing won't help the problem." Dad remonstrates, with Mum

"Sorry, dear."

"I don't why our car will not start!" Mum said, crossly

"I'll get the toolbox... see if I can find out what's wrong... then try to fix it." I said, firmly

Mum and Dad looked at each other with concern. I have been helping them fix their cars for about six months now, but they weren't sure that I could do it on my own yet.

"Are you sure you can, Cassie?"

"We don't want you getting hurt." said Mum, in a concerned voice

"I'm sure I can do it."

"I've watched you working on the cars and I remember what you did, the tools you used etc."

"I promise I won't hurt myself." I said, in a 'matter of fact' voice

"Umm...ok...Cassie, but I'll supervise you to make sure nothing goes wrong." said Dad

"All right Dad, but I've watched enough car programs to know how to fix things, I should be ok." I smiled at him

I went to the front of our car and Dad got the toolbox from out of the boot and handed it to me. I opened the bonnet and looked for any problems, underneath it.

"Dad, I think the crankshaft is broken!" I said

"You could be right Cassie."

"I'll pass you the extractor wrench so you can remove it and see." Dad said

Dad passed me the extractor wrench, I looked at the crankshaft and realise this is not going to be a quick job, this could take hours to fix!

"Dad, I know how to remove a crankshaft and put a new one in, but it's a big mechanical job, it requires the right equipment, and even then, it will take several hours to complete and I need a replacement part too." I said

"You're right, Cassie."

"Looks like we need to get it to a garage to be fixed up!"

"I'll check up to find one in Canberra." said Dad, getting out his iPhone

"I've found one Cassie!"

"City Car Care in Braddon." Dad said

"I'll give them a call, they are bound to have a towing service, they are a big repair garage!" Dad added

He dialled the number and arranged for a tow truck to collect our vehicle and get it fixed as soon as possible.

Whilst we were waiting for the tow truck service to arrive, Dad arranged for a car hire company to provide us with a hire car. Thirty minutes later the tow truck arrived to take our vehicle to the garage, and five minutes after that a hire car pulled up beside us.

Dad filled out the paperwork, got the keys from the man, and he jumped into his mate's car to go back to the car hire service centre. We now had a car to use for the day as we obviously will not be able to drive the three hours to Sydney... until our vehicle has been repaired.

"We shall have to drive to Sydney tomorrow, when we get our car back." said Mum

Luckily, we were able to book back in to our previous night's accommodation for one more night's stay.

In Braddon I spotted the Gelato Messina, what an awesome place to get a delicious ice cream! When we went inside there were gelati flavours like apple pie, chocolate fondant and strawberries and cream, there were sorbets of blood orange, lemon, salted coconut and mango salsa.

Mum, Dad and I, were giddy with choice, we could try several flavours if we wanted to. We could also try a flavour combo like Dulche de Leche & Apple Pie, if we want! Which flavour to choose? There are so many, I can't decide which one to try!

We finally choose our gelato flavours each and sit outside to enjoy them.

"I've always loved ice-cream."

"Vanilla has to be my favourite flavour of all-time!"

"When you add white chocolate to it Mum, it makes it even more delicious and wicked!"

"I never tried strawberry before, but now I'm enjoying extra flavours!"

"This is the first time I have tried gelato and I can't get enough of it!" I said, excitedly

"I also enjoyed ice-cream, growing up."

"Chocolate is my favourite flavour."
"I sometimes add sprinkles to it, to add a special touch." said Mum
"My favourite flavour would have to be banana."
"I like to add chocolate topping to make it special and tasty!" said Dad
"I will sometimes put cream on my ice-cream, and ice-cream on my bread during the summer." I said
"Yuck!"
"That sounds disgusting, Cassie!" said Dad
"It's gross, Cassie!"
"Another one of your weird food combinations!" said Mum
"Yes, it sure is!"
"It is appetising to me, but not so much for you two!"
"I've been experimenting since I was young...they are tasty to me."
"Whatever weird food combination will I come up with next?" I said, chuckling at the thought

Mum and Dad just groaned. We spent the day cruising around the sights of Canberra, then early in the morning after breakfast, we drove to the automotive repair centre, paid for the repairs to our car and got back on the road again to Sydney.

# Chapter Nine
# Sydney Harbour Bridge Climb

"Wow!"
   "I never knew Sydney was this big!" I said excitedly

We are in the central part of Sydney, it took us three hours to drive here yesterday, and now we are walking around this amazing city. There are so many shops, and buildings that are higher than those in Melbourne...like the World Tower and the Queen Victoria Building. There's even the Sydney Opera House! That's the world-famous Sydney Opera House... that was designed by the Danish architect, Jorn Utzon!

"Mum!"

"Dad!"

"Remember the reward I chose is climbing the Sydney Harbour Bridge!" I said

"Yes Cassie... we haven't forgotten!"

"We're going to climb it today... with some help from our guide!" said Dad

I looked at the Sydney Harbour Bridge for a moment... it is affectionately called the 'coat hanger' by Sydneysiders... because of its' shape!

*'Wow... it looks pretty big and very tall!'* I thought

"We'll walk around a little more until eleven, we might get something at the Sydney Chocolate Shop, there are plenty of items to choose from." Dad added

Shortly before eleven, we walked to the Sydney Harbour Bridge where we bumped into Sally and Tom Wilson, my aunt and uncle... my cousin Mia was also with them. I wonder what they are doing in Sydney?

"Tom!"

"I didn't expect to see you here!" said Dad, very surprised

"Neither did I, Daniel!"

"Nice to see you." said Tom

"Sally!"

"What a coincidence seeing you in Sydney." says Mum, taken aback

"What a surprise to see you in Sydney Mikayla!" said Sally

"Cassie!"

"I've never seen you in Sydney before!" said Mia, excitedly

"It's my first time and I didn't expect to see you here in Sydney... face-to-face!" I laughed

"What are you three doing in Sydney?" asked Dad

"We're staying here for a week... sightseeing and doing a bit of shopping."

"Sally and Mia do love their shopping!" said Tom, with a rueful grin

"We're staying for a few days... we are on our way to the Sydney Harbour Bridge climb!" said Dad

"We are here to do the same thing!" Sally laughed

"We've been to Sydney a few times... we've done the Bridge Climb the last two times we were here."

"This will be our fourth time...we just love it!" said Sally

"Mum and Dad have done it a couple of times... but this will be my first time doing it."

"I'm a bit nervous about it though." I said

"We will help you... with the guide's help you should be fine."

"Just let us know if you feel dizzy." said Tom

"Yes, Uncle Tom." I said

We walked across to the Sydney Harbour Bridge, where the bridge climb information is situated, it's going to be an exciting experience for me. I hope I can do it!

The climb base was the first part of our experience, we explored the area, what a good place to start your bridge climb! There's a visitor centre and a cinema, but there's no time for watching movies with a climb to be made!

After exploring, we went to the front desk to check-in with our reservation that we had booked two weeks before. Our climb is to start at eleven forty-five this morning, we check in with fifteen minutes to spare. The team at the front desk did a quick health & safety assessment to make sure we're ready and fit for the climb, we pass so it's on to the next stage.

"How many are there in your group?" asked the receptionist

"There are six of us, consisting of three family members each, in two families." replied Mum

"Names?" enquired the receptionist

"Mia, Sally and Tom... of the Wilson Family." said Tom

"Daniel, Mikayla and Cassie... of the Bontel Family." said Dad

"Good luck!" said the receptionist, smiling

"Thank you." said Sally

"You'll be provided with the all the outdoor gear you'll need for the climb."

"The weather looks fine... you will need to wear your sunglasses... enclosed comfortable shoes and bring a sense of adventure... we will provide the rest for you!" said the receptionist, cheerily

"We have all of that covered." said Dad

"That's good!"

"Head to the pre-climb area where your climbing gear will be fitted."

We met our guide in the pre-climb area... it's going to be so exciting, but I'm a bit nervous... I should be fine with help and support from my family.

"Hello, Bontel and Wilson families."

"I hear you're all ready for your bridge climb!" said Stan, one of our two guides for today's bridge climb

"Yes, we are!"

"We just need to do a couple of things before we start." said Mum

"That's right!"

"One of them is the gear that you need... the other is the guide rope that you will be linked to for safety, during the climb." Stan instructed

"Stan, before we start can we speak to you for a few minutes?" Dad asked

"Of course." said Stan

"Cassie, you stay with Sally, Tom and Mia, we'll talk to Stan for a few minutes." Mum said

"Ok, Mum." I said

Mum, Dad and Stan, walk a few paces away, I can't hear what they are saying, but I can take a guess...

'Stan... just so you know... our daughter Cassie has conditions called autism, hyperthymesia and anxiety... it's her first time climbing the Sydney Harbour Bridge... so guide her through the process one step at a time...help her when she needs it.'

'If she gets anxious... she uses anxiety techniques... but remind her about them... just in case.'

'She may have a fear of heights...please help her to overcome that fear in any way you can.'

'No problem Mr and Mrs Bontel... I've helped Mia to climb the bridge since her first time... as well as Sally and Tom... so there shouldn't be any problems with Cassie.'

"That would be great, thanks!"

I hear Dad say, as he, Mum and Stan, come over to the rest of us.

Stan gives us some instructions before we begin.

"You may get a bit dizzy when walking up the bridge... so I recommend you stop and take a few deep breaths before you continue."

"If you want to stop at any time... it's up to you." said Stan

"We have some items that need to be put in the lockers over there as they are not allowed on the bridge for safety reasons... these include iPhones and cameras."

"They will be safe in there won't they? asked Mum, anxiously

"Yes, they will be locked at all times!"

"Lauren my co-guide and I will take the photos."

"You will also get a group climbing photograph, a certificate of achievement, a Bridge Climb Cap and a free entry to the Pylon Lookout!" said Stan, proudly

"That's a good package!"

"We are ready to do the climb!"

"Let's do it!" said Dad, enthusiastically

"Good."

"We've got our gear on...now secure your ropes and clip on...we're ready to go!" said Stan

"Everybody ready?" Stan asked again

"Yes, Stan!" we all replied

"Well let's go then!" said Lauren

We started by walking through the purpose-built tunnel.

'It's really dark in here... but I'm brave... I'm used to it... I'll be fine.' I told myself

It was really dark, but it was part of the experience, the next part was climbing the bridge itself. Let's hope I don't get too dizzy, otherwise I may never complete the climb.

When we got to the other side of the purpose-built tunnel, we were near the steps of the harbour bridge. When I looked above me, I never expected the bridge to be that high up close, and so many steps!

*The Harbour Bridge is very high all right... it looks scary... but I have to be a big girl for Mum and Dad... I can do it.'* I thought, hopefully

"We're now at the start of the second part of the Sydney Harbour Bridge climb."

"Bontel Family, you go first."

"I'll lead...be careful." said Stan

Stan started climbing up the bridge and we followed behind him. I felt fine for the first section of steps everything was all right at the moment, I'm enjoying it so far.

The sky was mostly blue with a little bit of grey... then several steps later I start to feel dizzy... I couldn't bring myself to take another step.

"Oh dear... I don't' feel too good."

"Help!" I said
"What's the matter Cassie?" asks Mum
"I feel dizzy."
"I feel like the world's spinning around me!" I said, doing my best to remain steady
"We'll stop here for a few minutes, Cassie."
"Then you can decide whether to continue or not." Stan said
"Ok, Stan." I said, still feeling a bit dizzy
"Is everything all right up there?" asked Sally
"Cassie got a bit dizzy at the halfway point, but she will be fine after a few minutes." said Dad
"I'm sure she will be."
"The first time we climbed Mia was a bit dizzy... after a few minutes she managed to continue to the top and was happy that she completed the climb."
"I hope Cassie can do the same... but it's her choice." said Tom

I also felt anxious, but I knew what to do... Mum, Dad and Stan, helped me to keep steady...Mum and Dad warned me they were going to touch me... it was okay. After a few minutes when the dizziness had passed, Mum and Dad gave me a choice.

"Cassie, I know it's a difficult choice for you to make."
"Take a few minutes to answer this one." said Mum
"Do you want to continue climbing the Sydney Harbour Bridge or stop the climb and try again the next time we come here?"
"Take your time to answer." said Dad

For a few minutes, I thought about the question that I must answer.

*'I can stop climbing the Sydney Harbour Bridge and that will make me better... but I won't overcome my fear of heights and I may not get the chance to receive the photos if I do...but if I continue to climb the Sydney Harbour Bridge and reach the top... I will feel like I have conquered another fear... I will have the photos that I can treasure forever... I will be able to tell future generations... I must continue the climb... I know I can do this!'* I thought

"Mum... Dad... Stan."
"I thought about my answer... I have decided to continue climbing the Sydney Harbour Bridge!"
"I've started... so I'll finish!" I said, determined to try again
"That's the way, Cassie." said Mum
"You can do this Cassie!
"You can reach the top!" said Dad
"We know you can do it, Cassie!" said Tom, Sally and Mia
"Right... let's resume the climb!" said Stan

We resumed and continued to climb to the top, Sally, Tom and Mia started their climb.

*'I'm doing well after that dizzy break...the top of the Harbour Bridge is not so far away now... I'm almost there... it's like climbing Mount Everest... except you climb from the side and reach the top in the middle.'* I thought

"How are you going Cassie?" asked Mum
"I'm going well, Mum."
"It's getting a little bit easier now... I'm enjoying it a little more too." I said
"You are doing very well, darling."
"Keep going until we reach the top... we're nearly there." said Dad

"How are you three doing behind us?" asks Mum

"We're doing well thanks Mikayla." answered Sally

Mia, Sally and Tom's support and encouragement… as well as Mum, Dad and Stans' spurred me on… eventually we reached the middle of the top of Sydney Harbour Bridge! Whew! I had tried another challenge and this one had to be the hardest I've ever attempted before! Oh, yeah! Go Cassie! Go Cassie!

"Cassie, you have reached the top of the Sydney Harbour Bridge!"

"Congratulations!" said Stan beaming at me

"Thank you, Stan!"

"I have triumphed!" I said, fist pumping the air

"Well done, Cassie!"

You persisted and it paid off in the end!" said Mum, delightedly

"I'm so very proud of you, Cassie!"

"You did so well!" Dad said, with a grin from ear to ear

"So are we."

"You have conquered the Sydney Harbour Bridge!" said Sally

"You were very brave and you made it to the top!"

"Great job!" said Tom

"I'm so happy for you, Cassie!"

"Good on you." Mia said, smiling at me

"Thank you all for helping me through the process." I said gratefully

"Well done to all of you… for climbing the bridge!"

"Lauren and I will take the photos… you will receive them when you exit the Bridge Climb building." said Stan

After we returned to the building, we picked up our photos and looked them over, while we sat on the steps below.

"We look very brave and joyful." I said

"It looks like we're on top of the world!"

"It was fun doing it as a family." said Mum

"Would you allow me to give you a hug?"

"You deserve one after that amazing event." said Mia

"Mia, I'm not sure that I could allow you to do that."

"I dislike being hugged… maybe you might dislike being hugged too." I said, nervously

"Cassie, I have no problems hugging Mum and Dad since I was discharged from hospital after I broke my foot… when I dropped a pot plant on it when I was nine years old."

"I hugged them and told them I loved them too… they did the same back."

"You deserve a hug from me." said Mia

I wasn't sure whether to allow Mia to hug me. I dislike being hugged, (part of being touched… a sensory issue that I have), but since I did try a new activity, I allowed Mia to hug me.

"All right Mia, I do deserve one, let's give it a try." I said

We hugged each other, it felt good to hug Mia for the first time in years.

"How sweet is that? smiled Mum

"That's very good to see." said Dad

"Well done Mia for giving Cassie a hug… she hasn't hugged you for a long time… but with your encouragement she was able to do so." Tom added

"Thanks, Dad." said Mia, happily

"Cassie, you and Mia will become even closer now!"

"That's so sweet." said Sally

"We will." I agreed

Just then, we saw a female reporter and camera crew coming towards us. I knew the reporter because she had interviewed Mum, Dad and I, previously. The crew were from a celebrity magazine called 'Celebrity Guest' a magazine that features celebrities from Australia and around the world.

Mum, Dad and I, have been regularly featured since last year, we had our own section titled 'Unique Life with the Bontels'. Our family and friends are also featured now and then. I have been forewarned by Mum and Dad that they are going to interview me, so I know what to expect, I will try to answer their questions.

"Bontel Family, we've watched the whole thing unfold, we saw it all, this is a great triumph!"

"It will make an excellent piece for the 'Star Celebs' segment on 'Celebrity Guest'!"

"Cassie, you have scaled great heights to reach the top!"

"Mind if I interview you first?" asked Tania Garrison, the current reporter

"I don't mind at all." I replied

This is how the interview went after my first historic Sydney Harbour Bridge climb!

"Cassie... was this was your first time climbing the Sydney Harbour Bridge?" asked Tania

"How did you feel before that long climb?"

"Yes, it was my first time."

"I felt a bit nervous and excited all at the same time!"

"It was a challenge I wanted to experience on our road trip!"

"When you got to the halfway point of the bridge climb... you struggled there."

"What happened?" the reporter asked

"Well... I began to feel a little dizzy as you sometimes do when you reach that point on the Bridge."

"Everything was spinning around me and I felt a little bit nauseous...with Mum and Dad helping me and a five-minute break... I felt better and calmer."

"That's great!"

"When you made it to the top could you feel the excitement?"

"Yes, I did feel elated... the view was extraordinary!"

"I could even see the Sydney Cricket Ground and the Opera House from the top!"

Mum, Dad, Mia, Sally and Tom, were interviewed in turn. After all the excitement, we walked down the Opera House Steps.

"Cassie has shown bravery...the Sydney Harbour Bridge climb takes courage!" said Sally

"She's becoming braver every day, she might perform in one of the capital cities, even Sydney, with Daniel and Mikayla!" said Tom

"Imagine if they formed a three-piece pop band!"

"We could attend one of their concerts... I wonder what name they would pick?" Mia said

Then they heard a thud, and three 'oofs', from behind them! Mum, Dad and I, have missed our footing on the last step and fallen in a heap on top of each other.

"We missed a step that's all." said Dad, somewhat sheepishly

We picked ourselves up and dusted ourselves off. It was only the last step, we didn't get any scratches or bruises, it was a case of misjudging the step.

"Are you three all right?" asked Sally in a worried voice

"Yes, we're fine Sally." Mum assured her

"No bruises or scratches, we're ok." said Dad

"Our three-piece pop band, 'The Bontel Family' is doing well!" I said

"So that's the name of your band!" grinned Mia

"After that trip-up... I thought it might have been 'The Clumsies'." she added, cheekily

"'The Bontel Family' album was released in March this year." I told her

"It charted in the Top Ten in Australia and New Zealand!" said Mum

"That's a great effort for a debut album!" said Sally

"The album has thirteen songs, one about our diagnosis with the themes of acceptance, understanding and inspiration... also twelve cover songs." said Dad

"It has strengthened our bond as a family."

"Other countries around the world may release our album... if it's a hit on their music channels and radio stations!" I added

"May we come to one of your concerts?" asked Tom

"Of course!"

We've planned 'The Bontel Family' Australian tour starting in Sydney, it's our first concert of the tour!" said Mum

"We know...but remind us again who's playing what instrument... and who does the vocals!" asked Sally

"I play lead guitar and provide vocals, Mikayla plays drums and also does vocals, Cassie sings lead vocals!" said Dad

"Cassie do you play any instruments in the band?" asked Mia

"I play rhythm guitar in addition to lead vocals, I'm an aspiring popstar in the making!" I said, grinning

"You certainly are on the way to becoming a pop star with 'The Bontel Family' album release... maybe even a worldwide sensation!" said Tom, grinning back at me

"Maybe." I laughed

"The Bontel Family Band... is just the starting point of my popstar career."

"There will be two parts to our concert."

"One will be Cassie's solo... which is a cover song." said Mum

"Which song are you covering Cassie?" asks Sally

"I'm doing a version of 'Strawberry Kisses'... which was sung originally by Australian pop singer Nikki Webster." I replied

"That's a good song to cover... is it your favourite?" asked Mia

"Yes... I have a voice that sounds similar to hers." I replied

"We would love to hear that at your concert here."

"Can you tell us which cover songs you're each going to sing?" Tom said

"One of my favourite songs is 'Two Strong Hearts' by John 'Farnsie' Farnham!" said Dad

"Will there be any collaborations?" asked Sally

"There is one...with 'Quirky Service'." Mum replied

"Well good luck and we'll see you at the concert in Sydney soon!" said Mia

We said good bye to Tom, Sally and Mia and made our way back to our hotel.

"I'll look up concert venues... rehearsal rooms and performance locations... to see if any suit us." said Dad

There are few venues we could perform in such as... the Horden Pavillion...the Sydney Opera House... the Oxford Art Factory and the Metro Theatre."

"Which one shall we perform in first?" he asked

"I would like to perform at the Metro Theatre."

"It seems like a good place to me."

"It's well-decorated... colourful...with a myriad of music genres having played there." I replied

"I agree... it would be a great place to make our debut!" stated Mum

"Dad... when you are looking for rehearsal venues... can you look up some dance schools as well... see if you can get any backing dancers for my solo performance?" I asked

"Good idea Cassie... I'll see if there's any!" said Dad

Dad looked up some dance schools and found a special one which might have the backing dancers that I need for my performance.

"Here's one that might work, Cassie."

"What is that dance school Dad?"

"It looks very special." I added

"That one is called 'Pop Dance Music School'."

"It's a dance school for teens with special needs that includes mostly girls who love pop music and dancing, and who want to become singers and dancers."

"It includes teens with disabilities... such as Downs Syndrome... their parents help out."

"They are aged from between thirteen to eighteen years old... most of them aspire to becoming backing singers or dancers when they graduate from the school."

"It would be a great place to find your backing dancers!" said Dad, enthusiastically

"That would be a great place to find them!"

"What time do they have classes?" I asked

"They take three classes...first class is at ten in the morning and two classes in the afternoon at one and three." he replied

"Since it's a quarter to one, we'd better make a call and see if we can book them for rehearsals tomorrow... I will try to find a suitable rehearsal space!" said Dad

He dialled some numbers to make the bookings.

"Hello, is that the Pop Dance Music School?" Dad asked down the phone

"Oh good." he said, nodding his head

"I would like to book the pop dance girls dancing troupe for a special project."

"My daughter plans to do a debut solo performance at the Metro Theatre at the end of the week, we need rehearsals before the performance as well."

"Would you have anyone available?" he added

"Your class has five autistic girls that have performed at Sydney concert venues and they will be happy to perform with Cassie, that's great!"

"We will be rehearsing at the Metro Theatre at eleven in the morning...you have two breaks at eleven and two...you can meet us at eleven..."

"Eleven it is then, see you there!"

"Bye." Dad ended his call

"Well, that's sorted!"

"The Pop Dance Music School dancing troupe will meet us at eleven for rehearsals at the Metro Theatre, Cassie."

"We'll help you prepare, then it's your time to shine!" said Dad, theatrically waving his hands like a ringmaster

"That's great Dad!"

"The start of my popstar career!" I said, happily
Meanwhile Mum is 'cooking' something up and I don't mean food!
"I think I'll play a trick on my brother-in-law Glenn!"
"It involves the Collingwood and Sydney match that was played several days ago."
"I'm going to have fun!" said Mum, with a naughty look
Mum dialled Glenn's number.
"Hello Glenn... it's Mikayla here... oh bad luck." said Mum, in a very falsely sympathetic tone of voice
Then we all started laughing, she loves to tease him when Collingwood beats Sydney! Mum put Uncle Glenn on speakerphone.
"Very funny, Mikayla!"
"Wait until Collingwood loses to Sydney next time, they meet... then we'll see how funny that is!" said Glenn, fuming
"Like that's going to happen, Glenn!" said Mum, laughing
Then she cheekily hangs up the phone!
"That was a good one Mum... you're quite the comedian when you're teasing Glenn about AFL!" I laughed
"Why don't we visit Gary, my big sister Betty and Jacinta for tea?"
"I'm sure they would be happy to see us." Mum added
"We can do that." said Dad, agreeing
"It would be great to see them!"
"They used to have a big pool out the back to swim in and they used to have a karaoke machine too!" I remember
"They used to."
"They moved recently their old house used to have a steep driveway... their current house is just across the road!" Mum explained
"We have a few hours to do things before we visit there at around six this evening Cassie."
"We'll need some good accessories in our favourite colours, and some black designer sunglasses, to make us all look totally rad!"
"Let's go to the shopping centre to buy some necessities and browse a few stores!" Mum said, with a gleam in her eye
At one point, Dad and I nearly had to drag Mum away from the dress shop, she had her eye on a yellow sparkling dress, she was very keen to get it for our upcoming concert!
"Come on, dear."
"We can get it after we have a 'cuppa'." Dad tried coaxing
"You've got a couple like that back at our house... but if you want it... you can get it." I said, grinning
"Right...I do have a couple at home with similar sparkles...I'll consider after I've had a cup of tea." said Mum, grinning back at me
We chatted over our 'cuppa' about the things we loved about this road trip so far.
When we had finished, we spent the rest of the afternoon shopping, before we went to Aunty Betty's for tea.
"I'll text Kate, Adam, Amelia and Nicole to tell them that you did the Bridge Climb for the first time, is that ok?" asked Mum
"Yes, that would be good Mum." I said
Mum sent a text to Kate. Kate is twenty-nine and has long pink hair...it was originally ginger!

Mum's text read... 'Cassie has achieved something wonderful she climbed the Sydney Harbour Bridge for the first time today! She made it right to the top with just one stop along the way. She was very brave and rose to the challenge with our assistance.'

'Wow! My niece reached the top and what a bridge to do it on! Good on her for conquering the bridge climb!' Kate texted back

Meanwhile at Kate's place, she called out to the others to read her text from Mum.

"Adam, Nicole, Amelia, I received a text from Mikayla."

"It's about Cassie."

"Come and look at this!" said Kate

Adam, Nicole and Amelia ran to Kate's room to see the text.

"My goodness, Cassie did really well on the 'coat-hanger'!" said Adam

"That is so brave!"

"Cassie is becoming more inspirational with every day!" said Nicole, admiringly

"Cassie could climb the Eureka Tower in Melbourne if she wanted to!" said Amelia, excitedly

"Let's send our messages of congratulations to Cassie's iPhone to let her know how proud of her we are!" said Kate

Kate, Adam, Nicole and Amelia sent their messages of congrats which I received on my iPhone, One... Two...Three...Four!

Kate's text read... 'Congratulations, Cassie, my darling niece. You've reached new heights lol. I'm very happy for you!'

Adam's text... 'Very well done, Cassie. You've reached the summit of Sydney Harbour Bridge! Good job! You did well, to persevere to the top!'

Nicole's text read... 'You did so well, Cassie, sweetheart. You've scaled the bridge to reach the very top! I'm so proud of you for that.'

Amelia's text... 'You defied the heights to get to the top of the Harbour Bridge! I'm so happy for you. You can achieve anything you set your mind to!'

"Isn't that lovely, Cassie?"

"Getting all those congratulations from Kate, Adam, Nicole and Amelia." said Mum, smiling at me

"It is lovely." I nodded

"I appreciate them all... they make me feel good about myself." I smiled

"How about we invite them to our Sydney concert and have them perform with us on the track.... 'Help is on its' Way'?" said Dad

"That's a good idea." I replied, happily

Mum and Dad texted Kate, Adam, Nicole and Amelia, they replied with... 'The Bontel Family album charted in the top ten in Australia and New Zealand? Beauty! We'll definitely perform on the track... 'Help is on its' Way'... at your Sydney Concert!

We can't wait for that!'

## Chapter Ten
## 'Max and Smoochums'

Mum rang Betty at four o'clock to let them know we were coming.

"Hello, Betty, It's Mikayla." said Mum

"Hello, Mikayla, how nice of you to ring me."

"What are you up to?" asked Betty

At six we drove up to Betty and Glenn's house, it had a garage on the right side with steps leading up to the front door. There was an arch over the steps, with thorns poking through the gaps in the arches. We walked up to the door and I rang the doorbell, I could hear two dogs barking inside which made me feel nervous.

"Max!"

"Smoochums!"

"Settle down!"

I could hear Betty say through the door

"I'm not sure about Betty's dogs."

"They might bite me." I said, frightened

"It's all right, Cassie."

"They won't bite you."

"Just use your anxiety techniques." said Mum, soothingly

Betty opened the door she looks happy to see Mum.

"Mikayla!"

"How are you 'little sis'?" said Betty, hugging Mum

"I'm well thanks 'big sis'." said Mum, hugging her back

Mum and Betty get along well, Mum is the younger of the two, Mum sometimes plays pranks on Betty, she likes to wind her up like little sisters do! Since her mid-twenties, Mum has referred to Betty as cheeky 'Big Sis', even when they talk on the phone.

It's all in good fun, Mum gets along with Glenn… Betty's husband… and she shares a bond…a special one… with Jacinta my cousin. Mum helps her get around whenever she visits Sydney, when Betty is busy working as an administrator at a special needs school… Jacinta is blind, since she was born premature… she gets around with a cane.

Mum loves her big sister, they share a love of jokes and they both especially love Kevin Wilson, the Aussie comedian!

"How are you Daniel…you, handsome bugger?" said Betty, cheekily

"I'm fine thanks Betty." laughed Dad

"Cassie, how are you?"
"I'm well thanks Aunt Betty."
"I have a fear of dogs though!"
"Especially... Max and Smoochums." I said, eyeing them nervously
"It's all right."
"Max and Smoochums won't harm you."
"They're only playful and friendly." said Betty, reassuringly
"Okay." I said, though I was not strictly convinced yet
"We invited ourselves for tea Betty!"
"Thought you might need our scintillating company!" said Mum very cheekily, which made Aunty Betty laugh hard
"Yes... I'm sure we do!"
"Come in... Jacinta and Glenn are in the lounge room watching the news." said Betty

We went inside what a lovely house this is, there's a computer room where Glenn works, Betty and Glenn's room is on the left side and Jacinta's room is next to theirs. The bathroom is on the left side too, there's a lounge room, pool room and bedroom for guests staying over. They have a pool out the back like in their old house, but this one is slightly smaller than their old pool.

"Hello, guys.'
"How are you?" asks Glenn
"We're fine Glenn." Dad replied
"Hello, Uncle Glenn, nice to see you."
"It's nice to see you too, Cassie."
"Hello, Jacinta, great to see you again." says Mum
"Hello, Aunt Mikayla." Jacinta replies

She makes her way to Mum across the room and hugs her, Mum does the same.

"Hello, Jacinta." I said
"Hello, Cassie." Jacinta replied

Jacinta followed the sound of my voice and came to give me a hug too.

"Oh my, you've grown a bit since the last time I visited you!"
"You're about the 180-185 cm mark, aren't you?" asked Jacinta
"Yes... I'm 181 cm or five feet nine inches tall to be exact." I said
"Wow... you're taller than Aunty Mikayla and Uncle Daniel!"
"You are even taller than me!" said Jacinta
"Yes... I bet you're all shrinking!" I said, cheekily
"Cassie you always make me laugh... you could be a comedian." Betty smiled
"I might add comedy to my music in addition to the pop styles that I plan to use." I grinned
"You are going to be successful I can tell!" said Uncle Glenn, with a wink

I smelt a familiar smell... a smell that involves sausages, steak and onion! It's one of the smells that I love! It's delicious and mouth-watering all at the same time!

"Is that a barbecue I can smell?" I asked, hopefully
"Yes, it is!"
"We are cooking it for tea right now, it will be ready soon, would you like to help me cook the sausages, steak and onions?" asked Glenn
"Yes, Glenn... I sure would! said Dad, licking his lips

"I'll help you out, Aunt Betty." I said

"That would be good, thank you."

I helped Betty with the barbeque preparations as I have done before when family comes over, or when Mum, Dad and I, are having it for lunch or tea. I always enjoy helping and I'm careful not to burn myself, when the plates of hot meat are transferred from the BBQ to the table for eating.

"The sausages, steak and onions are ready to eat." I called

"I love a good barbeque!"

"I especially love a good steak." said Dad, grinning

"You certainly do love a good steak sweetheart I can vouch for that!" said Mum, stroking Dad's chin.

Whilst we are 'tucking in' to the barbeque we have a good chat about our road trip.

"You're doing a road trip?"

"That's so adventurous of you taking a big leap like that!" said Betty

"It is a great challenge for all of the family!" said Dad

"Goodness me!"

"Where have you been and what have you done so far?" asked Glenn, fascinated

"We visited a zoo in Melbourne where funny elephants squirted and soaked us with water, we went on a trail ride, and have been kayaking in Echuca." said Mum

"You must be having fun and plenty of laughs along the way!"

"I can see that you are bonding well with all your adventures so far!" said Betty

"We've eaten plenty of foods and guess what!?"

"We have even talked face-to-face without the use of technology! said Dad, laughing out loud

"How amazing is that in this day and age!" he added, with a grin

"It is amazing… in this day and age." said Jacinta

"I made a couple of new friends along the way."

"One of them was a young girl of eight… we had a great time building sandcastles together…it was such fun." I said

"I'm happy that you made a new friend… you may make many more during this road trip." said Aunt Betty

"I hope I do." I said

"Betty… our debut album 'The Bontel Family' is selling really well in Australia and New Zealand… it is becoming a smash hit album in both countries." I told her

"That's great news!" said Betty

"It definitely is!" Dad agreed

"Are there any concerts booked yet?" asked Glenn

"We've got a performance booked at the Metro Theatre… we are visiting the Pop Dance Music School to book and rehearse some backup dancers… for Cassie's solo performance."

"It's the start of 'The Bontel Family' band Australian tour." said Mum

"I hope you three do well with your debut concert performance."

"I wish you the best of luck." said Betty

"Thanks, Betty." Dad replied

"Daniel… Mikayla… I remember your three nieces Kate, Nicole and Amelia plus your nephew Adam came to our house in April 2009… you were here too with Olivia and Rebecca."

"We were all in the backyard having a barbeque and a few of us were having a swim."

"We were having a good time… laughing, telling funny stories and sharing jokes."

"The girls and boys were swimming in the pool... I came over with my towel to lay it down... Kate, Nicole, Amelia and Adam pulled on the end of the towel and I fell into the water!"

"We all laughed like crazy... especially as I was still fully clothed at the time! I shall never forget that moment!" laughed Betty

"That was a funny story Betty."

"I wasn't here... I stayed with a family member whilst Mum and Dad had a few days holiday in Sydney."

"They had a lovely time here... but I'm sure you had a lovely time at home as well." said Aunt Betty

"I sure did!"

"I made a phone call on the third day...I had fun with family too." I said

"Thank goodness for family members!"

"They help you feel safe when your Mum and Dad go away... they are your protectors... keeping you safe from scary things...you can trust them to love and care for you." said Betty

"That's a nice thing to say Betty...thanks for that." I replied

"That's all right Cassie... I appreciate your words to me too." she reciprocated

"Betty... your dogs' Max and Smoochums are lovely."

"How many times a day do you feed them?" asked Mum

"Glenn and I feed them twice a day... in the morning and in the late afternoon."

"Whoops!"

"I forget to give them their tea!" she said

"The barbeque got a bit busy... so we forgot!" added Glenn

"Why don't I feed them for you?" I said

"That would be helpful, Cassie." said Glenn

"To tell you the truth I have a fear of dogs since I was two."

"That's all right, Cassie."

"I'll help you feed them."

"They may lick your face... but it's their way of showing affection." Betty said

"All right, Betty."

Betty showed me where they kept the dog food, we got out Max and Smoochum's bowls and placed them on the veranda in the backyard. I crouched down, poured the right amount into both of their bowls and called.

"Max!"

"Smoochums!"

"Time for tea!"

Max and Smoochums raced up and licked my face, this time instead of fear I was laughing and enjoying myself.

"Who's a good little doggy?"

"Oh, yes you are!" I said to Max

I also said the same thing to Smoochums.

"There's lovely dinner ready for you two so eat up, it's very tasty!" I said.

"Well done Cassie." said Betty

I left them to eat their tea in peace and walked back into the lounge room.

"Cassie, we heard you laughing, it was a great thing to hear!"

"Well done." said Dad

"Good job, Cassie."

"You fed two dogs and were laughing doing it!" exclaimed Mum

"Thanks."

"Thanks for feeding them for us." said Glenn

"Mum sometimes helps me she is teaching me but you did it without any mess!" said Jacinta

"Thank you, Betty, for helping me to overcome my fear of dogs."

"Max and Smoochums, will be the starting point."

"That's okay, Cassie, I'm glad to help you and so are Max and Smoochums!" said Betty, laughing

It was later that evening, when Mum, Dad and I, got ready to return to our hotel. We said goodbye to Betty, Glenn and Jacinta, thanking them for the lovely time we had spent with them. It was the first time I had visited their new house and we will come to visit again! When we arrived back at our hotel, we showered and put on our pyjamas.

"Cassie, well done for interacting with Max and Smoochums!" Mum said

"Mum and I are so proud of you!" Dad said

"Now, who wants to watch a comedy film?"

"There's one on tonight and it's a family one!" Mum said

"We would!" said Dad and I together, we all love our comedy films

The next day Mum, Dad and I, arrive at the Pop Dance Music School at eleven for my solo rehearsals. This will get me warmed up for the performances tonight!

I've got a few practice sessions to work through…as the old saying goes… 'Practice makes perfect'! I am nervous and excited… it's going to be fun!

"Hello."

"I'm pleased to meet you… I'm Gabriella Fawthrop the owner and teacher at 'Pop Dance Music School'." said Gabriella

"We're pleased to meet you, Gabriella."

"I'm Mikayla Bontel." Mum replied

"I'm Daniel Bontel." Dad added

"I'm Cassie Bontel, their daughter." I said

"I know you are very busy with your shows."

"Let's get started with practice Cassie…first you need to meet my girls!"

"They are taking a break at the moment…I'll introduce you to all five of them." Gabriella smiled

The girls came back from their break and lined up in front of the dance mirror, they look so pretty with their coloured costumes and bows in their hair.

"Here are the girls!"

"They love pop music and are keen to practice with you!"

"There is Sarah who is sixteen and has mild autism, we have Petunia who is fifteen with high-functioning autism, Prunella is sixteen and has mild Autism, Macy who is sixteen and has Asperger's, and Dina who is seventeen and has savant syndrome."

"Girls, meet the Bontel Family!" said Gabriella

"Hello girls!"

"How are you?" asked Mum

"Good thank you." answered the girls

"Cassie has always loved to dance since she was two years old."

"Her first favourite artists were the Australian children's group, 'The Wiggles' and 'Playground Kids'."

"She would make up dance moves to 'Playground Kids' songs... then copy the moves of 'The Wiggles'... then giggle about it."

"Then when Cassie turned five, she used to dance to Elton Johns' 'Tiny Dancer' and Aquas' 'Barbie Girl'." Mum said, smiling at the girls

"I'm very pleased to meet you girls." said Dad

"So are we." giggled the girls

"I'm so excited to meet you all!" I said, shaking the girls' hands one by one

Dana was a little bit shy she had heard about me before but never seen me face-to-face.

"It's okay, Dana."

"It's Cassie... she's very friendly and nice." said Gabriella, reassuringly

Dana stepped forward to shake my hand.

"Hello, Cassie."

"I love your parent's music, Quirky Service, Katy Perry and Madonna."

"It makes me feel like I'm in the 'eighties'... with a rainbow full of colour."

"I love pop music too Dana... many pop genres around the world!"

"We're going to have lots of fun practicing for the performance tonight." I told her

"Yes, we will."

"It's going to be a fun session Cassie!" said Petunia

"Right then, girls!"

"Let's get this practice session underway."

"Take your positions please... form a part triangle shape."

"Cassie, take your position at the front please, stand at the point of the triangle." said Gabriella

We all moved into position, Dina, Prunella and Macy at the back, Sarah and Petunia in the middle and I am at the front, a perfect triangle shape!

"Good."

"Cassie, you like 'Nikki Webster' don't you?" asked Gabriella

"I sure do, Gabriella!"

"She is my favourite artist!"

"I have lots of other favourites too." I said

"That's fine, I think you will sing like her tonight!"

"I'll put on 'Strawberry Kisses' when I hand you the microphone... all right?" Gabriella explains

"All right... let's practice." I replied

Gabriella hands a microphone to me and turns 'Strawberry Kisses' on. I hear Nikki's voice *'I've been missing, wishing, missing ya strawberry kisses... I've been missing, wishing, missing ya strawberry kisses... come on... I've been missing, wishing, missing ya strawberry... oh-oh... I've been missing, wishing, missing your strawberry kisses... yeah-yeah'*

That was my cue to start singing, Sarah, Prunella, Petunia, Macy and Dana started their moves which they have been practising.

I sang the lines... 'I've been missing your strawberry kisses, coz nothing's as sweet, the taste still drives me crazy...I've been wishing your strawberry kisses, could fly through the wind to you from me.'

"Very good, girls."

"You did really well."

"Now let's do it again, this time with the karaoke version."

"Into positions please." Gabriella instructed

We all did very well with the karaoke version of 'Strawberry Kisses', my singing was on track, I have been singing since I was five years old.

"Good job, girls."

"Let's practice for fifty minutes, then we'll take a lunch break." said Gabriella

"Come on girls, we can do it!" I said, encouraging the dancing group

We practiced until lunchtime we were exhausted but our performance was coming together nicely.

Later that evening, after we had our dinner at the Metro Theatre at seven, the girls and I headed backstage to prepare for our performance. We called ourselves, 'The Sparkles' because it was a pretty name. As well as performing 'Strawberry Kisses', we will perform eight other pop songs recorded by various female artists and covered by me. It's going to be so much fun for us all!

## Here is the song list:

| Song/Original Artist | Lead Vocals | Composer/s |
| --- | --- | --- |
| 'Feelings of Forever' Tiffany | Cassie Bontel | Donna Weiss, John Duarte, Lauren Wood |
| 'Superstar' Jamelia | Cassie Bontel | Remee, Joe Belmaati, Mich Hansen |
| 'Baby one more Time' Britney Spears | Cassie Bontel | Max Martin |
| 'Wherever, Whenever' Shakira | Cassie Bontel | Shakira, Tim Mitchell, Ron Smith, Gloria Estefan |
| 'Holiday' Madonna | Cassie Bontel | Curtis Hudson, Lisa Stevens |
| 'Tik Tok' KeSha | Cassie Bontel | Kesha, Dr. Luke, Benny Blanco |
| 'Teenage Dream' Katy Perry | Cassie Bontel | Katy Perry, Lukasz Gottwald, Max Martin, Benjamin Levin, Bonnie McKee |
| 'Let's Get Loud' Jennifer Lopez | Cassie Bontel | Gloria Estefan, Kiki Satander |
| 'Strawberry Kisses' Nikki Webster | Cassie Bontel | Jeff Franzel, Andy Marvel, Majorie Maye |

Mum and Dad came backstage to prepare for our performance later, as the Bontel Family. This night is going to be an exciting one… filled with music and dance! There will be crowds and loud noises, but I will cope with that. This is my time to shine, step up onto the stage and show Australia what I'm made of!

"Cassie, it's going to be one exciting night, isn't it!" said Mum

"Yes, it sure is Mum!"

It will be a great debut I'm feeling a bit nervous and I know the crowd may be large with lots of loud noise… but I can do it!" I said, determinedly

"That's the way Cassie!"

"You will be our popstar daughter!" said Dad, with a wide smile

"Thanks Dad!"

"I am proud to have pop star parents like you!" I said, grinning back at him

"It's okay to be nervous Cassie."

"We all get nervous sometimes, even 'WE' did in our early years of Quirky Service, but once we're onstage, we sing and dance the whole night through!"

"Sometimes in our early years, we used to pretend the audience wasn't there whilst we were performing, until we overcame our shyness."

"I know you will do well Cassie in your solo debut, then we can all do well together later tonight, in our family band!" Mum squeezed my hand, and gave me a big smile

"I will do my best Mum!" I replied

"I don't need my headphones anymore." I said

Mum and Dad turned to look at each other, the look that passed between them was one of... *'Is she serious!!!'*

"Are you sure you don't need them, Cassie?"

"You might become overwhelmed and meltdown in front of the whole Sydney Metro Theatre!"

"I would be very unhappy if that occurred." said Dad, with a concerned look and worried tone in his voice

"We don't want you to get upset and spoil your solo debut."

"I would be broken-hearted if that happened." said Mum, holding my hands tightly

Mum always holds my hands when I get scared, upset, or when I'm about do something that she thinks will cause me to have a meltdown in a public place. Sometimes that includes my favourite activity, or the solo performance that I am about to do.

Mum is concerned about my safety, along with Dad who wants to protect me, as all parents want to do for their children.

They want to do what's best for me, so I can progress, survive, and feel safe in the world.

"Mum, Dad, I'm certainly sure I'll be fine."

"Don't worry about me!"

"I'm determined to perform well in my solo performance... no matter what it takes."

"I can step up those steps... onto that stage where I will entertain the crowd... just like they do in X Factor Australia." I said, with a determined look on my face

"Ok, Cassie, if that's you want to do."

"Dad and I, are very concerned about you performing in front of a big crowd without your headphones... but if you want to do this.... then it's all right with us."

"We would so be proud of you if you can manage that!"

"Good luck sweetie!"

"You have all our love and support." said Mum, letting go of my hands

"You can do this, Cassie."

"All your family and friends are behind you." said Dad, proudly

# Chapter Eleven
## Cassie's 'sparkly' Debut!

The MC walked onstage with a microphone in his hand ready to introduce us to the concert audience.
"Hello everyone, I should like to welcome you all to tonight's special music performance!"
"Tonight... we have two performances... which I guarantee you will enjoy!"
"The first musical event features sixteen-year old Cassie Bontel in her solo debut performance...with her backing group of five female dancers from the 'Pop Dance Music School'...from right here in Sydney... who specialise in students with 'special' needs."
"Sit back and wait for this aspiring new popstar to blow you away with her expressive voice... and her backing dancers with their amazing dance skills."
"Please welcome to the stage, 'The Sparkles'!" the MC shouted to the crowd

The 'Sparkles' walked onstage, we waved to the crowd and took up our dancing positions. There are so many people here, but for the first time I didn't mind at all. It felt good to be on stage! The people were so happy to see us, I saw a few people with banners in the crowd.

Mum and Dad were backstage, crossing their fingers for luck, hoping that I would do well and not get stage fright!

"Cassie would you like to say a few words to the audience?" asked the MC, handing me the microphone.
"Thank you." I said, taking the microphone from him
"Hello and thanks for making it here tonight!"
"I guarantee this night will be one you won't forget."
'The Sparkles' will perform nine songs... including 'Strawberry Kisses'... which we will perform at the end of the show!"
"Before we start... I would like to introduce myself and the dancers."
"I am Cassie Bontel... I am 'Blue Sparkle' and the vocalist of the group."
"My backing dancers are Sarah... she is 'Yellow Sparkle'... Petunia who is 'Green Sparkle'...Prunella also known as 'Silver Sparkle'... Macy is 'Orange Sparkle' and Dina is 'Pink Sparkle'!" I told the audience, pointing out each girl in turn

The audience clapped when Dina, Macy, Petunia, Prunella and Sarah each did a twirl to their name.
"Keep up the good twirls girls!" I said, laughing
"There will be sparkles in the air... are you all ready to dance and sing along?" I asked the audience
"Yes!" they replied
"I can't hear you!" I said, cupping my hand to my left ear
"YES!" shouted the audience enthusiastically
"That's the way!"

"Five...Four...Three...Two...One.... start the music!"

When the music started it was 'Feelings of Forever' made popular by the American singer Tiffany. The lyrics describe Mum and Dad's life when they were boyfriend and girlfriend, hopefully they will appreciate me singing it, to remind them of those times.

## These are the lyrics.

*If there was no tomorrow*
*then tonight would never end*
*If we could freeze*
*the hands of time*
*I would stay here in your arms*
*and not go back again*

*'cos all I want is for you to hold me now*
*And we can make it through this night together*
*All I need is for you to show me how*
*'Cos nothing can stop this feeling of forever*

*I've never felt this close to love*
*lyin' here face to face*
*Far beneath the silver skies*

*there's no one around*
*To chase this night away*

*'cos all I want is for you to hold me now*
*And we can make it through this night together*
*All I need is for you to show me how*

*'Cos nothing can stop this feeling of forever*

*The world is ours tonight*
*as long as we just believe*
*The feelings that we hold inside*
*are in every heart that beats*

*'Cos all I want is for you to hold me now*
*And we can make it through this night together*
*All I need is for you to show me how*
*'Cos nothing can stop this feeling of forever*

The next song we will perform is 'Superstar' made popular by 'Jamelia'... it describes us all... I hope you will enjoy it as much as we enjoy performing it." I said

*People always talk about (ay oh ay oh ay oh)*
*All the things they're all about (ay oh ay oh ay oh)*
*Write it on a piece of paper, got a feeling I'll see you later.*

*There's something 'bout this,*
*Let's keep it moving,*
*And if its good let's just get something cooking*

*Cause I really wanna' rock with you, I'm feeling some connection to the things you do.*
*I don't know what it is, that makes me feel like this,*
*I don't know who you are, but you must be some kind of superstar,*
*Cause you got all eyes on you no matter where you are,*
*(you just make me wanna' dance)*

*Baby take a look around (ay oh ay oh ay oh)*
*Everybody's getting down (ay oh ay oh ay oh)*
*Deal with all the problems later,*
*Bad boys on their best behavior.*

*There's something 'bout you, let's keep it moving,*
*And if it's good let's just get something cooking,*
*'Cos I really 'wanna' rock with you, I'm feeling some connection to the things you do,*
*(you do, you do).*

*I don't know what it is, that makes me feel like this,*
*I don't know who you are, but you must be some kind of superstar,*
*'Cos you got all eyes on you no matter where you are,*
*(you just make me wanna dance).*

*I like the way you're movin' (ay oh ay oh ay oh)*
*I just get into the groove and then (you just make me wanna play),*
*If you just put pen to paper (ay oh ay oh ay oh)*
*Got that feeling I'll see you later.*

*Make your move, can we get a little closer,*
*You rock it just like you're supposed to,*
*Hey boy I aint got nothing more to say,*
*'Cos you just make me wanna play,*

*I don't know what it is, that makes me feel like this,*
*I don't know, gotta be, gotta be a superstar,*
*All eyes on you.*

"This next song was made famous by Britney Spears and it's called 'Baby One More Time'."

*Oh, baby, baby*
*Oh, baby, baby*
*Oh, baby, baby*
*How was I supposed to know*
*That something wasn't right here?*
*Oh, baby, baby I shouldn't have let you go*
*And now you're out of sight, yeah*
*Show me how you want it to be*
*Tell me, baby, 'cos I need to know now, oh, because...*
*My loneliness is killing me (and I)*
*I must confess, I still believe (still believe)*
*When I'm not with you I lose my mind*
*Give me a sign...*
*Hit me, baby, one more time*

*Oh, baby, baby the reason I breathe is you*
*Boy, you got me blinded*
*Oh, baby, baby there's nothing that I wouldn't do*
*It's not the way I planned it*

*Show me how you want it to be*
*Tell me, baby, cause I need to know Oh, because...*

*Oh, baby, baby*
*Oh, baby, baby*
*Ah, yeah, yeah*

*Oh, baby, baby*
*How was I supposed to know?*
*Oh, pretty baby I shouldn't have let you go*

*I must confess, that my loneliness*
*Is killing me now...*
*Don't you know I still believe that you will be here*

*Give me a sign...*
*Hit me, baby, one more time*

*I must confess, that my loneliness, is killing me now...*
*Don't you know I still believe that you will be here*
*Give me a sign...*
*Hit me, baby, one more time*

"Our next song has Latin Pop and Worldbeat influences."
"It's called 'Whenever, Wherever' by Colombian singer/songwriter Shakira."
"She is one of my favorite artists… a vibrant vocalist… so let's get ready to 'shake our booty'…. with some Shakira inspired dance moves everybody!" I said
The audience cheered they were ready!

*Lucky you were born that far away so*
*We could both make fun of distance*
*Lucky that I love a foreign land for*
*The lucky fact of your existence*

*Baby I would climb the Andes solely*
*To count the freckles on your body*
*Never could imagine there were only*
*Ten million ways to love somebody*

*Le ro lo le lo le, Le ro lo le lo le*
*Can't you see*
*I'm at your feet*

*Whenever, wherever*
*We're meant to be together*
*I'll be there and you'll be near*
*And that's the deal my dear*

*Thereover, hereunder*
*You'll never have to wonder*
*We can always play by ear*
*But that's the deal my dear*

*Lucky that my lips not only mumble*
*They spill kisses like a fountain*
*Lucky that my breasts are small and humble*
*So you don't confuse them with mountains*
*Lucky I have strong legs like my mother*
*To run for cover when I need it*
*And these two eyes that for no other*
*The day you leave will cry a river*

*Le ro le le lo le, Le ro le le lo le*
*At your feet*
*I'm at your feet*

*Whenever, wherever*
*We're meant to be together*
*I'll be there and you'll be near*
*And that's the deal my dear*

*Thereover, hereunder*
*You'll never have to wonder*
*We can always play by ear*
*But that's the deal my dear*

*Le ro le le lo le, Le ro le le lo le*
*Think out loud say it again*
*Le ro lo le lo le lo le*
*Tell me one more time*
*That you'll live*
*Lost in my eyes*

*Whenever, wherever*
*We're meant to be together*
*I'll be there and you'll be near*
*And that's the deal my dear*
*Thereover, hereunder*
*You've got me head over heels*
*There's nothing left to fear*
*If you really feel the way I feel*

*Whenever, wherever*
*We're meant to be together*
*I'll be there and you'll be near*
*And that's the deal my dear*

*Thereover, hereunder*
*You've got me head over heels*
*There's nothing left to fear*
*If you really feel the way I feel*

"The Sparkles and I, will take ten minutes break…see you soon!" I waved to the audience as we left the stage
"You are doing so well, darling."
"You are coping with the crowds and your voice is wowing them all." said Mum, proudly
"Thanks, Mum."
"I know it's my first time on stage… but I feel more confident than ever before." I replied
"Mum and I are proud of you… performing with us as the 'Bontel Family'…is a big step!" said Dad
"Yes Dad, it's awesome!" I grinned

"How are you doing, girls?"
"Going all right?" asked Mum
"Yes, we're doing all right, Mikayla."
"Cassie is doing very well for a first performance." Macy smiled
"Have you always loved pop music and singing Macy?" I asked
"I always have." she replied
"I have some favorites and I play guitar like you… but I am too nervous to perform in public… not even at high school." Macy said, ruefully
"It's okay to be nervous…you will gain confidence the more you try." I told her
"I was in a similar situation for many years…now I feel more confident than ever before."
Macy you should follow your dreams and see where they lead you." I smiled
"Thank you for saying that to me Cassie."
"You inspire me to have more confidence." Macy smiled back
"You have helped me too." I replied
We are all ready to get back onstage for the second half of the show. The first song in our second set is 'Holiday' by Madonna.

*Holiday Celebrate*
*Holiday Celebrate*

*If we took a holiday*
*Took some time to celebrate*
*Just one day out of life, it would be, it would be so nice*

*Everybody spread the word*
*We're gonna' have a celebration*
*All across the world*
*In every nation*
*It's time for the good times*
*Forget about the bad times, oh yeah*
*One day to come together*
*To release the pressure*
*We need a holiday*

*You can turn this world around*
*And bring back all of those happy days*
*Put your troubles down*
*It's time to celebrate*
*Let love shine*
*And we will find*
*A way to come together*
*And make things better*
*We need a holiday*

*Holiday Celebrate*
*Holiday Celebrate*

*Holiday Celebrate*
*Holiday Celebrate*

*Holiday, Celebration*
*Come together in every nation*

> "Are there any Ke$ha fans in the audience?" I ask
> A few people put up their hands.
> "I'll take it!"
> "That's good!"
> "Ke$ha has some very good electro-type pop dance tunes, so dance and sing along to this one!"
> "Here is 'Tik-Tok'... let's party Sydney!" I call out to the crowd
> The audience cheered loudly and the music began

*'Wake up in the mornin' feelin' like P-Diddy (hey what's up girl)*
*Grab my glasses I'm out the door I'm gonna hit the city (let's go)*
*Before I leave brush my teeth with a bottle of Jack*
*'Cos when I leave for the night I ain't comin' back*

*I'm talking pedicure on our toes toes*

*Trying on all our clothes clothes*
*Boys blowin' up our phones phones*
*Drop top and playin' our favorite CD's*
*Pullin' up to the parties*
*Tryna' get a little bit tipsy*
*Don't stop, make it pop*
*DJ, blow my speakers up*
*Tonight, Imma fight*
*'Til we see the sunlight*

*TiK ToK, on the clock*
*But the party don't stop no*
*Whoa-oh oh oh*
*Whoa-oh oh oh*

*Don't stop, make it pop*
*DJ, blow my speakers up*
*Tonight, Imma fight*
*'Til we see the sunlight*
*TiK ToK, on the clock*

*But the party don't stop no*
*Whoa-oh oh oh*
*Whoa-oh oh oh*

*Ain't got a care in world, but got plenty of beer*
*Ain't got no money in my pocket, but I'm already here*
*Now, the dudes are lining up cause they hear we got swagger*

*But we kick em to the curb unless they look like Mick Jagger*
*I'm talkin' bout - everybody getting crunk, crunk*
*Boys tryna touch my junk, junk*
*Gonna smack him if he getting too drunk, drunk*
*Now, now - we goin' 'til they kick us out, out*
*Or the police shut us down, down*
*Police shut us down, down*
*Po-po shut us - (down)-man*
*Don't stop, make it pop*
*DJ, blow my speakers up*
*Tonight, Imma fight*

*'Til we see the sunlight*
*TiK ToK, on the clock*

*But the party don't stop no*
*Whoa-oh oh oh*
*Whoa-oh oh oh*

*Don't stop, make it pop*
*DJ, blow my speakers up*
*Tonight, Imma fight*
*'Til we see the sunlight*
*TiK ToK, on the clock*
*But the party don't stop no*
*Whoa-oh oh oh*
*Whoa-oh oh oh*

*DJ, You build me up*
*You break me down*
*My heart, it pounds*
*Yeah, you got me*
*With my hands up*
*You got me now*

*You got that sound*
*Yeah, you got me*

*You build me up*
*You break me down*
*My heart, it pounds*
*Yeah, you got me*
*With my hands up*
*Put your hands up*
*Put your hands up*

*Now, the party don't start 'til I walk in*

*Don't stop, make it pop*
*DJ, blow my speakers up*
*Tonight, Imma fight*
*'Til we see the sunlight*
*TiK ToK, on the clock*
*But the party don't stop no*
*Whoa-oh oh oh*
*Whoa-oh oh oh*

*Don't stop, make it pop*
*DJ, blow my speakers up*
*Tonight, Imma fight*
*'Til we see the sunlight*
*TiK ToK, on the clock*
*But the party don't stop no*
*Whoa-oh oh oh*
*Whoa-oh oh oh*

"Those of us that are teenagers have dreams… 'We live in America' singer…Katy Perry, proves no exception to that."
"Her songs explore youth and teenage love themes which I enjoy."
"Katy Perry fans can relate…I feel the same… so if you're ready let's sing 'Teenage Dream'."

*You think I'm pretty*
*Without any makeup on*
*You think I'm funny*
*When I tell the punchline wrong*
*I know you get me*
*So I let my walls come down, down*
*Before you met me*

*I was alright but things*
*Were kinda' heavy*
*You brought me to life*
*Now every February*
*You'll be my Valentine, Valentine*

*Let's go all the way tonight*
*No regrets, just love*
*We can dance, until we die*
*You and I, will be young forever*

*You make me feel*
*Like I'm livin' a*
*Teenage dream*
*The way you turn me on*
*I can't sleep*
*Let's run away and*
*Don't ever look back,*
*Don't ever look back*

*My heart stops*
*When you look at me*
*Just one touch*
*Now baby I believe*
*This is real*
*So take a chance and*
*Don't ever look back,*
*Don't ever look back*

*We drove to Cali*
*And got drunk on the beach*
*Got a motel and*

*Built a fort out of sheets*
*I finally found you*
*My missing puzzle piece*
*I'm complete*

*Let's go all the way tonight*
*No regrets, just love*
*We can dance, until we die*
*You and I, will be young forever*

*You make me feel
Like I'm livin' a
Teenage dream
The way you turn me on
I can't sleep
Let's run away and
Don't ever look back,
Don't ever look back*

*My heart stops
When you look at me
Just one touch
Now baby I believe
This is real
So take a chance and
Don't ever look back,
Don't ever look back*

*I'mma get your heart racing
In my skin-tight jeans
Be your teenage dream tonight
Let you put your hands on me
In my skin-tight jeans
Be your teenage dream tonight*

*Yoooouuu
You make me feel
Like I'm livin' a
Teenage dream
The way you turn me on
I can't sleep
Let's run away and
Don't ever look back,
Don't ever look back
No*

*My heart stops, when you look at me
Just one touch
Now baby I believe
This is real*

*So take a chance and
Don't ever look back,
Don't ever look back*

*I'mma get your heart racing*
*In my skin-tight jeans*
*Be your teenage dream tonight*
*Let you put your hands on me*
*In my skin-tight jeans*
*Be your teenage dream tonight*
*(Tonight, tonight, tonight, tonight, tonight, tonight)*

   "Jennifer Lopez aka 'J-Lo' is a wonderful singer from the USA."
   "With hot Latin influences in her music, she has become one of the best female singers of the 2000's."
   "'Let's Get Loud' is her biggest hit of the early 2000's... if you have got the Latin moves...stand up and show us your best Sydney!" I shouted

*Let's get loud, let's get loud*
*Turn the music up, let's do it*
*C'mon people let's get loud*
*Let's get loud*
*Turn the music up to hear that sound*
*Let's get loud, let's get loud*
*Ain't nobody gotta tell ya*
*What you gotta do*

*If you wanna live your life*
*Live it all the way and don't you waste it*
*Every feelin' every beat*
*Can be so very sweet you gotta taste it*
*You gotta do it, you gotta do it your way*
*You gotta prove it*
*You gotta mean what you say*
*Life's a party, make it hot*
*Dance don't ever stop, whatever rhythm*
*Every minute, every day*

*Take them all the way you gotta live 'em ('cause I'm going to live my life)*
*You gotta do it, you gotta do it your way*
*You gotta prove it*
*You gotta mean what you say*

*You gotta do it, you gotta do it your way*
*You gotta prove it*
*You gotta mean what you say*

*Let's get loud, let's get loud*
*Turn the music up to hear that sound*
*Let's get loud, let's get loud*
*Ain't nobody gotta tell you*
*What you gotta do*

*Life is meant to be big fun*
*You're not hurtin' anyone*
*Nobody loses*
*Let the music make you free*
*Be what you wanna be*
*Make no excuses*
*You gotta do it, you gotta do it your way*
*To gotta prove it*
*You gotta mean what you say*
*You gotta do it, you gotta do it your way*

"Our last song is a great favourite of mine... it's called 'Strawberry Kisses'... made popular by Australia's own... Nikki Webster."

*I've been missing, wishing, missing your strawberry kisses,*
*I've been missing, wishing, missing your strawberry kisses.*
*I've been missing, wishing, missing your strawberry kisses,*
*I've been missing, wishing, missing your, yeah, yeah.*

*From the bottom of my heart, boy, I gotta tell you this,*
*Since the day we've been apart, you're the only one I miss.*
*I'm like a tree with no roots, I just can't live without you, yeah-yeah.*
*Thought we were just a summer romance, nothing but a passing fling,*
*Seemed my heart had other plans, now I'm a puppet on a string.*
*Don't leave me dangling out there, boy, can't you tell how much I care?*
*Still see the sunlight in your hair, oh-oh.*

*I've been missing your strawberry kisses,*

*Coz nothing's as sweet, and the taste still drives me crazy..*
*I've been wishing my strawberry kisses,*
*Will fly through the wind to you, from me.*

*I've been missing, wishing, missing your strawberry kisses,*
*I've been missing, wishing, missing your strawberry kisses.*

*There's no question at all, boy, your tops on the list,*
*I'm falling head over toes at the thought of your lips.*
*I know you're no Cyrano, can't write those pretty words to show me,*

*How you feel deep inside, but oh-oh...*
*I've been missing your strawberry kisses,*

*Coz nothing's as sweet, and the taste still drives me crazy..*
*I've been wishing my strawberry kisses,*
*Will fly through the wind to you, from me.*

*I know what I'll do, once I find you, you're gonna make me your girl,*
*You're gonna be mine, even if I gotta search this whole world.*
*Strawberry kisses, strawberry kisses, come on, baby, now,*
*Strawberry kisses, gonna make you mine, oh, oh, oh-oh.*

*I've been missing your strawberry kisses,*
*Coz nothing's as sweet, and the taste still drives me crazy..*
*I've been wishing my strawberry kisses,*
*Will fly through the wind to you, from me.*

*I've been missing your strawberry kisses,*
*Coz nothing's as sweet, and the taste still drives me crazy..*
*I've been wishing my strawberry kisses,*
*Will fly through the wind to you, from me.*

*I've been missing your strawberry kisses,*
*Coz nothing's as sweet, and the taste still drives me crazy..*
*I've been wishing my strawberry kisses,*
*Will fly through the wind to you, from me.*

"Thank you all for watching the 'Sparkles'!"

"It isn't over yet though... there's one more surprise to go!"

"I'll head backstage to get ready, but please thank, Dina, Macy, Sara, Petunia and Prunella for their wonderful performances tonight!"

"Give them some appreciation."

Everyone clapped, I headed backstage and Dina, Macy, Sarah and Petunia shook each other's hands, said goodbye and went back to their parents who came to watch the performances.

"Well done Cassie."

"I'm so proud of you darling, for coping with the big crowd."

"I'm so amazed!" said Mum

"You did so well."

"Your solo performance was a triumph, I'm very happy for you." said Dad, beaming proudly at me

"Thanks Mum and Dad."

"I overcame another fear!"
"Our 'Bontel Family' concert starts in fifteen minutes, let's get ready!" I grinned broadly
A quarter of an hour later our instruments are on stage and Mum, Dad and I, are ready to go!
"Are you ready, Cassie?" asks Mum, nervously
"Yes, I am ready."
"Are you ready, Mum and Dad?" I countered
"Yes, certainly are ready Cassie!" said Dad, emphatically

# Chapter Twelve
# Bontel Family Band

The MC made his way to the stage and adjusted his microphone, here's hoping the 'Bontel Family' performance is equally as good as the 'Sparkles' concert!

"Ladies and Gentlemen, this is our second surprise concert for tonight!"

"The celebrity popstar family from Melbourne are here to perform in their debut concert as the 'Bontel Family' band, songs from their new chart-topping album!"

"Please, welcome to the stage, 'The Bontel Family' band!" said the MC

Mum, Dad and I, walked onto the stage waving to the audience as we approached the front. We are smartly dressed in our favorite colored clothes, and have our performance headsets on, ready to speak and sing to the audience.

"Hello, do you know what the surprise is yet?" I ask, excitedly

"No!" said the audience, waiting expectantly

"Well, the surprise is...this is our debut performance tonight... as the 'Bontel Family' band!" I said

The crowd cheered loudly, they are keen to see and hear how this band works. We are too! It will be my first performance with the Bontel Family band... Mum and Dad have been in pop bands and solo careers since 1982... so they are 'old hands' at it by now!

"We're playing fourteen songs we hope you will enjoy yourselves... first let us introduce ourselves...get to know us."

"I am Cassie Bontel... lead vocalist of the Bontel Family."

"I always enjoyed pop music growing up... I'm a musical child prodigy."

"I have been singing vocals since I was five... I learnt to play the guitar when I was seven."

"I experimented with pop genres, sounds and songs, my family always supported me, some of them were already popstars and they still make music today."

"I used to be too scared to perform for anyone else outside my family, but I overcame that fear and now I'm enjoying every minute of it!"

"Nikki Webster is my favorite artist... I really like her vocal style... it suits me." I told the audience

"I am Mikayla Bontel... I grew up listening to pop music and learnt how to play the drums at age six."

"I would practice three times a day for an hour and I also did vocals in addition to drumming."

"Madonna is my main influence... and one of my favorite artists... I really like her music." Mum smiled

"I am Daniel Bontel."

"Pop music was always in my life, when I first learnt to play the guitar at age six... I was born to sing!"

"When Mikayla and I formed 'Shyness'... later renamed 'Quirky Service'... my singing voice became one of the most well-known around the world... most of my fans were teenage girls back then... they would swoon at the drop of a hat!" said Dad, sheepishly

"I have a similar singing voice to Rick Astley." Dad added

The audience cheered wildly I could hear several teenage girls screaming as though they had seen his younger self! Dad didn't seem to mind at all... he was enjoying the moment.

"Thank you for your kind reception." Dad grinned

"Feel free to dance and sing with us... are you all ready?" I asked, excitedly

"Yes!" shouted the audience

'Louder!' I said

"YES!" screamed the audience

"That's the way!"

"Now let's do it!"

Mum and Dad moved to their positions, I stood in front so the audience can see us all. This is it! It's time to perform and shine!

We launched the concert with our own composition of 'A Family United', the first track off our album, and quickly move into the second 'Farnsy' classic!

| Song Title / Artist | Lead Vocalist | Composer/s |
|---|---|---|
| A Family United | Cassie Bontel | C.Bontel. M.Bontel. D.Bontel |
| Two Strong Hearts John Farnham | Cassie Bontel | Andy Hill, Bruce Wooley |
| The Boys Light Up Australian Crawl | Cassie Bontel | James Reyne |
| Bedroom Eyes Kate Ceberano | Cassie Bontel | Nick Launay, Raymond Jones |
| Heat of the Moment Asia | Cassie Bontel | John Wetton, Geoff Downes |
| Live It Up Mental as Anything | Cassie Bontel | 'Greedy' Smith |
| Eagle Rock Daddy Cool | Cassie Bontel | Ross Wilson |
| Boys in Town Divinyls cover | Cassie Bontel | Christina Amphlett, Mark McEntree, Jeremy Paul |
| The Loco-Motion Kylie Minogue cover | Cassie Bontel | Gerry Goffin, Carole King |
| What About Me? Shannon Noll | Cassie Bontel | Garry Frost, Frances Swan |
| Lift Shannon Noll cover | Cassie Bontel | Shannon Noll, Andrew Roachford, Bryan Jones, Adam Riley |
| Help is on its Way Little River Band Ft Quirky Service | Cassie Bontel | Glen Shorrock |
| Working Class Man Jimmy Barnes cover | Cassie Bontel | Jonathan Cain |
| This is Who I Am Vanessa Amorosi | Cassie Bontel | Vanessa Amorosi, Robin Mortensen, Niklas "Nikey" Olovson |

## Two Strong Hearts

*Well there's no need to analyze this kind of emotion*
*'Cos it comes naturally*
*A simple case of feeling love and devotion*
*So tell me tenderly*
*I wanna give my life to you*
*I wanna to feel my blood run through you*
*And oh... I want to touch you*
*Over and over and over again*

*We've got two strong hearts*
*We stick together like the honey and the bee*
*You and me*
*We've got two strong hearts*
*Reaching out forever like a river to the sea*
*Running free*
*Running free*

*I feel there's no need for compromising my reputation*
*When you lead me astray*
*I'm proud to be a part of this fascination*
*When I hear you say*
*I wanna be there to guide you*
*I'm gonna feel my love inside you*
*And oh... I want to touch you*

*Over and over and over again*

*We've got two strong hearts*
*We stick together like the honey and the bee*
*You and me*
*We've got two strong hearts*
*Reaching out forever like a river to the sea*
*Running free*

We follow next with Australian Crawl's classic...'The Boys Light Up'.
*Let me tell you about my mountain home*
*Where all the ladies names are Joan*
*Where husbands work back late at night*
*Hopes are up for trousers down*
*With hostess on a business flight*
*Taxi in a Mercedes drive*
*I hope that driver's coming out alive*

*The garden is a dorsetted*
*That lady - she's so corseted*
*She's got fifteen ways to lead that boy astray*
*He thinks he's one and only*
*But that lovely she's so lonely*
*She pumps him full of breakfast and she sends him on his way*
*What a sing song dance*
*What a performance*
*What a cheap tent show*
*Oh no no no no no*

*Then the boys light up*
*Then the boys light up*

*Then the boys light up*
*Then the boys light up - light up - light up*
*Then the boys light up*
*Then the boys light up*
*Then the boys light up*
*Then the boys light up - light up - light up*

*Silently she opens the drawer*
*Mother's little helper is coming out for more*
*Strategically positioned before the midday show*
*Her back is arched, those lips are parched*
*Repeated blow by blow*
*Later at the party all the MPs rave*

*About the hummers she's been giving*
*And the money that they save*
*To her it is skin lotion*
*For his promotion to*
*That flat in Surfer's Paradise with the ocean view*
*What a sing song dance*
*What a performance*
*What a cheap tent show*
*Oh no no no no no*

*Then the boys light up Then the boys light up Then the boys light up*
*Then the boys light up - light up - light up – light up*

Song number Four is 'Bedroom Eyes' made popular by Kate Ceberano

*After all this time can't believe that I'm about to take this ride*
*can't resist you no matter how I try*
*Said it was over decided we were through*
*I've convinced myself that somebody else could take the place of you*
*You're part of me my one obsession*
*And from this power you possess I need protection*
*When you're staring straight through me*
*With those eyes those bedroom eyes*
*I'm lost for words so hypnotized*
*I can feel it in my heart it's about to start*
*With those eyes those bedroom eyes*
*I made a promise to myself that I would erase you from my mind*
*Leave the past behind be done with you for good but then I saw you I knew that I had lied*
*I thought of just how much I crave your touch to keep me satisfied*
*You're part of me my one obsession and from this power you possess I need protection*
*When you're staring straight through me with those eyes*
*I must admit I'm not surprised*
*I can feel it in my heart it's about to start*
*With those eyes those bedroom eyes*
*You're a part of me my one obsession*
*I need you and from this power you possess I need protection*
*Hey what can I do there is no reason to lose my sight as long as I can see myself reflected in*
*those eyes bedroom eyes those bedroom eyes I'm lost for words so hypnotized*
*When you stare into my soul I lose all control*
*To those eyes those bedroom eyes bedroom eyes, those bedroom eyes,*
*I must admit I'm not surprised I can feel it in my heart it's about to start*
*with those eyes those bedroom eyes*

   Next, we heat up the stage with a song called 'Heat of the Moment' by a group named Asia.

*I never meant to be so bad to you, one thing I said that I would never do*
*One look from you and I would fall from grace and that would wipe this smile right from my face*
*Do you remember when we used to dance and incidence arose from circumstance*
*One thing led to another, we were young and we would scream together songs unsung*
*Cause it was the heat of the moment*
*Telling me what your heart meant*

*The heat of the moment shone in your eyes*
*And now you find yourself in '82, the disco hot-spots hold no charm for you*
*You can't concern yourself with bigger things, you catch the pearl and ride the dragon's wings*
*And when your looks are gone and you're alone, how many nights you sit beside the phone?*
*What were the things you wanted for yourself, teenage ambitions you remember well*
*Heat of the moment Heat of the moment The heat of the moment shone in your eyes*

I shout to the audience 'Let's Live it Up' as we launch into the song from the 'Mentals'

*How can you see looking through those tears?*
*Don't you know you're worth your weight in gold?*
*I can't believe that you're alone in here...Let me warm your hands against the cold*
*A close encounter with a hardhearted man...Who never gave half of what he got*
*Has made you wish that you'd never been born...That's a shame 'cos you got the lot*

*Hey there, you with the sad face*
*Come up to my place and live it up, you beside the dance floor*
*What do you cry for? Let's live it up*

*If you smiled the walls would fall down...On all the people in this pickup joint*
*But if you laughed you'd level this town...Hey lonely girl, that's just the point*

*Hey there, you with the sad face*
*Come up to my place and live it up Hey you beside the dance floor*
*What do you cry for? Let's live it up*

*Just answer me the question why...*
*You stand alone... by the phone...*
*In the corner and cry*

*How can you see looking through those tears?*
*Don't you know you're worth your weight in gold?*
*I can't believe you're alone in here...Let me warm your hands against the cold*

*If you smiled the walls would fall down...On all the people in this pickup joint*
*But if you laughed you'd level this town...Hey lonely girl, that's just the point*

*Hey there you with the sad face*
*Come up to my place and live it up*
*Hey you beside the dance floor*
*What do you cry for? Let's live it up*

*Let's live it up, live it up, live it up*
*Hey yeah, you with the sad face*
*Come up to my place*
*Come up to my place, baby*

*"Next up is every Australian's favorite song... here is 'Eagle Rock'... made famous worldwide... by Daddy Cool!" the crowd went wild*

*Now listen, who is steppin' out.*

*I'm gonna turn around, gonna turn around once and we'll do the Eagle Rock.*
*Oh momma!*
*Oh you're rockin' well!*
*Hmm yeah you do it so well,*
*Well we do it so well when we do the Eagle Rock*
*Now momma,*
*Yeah you're rockin' fine!*

*Why don't you give me a sign?*
*Hmm just give me a sign and we'll do the Eagle Rock.*

*Hey Hey Hey good old Eagle Rock's here to stay,*
*I'm just crazy 'bout the way we're movin',*
*Doin' the Eagle Rock.*
*Oh-oh-oh come on fast n you come on slow*
*I'm just crazy 'bout the way we're movin'*
*Doin' the Eagle Rock.*

*Go momma!*
*Well you're rockin' fine!*

*Why don't you give me a sign?*
*Just give me a sign and we'll do the Eagle Rock.*
*Oh baby!*
*Well I feel so free!*
*What you do to me!*
*What you do to me when we do the Eagle Rock.*

*Daniel's Guitar Solo*

*Now listen, now we're steppin' out.*

*Yeah, gonna turn around, gonna turn around once and we do the Eagle Rock.*

*Doin the Eagle Rock.*
*Doin the Eagle Rock.*
*Doin the Eagle Rock.*

"Now it's time for the boys to be back in town, this is a 'Divinyls' track everybody!"

*I am through with hanging 'round*
*With all the boys in town*
*Now I want a man around*
*Get me out of here*

*I am just a red brassiere*
*To all the boys in town*
*Put this bus in top gear*
*Get me out of here*
*I must have been desperate*
*I must have been pretty low*
*I must have been desperate*
*I must have been pretty low*

*I was always driving home*
*All the boys in town*
*But they never telephoned*
*Get me out of here*
*I think they're pretty phoney*
*You're not like the rest*
*You've heard of matrimony*
*They've all flunked the test*

*I must have been desperate*
*I must have been pretty low*
*I must have been desperate*
*I must have been pretty low*
*Oh, I'm tired, Oh, I'm wired Oh, I'm tired, Oh, I'm wired*
*Too much too young, Too much too young, Get me out of here*

"The next song will get you in the mood for dancing... it's called 'The Loco-Motion'".

*Everybody's doin' a bran' new dance now...C'mon baby do the loco-motion*
*I know you'll get to like it...If you give it a chance now...C'mon baby do the loco-motion*
*My little baby sister can do it with ease*
*It's easier than saying you're a- b- c-'s*

*So come on... come on...Do the loco-motion with me*

*You gotta swing your hips now...come on baby*

*Jump up...Jump back!*
*Oh well I think you got the knack wo-wo*

*Now that you can do it*
*Let's make a chain now*

*C'mon baby do the loco-motion*
*A chug-a chug-a motion like a railroad train now*
*C'mon baby do the loco-motion*
*Do it nice and easy now don't lose control*
*A little bit of rhythm and a whole lot of soul*
*So come on, come on...do the loco-motion with me*
*You gotta swing your hips now...that's right*
*Jump up...Jump back!*
*Well I think you've got the knack yay-yay*
*Move around the floor in a loco-motion...C'mon baby do the loco-motion*
*Do it holding hands if you get the notion...C'mon baby do the loco-motion*
*There's never been a dance that's so easy to do*
*It even makes you happy*
*When you're feeling blue*
*So come on come on do the loco-motion with me...You gotta swing your hips now*
*Come on, come on...Do the loco-motion with me*
*Yeah*
*Come on, come on...Do the loco-motion with me*
*You gotta swing your hips now*
*"Now it's time to slow it down a little for the next song."*

*Well there's a little boy waiting at the counter of a corner shop*
*He's been waiting down there, waiting half the day*
*They never ever see him from the top He gets pushed around, knocked to the ground*

*He gets to his feet and he says*
*What about me, it isn't fair*
*I've had enough now I want my share*

Can't you see I wanna' live
But you just take more than you give

Well there's a pretty girl serving at the counter of the corner shop
She's been waiting back there, waiting for her dreams
Her dreams walk in and out they never stop

Well she's not too proud to cry out loud
She runs to the street and she screams

What about me, it isn't fair
I've had enough now I want my share
Can't you see I wanna live
But you just take more than you give
So take a step back and see the little people
They may be young but they're the ones
That make the big people big
So listen, as they whisper
What about me

And now I'm standing on the corner all the world's gone home
Nobody's changed, nobody's been saved
And I'm feeling cold and alone
I guess I'm lucky, I smile a lot
But sometimes I wish for more than I've got

What about me, it isn't fair
I've had enough now I want my share
Can't you see I wanna' live
But you just take more than you give

"Now for another popular song from Shannon Noll entitled 'Lift'."

I know you're hurting
Feels like you're learning
'Bout life the hard way
And it ain't working
Seems like forever
That you've been falling

It's time to move on
Your life is calling, yeah
This was never meant to be the end
Close the book and start again

*Cause I know how hard it can get*
*But you gotta lift*
*You gotta lift*
*And sometimes that's how it is*
*But I know you're stronger*
*Stronger than this*
*You gotta lift*
*You gotta lift*
*When you can feel your*
*Whole body's aching*
*What's left of your heart*
*It won't stop breaking*

*You gotta let go*
*You took a hit*
*Time to pick up now*

*Move on from this*
*This was never meant to be the end*
*Close the book and start again*
*Cause I know how hard it can get*
*But you gotta lift*
*You gotta lift*
*And sometimes that's how it is*
*But I know you're stronger*
*Stronger than this*
*You gotta*
*Lift yourself up above all the hurt*
*Don't give up*
*Wipe your eyes and remember*
*You're better than this*
*Let them know*
*That they took their best shot*
*And missed*
*C'mon and lift*
*This was never meant to be the end*
*Close the book and start again*
*But I know you're stronger…Stronger than this… You gotta lift…You gotta lift*

"Now we have 'Help is on Its Way' made famous in Australia, by the 'Little River Band' and today, featuring 'Quirky Service'."

*Why you be in so much hurry*
*Is it really worth the worry*
*Look around*
*Then slow down*
*What's it like inside the bubble*
*Does your head ever give you trouble*
*It's no sin*
*Trade it in*
*Hang on, help is on its way*
*I'll be there as fast as I can*
*Hang on, a tiny voice did say*

*From somewhere deep inside the inner man*
*Are you always in confusion*
*Surrounded by illusion*
*Sort it out*
*You'll make out*
*Seem to make a good beginning*
*Someone else ends up winning*
*Don't seem fair*
*Don't you care*
*Hang on, help is on its way*
*I'll be there as fast as I can*
*Hang on, a tiny voice did say*
*From somewhere deep inside the inner man*
*Don't you forget who'll take care of you*
*It don't matter what you do*

*Form a duet, let him sing melody*
*You'll provide the harmony*
*Why are you in so much hurry*
*Is it really worth the worry*
*Look around*
*Then slow down*
*What's it like inside the bubble*
*Does your head ever give you trouble*
*It's no sin*
*Trade it in*
*Hang on, help is on its way...I'll be there as fast as I can...Hang on, a tiny voice did say...From somewhere deep inside the inner man*

Next a Barnsy' favorite, 'Working Class Man'.

*Working hard to make a living*
*Bringing shelter from the rain*
*A father's son left to carry on*
*Blue denim in his veins*
*Oh oh oh he's a working class man*
*Well he's a steel town disciple*
*He's a legend of his kind*
*He's running like a cyclone*
*Across the wild mid-western sky*
*Oh oh oh he's a working class man*

*He believes in God and Elvis he gets out when he can*
*he did his time in Vietnam*
*Still mad at Uncle Sam*
*He's a simple man*
*With a heart of gold*
*In a complicated land*
*Oh he's a working class man*
*Well he loves a little woman*
*Someday he'll make his wife*
*Saving all the overtime*
*For the one love of his life*
*He ain't worried about tomorrow*
*Cause he just made up his mind*
*Life's too short for burning bridges*
*Take it one day at a time*
*Oh oh oh he's a working class man*
*Oh oh oh he's a working class man*
*Oh yeah*
*Yes he is*
*Well he's a working class man*
*Oh*
*Ma ma ma ma ma ma ma ma ma ma ma ma ma ma ma*
*I tell you he's a working class man Working class*

"We will finish off with a Vanessa Amorosi song called 'This Is Who I am.'

*I spend my life, trying to do things right*
*but all I do is fall to my face with my hands on my head so many times*
*but then I learnt, after being burnt*
*to get back up and push straight on*
*stop the tears people move on, on*

*Well it's alright to be myself*
*now I've learnt to stand*
*well it's ok to be just who I am*
*I spent years really hating me*
*longing to be friends, now I hope that you can understand*
*This is who I am*

*Now when life gets tough*
*I'm quick to hurry up*
*I run all day, I run through the night*
*I break down walls, I hit up high*
*I don't care if I'm fat, or if you think my clothes are bad*
*'cos I can go to sleep at night, I'm a good person and I'll get by*

*Well It's alright to be myself*
*now I've learnt to stand*
*well it's ok to be just who I am*
*I spent years really hating me*
*longing to be friends, now I hope that you can understand*
*This is who I am*

*Are you someone, are you someone, are you someone, someone like me*
*you deserve, you deserve, you deserve to be free*
*cause the world will keep spinning, and you'll be trapped in it*

*Well it's alright to be myself*
*now I've learnt to stand*
*well it's ok to be just who I am*
*I've spent years really hating me*

*longing to be friends, now I hope that you can understand*
*This is who I am*

    The audience rocked out, they really had a blast at the concert and so did we onstage! Our debut performance knocked their socks off! We were very happy, it is one of the biggest achievements of my life, I'm so proud it all worked out well.
    "We would like to thank you all for coming tonight."
    "We appreciate your support!"
    "This was a spectacular night you have been a great audience!" Mum waved to the crowd
    "Before we leave... we'll sign some autographs."
    The crowd lined up in a long queue, ready for their autograph books to be signed, some of them had copies of our CD's to write on.
    I looked across the rows... my row was longer than Mum and Dads! I laughed to see that I had the most people waiting for a signature. Dad was going to have something to say about that! Hee Hee.

"Cassie, I have a bone to pick with you!"

"Oh really, Dad what's that?" I asked, trying not to grin

"Well... how come your line of fans turned out to be bigger than mine?"

"I thought I was the guitar playing 'swoonster' in our family?" Dad complained

I couldn't hold it in any longer... I laughed out loud.

"Ha, ha, ha!"

"Dad... your face was priceless when I looked at you...and you saw that mine was the biggest row of fans!" I laughed out loud

"Oh, Cassie... you have taken away Dad's popstar status and mine as well!"

"What will we do now?" asked Mum

"Mum... we can all be stars together... sorry Mum and Dad my fan base is awesome!" I said with a grin

Dad and Mum both laughed when I said that.

"Cassie that was a big achievement... you walked onto that stage with your backing dancers and your performance blew everyone away."

"It even blew us away!" Dad said in amazement

"Dad and I are very proud of you... we were concerned that you would get stage fright and meltdown... but you didn't!"

"You were brave and it all went very well... it was great to see you enjoy yourself throughout the night... it was so good to see." smiled Mum

"It was a risk going onstage facing the crowds and coping with the noise... but I challenged myself and it paid off big time!"

"The crowd seemed to like my music I think they can see the popstar potential in me!" I grinned

"Cassie... let me give you a congratulatory kiss." said Dad

"Dad please don't."

"I don't want a kiss."

"It's so gross!" I said, backing away a little

"It's okay Cassie."

"It won't be gross."

"It's to show my affection for you and my pride in your achievements tonight."

"It will be all right." said Dad, in a reassuring voice

I took three deep breaths to calm myself. Dad walked over to me, held my hands and kissed me on the left cheek. It felt good and made me smile like the sun.

"Thanks, Dad."

"I love you and always will." I told him

I summoned my courage and gave him a kiss back on his right cheek, it felt good as well.

"I love you too, Cassie."

"A father and daughter moment eh?" says Dad clearing his throat, with suspiciously bright eyes

"Yes, it is Dad."

"It's a great moment for me... and one to show my family love."

"I would like to give you a kiss too." Mum said

Mum held my hands and kissed me on the right cheek. It felt lovely and made my smile light up again.

"Thanks, Mum."

I love you too and always will." I said

"I will always love you too, Cassie."

"A sweet moment to share with mother and daughter... which brings joy and happiness to us both." said Mum, brushing away a happy tear

I gave Mum a kiss on her cheek... it was a sweet moment that I will treasure.

It has taken me many years to finally give my Mum and Dad a kiss. Although it took me a long time to show my affection for them... I have made big progress today! I used to lash out and hit them... or push them away... especially when I had a bad day. Now I can kiss Mum and Dad anytime I want to... including when I'm having a bad day... or overwhelmed by my sensory issues... which is great!

"Well after that breakthrough... and our concerts tonight... I think we should all get a good night's sleep!" said Dad

## Chapter Thirteen
## Newcastle, Beaches and Pizza

A day later I took a look out the window of our new hotel room.
   Wow!
What a wicked looking beach! The water looks crystal clear and the sun is shining. There are a few rock pools that I would love to explore. The city of Newcastle is big, we have a great view of the beach...it's sure to be fun here!
"Even Uncle Daniel did well too!" I heard Mum say
"Daniel... Kate says your guitar playing was brilliant." Mum relayed to Dad
"Thank you, Kate." Dad called across the room to Mum's phone, as she finished her phone call with Kate
"Right, we've got our bathers on... I'll put on some deodorant just in case it gets hotter later on." Mum mused, as we climbed down and claimed our spot on the sand
Taking out what she thought was deodorant...she sprayed it under both arms...but it wasn't deodorant at all!
"What the...shaving cream!" spluttered Mum, with her eyes wide at the frothing foam under her armpits!
I had switched her deodorant for shaving cream whilst we were setting up. I had pulled off another one of my famous pranks!
"Cassie!" Mum yelled
"Wait till I get my hands on you!" she said, shaking and pointer her finger at me
I was running down the sand laughing. Dad was laughing as well, he thought it was a hilarious sight.
"You think that's funny do you dear?" said Mum, ominously
"I'll shaving cream you if you don't look out!" said Mum, mischievously
"Oh... will you now?" chuckled Dad
Olivia arrived at the beach five minutes after we did... she walked up to Mum...she couldn't resist giggling at Mum's predicament.
"Oh no... what do we have here?"
"Shave-creamed Mikayla?"
"I've seen snowmen before... but never a snow woman!"
"It's quite a sight to see!" laughed Olivia.
"Very funny Olivia!" said Mum, sarcastically
"It's another one of Cassie's pranks!" said Mum, in exasperation
"Instead of deodorant Cassie swapped it for shaving cream!" Mum gasped
"Cassie is very tricky with her pranks." Olivia smiled
"Hmm...she certainly is... no matter how we try to be ready we still get fooled."

"We never expected to see you here, Olivia!" exclaimed Dad

"I didn't expect to see you three either!"

"I came for a week's holiday... isn't this a lovely place?"

"We arrived yesterday... we plan to try a few activities... we're also performing here as well." said Mum, wiping off the shaving cream with a towel

"How exciting!"

"I'll come to your concert!" Olivia said, enthusiastically

"That's great!"

"The more the merrier!" Dad said, with a big grin

"Where has Cassie disappeared to?"

"I haven't seen her for ages... I would like to spend some time with her too." said Olivia

"Oh, she's probably at the kiosk buying ice-creams... she ran that way laughing, (Mikayla pointed down the beach), after playing that prank on me." said Mikayla, rolling her eyes

"Hello, Aunt Olivia." I said, strolling across the sand towards her

"It's great to see you again."

"I haven't seen you in a while... what are you doing here?"

"Hello Cassie."

"I am holidaying in Newcastle for a week." she replied

"How are you?"

"I am having fun I have been exploring new cities... learning more about the history of Australia...I even made a couple of new friends along the way!" I told her

"That's great to hear."

"Have you seen today's paper?" Olivia asked, handing us her newspaper

On the front page there was a picture of us performing at the Metro Theatre in Sydney, the headline read... 'Celeb family band shines on debut in Sydney'.

"Wow!"

"That sure is a great photo of us!" I said

"Our album is charting and selling well... we're gaining popularity." Mum responded

We read the article together, it was a fantastic article, it was such fun to see me in a photo without sunglasses on for once!

'*A family pop band has wowed the crowd on their debut performance at the Metro Theatre! The recently formed Australian band, consisting of lead vocalist Cassie Bontel sixteen years old, lead guitarist and vocalist, Daniel Bontel, (Father of Cassie), and drummer and vocalist Mikayla Bontel (Mother of Cassie), amazed the crowd with their bright and dazzling tunes. They recorded their debut album last year in 2010 and released it in March 2011, they are beginning a tour to promote the album... whilst on a road trip around Australia!*

"*Our debut performance knocked their socks off...we played our hearts out tonight...the fans loved me more than Mum and Dad...my fan line was definitely the longest after the show...I hope they don't hear that!" said Cassie, giggling*'

I giggled again when I read that in the article, Mum and Dad pointed their fingers at me with grins on their faces... that made me giggle louder!

"Very funny, Cassie."

"You got away with that one!" said Mum, grinning

"That was very cheeky of you!" said Dad, trying to pretend that he was cross

"Yes, I did… and I am… it was hilarious!" I laughed out loud

We continued reading the article.

'Mikayla, who has been the drummer and vocalist, for 'Quirky Service' and 'Playground Kids' drummed her heart out the entire evening… 'I was born to be a popstar drummer, I'm still a legend on the drums'…said Mikayla, in true 'Rock-Star' fashion! This performance was electric… I'm still going strong after twenty-five years…I'll keep producing more music and I'll still be going in another twenty years' time!'

Daniel Bontel, the lead vocalist and bass guitarist of 'Quirky Service' and lead vocalist of 'Playground Kids' is still an awesome lead guitarist! "It's great being with my family, still making music, in the 'Bontel Family' band." "I'm still a guitar rock-god… I produce melodic tunes like the ones my daughter has been performing here tonight." he said grinning.

The Bontel Family will be performing in Newcastle next, so book your tickets now to see them perform live! A few lucky fans will get to meet them after the performance.'

"We've never been in the newspapers as the 'Bontel Family' band before." said Mum, impressed

"You must be very happy about that review!" said Olivia smiling

"Oh… by the way Cassie… I witnessed your trick on Mikayla just now."

"She will get you back!" warned Olivia

I grinned at her and Mum.

"We had a problem with our car before we got to Sydney." Dad told Olivia

"What happened?" she replied

"The crankshaft broke."

"Cassie was going to fix it but it needed special equipment in a garage situation." Dad told her

"We called a garage in Canberra, hired a replacement vehicle for the day…then drove to Sydney the next day, after our vehicle was repaired." said Mum

"I know Cassie likes cars… but I didn't know she had great mechanical skills like you Daniel."

"I learnt from watching Mum and Dad fixing their cars… I've also watched many automotive shows on how to fix mechanical problems." I told her

"She's becoming very good at it."

"Cassie probably learnt that from me." said Dad, proudly

"Now we are all ready, last one in is a rotten egg!" I yelled, running towards the water

"Hey… not fair… I wasn't ready yet!" said Mum, running after me

"Oy… I hadn't put my stuff down properly!" said Olivia, running towards the water too

"Hey…don't leave me behind!" said Dad, trying to catch up to us as we splashed into the waves

We all had a good time in the ocean, riding the waves and swimming together.

This is so cool, spending time with Olivia, alongside Mum and Dad on the beach at Newcastle. Olivia brought along her surfboard, so she also had fun surfing the waves too! It's a great day to be at the beach doing fun things, I could stay here all day! We emerged from the water soaking wet, but smiling.

"Who's up for pizza?" asked Olivia

"I am!" I said, hungrily

"Me too!" said Mum and Dad together

"I know where there's a Domino's Pizza place not far from here."

"Let's go… follow me in your car." Olivia said

We arrived at Domino's Pizza and pulled into the car park behind Olivia. We went inside and looked at the board… there were plenty of pizzas to choose from… as well as pasta and desserts. This is going to be a tough choice… but I know which ones I want to order!

I then noticed a poster next to the dessert menu, it said

*'Domino's Pizza Experience! Learn how our pizzas are made with assistance from our staff. Families... carers with clients... celebrity stars... are welcome anytime!'*

"We could learn how Domino's Pizzas are made!"

"That would be a good experience for us...especially if we get to eat the pizzas too!" I giggled

"Trust you to think of that Cassie!" sighed Mum

"Whaddya' mean Mum...you know I'm a growing girl." I winked at her and she cracked into a laugh too

"I'm with Cassie any chance to eat more pizza is a good one!" laughed Olivia

"Oh, you two...are as bad as one another!" said Mum, looking at Olivia and I in exasperation

"Sounds like a good opportunity to me." said Dad

"Well let's go and do it then!" I replied

We walked up to the counter and asked the cashier about the Domino's Pizza Experience.

"Excuse me."

"We would love to try the Domino's Pizza Experience." Mum explained

"Yes, of course."

"All you need are to put on Domino's aprons and hairnets for health and hygiene standards, and follow the instructions of our trained staff." said the cashier, handing us the aprons, hairnets and food handling gloves.

We put on all the clothing required and went into the kitchen... what a delicious experiment and awesome learning experience this is going to be!

"Right, we start by getting the bases and putting them on this rack in front of the toppings... then we spread the tomato pizza sauce onto the bases before we choose the toppings!" said the manager, who was demonstrating the procedures to us

We applied the pizza sauce to our bases.

"That's good."

"Now you can choose any toppings you want and then put the cheese on top."

"It doesn't matter what combinations you choose as you are creating your own special pizza!" smiled the manager

"Everyone's pizzas are looking great!"

"Lastly, we put them in the pizza oven... they will take about ten to twenty minutes to cook... the end result will be delicious I'm sure!" beamed the manager

While we waited for our pizzas to cook, we had a conversation with the Manager.

"What are your names?"

"You look familiar to me but I can't place who you are...do I know you?" said the Manager, with a puzzled look on his face

"I'm Cassie Bontel... lead vocalist in a band called The Bontel Family."

"This is my Mum Mikayla... popstar and TV presenter."

"Next to Mum is my Dad Daniel... popstar and TV presenter."

"Behind me is my Aunt Olivia... popstar, TV presenter and general store worker."

"Goodness me... that's a bigger CV than Domino's!" laughed the manager

"Now I know where I have seen you before... you were on the front page of my paper today!" said the manager, smiling

"You must love pizza very much!" said the manager

"I sure do love pizza...Hawaiian has always been a favourite of mine." replied Mum

"I love Meat-lovers Pizza!" I stated emphatically

"I love Aussie pizzas...'cos I'm an Aussie!" Dad replied

"Margherita Pizza has always been my favourite pizza of all time!" stated Olivia

"Wow...you really do love your pizzas!" the manager chuckled

Pizza was one of the first dishes I ever learnt to cook when I was five years old." I said, remembering

"Cassie has always enjoyed helping in the kitchen... she loves making her favourite dishes...especially Ginger Crunch."

Our pizzas were soon ready, we paid for them, thanked the manager for giving us a great experience and took them to the park to eat.

"How has your road trip been so far?" asked Olivia

"It's been great, Olivia."

"We've made some friends, helped Mr Samson an ALP MP find his briefcase, then got him to his meeting on time!" said Mum, smiling

"How's your store work going?" Dad asked Aunt Olivia

"It's going very well."

"The customers are friendly, most of them recognise me, business is booming and my boss Joanne is supportive, her daughter who works with children with disabilities, often comes into the shop." said Olivia

"That's great!"

"You're doing so well."

"Keep up the good work!" said Dad, smiling

"Thanks Daniel... will do!"

"Olivia, we have been looking for a long-lost family member." said Mum

"Have you?"

"Do you have any clues so far?" asked Olivia

"The clues we have so far, is that the long-lost family member is a man and he is one hundred and seventy-six centimetres tall!"

"That's all we know at the moment."

"I keep asking Mum to give me more clues... but she won't!"

"Mum is so tricky."

Olivia laughed.

"I hope you find him soon." she said

"I hope so too Olivia."

"Tonight, I will skype Mum and ask for another clue."

"Hopefully another clue will be the key to finding out who this long-lost family member of mine is." said Mum

"I wish you good luck with that!"

"I'm off back to my hotel." said Olivia

Later in the evening Mum got ready to skype Belinda.

"I hope you get that vital clue... otherwise we will have to keep looking!" I said

"I hope so too dear." said Mum

"We'll both help you whether Belinda gives you another clue or not." Dad said

"That would be great." Mum replied

"Hi Mum!"

"How are you doing on this fine day?" asked Mum

'I'm doing well thanks, darling.'
'How are you?'
'Not getting up to any cheekiness I hope?' said Belinda
"Umm...no Mum I haven't." said Mikayla, like a naughty schoolchild
'Oh... I think I might be the judge of that Mikayla.'
'I can see you trying not to laugh.'
'You can't hide it from me.' said Belinda, in her best 'Mother' voice
"I can so Mum." said Mikayla, sounding even more child like
'Mmmn.' said Belinda, in a tone that said... I don't believe a word of it
'I heard you performed in Sydney a few days ago... is that right?' asked Belinda
"Yes, we did."
"We rocked the house down there... Sydney loved our performance."
"A few fans were picked to meet us backstage...we all enjoyed the experience."
"They chatted with us, took photos and then we signed their autograph books for them."
"One of the girls was kind enough to give Cassie a lovely card from her Mum."
'What a great experience... lucky you Cassie.' said Belinda
"I thanked that lovely fan for her kind gesture." I said
'I'm sure you will treasure it forever.' Belinda said
"I will."
"I'll put in my treasure memories box... so that I can read it anytime I want to." I mused
"Earlier today we spent a couple of hours on the beach here...we had just finished setting up when Cassie switched my deodorant for shaving cream!"
"Olivia turned up at the beach as she is on holiday here for a week... she thought it was very funny!"
"Daniel did as well!" said Mum, scowling
'Looks like Cassie pulled a sneaky prank on you!'
'You fell for that one!' said Belinda, laughing
"Oh, hardy-ha-ha Mum!" said Mikayla, peevishly
"I will get her back somehow." Mum threatened under her breath
I grinned cheekily in the background when I heard that.
"Mum, I'm keen to hear the last clue."
"Pl-e-e-e-ase... reveal it to me." Mum pleaded
'Hmm... all right then.'
'The long-lost family member has a comb-over!'
'That's the last of the clues.' said Belinda firmly
"Mum can I just have one mo..." started Mum
'Nope!'
'Before you ask again... we are not skyping every day!' stated Belinda, in a final tone
"La-la-la... I can't hear you." said Mum, putting her fingers into her ears and pretending she can't hear what Belinda is saying
Dad and I cackled.
Belinda just raised her eyes to the ceiling and pretended she didn't hear Mikayla either.
"We are performing at the Great Northern Hotel in Newcastle soon."
"It should be a great place to perform in... it is decorated in the art deco period." Mum told Belinda
'That sounds a good place for live music...I'm sure you'll have a great time there.' she added

"We certainly will."
"We might explore the Hunter Valley if we get time, it looks like an interesting place." said Mum
'I'd better sign off.'
'I've got a cooking day tomorrow... I'm cooking for my friends.'
'It will be chocolate cake and some homemade scones.' said Belinda, tempting Mum
"Can you save a piece for me?" asked Mum
'Nope, I can't.'
'They're for my friends who are visiting me tomorrow.' Belinda said, winking at me
"Well can you at least save me a scone?" asked Mum
'Nope... sorry, they would all be stale by the time you got back from your trip, anyway!' said Belinda, winking at me again
"Not even..." started Mum
'No!' said Belinda, in a final tone
Dad and I lost it. Funny, funny, funny.
"That's fine."
"It's your cooking day."
"Cassie, Daniel and I are going to that Dad's month hideaway... no matter what you say!" said Mum, defiantly
'No, that is for the men only...it's a men's getaway...you are not invited Mikayla!' said Belinda, seriously
'Oh, is that so...I'm not scared of those men!' mocked Mum
'Is that right Mikayla... well you had better listen to your Mother or you will be in big trouble.' said Belinda
Dad and I looked at each other, we are not going to get in the middle of this one!
Mum took a deep breath and calmed herself down.
"OK, you win Mum." Mikayla said sweetly, but I'm sure I heard her say 'for now' under her breath
Dad and I looked at each other again with a disbelieving smile on our faces, we know Mum too well, she would never give up that easily! We may all be in for a bumpy ride!
'All right Mikayla, bye for now.' Belinda waved goodbye
"Bye Mum." she replied
Mum turned to us with a determined look on her face...we know that look all too well!
"Well at least I managed to get another clue from her about our long-lost family member...he has a comb over!" she said, triumphantly
We've got nearly enough clues, but we need at least one more... plus a visit to a certain family tree to identify who he is!" said Mum, in her best 'Sherlock Holmes' detective persona
"At least we're getting closer to finding the answers."
I just know we're getting closer." I said, excitedly
Mum and Dad found some old photos to show me of Olivia, Rebecca and themselves when they were young... having fun times on the beach at Stockton which is only twenty-five minutes down the coast from Newcastle Beach... which is where we are having fun today.
"Cassie, this one is of Mum, Olivia, Rebecca and I splashing each other in the waves at the beach in 1977, when we were seven years old."
"We went there for a few days holiday." Dad said
"Our parents were resting on beach chairs, so we decided to fill our buckets up with water and sneak up behind them...then we threw water all over them!"
"It was a funny beach moment, way back then!" says Dad, grinning at the memory

"That one was taken in 1980 when we were ten years old."

"We were all building a big sandcastle together."

"I was building... Dad was making the moat... Olivia and Rebecca were putting the shells on the walls."

"It was great teamwork creating our beautiful sandcastle... it was so big that we hid behind it on the beach when it was time to go!"

"Our parents were searching for us, when they heard a giggle coming from the sandcastle."

"We all had a laugh when they found us they were such fun times when we were young." said Mum fondly, reminiscing

Mum and Dad showed me photos of Mum, Dad, Olivia and Rebecca, throwing water bombs at each other when they were about thirteen years old, also one of Mum and Dad 'canoodling' when they were older teenagers.

"Those were funny photos...you shared some happy times then...didn't you?" I said

"That's right, Cassie."

"I still remember one funny story when we were seventeen." recalled Dad

"It was in 1987 and we were staying at Stockton Beach... it was during our second world tour as 'Quirky Service'."

"We were swimming and Olivia, Rebecca and I, decided to play a trick on your Mum."

"We swam quietly underwater to where Mikayla was swimming, and snatched her bathers!"

"We swam quickly away, then ran up the beach waving them above our heads like flags, whilst your Mum hid in the surf."

"She asked us to return her bathers, but we cheekily said 'nope you're not getting them back Mikayla!" then we stuck our tongues out at her and ran up the beach

"Your Mum shivered for a couple of minutes... then she walked up to us in her birthday suit... and got her bathers back!"

"We were laughing the whole time she walked up to us... to take her bathers back."

"I'll never forget that incident!" said Dad, chuckling

"It was very embarrassing at the time...eventually.... I saw the funny side!" Mum grimaced

"We were just young and foolish teens back then... having mischievous fun at Stockton Beach." Mum remembers

Dad played the sympathy violin.

"As for you, dear..." said Mum, playfully boxing Dad under the ear

Dad and I chuckled.

Let's hit the hay, our next destination is Tamworth, it will take us almost four hours of driving to get there." Dad said, as we turned in for the night

"Good night Mum and Dad."

"Good night Cassie, sleep well." said Mum and Dad

# Chapter Fourteen
## Tamworth

"Wicked!"

"This is great!"

"Tamworth is an awesome place to have a good time!" I said

We had arrived in Tamworth... the home of Australian country music! Artists like John Williamson, Lee Kernaghan and the Wolverines have performed here many times over the years. Mum and Dad have covered a few country songs with Olivia and Rebecca, also Kate, Nicole, Adam and Amelia... I think we may do a country album together.

"According to the tourist information we should just about see the Golden Guitar right over there!" said Mum

There it was... tall and shiny... the legendary Golden Guitar! It's one of the 'big' attractions in Australia... it's the first time I've seen one up close! It's amazing!

"Oh... my goodness!"

"That Golden Guitar is huge!"

"I've never seen anything like it before." I said, excitedly

"I'm glad you're enjoying it, Cassie."

There's a motel inn near the Golden Guitar that we can stay at... there's plenty of things to do here in Tamworth."

"We'll make the most of it while we are here!" said Dad, happily

We booked a room at the Golden Guitar Motor Inn and ordered some lemonade to quench our thirst after the long drive.

"Ahh, this is so refreshing."

"This is the life!" I said, with gusto

"Quite right, Cassie."

"Tamworth has a country theme...I love it!" declared Mum

"There are quite a few Australian country stars on the walls, The Wolverines, John Williamson and here is Graeme Connors." Dad said, impressed

"These are great Australian country singers they made country music in Australia popular...with melodic country tunes... and themes like romance, weather and family."

"I may write a country song in the future...I think I'll stick to pop for now." I said

"We love the themes and tunes of country music it makes us want to sing along and play our instruments too." said Mum

When we went to our hotel room, there was a big parcel on the bed with a note on it... it read...

'To the Bontel Family, inside you will find cowboy/cowgirl/country singer costumes to wear, if you choose to do a country song performance here at Tamworth, or even just exploring the town! Enjoy. Golden Guitar Motel Staff.'

"Well, why don't we open the parcel and try the costumes on." I said

We opened the parcel... the three country costumes were in our favourite colours.

We looked at them for a minute before we tried them on... we looked pretty smart now when walking around Tamworth... we were turning heads with our fancy gear!

"You three are lookin' good." smiled a passer-by

"Thanks for the compliment." I replied

"I have an idea."

"We can discuss it later... I will tell you all about it then."

Mum and Dad were curious to know about my idea... I could tell!

We continued to explore Tamworth, even signed a few autographs along the way. We also shopped at the City Plaza, where the cashiers asked for autographs as well.

Later, over a meal, I discussed my idea with Mum and Dad... it involves country music!

"Mum, Dad... my idea is that we form a one-off country band and perform covers of country songs mostly Australian country music artists...plus a couple from overseas."

"We make about ten tracks on Disc One, maybe another ten on Disc Two... then we record and perform them here at Tamworth during our stay."

"That sounds like good idea, Cassie." said Dad

"It would take a lot of organisation though." he added

"I agree, we would certainly need to extend our stay here in Tamworth, to get all that done!" Mum, laughed

A country music producer was seated nearby and heard us talking... he came over to our table.

"G'day."

"I couldn't help overhearing that you are thinking of doing a country album." he said

"That's right, we would like to try that." nodded Dad

"My name is Gary Rogers, the founder and owner of ACM Records, (Australian Country Music)."

"I've heard about your pop band 'The Bontel Family' I know you are doing really well."

"How about you come to my recording studio in a couple of days...we can record some cover songs there if you like the idea."

"However, you can't use the 'Bontel Family' band name...you'll have to choose a different 'monicker' for this one-off project!"

"I would suggest a name like 'Country Stars'."

"You don't have to go with that name if you don't like it."

"You will also need to cover the Country Rock genre, as well."

"Good luck, I'll see you at the recording studio in a couple of days." Gary waved as he left

"All we need is a name and twenty songs now!" I said, with a sense of trepidation

"We had better get back to the hotel quick smart and start working on this!"

We were deep in discussion about proposed names for our 'one off' country music project.

"How about the 'Country Bumpkins'?" said Dad

"No, that's not right... it's too awkward!" I said

"What about Country Pumpkin Stars?" asked Mum

"Oh NO Mum... that's so embarrassing!" I cringed, at the thought of it!

You're right Cassie, both names are no good!" said Dad

"Do you have a suggestion of your own?" he asked

"Well, my suggestion is Outback Family."

"Would you go with that?" I asked

"That's a much better name, Cassie."

"We will go with that indeed." said Dad, much happier with the choice

Next, we must choose our songs." said Mum

We took all of the next day to decide on the twenty songs that we wanted to record on our 'country' two-disc set. We made a list and decided on the order, setting it all out ready for when we go to the recording studio with Gary. We got a good night's rest that evening so that we would be fresh and ready for the studio the next day.

We arrived at the recording studio... I hope we do well... do Tamworth proud!

"All right Bontel Family, have you got your songs ready?" asked Gary

"Yes, we have."

"We're all ready to practice them." I said

"What name have you chosen for your country band?" asked Gary

"We have chosen 'Outback Family'."

"It has a country feel to it." said Dad

"That sounds like a good name." Gary replied

"What instruments will you be playing?" asked Gary

"I will be singing lead vocals and playing guitar... Mum will be playing drums and singing vocals... Dad will be playing keyboards and singing vocals as well." I told him

"My sister-in-law, Rebecca has been teaching me to play keyboards and piano for several years, even though I normally do vocals and bass guitar I've become very good at the keyboards as well." said Dad, enthusiastically

"That's great!" said Gary

"Are you ready to start a recording session now?"

"Yes, we are Gary." we all said together

## Disc One

| Track No/Name | Singer | Composer/s | Genre | Original Artist |
|---|---|---|---|---|
| Gonna' Ride All Night Long | Cassie Bontel | Darcy Leyear John Clinton Gizz Butt | Country Rock | Wolverines |
| Certain Circles | Cassie Bontel | Darcy Leyear John Clinton Gizz Butt | Country Rock | Wolverines |
| The Outback Club | Cassie Bontel | Lee Kernaghan Garth Porter | Country Rock | Lee Kernaghan |
| The Road Less Travelled | Cassie Bontel | Graeme Connors Mark McDuff | Country | Graeme Connors |
| Chandelier of Stars | Cassie Bontel | Keith Urban Monty Powell | Country | John Williamson |
| She's My Ute | Cassie Bontel | Colin Buchanan Lee Kernaghan | Country Rock | Lee Kernaghan |

| Track No/Name | Singer | Composer/s | Genre | Original Artist |
|---|---|---|---|---|
| Little Sisters | Cassie Bontel | Adam Brand | Country | Adam Brand |
| Days go by | Cassie Bontel | Monty Powell Keith Urban | Country | Keith Urban |
| Real Gone | Cassie Bontel | Sheryl Crow John Shanks | Country Rock | Sheryl Crow |
| Life is a highway | Cassie Bontel ft. Sunset | Tom Cochrane | Country Rock | Tom Cochrane |

## Disc Two

| Track No/Title | Singer | Composer/s | Genre | Original Artist |
|---|---|---|---|---|
| Better than a picture | Cassie Bontel | Darcy Leyear John Clinton Gizz Butt | Country | John Williamson |
| Achy Breaky Heart | Cassie Bontel | Don Van Tress | Country Pop, Country Rock | Billy Ray Cyrus |
| Not pretty enough | Cassie Bontel | Kasey Chambers | Country | Kasey Chambers |
| 4.The Captain | Cassie Bontel | Kasey Chambers | Country | Kasey Chambers |
| Courageous | Cassie Bontel with The Australian Country Girls' Choir | Melinda Schneider | Country | Melinda Schneider (Feat. The Australian Girls' Choir) |
| Rattlin' Bones | Cassie Bontel and Bill Greg | Kasey Chambers & Shane Nicholson | Country | Kasey Chambers & Shane Nicholson |
| So much trouble | Cassie Bontel | Warren H Williams | Country | Warren H Williams |
| Follow Me | Cassie Bontel | N/A | Country Pop | Uncle Kracker |
| True Blue (1986 version) | Cassie Bontel | John Williamson | Country | John Williamson |
| Be Yourself | Cassie Bontel | Melinda Schneider | Country | Melinda Schneider |

Over the next couple of weeks, we continue to work with Gary on our country album… right now we are getting into the spirit of the Tamworth Country Music Festival!

Mum, Dad and I are backstage at Toyota Park Tamworth, getting 'pumped' to enter onstage. With our colourful country costumes, our instruments already onstage, we are going to show Tamworth what we can do with our experimental album of country music classics!

"This is going to be one exciting concert!" I said

"Dad and I, have been here a couple of times… we really enjoyed ourselves… the first time will be one you will never forget darling!" said Mum

"You'll enjoy Tamworth even more when you take part!" said Dad, grinning

"I'm glad I'm experiencing Tamworth with you two!" I said, looking across at Mum and Dad, sharing the moment with them

"Tamworth has expanded my country music knowledge… just like the Murray River widens!"

"I shall remember this moment forever!" I said, with joy

"It will be lodged in our memories too Cassie." Mum added

The emcee walked onto the stage. I hope I'm ready to tackle this country music... it's too late to back out now! Let's do Tamworth proud!

"Ladies and Gentlemen, I'm introducing a one-off special performance today."

"This popstar family have come all the way from Melbourne... they also love a bit of country music." the emcee spruiked

"Today, they are performing fair dinkum Aussie songs and some country tracks from overseas artists too!"

"Please welcome to the Tamworth stage 'The Outback Family'!" yelled the MC

Mum, Dad and I, walked on waving to the Tamworth crowd. We picked up our microphones and made our way to the front of the stage.

"G'day Tamworth... how's it going?" I asked

"G'day." the crowd roared back

"We're the Outback Family, we will be playing some country and country rock for you today."

"There may be a little boot-scooting as well, if you're lucky!"

"Before we start, let's introduce ourselves."

"I am Cassie Bontel aka 'Outback' Cassie." I winked

"I'm lead singer and guitarist."

"I love tending to my cows and playing with the pigs when the day is done... I have a nice warm shower put my feet up in front of the fire... a lemonade in one hand and a farm cat curled up at my feet!" I said, giving another wink to the crowd

The crowd cheered and clapped.

"I'm Mikayla Bontel aka 'Outback' Mikayla."

"I'm the drummer and singer."

"I like tending to my horses and shearing my sheep... when the day is done I cook dinner for my family... then I read a good book!" said Mum, smiling at the crowd

The crowd cheered and clapped louder. It's a good start!

"I'm Daniel Bontel aka 'Outback' Daniel."

"I'm the keyboardist, guitarist and singer."

"I run most of the farm... occasionally I feed the chickens... when the day is over I like to kick back in a good armchair... watching the AFL or cricket." said Dad, with a grin

This is going to be one good country concert!

"Let's get this concert underway... Mum... Dad... are you ready?" I ask

"Yes, Cassie." they reply together

Our first set consisted of ten songs:

**Song 1:** Gonna' Ride all Night Long (Wolverines)
**Song 2:** Certain Circles (Wolverines)
**Song 3:** The Outback Club (Lee Kernaghan)
**Song 4:** The Road less Travelled (Graeme Connors)
**Song 5:** Chandelier of Stars (John Williamson)
**Song 6:** She's My Ute (Lee Kernaghan)
**Song 7:** Little Sisters (Adam Brand)
**Song 8:** Days Go By (Keith Urban)
**Song 9:** Real Gone (Sheryl Crow)
**Song 10:** Life is a Highway (Tom Cochrane)

The second set of ten songs were:

**Song 11:** Better Than a Picture (John Williamson)
**Song 12:** Achy Breaky Heart (Billy Ray Cyrus)
**Song 13:** Not Pretty Enough (Kasey Chambers)
**Song 14:** The Captain (Kasey Chambers)
**Song 15:** Courageous (Melinda Schneider feat. The Australian Girls' Choir)
**Song 16:** Rattlin' Bones (Kasey Chambers & Shane Nicholson)
**Song 17:** So Much Trouble (Warren H Williams)
**Song 18:** Follow Me (Uncle Kracker)
**Song 19:** True Blue (1986 Version) (John Williamson)
**Song 20:** Be Yourself (Melinda Schneider)

The Tamworth Crowd cheered wildly... this is so good I'm loving every minute and I'm sure Mum and Dad are loving every minute too... the Tamworth crowd have really enjoyed themselves at our 'country' concert!
"Thank you... thank you... we hope you enjoyed the 'Outback Family'?" I called out to the crowd
"YES...WE DID!" the crowd yelled back waving
"That's the spirit!"
"We would like to thank you all for coming along to this one-off Tamworth concert."
"You have provided much support and encouragement... which we very much appreciate."
We enjoyed singing and performing for you all."
"We'll be going now... thanks for everything Tamworth!" I shouted out
I then proceeded to take my hat off and throw it in the air with a, 'Yee-Ha' like I've seen cowboys and cowgirls do! Mum and Dad did the same! The crowd took off their hats and followed us with a huge 'Yee Ha'!!!
"Mum and Dad, that was a good county concert, it was awesome... I embraced the experience wholeheartedly!" I grinned
"It certainly was, Cassie!"
"Mum and I really enjoyed it... you did a great job well done darling." Dad said, proudly
"Great job sweetie." smiled Mum
"Thanks Mum, thanks Dad, I love Tamworth even more now... I'd love to come back again and bring Maria, Belinda, Darren and Jim with us." I said
"I'm sure they would love it."
"They love a bit of country music." said Mum
"Let's get a takeaway pizza...I'm hungry... I know where we can order one... a pub called 'The Pig and the Tinderbox'." said Mum
"The Pig and the what?" said Dad and I, confused
"The Pig and the Tinderbox."
"I thought it was a weird name at first too... but it's a good restaurant!"
"One of the region's first pubs'... set up in 1848...one hundred and sixty-three years later it's trialling a style where boutique bar... meets classic pub." said Mum, with a grin at our two astonished faces
"OK let's try it out!" said Dad, always ready to embrace a new food experience!
I found out lots of interesting facts about Tamworth along the way!
The Tamworth Country Music Festival is held each year in January, it celebrates country music culture and the Australian country music scene. The Country Music awards are held on Saturday of the Australia Day long weekend.

Lee Kernaghan and John Williamson regularly perform at this festival, and Keith Urban and Kasey Chambers started their careers from this very location! The 'Big Golden Guitar' that we saw when we arrived... is one of the big attractions in Tamworth... it was erected in 1988 at the location of the famous Longyard Hotel, on Sydney Road.

It has no strings because the Golden Guitar Trophies were modelled on it... the late renowned country singer Slim Dusty did the unveiling. It is an icon of Tamworth... since it opened an estimated three point six million photographs have been taken of it!

Tamworth became the first place in Australia to use electric street lights in 1888... thus earning the nickname 'First Town of Lights'! Wow!

Tamworth has become a lot brighter since that year!

After lunch we went to the 'Aussie Bush Leather'... a shop near Tamworth where they had cowhide leather products... from ladies' wallets... men's belts... backpacks and even UGG boots!

There are so many to choose from and to look at, I might add a wallet or handbag to the Minnie Mouse wallet that I always carry in my pocket when I'm out and about, or buy a pair of UGG boots that I could walk around in.

"I love this handbag."

"This one looks lovely!"

"It's so fashionable." said Mum, happily contemplating a purchase

"This belt would look good on my jeans."

"I could wear it with my cowboy hat and boots!" chuckled Dad

Mum and I giggled. It would make a good photo to show my special centre classmates and I'm sure our family and friends would love it too!

"I've got my eye on these pair of UGG boots!"

"I think they would look great on my feet and not only will they keep me warm during the winter months, I can parade around in my room with them, they feel so soft to touch." I said

"You will look good in them and I bet you will enjoy the feel of them on your feet." laughs Mum

"I sure will, Mum."

"They can take place alongside my blue shoes in my bedroom wardrobe!" I added

However, ... when we looked at the prices most of the items were over one hundred dollars! We looked at each other and decided not to buy any of them...it was a store well worth visiting...but you need lots of money!

A few days later Mum asked...

"Cassie, how do you feel about visiting the Powerhouse Motorcycle Museum today?"

"I feel excited about seeing the museum, Mum."

"I'm very keen to look at the motorcycles and learn all about them." I replied

"I can remember some of them." Dad said

"I owned a Yamaha before you were born Cassie." he added

"I used to take your Mum for a ride around the open Melbourne spaces."

"We felt the wind on us as we rode along."

"Gosh, those were fun times on my motorbike." said Dad, with a faraway look in his eyes

"Mum's older brother and my uncle John used to ride motor bikes too!"

"Many times, he would arrive at the Bontel-Macdonald mansion riding it... he would sometimes take me or Rebecca for a ride."

"We would laugh with delight as we rode with the wind." said Mum, remembering those days

"I have never had a ride on a motorbike."

"I blocked out the noise using my headphones because they used to upset me...but I'm keen to try now."

"Ok, Cassie."

"One day, I will get out my motorcycle and you can have a ride on it with me."

"You can put a motorcycle helmet on and a jacket, we'll have a fun time together riding on my bike." said Dad, grinning

"We sure will."

"Let's go and check out the motorcycle museum then!" I said

We went inside the Motorcycle Museum after paying the sixteen dollars entry fee. Wow! There were over fifty motorcycles from the decades of the fifties, sixties, seventies and eighties. Ducatis, Hondas and Laverdas were a few of the makes of motorbikes... among them was a rare limited edition F4 MV Agusta Series ORO.

All of the bikes have been immaculately restored to concourse condition, they are in pristine working order. We took our time checking the motorcycles out, including a 1969 Honda CB750 and a 1972 Triumph TR5 Trophy Trail.

Awesome! I never knew there were so many different types of motorcycles in my life!

They were all gleaming and polished to a high sheen they looked excellent to ride on.

I imagined myself riding on a Honda in the wide, open spaces of Australia... in full motorcycle gear with the wind blowing on me and the Wolverines song...'We're gonna' ride all night long' playing in the background. The sun was shining as I rode along and I checked out the views as I went! That was one awesome daydream!

We had complimentary tea... the owner took a few minutes to chat with us while we were drinking our tea.

"I see you've been enjoying the motorcycles in our museum."

"What do you think of them?" asked the owner

"They're awesome to look at."

"It brings back great memories to my wife and I of motor bike riding when we were younger." said Dad

"Fun times we had."

"We sometimes rode at sunset we loved the views when riding then." Mum added

"Do you love motorcycles too?" the owner asked me

"Yes, I enjoy learning about them." I replied

"My favourite would have to be the Honda."

"I'm keen to ride on one... one day when Dad teaches me how to."

"He might even take me for a ride on his bike." I said, excited at the thought

"One day... you will be riding around Australia... looking at the sights... feeling the excitement of motorbike riding." the owner grinned at me

"All I need is the motorcycle gear and the helmet and I will be ready."

"First...I will need to learn how to ride a motorbike safely... they are powerful machines!" I added

"That's our smart daughter... she loves learning about new things." said Dad, proudly

"I could teach her how to fix one if it won't start... she's great at fixing cars!" beamed Dad

"Good... it's always handy to have a mechanic in the family!" laughed the owner

"Yes!" Mum agreed, as she laughed too

That night as I was drifting off to sleep... I dreamt I was exploring small towns riding a motorcycle through the streets.

## Chapter Fifteen
## Country towns

Whist we are in Tamworth we decide to check out the small communities nearby... we drove to Kootingal which is fifty minutes away. The main attraction near Kootingal is the 'Big Chook'...another one of Australia's many 'big' things! I have never seen a chicken that big before! That's definitely winner-winner-chicken dinner! I think I might take a photo and send it to Nan Diane, (she's just learned how to use an iPhone), it takes a lot of getting used to!

"Woah, that is one very 'BIG 'chicken indeed!" we all agreed

"It will make a great photo!" I said

I took a couple of photos and sent them off to Nan Diane.

The next small town near Tamworth was Nundle, I've never heard of that town, but we decided to check it out

"Imagine if you take the second 'n' out of Nundle and replace the l with an i... what cheeky town name you would come up with." I giggled, naughtily

Mum and Dad both laughed

"Oh, Cassie, you do come up with some funny ideas." Mum said, laughing

"That was a classic...better than your one-liners Dad... or your embarrassing Dad jokes!" I said, grinning

Next, we decided to visit the Mount Misery Gold Mine Museum in Nundle. There's some interesting information for me to soak up, so it's time for me to learn more!

Nundle was the first location where reef gold was discovered... it was said that in 1849 alluvial gold was uncovered and discovered... reef gold was then found in 1852.

There is a one hundred and fifty metre underground tunnel to check out... it's a bit dark but I'm not going to let the dark stop me from the exploration! Mining and gold rush memorabilia is packed into the tunnel... we were enthralled by it all.

"This museum is giving me an authentic taste of the life and trials of the pioneers above the Nundle Gold Fields."

"I never learnt that during my Melbourne Secondary College years... I am fascinated by all of the shiny things that are here." I said, mesmerised by it all

"We've never visited an Australian museum quite like this one."

"The history of the pioneers is great to learn about... we are glad you are loving it as much as we do." Dad said

"There's a gold panning activity to complete the whole gold rush experience, would you like to do that, Cassie?" asked Mum

"No, thanks, Mum."

"I don't want to do that… just yet."
"Perhaps further along the road trip I will consider trying it." I replied
"Ok, Cassie."
We checked out the newspaper extracts from the gold rush era and we learnt about the local characters and events occurring at that time in Nundle. After all that exploring, Mum, Dad and I are feeling peckish so we go to find a café for some lunch.
There are mouth-watering home cooked meals and tantalizing treats, which ones shall we choose?
We sat next to the fire and ordered our meals and we talked about the day so far.
"Mum, Dad, I really enjoyed the Mount Misery Gold Mine Museum."
"It was like stepping back in time into the gold rush period, learning about Nundle's gold era."
"I was like a six-year-old discovering a favourite toy in a toy shop." I said, happily
"We enjoyed it too, Cassie." said Mum
"This museum we won't forget!"
"This café is great too… with home-cooked meals and the fire adding a nice warm location." said Dad, contentedly
"It reminds me of the visits to Maria and Jim's house, sitting in front of the fireplace on a winter's day… reading my books and doing my magazine puzzles." I remember
"Nundle is a great small town to visit."
"Besides visiting major towns we've started discovering small towns and finding a gem or two."
"I think I would like to stay here for the evening."
"What do you think, Mum and Dad?" I asked, hopefully
Mum and Dad looked at each other.
Then Mum answered…
"All right, Cassie… we can."
"As it's less than an hour from Tamworth, we can collect our stuff and book in for an overnight stay."
"There's some home cooked cakes, slices and biscuits over there, we could buy a few to eat on our journey back to Nundle." I said
"Sure thing, Cassie."
"We haven't had slices and biscuits for a while, so we might stock up on a few." Dad agreed
We bought some of the local goodies, including honey. I plan to spread it on my biscuits! Later, when we arrived back in Nundle we chose to stay at the 'Peel Inn', it looks like an awesome inn to stay in for the night!
It's over one hundred and fifty years old…still it boasts all the features of a modern pub!
I will have fun staying here I can't wait to sleep in the stylishly renovated rooms.
"Hello, we'd like to book a room for the night." said Mum, to the receptionist
"Of course."
"Hmm…are you the Bontel Family?" asked the receptionist
"Yes, we are the Bontel Family." said Dad, smiling
"Welcome to Nundle Peel Inn."
"We have two bars… or you can enjoy a delicious meal in our restaurant."
"There is local produce, including mouth-watering local trout, succulent steaks, tender roasts and our celebrated Nundle pies."
"You can sit under the forty-year old grapevine whilst enjoying your meal… if you wish."
"There are also daily specials and complimentary breads."

"When you wake in the morning you will hear the birds singing before beginning your next adventure." said the receptionist

"Oh, my goodness!"

"That all sounds awesome!"

"Especially the bit about the foods...I can't wait to try!"

"I'll certainly enjoy the views while sitting on the veranda... watching the world go by."

"I love hearing the birds sing it makes me feel relaxed in the mornings and afternoons."

"I've never stayed here before but I shall make the most of it with Mum and Dad!" I said, full of excitement

"I'm sure you will, Miss Bontel."

"Here is your room key."

"Enjoy your stay." smiled the receptionist

"We will." said Mum, happily

Our room has damask bed linen. I hope I feel comfortable sleeping on it, there is an antique washstand, cane bottomed bentwood chairs from the original dining room, tongue and groove timber ceilings and timber shutters.

I touched the damask linen it feels comfortable enough, although it will be my first time sleeping on that fabric.

I checked out the bathroom and thankfully there was a shower to practice my singing in.

Maybe I could try singing a country song or two!

"Mum, Dad."

"I'm starting to like this room already."

"The damask feels comfortable to sleep on and the ceiling is nice."

"The country pub experience is embracing me, it's a great feeling."

"We can see that you are liking it, Cassie"

"We are loving it too!"

"The wallpaper is lovely in this room." said Mum, smiling

"Our family and friends would love this place."

Cassie, you're going to love the views." said Dad

"I bet... I think I will try the Nundle pie."

"I don't know what flavour it is... but I will give it a go!" I declared

"Good on you, Cassie!" said Mum

"You are becoming more adventurous with your food choices as we go along, it's good to see!"

"Thanks, Mum."

"There is a long way to go, though."

"I'm getting there with your help and encouragement." I added

We made our way outside to the beer garden, looked over the menus and ordered our meal.

There was Peel Inn pie... a two-hundred-gram Scotch fillet with beer battered chips...or a Steak burger! It was a pity there wasn't a dessert menu... I would have liked to order a nice chocolate cake... with white chocolate icing on top and white chocolate sprinkles! That is my ideal dessert, mmm! Don't tell Mum that though she'll be envious and probably vanish it away from me. Hee hee.

We looked at the views... the colours and the sights relaxed us.

"I imagine I'm walking in the botanical gardens with orchids... admiring the flowers all the way through." I said, smiling dreamily

"Dad and I used to walk through botanical gardens when we were dating."

"The colours and aromas were beautiful... we would spin around and run through the flower laden paths."

"Fun times for us." said Mum, recalling

"That makes me think of when I used to skip and twirl around in the backyard in my... but I'm not revealing anymore... there are other people around who may be listening." I said, blushing

"We're glad you stopped yourself before you revealed the X-rated part of that story!" said Mum, relieved

"Nearly got myself into 'hot water' there!"

"Changing the subject... the Peel Inn pie... is quite delicious!"

"My tastebuds went a bit wild... but they settled down once I started eating it." I said

"Good job, Cassie."

"You're doing well with trying new foods so far on this road trip."

"That pie would not have been on your 'acceptable' list before." said Dad, grinning

"Who knows I might try a pot pie next time, Dad!" I said, with a grin

Later that evening, I needed a shower so I placed my iPhone near the sink and my pyjamas on the seat before I went in the shower to practice my singing.

It happened that at the same time Dad had decided to send a romantic text to Mum. He does that when he is in a romantic mood sometimes. Mum sends the same kind of thing to him.

This is how I came to receive the following text...

*Oh, darling. To me, you are a lovely rose in a meadow field. We could lay down there and I would kiss you and make love to you while the sun shines down on us. You're my Madonna sweatheart*

Unfortunately, ... (for me) ...he messaged the wrong person and sent it to me instead of Mum! Also... sweetheart got changed to... sweatheart!

I had just turned off the shower when I got the text!

I dried myself off before I picked up my iPhone... I didn't want to get it wet. When I read the message...I cringed. I don't know how Dad's romantic text got on my iPhone but it is gross! Yuck!!!

I sent a reply to Dad... *"EWW! DAD! WTF? It's disgusting and gross what you sent to me!"*

Dad went bright red with embarrassment... I could tell ...when he messaged me back.

*Oops! Sorry!! I meant to send that to your Mum! I don't know how it got on your iPhone!* I could hear him muttering in the next room...I was trying to say sweetheart! Stupid autocorrect!!!

I can imagine Mum frowning at Dad... she wouldn't think that was funny... and now Dad doesn't think it's funny either!

Mum made several autocorrect mistakes when she got her own iPhone and so did Dad.

That text was gross, I won't forget that bad mental picture in a hurry!

I sent Dad another message...

*'Dad, I'm going to send this to everyone, so they can get a big laugh out of it. I'm also going to send this to the 'Damn You Autocorrect' website! By the way, I bet you are in big trouble with Mum at the moment! LOL*

Dad replied...

*"I knew you were going to do that! I guess I am in big trouble with Mum, she's frowning at me. How embarrassing!*

I emerged from the bathroom and walked to my bed... about to call Ivy.

"Cassie... before you make that call you need to put your pyjamas on!" said Mum, disapprovingly

I looked down and oh dear, I haven't got my pyjamas on! Oh No! I have forgotten my clothes again!

I feel so comfortable without them on, I would rather be without them all the time...but I know that's not acceptable now that I am no longer a little child.

I have committed a social faux pas...lucky it's only Mum in the room to see me!

"Please excuse me." I say, blushing and covering my modesty, as I race back to the bathroom to quickly put on my pyjamas

"You need to remember that lesson Cassie." said Dad, firmly as I scooted by

"Yes, Dad." I replied

I then called Ivy to tell her about the Peel Inn.

"Hello, Ivy."

"We're currently staying at this lovely, awesome inn… it's in a small town in New South Wales."

"It's called the Peel Inn."

"It's a brilliant place to stay."

"We had our meals in the beer garden"

"I tried the Peel Inn Pie… let me tell you my taste buds went wild…but they got used to it!"

"I've never tried a meal like that before in my life, it was delicious."

"Whilst I was having my shower earlier on, Dad tried to send a romantic text to Mum but he accidently sent it to my iPhone, then the autocorrection had the nerve to change it from sweetheart to sweatheart…I cringed when I received the message… I can tell you!"

"I didn't find it funny initially…I messaged him to let him know what I thought… then told him that his mistake is going on the 'Damn You Autocorrect' website!"

"That autocorrection feature is a pain in the arse!"

"We explored the Mount Misery Gold mine in Nundle earlier in the day… we had to walk through a tunnel where we saw some gold memorabilia and then learnt information about life back in the gold rush days."

"You should recommend it to Nina, George, Zoe and Peter, they might like to come next time if we do it again."

"I'd better go now."

"I'm going to enjoy sleeping in this damask bed!"

"I'll make sure to send a few photos of the Peel Inn, so you can see what it's looks like."

"Bye."

Now that Dad is in a 'sticky situation' with Mum, he is trying to get back into her 'good books' after the autocorrect blunder! Mum will get him to make a cup of tea for all of us and then she will make him tidy the room in the morning! Dad knows there is no arguing with Mum… so he goes to make the tea. I thought it was funny… but wisely kept my mouth shut!

We read our books for a while and then turn in for the night. The damask was new to me, as my bed has always had cotton sheets, blankets and pillowcases. I will need to get used to sleeping in beds of other fabrics during our trip.

The next morning, I heard the sound of singing birds as I awoke. Chirping and singing birds always soothe me… in the morning I have an alarm which has chirping birds. It's a great start to the day… Mum, Dad and I, drive to our next destination.

Barraba is the last small town we chose to visit it will take two hours to reach from Nundle, there are plenty of things to do when we arrive.

I found out that in 1889 copper was discovered at Gulf Creek… the first mine was established in 1892. Two hundred men were employed at that site in 1901… which at the time was one of the largest in the state. A village was developed… which included bark-hut residences…stores… a school… a hotel and a post office.

However, … in 1911 a major company had to pull out and the mine only had a handful of employees left… though it managed to struggle on for some years… the school was closed in 1957 and the post office followed nine years later.

The Kamilaroi Aborigines occupied the site before the white people came.

Allan Cunningham crossed the Manilla River in 1827 and named it Buddle's Creek... which is located a little to the west of the present-day townsite. Barraba's name derives from an Aboriginal term... meaning 'camp by the riverbank'.

A Scotsman named John McKid opened the first store on this future townsite in the mid 1840's...which would later be surveyed in 1852. Gold was discovered in the areas of Woods reef, Ironbark Creek and Crow Mountain. At this time, Woods reef was a vital village... but when the gold was exhausted in the late 1860's... the village became extinct.

We decided to a bit of bird watching... Barraba's information centre at 114 Queen St...was the place to get material about 'bird routes' and the best places to watch out for them. The regent honeyeater and the turquoise parrot are a couple of rare bird species... so we will need to use our binoculars and keep very quiet...we don't want to scare them away.

Mum, Dad and I got some snacks and took our binoculars with us, we began to look around for those two rare birds.

Twenty minutes passed...

"Do you see any of the rare birds, Mum...Dad?" I whisper

"Not yet, Cassie." Mum whispers back

"Me either, Cassie."

"We'll just have to keep looking." Dad's whispering voice joins in

Another twenty minutes passes by. I look around again and guess what I see?

A regent honeyeater has just landed close by. It has yellow, black and white feathers, the rest of its body is black.

I thought... *'Oh gosh! That's one very pretty regent honeyeater! I would love to take a picture of it.'* Mum and Dad saw it too.

It was another fifteen minutes when a turquoise parrot came into view. It was coloured green, yellow and blue all over its body with a tinge of red.

"Mum, Dad, look how beautiful this parrot is."

"What gorgeous colours."

"That's a beautiful bird to remember."

"I've seen a similar bird... I remember that my aunt had a parrot with those colours... I loved looking after it when I visited her." said Dad, quietly

"It would make a great photo... but we'll let it roam the area."

"That's one colourful bird indeed." whispered Mum

Then the turquoise parrot flew up into the air and landed on my head. Luckily it was small...or I would have freaked out if it was much bigger.

"Um... Mum and Dad."

"Why is the turquoise parrot sitting on my heard?" I asked, nervously whispering

"It's all right, Cassie."

"Don't be scared."

"It's just resting... checking out the views from there." said Mum, reassuringly

"Oh... ok." I said, not entirely convinced

Dad got his camera out...I gestured not to take the picture. I don't need to be embarrassed... my friends would laugh at me if that photo was taken!

The parrot then hopped off my hair and onto my arm… this time I gestured silently for Dad to take the photo. He took it… then the parrot flew away.

"I enjoyed looking at those birds."

"They were beautiful to see… we've got an awesome photo of the turquoise parrot to show everyone."

"It was a great activity for us to do… Barraba was another interesting town to visit!"

"I would come again." I said, joyfully

"We loved this small town too Cassie."

"Bird watching is a great activity to do as a family." said Mum, happily

"You're opening up to new activities since we began our wonderful road trip around Australia!" said Dad, enthusiastically

"Thanks, Dad."

"What new activity will I try next… it's anybody's guess!" I stated, with a laugh

We strapped ourselves into our vehicle and drove another two hours to our next destination…Moree.

"Here we are in Moree!"

"It seems like a picturesque place to stay for a while."

"If I remember rightly there's a picnic spot at Terry Hie Hie that your Dad and I went to when we were nineteen." said Mum

"It will be a good place to have an awesome picnic." I said

"That's right, Cassie." says Dad, ruffling my hair

"Dad stop it!" I said, a little embarrassed

"It's all right Cassie."

"It's just another form of affection." said Dad, laughing at my scowl

"Oh…ok…thanks for that." I said, not very convinced

The Winchester Motel in Anne Street seemed like a nice place to stay, so we booked our room there and then drove another forty-five minutes out to Terry Hie Hie for a late picnic lunch… consisting of cheese… crackers… pasta and potato salad… and a carrot cake.

"Cassie, when Dad and I were nineteen we were here during our 'Fun and Games' tour of Australia and New Zealand."

"We had a picnic… then we visited the graves of some family members in the area."

"We explored a bit of history which was fascinating to learn about… then later we even tried some Thai food at a restaurant back in Moree…called Moree Thai Cuisine!" said Mum, remembering

"How was the Thai food back then?" I asked

"It tickled our taste buds…the dishes were so tasty we had to order them again the next day!" Dad chuckled

"Here we are in a quiet spot… a nice place to have a family picnic!"

"I get to spend this day with you Mum and Dad… family time is what matters most!"

"That's true, Cassie."

"We appreciate it and love spending time with you." said Mum, smiling

"We're enjoying this road trip as a family… learning new things together as we go to even more destinations… we'll uncover further discoveries."

"Terry Hie Hie is an Aboriginal area of significance for the Kamilaroi people… the picnic area is close by to a ceremonial corroboree ground." Dad told me

"Why don't we go to the Moree Cemetery later to pay respect to our family ancestors?" I said

"We sure can Cassie... it'll be good to pay our respects and remember our family from generations before." said Dad

Later... when we had finished our picnic lunch and enjoyed the surroundings... we drove back to Moree churchyard and made our way to family graves.

"That's my great-Aunt Judith."

"She was born in Manchester, England... she came to Australia when she was five years old."

"Her family settled here and many years later she worked as a staff member at a clothing store... she was known for introducing a new dress line that became popular around the world... women wore that dress line for their weddings." said Mum

"What brand was that, Mum?"

"It must've been very popular." I added

"The line was called 'Flower'."

"My grandmother passed on her white wedding dress to my Mum in 1968... and then my Mum passed it on to me in 1990."

"Flower still continues to be popular today... there are about sixty-two stores in Australia at the present time." said Mum

We walked over to another grave as Dad recognised a family members name.

"That was my great-uncle Barry... he came to Australia from Dublin, Ireland on a convict ship... he worked as a blacksmith... he made a gift for his future wife Maxine... using the blacksmith tools he had when he was twenty-two years old."

"They married two years later in Melbourne... Maxine gave birth to a son and he later became Edith's husband." said Dad, smiling

"Edith is my Nan and Maria's Mum!"

"How great is that!" I said

"Cassie you have Irish heritage on your Dad's side and English and Scottish on my side... that's something you have just discovered!" said Mum, grinning

"I didn't even know that!"

"That's wicked!" I replied

We started to walk out of the Moree cemetery when we saw a familiar looking woman... probably in her late sixties... in a purple hat with a daisy flower on it and a green and yellow scarf.

"Who's that over there?"

"Is that?"

"No, surely not." said Mum

"I would recognise that woman from a mile away!"

"She's related to us." said Dad

"I've seen her a few times... I know who she is... especially with that purple hat!" I laughed

We walked over to the familiar figure she turned to say

"Mikayla Bontel... my lovely niece!"

"How are you?"

"Aunt Mabel...my beautiful aunt!"

"I'm doing well." said Mum, excitedly

They hugged each other tightly because they hadn't seen each other for a long, long time.

"I haven't seen you in about eleven years, Mabel."

"We didn't expect to see you here at Moree!" exclaimed Mum

"Neither did I."

"I'm just here on a holiday for a few days... I've been paying my respects to Dad who passed away recently." said Mabel

"We're sorry to hear that." Mum said, sadly

"It's all right... let's not let sadness get the better of us... we must have positive thoughts and move forward." said Mabel

"That's true." Dad replied

"Shall we go to the park nearby... have a bit of a chat and catch up? asked Mabel

We drove to the park and sat on one of the benches to chat with Mabel.

"How's that lovely Daniel going?" asked Mabel, with a twinkle in her eye

"I'm doing great thanks Mabel." said Dad, cheerfully

"What about pretty Cassie?" asked Mabel

"I'm fine, thanks." I said, with a smile

"Would you like to give me a kiss?"

"I haven't seen you for such a long time." said Mabel

"Ok." I said

I gave Mabel a kiss and she gave me one back... it was similar to my grandmother's kiss... but it was not too bad.

"How do you find Moree on this cold, but fine day?" asked Mabel

"We like it so far we are showing Cassie some of its history." said Mum

"I'm enjoying learning!"

"It's like a travelling classroom, learning even more about the country we live in."

"Mum and Dad are the best teachers... every place and new environment we go to is a learning and exploring experience!" I said, enthusiastically

Mum and Dad smile, they know that I love learning more about Australia than I've ever done before, they are helping me to progress through the tougher areas and I'm becoming more independent.

"We are broadening her education... navigating the challenges together as a family... helping each other through... because that's what families do!" said Dad

"It's good to hear that you are all doing so well."

"I love hearing about the road trip that you are taking around Australia... keep up the good work!" Aunt Mabel said, smiling at us

"Thanks, Mabel."

"Thanks for the encouragement!" Mum gave her a hug

We are trying to find out where my Dad is taking his men's month holiday!"

"Every time I ask Mum where they are all going... she won't reveal the location to me!" said Mum, petulantly

"Hmm...we always share secrets... she won't reveal your Dad's location to you... that's for sure!"

"However, ... I can tell you where the location is!" Mabel said, winking at Mum

"Come with me and I will tell you where they are." Mabel beckoned us towards her car which was in the car parking area.

We got into Mabel's car, so no one else could hear the location that Mabel is about to tell us...

# Chapter Sixteen
# Gold Coast

"I never knew that the Gold Coast would be so big!" I said, full of excitement
We have arrived at the Gold Coast after a long six-hour drive... Mum is telling us about how we are going to pull off a prank later, during our stay here in Queensland...at the Dad's holiday retreat in the Brisbane Holiday Village...where they are staying.

Two hours ago, we stopped at Stanthorpe Museum to find out some information about our long lost relative... Mum was closing in on that elusive family member!

There is SeaWorld, Dreamworld and Burleigh Heads beach to see! We are going to stay at the Sheraton Mirage Hotel for about two weeks... maybe a bit more. No matter how long we stay here... we are going to have loads of fun!

"I'm not sure about the rides...they make you go weak at the knees!"

"Too scary!" I said, shuddering

"I agree, Cassie!"

"They are too scary for us, especially the Big Drop!"

"I can't see myself going on that one!"

"I might get queasy!" said Mum, uneasily

"Me either!" said Dad

"How about we start by visiting 'Ripley's Believe It or Not'?" said Mum

"I've read a couple of those books... some of the content freaked me out!"

"I'm happy to take a look and check out the unusual, weird and unbelievable stuff!" I said, grinning ghoulishly

"Well then... let's go there and check it out."

"I'd bet there is some cool stuff that will amaze the three of us!" said Dad, enthusiastically

Upon entering inside we were fascinated... amazed... and shocked... with what we found and saw! There was the world's tallest man R.Wadlow, he grew to be two point seven-two metres tall! Wow! He was unbelievable... we had to crane our necks up to see his face!

Next... we viewed some shrunken heads which 'creeped' us right out!

"Eww!"

"Those heads are gross!"

"They disgust me!" I said, cringing at the sight

"They look disgusting to me too!" said Dad, grimly

"I think we should move away from this display and look at something less gruesome!" Mum added, hurriedly

"Good idea, Mum." I said, relieved to be moving away from those 'heads'

Next... we viewed something nicer and much more amusing. It was a wedding dress made of toilet paper! What an ingenious way to create a dress for your big wedding... whoever thought that one up must be a clever, cheeky creator! What a fashion statement it makes!

"Ha, ha!"

"That is the funniest Ripley's item I've seen so far!"

"It will make a great photo!" I said, giggling

"That's quite a dress!"

"I've never seen anything quite like it before."

"The bride who wore it must have been a hit at her wedding!" laughed Mum

"It is indeed an unusual dress."

"It's an imaginative use of toilet paper...it's kind of lovely too." Dad said, thoughtfully

"It's definitely one of a kind Mum...I would love to see you wearing a similar one for your next wedding anniversary!" I said, very cheekily

"Cassie that will not be happening!"

"You... cheeky miss!"

"Everyone would laugh at me... Mum and Dad would not approve of me wearing a household toilet item for a dress!" muttered Mum

Dad laughed out loud at the idea of Mum wearing a toilet paper wedding dress at their next wedding anniversary celebration!

"Mum... if that ever happened... I would take a photo of it and upload it to my iPhone to show all my friends... it would go viral on YouTube in no time!" I said, chuckling at the idea

"You will do no such thing, Cassie Annabelle Bontel!" Mum fumed, turning to speak to Dad next

"Daniel... it's not funny!"

"There will be no toilet paper wedding dresses in any of our anniversary celebration photographs!!!"

"Has everybody got that quite clear!" said Mum, glaring at us both

Dad and I just sniggered.

"You two are always trouble when you plot together."

"I don't know where you get these ideas from!" she muttered, which made Dad and I laugh even louder, because everyone knows Mum is the worst prankster of all

We decided to do some shopping at the Pacific Fair, set amongst a tropical landscape with a unique outdoor ambience. We felt like we were shopping in a jungle paradise, just like Hawaii ... even though that's far away from Australia.

We saw luxury brands like Louis Vitton... Gucci and Prada... global mega brands like H & M... Sephora and Zara! Mum likes those brands and I'm starting to as well... maybe Mum and I will weigh up our options... before deciding what to buy! Dad probably won't buy anything... maybe a Louis Vitton...he might buy something if he finds a men's brand that he likes.

"Mum, these brands are so luxurious!"

"I would love to get my hands on a Gucci handbag!" I said, imaging myself 'swanning' around like a posh young lady

"I bet you would, Cassie!"

"I love my Louis Vitton and Prada."

"I own a handbag and shoes in those brands... I simply love Prada!" said Mum, dreaming of herself walking in her Prada shoes

"Hmm... I think I would like to buy a luxury brand or two myself!" said Dad

"Sorry Dad."

"It's mostly marketed towards women... tough luck." I said, pointing at him

"Well, okay then."

"I'll see if I can find a men's brand to look at and maybe buy!" said Dad, dejectedly

"Imagine me walking down the streets... with a Louis Vitton handbag and Gucci shoes... combined with a sparkly blue dress!"

"I will turn heads and be the talk of the town." I said, in a dreamy tone

"My darling girl will be a fashionista soon!" laughed Mum

"I have started to embrace fashion more than ever before!" I replied

In the end, we decided not to buy anything due to the high prices of those luxury and global items... but there is no harm in window shopping and that's fun too!

We were feeling peckish so we went to have a bite to eat at the food court. We talked as we munched.

"Cassie, what do you think of the Gold Coast so far?" asked Dad

"I think it's vibrant and cool!"

"Even though we have just arrived I'm enjoying it very much.

"I loved shopping and 'Ripley's Believe it or Not' is just a wicked place!" I said

"We love the Gold Coast too, Cassie." said Mum

"The attractions are amazing and we can explore the city together, there are lots of activities that we might try." Mum added

"I would like to perform with you two during our stay... I think I would like to try a new activity too." I commented

"What new activity would you like to try Cassie?" asked Dad

"There is a place called Planet Chill and I am keen to try ice-skating!"

"I've never been before... but I'm open to giving it a try!" I said

"Mum and I have been ice-skating before in a few countries and we enjoyed it."

"One time in Melbourne in 1989 along with Olivia and Rebecca we were ice-skating at the former Melbourne ice rink... we were doing some brilliant ice-skating moves inspired by Torvill and Dean!"

"We had made up a special to move to finish our routine... we skated to opposite corners and skated up to each other... held each other's hands and then whirled around the rink three times... before finishing with a twirl and a bow."

"That was a fun ice-skating time for us all... we had been practicing it for months!" Dad said, proudly

"That sounds like a really fun time for you back then... I hope I can skate with you in some wintery countries overseas someday."

"I think ice skating will be a lot of fun for us to do together tomorrow afternoon!"

We will need to rug up...the ice will be very cold!" I said

The next day after a late start... we dressed in our winter gear and made our way to Planet Chill... we paid twenty dollars for the skate hire and helmet... then went to meet our instructor. We are having a two-hour session on the ice, so I hope I can learn the basics in that time!

"Hello"

"I hear you're very keen to do some ice-skating."

"Are you excited?" asked our instructor Nadine

Nadine was dressed in an ice penguin's outfit.

"Yes, we are Nadine!"

"Daniel and I have been ice-skating before... but this will be our daughter Cassie's first time!" said Mum

"She looks excited." said Nadine

"Yes, I am very excited... although I have to admit I am a little bit nervous too... in case I fall over on the ice!"

"Can you help me to learn the basic moves...then I can become an ice-skater like my Mum and Dad." I said

"Yes, I can."

"I'll do my best to teach you and refresh Mum and Dads' moves too!" said Nadine

Before we started, Mum and Dad talked to Nadine while I stood at the side looking around and observing a few teenagers playing a couple of games, like air hockey and foosball in the 'Chill Zone'.

"Nadine... Cassie has a condition called mild autism and also has anxiety."

"Cassie is more open to trying new activities these days but she is a little nervous...teach her one basic move at a time... so she understands what steps she needs to make."

"If Cassie becomes anxious, she can use her anxiety techniques to calm herself down...just remind her."

"No problems, Daniel and Mikayla."

"I have taught several special-needs children how to ice-skate...it shouldn't be too hard to teach Cassie." said Nadine

"Are you ready?" Nadine asked

"Yes, Nadine."

"Good!"

"Cassie...let's start with you."

"The first thing is to practice falling."

"Don't worry... it's all part of this sport...it will happen naturally."

"If you practice the right way to fall on the ice...then hopefully... it will help to keep you from getting injured."

"First... you bend your knees and squat into a dip position."

"Then you fall sideways... lean forward and put your hands on your lap."

"When you want to get back up... roll over onto your hands and knees... place your feet between your hands and knees one at a time... and gently push yourself back up." instructed Nadine

I listened to all the steps that Nadine had told me and did them all until I felt comfortable.

"That's one basic step out of the way, Nadine."

"There are a few more to go... right?" I asked Nadine

"Right."

"Next you need to learn basic gliding."

"It will help you to move over the ice."

"Take two steps marching forward and glide forward slowly."

"Once you feel comfortable with that... pick up one foot as you glide." Nadine demonstrated

I tried all the basic gliding steps it wasn't easy to do and I fell over a couple of times.

"OOF"

"Are you alright, Cassie?" asked Dad, as he and Mum helped me up

"Yes, Dad."

I'm alright... just a little embarrassed that's all!" I said

"You'll be okay, Cassie."

"You will eventually get the hang of it."
"I will... Nadine."
"I'm determined to learn all the steps and have fun skating." I said
"That's the way, Cassie."
"The next move to learn is called swizzles."
"This is a very tough move to master, are you ready, Cassie?"
"Yes, Nadine... I am ready!" I said, pumped up
"Great."
"You start by placing your heels together... then you slide your feet apart... next you point your toes together."
"If you put them together one at a time... you leave an hourglass figure in the ice."
"Make sure you keep your feet on the ice as you do this." said Nadine
"I got all that, Nadine."
"I'll do my best." I said, a little nervously
It was a difficult move...I managed it after lots of practice.
"Those swizzles were difficult...I think I have the hang of them now!"
"You're doing a great job." Nadine said
"The last thing you need to learn is how to stop."
"To do that... you need to stand with your feet together."
"While skating you push your feet apart and stick one skate out sideways."
"Some frost from the ice will be pushed off and make you come to a sudden stop."

I listened to every instruction that Nadine gave me, I tried gliding and swizzle moves. I was enjoying myself so much that I nearly forget to use my stop moves. After five minutes, I had to apply my stop moves, I pushed my feet apart and stuck my right skate out sideways, I stopped right next to Nadine.

"Yes!"
"I did it!"
"I learnt how to ice-skate!"
"I am woman... hear me scream!" I said, excitedly
We all laughed together at that!
"Well done, Cassie."
"We're proud of you... learning all those new skills!" said Mum, beaming
"You'll be skating with us in wintery countries soon, darling."
"You did very well, trying ice-skating for the first time." said Dad, grinning at me
"You've been a very good student, Cassie."
"You have mastered all the moves... you are ready to try skating with your Mum and Dad."
"Isn't that great!" said Nadine
"It is awesome and cool Nadine!"
"You are a great teacher... it wasn't easy for me to learn all the moves...with your help I did them all!"
"I do enjoy ice-skating... that's for sure!" I said, shaking Nadine's hand
"That's great Cassie!"
"I could see your determination when learning the moves and also when you fell over a couple of times."
"You should be able to skate for the rest of the session with minimal fuss now."
"You've got plenty of time before your session ends... so skate away and have fun everyone!" Nadine said, as she waved us off onto the ice

Mum, Dad and I skated for the rest of the session, putting our moves to good use. We laughed and had a fun time together as we skated around the rink. It was cold but we weren't going to let that stop us from having an awesome time!

We thanked Nadine for teaching us how to ice-skate and walked back to the Vibe Hotel.

"Cassie, we're proud of you for giving ice-skating a go."

"We could see you starting to enjoy it as the session went along, which delighted us." said Mum

"You were a bit nervous to start with but Nadine helped you to learn all the basic moves you needed to try ice-skating and you managed them all…so that's great." Dad smiled

"Thanks, Mum and Dad."

"I enjoyed ice skating… it was so much fun."

"It has become my new favourite activity!" I laughed

"It was so cold at Planet Chill, but I didn't even feel it!"

"I need some hot food after spending all that time on the ice." I said

"Yes, let's get some hot food to warm us up." agreed Mum

"There's a place called 'Bounce' in nearby Robina."

"There are fifty interconnected trampolines… we can channel our Michael Jordan aerial basketball manoeuvres." I said

"It sounds like a good place to bounce."

We can drive there after we have something to eat… it will take us an hour to get there." Dad said

The first hourly session cost sixteen dollars and ninety cents, we paid our money and read the warning signs which said 'Stay safe and have fun' pointed out to us by the supervisor, then off to have an hour full of bouncing fun! Bouncing on the trampolines and off the walls, I channelled my inner Michael Jordan in the slam dunk and did some fantastic b-ball moves! I pretended to slam the ball into the basket, laughing gleefully like a kid, thoroughly enjoying myself.

I noticed Mum and Dad enjoying themselves too, laughing like teenagers as they bounced around. We are having so much fun, I wonder what our family and friends would think of it…we can recommend it to them!

"Are you enjoying the trampolines, Mum and Dad?"

"We sure are, Cassie." laughed Mum and Dad

After an hour, we had a break.

"I remember jumping on my trampoline in the backyard… I would laugh with sheer delight!"

"I used to jump on a small trampoline in the ground when I was young, then I graduated to a full trampoline when I was five."

"I remember when I was thirteen… you installed a trampoline with a safety net around it… so I could jump safely without bouncing off and hurting myself."

"When I jumped up and down… I could see the whole backyard garden… our house and the neighbour's houses around me."

Sometimes… I would lie down on the trampoline and look up at the sky… I would watch the clouds and sun…with my sunglasses on."

"I still jump on the trampoline whenever I get the chance… it's one of the things that helps me to unwind at the end of the day." I said

"We used to hear you laugh when you were jumping on the trampoline enjoying yourself." said Dad

"We used to have one in the Bontel-Macdonald house, but we had to get rid of it because it was getting too old, we had a great time on it for many years!" said Mum, remembering

"It might be a good evening to go to the Miami Marketta."

"There will be delicious street food from tapas to gelato to French crepes… plus there's live acoustic music from five to seven… then the live band starts from seven-thirty and goes till ten o'clock at night!"

"What more could you ask for?"

"What do you think?" I said

"It's a great idea Cassie…it's only fifteen minutes to drive to Robina."

"It sounds like a lot of fun." said Mum

"I can't wait!" I said

A short time later we arrived in Miami… Queensland!

We found a parking spot, locked up our vehicle and walked to the evening Marketta.

"I've never tried tapas before…I'm a bit wary."

"What if I don't like it? I say, screwing up my face

"It's ok, Cassie."

"You don't have to try them… if you don't want to." said Mum

"Take your time Cassie." Dad said

I looked at the tapas.

It was a cold plate consisting of mixed olives and cheese. It looked awful to me at first glance… those two ingredients that go to make up a Spanish appetizer or snack. Still… I thought about the other new foods that I've tried lately… I decided to try a selection. I ate and felt the flavours of the mixed olives and cheese and bread as well. My tastebuds were going crazy at the texture of the new food… but I managed to eat it all… I had a big smile on my face when I finished.

"Mum, Dad, I've done it!"

"I enjoyed eating tapas."

"I might try them in Spain… Latin American countries… or even Mexico now that I've experienced eating some!" I said, excitedly

"That's great to hear, Cassie." Dad said, smiling

"I might be able to try a Korean potato like I've seen at the Melbourne Markets and maybe visit some more food markets and try various samples there too." I said, happily

After we sampled the donuts and cronut desserts, (they were delicious), we sat at the reservations bar, while we waited for the live band to begin.

However, … there was bad news as the MC made an announcement.

"The main band can't be here tonight due to one of their members being injured earlier in the day."

"I'm afraid the concert is off… unless a substitute band can be found… which seems unlikely at this late stage." the MC told the audience

The crowd groaned and so did we.

This could be a great opportunity for us. We could perform and fill in for the main band…it could be the chance for an impromptu gig if all goes well.

I put my hand up and shouted…

"We are in a pop band… we would like volunteer to fill in for the band that can't make it tonight."

"Hmm…you three can come on stage.' motioned the M.C.

"What is your pop bands' name?"

"We're the Bontel Family."

"We've performed at a few concerts and we'll be more than happy to perform tonight." said Mum

"I'll be more than glad to let you three perform."

"The audience was looking forward to the main band tonight...you might just save the evening's entertainment." said the MC gratefully

"We'll rock the night away and amaze this lovely audience." Dad said

"We won't let the audience down. I added

It was quickly arranged through the MC, that we were able to borrow the missing band's equipment for the evening to play on... which had already been set up earlier in the day.

"Hello everyone!"

"Are you all doing well?"

"Yes, we are!"

"We would like to perform some songs from our debut album for you."

"As a bonus, we will play an acoustic version of our smash hit, 'A Family United'."

"Please enjoy yourselves and feel free to dance if you want to."

The audience loved our music... there were about three hundred people at the Marketta... it took a long time to sign autographs after the show...Mum, Dad and I have really enjoyed the night. It was late by the time we finished and drove back to our hotel in Brisbane for a good's night sleep.

The next morning after we had breakfasted, we found our way to the Brisbane Holiday Village where the Dads' are taking their vacation. We scouted around until we saw some familiar vehicles parked next to some cabins and caravans. We caught a glimpse of some of the Dads' going about their morning camping routines.

We kept well-hidden and out of sight, as we planned our strategy.

"The Dads' all love soft drinks so when they go to get some snacks... we can sneak in and shake up their tins."

"When we hear them coming back from the village shop... we hide behind these caravans and wait to see what happens!" whispered Mum, trying not to giggle

"I think we know what's going to happen." Dad said, winking

"It's not going to be pretty!" he added with a 'devilish' grin

"The 'Dads' are not going to know what's hit them!" I said

"If we can execute this one without being busted... we will be lucky indeed!"

We crept behind a caravan... the one where Patrick Jones, Zoe's Dad was staying... we peeked out from the right side and saw the Dads' were now sitting around their campfire.

They were all wearing 'daggy' Dad shirts... the type that Dads' wear to embarrass their kids!

"Eew!!"

"Do you see what my Dad is wearing!"

"A sixties style 'nerd' shirt with a 'science' man and woman on it!"

"It says 'Science is fun be a nerd'." said Mum, groaning

"Yes, I saw it!"

"My Dad is wearing a daggy shirt that says VB the funny beer that makes you feel sneaky."

"Aargh." says Dad, putting his hands over his eyes

"I love my Grandads' but when they wear those daggy shirts... they are very embarrassing!"

"I can't imagine what is on the other Dads' shirts!" I said, shaking my head

We peeked out again, the Dads' were swapping stories and telling of 'funny' times that they have had over the years... as all family members do when they get together!

We listened behind the caravan and this is what we heard...

"Mikayla is such a funny daughter... when she was five, she put salt into Belinda's tea and mine also... when we sipped the tea we instantly spat it out!"

"We didn't know who had put it in...then we heard Mikayla giggle and we couldn't find her."

"It was so funny to her... I said to Belinda... that Mikayla is a cheeky little monkey, she is going to be trouble!" Darren chuckled

John Smith... Jessica's Dad, replied with his story.

"Jessica could be a cheeky little angel when she was young too... when she was six... I was making lunch with Josephine when we heard a monkey noise from the backyard where she had been playing."

"I looked out the window, where she was playing a monkey game with Jacinta and Joseph, they had made up a game and they were all being monkeys together."

"I smiled and laughed at that funny sight... Josephine did too!"

"Caroline was a cheeky little thing back in her younger days as well." said Dean

"When she was five, she had her eye on Carol's diary... she wasn't interested in reading it... she was planning on hiding it from Carol!"

"When Carol wasn't looking... Caroline took it and hid it in her room."

"Carol said...Caroline, where's my diary?"

"Caroline replied...don't know Mummy."

"Carol eventually found it in Caroline's room, Carol tried not to laugh but she couldn't help it."

"Earlier in the day at lunch-time she had dumped her spaghetti lunch on Carol and laughed... Mummy's got spaghetti hair!"

"Kimberley and Brian laughed as well... Carol told her... the spaghetti is supposed to be in your bowl... not on my hair!"

"We sure have had some funny moments with her."

Just then Patrick turned up at the campfire.

"Sorry I'm late." he said

"We haven't got the snacks yet."

"I found a good 'stash' though at the village shop... there are chips and chocolate... as well as salty peanuts!" said Patrick

The Dads' followed Patrick to the village shop to get their holiday snacks. This was the opportunity we had been waiting for to execute our prank! Mum, Dad and I, crept over to their drink cans that they had left on the picnic table. We started to shake up all the cans.

"This will be priceless!"

"The Dads' won't know it's us." Dad, sniggered

"Wait till we tell everyone back in Melbourne." says Mum, giggling

"This may be one of our top ten pranks, if we can pull it off!" I said, happily

I looked up and saw the Dads' coming back in the distance!

Uh Oh!

"Quick!"

"They're coming back!"

"Let's hide behind this caravan." I said

Mum, Dad and I, hid behind Dean's caravan just as the Dads' strolled back to their campsite.

"We've got our snacks to go with our refreshments!"

"Let's get straight into them... relive our childhood memories of all our favourite treats!"

"Cheers!" said Jim, raising his can and getting ready to open the lid

"Cheers!" said all the Dads, as they starting opening the tabs on their tins
Mum, Dad and I, were doing the countdown behind the caravan.
"One...Two...Three." we whispered giggling
'WHOOSH'... the sound of exploding liquid bursting out of cans could be heard everywhere.
Then yells and cries as the men were all covered in sticky, sweet, frothing, fizzy drinks!
"What was that!"
"What happened."
"What the..."
"Maybe we left them too long in the sun..." began one
"There's something fishy going on here..." said another
"Someone has been shaking these drink tins... that's why we got a soaking!" stated Darren
"I reckon' I might know who it is too!" said Jim, suspiciously
We tried to sneak away at this point...only Mum couldn't stifle her giggles.
"I know that giggle anywhere in the world!"
"That laughter belongs to Mikayla!"
"Mikayla Natalie Bontel!!!"
"I know it's you... reveal yourself at once!" said Darren, loudly
"Time for me to face the music." Mum whispered
Mum emerged from behind Dean's caravan, with a sheepish grin on her face. She knows the game is up... there's no hiding now!
"Err... hello everybody." says Mum cheerfully, trying to bluff her way through
"Mikayla, did you shake our drinks?" asked Darren
"May...be." she replies cagily
"I think you did!"
"You look guilty to me!"
"You cannot escape my gaze!" Darren said, accusingly
"I nearly got away with it... but I couldn't help giggling... that's what gave me away!" said Mum, ruefully
Dad and I, couldn't help laughing at Mum's predicament
"AHA"
"The plot thickens!" said Jim, triumphantly
"Daniel Fred Bontel!"
"Cassie Annabelle Bontel!"
"Show yourselves!" he added
"You two might as well come out... the Dads' have rumbled us." Mum called out to us
Dad and I had no choice but to reveal ourselves. We walked out with guilty grins on our faces. Mum, Dad and I, were like three naughty schoolkids about to 'fess up' when caught in the act!
"Daniel, Cassie, were you in on this escapade with Mikayla?" asked Jim
"Err... we definitely were." I replied, sheepishly
"We thought we were going to get away with it...we couldn't help laughing at the mess Mikayla was in... which gave us away." said Dad, equally sheepishly
"You three are the biggest practical jokers we know!"
"We would give you three a clip under the ear if we could!" said Darren, crossly
"We apologise for our prank." Mum said, sincerely

Then Mum noticed a bar of chocolate sticking out of Darren's pocket, she recognised the Cadbury wrapper... it's white chocolate too!

"Dad... what's that in your pocket?" asked Mum, in an innocent tone

"Nothing, darling." said Darren

"I can see the white chocolate... sticking out of your pocket... hand it over please Daddy." pleaded Mum

"Nope... you can buy your own!" said Darren

"Come on..." Mum wheedled

"No way... it's my chocolate!" Darren said

I crept around behind Darren and pinched the white chocolate bar from out of his pocket

"Hey!"

"Cassie... give me back my chocolate!" yelled Darren

"Sorry Darren... you can't have it all... I'm afraid." I quipped, cheekily

Then I ate two rows and let out a loud belch!

Everybody laughed!

Mum and Dad tell me that belching in a public place is not appropriate...especially when I say things like...

"Wow!"

"That was loud!"

I understand the rule...this time I do it anyway.

"Very funny, Cassie."

"You're even worse than your Mum."

"She used to do that when she was three!" said Darren, glancing at Mum

"I used to do it from when I was three to seven years old."

"I knew it was inappropriate when I was six... but I kept doing it for another year." said Mum, grinning from ear to ear

"Since you are all here, why don't you join us for a couple of hours?"

"There are plenty of chips, chocolate and salty peanuts to go around." Darren said

We spent a fun two hours with the Dads'... telling dirty jokes... funny stories... and eating lots of snacks that the Dads' had bought.

"Mikayla once dressed up as a fairy when she and Rebecca turned twenty."

"The party was very lively... with backyard sports... playing games... also Mikayla and Rebecca made the birthday cakes themselves."

"That was good, because normally Maria and Belinda baked the cakes."

"When we gathered around the table, Belinda cut the cake and it deflated like a balloon!"

"It turned out Mikayla and Rebecca switched their cakes as part of a practical joke!"

"They emerged with smirks on their faces and started a food fight!"

Mikayla shouted...

"Let's get this FOOD FIGHT started!"

"Then there were sweets and cake everywhere!"

"It was hilarious... all their friends joined in!" said Jim

"Rebecca and I played a similar trick on our twenty-first birthday...instead of cakes we threw water bombs through the window... drenching the guests and the staff."

"It was all in good fun though... we had a good time!"

"How is your road trip going?"

"You must be having fun." said Jim

"Yes, we certainly are."
"That's good… we heard on the news that you and Daniel tried to steal Cassie's fans!"
"That didn't work out… did it?" asked Jim
"It didn't work out for US!"
"Despite disguising ourselves as Madonna and John Farnham… Cassie was on to us disguising herself as Nikki Webster and busting us at a concert… just as we were talking to the fans that we had lured away from Cassie!" said Mum
"Oh, ho!'
"She was on to your plan then?" said Dean, smiling
"I sure was!"
"I overhead them planning the prank… so I planned a prank of my own to counter it." I added, grinning
"That's my darling grand-daughter!"
"Always having a practical joke… just like her Mum!" said Darren
"Yes, I passed it on to Cassie and Rebecca as well!" said Mum, very pleased with herself
"Darren… Mum was snoring a few nights ago…Dad and I recorded her in secret…then we played it back to her the next day."
"Mum had to own up to the fact that she does snore… you know she is the loudest snorer out of the three of us!" I said
The 'Dads' thought that was hilarious… but I'm not sure that Mum did!
"Mikayla, you're so funny when you snore!" laughed Darren
"Ok…OK!"
"I am funny when I snore!"
"Daniel and Cassie have to wear earplugs to get any sleep, when I start snoring."
"I will completely deny it the next morning…today I had to face up to it when Daniel and Cassie recorded it and played it back to me!"
"How embarrassing!!!" Mum said, blushing
"Mikayla… it's okay if you snore loudly… lots of people do."
"It can be funny when you talk in your sleep too… if you are having a hilarious dream." said Darren
"I used to do that, but I haven't since I was twenty years old." Mum replied
After a couple of hours, Mum, Dad and I, get ready to go back to our hotel.
"Bye, Daniel, Mikayla, Cassie."
"I hope you all have a wonderful trip… send us some photos if you can." said Jim
"Bye."
"Have fun for the rest of your stay in Brisbane." added Darren

## Chapter Seventeen
## Bris-Vegas 'High Rollers'

The next morning, we were walking along Kensington Parade admiring the various buildings and all the sights.
"Isn't bris-vegas astounding?"
"It's a great view!" I said
"It is, Cassie."
"It's very vibrant… look at that Korean restaurant called Madtong San II."
"I would love to taste some of those Korean dishes! Dad added
"Me, too!" I agreed
"That would be excellent." Mum agreed

Suddenly, Mum saw Maria and Belinda in the distance. The 'Dads' may have informed them of our prank…we could be in trouble here!
"Oh No!"
"Mum and Maria are here!"
"We can't let them see us."
"Let's hide somewhere." said Mum

Mum, Dad and I, hid behind some bushes, hoping Maria and Belinda won't bust us!
"Daniel, Mikayla and Cassie, are up to their old tricks."
"They played a prank, this time at the Dads' holiday retreat!" said Maria, crossly as they passed by
"Hmm."
"They are the practical jokers, all right."
"I wonder how they found out the location." said Belinda
"I don't know, but we'll find out soon enough!" said Maria, in a determined voice
"They're here somewhere, I can feel it!"
"Let's go to the 'Treasury Casino and Hotel' for lunch." Belinda decided

When Maria and Belinda were out of sight, Mum, Dad and I, emerged from the bushes brushing the leaves and twigs off ourselves.
"Whew!"
"That was a close one!"
"Maria and Belinda nearly saw us!"
"How can we prank them… without them knowing it is us." Dad mused
"I've got a great idea and a plan I'll tell you all about…back at our hotel." said Mum

Later back at our hotel… Mum tells us her plan.

"My idea is to prank Mum and Maria at the casino…here is the plan."

"First, we sneak into the hotel… let them know what we are planning…before Mum and Maria get there for lunch."

"We get changed into our disguises in the rest rooms."

"I will pose as a barmaid… Daniel can be a casino dealer…you will have to wear a hat to cover your 'Rick Astley' hairstyle!"

"Cassie, you can dress as a professional pool player with a wig on… then we shall all adopt different names and 'personas'…then Mum and Maria won't suspect who we really are!"

"When Mum and Maria are sitting down at their table Cassie and I will appear as waitresses… Daniel you will be the drinks waiter".

"When they order their lunch and a pot of tea… we will replace the sugar in the sugar bowl with salt…an oldie but a goodie!" Mum sniggers

"We shall be hiding behind the bar to see what happens when they put what they think is teaspoons of sugar into their cups of tea!"

After they have taken their first 'delicious' mouthful… we will go back to their table and reveal our identities!" said Mum, chortling at the idea

"We need to keep a low profile like we did yesterday to pull this one off." I said

"It's eleven-thirty we should get there before Mum and Maria do!" said Mum

We drove to the hotel and crept inside to let the staff know about our prank… they gave us their approval after we assured them that nothing will go wrong. Then, we changed into our costumes in the rest rooms.

The prank is underway!

"Daniel, you go to the poker machines and games room."

"Cassie, you go to the pool tables…I will go to the bar and serve drinks." said Mum, planning our movements like a military exercise

"Yes sir!" said Dad and I, saluting Mum together

"Then let's execute this prank!" Mum replied, smartly

Mum went behind the bar… Dad went to the poker machines and games room… he will be supervising the blackjack game… I go straight to the pool table.

'Hope this goes well…' I think

At noon Maria and Belinda stroll in… Mum in her role as barmaid checks her watch and thinks… 'Yes, here they are now…they are about come over to the bar…they will ask if I have seen Daniel, Cassie and myself… It's time to play the part… I will use one of my 'accents'…here goes.'

"Hello, you must be new…we haven't seen you here before?"

"Yes, I'm Betty… I've just started working here." said Mum, in a 'posh' British accent

"The environment is sophisticated here." Maria said

"Yes, we don't get many silly drunks."

"I'm sure that's true." replied Maria

"What drinks are you serving today?"

"There is lemonade for the children…assorted beers for the men…cocktails for the women." Betty replied

"I hope you do well on your first day Betty."

"By the way have you seen Daniel, Mikayla and Cassie Bontel, anywhere?" asked Belinda

"No, I haven't." Betty answered

"Well if you see them… please let us know." said Maria

"I certainly will Mrs Bontel, and Mrs Macdonald."

Maria and Belinda then walked to the casino machines. Mum was thinking,
'Good luck finding them...it's a good start... I hope Daniel does his part well.'
Whilst silently chuckling to herself.
"Let's play in the casino, Belinda."
"We're never too old to play a bit of blackjack." said Maria
"Yes, let's do that."
"We'll have a good time playing and we might win a bit of money... if we're lucky." chuckled Belinda

Dad, is wearing a red and white casino style suit, with a light brown wig, he sees Maria and Belinda coming towards the blackjack table.

'Maria and Belinda are here to play a bit of blackjack...we'll see who is the luckiest out of the two...time to execute my role'
"Hello you must be the latest casino dealer?" said Maria
"I certainly am Ma'am...I'm Darryl your dealer... I've been working here for a few hours now... I'm working the afternoon casino session.' said Dad, in his best southern American drawl
"That's a good job to have, Darryl."
"What casino games do you favour?" said Maria
"I excel at poker and roulette, but my favourite is blackjack."
"Mine too!" laughed Belinda
"You must be an expert Darryl!"
"I sure am lil' lady!" said Dad, getting into his role
"We'll play a few games of blackjack... we're very keen!" smiled Maria
"That's good... take your seats we'll be starting in two minutes."

After a few games, Maria and Belinda won a bit of money.... it was close between the two of them but Maria won just a little more.
"Thanks, Darryl for letting us play a few games of blackjack." said Maria
"It was my pleasure ladies."
"We loved your sense of humour."
"Have you seen Daniel, Mikayla and Cassie in here?"
"Nope, not me." he replied
"Well, let us know if you see them?" said Belinda
"Okey-dokey, ladies." 'Darryl' nodded

Maria and Belinda walked over to the pool tables... Dad was watching and thinking...
'So far, so good...Mum and Belinda are going to play a bit of pool before they order their food...Cassie will hopefully play her part well.'
He silently smiled to himself and gave the other patrons the thumbs up, they quietly reciprocated.
"They were good games of blackjack."
"Now, how about a couple of games of pool before we eat?" Maria said
"Sure!"
"A couple of games will give us an appetite!" grinned Belinda
They walked to the pool tables and chose a vacant one.
'Here come Maria and Belinda about to play some pool with me... they won't suspect it's me...I've got a wig on and my pool player costume too...it's time for me to execute my part...here I go'
"Hello young lady."
"You must be the new pool player here?" say Maria and Belinda, introducing themselves

"I definitely am." I reply in my best 'Scottish' accent

"I'm Ava Pool... I come from Edinburgh in Scotland... I've been junior snooker player for the world girl's section since I was thirteen years old."

"My goodness!"

"You seem to excel at pool... I see a couple of titles on your snooker shirt."

"When did you win those?"

"I won my first title when I was fourteen... beating a British teen pool player aged sixteen... I won my second title when I was fifteen... beating a Welsh teen pool player aged seventeen."

"I have earnt fifty thousand pounds in winner's prize money."

"Strewth!"

"You have worked hard to earn those titles, as well as the prize money."

"Does staying calm and being professional, help you to succeed?" said Belinda

"Yes... it does."

"I'm very collected under pressure...especially when a snooker match is close!" Ava stated

"That's very good advice."

"Belinda and I, might play a couple of games with you if that's all right." Maria said

"That's fine by me."

"Maria you're up first."

"This is how we play." Ava instructed

"Here are the red pool balls and these are the yellow pool balls."

"If player number one hits their chosen coloured ball, but it doesn't go into the pocket...then player number two gets a shot."

"If player one hits their ball but misses... player two gets two shots."

"One player must pocket all their balls... before they attempt to pocket the black ball."

"If a player pockets the black ball before the other player pockets all their coloured balls... that player wins the game."

"If, of course... at any point during the game... one player somehow pockets the black ball...then the other player automatically wins."

"Have you got all that, Maria?" said 'Ava' mischievously

Yes... I think I got all that Ava."

"Same for you too Belinda."

"Yes, thank you Ava."

"Maria, let's get this pool game started!"

I beat Maria in that game, pocketing all my balls and the black ball before Maria can pocket her last two.

"Well done Ava, you were too good for me in that game."

"I sure was."

"Thanks for a good game Maria."

"Belinda it's your turn to take me on now."

"Are you ready?"

"I'm up for it."

"Let's get started then."

I was too good for Belinda as well, pocketing all my balls as well as the black ball, before Belinda pocketed her last one.

It was so close to going into the middle pocket, but I was able to pocket the black ball in the corner pocket!

"Ava you are a champion pool player!"

"Thanks, Belinda." I said, shaking her hand

"Just before we go, have you seen Daniel, Mikayla and Cassie anywhere?" Belinda asked

"No, sorry I haven't seen them."

"Give us a shout if you do please."

"I certainly will."

Belinda and Maria went to the table they have booked in the bistro, I met up with Mum and Dad in the restroom.

"Part one of our plan is executed."

"It all went well and now on to part two!"

"We have our 'waiting' costumes ready... part two of our plan ready to commence!" I said

"We'll change in to our new costumes and then go up to Maria and Mum's table, to take their orders."

"Cassie, you put the salt in the sugar bowl... Daniel you and I will serve the food."

"Then we will take cover behind the bar and reveal ourselves when they drink their tea." sniggered Mum

"We've got our accents ready for the part." Dad grinned

We giggled and shushed each other.

We put our waiter/waitress costumes on... Dad's came complete with a false moustache... we walked up to the table where Maria and Belinda were sitting.

"Are you our waiting staff?" asked Belinda

"Oh yes madame, we are." said Mum, in a French accent

"I am Madame Nina... I come from France to serve 'le tourists' that come to this 'magnifique' restaurant."

"I am Jean-Pierre, I come from France with Madame Nina also... I help her serve 'le tourists' with their aperitifs." said Dad, also with a heavy French accent

"I am Mademoiselle Chantal."

"I arrive with Madame Nina and Monsieur Jean-Pierre."

"The people here are having an excellent time." I said, doing my best impersonation of a young French waitress

"My word... what do you have on your menu today?"

"We have 'Chicken Parisienne', 'Steak fondue with French fries', and 'Shrimp a la barby' with vegetables."

"We have 'French Limonade' and Champagne to drink." said Jean-Pierre

"Please let me know when you have decided on your order."

"For dessert we have fruit sorbet with many delicious sauces to choose from... we have patisserie... and the 'magnifique' dessert of the day!"

"Wow!"

"There are so many choices on this menu."

"Yes, we have a superior selection!"

"What would you like from la section principal?"

"I'll have 'Chicken Parisienne' please." said Maria

"I'll have 'Steak fondue' with a side of vegetables please." said Belinda

"What will you have from la section des boisson?" said Dad with a flourish

"I'd like to order tea." said Maria

"I'll order tea too." said Belinda

"If you have some room for dessert... what would you like from la section des dessert?"

"I'll have a 'Madelaine' to go with my cup of tea." Maria smiled

"I'll order fruit sorbet with strawberry sauce." said Belinda, licking her lips at the thought

"Your food will be ready shortly." I replied

Mum, Dad and I, went into the kitchen, where the chefs began preparation of the menu orders, one of the staff members gave me the salt, which I filled the sugar bowl with. When the food was prepared, we took the meals, and the pot of tea, teacups, milk jug and 'sugar' bowl on a tray to the table.

"Here are your meals ladies." said Madame Nina

"Thank you." said Maria

"Here is your pot of tea for two ladies." said Jean-Pierre, as he placed all the items on the table for the ladies to enjoy their tea

"Thank you."

"We will bring out your desserts, a little later."

"Bon appetite."

Mum, Dad and I, then went behind the bar and hid. Maria and Belinda poured their tea into their tea cups from the teapot... added some milk from the milk jug... then put their teaspoons of 'sugar' into their cups of tea and stirred them.

Next, they lift their cups to their lips, (and being quite thirsty after all the games they have been playing earlier), take a big gulp of tea together!

"Blah!" said Belinda spluttering

"Yuck! said Maria spitting out the tea all over the table

"Someone has put salt in the sugar bowl!"

"Who did that?"

Mum, Dad and I, giggled and high-fived each other! We walked over to Maria and Belinda's table.

"Is something wrong with your tea?" said Madame Nina

"Yes, there is!"

"Someone has put salt in the sugar bowl!"

"It tastes terrible!"

"Would you care to find out who switched your sugar?" said Jean-Pierre, casually

"Yes, we would!" said Maria, crankily

"Just one moment... we will find them!"

With a flourish Mum, Dad and I, ripped off our costumes to reveal our true identities. Everyone in the pub was laughing... Maria and Belinda were red-faced with embarrassment.

"Daniel! Mikayla! Cassie!"

"We should have known." Maria said, grimacing

"Yes, it was us!"

"You didn't suspect a thing!" I smirked

"No, we didn't...you completely fooled us!" Belinda, frowned

"The looks on your faces were priceless!" laughed Mum

"Why don't we tell you how we did it... over lunch?"

"We can also tell you about the disguises and personas we used." Dad said, enthusiastically

We ordered some meals and when they had been served, Mum, Dad and I, told Maria and Belinda about our prank plans... later we also told them about our road trip.

"We performed on the Gold Coast recently... it was awesome!"

"The families had the best time and we had great fun too."

"That's very good, you must be having such fun performing to all the families who are on holiday." said Maria

"I certainly am!"

"The atmosphere was vibrant filled with families having fun.

I loved seeing them... it reminded me of fun times when I'm making music with my family and performing on my guitar." I said, happily

"You have come a long way since Maria and I saw you last."

"You have matured a lot since then."

"Come and give me a hug." Belinda added

I walked over and gave her a hug.

*'Even if you do still play pranks on me'...* she whispered in my ear, that made me giggle again

Then I hugged Maria too, I felt the relief and warmth of their hugs, feeling happy and proud of myself. We ate and talked a little more...owning up to pranking the Dads' as well!

"How did you find about our holiday prank on the Dads'?"

"They told us about all that, earlier!"

"You were very sneaky to find out their location, Mikayla."

"Who gave the location away?" Belinda asked

"It was Aunt Mabel who gave us the location... she told us not to tell you." said Mum trying not to grin... but failing

"That Aunt Mabel!"

"I told her not to reveal the location!" Belinda, fumed

"I've heard that you've tracked down our long-lost family member Mikayla."

"Where did you find him?" asked Maria

"Daniel, Cassie and I, used the clues we had, then with the information we gained with the Stanthorpe Historical Museum's help, we located him at Robinson Lane, Coolangatta... it was Steve Roberts, my cousin!"

"How was he?"

"Did you have a good time catching up with him?" asked Belinda

"Yes, we did."

"We had a good old chinwag, just like in our younger days, we ate and drank together, he hasn't changed a bit!" Dad said

"I remembered that he was a 'Holden' man...he still is!"

"He would visit us twenty years ago... he would drive his Holden to do the shopping for me when I was busy." said Maria

"He's a very good cousin."

"I had never met him before...he was funny and nice... he and I have one thing in common...cars... Holden cars... that is!" I said

"It sounds like you three had a good time with Robert."

"I'm glad you've found him and he was happy to see you again." said Belinda

"Yes, he was." Mum agreed

When we were leaving the pub, Belinda said...

"Maria and I will visit Robert in Coolangatta... before we leave Brisbane."

"He'll be glad to see family members he hasn't seen for twenty years...it will be nice." Maria said

"It will be."

"Have fun, you two!"

"Have fun on your road trip… Daniel thank you for showing me the photos… they were lovely." said Belinda

"That's all right Mum."

"I enjoyed taking them and Mikayla helped out too." said Dad

"Cassie… we hope you overcome more obstacles as your road trip continues."

"We know you will do us proud, sweetie." Maria said

"I will never give up… until I have achieved all my goals!" I grinned, as we waved goodbye

# Chapter Eighteen
# Brisbane River Emergency

Mum, Dad and I have decided to walk along the Brisbane river today, the fresh air will be good for us. The bridge is very long, there are fifteen bridges altogether and you can drive on them all.

"Queensland is such a nice place... the sun is shining it magnifies Queensland's proud boast... as the 'Sunshine State' of Australia!" I said

"It sure does Cassie." agreed Mum

As we are walking along someone shouted out...

"Help!"

"Someone, please help!"

We rush to see what's wrong.

"What's the matter?" Mum asks

"My four-year old daughter has fallen into the river... she cannot swim... she is struggling to stay afloat!"

"Please hurry!" the mother called

I look over towards the river and see the little girl struggling in the water, I take my shirt off and run towards the edge of the riverbank.

"Be careful, Cassie!" said Mum, fearfully

"Remember safety first Cassie... we don't want anyone else falling in and getting into trouble?" shouted Dad

"It's all right Mum and Dad... I'm going to use my shirt to pull her in if I can." I called back to Dad

I ran up to the edge of the river... lay down on my stomach and holding on to one arm of the shirt... threw it into the water towards the struggling girl.

"Grab hold of the shirt sleeve if you can and I will pull you in!" I shouted to the little girl

The little girl tried but missed. I pulled in the shirt quickly and tried again, encouraging her all the time.

"That's right!"

"Grab it and hang on tightly!"

This time the little girl got the sleeve and held on with both hands. Now Mum and Dad had reached the riverbank beside me and were able to help me pull her to the edge. We all spoke encouragingly to make sure she was holding tight.

"It's all right, we will get you out." I told her

"Good girl... hold tight." said Dad

"Nearly there, sweetie." said Mum

Finally, she was at the river's edge... Dad leant over and scooped her up... as Mum and I kept a tight grip on the shirt in case she was too tired to hang on any longer and slipped back towards the water. It was tricky... but by using teamwork we managed to get her out of the water safely.

Dad told Mum to call triple 000... the little girl seemed to be all right but she had swallowed a lot of water... she could also be in shock or have hypothermia from the cold water...so it was best to have her checked out in hospital... to make sure all was well.

The ambulance arrived on the scene and the ambulance officers took the girl to the hospital to be checked over by a doctor. When the attendants were loading her into the ambulance one of them said...

"Well done...you worked well together... I think she'll make a full recovery thanks to your quick thinking... calm assistance and teamwork!"

"You all did a great job!" he said, with a big smile on his face

"Thank you... we just did what needed to be done." I said

"Thank you all... you saved my daughter's life"!

"How can I thank you?" said the little girl's mother

"We have all the reward we need... knowing that your little girl is safe and well." said Mum, gratefully

"I must follow the ambulance to the hospital now... my daughter will need me close by... so that she feels safe."

"Goodbye and good luck on your holidays." she called, as she waved to us

"Thank you." I said

"Well how about that!" exclaimed Dad with a big smile on his face

"We saved a little girl's life and worked together as a family team to do it!" said Dad, proudly

"Cassie, you did really well."

"That was really quick thinking... using your shirt as a rescue item!" said Dad

"Yes Cassie, that saved the day!" added Mum, with admiration

"Thanks Mum and Dad."

"I remembered my water safety training from swim and survive lessons at the pool."

"It's always better to try and use something to pull someone in to the edge if you can... rather than jumping straight in... or you could end up with two people in trouble in the water!"

"I'm just super glad that everything turned out all right in the end!"

"I'm starving!"

"It must be all that adrenaline!"

"This calls for a well-earned lunch... I'm sure I can find a good place to eat in Brisbane!" I said

Then we all laughed together.

After lunch we decided to see some more sights.

"We could see the Old Windmill... or maybe go for a swim... it's your choice Cassie." said Dad

"The Old Windmill seems like an interesting place to see and learn about... let's go there."

"O.K." Mum agreed

The Old Windmill was very interesting indeed. I learnt a few facts, like it was built in 1928 in colonial times and convicts used it to grind grain like wheat and maize.

It originally had wind-powered sails, the treadmill was used to grind grains for four years from 1938 till 1942 when the convict settlement closed down and the treadmill was dismantled.

It was then used as a weather tower for many years and is now currently in service as a weather observatory. We read the heritage notice at Wickham Park which told us all about the Old Windmill's history.

We decided to have a good workout later in the afternoon, we made our way to the Brisbane YMCA where we signed in as guests. Mum, Dad and I, went into the changing rooms to put on our bathers.

Then I remembered a memory from my high school years, I became too scared to change out of my clothes instead I hid in the nearest cubicle. I had nervously stripped down to my bra and knickers but I was too scared to come out in case the other women saw me changing. I peeked out a little, and gestured for Mum to come to me.

"Cassie, what's wrong?"

"Are you all right in there?" asked Mum, with a concerned look

"No Mum."

"I'm not all right in here."

"I'm too scared to come out of the cubicle." I said, nervously

"It's okay darling."

"Would you like to talk with me about what is scaring you?" asked Mum

"Yes Mum."

"Not in here though."

"I'll tell you about it in the lobby."

"Just let me put my clothes back on first." I said

After I put my clothes back on Mum and I went out to the YMCA lobby to have a talk about what is scaring me.

"Mum when I was in there... I had a flashback to a memory from when I spent three years at Melbourne Secondary College." I said

"What was it, Cassie?"

"Can you tell me what it involved?" asked Mum

"The memory involved Physical Education class."

"I would refuse to get changed in front of the other female students... because I was self-conscious about something to do with my body." I said

"What is it that you were self-conscious about, Cassie?"

"You can tell me."

"It's okay... I'm your Mum."

"Since I was thirteen in year seven at Melbourne Secondary College, I felt self-conscious about my small breasts."

"I saw the other girls and thought."

*'Why are my breasts smaller than the other female students? It's not right, not right at all! I'm probably the student that has the smallest breasts in Melbourne Secondary College, I'm not happy about it! Argh!'*

My female teachers had to be with me, my full-time female aide always had to be with me, and in extreme cases you Mum, had to be with me too!

I did not want to discuss it with you... because I was too scared to bring it up...then when you tried to discuss things with me...try to show me books about puberty... I would get frightened, refuse, and run to my room... then not come out for an hour or two with a meltdown.

I just didn't want to talk about it as it was too awful and scary for me then... but now I have found the courage to talk about it with you." I said

"I'm so glad you've found the courage to tell me about it."

'I'm very proud of you for sharing it with me."

"Give me a hug, sweetie." Mum said

I did and I felt relieved and more confident now that I have spoken up about something that I was too scared to talk about previously... I'm glad my Mum can now help me to talk this through.

"Thanks, Mum."

"Remember Cassie... we are all shapes and sizes in this world... it's not one size fits all...you are the size that is just right for your body."

"Also... your body is still growing and changing."

"I feel so much better now that I have finally opened up to you."

"That's good Cassie."

"I always want to help you in any way I can... hopefully one day you will be able to help others too... especially young girls and women with autism like yourself." smiled Mum

"I will certainly try my best Mum." I said

Mum and I, went back into the women's changing rooms, we decided to go to the gym first and swimming afterwards.

We're ready to hit the YMCA gym."

"Is everything all right?" asked Dad

"Yes... eventually it was."

"I spoke with Mum about a problem I was having."

"It was a 'girl' thing!"

"Just a part of growing up... I was self-conscious about my 'boobs'... but I'm not anymore!" I said, with a grin

"Well I think you spoke to the right person about that particular subject!" said Dad with a nervous grin too, seriously relieved I didn't ask him any questions

"You're not wrong there, Dad!" I said giggling at the slightly uncomfortable look on his face

"Now let's hit the gym and work on our endurance." I said, happily

We entered the gym to find plenty of exercise machines. There was the lateral-pull-down leg press, the chest press and even a few treadmills and cross-trainers.

I am keeping at a healthy weight and exercise by walking, and using my Wii Fit too, these machines certainly test endurance levels and muscles. I grab my bottle of water ready for later... when I need rehydration!

"Cassie, this is the program you are going to try today."

"Two lateral-pull downs, One leg press, One chest press and five minutes on the treadmill".

"It's a trial program, we'll give it a go and if you like it we'll try a similar program in Melbourne when we get back." Mum said

"It sounds a good program to start with."

"I've never tried these machines before... I'll be fine though... I can use them to help me become stronger and fitter."

"I'll be your personal trainer for this trial session." Mum said

"Don't get any cheeky ideas about slacking Cassie... or I'll make the workout harder!" Mum asserted

"I won't Mum, I'll work hard at exercising today." I said

"I'll be doing my work out if you need me." Dad said, as he strode away to the machines

First, I did the leg press... I was a bit cheeky and put my legs on the leg press bar instead of under it.

"I saw that Cassie."

"Put both your legs under the bar please." said Mum, like a trainer

I did that but I put my right leg on the bar.
"Right leg under the bar, please." said Mum, firmly
Then I put my left leg on the bar.
"Cassie!"
"Left leg under the bar!" Mum said, in an exasperated tone
I sensibly put my legs under the bar, ready to do the leg presses properly.
"Good!"
"Now can you please do fifteen presses for me." Mum said
I managed to do the fifteen presses... some of them were a little lower... but I finished all fifteen.
"Good start, Cassie."
"You need to do some of your leg presses a little bit higher... but good job for a first time try." Mum approved
Then we moved onto the lateral pull-down.
"Hmm."
"I know how it works but can you give me a refresher on how to use it Mum?" I asked
"Of course, darling."
"You put your left hand on the left side of the bar and your right hand on the right side of the bar like so...sit down on this seat and pull the bar down to your chest about ten centimetres...not too close."
"I would like you to do fifteen repetitions for me please.
Mum set the weight to twenty-two kilograms as I am using it for the first time. When she turned to write my progress, I changed it to eight kilos. I am about to pull the bar to my chest when she said.
"Cassie... did you change the weights?"
"Err.... no." I said, cheekily
"I think you did!"
"Nice try but I'm on to you like a hawk!"
"You can do thirty reps for that!" said Mum, crossly
I cheekily changed it to fifteen kilos.
"Forty!"
"Fifty!"
"Sixty!"
"One Hundred!"
"CASSIE!"
"Stop mucking around will you please?"
"Crikey!"
"I don't what I'm going to do with you!" said Mum, crankily
"Nothing Mum!" I said, giggling
"I don't know what's going on...but you two are loopy." Dad said, shaking his head as he jogged on the treadmill
"I'm not... it's Cassie!" said Mum
"Are you keeping an eye on us Dad?" I asked, giggling
"You bet I am!" said Dad, trying to jog and tell me off at the same time
I started to do the fifteen pull downs... I was getting tired but doing well.
"Great Cassie."
"Now we'll move on to the chest press." said Mum

Mum put it at twelve kilos and I sat down in the chair. I put one foot on the chest press bar and the other on the gym floor.

"Nice try."

"Now put both of your feet on the floor please." said Mum in her personal trainer voice

I mischievously swapped foot positions around giggling.

"Cassie both feet on the floor, please."

"I'm not starting the count... until you put both of your feet on the floor!" Mum re-iterated

I put both of my feet on the floor but I stood on Mum's right foot with my right foot.

"Ouch!"

"Cassie, would you mind getting your foot off my foot." Mum said sharply

I smirked... took my left foot off and stepped on Mum's left foot.

"Ouch!"

"Cassie, do you mind getting your left foot off mine!" Mum repeated

I smirked and stuck out my tongue... then blew Mum a 'raspberry'.

"Oh, very mature Cassie." Mum said, crossly

"I shall just make you work harder if you keep up that cheek!" said Mum

I decided to do the fifteen chest presses properly.

"There's one more thing to do on your trial program, Cassie."

"It's the treadmill."

"You will walk for five minutes... and if you want to... you can run for one minute."

"It looks like they are all vacant at the moment... so go and choose one and I'll be there in a few minutes."

"Ok, Mum." I said

I went off to the treadmills and noticed that they were trialling some new settings. They had settings such as manual, ten-kilometre walk, and additional languages like French, Spanish, German, Italian and Japanese.

Any overseas tourists who are keen to use a treadmill can try one out in their own language...then choose the mode that suits their fitness levels and abilities. A big grin spreads across my face...I'm going to have some more fun with Mum. Hee hee.

I sneakily reached across to the treadmill next to me and was about to change it to French when Mum walks up.

"Ah ha!"

"I caught you Cassie!"

"Trying to change the language on the treadmill I was about to use eh?" says Mum grinning, happy to have caught me out

"Erm... no I wasn't." I tried, innocently

"You were about pull one on me... but I saw you sweetie."

"Busted!" said Mum, happily

"You caught me Mum." I said, stubbornly

"I nearly tricked you." I said, resigned to the fact that Mum had been too quick for me this time.

"Come on let's do our five minutes on the treadmill." said Mum, grinning

Mum and I adjusted the speed and set the treadmill level to two... it is just about right for me for my first time. Here I go!

When I finished the walk, I was exhausted but it was well worth it!

"Cassie, did you enjoy the trial gym program that I set for you?" Mum asked

"Yes, I did."

"It was challenging... but I got plenty of exercise!"

"These gym machines were hard to use at first, but they are brilliant to exercise with." I commented

"I'm glad you enjoyed them." Mum replied

"Would you like to try the gym back home in Melbourne for a few weeks, see how you like it? asked Mum
Yes, I would like to try that."

"It could become part of my routine." I said

"How was it."

"Did you get a little fitter?" Dad asked us

"Yes Dad."

"The machines were fun to use once I got used to them, I've enjoyed the YMCA." I added

"I'm happy Cassie had fun getting fit, despite being cheeky to me throughout the whole trial session!" said Mum, gesturing at me

"When we get back to Melbourne, Mum and I will arrange with the Melbourne YMCA to get you a YMCA pass card with twelve sessions on it... that way you can use it any time you want to." Dad said

"That will be good Dad."

"A new challenge for me to face." I replied

# Chapter Nineteen
# Triple M FM

We were having breakfast the next day in our hotel room, when there was a knock at the door.
"Who could it be knocking on the door at this hour of the morning?" wondered Mum
"I'll answer and find out." I said
I opened the door and a messenger boy stood in the door way, he had come to deliver a message to our room.
"A message for The Bontel Family." the boy said
"Thanks." I said taking the folded note
I opened the note which read.
Bontel Family,
*You are doing very well with your debut album and tour it has been most popular in Australia. I would like to invite you to two radio interviews... you can choose any subject you want to talk about including autism. I hope to see you here. Please contact us at DJ's Triple M FM 104.5*
"Awesome!"
"We get to do two radio interviews on Brisbane Triple M FM 104.5."
"I have never done a radio interview before I feel a bit nervous about this situation." I said
"You'll be okay with us Cassie."
"We'll arrange with Triple M FM to give you a tour of their radio studio to see how it all works."
"You will gain confidence doing the interviews... we'll help you through." Dad said, reassuringly
"Okay we'd better get ready for them."
"The note also adds the first interview will start at twelve-thirty after the lunch break."
"We'll relax for a couple of hours then start getting ready."
"Clean coloured clothes required... brush our hair... clean our teeth... put on deodorant so we don't stink out the studio!" I said, laughing
"Good thinking Cassie."
"We'll be ready then!" said Mum, grinning
Dad phoned the studio to let them know that we accepted their invitation.
I'm so excited!
A bit nervous though about doing my first ever radio interview!
I've heard my family, including Quirky Service, on the radio before, so I should feel confident... but that was them... not me!
What topic will I choose for my solo radio interview?
What topic will Mum, Dad and I decide on for our family interview?

Will our family, friends and fans listen in?

All these questions and more are buzzing round in my head like a swarm of busy bees!

"I have decided on a topic for my solo radio interview, I am going to talk about my autism." I said

"That's very brave of you to choose that topic Cassie."

"It is a risk… but I'm sure you can manage it."

"I'm not sure I want to talk about my Hyperthymesia though."

"It's rarely known about in Australia." I remarked

"Maybe you can explain it in addition to your autism… it might raise awareness of a little-known condition." said Mum

"I can try."

"It's eleven-thirty we'd better get ready to be there on time!" I said

We made our preparations and found our way to Brisbane Triple M FM with ten minutes to spare. We knocked on the door, the radio interviewer introduced himself as Bert he showed us around the studio. We saw control consoles, mike stands, headphones, and walls of records. This is an awesome place it's going to be one wicked radio interview!

"What do you think of the radio station and our studio?" asked Bert

"It's got great gadgets!"

"It's a great place."

"I think I can do a wicked radio interview here!"

"Well that's just what we are going to do young lady!" said Bert

"We've got about ten minutes before we start."

"If you go into the radio interview room over there… you can get yourselves set up."

"Who's doing their interview first?" Bert asked

"I am Bert." I said

"What topic have you chosen Cassie?" asked Bert

"I have chosen to speak about my diagnosis of mild autism and hyperthymesia."

"I hope to start raising awareness of both conditions." I said, calmly

"It will be great to talk to you about those, Cassie." said Bert

"We will be ready to go in about nine minutes… so be prepared." Bert instructed

Mum, Dad and I, went to the interview room and checked it out. We sat down in our chairs, I saw that my chair had a handle that you could turn clockwise to make it go up, and counter-clockwise to make it go down. I cheekily turned it clockwise and up went my chair!

"Up she rises!" I laughed

Then I noticed Mum and Dad giving me withering looks… I can tell that they are mentally saying,

"Cassie!"

"Put your chair down to its proper position and behave yourself!"

"Sorry Mum and Dad."

"I really shouldn't do that on live radio."

"Don't want to embarrass us!" I said

"We'll be red-faced if we stuff up!" said Mum

"At least no-one will be able to see that on radio!" Dad added, with a cheeky grin

When my solo interview is about to start, I put the radio headphones on so I can hear Bert's questions and comments. Here I go!

"Hello and welcome to Brisbane Triple M FM."

"This afternoon we have got the first of two special interviews."

"The first interview will be with Cassie Bontel… lead singer of the 'Bontel Family' band… Cassie is also a songwriter too.

"Cassie is going to talk today about her diagnosis of mild autism… plus the rare condition known as hyperthymesia."

"Welcome Cassie."

"Thanks Bert."

"It's great to be here."

"Cassie you have mild autism which is on the autism spectrum."

"Can you tell us… how does having mild autism affect you?"

"It used to affect the way I see the world… it would make me act differently from other people."

"I have fewer problems fitting in the world these days… but sometimes I have to stay in my comfort zone… which is my house… before I can take a big step and face the 'unfamiliar'… head on."

"Cassie how many of your five senses are affected by your mild autism… can you tell us what kind of challenges you have had to face?"

"All of my five senses were affected."

"I was sensitive to loud noises, from fire drills, other kids…including babies… sirens… to heavy metal music."

"These sounds were like someone was screaming at me… I would become overwhelmed with sensory overload."

"This would cause me to lash out at the person or persons who were causing the loud sounds."

"I listen to pop music and cover some songs myself these days… and that's fine now."

"I was sensitive to bright lights… with the same reaction as to loud noises… I always wore dark black sunglasses whether I was in my house… or when I went out somewhere."

"I would also wear my sunglasses whenever I had my photo taken… because I was sensitive to the camera flash."

"Certain smells would overwhelm me… such as perfume and petrol fumes… it could sometimes cause me to vomit… I would become upset or angry with the person causing the smells…such as the person cooking food."

"The taste or texture of food was troublesome… for many years I could only tolerate smooth foods… like smooth peanut butter…I would refuse to eat those with texture… including fruit and vegetables because they made me gag… or I would become overwhelmed by the texture."

"I have a long list of foods that are acceptable… and a list of those that are not… that my family and support network must follow."

"The foods that I like must be prepared a certain way or I am unable to eat them."

"I may have a meltdown if I'm served a food that is not on my acceptable list."

"It can be difficult to eat out at a restaurant… if I order a dish and they get it wrong… this is likely to trigger a meltdown."

"Lastly… for many years I was sensitive to touch either by feeling or skin contact."

"When I got touched… even by someone I knew… I would get frightened or overwhelmed."

"This caused me to become angry or upset… to hit out at the person that touched me… I even did it to my Mum and Dad when they tried to show their love and affection for me… it was very hard for them."

"I wore gloves to touch things that I didn't want to touch like rubbish bins or my parent's skin… because the feeling was gross to me…I would never touch insects because they frighten me…even a picture of an insect would scare me!"

"Thank you for speaking about these issues with me." Bert said

"You haven't had an easy life with these sensory issues!"

"No… I haven't."

"Fear of crowds didn't make things easier either…I got through it with the love… help… support… and encouragement of my Mum, Dad, family and support network."

"They are my heroes and inspiration in life… they continue to be."

"That's great that you have your family and friends to help you navigate your way through the world."

"Yes… it is!"

"Without them… I wouldn't have made the progress to get to where I am today!" I told Bert and the listeners

"Let's keep building on those positives Cassie!" Bert replied

"You have had no problems with empathy, sympathy and compassion during the past ten years…which is wonderful."

"Can you relate to our listeners a time when you needed to use these qualities… in your everyday life?" Bert asked me

"I sure can Bert!"

"During our road trip when we were leaving Echuca… something fell on the roof of our car."

"It turned out to be a magpie with an injured wing."

"I carefully tended her injured wing… checked her for other injuries and then we drove her to a local vet."

"We named her Margaret after Mum's grandmother."

"We took Margaret to the Family Vet Centre in Wodonga… then the next day we picked her up and delivered her to a lady named Valerie Kingston at her bird sanctuary… called 'Caring Bird'."

"We said goodbye to Margaret and left her in kind, caring hands to mend."

"That's great Cassie!" Bert said, smiling at me

"Kind, caring and compassionate actions from you… and your family!"

"Thanks Bert… it felt good to be doing the right thing… as Mum and Dad have always inspired me to do… with their actions."

"Now Cassie… can you tell me something about this condition called Hyperthymesia?"

"Yes Bert… as well as autism I have a rare condition which is not well known here in Australia… called Hyperthymesia."

"It means that I can remember every day of my life… except for the day I was born."

"Wow Cassie!" Bert exclaimed

"That's just incredible!"

"I can use language… emotions… words… descriptions… and visualisations… to describe what happened on a particular day and date during my life."

"Well that seems like it would be a very positive and good thing to have total recall." said Bert, enthusiastically

"You would think so Bert… but it can get you into hot water too…especially if others don't remember the events or conversation of the day… in the detailed way that I do!" I grinned

"I didn't think of that Cassie…you're right it could get very tricky…people sometimes like to remember things with 'rose-coloured glasses on… don't they?" Bert laughed

"You are one smart cookie Cassie!"

"Yes, I am Bert… I have an IQ of one hundred and ninety-seven which makes me a universal genius!" We all laughed loudly at that statement

"I hear that you are also a child prodigy when it comes to music?"

"What instruments do you play?" Bert asked

"I have been playing the guitar since I was six and singing since I was five."

"I have been writing my own songs since I was ten... I also cover songs from around the world including... Australia... Europe... Asia and North America."

"You love pop music and your voice has been likened to Nikki Webster I'm told?"

"Yes... her song 'Strawberry Kisses' is my all-time favourite song!"

"The album it appears on which was 'Follow Your Heart'... was released in 2001 as her debut album." I told Bert

"That album was given to me on my eighth birthday in 2003 by my Aunt Kate."

"She knew how much I loved pop music so she bought it for my birthday and I was so excited when I received it."

"What a special memory!"

"Now... how about your school life."

"What schools did you attend?"

"I originally attended the Melbourne Special Centre for girls with autism from 2001 when I was five until 2007 when I was twelve. Although I didn't directly make friends... I was more than happy to play with everyone and I gained lots of skills during my time there."

"Then I made the transition to Melbourne Secondary College which I attended from age twelve in 2007 to age fifteen in 2010."

"It was a mixed school... whose students were 'neurotypical' and not like me!"

"I refused to socialize with the other students throughout my three years at Melbourne Secondary... I had a hard time getting used to strangers there."

"I had a full-time female aide to help me with socialization and my work... but despite all her efforts... I was still unable to make any friends."

"I did not attend any social skill classes... I refused to do any group work."

"The other students didn't want to work with me... because they thought I was... that 'freaky chick weirdo'... or... 'princess dumb-arse'!"

"When I was fifteen and in Year 9 in 2010 I was in the library studying at lunchtime as I always did during my years at Melbourne Secondary... my aide who was named Dina...was concerned for me and encouraged me to go outside and make some friends.

I flatly refused saying...

"Making friends my arse!"

"I'm enjoying being by myself!"

Dina knew it was better to let me be by myself.

"It's your choice, Cassie."

"No need to get angry with me."

"Calm down please."

"Fire drills were one of several loud noises that overwhelmed me... I refused to play team sports in P.E... including 'battleball'."

"The integration office became my classroom... after I had a big meltdown during the fire drill in the second half of year nine!"

"However... there were a couple of positives to come out of that situation... as in those three years I got all straight A's in every subject...I also won the year nine UNO tournament against Mrs Petunia... my year nine teacher."

"I had a special graduation in the integration office, not with the other students... which included Mum, Dad, and the office integration ladies."

"After having a 'run' of bad anxiety issues throughout the summer of 2010/11 for which I was prescribed Fluoxetine and Risperidone... I returned to the special centre for girls with autism again where I made my first official friend... named Jenna Williams in 2011."

"Jenna, has Asperger's."

"The other students recognized me on my return and were happy to see me again."

"I remained at the special centre until the middle of the year in June 2011 when I had a special graduation at the MSC and finished school...Mum and Dad announced that we were going on a journey around Australia... which is the road trip that we are taking right now!"

"That's incredible!"

"What a lot you have experienced in your sixteen years so far Cassie!"

"Thank you...Bert."

"It does seem like quite a lot when I think back over it all with you today!"

"Now, you are currently the lead singer of the 'Bontel Family' band touring Australia and promoting your self-titled debut album 'The Bontel Family'."

"How it's going so far?"

"It's going great."

"The album is selling well and has hit top ten on most of the world charts... including number one in Australia and number four in New Zealand."

"It's amazing what a top selling album can do for your music career!" said Bert, enthusiastically

"Our fans loved it and our concerts have been wicked!" I agreed

"I'll never forget the Gold Coast concert where Mum and Dad tried to steal my fans... but I was on to them... planning a prank of my own and they were red-faced big time... when they found out it was me after I grabbed their wigs!"

Bert laughed and said

"I listened to that a few days ago and it was very funny."

"It'll probably be featured on some compilation blooper specials or something."

I laughed too

"Yeah... it probably will be."

"Mum and Dad will be embarrassed to watch it!" said Bert, chuckling at the thought

"Guess they will have to get used to it." I said, giggling again

"Cassie you have been very open about your autism diagnosis... is this because you want to raise awareness in the public about these conditions?" asked Bert

"Yes Bert... I plan to do more concerts and talk about autism with my audiences... also I want to attend autism events in Melbourne... where I shall be writing a song about autism."

"I intend to perform that song very soon...I will probably release it as a single in the middle of next year."

"So, listeners...you heard it right from the horses' mouth... so to speak!

"We look forward to hearing that new single Cassie and thank you so much for a fascinating interview here today."

"We'll close this solo interview now but please come back and join your Mum and Dad for their upcoming interview in the second half of the show."

"To take us to the break please choose a song for us to play Cassie."

"I choose 'Jessie's Girl'... by Australian singer/songwriter turned actor... Rick Springfield."

"It's a great song and he was quite 'hot' back in his singing days!" I added, with a grin

"This is Bert Jenkins of Brisbane Triple M FM... taking you into the break with Rick Springfield's... Jessie's Girl."

"We continue with our second interview speaking to the members of the 'Bontel Family' band in the second half of our show listeners...don't go away!"

Bert flicked the switch and the music played.

"That was a very cheeky statement about Rick, Cassie." giggled Mum

"Ye-e-s... I was listening to that bit very closely." Dad said, giving me a look

I gave Dad a cheeky grin.

"You did very well... speaking about your autism."

"You were brave and confident and spoke clearly... like you do when you are talking to us."

"What a great job!" said Mum, proudly

"Thanks Mum."

"I opened up to the whole of Australia!"

"I hope our family and friends tuned in to listen... I would feel honoured if they did." I added

"I'm sure they will have."

"They would be proud of you."

"They might even want to talk to you about the radio interviews afterwards... so be ready to answer all their questions next time they see you... or talk to you on the phone." said Dad, cheerfully

"Thank you, Dad."

"I am definitely proud of myself."

"This is a biggest achievement I have made on the road trip so far... and thanks for encouraging me to try it."

"It has been a real confidence booster!"

"Would you like to do a bit of radio presenting in the future Cassie?" asked Mum

"I would... yes."

"I used to listen to Quirky Service and Dan and the Cheeky Babes... plus relaxing music on the radio... so I would feel like somebody was at home looking after me whenever you two were away."

"Mum and I, have been doing radio interviews for many years... you will get plenty of practice as we continue on the tour." said Dad

The second interview started... Mum, Dad and I, were talking about our music and the 'Bontel Family' Band.

"Welcome back to Brisbane Triple M FM... this is the second interview with the 'Bontel Family who will be talking about their music careers and the 'Bontel Family' band."

"Daniel we'll start with you." Bert began

"You're best known as the original lead singer and bass guitarist of 'Quirky Service' and a big hit with the girls."

"Did you enjoy being so popular in the eighties and nineties?" Bert asked

"I really enjoyed the worldwide experience back in those decades... Quirky Service rose to the top from 1986 when 'Quirky Service' our second album was released... our fans and our families supported us throughout that entire time."

"It was an excellent experience seeing the countries we visited on our world tours... we made lots of new friends along the way too!" Dad replied

"Mikayla you were the original drummer and singer of Quirky Service... what was that whole experience like for you during the eighties and nineties?

"The whole experience was a blast!"

"We started out at fifteen years old in 1985... we were teen-pop sensations then became successful worldwide through our albums sales... our fans were mostly teenage girls who loved our music."

"Even teens with disabilities... such as Autism and Downs Syndrome loved the music and several of them sang with us at special events... in many countries."

"I enjoyed their love and support as much as Daniel did."

"Cassie... you have been writing songs since you were ten years old." said Bert

"What themes and inspirations do you use for your songs? he added

"The themes and inspiration I write about... are mostly those of a teenage girl like me Bert...parties... dancing... family... friends... life... desserts... technology... beaches...etc." I grinned, as I listed them off

"I mostly write positive lyrics and in a few of my songs I have mentioned Mum, Dad or other family members... which they appreciate."

"Daniel"

"Mikayla"

"Do you love that Cassie puts you into her songs sometimes?"

"Yes, we do."

"We feel appreciated when Cassie mentions us in a song."

"Maybe she will release them one day for her debut album."

"Cassie wrote one for me and one for Daniel which was lovely... it was beautiful to hear her sing them to us...then to our family later on."

"She has all her solo songs ready to sing onstage during our tour... in case Dan and I get held up...it hasn't happened so far." Mum smiled

"Let's hope she gets the opportunity real soon!" says Bert, giving me a wink

"Daniel you were also known as the lead singer of the Australian children's band 'Playground Kids'."

"What was the experience like performing in that band?"

"It was a wonderful experience recording music and performing for kids with disabilities... they enjoyed seeing us 'live'... in between our university commitments."

"We connected really well... the parents enjoyed seeing us too...some of them recognized us from our 'Quirky Service' years." grinned Dad

"Mikayla... you were the original drummer and vocalist of Playground Kids."

"You are always great with kids... along with Daniel, Olivia and Rebecca... especially with your target audience of children with disabilities." Bert relayed to the listening audience

"Playground Kids were a brilliant band to be part of... our music was popular with the children and we loved the music we performed for them... despite being busy at Melbourne University at the time."

"Our audience loved the albums... watching our videos... and especially the 'live' performances when they could join in."

"Mikayla what was the most memorable moment when you were with Playground Kids?"

"That would be back in 1998… we had just finished performing in Geelong."

"We were signing autographs and we had just said goodbye when an eleven-year-old autistic girl ran over to Olivia and wrapped her arms around her… hugging her."

"Olivia was surprised but hugged her back and smiled."

"The audience found it heart-warming… it was a very special moment."

"They hugged two more times and Olivia walked back to us."

"I'll never forget that moment Daniel, Olivia, Rebecca and I… had tears in our eyes."

"What a wonderful moment, Mikayla."

"Yes… just the best Bert!" Mum said, with her eyes shining

"You three formed your new pop group the 'Bontel Family' band last year."

"You recorded your self-titled debut album the 'Bontel Family' and released it in March this year."

"It's selling really well… it has reached the top ten in most countries."

"You are also currently touring around Australia… with more and more fans coming to see your concerts and listening to your new debut album."

"How do you feel the tour is going so far?"

"It's going excellently!"

"Our fans love our album… so far all of our concerts have been sell-outs!"

"We have been meeting a few of our fans in meet and greet sessions after our shows…one fan in Canberra even stopped me to give me a card with a positive message… telling me that I'm doing well and to keep up the good work!" I told Bert

"Well that's encouraging Cassie!" Bert grinned at me

"Do you plan to release any follow-up albums after you finish your tour?"

"Maybe… but we're not giving anything away yet."

"We'll consider it once we finish the tour first."

"Thank you for what has been an excellent interview."

"You have all been great, and good luck with the rest of your Australian tour."

"Thanks Bert." we all chorused together

"We'll send you into the break… with Kate Ceberano and 'Bedroom Eyes'."

"We'll be right back on Brisbane Triple M FM".

We said goodbye to Bert, thanked him for the awesome interviews and we went out to McDonald's for a reward, mostly for me.

Cos'…

"I 'aced it!" I said, high fiving the sky!

"Cassie, you did so well during those radio interviews."

"You were brave… confident… and more open than you have ever been." said Mum

"I definitely enjoyed those interviews!"

"I think I'll consider doing a bit of radio work during my career… I can speak about autism as one of my topics." I said, impressed

"Well done." said Dad

# Chapter Twenty
## Charleville, Blackall & spare tyres!

As it was over eight and a half hours drive to our next destination of Charleville, we decided to break up the journey with an overnight stop at Miles the following day. We arrived around midday and booked into the Starline Motor Inn for one night's stay. After we had some lunch, we spent a pleasant afternoon walking through Miles Historical Village attraction.

Early next morning, we left on the next four hours stretch of our drive to Charleville, when we arrived, we went straight to the historical museum located at 87 Alfred St, which was built in the year 1888.

Inside we found historical artefacts... photographs... furniture... old vehicles... and newspapers. There was also an amazing collection of early machinery from the olden days... including an original Rail Ambulance... a Denis Fire Engine... a Marshal Portable Steam Engine and can it be a replica Cobb and Co Coach? Wow!

"When Dad and I were young... we used to go to our friend's place... where they had a couple of old vehicles similar to these ones."

"We admired them and learnt a lot about them."

"They were fascinating vehicles and very useful too!" Mum added

"Did you enjoy the museum, Cassie?" asked Dad, sometime later

"Yes Dad."

"I loved the artefacts... I also enjoyed the early machinery."

"Those machines were put to good use in the olden days... even though they have been replaced with more modern versions now... I still enjoy learning about the traditional ones!"

"Learning history in a museum like this... is much better than a normal classroom!" I decided

"You have a good point there Cassie!" Mum grinned

"I soak up the information and learn about things without needing to look it up on the internet."

"That's good Cassie."

"You can always ask questions of the museum staff... if you want to know about a particular item." Mum added

"I'm good at that!" I winked

As we were leaving the museum I piped up.

"Heinemann's Bakery sounds good for a bite to eat!"

"Our stomachs will be filled for the next destination!"

"Sounds good to me too!" grinned Dad

"I agree." Mum laughed

"Mum, Dad, we are proud to be true-blue Australians... aren't we?" I asked

"Yes... we are Cassie." said Mum

"Australia is our home."

"It's close to our hearts."

"It's the spirit of it." said Dad, proudly

"Cassie... what is it about Australia that you like?" asked Mum

"I love the attractions!"

"I've been to favourite ones many times in Melbourne... the MCG... the Royal Botanic Gardens... but on our road trip it's so lovely and beautiful to see and learn something new...every place we go to!" I said, happily

"The one thing about Australia that I like...would have to be the people!"

"They are the friendliest people I've ever known!"

"They help you with directions if you need to find a place... in cafes and restaurants they give great service... and serve good quality food!" said Dad, smiling

"The one thing that I like about Australia... would have to be the animals and the wildlife!"

"Koalas...Dingoes...Platypus...Emus...you name it...we've got it!" said Mum, enthusiastically

"Then there are the important historical events our country has played a part in as well." Mum added

"Hey... there are four more things we all like!"

"What are they...?" said Dad, expectantly

Mum, Dad and I, put our hands one on top of each other's and said in unison.

"TRAVELLING, SINGING, WRITING AND SHOPPING!"

Then we high-fived each other! Our next destination is Blackall... so on we drive.

We have three hours before we will reach Blackall, so Mum hands the trivia book to Dad as she is driving this session.

"Cassie, you are doing so well on the Australian trivia questions."

"You have got every one of them so far!"

"Well done 'brainiac'!" Dad grinned at me

"Thanks, Dad." I grinned back

"Righto."

"These next three questions might be a little tricky... so take your time before giving me an answer." Dad said

The original 'Black Stump' marks what Station established in 1887?" Dad asked

"It is the original Astro Station."

"Which refers to places beyond the Black Stump." I said

"Which state school was opened on September the tenth 1877... destroyed by fire on the fifth of October 1964... and subsequently rebuilt?" Dad said

"That is the Blackall State School." I replied

"What is the dominant industry in Blackall?" asked Dad

"The dominant industry has to be grazing." I said

"Crikey!"

"You answered them all correctly."

"I thought at least one of them would 'stump' you... but you knew them all." grimaced Dad

"I'm just too good!"

"You just can't beat me... no matter what trivia questions you ask me... I know what the answers are." I said

"Oh, can't we?"

"Just you wait!"
"We're sure to find a question... but you might use Google to look up the answer." Mum mused
"Google?"
"What's that?"
"I don't Google to look up the answers!"
"I just answer them."
"I may be tech-savvy... but you two seem to be out of touch with the Australian trivia questions!"
"Old and New!" I grinned, knowing that would 'rile' them both up!
"Ha...ha...ha."
"That's what you think Cassie!"
"We'll find a question don't you worry about that!" said Mum, chuckling
"We will see... maybe I will 'stump' you two with a question!" I said, playfully

We arrived at Blackall... it seems like a nice town to stay in for a night or two.

"I have been looking at activities in Blackhall... the only one we can do today... is to shear sheep at the Wool scour!"
"Do you want to try that?"
"Yes!"
"I want to do it!" I said, excitedly

The tour was ready to start when we arrived at Blackall Wool scour... we were very lucky to grab the last three spots available.

"I know you don't need your headphones anymore... but you may want to put them on in here... as steam driven machines can be very loud." Mum said
"Ok, Mum." I nodded

As we went inside, I put on my headphones. Each stage of the wool processing was very interesting... the 'yarns' along the way were great and I understood them... even though they were new to me.

We learnt that the local shearer John Robert Howe 'aka' Jack "Jackie" Howe held the record for shearing three hundred and twenty-one sheep in seven hours and forty minutes! It's a record that still stands today. Phew! What hard work for him... he did well to earn that record! Now it was time for us to try our luck at hand shearing and to test our skills at wool classing!

We will give it a try... are you sure we won't be hurt?" I asked
"No... it won't hurt you."
"Just use it properly and you'll be all right... stand well back from the Hargan saw so you don't get cut." said the tour guide
"I'll give it a go first... I need some help from you Mum... since it's my first time shearing." I said, a little nervously
"I will help you Cassie... you're okay." said Mum

My hands were shaking... but with the help of Mum I managed to shear one sheep!
"We did it, Mum!" I said, excitedly
"We did well darling!" Mum said, relieved

Lastly, it was Dad's turn... he was shaky too... but he did great!
Well done... Dad." I said, as we left
"I've booked a caravan for the three of us." Dad says
"We've never stayed in a caravan... it will be another fun family activity for us to try." Mum said, laughing
"I think that's a good idea." I agreed

"I would never stay in a caravan before... because of unfamiliar smells... unfamiliar environment... and the possibility of insects being around me."

We made our way to the Blackall caravan park and who should we see... but our friends... the Smith family!

There is Jessica and Jason...who is Jessica's husband and has Savant Syndrome... their two daughters... Zara who is eighteen also with Savant Syndrome... and Melinda who is sixteen and has Asperger's Syndrome.

We decided to play a trick on them using a fishing rod with a mechanical gripping tool on the end of it that can pick things up. They went inside their caravan, so we hid behind some bushes, Mum tried to pinch a cake that they had left on the camp table outside their caravan.

She had to do it carefully and gently, to avoid attracting attention. We giggled a little, but hushed each other.

The family came back out and realised the cake was missing!

"Hey?"

"Where's the cake gone?"

"Did you move it, Jason?" asked Jessica

"No... it wasn't me." Jason replied

"Did you do it sweetie?" Jessica asked Zara

"No Mum... it wasn't me." said Zara, innocently

"Did you move the cake darling?" Jessica questioned Melinda

"Nope... it wasn't me, Mum." said Melinda

We sniggered quietly... or so we thought.

*'I recognise that sound!'* thought Jason, suspiciously

"We'll get them back." whispered Jason, to Jessica

"Pass me that big mug please?" Jessica said out loud to Jason

Jason passed the mug to Jessica.

"This will be big enough." he smirked

"Zara... please pour the water in here."

Jessica held out the large mug and Zara filled it to the top. I'm not sure what they wanted it for...I guess they are going to 'brew' a cuppa.

"Melinda, please put some cushions on those extra chairs."

"If we have any visitors... we want them to feel comfortable." Jessica added

Melinda put the cushions on the three spare chairs.

"Everything is ready." said Melinda, with a big smile

Then they strolled around the area chatting to each other.

Jessica strolled nonchalantly over to the bushes...the ones we were hiding behind... she began speaking out loud. What was she up to?

"This bush needs a little water to survive through the summer and winter." she said, then promptly threw the large mug of cold water all over the bush, drenching all three of us

"Whaa"

"Hey!"

"Glu!" we all spluttered as the very cold water went all over us

"Ha, ha!"

"We have the culprits now!" shouted Jessica, triumphantly

"Mum, Dad and I, stood up from our hiding place... dripping wet and red-faced."

"We have been out-pranked by our friends...oh the shame of it!"
"Daniel, Mikayla, Cassie."
"So... you were the ones that pinched our cake." accused Jessica, pointing her finger at us
"Err...err...No." Mum said with a sheepish look...nobody was going to believe that one
"We knew it was you."
"We can tell by the sheepish looks on your faces!" said Jessica, giggling
"All right... it was!" said Dad, 'caving in' immediately
"We definitely pinched your cake." he blabbed
I groaned... I was definitely going to need to have a talk with Dad about solidarity under fire!
"You were missing... so we took the opportunity." I admitted, now that Dad had blurted it all out anyway
"What a sneaky lot you are!" said Jason, admiringly
"What's that behind your back Mikayla?" asked Zara, seeing the fishing rod
"Err...nothing." said Mum, trying not to laugh.
"I see something behind your back!"
"That's a fishing rod with a 'contraption' on the end to pick things up with."
"I'll take that thank you!" said Zara, walking up to Mum and grabbing the fishing rod from behind her back
"Well would you believe it... that's a fishing rod all right... now how did that get there?" Mum said, a picture of innocence

Meanwhile, I'm thinking... *give it up Mum, that duck has no wings!*
"Well now that you are here why don't you come and sit down and have some lunch with us?" said Jessica.
"We would love to." said Dad

We walked over to the 'prepared' chairs and sat down. There 'erupted' three enormous 'fart' noises from beneath our bottoms!!!

Jessica, Jason, Zara and Melinda completely lost it they were rolling around on the ground holding their sides. Mum, Dad and I, were like 'stunned mullets'... a deep shade of puce spreading over our faces!

"Who does this belong to?" I asked, holding up what turned out to be a 'whoopee' cushion hidden underneath

Melinda, who had finally recovered her breath whistled innocently as though it wasn't her. I walked up to her and pointed the finger.

"Melinda... it was you that put the whoopee cushions on our seats, wasn't it?" I said, my turn now to be the judge in the court case
"Err... maybe?" Melinda, said winking
"You are so cheeky!"
"I will get you back you know."
"Soon!" I threatened
"Oh... will you?"
"I've got my eyes on you." Melinda grinned
"I've got my eyes on you too." I countered
"You two girls are funny." said Jessica
"Let's have lunch."
"Jessica... the girls... and I... have created a special lunch." said Jason, theatrically

The special lunch consisted of fairy bread, with cupcakes, scones, fruit and a white chocolate cake. Mum and I couldn't resist gawping with excitement at the sight of the white chocolate cake!

"I knew that would make you excited."

"You two sure do love your white chocolate, don't you?" Jessica said

"Yes, we do!"

"I have had a love of it since I was six!" Mum said fondly at the thought

"Mum passed her sweet tooth on to me... so now I share that love!" I said, grinning

"We have scones and cupcakes to compliment the white chocolate cake, the fairy bread to add a lovely touch, and fruit to balance our picnic lunch, we hope you enjoy it." said Zara

"I'm sure we will!" said Dad, appreciatively

"You four are very busy... but you always find time to picnic together and share funny stories." Mum said

"Jessica... I still remember the time I put a snake in your caravan bed!" said Mum

"I do too!" said Jessica, emphatically

"You, Daniel, Olivia, Rebecca, Jason and I, were camping in the Grampians."

"We were sitting around the campfire talking about our music... and our upcoming tour of Asia."

"We went to our tents to sleep and you hopped into your bed before you noticed a snake in it...you shrieked like a wuss!"

"I revealed myself as the culprit and we all laughed."

"We enjoyed our stay... we all had a go on the flying fox we had a grand time on it." Mum remembered

"That rubber snake gave me a terrible fright... but I laughed about it later!"

"Much later!"

"I got you back with Jason's help... by placing a rubber mouse in your bed the next night... and then YOU screamed like a wuss too!" said Jessica, like the cat that got the cream

"Hahaha very funny." said Mum, sarcastically

"I've got a funny story of my own." said Dad

"The year was 1983."

"Mikayla, Olivia, Rebecca and I, were staying at a Sydney hotel during our family holiday there."

"One night we were all returning to our hotel rooms with our parents after dinner in the restaurant... there was a knock at our door."

I said...

"I'll see who it is."

"Might be a relative coming to see us... who knows?"

"However, ... when I opened the door there was no one there... except a bucket of water suspended above the doorway... which poured all over me!"

"Mum, Dad and Olivia cleaned up the mess... whilst I got changed into dry pyjamas!"

"I knew who was responsible for that prank... I could hear her giggling from next door!" Dad said, smiling at Mum

"Yes... it was me who put the bucket of water on the door."

"I couldn't resist it!"

"I had Rebecca helping me of course!" sniggered Makayla

We chuckled at that funny memory... Mum was quite the practical joker in her day... even on holiday! You have to watch out for her all the time!

"What is your next destination?"

"I hope it's a great place!" said Jessica

"Gladstone is the next place we are going to."

"We can dive...snorkel... swim with turtles... fish for Barramundi and Mangrove Jack... walk in the footsteps of explorer Captain James Cook... or even check out Fitzroy Island by hiring a private vessel." I said

"That's sounds wicked."
"You will all have an awesome time... I'm sure of that." said Melinda
"We sure will."
"We'll send you some photos." Dad added
"That would be great!"
"We'd better get to bed... if we want to make an early start in the morning." Mum replied
In the morning after breakfast we said our goodbyes to the others.
"We're staying for a few more days...we wish you luck on the next stage of your road trip." said Zara
"Thanks...bye." Dad waved
Six hours and seven minutes later we heard a hissing noise and a clunk! That doesn't sound good!
"What the 'heck' was that?" asked Mum
"It sounds like something's blown... I know that sound."
"I definitely know that sound, it's not good!" I said
That won't be too bad...there's always the spare we can use to fix it!
Mum, Dad and I, jumped out of the car to investigate what had gone Psshht! It was one of our tyres... but which one? We soon found out. It was the left back tyre! This is not looking good we need cool heads to get us through!
"Oh drat!"
"The left tyre has blown!"
"We are going to need the spare!" said Mum
"I'll go and get it dear." Dad said to Mum
He went to the back of the car, opened up the tyre well... but no spare tyre!
"Sorry...we don't have a spare tyre." Dad said, quietly
Mum and I went to the back of the car to check it out... Dad was right... there was no spare tyre in the boot!
Dad... you forgot to check the spare tyre!!!" I said, shooting daggers at him with my eyes
"I forgot!"
"I thought we had everything we needed... the spare tyre was one thing we do need in an emergency...I messed up big time." said Dad, miserably
Mum gave Dad the 'evil eye'... she had her arms folded which was not a good sign!
"Now we're stuck here... two and a half hours from Gladstone with no spare tyre!!!"
"Flaming hell!" said Mum, getting worked up
"Let's all keep calm." said Dad, hurriedly trying to placate Mum before there was an explosion of epic proportions
"I'll phone some tyre places in Gladstone." he added, getting out his iPhone and searching for numbers
Unfortunately for Dad... it's late on a Saturday afternoon by now... and all the tyre places are closed for the weekend!
"Looks like we're stuck!" said Dad, unhappily
"This is not what we expected at all!"
"I'll be fine though I can get through it." I said, more to reassure myself, than Mum and Dad!
Mum and Dad smiled a little at each other thinking... *'If Cassie can cope, then so can we'*.
Mum put her hand on my shoulder.
"We will all be fine." said Mum, with a smile
Suddenly... a lightbulb lit up above me... just like in the cartoons.

"I've got an idea!"
"The Smith Family have got a spare tyre on their four wheeled drive!"
"Yes?" says Dad, with a puzzled look
"Well, why don't we call them and ask if they can bring the spare tyre to us... we can fit it to our car... then we can continue on to Gladstone!" I said, excitedly
"Great idea Cassie!"
"I'll call them and tell them what's happened." Mum added
Mum got out her phone and called Jessica's number. I hope the Smith family can help us. They are our friends... I'm sure they will help just like we would help them if they were in trouble. The Smiths' were cooking a late BBQ lunch when Mum rang Jessica.
"It's Mikayla ringing... I'll keep cooking while I answer her." Jessica said
Jason was busy laying the table with Zara and Melinda. Jessica answered her phone.
"Hello, Mikayla."
"Of course."
"What's the problem."
"Oh, dear."
"That's not good."
"What's that?"
"You haven't got a spare tyre!!!"
"Yes, we have some spare tyres... we'll bring them as soon as we have had our meal."
"We'll be there as soon as we can."
"We won't get to you till later this evening... so we will all have to pitch in then."
"We'll see you in five or six hours."
Mum spoke her reply on the phone...
"We'll see you later...bring some food please we shall be starving by then!"
I heard Jessica laugh... then Mum said...
"Stay safe, too."
"We don't want anyone to get lost on the road."
"Well, thank goodness for Jessica!"
"They will all be coming with the tyres!" Mum said, relieved
"We don't have to spend the night in the car!"
"Our friends know we're in trouble... and they are on the way." I said, happily
"All we have to do now is wait for them."
"We can read... look at the views... use our iPads or iPhones... whatever we want Cassie."
"I know the Wi-Fi won't work out here... but you can still listen to music on your iPad... or read your 'Twilight' books... or you can even chat to us!" said Dad grinning wryly, now that he was off the hook
"Ok, Dad."
We managed to push our car off to the side of the road to wait for our rescuers.
During the next few hours Mum, Dad and I, chatted to each other about our road trip so far and the discoveries we have made. We also listened to music on our iPods and read books which we brought along for the trip. Dad yawned at one point and I made a joke...saying...
"You'll catch flies in there."
"Hahaha very funny, Cassie."
"It's not fly season yet!" laughed Dad

"Is that the Smith's car, I hear?"

"I hope so." Mum said

The car sound came closer and... it was the Smith's car!

"Hooray!"

"We might've ended up spending the entire night here... but thank goodness we don't need to!" I said with great relief

"Hello... we finally made it!" smiled Jessica

"You called and we're here!"

"Here's what we're going to do."

"I will take off the flat tyre and put on one of the spare ones using my tools... while Jessica fixes the other spare... if she can...with Zara's help."

"Melinda will take the flat tyre and put it in the back of our Holden Colorado... then Zara and Melinda will give you the food we've brought when we've finished... then you should be all right to continue the last couple of hours on into Gladstone for the night." Jason said, very pleased with his plans

"Thanks."

"We're so grateful to have friends that help each other out... you four are just 'those kind' of people!" said Mum with a broad smile

"Of course, ... we are happy to help." Jessica returned the smile

Jason took out the flat tyre and using his tools, put the spare tyre carefully in place, while Jessica and Zara put the other spare tyre on the back of our Holden. Then Zara and Melinda kindly brought us some food that we needed for the rest of the drive to Gladstone.

"Thanks so much, you two!"

"We will survive!"

"We were getting very hungry." I said

"Let's face it...Cassie is always hungry!" said Dad, with a big grin

"Hey!" I said, but grinned back at Dad... because it's so true

"Here's some water too." said Zara

"Well, your car has a new tyre so it's ready to drive again...and you have a spare tyre in the boot... just in case it happens again!" said Jason, grinning

"Thank you so much...you are life savers!" replied Mum

"That's all right, we will always help you out, whenever we can." said Jessica, smiling

"Cassie managed to remain calm throughout the whole situation." said Dad

"I sure did!"

"Luckily our games and books helped to pass the time."

"Then once I knew I wasn't going to starve to death... I was fine!" I said, happily

Everybody laughed their heads off when I said that...I can't understand why...I take eating very seriously!

"Good on you Cassie!"

"You're getting braver by the minute on this road trip!" said Jason admiringly

"Thanks Jason."

"Thanks Zara and Melinda...you two are good friends to me." I gave Zara and Melinda a big hug

"Well we'd better get back to Blackall... enjoy the rest of your tour and the 'Bontel' family road trip!"

"We're enjoying the album and watching you on live TV!" Jessica added

"Thanks...enjoy the rest of your Blackall caravan stay."

"Goodbye." Mum waved them off

# Chapter Twenty-One
## Mackay and Magnetic Island

We booked in to the Metro Hotel Gladstone for the night... now that we are back on the Queensland coast... we plan to explore the coastline and some islands as we go.

"How would you like to go to the Great Barrier Reef?" asks Mum, cheerfully

"I would love it!"

"That would be awesome!" I said, excitedly

"There are fish and coral species on the reef, that are amazing!" said Dad

"I'm sure I will love exploring the Great Barrier Reef!"

"I've researched the area, it looks great!"

"We can also take a family adventure on Magnetic Island."

"That could be fun?" Dad added

"That would be wicked!" I said, excitedly

"There's golf... snorkelling... jet skiing... as well as live entertainment."

"What would you like to see first Cassie?" asked Dad

"I would love to go to Magnetic Island, please!" I said eagerly

"I love Magnetic Island." Mum said, happily

"I've been a few times with Dad and Olivia... Rebecca has been there a few times too... we've all enjoyed it there." said Mum, smiling

"It will take us a few days driving up the coast... it's over nine hours from Gladstone to get to Townsville. We can break the journey halfway and take our time to enjoy the scenery on the way."

"Tomorrow we can make our way towards Mackay, which is halfway, let's get some much-needed rest after our eventful day!" Dad said, as we settled in to our accommodation

The next morning, we breakfasted in the 'Rock salt Restaurant' at the Metro. We decided before we left Gladstone to take a trip to see HMAS Gladstone II... a decommissioned navy patrol boat that has been turned into a museum. We booked in to take the one-hour tour onboard at Flinders Parade.

"That was very interesting Dad!" I said

"It sure was Cassie... I enjoyed it very much."

"Let's get back on the road now...I will take the first driving stretch." said Mum, starting the engine

A couple of hours later, we had a quick bite to eat at Marlborough and changed drivers, another couple of hours passed and we arrived at Mackay at three thirty in the afternoon.

We booked into an apartment at the 'Quest Mackay On Gordon'.

Time to stretch our legs and get some fresh air!

We had arrived in time to take a city centre guided 'Art Walk Tour' at four-thirty. The tour is being led by Artspace Mackay's gallery director, and takes in the art installations through the Mackay city streets... ending up at Bluewater Quay. We had a great time looking at all the quirky art installations along the way... we also got to stretch our cramped leg muscles from all the car travel!

The tour worked out perfectly for us, as it ended at the 'Mackay River Street Twilight Market'... which just so happened to be open from four in the afternoon to eight in the evening.

Not only would we have somewhere to buy our evening meal, but also a night's entertainment browsing the market stalls and listening to the local music. We had a lovely time and ambled back to our accommodation when it was finished.

The next morning, we left early... Dad was driving.

"We will need to make our way to Townsville and catch the ferry across." said Dad, as we continued up the coastline

Four hours later we drove in to the ferry terminal at Townsville... then on board the ferry which takes cars and passengers across to Magnetic Island several times a day. Magnetic Island, here we come!

Once we have driven onboard, we can stay with our vehicle ready for disembarking at the other end... or we can get out and look over the side at the views of the ocean. It doesn't take very long to make the crossing over to Magnetic Island... so we decide to stay in our vehicle ready to make a quick exit at the other end and get into our exploring for the day!

We discuss what we can do when we get on the island.

"Magnetic Island is going to be a great place to spend our time together." said Dad

"This is one holiday stop we will never forget."

"We can enjoy the beauty... swim in the water... and dance to live music." Dad added

"We can drink cocktails on the beach." I said, mischievously

We looked at each other and shook our heads.

"No."

"We can't drink cocktails... we don't know what's in them."

"We'll stick to water!"

"Remember Cassie you are only sixteen... no alcohol for you...young lady!" said Dad, wagging his finger at me

"Mum, Dad, I've never been on a boat... ship... or ferry... before."

"What if I get seasick?"

"What can I do if it happens?" I asked

"Well... let us know... and we'll get a bucket for you and you can throw up into it."

"I am very hopeful that you won't get seasick during this trip to Magnetic Island and back... it's not very far Cassie." said Mum, grinning

"I don't want to ruin our Magnetic Island holiday break... before it starts." I said, sheepishly

Twenty minutes later... Magnetic Island was straight ahead. Wow! What a beautiful island! Magnetic Island looks so bright and colourful...there are holidaymakers everywhere having a special time.

"Land Ho."

"I see Magnetic Island up ahead of us... my it looks beautiful!" I commented

"It does indeed look beautiful, Cassie."

"It hasn't changed a bit... since Dad and I last visited." said Mum, happily

The ferry pulled alongside the terminal dock and when the crew had prepared the landing procedure the cargo doors were let down for the vehicles onboard to drive off safely to the island. The sand is pure white... the trees are a lush tropical green... as the sun shines through the clouds I soak it all up... I'm loving Magnetic Island already! There are many fun activities to choose from... I don't know where to start! I pretend to kiss the sand and Mum and Dad grin at me.

"The first thing I want to do is snorkel...it's a wonderful place to immerse yourself among the coral and learn more about the Great Barrier Reef."

"We can find out what we can all do... to help save our corals from bleaching and climate change... so that Australia's wonderful treasures... will still be here for everyone to come and see... for generations to come!" I said, enthusiastically

"Dad and I, and all our family have been snorkelling... swimming... and diving over many years... and we want that to continue always." Mum said, as Dad nodded in agreement

"We can take some photos with underwater cameras... we will need wetsuits." Dad added

"We need three snorkels too!" I reminded him

We went to the Magnetic Island dive shop where we can hire all the equipment we need to snorkel or scuba dive...at the shop they also hire out diving instructors for lessons on snorkelling... scuba diving... water safety and swimming.

There was one other thing we had to do!

"We need a boat to take us onto the reef... we can't swim all the way there ourselves." I said, laughing

"Good point Cassie."

"Hello."

"Welcome to Magnetic Island."

"How may I help you?" asked the owner of the Magnetic Island Great Barrier Reef Office.

"We're here to explore... snorkel... dive... and swim the Great Barrier Reef... as a family."

"We're very excited to be here." Mum said

"It's Daniel and Mikayla Bontel... isn't it?

"I thought I recognised your faces!"

"You've been here before and had a good time."

"Partying... exploring... and having fun."

"You stayed safe...I remember you told us that you don't drink any form of alcohol... that's great... because alcohol and swimming don't mix!" he said

"We drink lemonade and still have a fantastic fun time together!" said Dad

"Ah good times!"

"Who is this lovely young lady."

"I am Cassie... lead singer of the 'Bontel Family Band'."

"I've never been to the Great Barrier Reef before... but I'm keen to swim alongside the aquatic creatures... and to explore everything!" I said, excitedly

"That's great!"

"All you need to do is get changed into your swimsuits... take all your equipment with you...plus your dive instructor... hire a boat... and you're good to go!"

Mum, Dad and I changed... picked up the underwater cameras and went to look at the boats. We selected the best looking one we could see...we were all set to go!

"Hello."

"Ready to dive onto the Reef?" asked the skipper

"We're ready to dive the Barrier Reef, skipper." I said giving him the 'thumbs up' sign

"Good."

"Be careful, stay safe and follow the instructions of your diving instructor."

"I would love to see some of the photos that you take... when you are finished."

"Oh... and just one more thing... remember to keep an eye on your oxygen tanks... when they get to three quarters empty then swim to the surface... so you will have enough oxygen left to get you there, safely."

"I hope you enjoy this brilliant experience." the skipper said

"We certainly will... we'll enjoy it guaranteed!" said Mum, joyfully

Mum, Dad and I, put our snorkel masks on and fell off backwards...that's how scuba divers do it when they are diving... and we started exploring the Great Barrier Reef!

The reef was most definitely awesome... I was amazed at all the colourful corals that covered it... orange... pink... green... yellow... as well as blue. *'Ooh, these corals are so beautiful, I must take a few photos of them so I can show my classmates at the Special Centre.'* I thought, happily

Mum was delighted by the fishes... particularly the clownfish which were her favourite... and a turtle that came swimming up to her... *'Wow!... that turtle is very special indeed.... how cute is he... I'll take a couple of photos of him.'* Mum was thinking

Dad noticed a dugong swimming past he was amazed by the size and the sight of it... *'Strewth!... that's one amazing dugong all right... it looks enormous, what a rare creature to sight...I'll take a few photos of this... it will be good to show to our family and friends.'* Dad thought

We swam around taking photos, I took several of fish whilst looking at the coral and plants that were growing on the ocean floor. This is so awesome, swimming in such a unique Australian location like this, seeing the aquatic locals up close! I will treasure this adventure for a lifetime, so will Mum and Dad!

We checked our oxygen tank levels they were nearly half empty. We had a look around, taking more photos in each different area that we explored. Next time we checked our oxygen tanks levels they were three quarters empty... it is time to surface. We swim back up to the side of the boat, we can't wait to report on the creatures that we've seen below!

"Mum... the corals were so pretty!"

"Just wait till you see the photos I took of them!" I said

"The dugong I saw was quite amazing!"

"I just can't wait to see the photos I took of him!" Dad chuckled

"I took my first underwater 'selfie' with a turtle!"

"Wait till you see it!"

"Our family will be amazed at these photos!" laughs Mum

The skipper leans over the boat edge.

"You three sure had a grand old time on the reef."

"Come up into the boat... I'll take you to the shore and you can show me the photos you have taken."

"I would love to see them." said the skipper

Mum, Dad and I, pulled ourselves into the boat with help from the skipper, we made our way back to shore, where we showed him all the pictures we had taken whilst underwater on the reef.

"These are brilliant photos... Bontel Family."

"You even captured the rare and vulnerable dugong which is excellent."

"You will be able to show these photos to your friends and family... they will be 'wowed' by what they see!" said the skipper

"You bet they will be!"

"Especially my underwater 'selfie' with a turtle!"

"I'll never forget that!" said Mum, happily

"Thanks skipper… for taking us onto the reef."
"It was my first time and it was wicked!!!"
"I saw some coral and fishes… and creatures that I have never seen before… it was excellent!"
"Fortunately, we didn't see any 'SHARKS'… and we stayed safe." I giggled
"Well good for you!"
"Enjoy the rest of your Magnetic Island stay." said the skipper
"Thanks, Skipper… will do." said Dad
At the Arcadia Village Motel Mum asked…
"Cassie… since you have overcome your fear of being touched… how about we go for a massage tomorrow… at the 'Massage on Magnetic'?"
"Yes… that seems a relaxing place to go to." I said
"Would you like your Mum to practice on you… so you can get an idea of what a massage feels like?" asks Dad
"Yes please."
"It would be good to practice… before I attempt the massage."
"Cassie, remove your clothing except your underpants and lay face down on the bed…then I can get started with the practice." said Mum
I stripped off and lay down on my stomach.
"Where would you like me to start the massage Cassie?" enquired Mum
"You can start with my scalp." I replied
"I'll put on some classical piano music to provide a calm and relaxing atmosphere." said Dad, helpfully
Mum massaged my scalp… my temples… my neck muscles. It felt relaxing with Mum's gentle hands running through my hair and massaging my scalp underneath.
I love that relaxing feeling… it's so soothing to the mind. It's a bit cold in the room… but I am fine.
"That's so relaxing, Mum."
"It reminds me of the many times when I was sleeping at night in my bed with warm fleecy sheets in wintertime… with you holding my hands and rubbing them when I got upset." I said
"This has calmed you down and relaxed you when you have been upset… anxious… or overwhelmed."
"You are becoming more 'neurotypical' these days…we love you with… or without… your autism and hyperthymesia." said Mum, fondly
"I know there is no cure for autism… I wouldn't take a cure for it."
"Mum… Dad… would you two take a cure for autism if there was one?" I asked them both
"No… we wouldn't Cassie."
"We're fine with our autism and hyperthymesia… we are living life to the full as a family that sticks together!" said Dad
"There's a saying… 'a family that plays together - stays together'!"
"That quote certainly describes the three of us… we are inspired by it… we can overcome barriers… take on the world performing and wowing our fans as we go." I said
"You're quite right Cassie!"
"Here we are performing as the 'Bontel Family' band." Mum said
"We love music and hope to inspire Australia and the world… with happy and positive songs."
"We hope you can do the same with us." said Dad
"I will certainly do that!"
"If music can't inspire Australia and the world… nothing will!" I said, passionately

Mum then massaged my back... it felt really good... so much so that I completely relaxed
"How does that feel Cassie?" asked Mum
"It feels so relaxing and with classical music playing... it's even better." I said, dreamily
"I'm glad you are enjoying it, Cassie."
"How about you try massage with us... back home in Melbourne...when there are no clients?" said Dad
"Yes, I could try that." I said
"You might even take over from one of us... as a job... in addition to your successful music career."
"Would you like that?" asked Mum
"I might do, Mum."
"Let's just see how our music career goes first!" I said, smiling
Mum then moved on to massaging my feet.
"Ha! Ha! No! No!
"Stop it, Mum!"
"That tickles!" I wriggled around trying to get my feet away
"Sorry Cassie."
"Are your feet ticklish?"
"Yes... very ticklish." I giggled
"I'll just do your arms to finish."
When she was finished massaging me Mum asked...
"How was the massage, Cassie?"
"Did you feel relaxed the entire time?"
"Yes, except for the feet!" I said
"That's good, Cassie."
"You have got the idea now... what it will be like when we go for a massage at the Massage on Magnetic."
"Now we can book ourselves in for tomorrow." said Dad, smiling
"OK Dad." I agreed, as I went to get some sleep

Over the next few days, we walked along the Nelly Bay walking track looking at all the wildlife... swam in the sea and lazed on several beaches soaking up the late winter sunshine...and we also tried some beachcombing along the way.

Despite the weather getting cooler... one seventeen-year old teenage boy tried 'hotting things up'... by telling me that I looked beautiful and asking me whether I would go out with him!

I politely blocked his advances... so he quickly went off to find another conquest on the beach!

Mum, Dad and I, finished off our stay by visiting an art gallery... a cultural display... and then seeing some live entertainment. I can't wait to go back to Magnetic Island again! I had an awesome time there with Mum and Dad!

We are now back in Townsville after a week of fun-filled days on Magnetic Island.

It's time for our Townsville concert... we arrive and make our way onstage ready to perform. The audience are pumped and ready to go...so are we!

This is going to be an excellent night I'm sure of that!
"Are you ready, Townsville?" I call out
"YES!" the audience shouts back
"Then let's go!"
The Townsville concert was brilliant!

We had arranged another backstage meet and greet… this time for four autistic teenagers aged between fifteen and seventeen… there were three girls and a boy. Three had mild autism and one savant syndrome.

They are fans of the 'Bontel Family' band, and they are also siblings who have formed a local band based in Townsville. I can't wait to see them. Mum and Dad are excited too!

The four autistic teens came backstage they were very excited to see us… they nearly bowled me over!

"You four are the most excited fans I've seen since a Daddy Cool concert from 1972!"

"How are you?" I asked them

"We're great Cassie!"

"We're so excited to meet you!" said the eldest autistic teen girl, shaking my hand

"So am I."

"What are your names?" I asked.

"I'm Heather Larson… I am the eldest at seventeen… I have mild autism." said Heather

"I'm Felicity… I'm sixteen and I have mild autism as well." Felicity said

"I'm Sophie… I'm sixteen and I have savant syndrome." said Sophie

"I am Vince… I'm fifteen and I have mild autism." Vince added

"It's wonderful to meet you all!"

"Over there is my Mum Mikayla… and my Dad Daniel." I said shaking their hands one by one and pointing to where Mum and Dad were standing

"It's an honour to meet you Daniel and Mikayla."

"We've heard so much about you… we would like to say you are doing an excellent job with your music." said Heather

"Thanks darlings…that's so nice." said Mum, smiling

"Much appreciated… we're glad you're enjoying 'Quirky Service' and the 'Bontel Family' music." said Dad

"I heard you four have formed a local band."

"That's great!"

"What is the name of your band?" I asked

"The name of our band is 'Sunshine Sky'."

"It's a good name… I was the one that came up with it… because our music represents the sun shining in the big blue sky on a sunny day." said Felicity

"That's definitely a great name."

"Have you recorded an album yet?" I asked

"We are in the process of recording our debut album… which is self-titled, the 'Bontel Family' album has inspired and influenced us." said Sophie

"That's a big commitment… are you are doing well with your plans."

"How many songs have you written for the album?" asked Mum.

"We have recorded eleven songs."

"Nine are written by the four of us as co-writers… and two are 'Quirky Service' songs."

"When it is released… we'll consider a tour of Australia and possibly New Zealand." said Vince

"Great!"

"Good luck with that… if you want us or 'Quirky Service'… to play at your first music concert then contact us…we will see what we can do." said Dad

"We will… that would be so much fun!" said Heather, excitedly

"We'll sign your autograph books now and give you a remastered copy of 'Quirky Service's' 1986 self-titled album."

"These twelve songs have themes that describe our teen lives... hopefully they will inspire your music to break barriers... just like we did with 'Quirky Service' and the' Bontel Family' band."

"We hope you will love listening to it... as much as we loved making it."

We signed Sunshine Sky's autograph books and gave them signed recording photos of us from our self-titled album.

"Keep trying until you reach the top...don't forget to relax and have fun along the way."

We wished them well as we left the concert venue for our hotel... I'm sure they will go far!

"Cassie." whispered Dad the next morning

"See this 'Skyhooks' CD that I've got here?"

"Yes, Dad."

"I see you're planning another prank on Mum... aren't you?"

"Yes, I am and you can help me pull it off!"

"Here's what we do."

"While she is having her shower... we sneak down to our car eject Madonna's 'Like a Virgin'... and put 'Living in Seventies' in... then select track number four 'Horror Movie'!"

"Then we make sure we are nowhere around when she goes to turn it on!" whispered Dad, conspiratorially

"OK we can give it a try." I shrugged my shoulders

Dad and I crept down to the car... switched CD's...then I took the remote and waited for Mum. We packed our luggage and put it in the car. Mum finished showering, dressed and came out of the room with her luggage packed and ready to put in the boot. She noticed us standing nearby.

"What's going on?" asked Mum, with a suspicious look on her face, she thinks we are up to something

"Erm...nothing." I say with an innocent look

"Everything's fine." Dad said

"Hmmm...if everything's fine I'll get the car warmed up then." she replied

As she got in the car... I held up the remote ready to press the CD player on.

"Is that the remote..." starts Dad, before laughing

"Yes, it is!" I said, laughing back at him

"Mum has started the car... so... Three...Two...One."

I switched the track on using the remote control. It was just above medium level volume and 'Horror Movie' started playing.

'Skyhooks' is a band that Mum dislikes!

Dad, Olivia and Rebecca, would play their songs as pranks on Mum! Afterwards... she would get them back... by turning the tables on them by playing their least favourite artist.

"Oh hell!"

"Who did that!"

"It's that awful song!" said Mum a little annoyed, Dad and I are laughing hysterically outside the car

After quickly turning the radio off Mum emerged from the car and gave us her famous 'glare' Dad and I grinned sheepishly. Oops!

"OK."

"Who switched my Madonna CD with the Skyhooks CD?" asked Mum, holding up the 'Living in the Seventies' CD

"As if I even need to ask!"

"It was him/her!" said Dad and I, pointing at each other and trying to pin the blame

"Come on."

"Own up."
"Who is behind this prank?" asked Mum
Dad and I tried not to laugh but it was no use!
"I thought so!"
"You were both behind this prank!"
"You know how much I dislike 'Skyhooks'... I also dislike that lead guitarist... Red Symons too!"
"Olivia is a much better lead guitarist than him." said Mum
"Yes... she is a better lead guitarist than Red Symons."
"I bet you won't get us back for that prank." I said, mischievously
"Oh, I won't...won't I?"
"'We'll see about that!" Mum muttered, ominously
"You two had better watch out." she added, teasingly
"We certainly will!" said Dad, rubbing his chin thoughtfully
We all got in the car and Mum drove away on the next leg of our journey.

# Chapter Twenty-Two
## Fitzroy Island

We had arrived in Innisfail on our way to Cairns and were taking part in the amazing local attraction called a skywalk.

"What a spectacular vista it is from the Mamu Tropical Skywalk!"

"A mixture of green and yellow plants all around us in the tropical rainforest."

"It's an amazing view from the Skywalk!" I said, enchanted by the views

Mum, Dad and I, are high above in the canopy of the Mamu tropical rainforest on the Skywalker... at Paronella Park.

"The rainforest is such a relaxing place to be."

"Do you remember your tropical rainforest relaxation CD that you listened to in your holidays?"

"You loved it and it helped you to relax." said Mum

"That CD helped me to visualise myself in the rainforests of the Amazon... on a sunny day with toucans and large tropical parrots."

"I imagined I was holding a lemonade in one hand... wearing my sunglasses... and dressed in my blue bathers!" I said, remembering

"That sounds like a great visualisation, Cassie!"

"Mum and I loved the picture that you drew of it... with lots of excellent details and colours." Dad reminded me

"That bought lots of positivity to my day." I said, smiling

"We have loved your sketches on the road trip so far... we can't wait to see what you sketch next!" said Mum, proudly

"It may be a view of the Mamu Tropical Skywalk... I haven't decided yet." I grinned

I took a few photos of the spectacular views and sent them to Mia. She loves views like this one, I know she will love them. We were getting hungry after all that walking, so Mum checked on her iPhone, to see if there were any pubs in Cairns where we can have our lunch.

When Mum saw one option she started laughing. Dad and I looked over her shoulder to see what was making Mum laugh.

"The Cock and Bull." I read, before bursting out laughing

Dad had a cheeky grin on his face too... when he saw the name of the pub.

"The tourists get a chuckle out of that name every time they see it." said the guide, when we explained why we were all laughing

"I'm sure they do." Mum replied, still grinning

We left Innisfail and drove to Cairns, arriving an hour or so later.

We eventually chose... P.J. O'Brien's Irish Pub... we could smell the hearty pub grub as we walked in the door. Dad ordered three lemonades at the bar.

"Coming right up." said the barman, in an Irish accent

"What a nice atmosphere and authentic feel."

"There could have been a few 'shenanigans' going on here... if your Irish ancestors and relatives were in this awesome pub!" I said, smiling

"There certainly would be!"

"There would be eating... drinking... telling jokes... sharing stories... and making music till closing time!" said the bartender, laughing

"Mum and Dad are planning to come here on their forty-fifth wedding anniversary in a couple of years... we shall be here for that exciting event!" said Dad

"I will discover a bit more of my Irish heritage on your side, Dad."

"Then when we travel the world on our future music tour... we can go to Ireland for a bit of Irish 'fun and games'." I said, winking at Dad

"Our plan is to do all that in maybe three or four years from now." said Dad, smiling happily at the thought

"We will have lots of preparation time before that happens."

"I'm sure you will cope well and have fun with your Dad's Irish side of the family!" said Mum

"People who visit this pub are likely to discover the 'craic' and stay a long time enjoying it!" said the barman, grinning

I spat out my drink in shock! I know what crack means in Australia at least two versions anyway, but I don't think the barman is referring to... no...it couldn't be... he can't possibly mean 'that' version... it would be 'TOO' gross! I think we have our wires crossed somewhere!

"What?"

"Oh, sorry."

"We're staying for lunch...we'll have a good time here for a couple of hours." Dad said

"When you are ready to order, I guarantee the meals on our menu will be mouth-watering."

"P.J. O'Brien's have hearty meals I can tell you!" said the barman, smacking his lips at the thought

After we had ordered our drinks, we ordered our meals. When they were delivered to our table they looked delicious we had just started eating when a tourist walked up to us with a smile on his face.

"Do you three want to hear an Australian joke?" he began

"Look sir... before you start... I will tell 'YOU' something."

"We are 'Australian' musicians in a family band... this is my wife and daughter and we are having a family meal together."

"Now are you sure you want to tell us your 'Aussie' joke?" asked Dad, politely but firmly

"Nope!"

"I think I'll tell it to someone else." said the tourist

"Good choice." said Dad

The tourist went off and Mum, Dad and I, laughed and high-fived each other.

"Good one, Dad!"

"He decided not to tell his Aussie joke!"

"It definitely was not the best time to approach someone with a joke... whilst they are sharing a meal with their family or friends!" I said

"You were calm and professional... as you always are... with a witty counter-attack of your own." said Mum, admiringly

"It's my natural talent." said Dad, with a wink

"I learnt it from 'Dan and the Cheeky Babes'… our comedy pop group from the nineties."

"I have been giving you the benefit of my instruction for years Cassie… it certainly paid off at the Gold Coast concert!" Dad said, as he winked at me

"Thanks for those lessons Dad!" I said, laughing and winking back at him

"I hope I can remember them on our overseas tour!" I said, grinning

Our pub meals were delicious… I tried traditional Irish stew… Mum and Dad enjoyed P.J's pork sausages. The meals were very hearty, I would definitely try more of those again soon!

After lunch we made our way to the docks and caught the ferry from Cairns to Fitzroy Island where we booked in to the Fitzroy Island resort. In our hotel room, Mum showed me a photo of her and Dad.

"This was a good holiday photo taken on Fitzroy Island with Dad and I in January 1995… that was before this luxurious resort was built." said Mum

"You two look lovely in that photo… you look 'hot' as well on the beach." I said, mischievously

"Yes… the temperature was very high that day." said Mum, innocently

I groaned.

"Aaw… Mum…you know I wasn't talking about the temperature!"

"I meant that you and Dad look like two beach babes." I said, giggling

"Mmmn." said Mum, but I looked across at Dad and he was grinning in a pleased way, Mum continued telling me about the photograph

"I was lying on my sunshine yellow towel on the sandy beach at Fitzroy Island… with my sunglasses on and wearing my yellow bathers."

"Dad was next to me on his grass green towel… in his green bathers… his hand was on my stomach."

"Gosh we were definitely a lovebird couple I was pregnant with you at the time this photo was taken."

"He was saying… 'I can feel our child'."

"I replied… 'she is enjoying this holiday with us… one day we will take her to this very special location and tell her all about it'." Mum remembered, fondly

"Wow that's awesome!"

"You two were having a great time as 'parents-to-be' on Fitzroy Island!"

"Where was Olivia and Rebecca?" I asked

"They were doing girly shopping and getting a makeover in Cairns… they had hair spangles put in their long hair and make-up applied."

"Your Dad and I were amazed when we saw them."

"They bought tropical rainbow clothes for us and we danced with the locals." Dad added

"There was an old bar where you could listen to live music at night."

"We could have a grand old time there." I said, happily

"That's a good idea Cassie."

"It'll be good for us… we might even put on a performance… have good times aplenty." said Dad

"I can't go to that because I've got a cold." said Mum, out of the blue

"Come on, dear."

"You don't get out of it that easily."

"It will be so much fun to do together as a family." wheedled Dad

"All right then."

"We'll go there tomorrow evening."

"I wouldn't go to an event like that years ago… because I was too shy and so were you!"

"You've got a point though!"
"We will have fun together!" Mum said
"Well this is a wicked... awesome... island!"
"Fitzroy Island is a brilliant place to be... we will have fun times together in this special place." I said, excitedly
"We definitely will have fun times Cassie, sweetie."
"I love creating memories with you and Dad... especially when I get to be involved with them." I said
"We are planning to do a bit of surfing later."
"Would you like to come with us Cassie?"
"You don't have to if you don't want to." added Dad
"Not just yet."
"I have never surfed before in my life...I wouldn't want to go on a surfboard!"
"I might consider giving it a go...... later.... *much later.*" I muttered under my breath
"Okay."
"We'll let you think about it."
"Let's get started on those family memories!" said Mum

We chose to take the walking and hiking trails first. I was assured that we would be safe from any creatures we may come across. We put on repellent... just in case of mosquitos...I don't want any mosquito bites at all! As we were walking among the trees along Lighthouse Road, a mango dropped on the ground and splattered.

"That's a mango... I hear they taste good in drinks and tropical meals."
"I don't know which tree it fell from though." said Dad

As he finished talking another mango...this one was rotten... fell on his face splattering him... and a bit of it got in his hair. Oh, dear! Ha, ha!

All of us laughed...I couldn't resist taking a photo of it.
"Look at this everybody!"
"What do we have here?"
"Dad being tree-mangoed!" I giggled
"Very funny Cassie." said Dad, wiping squashed rotten mango off his face
"Ooh how romantic."
"You look very fruity dear." said Mum, laughing at Dad's look
"Ha! Ha!" said Dad, very un-impressed

We managed to finish the walking trails without getting bitten by any mosquitos, we avoided the little creatures along the way, and we had plenty of exercise and fresh air!

After we had lunch at the Fitzroy Island Resort, we went to a beach area and laid down on our towels in our bathers, we planned to have a little swim later. We put sunscreen on so we would not get sunburnt, we didn't want to end up looking like boiled lobsters!

"Ahh, this is the life!"
"Relaxing on Fitzroy Island, wearing your dark sunglasses, the sun shining down, the gentle sound of the ocean lapping nearby."
"Best of all, you don't need any kind of technology, just some fresh air and a good novel." I said, happily
"Too right, Cassie!"
"In our time we grew up a with a bit of technology... but we only used it when we needed to."

"We 'socialised' at gatherings... played games with each other during the seasons... on holidays we had fun together in Victoria and other states... even overseas when we were on tour."

"We took books and read them at the beach... usually after long days of performing."

"It's good that you can relax with a book." said Mum, smiling

"This is a great place to spend time with your family, I'm glad we're all having a good time here together." Dad said

"I'm really enjoying this place the longer we stay the more I feel like I never want to leave." I said, happily

Later, after our swim we made our way to the store.

"Let's go and get some provisions from the general store."

"I've never seen a general store quite like this."

"Look at all the stock available here!"

"It has just about all the basic shopping you need for a stay on Fitzroy Island."

"Some things look so tempting." I said

"Some look useful... what are we waiting for?"

"Let's shop!" Mum commanded

"We'll get what we need dear." Dad said, looking a trifle worried about Mum's combat approach to shopping!

The Fitzroy Island general store was unlike other stores that I have seen. It had the various items that you need for your shopping, as well as necessities for camping and household items too!

Mum, Dad and I, were delighted to see some of the curious pieces they stocked. We bought a few items and some food too... because if we're going to stay a few days more... we will need more food!

"This store is so efficient, the items here are excellent!"

"I am loving this shop already!" said Mum, cheerfully

"Thank you very much... the people that stay on Fitzroy Island all come here for their shopping...we try to stock as much as we can for them." said the cashier

"It's our first time here and we have all the items we need for our holiday." I said, very pleased

"You're enjoying Fitzroy Island, aren't you?" asked the cashier

"Yes, we are!"

"It's a magical place... we are escaping city life... forgetting our worries to enjoy the fun and relaxation here." said Dad, smiling

"It definitely is a magical place."

"Enjoy the rest of your stay."

"We will." Mum replied, as we left the shop

We went to the Fitzroy Island restaurant facility, it looked very nice. We were all hungry so this seemed like a good place to eat. The dishes sounded very temping, we ordered a few and boy did we enjoy them! Mum recalled a memory which made her smile with happiness.

"I remember a time when you were five years old, Cassie." she started

"We were at our usual beach near Melbourne playing on the sand, you were making sandcastles and I was helping you to decorate them with seashells."

"I went back to reading my Danielle Steel book, and Dad was asleep on his towel."

"You decided to cover your Dad with sand, all over his body with your bucket and spade, I smiled mischievously, when I saw what you were doing."

"You even put some seashells on him for artistic decoration, you were trying not to laugh while doing it."

"When it was time to leave, I said to you 'Cassie where is your father'?"

"He's around here somewhere I know he is."
Then you replied to me
"I don't know Mummy."
"Oh, there he his."
"He looked like a sand sculpture."
"Dan, you were so surprised when you woke up and teasingly quizzed Cassie about it, but she just giggled and we all laughed."
"That memory still makes me smile today, when I bring it up or think about it." Mum said
"I was mischievous that day, I covered Dad all over with sand, except his head!"
"Dad we were going to leave you there, but when Mum asked me where you were, I couldn't help giggling."
"You did not expect that from me... you didn't know what tricks I could play on you even back then." I said
"You are right!"
"I never expected that trick... you were a cheeky little thing... and you still are...only bigger!" said Dad
"Very funny... Dad!"
I would like to recreate that memory with you... it was an excellent trick!" I said
"We can do that... Fitzroy Island has plenty of sand!"
"Only this time I shall be awake... to see what's going on!" Dad grinned
Meanwhile... during our dinner... some of the peas rolled off my fork and onto the floor... Dad couldn't resist making yet another one of his Dad jokes!
"Oh, no!"
"Esca...peas!" laughs Dad
"Dad!"
"Stop it!" I groaned, putting my head down with embarrassment
"It's an oldie... but a goodie." laughed Mum
"How embarrassing!" I groaned
Yet... it was funny all the same.
After dinner we went back to our hotel.
"Cassie I've got something for you." Mum said
"You can wear this if you want to... if the room is too bright for you." said Mum, handing 'something' to me
"A sleeping mask"
"I could wear this some nights."
"Thanks Mum."
"Did you use it on bright nights?" I asked
"I used to."
"I would wear it whenever I needed a good night's sleep."
"I hope you enjoy wearing it... if you need it."
"Of course, Mum."
"I hope I don't snore as loud as you." I said, cheekily
"You might be a louder snorer than me!" stated Mum, (but I think it was wishful thinking on her part, if you ask me)
"That would be funny to hear." chuckled Dad
"Nice try Dad... but NO!" I said, emphatically

Mum, Dad and I, were relaxing on Fitzroy Island beach again... this time I had my MP3 player with me and I was listening to eighties music. I have five genres of music on my player Bubblegum, Eurodance, Eighties, Favourites and Classical.

Mum was relaxing, Dad was reading his 'Jo Nesbo' book... 'The Snowman'.

I am loving Fitzroy Island it's such a good place to stay and relax, away from busy city life. It'll be sad to go back to Cairns tomorrow, but I'm glad I spent a week here with Mum and Dad and made some memories with them. It's been rad!

I've got one more memory to make, it involves something that I did in the year 2000 when I was five years old! When my eighties playlist finished, I got my bucket and spade and starting putting sand on Dad's body. So much for Dad being awake this time... he has fallen asleep again in the warm sunshine whilst reading his book!

I am ready to create another sand sculpture memory. A couple of kids came over to see what I was doing and helped me to put shells over the sand body. Dad is going to get another surprise when he wakes up again!

"Mum... I have thought about it and I'm ready to give surfing a go." I said

"That's good, Cassie."

"Let's hire some surfboards and hit the waves."

"Cassie where's Dad."

"We can't go surfing without him." Mum said

"Well we better find him then." I said, giggling

I moved aside and Mum could now see that Dad was a piece of beautiful 'beach art', with most of his body covered in sand!

"Here he is Mum." I said, proudly displaying my handiwork

"He looks like a sculpture... created by none other than me." I said, with a flourish

"Oh, my."

"He certainly does!"

"You had fun recreating that memory." said Mum, sniggering

"I knew you would appreciate my artwork Mum." I said chuckling

"Dad!"

"Wake up it's time to go surfing." I said loudly

Dad woke up with a start... only he didn't seem to have any arms... legs... or body...just a head!!!

He tried to swivel his head from side to side... to work out what was wrong... then he could see that he was covered in shells... and underneath that sand all over him!

"Cassie!" he yelled

"Yes... Dad." I replied, sweetly

"Get me out of here...I can't move!"

"Uh Oh!"

I think we might have overdone it with the shells!

"It wasn't me, Dad." I said, hurriedly

"Mum was the one that did it!" I said, 'shopping' Mum

"It wasn't me... it was Cassie!" said Mum indignantly, after being 'dropped in it'

"I know WHO was responsible and she is going to get a clip under the ear in a minute!" Dad glared

"All right Dad... I'll help you to get out."

"Even if it is going to ruin my lovely beach artwork." I sighed, dramatically

"You know Dad... you would look good in a beach photo shoot... in a Fitzroy Island Magazine... in the 'hotness beach celebrity' section." I told him

He wasn't looking too thrilled with that idea at the moment... so I decided that maybe I should quit while I was ahead...or even funnier... while Dad was just a...head!

Time to start digging him out before he turns puce like Mum did...oops!

It took me a long time to get all the sand and shells off Dad... I forgot how much I had grown since the last time I covered him... there is a lot of difference between how much sand can be shovelled by a strong sixteen-year old teenager... and a little girl of five years!

"Phew!!!"

"I'm exhausted... I don't think I will try that again in a hurry!"

"Well... I'm very glad to hear that!" piped up Dad, who had been patiently waiting to be dug out for the last twenty minutes!

"Sorry Dad... I forgot how strong I am...I must have shovelled half the beach over you!"

"You don't say!" said Dad with a grimace, as he tried to get the sand out of all his 'nooks and crannies'

"I really need to get in the water now to wash myself off!" he complained

Mum and I went to get the surfboards... whilst Dad did the best he could in the water to get all the sand off himself. We made our way to a good surfing spot and laid the surfboards down. Mum and Dad showed me a few basic moves to start off with.

"The first thing you need to know Cassie... is how to stand up on the board." said Mum

"Watch how I pull myself up onto my knees... then jump up onto my feet and stand in the middle of the board with my knees bent...arms out-stretched to balance me in a surfing stance." Mum said

I tried to copy Mum...but it was not as easy as she had made it look... and I was a bit nervous.

"It's all right Cassie".

"There's no one else around but us." said Mum

I tried the sequence of moves again... it was going to take a lot of practice... and we were still only on dry land!

"Good try Cassie."

"Now before you stand up on the board to catch a wave... you have to lie flat on your stomach on your board in the water...then use your arms to paddle it out to where the waves are." Dad said

I practised lying flat on the board and paddling. Then I put the two movements that Mum and Dad had shown me together. It was very hard work! Now it was time to try and put it all together in the water!

"Good job, Cassie."

"Now, let's try to catch a couple of small waves to start off with and see how you do."

"Let's go." Mum called, as she ran into the water carrying her board

Thankfully, the waves were quite small... Mum and Dad surfed beautifully... I tried to make the moves in the shallow water as well. It takes a lot of practice and lots of falling off... before you get better!

I didn't mind falling off though... it was all part of the fun...I enjoyed every minute of it!

I may not be 'Layne Beachley' yet... but who knows how good I might become if I keep trying!

"How did you enjoy your first try at surfing, Cassie?"

"Was it fun?" asked Mum

"It was awesome... Mum!"

"I had a blast!"

"Thanks, to you and Dad, for helping me learn."

"I had so much fun."

"That's great Cassie." said Dad

"I can't wait to tell everyone what I learnt... and to show them too." I said

"Let's get showered and dressed... then we can try out the games room... we've never been in there before and I'm very keen to try some of the games." I said

After much fun on Fitzroy Island we caught the ferry back to Cairns and resumed our journey to the middle of Queensland... on our way to the Northern Territory.

# Chapter Twenty-Three
## 'Tism' Talk Time

We travelled back down to Townsville and across to Hughenden, where we stayed at the Royal Hotel in Moran Street for the night, on our way to Longreach.

In the car the next day Mum is giving me trivia questions as Dad drives.

"Longreach is on the Tropic of what?" asks Mum

"It's on the Tropic of Capricorn." I reply

"The worst locust plague in three decades occurred in which month of 2010?"

"That was in April 2010... I have a fear of insects and locusts are one of them!" I state

"The 'Australian Stockman's Hall of Fame' was opened in 1988, by which British Royal Family member?" Mum said

"That would be Queen Elizabeth II." I replied

When we arrive at Longreach in the late afternoon, we drive to the Jumbuck Motel where we are given unit eighteen. The facilities at the Jumbuck Motel included a pool, playground, Qantas history room, picture gallery and much more. They have great facilities...we might get a swim in if we have time and the weather is good! We have a snack of baked beans. Mum and Dad watch TV for a while, I read 'Twilight' the first book in the Twilight series by Stephanie Meyer.

Mum and Dad are in the mood for love!!!

"Come here you 'big missy'." said Dad to Mum

"Yes, my 'mister handsome'." said Mum to Dad

They were in their bedroom... but I could still hear what was going on through the bedroom walls... whilst I was trying to concentrate on reading my book! I could hear them doing 'IT', no matter how much I was engrossed in reading 'Twilight'!

"Why don't you two just get a room!" I said, banging on the wall

"*Eee...uw!*" I muttered under my breath to myself

"We 'ARE' in a room!" replied Mum, giggling

"I think I would prefer it if you were in a room in another BUILDING!" I called out, from my bedroom next door

Dad laughed and called out...

"It's only nature Cassie." but I noticed things got a lot quieter after that...THANK GOODNESS!!!

Sometime later, I asked Mum if I could make a phone call.

"Mum... can I use your iPhone to make a quick call to Nan Diane?" I asked

"Yes of course you can Cassie." she replied and handed me her phone to use

'Hi Nan... we are in Longreach.' I replied to her question of what I was doing

'In Blackall we learnt each stage of wool processing and even tried a new thing... shearing some sheep!'

'Thanks Nan... yes we were very proud of ourselves too... for having a 'go' at shearing!' I replied

'In Charleville, we visited the Historical Museum where we saw old vehicles... old newspapers... furniture and machinery.'

'Yes... I did enjoy it... it was very interesting.'

'Our family band is doing well.'

'We're currently in Queensland as part of our Australian tour... promoting our self-titled debut album.'

'It's selling well all over the world... not just in Australia.' I told her

'Yes Nan... we will be doing some charity concerts too... we like to help support those in need...it's a really worthwhile thing to do and it's fun as well!'

'Nan... I have a question to ask you?'

'Be warned though.'

'Do you think I'm weird?' I asked her, seriously

Mikayla and Daniel overhearing from their room looked at each other in shock. Mikayla was thinking... *'Oh, did I hear that right?... she thinks she's weird... she's not... she never is! She is starting to become aware that she is different to other kids.'*

Daniel was thinking... *'Oh my Goodness! We definitely weren't prepared for that. How are we going to tell her about her autism diagnosis? This has caught us off guard... we'll have to explain to her that she may be different from other kids... but she is our loved daughter regardless...we had better prepare ourselves.'*

Nan Diane tells me that I am smart and cute... that I am her unique and darling granddaughter... she says that everyone is different... and it doesn't make them weird.

'Thanks for that Nan.' I said, happily

Mum and Dad looked at each other nervously

'I'm going to have my dinner now and watch a classic movie.' Nan tells me

'Bye my darling Cassie.' she says

'Bye Nan Diane.' I said, ending the call

Dad came up to me and tried to start a conversation.

"Err...um... Cassie it's not easy for Mum and I to ask you this..." he started, but petered out before he got anywhere

"Aah... Cassie...what Dad is trying to say is...well..." Mum didn't get any further than Dad did with the conversation.

I've never seen them so nervous in all my life! They didn't know what to say in case they might upset me... I'm sure I could almost hear them sweating! I could tell by the nervous looks on their faces that they didn't know where to start.

"You can do it... Mum and Dad."

"Take your time."

"I don't mind." I said

Mum and Dad sat down on their bed... I sat opposite them with my hands on my knees ready for the 'Autism' talk!"

"Cassie... why do you think you're weird?" asked Dad, tentatively

"Because autism makes me different." I said

"Autism... including mild autism... makes you feel... think...act... differently... to other people." Dad said carefully

"Yes." I agreed

"It also makes you unique and special." Mum added, quickly

"Yes… I agree." I replied

"Let's get the hard part of autism out of the way first!"

"Let's discuss your sensory issues." Dad said

"You have always been sensitive to loud noises… you would become overwhelmed…which is called sensory overload…you would cover your ears and lash out at any person that caused the loud sounds."

"We had to buy you noise-reduction headphones… so you could cope with the loud sounds in public places… like restaurants and supermarkets."

"You did the shopping once at fifteen years old without your headphones… it was a rare occasion when you coped and didn't become overwhelmed."

"You tolerated pop music including songs you played on your guitar… later music would become a part of your life." Dad added

"When I was exposed to loud noises… it felt like screaming to my ears." I told them

"That explains why I covered my ears if I didn't have headphones available."

"Fire alarms… babies… children… heavy metal music… blenders… hair dryers and car alarms… are only some of the many loud noises… that I have had to endure since I was born."

"Then… when I went on that Sydney stage without my headphones… I felt like I escaped from the clutches of the loud noises that overwhelmed and suppressed me before."

"Music has contributed to my relief… as well as your loving support." I told them

"Then there was your sensitivity to smells." Mum said

"You would become overwhelmed by smells… from rubbish… perfumes… foods… this in turn would cause you to vomit… then you would get angry or upset with the person you thought had created the smells."

"I'm sorry if my perfume overwhelmed you over the years." said Mum, with a wry smile

"That's okay, Mum."

"You remember Mum… I had to wear a surgeon's mask whenever I took the bins out… 'Dove' shampoo and soap were the only type I could tolerate to use… when I finally overcame my fear of showers!" I grinned

"Then there's your sensitivity to bright lights and camera flashes!"

"You had the same reaction to those as when you were exposed to loud sounds."

"You always needed to wear your sunglasses whether at home or out in public…you would refuse to take them off… even when there was only one bright light in a room." Dad mused

"Right."

"When I was exposed to bright light… it felt like the sun was shining full-beam on me…even on the coldest day."

"I also thought someone was trying to blind me with a camera flash!"

"At times people would think I was being a temperamental popstar… rather than a teenage girl with autism."

"Now I don't mind camera flashes when I'm performing…as long as I'm wearing my sunglasses… but sometimes I tell my fans not to take pictures of me when I'm in a bad mood… or when I'm busy." I said with a grin

"Next… your food sensitivity."

"For many years the only type of food you could tolerate was smooth, like peanut butter… SMOOTH only… you would refuse to eat food with texture… including fruit and vegetables."

"It was a nightmare trying to get you to eat them!"

"We tried various ways… including disguising the food and putting in vitamin pills… but somehow you always managed to find out!"

"When you were six… we started writing up a long list of your food likes and dislikes… we added to them over the years… for us… our extended family… even your support network to help us all!"

"The foods you liked… must also have been prepared in a certain way… otherwise you wouldn't eat them!"

"For example, you like roast chicken."

"However, you only like it roasted and drizzled in BBQ sauce… not tomato sauce!"

"If we… your support network… or your carers… served a food that was not on your list… you would have a meltdown!"

"It was very difficult when we were at a restaurant… or at a relative's house… but slowly the relatives remembered your list." Mum said, painfully

"Right of course."

"Those foods on my 'dislike list' were unfamiliar to me… I would not eat them no matter how hard you tried."

"I would throw them… I employed tricks of my own using stealth and sneakiness…so you wouldn't find out."

"Since I started eating fruit and vegetables in Echuca… I am becoming more open to trying new foods."

"Even trying Italian and Korean dishes… as well as café and takeaway foods which I now eat with vegetables… and I'm retaining a healthy weight." I said, very pleased with myself

"You need to stay at a healthy weight which is good… but we don't want you to lose too much weight." Dad grinned and so did I… he knows there is no fear of that…'cos I love my food

"Next on the list… is sensitivity to touch."

"You did not like being touched… either by hand… or skin contact."

"Whenever you got touched… including by us, you got frightened or overwhelmed… which made you angry or upset… then you would hit the person that touched you."

"It was very hard for us when we were trying to show our love and affection to you… especially if you had hurt yourself."

"You wore gloves all the time so that you could touch things you didn't like to touch… like the bins… or us!"

"Wearing the gloves was a way for you to touch things without distress… you insisted on wearing them all the time….as there were many things you didn't like to touch." Mum recalled

"When I got touched either by someone I knew, or someone I didn't know…it felt like a knife was stabbing me… I would hit out at the person to get rid of the horrible pain."

"I wore gloves because touching things I didn't want to… felt gross… it was too awful to feel them."

"When I touch you with gloves on… it is one way that I can show my love and affection for you, without causing me distress…I never liked being kissed or hugged for that reason also." I explained

"We understand that now." Mum and Dad said, smiling at me

"You went through many phases of routines and rituals… at different ages… as you began to grow up."

"I remember when you were two… you went through a phase of opening and closing doors, all the doors repeatedly… then when you were three… you went through a phase of flicking the lights on and off!"

"It nearly drove your Mum and I 'MAD'…no matter what we tried to stop it happening, including the advice of an 'Autism' expert, you would resist us by mostly striking out…we helped you through…eventually you overcame those phases!"

"Also, from age two… you would rock back and forth when you were distressed… this was usually accompanied by sobbing, groaning or moaning."

"Then when you were seven the rocking back and forth stopped… you used a rocking chair instead… sometimes your Grandma's rocking chair as a substitute for four years… until you were eleven." Dad remembered

"Those were two of the many rituals and routines that I had in order to feel safe and gain control of my anxiety… which hadn't been diagnosed at that time."

"They helped me to maintain control of my environment, I followed them in a certain order that made me feel much better and calmer when I did them."

"If I didn't follow my rituals and routines… I would meltdown for hours… it would be very embarrassing and harrowing for you both to witness." I recalled

"Let's talk about those routines… meltdowns… and anxieties." said Dad

"One of your 'routine' examples… is that you insisted we go along the same route no matter what place we were going to."

"If we had to change the route…because of traffic or road closures for example… you would kick the seat… shriek and have a meltdown…sometimes with a little swearing thrown in for good measure!"

"We would cringe with embarrassment… we would have to go back to the familiar route… as you would only calm down then."

"If we couldn't get back to familiar roads… you would continue kicking… shrieking… and crying… until we reached our destination." Dad said, 'shuddering' slightly at the memory

"I still remember all that!" I grimaced

"When you went down a different route…I felt to me that we were going down an unknown scary road… I couldn't find the words to tell you… because I didn't start talking until I was four years old."

"I was thinking… *'Get me off this route! It's too scary for me!*"

During the last two years… I have had no problems with that… thanks to therapy and your help."

"Whenever I'm in the front seat… I become the GPS… then when you are driving in a new area… I'll tell you where to go to get to our destination… I visualise the area before we start the drive there."

"The painful routine is gone… replaced with a positive one… which is a relief for all of us!" I commented

"It sure is!" said Mum and Dad together, with happy emphasis

"Let us tell you how it was for us when you had a meltdown." Dad said, softly

"When you had an 'autistic meltdown'… you would throw yourself on the floor onto your stomach… thumping your fists and kicking your legs… this would be accompanied by shrieking and crying… but no words involved."

"Other times… you would sit down with your hands on your knees and your head on your hands crying… you never spoke… you would hit out at us if we tried to calm you."

"You stomped your feet and shrieked… stormed off to your room… where you would shriek and sob into your pillow."

"Many times… you lay down on the floor and sobbed… we would lie down next to you and try to calm you down."

"We used techniques such as the weighted blanket… which always worked well… encouraging you to use your anxiety techniques… rubbing your hands… reassuring you that you are safe with us."

"It was a bit embarrassing in public… so when that happened… we would take you back to the car… or to a quiet place to calm you down."

"It was heartbreaking for us to see you like this... and at times we didn't know what to do... so we just stayed with you until you felt better."

"Since you turned fifteen in early 2011 you've been meltdown free... it now only consists of tears streaming down your face... remaining silent and looking down at the floor or ground...usually while sitting down." said Dad

"Mum and Dad... let me tell you what those meltdowns were like for me." I said, quietly

"When I was in the middle of those meltdowns... I felt like I was on the edge off a cliff... about to fall off it."

"I was trying so very hard to express myself during those times... but the words would not escape me... I could only scream and shriek and cry."

"When it happened in a noisy, crowded and bright place... I couldn't use my anxiety techniques... because there were too many things happening around me."

"The car... quiet places... and my house... are the only places that I can use them effectively."

"I felt helpless in those terrible times... I was in a dark place where you couldn't reach me."

I felt so glad when I broke free of the meltdowns... I still get upset but silently now... you can help me when that happens." I said, with relief

"At fifteen you went through a puberty adjustment phase... where you would 'snap' and lose your temper for no apparent reason!"

"That would usually be accompanied by swearing and a meltdown... so we had to be very careful to avoid things that may set you off."

"We would have to calm you down... you would go to your room and if any family came visiting... Dad and I would have to warn them that you didn't want to talk at the moment... for fear of an explosion!"

"During this 'period' of time... if we served your food not in the way you wanted it... you would shout at the top of your voice...'THAT'S NOT HOW MY MEAL IS MADE, I WANT MY MEAL MADE THAT WAY, YOU ...BLEEP!'... then you would swear and meltdown."

"We would have to soothe you and make sure your meal was the way you wanted it."

"Also, during that period of adjustment time... you had to take several days off from Melbourne Secondary... for fear you would snap at the other students, teachers and your aide!"

"Thankfully you got through that phase and apologised to us for causing us grief at that time... we forgave you." said Mum, shrugging her shoulders

"It was frightening and scary going through that temper phase."

"When I seemed to be losing my temper for no reason at all... I felt angry... mad... upset and fearful... all at the same time!"

"You two both had to calm me when it happened... I would swear and meltdown... I felt filled with rage... upset and wanting to hit something!"

"I had to go to my room to cool off and calm down... everyone had to be so careful not to trigger me and set off my temper again."

"It was a terrifying phase... I'm so glad I got through it... and I'm so sorry that I caused you grief at the time." I said, from my heart

"We know you are Cassie... it was terrifying for us too." Dad remembered

"We are just so happy that we were able to help you work it out." said Mum, gratefully

"When you were going through puberty and you had your first period at fifteen you freaked out... dashed into your bedroom and closed the door."

"You didn't want us to see that happen to you... I was so concerned for you and opened the door to find you lying on the floor with all your clothes off... sobbing!"

"I wasn't sure what had happened... so I took you to the bathroom to get you cleaned up and you said to me...

"That's period blood, isn't it?"

"Yes. Cassie it is." I answered you

"It's okay... you're not bleeding because you are hurt... that is just part of being a female who is going through changes... to eventually become a woman."

I remember you told me that...

"It's nothing to worry about... it's completely natural for 'us ladies." I said, smiling at Mum

Then I said...

"Come on let's have a Mother/Daughter talk about it." Mum laughed, as we recalled those times

"After you had put some fresh blue clothes on... we had a talk about periods... how to manage them some days when they are painful... by laying down on the couch or bed with a hot water bottle to relieve the pain." Mum reminded me

"That was a tough thing to learn about... some days the pain hurts like 'BLEEPING' hell!"

"Like someone is squashing me!" I used to say

Then you would say...

"You will get through this Cassie... Mum is here for you."

"Don't cry... I will help you...' all the while, rubbing my hands.

"That certainly helped me to feel calmer... so I could work my way through it." I said

"In year nine when I was fifteen years old... Mrs Dina was concerned about me not having any friends. In reply to that comment I said...

"Making friends."

"My arse!"

"I'm enjoying being by myself!"

Dad piped up...

"You are excellent at using sarcasm... you definitely have an understanding of how it works."

"You don't take everything literally... you have no problems working out what things mean... including idioms...it's amazing!"

"Yes... I have a talent for them as well...I used them on the bullies at Melbourne Secondary College... they were baffled and confused... they eventually gave up and moved on to target somebody else!"

"One of your issues has been crowds." Mum said

"When you came across a crowded public place by accident... you would cover your ears and try to hide somewhere... before 'melting down'."

"We would take you to a quiet place to calm you down."

"Mum and I would plan carefully to avoid crowds... also giving you some forewarning if we could... and an escape route if we needed one for any reason." said Dad

"Special occasions... including birthdays and Christmas... would have to be quiet occasions... only a few people... because you would get overwhelmed if we gathered too many people together."

"Your problem with crowds has gone now and your concerts have been successes... talking and interacting with the audience has been a joy for us to witness!"

"We're very proud of you for overcoming your fear, sweetie!" Mum said, with a big smile

"I'm proud of myself... for overcoming it too!"

"The crowds were like strangers... I didn't want to be near them... only family."

"In comparison... the crowds were like cats... and I was a small mouse!"

"I was afraid they were coming to catch me and eat me all up!" I laughed at myself

"The strategies you two thought up for coping with crowds... along with encouragement...support... and help got me through... although it took some time."

"My house was a comfort zone where I could escape from crowds, if it got too much!"

"When I was ready to face them head-on... I had to be a big girl... brave enough and strong enough for whatever crowd event we attended."

"I enjoy crowds now... they don't bother me anymore... I like talking to audiences and interacting with them during our concerts."

"It's another barrier that I have broken and I'm happy to be doing it with you two!" I said giving Mum and Dad the 'thumbs up' signal

"So are we Cassie!" said Mum and Dad together

"Let's review our family history up until now." said Mum, thoughtfully

"Dad and I met at a special centre in 1975... ten years later we became boyfriend and girlfriend."

"We were always the ones for each other...we got married in a private ceremony at Wilsons Promontory Lighthouse on the ninth of June 1990... later we held a reception at the Melbourne Town Hall."

"During my pregnancy with you I craved chocolate...especially white chocolate... Dad had to hide it from me in various places so I wouldn't eat too much!"

"I once managed to find some and was about to eat it when your Dad busted me, I had to hand it over to him and eat fruit instead... which did me the world of good!"

"On April the twenty-first 1995... I gave birth to you."

"Your middle name of Annabelle was your Dad's idea... we brought you home a week later on April the twenty-eighth 1995."

"The next day we invited our family and friends to meet you."

"You were quiet and rarely fussed... we had no problems taking you out."

"We had a party for your arrival... we were attending Melbourne University and also in our first year of 'Playground Kids'... the children's band we formed from 1995-1999."

"We went on a few dinner dates with our friends...you came along too."

"When you were about eighteen months... we knew something was wrong."

"You didn't talk and you were lining up your toy cars in order of colour and size."

"I suspected something wasn't right."

"I thought I recognised a couple of autistic behaviours."

"You would meltdown over trivial things... whenever your routine changed... or when you were being touched."

"You would hit... kick... scratch... roar... and shriek like an animal, whenever those things occurred."

"The supermarket was the one of the worst places for this to happen!"

"At two years of age you still weren't talking...more symptoms were showing up."

"We took you to Dr Hannah where we filled out a form of ten questions about autism... the symptoms that you were displaying... your behaviours and preferences."

"When you were officially diagnosed with mild autism... we went straight into early intervention...we tried several programs which didn't go so well."

"We taught you AUSLAN...Australian Sign Language... until you learnt to talk and became fully verbal at age four."

"Whilst we were trying all these things, we taught you at home... skills such as empathy and other life skills... until you attended a special centre for girls with autism, from age five until you were twelve."

"You had no problems communicating and socialising with us, despite your sensory issues…all your senses were affected."

"We wrote you social stories from the age of four for various events and situations."

"They helped to make the transitions a little easier… despite some days being tough." Mum added

"At age twelve we decided to try sending you to Melbourne High School… in order to make friends… despite having a full-time aide, Mrs Dina, to help out… you refused to socialise with the other students… much to our dismay."

"By late in year nine your social skill worker and the Melbourne Secondary College counsellor gave up and wouldn't even go near you!"

"For the rest of year nine after you had that big meltdown during the fire drill… the integration office became your classroom and one of the integration ladies…your teacher."

"You finished year nine in 2010 and we held a special graduation in the integration office, with no other students."

"Then from January 2011- June 2011 you attended the special centre for girls with autism again which was much better for you… and for us."

"Mum and I, were happy for you when you made a friend named Jenna Williams who had Asperger's… she had been through the same challenges as you…she was mature, compassionate, empathetic and willing to help you out when she could… because she understood you." said Dad

"During Summer 2010/2011 you went through what we call your… 'Anxiety Run.'" Mum said

"About two days after New Year's Eve 2010… you became extremely anxious and too afraid to leave the house… we had to get family members to come to our house instead."

"You were afraid of most things… you didn't want to go near us… thinking we were…. 'monsters with scary hair and eyes who are coming to frighten me'."

"You got upset and had meltdowns most days… we would spend hours trying to calm you down."

"You hid under your bed or blankets when you got frightened… insisted on leaving the lights on every night because you were afraid of the dark… something which hadn't happened since you were five years old."

"You couldn't find the words to tell us what you were going through… we were so concerned you wouldn't come back to us."

"Near the end of January, we booked an appointment to see a doctor in Warrnambool… it took a lot of reassuring and comfort but with your dolphin soft toy in hand… we got you there… and then you couldn't speak to the doctor."

"You managed to write down what you had been going through… you used descriptions…words…language and experiences… to associate with what you had been experiencing."

"The doctor understood and praised you for helping us all to understand through your writing."

"He prescribed Fluoxetine to take in the mornings and Risperidone at night, to keep anxiety at bay."

"By early February you felt happier and calmer… you told us what had happened that you couldn't tell us before…you apologised for putting us through that ordeal… which we accepted and told you it wasn't your fault." Mum explained

## Chapter Twenty-Four
# Revelation & Writing

"Now let's focus on the positives!" said Mum decisively

"Things about your diagnosis of mild autism and hyperthymesia...that help and enhance."

"You see details that others miss... like a detective finding a crucial piece of evidence... for a vital case that needs to be solved."

"You can sing and cover a song on your guitar after hearing the lyrics only once."

"You have an IQ of one hundred and ninety-seven... with a classification of universal genius."

"This makes you talented in music... a child prodigy."

"You have been very good at the guitar since you were six... and excellent at vocals since you were five years old."

"Hyperthymesia... makes you recall almost every moment of your life... except your birth...with accurate attention to detail."

"You remember personal events that hold personal significance to you... both negative and positive."

"When any of us ask you about what you did on a particular day or date... you describe to us what happened... using emotions... experiences... words... language and visualisations... as they occurred on that day."

"You are knowledgeable about almost every subject and can easily pass tests with a 99.95 % accuracy."

"You love answering quiz questions when watching quiz shows as you take the part of the contestants."

"Every quiz and board game that you have played with your Dad and I... usually ends up with you winning!"

"You are a very good quiz player." Mum stated

"I am passionate about quiz shows... my main interest is Australian History... Dad I might become better than you at quizzes." I said, winking at him

"I thought I was the best Australian and World Quiz Champion... out of Mum... Olivia... Rebecca and I?" said Dad, listing his opponents in the family for top quiz scores

"Hang on...I thought I was the best Australian and World Quiz Champion!" Mum grinned back at us

"Sorry Mum and Dad... I'm better at quizzes than you two... I might participate in an Australian or World Quiz Championship and beat you both!" I said, giggling

"Sometime soon... why don't we take you to a pub quiz and enter as a family?"

"It would be good fun to do...we might even have a chance of winning a prize?"

"I would love to try that... I have never done one before...it will give me a chance to test my quizzing knowledge against other people." I said, excitedly

"We can arrange that."

"Right... next on the list of positives... you are good at cricket and basketball."

"You can name all the cricketing nations and players from past to present… you're very good at batting and bowling… since you were seven years old."

"It certainly showed when you were in year nine and scored fifty-seven not out… taking six wickets for thirty-one runs… against the Bendigo High School Mixed Team."

"You still played cricket when you attended the special centre… right up until we took this road trip."

"I was the female version of Shane Warne and Steve Waugh!" I said, laughing

"The high school mixed teams couldn't get me out in most of the matches… they were too slow to beat my bowling."

"In the final I earnt my teammates respect… despite not making any friends."

"You're also good at basketball."

"We would practice in the backyard since you were eight… just for fun!"

"It would greatly improve your motor skills for things like opening jars…increasing your muscles for moving heavy items around like tables and chairs."

"Your favourite player has always been Lauren Jackson…you did an assignment on her at the special centre when you were ten years old." Dad reminded me

Yes… I loved basketball as well… I played two times a week for exercise when I wasn't playing cricket."

"I mastered the basketball twirl on my finger when I was eleven years old… I'm still good at that!"

"I was never interested in playing for the Melbourne High School mixed basketball team…I still play basketball whenever I get the chance."

"We have had some funny moments over the years with you too Cassie!" said Mum, smiling

"Let's talk about some of those funny moments."

"I recall one when you were little in 1999."

"I was giving you a bath…you had a fear of getting your hair wet back then… I was playing a game with you and you were laughing like mad."

"I was getting some special shampoo that you used to love… designed to be put in the bathwater… when you got out your little water pistol and squirted it at me!"

"I signed to you… 'Cassie, did you just squirt me'?"

"You giggled and shook your head NO."

"I recall I said… 'Oh I thought there was someone squirting me'… I put the special shampoo in the bath turning to get the bubble bath, it happened again!"

"I signed 'Cassie you just squirted me…didn't you!"

"Then you signed, while laughing… 'Silly Mummy it wasn't me… it was Daddy'."

"I replied… 'Oh was it'?"

"He must've sneaked in here and got me!"

"Daniel… did you squirt me with the little water pistol?"

"Dad said… 'No, it wasn't me'."

"Cassie did it to you!"

"You know how sneaky Cassie can be… especially with her water pistol'!"

"I signed to you… 'Cassie you cheeky little giggle-girt'!"

"You 'ARE' the one that squirted me!"

"You need to burn some more energy… before I can get you out of that bath!"

"Think it's funny, do you?"

"Then you just laughed excitedly and flapped your hands… it was such a funny moment that I still remember it today." Mum smiled fondly, remembering

"It was one of my best pranks at that age!"

"I tried to blame Dad... but you knew I did it... it's still funny." I laughed

"When you were four years old you went to kindergarten...you didn't last long there!"

"You were painting a picture away from the other students and enjoying it... then you proceeded to paint all over yourself including your hair...the teacher Mrs Joanne couldn't catch you because you were too fast for her!"

"That was funny for a moment."

"On that day the kindergarten photos were being taken... you filled up a bucket of water and proceeded to pour it all over the girls which made them scream... then you did the same to the boys!"

"Nobody caught you... even though we know it was you that did it!"

"We took you home to wash your hair in the bath."

"You screamed and fought... but eventually we got it all out which was a relief!" said Dad, grimacing

"It was funny when I painted all over myself and threw the bucket of water all over the other students."

"I was always too quick, to be caught for pranks like those... but it wasn't funny when you two washed my hair to get all the paint out!"

"It was all good when the paint was gone." I grinned

"When you were fifteen years old you scared off a female carer you didn't like... by taping ghost noises and horror sound effects and placing the tape recorder near the chair where she was sitting reading her book."

"When you played the tape... she got such a fright that she packed up her stuff... loaded it into her car and sped off!"

"When your Dad and I got home we saw that she had gone."

We asked...

"Where's Janet, Cassie?"

"Did you scare her off?"

"You sneakily denied it... but confessed to it later."

Mum said...

"You scared off another carer"?

"I can't believe you did that again."

"I did scare those carers off giving them a fright...they wouldn't look after me again." I laughed

"Isabelle was the only carer I trusted."

"I don't need carers to look after me anymore... I can look after myself."

"You two can trust me to be by myself... to look after the house and make my own meals...to clean up after myself.' I said

"Are you sure about that Cassie?"

"We don't want you feeling scared or frightened when we go out." Dad said

"In June 2011 we announced to you that we would all be going on a road trip... we held a 'graduation' at the special centre... before commencing our adventurous journey together."

"We went to the Melbourne Recording Studio to record the songs for our debut album... 'The Bontel Family'... which included one song we co-wrote called 'A Family United'...plus thirteen cover songs.

"In between tracks we taught you how a recording studio works and how to record an album...with the help of the sound engineers."

"We released the album in March 2011...then we decided to tour around Australia promoting it whilst taking our road trip... which is of course what we are on right now!" said Dad, cheerfully

"That was so much to take in Mum and Dad...but thank you for giving me 'the talk'!" I said, pretending to mop my brow

"That's all right, darling."

"We're happy we've 'manned' up to do it...we're pleased you took it all in so well!" said Mum, obviously glad that went off without a hitch

Now the 'Autism Talk' is done...let's have a good dinner and dessert!" I said, hungrily

"Good idea, Cassie!"

"We all deserve a good 'feed' after a talk like that!" Dad winked at me, as he grinned

"I'm glad you told me and I understand it all now...but last year in 2010 when I was fifteen... I looked up my autism diagnosis!"

Mum and Dad looked shocked for a moment. They did not see that coming!

"Did you really?"

"How did you do it without our knowing?" asked Dad, in awe

"When you two went out to dinner one evening and trusted me to be home alone... because you couldn't find a 'carer'."

"Isabelle my regular carer wasn't available that night... so I took the opportunity to look it up... I searched through the sections and read them carefully... I checked out your blog and confirmed why I was different from the other kids...all the symptoms described me to a 'T'!"

"I did that after I observed the other students playing a game which I feared and never played... called 'Battleball'... also known as a variant of Dodgeball."

"When you two came home I decided not to tell you until the time was right... which is now."

"I'm sorry if I kept it quiet... but I knew what I had to do." I said, smiling

"That's all right, Cassie."

"We understand."

"If we talked about your autism a couple of years ago you would have got upset and depressed... wouldn't you?" asked Mum

"Yes... I would have."

"I would have been upset... I would not have left the house for a long time."

"From when I looked it up... I had to be strong for you two... I waited for that right moment to let you know that I knew... I'm glad the right moment has come you two have been strong for me through thick and thin." I told them

"We have helped each other through tough times...we have had help from your support network and our relatives too." said Dad, thankfully

"Because we're your parents we both work hard to put food on our table... you contribute by studying... navigating... and working... then the three of us can relax and laugh together."

"Despite the hard times we sometimes have to face... we always love you... always... as you love us." said Mum

"Thanks Mum and Dad... you two are great supporters through all the obstacles we have faced together."

"I have something to show you two." I said

I took out a piece of paper and showed it to Mum and Dad, it was neatly drawn and coloured.

"I drew the colours of the rainbow... each of the colours represents an autism spectrum condition".

"The Violet represents classic autism... Purple stands for severe autism... Blue is low-functioning autism... mild autism is represented by the colour Green... Yellow stands for high-functioning autism... Orange is Asperger's syndrome... and Red is savant syndrome."

"The arrow points to the colour Green... which is where I am on my... 'Autism spectrum condition' rainbow." I said, smiling

"That's amazing Cassie... it's very well-drawn." Mum said, admiring my picture

"Thanks Mum... I also wrote a letter to you both when I looked up my diagnosis."

"Take your time to read it."

Mum and Dad took the letter to read... this is what it said...

'Mum and Dad,

As you are now aware, I realised I was different from the other kids. I have had to navigate through the world with your help, encouragement and support. When I became more independent, I was able to navigate more on my own, with occasional assistance.

Loud noises overwhelm me... like strangers shouting, but I'm getting better at coping with that. Bright lights shine too hard on me... like the sun in Egypt, but I'm slowly getting used to the glare! Crowds scare me... like I am going to be swamped, but little by little I'm gaining confidence with help from you.

Melbourne Secondary College was a time when I didn't socialise. It's not that I have problems socialising and communicating with you, and our family... it's that the other students were not like me. The teachers and integration staff understood me, they helped me through years seven, eight and nine. The other kids I referred to as, 'Strangers from Planet Stranger', I didn't trust them, and they didn't trust me!

Despite all that, I managed to enjoy myself and spent plenty of family time together. Looking up my diagnosis made me more relieved, I can wait till the time is right to let you know that I know! I hope you read this soon, I will be ready to talk about my autism then.

From your loving daughter Cassie!'

"Cassie that was very well-written and heartfelt." said Dad, looking at me proudly

"That certainly describes what you have been through." Mum agreed

"I wrote that letter while I was reading about my diagnosis... remembering all the experiences that went with it."

"I didn't want to show it to you yet... but I'm glad I bought it out when I needed to."

"It was mostly easy to write... then I hid it in a safe place in my room." I added

"Well... you did the right thing... good job for writing to us and explaining how you felt."

"For remembering all those experiences and letting us know in your letter."

"Well done, darling." said Dad.

"When you hugged us in Sydney after your solo concert, our first 'gig' on 'The Bontel Family' tour... that was a big breakthrough for you!"

"You don't mind us hugging or kissing you affectionately now... but like any teenager you get embarrassed in public... especially in front of your new friends!"

"Yes... I think I said something like

"Mum!"

"Dad!"

"You are so embarrassing!"

"Not in front of my friends!"

"Then my new friends would laugh... but I don't mind it now." I said, screwing my face up a bit

"It's okay to be embarrassed when your Mum or Dad kisses you in public... just tell us to stop it!" Mum laughed

"Ok... I will then." I said, relieved

"We have a story to tell you Cassie."

"Dad and I were driving along a Melbourne Bridge… which had a pedestrian path for people to use when crossing the bridge."

"It was 1995, a rainy day and we were driving a 'Holden' with a sunroof."

"I was wearing a yellow dress with a yellow bow in my hair… Dad was wearing a green suit, a green tie and green shoes."

"We noticed a girl of about sixteen who looked just like you standing on the side of the road signalling for us to pull over."

"We pulled over and asked where she was going."

"The girl said… 'I have two destinations that I need to go to… one of them is to the music store to pick up my guitar that I need for a concert."

"Hop in… we'll take you there."

She got in to our car and we drove to 'Tune Stop'… we noticed she was wearing a shiny diamond blue dress… with a blue headband on her head and shiny diamond blue shoes… we also noticed she was wearing a blue diamond ring on her left finger… she had long black hair that reached down to her shoulders.

"We've never seen her before… but somehow I can tell she is a celebrity!" Dad said

"She is a definitely a celebrity… but I don't know who she is." Mum added

"How can we find out her identity?"

We dropped the girl off at the music store, while she was inside, we noticed she had dropped a card out of her bag on the back seat. It was an identity card, as well as her name it said that she was autistic. She came back to the car carrying a guitar inside a guitar case in her right hand, we put the I.D. card back in her bag as she climbed in the car.

I asked her where she needed to go next.

"What's the second destination you want to go to?"

She told us an address that Dad and I had never heard of, she gave us directions and when we got to the destination there were two roads ahead. One way was to Henry Street, which we knew and loved, the other was unknown. A choice had to be made. Which road would she choose? It was a crossroads in her life! After a long hard think, she decided to take our road, and we took her in."

"That's an excellent story Mum."

"That sixteen-year-old autistic girl in the story is me… and the couple in the story is you and Dad!"

"It's a great example of a crossroads situation!" I said, smiling

"Cassie… Dad and I… are going to write a book about you!" Mum said

"Um… ok."

"Why would you want to write a book about me?" I asked, puzzled

"We want to raise awareness of autism through this book… you will be the 'voice' of the book." Dad explained

"That would be great!"

"What is going in this book… if it's about me?" I asked, curiously

"Your life… funny moments… worst moments… achievements… interests… and music…will be among the things in there!"

"Dad and I will try make this book as positive as we can… not too much negativity." Mum added

"That's good."

"Can I write my comments in there?"

"It can be about my experiences and achievements… as well as advice." I said

"Of course, you can, Cassie."

"It would be excellent if we had your input!" Dad said, enthusiastically

"I will certainly put my contribution in there."

"Are you sure you two won't embarrass me?" I said, cautiously

"Course we won't, Cassie."

"We wouldn't do anything like that!" said Mum

"We won't put anything in the book to embarrass you darling." Dad agreed

"That's fine then." I replied, with a wink

"I'm glad I'm 'myself'…despite being 'different' from other people… I always love you both." I told them happily

"That's a nice thing for you to say Cassie."

"Come here and give me a big hug." said Mum, reaching out her arms

I walked up to Mum, reached my arms out, put them around her waist and hugged her hard!

"Whoa Cassie!"

"That's the biggest hug you have given me, since Sydney!" said Mum, surprised

I also kissed Mum, and hugged Dad too.

"Whoa!"

"That's some hug Cassie."

"I didn't expect that!" he said, amazed

"I know Dad."

"I didn't know my own strength!"

"We're getting used to it though." he smiled, happily

"Now let's get to that food!" I added hungrily

Mum and Dad both laughed out loud together.

## Chapter Twenty-Five
## Winton & Mt Isa

The next morning after we had finished our breakfast, we made plans for our next destination. We intend to drive to Winton next, stopping at the Australian Age of Dinosaurs Museum on the way, as it's twenty-four kilometres outside of Winton on the road from Longreach.

"Cassie we're out of drinks... except water."
"What would you like?" asks Dad.
"I'll have a VB thanks Dad... I'm not driving." I said, mischievously
We all laughed together.
"Just kidding!"
"I got you going though... didn't I?" I laughed
"You got us laughing all right." chuckled Mum
"You can get your learners permit at sixteen years old these days." said Dad
"Can you really get your learners licence at sixteen?" I asked
"Yes darling... really." said Mum
"We can learn all about dinosaurs soon at the Australian Age of Dinosaurs Museum."
"Won't that be fun?" Mum asked
"I used to have a fear of dinosaurs, years ago, even kids playing like a dinosaur would make me meltdown, but I'm very keen to learn about them now."
"I remember lots about them too."
We arrived one hour and a half later at the Australian Age of Dinosaurs Museum, where there were plenty of dinosaurs to learn about... including an Australovenator (Banjo) and a Diamantinasuarus (Matilda). What unusual names for dinosaurs... but very Australian!
We saw the fossil preparation laboratory... the collection room... and the dinosaur canyon tour... which took us three and a half hours altogether.
When we were finished, we drove the final half hour in to Winton just in time for lunch and to find some accommodation for a couple of nights.
"We can stay at the Matilda Country Tourist Park." I said, checking it out on my phone
"Once we have booked in at the tourist park for a couple of nights... let's go to the Balamara Bakery in the main street and get our lunch." I added
We picked up some sandwiches and scrolls at the bakery to take with us.
We chose our camping site and set up the tents in the tourist park.
"Let's go and check out Winton's famous musical fence... it sounds like fun." said Mum
"There are several things to discover here." said Dad

"Winton is the home of 'Waltzing Matilda' and QANTAS."
We found the location of the fence and decided to give it a try!
"This musical fence seems well tuned… I reckon I could play a couple of melodies on it."
"This drum kit looks good to play on too… it's well set up." added Mum
"Either of those will suit me fine."
"There are a few songs I can try." Dad smiled
"Those were two good tunes you played there Cassie." commented Mum, a short time later
"Thanks Mum… it's a very melodic fence!" I laughed
Then Mum tried the musical fence and made some great sounds.
"Those were two groovy tunes… Mumma." I said
Mum spluttered with laughter.
"I'm a groovy Mumma… am I?"
"Funny you… Cassie." laughed Mum
Dad was the last one to play the musical fence and he also produced a couple of fine tunes.
"That's awesome… 'Daddio'! I said, giggling
"Daddy - Who?"
"Very funny Cassie." said Dad, grinning
Mum and I looked at each other and burst out laughing again!
We made our way over to the drums… as Mum is the drummer… she will definitely want to try these out!
"I'll be able to make some fine beats on these drums… they are very well made." Mum said
"We'll film you playing them, it will make good footage to show our family and friends." I said
Mum went ballistic on the drums and Dad and I filmed her on our iPhones! We got some great footage. Dad uploaded it to his to Facebook page and I uploaded mine to Jenna's iPhone…that way she can show it to Caroline, Andrew and our special centre classmates! I hope they like it.
"You've still got it Mum!"
"You're drumming is smashing it… even on tin drums." I said, admiringly
"Thanks Cassie, I'm smashing my heart out today!" said Mum, happily… she's always happy when she's playing drums!
Dad and I both tried the drums and uploaded each other's footage to Mum and Dad's Facebook page and also to Melinda's iPhone.
"I hope all our family and friends love this drumming footage."
"We've smashed some great tunes out and hopefully it will inspire them to try some drumming… or even visit Winton sometime." I said
"It was great fun to make music on that fence."
Later, back at our campsite getting the BBQ ready for dinner, we had a visit from two fellow campers that strolled over to our campsite, they had seen me on a news item earlier that day and recognised me.
"Cassie Bontel!"
"How nice to see you in Winton." said the female camper
"Hello." I replied
"The 'Bontel Family 'band is fun."
"We love listening to the band." added the male camper
"Why thank you for the lovely compliment." I said
"You're very beautiful and a sweet singer… your voice is lovely." the young girl said

"Thank you."
"That's very nice of you." I replied
"Would you sign our autograph books?" they ask
"Yes, of course I will."
"I would be glad to sign them for you."
Mum, Dad and I, signed.
"Would you like some of our BBQ dinner?"
"There's plenty to share." I offered
"No thank you... we have plenty of food back at our campsite... but thank you for asking."
"OK." I said, waving goodbye to them
Later that evening... I got a glint in my eye and decide to plan another prank on Mum and Dad. I got a rubber mouse... crept into their tent and hid the mouse amongst their bedsheets...I went back to my tent smothering a giggle.
Fifteen minutes later...
"Holy.... bleep!" shouts Mum
"S...t... bleep!)" shouts Dad
I allowed myself a straight out laugh this time! Nice one Cassie, I congratulated myself.
"Whoever put that rubber mouse in our bed is going to be in big trouble in the morning!" said Mum, in her loud and cranky voice
Mum, Dad and I, were having breakfast... eating little packets of cereal with strawberries on top.
"Did you two have a good sleep?" I asked, craftily
"We eventually did!"
"SOMEONE... put a rubber mouse in our bed last night and gave us a fright."
"You wouldn't happen to know anything about that... would YOU?" said Mum, glaring at me
"Umm...err...maybe...." I muttered, with my head looking at the ground
"I knew it!" said Mum, triumphantly
"I'm sorry Mum and Dad... but it was very funny." I sniggered
"Maybe for you, young lady... but your Mother nearly had a heart attack when her toes touched it in the bed." said Dad, trying to sound cross, but I could see the twinkle in his eyes as he tried to keep a straight face
"All I can say Cassie... is payback will be sweet!" said Mum, in a huffy voice
Uh oh, looks like Mum is on the warpath! I'm going to need to keep my wits about me.
Today, we have decided to drive back out of Winton to explore an attraction called the 'Jump-Up', which is on top of a huge mesa plateau. It's going to be a wicked place to explore! As we walk through huge rocky outcrops, cliffs and canyons, I am enthralled at all the awesome vistas... Mum and Dad are having a great time too.
"This is totally wicked!"
"The huge mesa plateau is awesome to see... the Austral and the Diamantina were amazing dinosaurs to learn about yesterday."
"It's hard work walking these trails... especially when the weather is starting to warm up... but I don't mind at all." I said
"That's good Cassie... Mum and I, are enjoying it too."
"We've never seen a plateau quite like this before... it's a beauty of a sight." Mum said
"The cliffs and canyons are excellent... it feels like we are nearly on top of Australia!" said Dad

We spent the day hiking the trails and taking pictures of the wonderful vistas. Late in the afternoon we drove back to the tourist park to make our evening meal... then off to bed as we plan on making an early start the next day.

We booked ahead to stay at the Blue Heeler Hotel in Kynuna...we planned to explore the Combo Waterhole from there... as camping is prohibited in the Combo Waterhole Conservation Park. It took us two hours to get to Kynuna and check into our accommodation at the Blue Heeler Hotel. We checked the road conditions with the Queensland Parks and Wildlife department and drove out to the waterhole in our four wheeled drive vehicle.

Some people believe that Combo Waterhole is the setting for the 'Waltzing Matilda' story... or part of the inspiration that comes from it.

In 1895, a bushman named Andrew Barton (Banjo) Patterson visited Combo Waterhole while he was staying at Dagworth Station. He had the inspiration to write the words that would later become one of Australia's most famous songs of the bush.

A song which would capture the spirit of Australia... that song came to be known as "Waltzing Matilda!"

"Wow!"

"Look at all these unique flagstone overshots!"

"Cobb & Co serviced this area and the flagstones helped them on their way." I said, excitedly

"They certainly did Cassie!"

"They were a famous coach company back in the olden days...most Australians still remember the name... through family history." said Dad

"We all remember learning about it in history classes at school...Dad and I visited a museum that featured a coach during one of our world tours... it was very interesting to learn about our cultural heritage." Mum agreed

I looked around for some shady picnicking spots that we might use as we got our picnic basket ready and I found a nice one. The sun was shining brightly and the waterhole was sparkling in the sun as we ate our picnic.

"What a nice spot this is."

"The Combo Waterhole is lovely to sit by and see the beautiful trees all around you as you eat and talk together."

"You can soak up all of the beautiful nature around... relax and watch the clouds drifting by." I said

"Another memorable place." said Dad, happily

"You and Mum visited this waterhole previously in 1992... didn't you?" I asked

"That's right, Cassie."

"Dad, Olivia, Rebecca and I, came to the special waterhole during our trip."

"We spent a week in the area."

"We came away with special memories of our time here." Mum remembered

"Those were great times for you two back then and now we are having great times right now!" I said, happily

We couldn't leave the waterhole without taking a few photos each... so we did... and then drove back to Kynuna.

"I recall another trip back in 1991." Mum reflected

"We were camping at the Plantation camping ground, near Halls Gap."

"We took our vehicles over the unsealed Mt Zero Road to get there, then we set up our tents... Olivia, Rebecca and I in one tent... and Daniel in the other."

"One day we walked to the Northern Grampians range... where we saw Aboriginal rock art... it was so fascinating to learn about the history behind it."

"Another day... we drove to Heatherlie Quarry and learnt about the stone that was mined there and used for many important buildings that became part of Melbourne... like Parliament House... and the State Library."

"We also took a bushwalk next to Mount Difficult and admired the spring flowers... colourful wild flowers... as well as going to the 'Wartook' gardens."

"In between all our activities... we had picnics...played card games... and also read our books."

"On the fifth day... Dad crept into our tent and put a rubber mouse in there."

"He got into his sleeping bag to wait for the commotion to start!"

"When we noticed the mouse... we shrieked with fright and spilled our drinks... later that night we got him back by placing a rubber snake in his tent!"

"When he saw what he thought was a live snake... he dropped a 'swear bomb' in fright... and we all ran to our tents laughing!" giggled Mum, at the recollection

Rebecca said...

"You put that rubber mouse in our tent, didn't you?"

Dad laughed.

"Nope." he said

"We think you did... you're tidying our tent up for that prank!" we said to him

He laughed even harder for a few minutes...then he decided to tidy our tents up... whilst we just sat in our chairs drinking tea and watched him do all the hard work.

"That's a funny story Mum." I said

"I thought I got away with it but my chuckles got me busted!"

"It was a fair cop." said Dad, smiling

We arrived back at the hotel... after we had cleaned up in our rooms... we had a pub meal that evening and packed up ready to leave in the morning.

McKinlay is the next stop on our journey. Although only an hour or so down the road, we have decided to drop into the local pub at McKinlay for a pub lunch on the way to Mt Isa...it is famous for being the 'pub in the movie... 'Crocodile Dundee'! The name of the pub is 'Walkabout Creek Hotel'.

The next morning after a leisurely breakfast... we packed the car and got on the road to McKinlay... which has a population of one hundred and seventy-eight!

We arrived in McKinlay at about eleven in the morning and went to scope out the now famous Walkabout Creek Hotel. We took plenty of photographs of the interior and the exterior as well... we want to send them to our friends and family as they are fans of the Crocodile Dundee movies... too.

After having a pub lunch, we drove to our next destination Mt Isa... which was two and a half hours away... we arrived at about four thirty in the afternoon. We booked in to the Isa Hotel in Miles Street, Mt Isa.

Once we had put our belongings in our rooms, we decided to check out the shopping facilities nearby. We went to the Mt Isa Village to explore the surroundings and pick up some more supplies for our journey.

After a good night's sleep Mum and I woke up early the next morning... it's Father's Day today!

We are planning an activity for Dad he will love it I am sure of that! I can't wait to see the look on Dad's face when we tell him what we have arranged!

"Cassie come outside with me for a moment." said Mum

I followed Mum outside, she quietly closed the door and whispered in my ear.

"Father's Day today... I know Dad will love his gifts... I have arranged a little surprise activity and a lovely steak dinner... for later in the day." Mum whispered

"That will be great Mum!" I replied

"It will be a special treat for Dad... he loves steak!" I whispered back

"He sure does!" Mum agreed

"Now let's wake him up."

Mum and I, went back to our hotel room and woke up Dad.

"Happy Father's Dad!" I beamed

"Thanks Cassie." Dad replied, sleepily

"Happy Father's Day dear." said Mum, grinning

"Thanks, dear." Dad returned her grin

"What do we have here?" asked Dad

"That's my gift for you Dad." I said, smiling

"I know you're going to love it." I said in anticipation

Dad opened his gift... it was....

"Trevor Marmalade's Footy Show Jokes."

"Great!" said Dad, enthusiastically

"I loved watching 'The Footy Show' with Trevor as the comedian behind the bar." he added

"Thanks Cassie."

"I will enjoy reading the comments he made about the seven series!"

"Give me a kiss." said Dad

"I just knew you would love it Dad." I said, giving him a kiss

"Daniel dear... here is a Father's Day gift from me too." said Mum, handing Dad a package

Dad opened Mum's gift... it was...

"A Richmond Tigers soft drink/stubby holder!"

"Beauty!" said Dad, looking very pleased

"I'll enjoy the next Richmond game with my drink in this 'stylish' holder... thanks dear!" said Dad, giving Mum a kiss

"Dad we've got something planned for you today... we'll take you to it." I teased

"Can I guess what it is?" asked Dad

"Nope." I said, wagging my finger at him

"After lunch we can go there."

"Later today... you and I will wish our Dads' Happy Father's Day on skype... we'll buy them Father's Day gifts later... to give to them on our return from the road trip." Mum said

"Let's have breakfast in the 'Mount Isa breakfast restaurant'...we'll order a nice Father's Day breakfast for you Dad." I said, laughing

When breakfast was over, Mum and I took Dad to his surprise Father's Day location. We drove out to Lake Julius... which was constructed in 1976... Julius Dam was made for irrigation and town water storage purposes...from its construction Lake Julius was formed. The Leichhardt River and Paroo Creek are located below it... seventy kilometres north east of Mount Isa.

"Dad these are the activities for today... viewing Lake Julius and later visiting the Riversleigh Fossil Centre." I said

"Wonderful!"

"Look at the structure of that dam!"

"I've seen plenty of man-made dams overseas... this one can rival them!" said Dad, impressed

"Let's enjoy the view."

We studied the lake... we were lucky to have good weather.

"This reminds me of a beautiful spring with your Dad in 1989... we were running errands down the street... Dad had an extra something to do."

"He went into a perfumery shop and came out with some lavender perfume for me."

"I was so happy to receive such a nice spring present... that I sprayed a little bit of it and I kissed him on his cheek!"

That was the year before we got married... it was one of those romantic moments that we 'ladies' like to remember." said Mum, with a dreamy look on her face

"That's a lovely story Mum."

"Do you think I could try one of your perfumes soon... Mum?" I said, hopefully

"I think so... soon I'll get them out and you can choose one to try." said Mum, smiling

We continued looking at Julius Lake for a while... watching the water gushing out of the archways and all the way down to the body of water. It was so enchanting to see the water wall... I could watch it for hours.

After viewing the lake and water constructions, we drove back to the hotel for lunch and to skype the Dads' for Father's Day. First Mum skyped her Dad Darren, to wish him a Happy Father's Day.

"Hi Dad... Happy Father's Day!"

"Thanks darling... how are you doing today?"

"I'm good thanks Dad."

"We're having a great time in Mount Isa... we took Daniel to view Lake Julius where we had a lovely time."

"What presents did he receive for Father's Day?"

"Trevor Marmalade's Footy Show Jokes' from Cassie, and a Richmond soft drink/stubby holder from me... he will enjoy watching Richmond games with that in his hand."

"He'll enjoy those gifts... he's always proud to wear the yellow and black of Richmond!"

"Cassie and I are also planning a steak dinner for him later this evening... we know how much he loves his steak!"

"Dad... we are also about to take Daniel to the Riversleigh Fossil Centre this afternoon."

"We will learn about the prehistoric habits of outback Australia and see fossils and dioramas."

"Hope you have a fun time learning there."

"We will!"

"Happy Father's Day... I'm buying a late Father's Day gift for you during our road trip."

"Thanks darling... I can't wait to see what I get"

"Bye Dad."

"Grandad is having a good fathers' day... isn't he Mum?"

"It was good to skype him and see his face on Father's Day!"

"Later... we can buy him a gift... while we are still in Mount Isa." Mum added

The Riversleigh Fossil Centre was heaps of fun to visit, it was exciting, scientific and interesting to see the display of fossils which were fascinating... it showed us accurately what the remains of the ancient world looked like. We took a guided tour... we saw how the fossilized bones of the extinct creatures were formed in the limestone layers.

"Dad... all this looking at bones has made me hungry!"

"I think 'Red Earth' would be a very good place to have our steak dinner!" I said, grinning at Dad

"They will have the nicest steak you could ever eat... with several different sauces to choose from... to drizzle over your juicy steak!" I said, winding Dad up

"Stop it Cassie... you are making my mouth water." said Dad, licking his lips at the thought

"Mum and I guarantee it will be the best steak meal you have ever eaten!" I said, grinning

"I can't wait to see what steaks they have!" said Dad, 'champing' at the bit

"Hold that thought dear... you need to skype your Dad first." said Mum, smiling

Back at our hotel... we dressed for dinner and Dad set up his skype connection on the Internet.

"Hello, Dad."

"Happy Father's Day!"

"Are you having a good Father's Day?"

"Thanks son... I am!"

"Were you spoilt rotten?"

"I'm about to be...Mikayla and Cassie are taking me to 'Red Earth' steakhouse in Mount Isa for dinner... so I can enjoy a big juicy steak topped with any sauce I choose!"

"Mmm... that sounds tasty!"

"When I first put a steak in front of you at six years old... I knew you would always love it...that's why you usually choose steak when we go out to a restaurant... or at a family BBQ!"

"Mikayla knows how much I love steak... every time I order she says... you do love your steak dear...usually accompanied by a big grin."

"What can I say... I'm a lucky man Dad!"

"We've been to the Riversleigh Fossil Centre in Mt Isa... it was amazing to learn all about the fossils and see the bones."

"You had a fun time then!"

"We all did!"

"Seeing all those bones gave Cassie an appetite...she's starving!"

Everybody laughed at that comment!

"Anyway... we'll be off to 'Red Earth' soon."

"I'll buy a Father's Day gift for you during our road trip."

"You do that son... I'll be keen to see what it is!"

"Bye Dad."

"Bye Daniel."

"I'm sure Grandad is having a good Father's Day too." I said, happily

"He certainly is!"

We arrived at Red Earth at six...where we were shown to the table that Mum and I had booked earlier. We ordered our meals, then chose our drinks.

When Dad's steak arrived... he was stoked!

"Wow!"

"That's a huge T-bone... it's going taste delicious!" said Dad, with his eyes wide

"You can choose a sauce for extra flavour." Mum suggested

"With veggies on the side... you have an excellent Father's Day meal Dad... enjoy!" I said triumphantly, as if I was the one who had prepared and cooked the magnificent meal

I winked at Dad but he was too busy 'tucking' in!

After he had finished the meal Dad made a comment.

"Well that was a delicious starter...what's for dinner?" he said, innocently

"What's for dinner!!!" I covered my face with my hands and muttered under my breath with embarrassment
"Behave yourself Dad!" I said, putting my finger to my lips and giving him the 'serious' look
Mum laughed out loud at Dad's joke and I groaned in embarrassment again.
"Don't encourage him Mum!" I implored, as I rolled my eyes to the ceiling
Mum just laughed even harder.
Mount Isa is a good place to stay... we're going to visit the Northern Territory next.
After our fabulous feed, we made our way back to the hotel and turned in for the night.
Tomorrow we can plan the next stage of our journey into the Northern Territory!

# Chapter Twenty-Six
## 'Freddie', 'Rob' & Redbank Gorge

"Alice Springs is a good place to start in the Northern Territory... I would love to see the reptiles there." I said

Well it is almost fifteen and a half hours driving time to get us from Mt Isa to Alice Springs!" Dad replied

"There is only one place that we can stop on the way too...the Dangi Pub." he added

"That means we need to get our petrol... water... and food supplies... in Mt Isa... before we leave this morning."

We stock up the four wheeled drive and head on the road to Urandangi... it's a hot dusty drive and we arrive five and a half hours later. We book in to the Dangi pub for one night... intending to leave early in the morning... before the sun gets too hot. We have twice as far to travel tomorrow and won't arrive in Alice Springs until late afternoon.

We are going to camp in the West MacDonnell National Park... which is about ten minutes driving distance from Alice Springs. On our long drive the next day... we discuss the different places we may go... when we eventually get to Alice Springs.

"There is Alice Springs Desert Park, where we can explore the environment and learn about the flora and the wildlife there." suggested Dad

"There's also the Alice Springs Reptile Centre... where we can get up close to a variety of snakes... lizards... and even a salt water crocodile!"

"I won't be going near the crocodile though!"

"It's a bit creepy." said Mum, screwing up her face

At West MacDonnell National Park... we can camp... explore the canyons... and learn about history and nature too." I said, eagerly

"We will be camping there... Cassie!" said Dad

"Mum and I went camping there a couple of times...once with Olivia and Rebecca... and Kate... Nicole... Adam... and Amelia... have been camping there a few times too."

"I'm sure you will enjoy it for your very first time there." said Dad

"I sure will Dad!" I said, happily

"I've seen photos of it online... I will have plenty of fun in that national park!" I smiled

We finally arrived at the national park and set up our campsite for the night... we were tired and ready for bed... by the time we finished and fell into our sleeping bags...we went straight to sleep.

We woke refreshed... bright and early the next morning we took a trip into Alice Springs to pick up some breakfast supplies. As Mum, Dad and I, walk out of the general store we spot a breakfast show 'Rise and

Shine' weatherperson... who also spots us! I recognize his badge from the breakfast show we watch every morning... he's from Melbourne. I think we are going to be on TV!

"Bontel Family... hello... I thought I recognized you."

"Your music is doing so well around Australia." he commented

Mum and Dad recognized him too... as Oliver Dermot... they were surprised to see him.

"Oliver!"

"We remember meeting you on 'Rise and Shine'... after we received our medals in Canberra."

"We were honoured to be interviewed on the show...very proud to present our medals to the Australian public." said Mum

"We have a family activity organised on 'Live TV'... if you would like to take part this morning?" Oliver asked

"It will take place after the nine o'clock weather report... are you willing?" he added

"Yes... we certainly are."

"Bring it on!" I said

"Good... then meet me at the Alice Springs Reptile Centre at nine."

"No time to go back to camp and cook breakfast now!" said Mum

As we drove to the Alice Springs Reptile Centre... where Oliver... a camera man... and several other people met us... I thought... *I don't know what the activity is...we'll do it together... or solo... whatever it is!*

"Hello everyone."

"Here is your activity!"

"You will each be given a frog to hold... for a few minutes."

"If you have a fear of frogs...you must do your best to try and overcome it."

"When 'Rise and Shine' cross live to me... I shall explain to the audience watching at home... what is happening."

"Then I will cross back to the weather report." Oliver instructed us

"OK." we answered

"Do any of you have a fear of frogs?" asked Oliver.

Mum and I put our hands up.

"We both do." said Mum and I together

"I have a fear of frogs since one landed on my head when I was three... after I took it outside... when Mum wouldn't allow it in the house."

"Ugly creatures... Ew!" said Mum

"When I was three... a frog jumped into my bucket in the backyard whilst I was playing...it frightened me and since then I have had a fear of frogs!"

"That's why I refused to do biology in my Melbourne Secondary College years!"

"Eurgh!" I said, disgustedly

"I'll do my best to go gently with your frog handling." Oliver smiled, at our 'screwed up' faces

"Bob is finishing up his sports report... I'm ready to go with the frog taming segment... or should that be Bontel taming? Oliver grinned and winked at us

"Are you ready?" asked Oliver

"Yes Oliver." said Dad, grinning

"Yes." said Mum and I, dubiously

Co- host Adrian opened the airwaves...

"Now, let's cross 'live' to Alice Springs where Oliver is about to do some crazy frog bonding... with none other than... 'The Bontel Family'!"

"What's happening over there Oliver?"

"Well Adrian... I'm planning to 'show off' some of our wonderful reptiles at the Alice Springs Reptile Park... to Daniel... Mikayla... and Cassie Bontel... those musical sensations from the Bontel Family Band!" Oliver replied, in his best 'commentator' voice

"To begin... I'm helping Mikayla and Cassie... to overcome their fear of frogs... with...wait for it... a bonding session!" Oliver grinned down the barrel of the lead camera as he spoke

"Look out girls... here come the frogs... after our local weather forecast!" Oliver looked our way

"That's it for today's weather forecast..." Oliver finished, and our fate was sealed

"Right Mikayla... you are first cab off the rank... so to speak." Mum didn't look too impressed with that dubious honour

"Are you ready to meet 'Freddie'... Mikayla!?" Oliver said like a 'maniacal' gameshow host

"Errr... I guess so." said Mum, with very little enthusiasm

"Great!" smiled Oliver to the camera

"Vincent... bring out Freddie will you please?"

Vincent came over with Freddie and handed him to Oliver. He looked cute and creepy all at the same time. Let's hope I don't freak out on Live National TV!

"Thanks...Vincent." said Mum, to tell you the truth... she didn't sound very thankful

"Mikayla take your time to hold him and don't be scared."

Oliver placed Freddie in Mum's hands... she looks nervous and faintly horrified to see what she is holding.

"That's great Mikayla... you did really well!"

"Thanks Oliver." what Mum really meant, was... thank goodness it's Cassie's turn and I don't have to hold this frog any longer

"Now Cassie it's your turn."

I look at Freddie and Freddie looks at me... he seems cool but at the same time I find him scary and creepy too! My internal monologue in my head is saying... *'Eurgh, I don't want to hold him in case he might jump on me and freak me out on live TV'!*

When Oliver placed Freddie into my hands... I stiffened up a little bit... somehow, I managed to remain calm until the time was up. I don't know how I did it...but I did!

"Well done Cassie."

"You both did great!"

"Let's hear a big cheer for Cassie and Mikayla!"

Whilst Oliver is busy planning his next event... Mum and I whisper... then sneak up behind him... we gently place Freddie down the back of Oliver's shirt... which makes him hop around like a 'frog' trying to get Freddie out! Mum, Dad and I dash out laughing... whilst everyone in the vicinity are hooting too! We jump into our car and drive back to the campsite.

"Ha, ha that was hilarious!"

"Putting a frog down Oliver's shirt." laughs Mum

"That was our first ever live TV prank!" I laughed

"I bet the 'Rise and Shine' viewers were all laughing hysterically at home... too!"

"Oliver will be very wary around you two... from now on." chuckles Dad

The West MacDonnell National Park was spectacular with its majestic beauty and scenic gorges. We learnt that the 'Tjoritja' people are the traditional owners of this park and they continue their cultural practices... the local Arrernte Aboriginal culture, which has a highly significant connection to the land there. We need to respect Aboriginal culture and land like the park... we have to make sure we care for the land as they have always done.

Mum, Dad and I, looked over the map to find the designated camping areas. After we went to the Visitor Information Centre and listened to the introduction... we made our way around the sites... we decided to start at Simpson's Gap... the site of the 'Arrernte' people.

There was also Ormiston Gorge. We saw many vegetation areas within Simpsons Gap, they were very interesting to see.

"These large stands of Mulga are wicked!"

"The 'Arrernte' are protective of them... so that they will be here for many generations of visitors to see." I commented

"You are always keen to learn about Australia's history." said Mum, approvingly

"Over the next few days we may learn more about the surprises and sites here at West MacDonnell."

"Who knows what hidden gems we may discover?" said Dad, philosophically

We journeyed to the towering cliffs of the Simpsons Range...where I can see the Simpson Gap for miles around! There are gorges everywhere I look... I can even see the permanent waterhole from a distance!

I'm really enjoying this moment with Mum and Dad. I could take a couple of photos, but I don't want to do that just yet... I'll savour the moment for now.

"This permanent waterhole is awesome!"

"It's a part of the land... it looks so special."

"We can't swim in there... but we can learn all about it." I added

"It's a great area of the National Park." said Mum

We finally got around to taking a couple of photos and then headed back to our campsite, we chatted about the day's views whilst we ate our meal.

"Simpsons Gap was a wicked area to explore... I loved the towering cliffs!"

"This may be one of the best views I have seen of Australia so far." I said

"The permanent waterhole was excellent to see, it was crystal clear, similar to the oceans at the beach."

"We may choose to swim somewhere like the Ellery Creek Big Hole... Ormiston Gorge... or the Glen Helen Gorge... as the weather is getting hot." said Mum

"I liked the gorges!"

"We explored most of them and saw some Aboriginal art on the cave walls... there is a little story behind each one of the drawings."

"It's only our first night here... but we have learnt lots about Simpsons Gap." Dad said

"We've all had a brilliant day... we need a shower after a long hot day like today."

I'm 'bagging' the first one!" I crowed

"Cassie you can have the first one...only don't waste the water!"

"The other campers need some too!" said Dad

"Ok Dad I won't waste the water." I replied

We all had our showers and walked back up to our campsite. We looked over the photos we had taken during the day... we read our Kindle Books and wound down for sleep... because it's going to be a lot hotter tomorrow!

Later that night, Mum and Dad crept out of their tent and walked towards mine with a rubber snake in tow! They were hoping to get me back for the rubber mouse prank!

"Dan... Cassie will get a fright when she sees this snake we are going to put in her tent"

"This will be priceless." sniggered Mum

"It will be priceless… Kayla!"

"The rubber mouse gave us a fright… so let's get even with the rubber snake." chuckled Dad

They shushed each other silently so as not to wake me. They quietly opened my tent and Mum gently put the rubber snake near my right hand and crept out of the tent… Dad closed the flap… but when they turned around…

"Guess who?" I said, cheekily

"Holy… bleep!" shrieks Mum, falling over

"Arrgh…bleep!" shrieks Dad, falling over Mum

"Thought you could put a rubber snake in my tent and get away with it…did you?"

"Not a chance!" I laughed

"But… we thought you were in your tent!"

"How can you be in two places… at one time?" asks Dad, flabbergasted

"I bought a mannequin… and I put it in my sleeping bag."

"The decoy worked out great… didn't it." I grinned

"Yes… we thought it was you!"

"Where were you the entire time?" asked Mum, in amazement

"I was in our car watching you… and when you went into my tent… I hopped out and walked up behind you… waiting for you two to come out!" I said, grinning from ear to ear

"You nearly gave us both a heart attack… Cassie!"

"You foiled our prank… yet again." said Mum, crestfallen

"Indeed… I did!"

"Mum… would you like to touch the snake?"

"His name is Rob." I said, dangling the rubber snake under her nose

"Um… no thanks."

"I'd better get back to sleep." said Mum, running back to her tent quick smart!

"Okay."

"Dad… would you like to touch Rob?" I asked

"I'll pass on that one!"

I've got some sleep to catch up on too." said Dad, also beating a hasty retreat back to the tent.

"That's fine."

"He'll be safe with me" I giggled

The next morning… we have a couple of water bottles each… some bananas… and a box of BBQ shapes… so we are ready for the trek!

We're at Redbank Gorge and it's just amazing! It's taller than the three of us combined and there are great formations and colours all over the gorge! We could either walk along the creek bed… then embark on section twelve of the Larapinta Trail… or hire an airbed and float down the glorious sparkly waters of Redbank Gorge.

"Mum!"

"Dad"!

"Why don't we float on the airbeds through Redbank Gorge?"

"I certainly would love to give that a go." I said, excitedly

"Of course, Cassie."

"We've got our bathers underneath our clothes... we'll put our clothes in a plastic bag... give it to a staff member who gives out the airbeds... and we'll be floating down the Redbank Gorge with no trouble at all." said Mum, confidently

"Whilst we are floating... we can look up at the gorge walls and the bright blue sky... appreciate all of nature around us... it will be so relaxing." said Dad, smiling at the idea

We hired three airbeds... put them on the water and gently sat on them... lying back on the lilos... we paddled and floated down the Redbank Gorge.

"It's so relaxing looking up at the sky and floating."

"This is bliss!" I said

"It definitely is!"

"It's one of the most relaxing things we have done... I'm loving it." said Mum, happily

"This is a great view of the Gorge... the sides are so very tall."

"Would you like to take a photo of them Mikayla?" said Dad to Mum

"I certainly would!"

"They will be great to show family and friends." she answered

"I remember when Zoe and her family used to drag you and Dad in a round rubber tube...bouncing up and down behind a hire boat... in Bridgewater Lakes... between Mount Gambier and Portland."

"I thought it looked so scary and terrifying... I preferred to watch... I laughed when you sometimes fell off... I would play in the water area near the reeds."

"We remember those fun days with Zoe and her family... we all gave it a go...we understood you when you didn't want to try it."

"It would have caused a big 'meltdown'... if we had forced you to have a go on it."

"If we choose to go to Bridgewater Lakes and Zoe and her family are there using the boat and round rubber tube... would you like to have a try now Cassie?" asked Mum

"Yes, I think I would... Mum."

"It's time I tried something new...who knows... I might like it!" I answered

"That's the spirit, Cassie."

"Sometime... when we are travelling between Mount Gambier and Portland... I'll give Zoe a call and see if... Peter... Ivy... Nina... and George... can meet us there to have some tube fun." Dad said

We walked along section twelve of the Larapinta Trail and everywhere I looked Redbank Gorge's natural beauty of flora and fauna surrounded us. There were many great things to see, we must respect and appreciate them all, it feels great to be walking amongst nature in this wonderful Australian landscape, which I love.

"We are getting exercise and keeping fit... the sun is shining...we have water to drink in case it gets too hot." I said, contentedly

"We are always happy to see and enjoy the Australian landscape and nature with you, Cassie." Mum nodded

"It's a wonderful country and a great environment to live in." said Dad

"I hope this beautiful environment... the nature... the flowers... the animals... remain for future generations to see and enjoy too." I fervently added

"We hope so too... Cassie!" said Mum and Dad together

"We can take photos to show our family and friends when they come over to our house." said Mum

"This will be another memory... for us to share in the years to come." said Dad

We all took some photos of the flowers as we walked the trail walk… it was well worth the effort and we saw plenty of interesting things along the way. It was around thirty-two degrees…I had a good day and Mum and Dad did too.

After our stay at Alice Springs we packed up all our camping gear and headed for our next destination… which was to be Darwin. The trip to Darwin is another long haul, so we must break it up with some stops on the way. First, we will drive to Tennant Creek and take a quick lunch break there, then drive on to Daly Waters.

We passed the Devils Marbles on the way, to Tennant Creek the next day. We took some photographs and laughed at the funny shapes, which reminded us of other things, besides marbles!!!!

The next day it was time to visit the town of Daly Waters which has a population of only twenty-three people! I didn't know there was a town that had that number of people in it! The most famous feature in Daly Waters is the pub! It was built as a drover's rest in 1893, a mob were always staging for stores and the boys would have a night out before taking on the Murranji leg. It is one of the Northern Territory's oldest buildings. I never knew a building that old existed in Australia!

John McDouall Stuart named this tiny settlement during his third courageous attempt to cross Australia from north to south. He named the springs after Sir Dominick Daly… governor of South Australia, at the time.

We saw the 'Stuart' tree which has a plaque by it saying… 'The explorer John McDouall Stuart is presumed to have carved the initial 'S' on this tree, on the twenty-third of May 1862, during his successful journey from Adelaide to Darwin, erected by the Northern Territory Forces in 1944.

Stuart was a legendary explorer during the early 1860s and it was a delight to discover the plaque, and read about his history.

We saw a few trucks as we drove in to the Hi-Way Inn caravan park. I wonder what they were doing here? I think they were probably taking a break from all their driving, before resuming again the next day.

"Cassie, are you having fun?" asked Mum

"Yes I am."

"I'm learning so much history as I go!"

"I love staying in motels and camping now."

"Sometimes… you don't have to stay in motels or hotels all the time… camping can get you back to nature and you can chat and do family things that you might not do get a chance to do at home."

"It's just the simple things and fun activities that makes memories together!" I said, smiling

"That's so true, Cassie." Dad smiled back at me

"We love the variety of staying in motels and hotels… camping… getting back to nature… trying new activities together… it's all so much fun!"

"We are all very lucky to be undertaking this journey together… seeing our beautiful country… its' amazing flora and fauna…its special places and wonderful scenery… 'Aussie' characters… and truly inspiring stories all along the way." Mum said to me

"I love you two…how you help me when I need help… especially… to overcome barriers and obstacles."

"We've still got a long way to go… let's continue to make more memories and find even more amazing places." I said, happily

We held each other's hands and smiled… we're one proud celeb autistic family… this journey is the… 'trip of a lifetime'… for the three of us!

Next day, I woke up and looked out the window as the sun was rising. It made me think of… *'A warm fire that breaks through the morning chill on a cold winter's day.'*

I took a photo of it... Mum and Dad had woken up by then.

"Morning, Cassie."

"Did you have a good sleep last night?" asked Mum

"Morning, Mum and Dad."

"Yes, I did have a good sleep."

"I watched a lovely sunrise this morning and I took a photo of it to show to you." I said, showing Mum and Dad the photo

"That's a beautiful photo, Cassie."

"I might change the cover photo on my iPhone... it will remind me of all the 'sunrises' we have seen... since coming on our road trip!" said Dad, happily

"I enjoy the sunrises too... it's always a good start to a morning." I said

Even though Daly Waters has only twenty-three people in its population, I am enjoying staying here. I look around, it's very quiet and peaceful at this time. The only sounds I can hear is the inn running and the odd car driving past. I will be sorry to leave this little town I have had lots of fun here.

As we pack up our stuff, I wonder what it would be like driving one of the trucks and making deliveries to the locals in nearby towns, seeing the sights out of the truck window. I would love to have a ride in a truck one day... I recall that Darren once had a truck that he used for his former work at a Melbourne depot... when he was not working as a 'special needs' worker.

He still owns the truck and has just restored it. If I ask him... he might be able to take me for a little ride in it... I'm getting excited at the thought of having a drive in one... I would even love to drive one myself and decorate it too!

"Do you remember that carving on the tree, Cassie?" said Mum

I nodded.

"We'd like to tell you a little love story."

Uh! Oh! I know what's coming next.

"Dad and I went to our favourite field full of trees near Melbourne when were eighteen."

"Dad thought it would be nice to carve our names into the trunk of a tree."

"He took his time to carve a heart shape and his name and mine."

"I thought it was a sweet thing."

"I kissed him on the right cheek and we ran through the nearby fields... we lay down in the grass... laughing and kissing."

"It was a lovely time for lovebirds." said Mum, with that faraway look in her eyes

"Thanks for telling me that story Mum... even if it was a bit mushy for me!"

"Our American counterparts... Mirabelle and Ian Baker did a similar thing in their favourite park in New York."

"Maybe... if we get the chance to see them... they can show us where Ian carved that heart with his and Mirabelle's name." said Dad

"I would love to do a similar thing with a boyfriend...eventually."

"For now, I'll stick to being single... that's fine with me." I said

"That's fine with us too, Cassie." said Mum

"Thanks Mum... I'm happy being single at the moment." I replied

As we were walking down the street and talking a Daly Waters local approached us.

"Hello... are you enjoying Daly Waters?" he asked

"Yes... we are."

"It's the quietest town that we've ever visited... and the locals all know each other."

"I think the same thing every time I reflect on my home town."

"I appreciate the things that we have in a small town...we get by without complicated technology... or traffic jams... like you get in a big city."

"We get by each day helping each other... spending family time together and appreciating what we have."

"We are teaching our daughter those lessons." said Mum, smiling

"I'm glad to hear that."

"Let me tell you something... when you visit small towns and encounter people who are less fortunate than you...it's good to think about what you can do to help them if you can."

"Think about what they are going through...put yourself in their shoes."

"That way you will remind yourself that some people are not so fortunate as others...we can all help each other out at times." said the old man wisely

"My wife and I have been doing that since we were young... Cassie our daughter... is being taught those lessons too."

"It makes us feel appreciated when we are helping out those in need." said Dad

"Great work." he nodded

"Well... I'd better have some breakfast."

"I wish you three well with whatever you are doing." the old man waved goodbye

"Thanks for the advice... we will remember it." I said

Mum and Dad have given me lots of advice over the years... and with help... I have put these pieces of information to good use in certain situations. I feel grateful and lucky to have loving... caring... and understanding parents... despite my autism. I remind myself that they are helping me through life's obstacles... to become independent and brave... so that I can face future challenges... like having children and becoming an autistic Mum in the future.

After our morning walk, we made our way back to the caravan park to rustle up some breakfast, before continuing our journey.

We pass through Mataranka a couple of hours later on our way to Pine Creek.

The writer, Sumner Locke Elliot wrote this passage about Mataranka... 'This lonely strip of barren and seemingly endless sandy waste of ant-hills and stunted trees, thick hot red sand in the winter time, and a sea of mud during the dreaded 'wet'.

It seems a bit harsh to me!

Another couple of hours later and we make it into Pine Creek.

Pine Creek was formed in the late 1500's when one of the linesmen of the Overland Telegraph Line uncovered gold. Even today, Pine Creek needs mining to survive, the surface gold was gone quite quickly, but the Chinese miners entered the area in considerable numbers and kept the goldfields active.

The area is also known for its mango production, the mango season starts in early September. The first box of mangos for the season is sent to Sydney to be auctioned off for charity.

The mango season officially opens when the first box of mangoes from Pine Creek is sold. In one year... the Sydney Children's Hospital received twenty-five thousand dollars... thanks to the mangoes!

One attraction is the 'Old Bakery' built in 1908 at the location of Mt Diamond and originally used as a butcher's shop... it was re-erected in 1915 on its present site.

You might look the ant bed over which dates from 1922...until World War Two it operated as a bakery. These are a few 'quirky' facts I can tell you about Pine Creek... I can recommend a visit to this town if you are interested in history... like me!

The Pine Creek Railway Resort where we are staying has an excellent pool for us to swim in... a great menu for us to check out and nice rooms. It's not quite a holiday resort but I will enjoy staying here for the next two days, to check out their facilities.

"What a nice menu you have." I commented

"Thank you."

"We have an all-day breakfast menu... dinner is from six to eight-thirty in the evening."

Before we get ready to go to dinner... I decide to make a phone call to Melinda to tell her where we are and to send a couple of photos of the Railway Resort to her.

"Hello, Melinda."

"How are you?"

"We're in a small Northern Territory town called Pine Creek."

"I've never been here before, but I'm enjoying it and its history."

"I love my Australian history and I'm learning heaps more than I found online."

"The weather is quite hot, but I'm coping well... I have my cold, water bottle to sip on."

"There are two pool tables... so we might get a game or two in whilst we are here."

"I might even go for a swim in the pool whilst we are staying here that will help me to cool off!"

"I'm about to have dinner at the Pine Creek Hotel Restaurant."

"I'll send you a couple photos so you can see what it looks like."

"Tell Jessica and Jason that I said hello and Zara too!"

"Bye."

# Chapter Twenty-Seven
## Kakadu, mozzies & Darwin

After we have spent a couple of days in Pine Creek, we move on to our next destination...which is Jabiru in the Kakadu National Park.

"Cassie, would you like to see the Nanguluwu Rock site?" asked Mum

"I would love to do that, Mum!"

"The rock art sounds like it would be very interesting to see... I wonder what materials they used to paint them?"

"We may see some unusual birds and wildlife along the way... I might get some good photos!" I said, happily

"We'll need plenty of water... some food... and good sturdy hiking boots... to manage the three kilometres walk!"

"We'll need our cameras too!"

"Is everybody prepared?" said Dad

"Yes... we've got it all." I replied

"Yes dear... we've packed our supplies." said Mum

"Let's get walking then!" said Dad, taking the lead

The track is easy to moderate, so we will be able to take our time to appreciate the many forms of rock art as we pass by each site. I hope we have the right boots for our trek...otherwise we could end up with blisters... they can be painful and itchy!

We certainly don't want that to happen!

We pass through the spinifex, looking at nature all around us as we go. We were told to keep an eye out for a rare species called, the white-throated grass wren. If I see it, I need to be very quiet and takes its photo discreetly, so as not to frighten it.

"Mum, Dad."

"I've seen a native bird or two...I really hope to catch a picture of the white throated grass wren!" I said, eagerly

"If I can get one... I will upload the photo and send it to Zara... she loves birds like I do."

"Cassie... Zara would love that."

"Make sure your iPhone has plenty of power." added Mum

"Yes, Mum."

"I checked before we left... it has plenty of charge." I said

Just then, we heard a tiny noise... we turned to the right to see... a white-throated grass wren! Oh Wow! It is so close! It's time to take that photo.

I quietly take out my iPhone... but it won't load... then I realise that right at this crucial point my iPhone has run out of power! Oh, blast it!

"Aargh!" I hiss through gritted teeth

"My iPhone doesn't have any power left." I whisper

"Well... there goes my photo opportunity." I say, disheartened

"I thought I had enough power... but somehow it just ran out on me."

"How frustrating."

I sighed with disappointment... looking up at the sky

"I know it's frustrating, Cassie."

"Don't be sad."

"I'll take that photo for you... if you like." said Mum, trying to cheer me up putting a hand on my shoulder

"That would be great, Mum."

"It's the first time it has happened."

"It will be great if you would do it for me." I said, gratefully

Mum took the photo and uploaded it on to my iPhone... I sent it through to Zara. She responded a few minutes later with... *'Awesome! I never knew there was this kind of bird in Australia. Thanks, Cassie. You know how much I love birds this one is very rare.'*

We eventually arrived at the cave site and observed the wide range of subjects and styles of rock art. There were hand stencils... dynamic figures in large headdresses carrying spears...boomerangs... and representations of 'Namadi' spirits...with mythical figures like 'Alkajko'... which is a female spirit with four arms.

I became emerged in that world for a moment... doing some dancing which made Mum and Dad laugh... I also made an impression of a mythical figure. It was great fun seeing it all...maybe we will have a chance to bring the rest of our family along... to see it sometime.

"How was it, Cassie?"

"Did you enjoy all those artworks and finding the grass-wren?" asked Dad

"I sure did, Dad!"

"I loved the artworks and I am so happy that Mum managed to get a picture of the grass-wren!"

"It's been another visual history lesson!"

"That's two rare birds I've seen now... I'll be able to start a scrapbook for rare birds!" I said, happily

"That's a good idea, Cassie."

"You can put your photos in it and show them to everyone." Mum agreed

"I'll put my photos in and do a bit of artwork as well."

"My title would be... 'Cassie's Rare Birds Scrapbook: Australia and World Travels'." I said, giggling

"You can show your future children, and generations the photos, it may inspire them to go on travels with you and find more rare species." said Dad

"I could do that, Dad."

"It's been a great day!"

"I'm feeling very hungry... let's go to the 'Jabiru Sports & Social Club'.

"They have regular sport shows on the TV... so we can catch up with the world of sport...whilst we have our meals!" I said, grinning

"It sounds like a great pub!" said Mum, who is always interested in sport

"Let's get ready... dinner will be served in an hour or so." I said

It is still hot... so we decide to sit in the air-conditioned restaurant.

When the waiter served our meals... he turned to me and said.
"You're looking very pretty tonight Miss... your headband compliments your dress."
I could tell he was making a compliment, so I responded with.
"Thanks." whilst blushing
I went to get my drink and the barman chatted to me.
"Hello, Miss."
"Are you enjoying the Jabiru?" asked the barman
"Yes... I am."
"I'm visiting places on the road trip that I'm taking at the moment." I told him
"That's nice."
"I bet you're enjoying the history of this big country." the barman smiled
"Oh Yes."
"I love learning about each towns' history."
"We love our sports at the Jabiru Sports and Social Club... the regular customers rock up in their AFL or cricket garb... to watch their two favourite sports on the big TV's."
"You can hear all the barracking as the matches are being played." said the barman
"I love my AFL and cricket!"
"I'm a big Carlton Blues fan since I was three."
"I have never attended a game before...I will get the chance one day."
"I support the 'Blues' through and through... even when they lose."
"Cricket has been a big part of my life... I'm an excellent all-rounder with the bat and ball and I love watching it during the summer... I would like to attend a game one day... possibly whilst I'm travelling."
"I'm a sporty type of person as well as musical one... you see." I said, laughing
"You're an all-rounder person!"
"I might follow in my Mum and Dad's footsteps and do cricket commentary... like they did years ago in the 1993-1994 South Africa tour of Australia... and the 1994-1995 ashes series in Australia."
"I could even commentate a world cup... the next one is due to be held in Australia and New Zealand...I'll wait and see what happens." I said, grinning
"Carlton are out of the finals this season... having lost to West Coast Eagles in a close one by three points... which was a bit disappointing...still there's always next year."
"Richmond didn't make the finals... finishing twelfth... tough luck to my Dad!" I said
"I heard that Cassie...just wait till next year!" Dad, said hopefully
"Collingwood are due to play Hawthorn and hopefully for my Mum... Collingwood will go through to the Grand Final."
"C'mon the maggies!"
"They can win another premiership like last year!" said Mum, pumped
"That's my family for you."
"We do love our AFL!"
"I'd better go and finish my meal."
"It's a nice club to have a wicked meal and a drink."
"Bye." I said
"Bye... have a good time in Jabiru for the rest of your stay." the barman replied

When we went back to the Mercure Kakadu Crocodile Hotel and entered our room, I felt an itch on my leg. I looked down and was horrified to see that I had been bitten by a mozzie! There was a little red 'mozzie' bite on the front of my leg.

Now most people would say it's only a little mozzie bite and not worry about it!

You would probably say that...but not ME I hate insects!!!

"Mum!"

"Dad!"

"I've got a mozzie bite on my leg and it itches like hell!" I said, yelling

"Oh, dear."

"It's only a small one, Cassie."

"I will put some cream on it to soothe it... sit down on your bed." said Mum

I tried not to scratch the bite because that only makes it worse... I was nearly in tears but I need to stay calm so Mum can apply the cream.

"Don't scratch it Cassie." said Dad

"I'm trying not to, Dad."

It itches like 'billyo' though!" I cried

"Ok Cassie... hold still while I put the cream on." said Mum, reassuringly

Mum puts a bit of cream on her finger and goes to put it on my leg...I recognise the cream and freak out.

"Don't, Mum!"

"Don't let it near me!" I shriek

"It's okay, Cassie." Mum says

"Don't touch that bite, Mum!"

"It might be freezing and it will make it itch more!" I yell

I'm sure people in the nearby rooms can hear my shrieks thinking... *'Who the hell is making that racket!?!'*

"Hold still... Cassie."

"I'm trying to help you!" said Mum

"Cassie... why don't I hold your hand and stroke it... while Mum puts some cream on your bite?" suggests Dad

"That might help, Dad." I said

Dad put his hand over mine and stroked gently... Mum put the cream on the 'mozzie' bite...I could feel the cold sensation of the cream... thanks to Dad I remained calm and relaxed.

"There... all done Cassie." Mum concluded

"Thanks Mum... I was afraid the cream would make the bite itch even more!" I said

"Well... it should soothe the bite and it will heal sometime soon."

"In the meantime, try to resist scratching it!"

"If you can do that... it should go down." said Dad, firmly

"Thanks, Dad."

"It was frightening but you helped me through... even though the cream freaked me out a bit!"

"I won't let a mozzie bite stop me from having fun on our journey." I said

"Exactly, Cassie!"

"We shall continue to have fun together."

"If you get another mozzie bite... you know the procedure now." said Mum

I sure do Mum and Dad." I said, happy it was all over

I gave Mum and Dad a hug and a kiss, thankful for that episode to be forgotten!

Just before bed, I went to take a shower.

"Cassie, this time remember to put your pyjamas on before you come out of the bathroom." Mum reminded me

"Ok Mum, I won't forget this time." I promised

After a few lovely days spent in Kakadu we moved on our way towards Darwin... next stop was Hayes Creek... where the Tjuwaliyn (Douglas) hot springs were nearby.

This attraction is owned by the 'Wagiman' people in co-operation with the Parks and Wildlife Commission... the traditional owners have the right to close it for ceremonial purposes.

"Since it's a sacred site... we can't swim in it and neither can we swim in the springs as they are too hot especially at the point where they flow into the Douglas River."

"I guess we will have to go to one of the pools downstream where the springs have mixed into the cooler part of the Douglas River and relax." I said

"We might as well, Cassie."

"We need to relax after our drive." said Mum

"It will be invigorating and rejuvenating for us...we will be soothed from our traveller's woes." said Dad, going all 'poetical' on us

"After all that driving... it will be good to unwind." he mused

When we arrived, we spent an hour relaxing in the warm soothing waters. It was my first time in a hot spring.

"Cassie... what do you think of the hot springs?" asked Mum

"It feels like I'm relaxing in a nice warm bath before bedtime."

"That's another discovery I have made... it reminds me of the spas I've relaxed in... I certainly needed that." I said, feeling content

"There are many benefits to be had from relaxing in warm water...all those aching muscles rejuvenated... ready for the next adventure!" said Dad, very pleased with himself

"When we are far away from here... or when the weather has turned colder back in Melbourne... I am going to use this place as a visualisation... it will go something like this."

*'I will picture myself walking to the hot springs with a towel wrapped around me... as I get closer to the water, I take off my towel to reveal my swimsuit in my favourite shade of blue... I step into the springs and sit down in the water up to my waist... I feel the water gently soothing my aching muscles...as I relax all the troubles of the day will slip away...'*

"That's a lovely visualization, Cassie."

"We might install a spa at home, so that you can relax after a long day of performing, working out and socialising."

"Do you like that idea?" said Mum

"Yes, that sounds great Mum!"

"That would be so good to have in the house!"

"I can't wait to try it out!" I said, excited at the thought of my own private spa

Just a couple of hours more and we arrived in Darwin.

"This is awesome!"

"Darwin seems like a great city to be in... despite the hot weather." I said

We decided the first thing to do was visit the Museum and Art Gallery of the Northern Territory. There were several collections of specimens making up most of the Museum and Art Gallery... from fishes...to birds...to mammals. Gosh, there are so many... I don't know which ones to look at first!

"These butterflies look so colourful… a few of them have got the same colours as our clothes."

"I've always loved butterflies, I used to chase them around our backyard whenever I saw them, I would laugh and squeal with joy!" I remembered

'Yes, you always loved butterflies… I would film you in the garden to show to our parents."

"They loved watching the films and so did you!" Mum said

"I loved watching you chasing the butterflies… you would get upset when they flew away out of your reach."

I would say…

"Don't cry, sweetie."

"Your butterfly friends will return tomorrow and play with you again." said Dad

"I remember those fun times." I said

"I'll buy you a butterfly bracelet sometime soon." said Mum

"That would be beautiful Mum." I said, happily

Next, we went to take a look at the indigenous art, and Northern Territory rock art.

The indigenous clans painted pictures to represent their life, and to demonstrate their traditional culture and art. We respect their culture which is thousands of years old… I studied the indigenous art carefully… I see several indigenous people sitting around in a semi-circle with two people in white shirts in red ties talking to them.

There are also two vehicles in the background and the whole picture represents the indigenous culture as well. It's the most amazing piece of artwork that I've ever seen.

We also saw some other Australian artists I've painted artwork that is similar. My artwork once won a prize when I was ten years old, I drew the city of Melbourne and added lots of colour to it. I also drew my house with Mum, Dad and myself in front of it, I added positive colours to make a lovely picture. There weren't many people at the art awards, so I was able to collect my award without getting overwhelmed.

"That was a great place to learn about the Northern Territory!"

"The art was fascinating to look at, I loved looking at all the collections!" I added

"We did too, Cassie."

"We had a good time viewing the different collections, the southeast Asian artefacts were similar to those that Dad and I saw, during our music tours of Asia." said Mum

"The sacred objects remind us of the Aborigines ceremonial life, watching Aboriginal films, learning a lot about their culture and stories, gives us great respect for them." Dad said

"They are a big part of Australian history and culture… they have contributed to Australian society in many ways… we must try to trust and understand each other." I said

We decided to go to the Northern Territory Library, where there were many books… magazines… newspapers… and E-books… so many to choose from! I could read them all if I wanted to and had several years to spare!

"Guys… there's one about how the Northern Territory was founded."

"That might be a great read." replied Mum

"There's one about notable Northern Territory people who contributed to towns, sports and social events."

"I definitely would read that one… it looks very interesting to learn about." says Dad

"Mum, Dad, there's a book about the music of the Northern Territory."

"This will be fascinating... to learn about the music of the Northern Territory and the famous musicians they have produced." I said

"I'm glad you three are enjoying the library... is it your first time here?" asked the librarian

"Yes, it is."

"We are bookworms, particularly Dad!"

"He loves a good read"

"I sure do!"

"I have lots of novels at home... particularly 'Jo Nesbo'!" Dad said, enthusiastically

"Well you are sure to have a good time here then!"

"Take your time to look around... there's plenty to learn about the Northern Territory's history here." the librarian said

We had a good look around the library, learning more about the Northern Territory's history along the way. I was amazed at the information and facts that I didn't know, about the only territory in Australia, the same went for Mum and Dad.

Apart from the Melbourne Library, that I regularly visit... this has been the best library in Australia I have seen so far.

'Elsey Station' was the subject of Australian novelist... teacher... and RSL volunteer... Jeannie Gunn (OBE)... in which her account of her autobiographical novel... 'We of the Never-Never'... tells of her experiences on the local station.

There was a film based on the novel, which was released in 1982, and shot here in the Northern Territory, it is a classic Australian novel and film.

We drove back to the hotel for a wind-down, it was a little less hot but the sun was still high in the sky, so I stripped down to my bra and knickers, got out a few photos and sat down on the couch.

I looked at a photo of me, Mum and Dad, in Sydney before we climbed the Sydney Harbour Bridge... with Tom, Sally and Mia. I smiled at the memory of it... it was a great achievement for me... despite getting dizzy and anxious halfway.

I looked at another photograph. This one is me playing in the swimming pool when I was six years old, I was laughing and having fun. It reminded me of home. I lay down on my side on the couch, my head on the pillow with my right hand supporting my head, a couple of tears fell down my face. A tear dropped on the photo and glistened on the surface.

Mum came in, sitting down next to me with a worried look she said...

"Cassie, are you ok?"

"Can you tell me what's made you sad?" she asked

"Mum... I had a look at the photos and I smiled at the Sydney Harbour Bridge photo... which was fun."

"Then I looked at the photo of me swimming in the swimming pool when I was six years old... it reminded me of home and I got homesick all of a sudden." I sniffed

"It's okay Cassie."

"We all get homesick every now and then... even when we are having fun on holiday sometimes."

"Since you were three years old, we started taking you on little holidays in Victoria... such as Ballarat for a few days... by day three you got homesick but over the years you managed a few days... then a week... occasionally you were homesick... but you still managed to enjoy our holidays." Mum added

Mum held out her hand to me, I placed mine in hers.

"I enjoyed those little family holidays...when I got homesick, I was missing my home... but thanks to you two and also with help from therapy and family members... I also enjoyed staying at places like Ballarat... Bendigo... Geelong... and Colac for a few days or a week."

"This road trip I have broken the record... I'm doing so well despite a couple of anxiety filled teary moments...we're halfway there and I thank you for helping me through... I appreciate it!"

"Thank you, Cassie... it's nice to be appreciated." smiled Mum

"We hope you can enjoy the entire road trip with us, sweetie!" said Mum, rubbing my hands gently

Mum's soothing hands calmed me down.

"Thank you, Mum... I feel better." I said, happily

"You are a good role model to me Mum... you inspire me to keep going and never give up!" I said, appreciatively

I sat up and hugged her with tears on my face...they were tears of thankfulness now.

Mum held me quietly, stroking my back softly and whispering.

"Ssh, shh... it's all right Cassie."

"You are doing so well on this road trip...Dad and I, are so proud of you."

"You have done some amazing things... had some funny times... achieved many milestones and made progress... in big strides." said Mum, proudly

Mum gave me a handkerchief and I wiped away my tears and kissed her.

"You're a great Mum!" I said

"You give me confidence to do big things like this... you are the best role model and I look up to you." I said, gratefully

"I always love you...you help me through tough times and so does Dad as well."

"You are always here for me...I can be here for you when you need me too." I told her

I hugged Mum and she hugged me back.

"Thank you for saying such lovely things Cassie."

"I will always be there for you and so will Dad."

Dad came over and hugged me... I hugged him back.

'I will complete this road trip with you both... no matter how long it takes us.' I said

"That's the spirit... you are doing so well Cassie."

"You are becoming more confident and so much braver in trying new experiences."

"I'm very happy for you."

"This road trip is changing our lives for the better."

"I hope you make more and more progress as the journey continues." said Dad, with a big smile

"I do too Dad!" I agreed, heartily

"Would you like some lemonade, Cassie?"

"It will help you feel cool and refreshed in this hot Darwin weather." Dad added

"Yes, please Dad!"

"That would be a great idea!" I agreed, enthusiastically

Dad got me a can of lemon drink and I went out on the balcony of our suite. I sat down on a seat and sipped my drink, looking out at the whole city of Darwin. It is a great city I can spot the Alexandra Lake from our balcony.

There's plenty more to see, we might even see Kate, Nicole, Adam and Amelia along the way, who knows? There are more performances to stage for 'The Bontel Family' tour, so more fun and fans to meet too!

Mum called the Darwin Theatre to arrange some of the coming performances.

'Hello is that the Darwin Entertainment Centre.' Mum spoke down the phone
"I would like to arrange the three performances of 'The Bontel Family' pop band."
"Tuesday, Wednesday and Thursday would suit us."
"That suits you as well ...oh good!" Mum responded
"We shall see you on Tuesday."
"Bye.
"I have arranged three performances for Tuesday, Wednesday and Thursday next week."
"We'll have plenty of fun, I'm sure we will see plenty of our fans there!" said Mum, smiling
"That's excellent Mum!"
"It will be a great venue to perform our Darwin concerts in... it will be as exciting as the Sydney Metro Theatre where we performed!" I replied, excitedly
"That's great dear... we'll get plenty of practice in before those dates... so we'll be ready for some great concerts." Dad said, happily

I went to have a shower. I noticed that there was a bar of soap and two bottles of shampoo and conditioner in the bathroom, but I've got my toiletry bag with me, so I use my own soap instead.
"Isn't it lovely to hear Cassie singing in the shower?
"She's loving it since she overcame her fear of showers when she was fifteen."
"It's her practice before a concert too, it soothes her before a show."
"I hope she doesn't overdo it!"
"We've got a busy week ahead of us!" said Dad
I spent a few minutes singing in the shower... before Mum knocked on the door.
"Cassie, don't take too long in there... will you?
"I don't want you to waste all the water." Mum said
I decided to be a bit cheeky.
"Cassie is not available right now... please leave a message after the tone and I will get back to you... Beep!"
Mum laughed.
"You are so funny Cassie... out of there I need my shower!"
I got out of the shower and put on my underwear I didn't want to sweat in pyjamas in this weather... I wanted to feel a little cooler and free.
I sat down on the couch got out my 'One Direction A-Z' book and read it. Jenna gave me the book for my sixteenth birthday... she is a fan of 'One Direction'... they are one of her favourite bands... I have enjoyed reading about them and becoming a fan too!
"Cassie, aren't you cold?" asked Mum
"No Mum."
"All right sweetie... don't forget to put your pyjamas on if it gets cooler."
"If you want to sleep the way you are its fine." said Mum, with a giggle to herself
Dad offered me a refreshing glass of water with some white chocolate cookies which I accepted.
"Daniel... I hope those are not my white chocolate chip cookies... you're in big trouble if they are." said Mum, teasingly
"Err...of course not dear." said Dad, wiping an imaginary bead of sweat off his brow, whilst winking at me
Mum came over and spied the cookies.
"Cassie... what are you doing with my special white chocolate chip cookies?" asked Mum

"Err... I was about to eat them... but I've decided to hide them in a place where you will never find them." I said, annoyingly

"Come on... hand them over." said Mum, putting her hand out for the biscuits

"Sorry... you can't have them... get your own." I said, giggling

"They are my own!" said Mum, glaring daggers at Dad, who was trying hard to look like he wasn't part of this at all

"Nope" I said, giggling.

"Cassie... please let me have at least one of my own biscuits that your Dad pilfered for you." pleaded Mum

"Ok, Mum... you can have one." I said, magnanimously

"Thank you, Cassie...I've got my eye on you 'Mister'." said Mum, pointing her finger at Dad, who rolled his eyes at me for getting him in to trouble with Mum, I grinned back at him

We watched a family comedy movie one of Mum's favourites... (I think Dad was trying to get back in her good books) ... then we decided to have an early night.

I didn't want to wake up in the middle of the night or morning with my bed or pyjamas covered in sweat, (that would be frightening for me), so I decided to leave my knickers on but took off my bra so I wouldn't be uncomfortable whilst sleeping.

As I lay down on the cool sheets, I thought... *'Ahh, this is delicious and much cooler for me to sleep peacefully.'*

I felt relaxed... I would sleep soundly all night... ready to face the new day whatever came my way.

# Chapter Twenty-Eight
## The 'Ghan'

The next morning, Mum and Dad have something good to say to me when we are having breakfast from the look on their faces, something exciting is about to happen!

"Cassie, we have something for you to learn today."

It's something we learnt when we were eighteen." said Dad, mysteriously

I wonder what it is?

"It is something special!" said Dad, importantly

"What is it, Dad?" I asked, intrigued

"Today... we're going to give you your first driving lesson!"

"It's a big step in your life...we want to help you to get there." said Mum, excitedly

I spat out my drink in shock... it went all over Mum!

"Sorry about that Mum."

"I didn't expect that news." I said, nervously

"That's ok Cassie." said Mum, laughing

I was a little bit nervous... but excited too!

"I get my learners first up... then progress to P-Plates... if I work hard, I can get my full licence after that!" I said, getting carried away at the thought of being able to drive

"Of course, I shall have to take driving tests for the last two, it will be worth it to have my own driver's licence at the end!" I chattered on excitedly at the prospect

"It sure will be Cassie... remember it takes lots and lots of practice and time though...to become a proficient driver." Dad said

"We'll have to find some nice quiet roads around Darwin for you to practice on... with as little traffic as possible... to start with."

"It will take many... many... lessons to become a competent and confident driver...we will start off slowly and build up your skills and confidence." said Dad, encouragingly

"I like that idea."

I have a car in mind for the future... when I get my licence." I said

"What car do you have in mind, sweetheart?" asked Mum, innocently

"A Ford Falcon is what I'm aiming for!" I said convincingly, and waited for the 'fallout' with a mischievous smile to myself

"Not a Ford Falcon!"

"That's my least favourite car!" said Mum, with a frown

"No, no, no!"

"That's no good!"
"You can't get that!" said Dad, in horror
"Ha, ha!"
"I got you two... bigtime!"
"I'm really aiming for a Holden Commodore!" I said, grinning back at them both
"The one with no roof... I would wear my dark black 'Hawkers' sunglasses... some snazzy brown leather driving gloves... a lovely shiny necklace from the jewellers and away I go!"
I will drive down the Melbourne streets and if I see any cute boys...especially autistic ones... on the footpath I will stop beside them... pull down my sunglasses and say...
"Hello, boys...do you want a lift in my speed machine... baby?"
Then they would say...
"Yes please... babe!"
"Then we would 'cruise' around town having fun together!"
Mum, Dad and I, broke into fits of laughter... tears running down our faces as we imagined that scene!
"Cassie... you crack me up with your flights of fancy!" Mum giggled
"I can just imagine you in your Holden Commodore!"
"Maybe you can chauffeur us and wear a special uniform with a stylish cap!" said Dad, with a big grin
"You never know Dad."
"I could be a celebrity driver!"
"Well... you will need to learn how to drive first!" said Mum, with a practical tone bringing us all back down to earth
"After breakfast, we'll take our car to a quiet place and we can begin your first lesson?"
"OK Mum... I can't wait!" I said, nearly too excited to eat breakfast
Mum and Dad have found a quiet spot with no traffic and I'm ready to learn to drive. I'm a bit nervous, but I'm excited that I'm taking another big step forward in my life. I hope I can do it well.
Wish me luck!
"Cassie, we know you know a lot about how a car works...so we'll give you a refresher on the parts of the car you need to use for driving?" said Dad
"Ok... I am ready to learn!"
"This is the accelerator."
"You press it with your foot when you want the car to go faster."
"These are the visors."
"When you are driving, they will stop the glare from the sun shining in your eyes... when you pull them down you can see the road properly...especially needed when it's very sunny." Mum added
After Mum and Dad had gone over many parts of the car such as the brakes... the ignition... the handbrake... and the clutch... the first lesson was about to begin.
"Cassie... this is what you do to start the car."
"You put the car key into the ignition...don't turn it yet... identify the clutch, the brake and the accelerator... make sure the car is in neutral and turn the key." said Mum, demonstrating each step as she instructed me
"Now Cassie... you try." said Mum
I went through all of the processes step by step.
"Good, Cassie."
"You remembered all the processes... that makes you one step closer to driving a car for the first time."
"Thanks Mum."

I think I am ready for part two now." I said

"Well... part two is driving the car!"

"It's a big step towards driving safely and confidently... are you sure you're ready to begin Cassie?" asked Dad

"Yes... I sure am Dad!"

"I can do it." I said, confidently

"First, you press down fully on the clutch."

"Then you put the gearstick into first gear."

"You have to move it left and up... to get to the number one position."

"Then you slowly lift your foot off the clutch and keep lifting your foot until the rpm's start dropping and the car starts moving forward."

"You need to be slowly pressing down on the accelerator at the same time... very slowly and gently... until the 'biting' point is reached and the gear is engaged to move the car forward."

"There's an important thing to watch out for."

"It's called stalling!"

"The car will 'stall' if you release the clutch too quickly...then you'll have to start all over again from step one."

"Don't fret... you're bound to stall any number of times... when you are learning to drive a car with a manual transmission."

"It takes lots of practice to find the perfect balance."

"Mum and I, know that you will get there eventually... it's the same process for every person who first learns to drive a car."

"When the car begins to race...around 2500-300 rpm... depending on the car... use your left foot to fully depress the clutch and move the gearstick down to two which is second gear." Dad said

Dad demonstrated each step, whilst I observed and listened carefully to make sure I don't miss any crucial points.

"Now... can you try all of that, Cassie?" asked Dad

"I can Dad... there should be no fuss." I said, hopefully

I followed all the steps and everything went smoothly.

"Good job Cassie."

"You're doing a great job." said Dad

"Thanks Dad."

"Is there a part three to this process?" I asked.

"There are many parts to driving Cassie."

"Next, we will practice hill starts."

"This is a measure to prevent your car from rolling backwards on an incline."

"When you are using the brake pedal, use your left foot to depress the clutch and your right foot to depress the brake." Mum said

Mum also taught me to use the hand brake when performing a hill start, she demonstrated all the steps and I copied her carefully without incident.

"Well done Cassie!"

"My pop 'superstar' daughter will soon be driving a snazzy Holden Commodore like me!" grinned Mum

"Me too!" said Dad, not wanting to be left out of the equation!

"It will be better than your cars!" I said, cheekily

"What!"
"Very funny." Mum quipped
"Ours are the best!" said Dad punching the air
"I will have a blue car... with yellow stars and green hearts on it." I decided
"Oh... we're so jealous!"
"We shall have to get similar ones in our colours!" Mum fires back
"Come on cheeky... let's drive to see someone we know."
"You can practice driving all the way there."
"Mum and I, have arranged for them to meet us in Darwin." said Dad with a grin
I was gaining confidence in my driving...I put it to the test by driving to a quiet area near Darwin.

There I see two people that we all know! The old woman is wearing a sixties style flower dress and a sunhat, the old man is wearing a green, red and orange striped jumper... he has glasses on and a leather hat on his head.

"Hello Grandma!"
"Hello, Grandad!"
"It's so lovely to see you both!" I said, hugging them
"Hello Cassie sweetheart."
It's lovely to see you too." said Grandma Georgina, hugging me
"Hello Cassie."
"How nice to see you again." said Grandad Lucas, hugging me close
"Hello Daniel and Mikayla, how nice to see you two."
"It's lovely to see you too Grandma and Grandad Macdonald." said Mum, hugging them both
"It's great to see you two... after such a long time!" said Dad, hugging them tight

Grandma Georgina is my Mums' grandma and Belinda's mother... she was born in Edinburgh, Scotland and is known to our families as Grandma Macdonald. I've visited her a few times and she always make ginger crunch for Mum and I, when we visit her.

Years ago, she would let me play with her cotton blanket, it was the only fabric I could tolerate.

Grandad Lucas is my Mum's grandad and is Darren's dad, he was also born in Edinburgh, Scotland. He is called Grandad Macdonald by our families. He has a collection of model vehicles including cars...he would often let me look at them, but would warn me not to touch them. He told tell me the history behind every vehicle and interesting facts about them.

"How are you three?"
"Are you having a good time in the Northern Territory?" asks Georgina
"We definitely are."
"Daniel and I have just started teaching Cassie to drive... she is doing very well."
"We are very proud of her." says Mum
"Well done Cassie." says Lucas
"I drove here today... for my first 'trial' drive."
"That gave me a lot of confidence." I told him
"Learning to drive at sixteen years of age... how exciting!" he replied
"You two must be good teachers." he said, nodding at Mum and Dad
"Cassie, you are doing well to learn an amazing new life skill."
"I've got something that you can share with Mum and Dad." says Georgina
"I'm very keen to see what you have brought with you Grandma." I said, eagerly

"I'll show you when we get back to our hotel."
"We'll follow you there."
At the hotel, Georgina showed us what she had brought for us to share.
"I've baked them for many years and won several ribbons for them."
"I passed my baking skills on to Belinda...she in turn passed them on to your Mum and Rebecca."
"You have always loved these treats when your Mum, Rebecca, Diane and I, made them...especially when you came to visit."
"Here they are." said Georgina, smiling
She handed me a box full of ginger crunch which she baked before they arrived in Darwin...they smell lovely.
"Thanks Grandma!"
"They look like they're going to taste really good!" I said, licking my lips at the thought
We took two each and started a conversation together, as we haven't seen each other for a while.
"How is your road trip around Australia going?" Georgina asked
"It's going great so far."
"We have been to the library... and we've seen the Northern Territory Museum... we've also been learning about the artwork that is a part of the Northern Territory's culture." I replied
"Great!"
"You've been learning a lot about the Northern Territory then."
"You're a smart grand-daughter... Mum and Dad can teach you a lot too." said Lucas
"We are all learning new things that we didn't know about Australia...we are loving every minute of Cassie's first trip!" Dad answered
"It's good to explore and have new experiences together... tasting the local dishes and meeting new people." Georgina smiled
"I am embracing new experiences and enjoying them."
"I'm eating new foods... so that when we travel overseas... I will be able to try some international cuisine too!"
"I wonder if Mum would try an edible bug dish." I giggled, as I looked sideways at Mum
"Ergh!"
"Don't even go there... Cassie Bontel!"
"They look disgusting!" Mum shuddered
"I'm sure you could at least try one... Mum." I said, slyly
"No!" Mum said, with full force
We all laughed together... at the horrified, screwed up face of Mum... as she imagined having to eat an insect!
"I tasted all of them and they tasted good." Dad laughed, good naturedly
"I always try any dish... even edible bugs!"
"Mikayla, Olivia and Rebecca wouldn't go near them...I went for it every time!"
"Daniel you have always been an adventurous eater!"
"You would try anything!" Georgina grinned
"Yep... that's me!"
"Yesterday, I looked at a photo of my six-year-old self-swimming at the Melbourne Pool."
"It reminded me of home and I got homesick and cried...Mum was there to comfort me."

"She told me that I was very brave for going on this road trip… I told her that she was a great Mum for helping me through tough and scary times."

"I chose to continue on this road trip… if I quit… I would have wasted the chance to make some wonderful new memories with my family."

"You were very brave speaking to your Mum and Dad about what upset you… that's great news to hear that you chose to continue the road trip!"

"Lucas and I, want to see all your pictures and hear all about the memories being made by you three."

"We shall make more with each stage of our journey."

"Who knows what we might find along the way!"

"When we came to Darwin for a four-day holiday trip… we certainly didn't expect to see you here!"

"We didn't expect to see you either." said Dad, laughing

"I've got another batch of ginger crunch here…these ones are ours." said Grandma

"We're off to the shops now… we'll be back in a little while." said Lucas

I noticed Georgina had put the second batch of ginger crunch on the bench. With a gleam in my eye I picked the box up and passed two biscuits to Mum and we started eating them.

A short while later Dad noticed that Georgina and Lucas were on their way back.

"Uh Oh."

"Quick you two!"

"Hide somewhere… where Georgina and Lucas can't see you." whispered Dad

"Daniel… we've got you, Mikayla and Cassie, some…"

"Someone ate my second batch of ginger crunch!"

"Daniel did you eat them?" asked Georgina

"Err…no Georgina."

Georgina glared at him.

"Come on… own up." said Georgina, crossly

Mum and I, can't help giggling at Dads predicament.

"Ah, now we know who ate Georgina's entire ginger crunch!"

"Mikayla, Cassie, come out!" said Lucas in a stern voice, but his eyes were crinkling up at the corners

Mum and I, emerged with crumbs dropping off us and guilty faces.

"Erm…it wasn't me."

"It was Mum." I said sheepishly, pointing at her

"It was not me."

"Cassie was the one that did it." said Mum, pointing back at me

"You two are both as bad as one another." said Georgina, pointing her fingers at both of us

"Yes… we are." I admitted

"Yes… I started this act with Rebecca… many years ago." said Mum, ruefully

Georgina glared at us, it looked like she was going to give us a clip under the ears, Mum and I, are in big trouble!

"You two may think it's hilarious to pinch and eat my ginger crunch…it's not!"

"If I catch you at it again, I'll give you both a clip under the ears!" said Georgina, severely

"Ooh, we're frightened." I said, in mock fear

"Very frightened indeed." added Mum, in the same vein

"Daniel, can you keep an eye on them both… please." said Georgina, appealing to Dad

"I certainly will… Georgina!"

"I'll keep them in line for you." said Dad

"Good on you Dan." said Georgina, satisfied that Dad will keep an eye on us

"We have been travelling on the Ghan from Adelaide to Darwin."

"If you have time… take a side train trip on it… stay in Adelaide for a day or two… then return on the 'Ghan' to pick up your car in Darwin and continue your road trip."

"It takes about fifty-six hours each way…you will absolutely love the journey." said Lucas

"The Ghan travels two thousand, nine hundred and seventy-nine kilometres, in either direction and it stops at Alice Springs for four hours… before it resumes its journey." I said

"That's right Cassie."

"You sure know lots about Australian history… have Daniel and Mikayla been teaching you?" asked Georgina

"They sure have!"

"They have travelled around Australia and learnt more about it each time."

"I also learnt some information on the Internet and during our journey." I said

"Well, we intend to spend at least three more days here at this hotel."

"I hope you have fun on 'The Ghan'… send us some photos when you finish the journey." Lucas said

"We will, have fun for the rest of your stay in Darwin." Mum added

A few days later, Mum, Dad and I, are at the station ready to board 'The Ghan'!

This is going to be one fun train ride I'm not going to forget. I learnt a lot about the Ghan before coming here…now I'm going to learn even more about it. I might make a new friend whilst I'm aboard!

"Cassie, we're going to have so much fun… I hope you enjoy it." Dad said, excitedly

"I definitely will!"

"We get private cabins… we can make new friends… and view magnificent landscapes."

"What's not to love!" I laughed

"We'll have plenty of time to do puzzles and chat and to learn about the Ghan."

"We've got plenty of old photos that we can show you too!"

"They're of me… your Mum and our family and relatives… on their Ghan journeys." said Dad, happily

"So, what are we waiting for… let's get on 'The Ghan'!" I said, enthusiastically

Mum, Dad and I made our way to our private cabin.

"Is this your first time on The Ghan?" asked the porter.

"It's another visit on the 'Ghan' for Daniel and I…it's our daughter Cassie's first time." said Mum

"I hope you enjoy it young lady."

"There are restaurants for dining… and sleeping beds in your cabins… for the four days and three nights journey to Adelaide."

"You will also learn about the history of the 'Ghan' during your journey."

"I hope you will enjoy your trip aboard the 'Ghan'." said the porter, smiling

"We sure will!" I said, happily

I noticed the 'Ghan' logo was shaped like a camel… one hundred and fifty years ago pioneering cameleers blazed a permanent trail into what is known as the 'Red Centre' of Australia.

According to the outback lore of the 1800's, Afghans, 'Ghans' came from the mysterious outpost of the country of Afghanistan in Asia.

The original Ghan line was similar to the route of explorer John MacDouall Stuart. The first Ghan train was farewelled on Sunday the fourth of August 1929. There were lots of excited people gathered around to see it off... it had one hundred passengers and supplies on board... the first destination it went to was Stuart... which was Alice Springs' original name.

Two days later on August the sixth... the silence of the MacDouall Ranges was pierced by the train's whistle as it arrived at the station. The Ghan has put up with problems over the years... from flash flooding... to intense heat... and termite damage!

According to legend, 'The Ghan' was stranded in one spot for a period of two weeks... the passengers were very hungry by then... so the engine driver had to shoot wild goats to feed them whilst they were stranded!

Mum and Dad told me that story... just the day before we were to go on our journey onboard!

I wonder if they were pulling my leg with that story?

It sounds a bit extreme... but in a situation like that you have got no choice... if you want to survive and hopefully get rescued... I guess!

"This is a beautiful landscape!"

"You can see the red earth...wide, open horizons... and a few trees."

"It's awesome!"

"What a great train the 'Ghan' is." I said, excitedly

"The 'Ghan' is definitely a great train, Cassie."

"We are glad you are enjoying it."

"In years to come... you will remember this journey." said Mum

Mum shows me a photo from 2006, it shows Mum, Dad, Aunt Betty, Uncle Glenn and cousin Jacinta at the Ghan restaurant... eating and having fun.

"This is a good photo."

"They have great meals at the Queen Adelaide Restaurant!"

"Mum was eating kangaroo... Dad had barramundi... Betty was eating lamb... Glenn was eating saltbush with Margaret River cheeses... and Jacinta was eating the wild rosella flower."

"I would love to try any of them... they all sound delicious to me! I said, working up an appetite just looking at the photo

"We've booked into the Platinum Club... we're going to enjoy the restaurant there."

"There's plenty of good food." said Dad, grinning at me, he knows how much I like eating these days

The cabin we have booked is a private lounge during the day... it has a movable table and two ottomans... there's plenty of room to entertain or simply relax and enjoy this magnificent view.

Dad took out another photo and showed it to me. This one is of Mum, Aunt Rebecca, Betty and Jacinta in front of 'The Ghan' in 2009. Mum and Rebecca were wearing their favourite clothes... Aunt Betty was wearing a sunny dress and Jacinta was wearing a summer dress with flowers on it... they were all going on a picnic.

"It's a great photo!"

"What colourful clothes you were wearing in the hot sunny weather."

"It looks like you had a fun time." I said

"We certainly did have fun."

"We packed sandwiches, drinks and a couple of our favourite chocolates as well as a pavlova cake."

"After that photo was taken... we got on the Ghan... we read books, told stories from the past and funny jokes."

"We learnt a bit about the Ghan's history and visited Katherine and the Northern Territory... we went on the Adelaide River Jumping Crocodile Cruise...we were too scared to go near the crocodiles."

"Betty and Jacinta were braver than Rebecca and I."

"We also visited the Wetlands Visitor Centre and enjoyed viewing the Marrakai Plans."

"We finished off the last two days by joining the Litchfield Waterfalls tour and exploring Darwin."

"Dad and I, did the same thing in 2006 and you will get to see all those highlights with us this time." said Mum

"I will enjoy doing that."

"The Litchfield Waterfalls seems like a good place to view and Katherine will be a wicked town to visit."

"Mikayla dear... can I come on the next women's holiday on the 'Ghan' if you choose to do another?" asked Dad

"I'm afraid you can't dear."

"No men allowed on the 'ladies trips'... you know that!" said Mum, grinning

"Not even..." starts Dad

"No!" says Mum, firmly

I cackled at that one! Poor Dad not being allowed on Mum and her women's Ghan Train holidays!

Later that evening, we made our way to the Platinum Club, where we were given a nice welcome.

"Hello, Bontel Family."

"Welcome to the Platinum Club."

"We hope you will enjoy the delicious meals our well-trained chefs will make for you."

"Drinks will be served to you at your table... once you have chosen and ordered."

"Make your way to your seats at the Captain's table, I hope you have a pleasant evening." said the Ghan Platinum Club porter.

"We sure will." I said

"Ooh, we get to sit at the Captain's table."

"It doesn't get any better than that... does it?" asked Mum

"No, it doesn't!" I agreed, emphatically

"We get to choose fancy meals and enjoy them with the Captain!"

"What more could we want?" says Dad, very impressed

We sat down at the Captain's table and perused the menu. The dishes on the menu were very fancy and very tempting. I didn't know which one to start with, there were so many delicious options to choose from, I decided to be brave and try a new one!

"Cassie we've decided on the dishes we want."

"What are you going to choose?" asks Mum.

"I have decided, and it's going to be delicious and fancy!" I said, with a flourish

When we had ordered our dishes, I looked around the Platinum Club. It had a sophisticated Australian design... the tables had quartzite tops... the floors were made of timber... there were brass fittings and the leather banquette lounges were in tones of ash... moss... and sepia... which were beautiful, adding a fancy touch to the club.

"The Platinum Club is so fancy."

"There are many tempting dishes and the lounge looks like a great place to sit and chat."

"Yes."

"This is a lovely section of the Ghan... they didn't have this club back in 2006... it's great!" said Dad, totally impressed by what he saw

"The views are spectacular from here, with all the rock formations and desert scenes."

"Mum and Dad would have loved this they would have been astonished at the beauty of the Australian landscape." Mum looked in amazement through the viewing windows

"Look… I can see the Captain coming towards our table."

"He might become our new friend." I said

"He might."

"He seems very friendly and professional."

"Hello Captain."

"Why don't you come and sit with us?" Mum said

"I would love to." the Captain replied

He sits down…doesn't he look handsome in his Ghan uniform! He is wearing a blue and white train driver uniform with The Ghan logo on it and a few award decorations… which he probably earnt for the 'Ghan' and tourism services.

"Is that…. no surely not."

"It is!"

"It's the 'Bontel' family… isn't it?"

"I didn't expect to see you in the Platinum Club." said the Captain

"Neither did we."

"Daniel and I, have been on the Ghan before in 2006… I also travelled again in 2009."

"It's the greatest train that we've been on… the views are beautiful." Mum said

"Yes, all the views are spectacular from the 'Ghan'… it's our beautiful country!"

"Now would this be 'Miss Cassie Bontel' sitting next to me?"

"She looks like she would make a good Captain's assistant." the Captain smiled

"I sure would Captain!"

"Travelling on the Ghan is part of our road trip round Australia that we are taking."

"This is one of the highlights so far… we plan to make as many memories as we can." I told the captain

"I'm so glad you are enjoying the Ghan journey."

"I've been working here for about three months… it's a great job, with many responsibilities."

We ordered our meals and continued talking with the Captain.

Mum and Dad showed the Captain their medals… he was amazed.

"How proud you must be."

"What a great achievement." said the Captain.

"Daniel and I earnt them for services to disability… TV and music… also changing the way Australians think about disabilities." said Mum

"That's fantastic!"

"Keep up the good work… you might earn an Order of Australia… or a CBE one of these days." smiled the Captain

"After this journey to Adelaide… then back to Darwin… we plan to go to our next destination for a concert… on 'The Bontel Family Tour'."

"It's been awesome so far!"

"I've been more popular than Mum and Dad… but we have decided to share our fans… which is better for all of us." I said

"That's excellent Cassie!"

"We might even put some of your debut album over the speakers at some point… wouldn't that be good?" said the Captain.

"That would be good, Captain." said Mum

Our dishes arrived and we 'tucked' in... they were delicious!

"Let's drink to your road trip journey."

"Cheers!" said the Captain

"Cheers!" said Mum, Dad and I

We 'clinked' our glasses together and drank to the continuing road trip ahead.

Later that night Mum and Dad got into their double bed... I got into my twin bed in our cabin. I have never seen a cabin like this before... it converts into a bedroom at night and back into a normal room during the day... just like magic!

"Mum."

"Dad."

"I have an idea!"

"Why don't I sing with various Australian children's groups and children's tribute bands?"

"I can sing lead for them... occasionally play guitar or keyboards... they can play their instruments and sing vocals too."

"The audience would either be children with disabilities and their families... or our fans... or a mixture of both!"

"It doesn't matter which... I will have an awesome time performing with them." I said excitedly

"That's an excellent idea Cassie."

"What are you going to call this lovely project?" asked Mum

"I'm going to call my awesome new project... Cassie and Friends." I said, grinning

"That sounds like a great project, Cassie!"

"We'll help you in any way that we can."

"We need to select a destination for this project... then we can call some children's bands to arrange for rehearsals with them." Dad said

"I'll have fun with children's groups and the audience if it goes ahead... whatever happens with my new project... I'll still do a solo performance during our shows."

I lay down on the cabin bed, the sheets and blankets are cool and summery. It reminded me of summer nights in similar sheets. I feel the comfort of the blankets relaxing me, just like my weighted blanket that I used when I got upset and melted down.

It felt like the comforts of home, whilst being on the Ghan. I drifted off to sleep and I dreamt of driving 'The Ghan' from Darwin to Adelaide and back, waving to the local wildlife as I passed them by.

# Chapter Twenty-Nine
## Adelaide

We arrived in Adelaide around lunchtime the following day. Mum, Dad and I, stepped off the Ghan, there were spectacular buildings all around the Adelaide Convention Centre, Adelaide Aquatic Centre and the Big Rocking Horse. There was also the AAMI Stadium, which is the home of the Adelaide Crows Football Club. We only plan to stay overnight, so we'll just select a couple of places to explore.

"It's about twenty-eight degrees."

"Why don't we go to the Adelaide Aquatic Centre for a swim later?" I said

"Let's find a café for lunch." said Dad, looking at his phone

"There is Brunelli's Café...let's try that one."

We arrived at Brunelli's Café and chose to sit in the outdoor area. When we had ordered our meals, Dad decided to skype Maria.

'Hello son, how are you doing?'

"I'm doing well Mum."

"We have just travelled on the Ghan."

"We are in Adelaide."

'Wow, you've been on the 'Ghan'!'

'That's wonderful!'

'How was the trip?'

"It was good Mum."

"We booked the Platinum Club and got to sit at the Captain's Table."

'Lucky you!'

'You must've had an excellent dinner with him.'

'He's so handsome.'

"Fancy you noticing that, Mum!" Dad chuckled.

"We had a good time, chatting and telling jokes, he used to work at his family's holiday resort as the holiday activities captain, he's been working on the Ghan for about three months now."

'He's an excellent captain, I'm glad you had a good dinner with him.'

"Cassie has another achievement that she is working on."

'Goodness!'

'What's that?'

"She had her first driving lesson!"

'That's wonderful!'

'I'm so proud of her!'

'Cassie I'm so happy that you are learning how to drive, you might be able to take Jim and I to the shops one day.'

"I sure will Maria."

"I would be happy to do that for you and Jim anytime, once I get my licence."

"It will take a lot of hard work, but she can get there, the key is lots of practice!"

"This afternoon we are planning to go to the Adelaide Aquatic Centre for a nice swim, it's about twenty-eight degrees here!"

'Have fun in Adelaide and good luck with the rest of your music tour around Australia.'

'Bye, son.'

"Bye, Mum."

The conversation at the table turned to footy, as we waited for our meals to arrive.

"Collingwood have made it to the 2011 AFL Grand Final against Geelong!"

"They will play on the first of October 2011, to see who wins the AFL Premiership." said Mum

"I hope Collingwood wins that match!"

"Last year on the twenty-fifth of September 2010, they drew with St. Kilda in the first 2010 AFL Grand Final... the score was 9.14 (68) to 10.8 (68)."

"Then they played again the following week... that time Collingwood won 16.12 (108) to 7.10 (52) ...for a fifty-six points victory and their fifteenth premiership!"

"Scott Pendlebury won the Norm-Smith Medal for best on ground performance... gosh he played so well." I said, admiringly

"He's one of my favourite players...but of course Tony Shaw is my all-time favourite Collingwood player!" said Mum, fervently

"Let's hope Collingwood wins it for you dear." Dad smiled

"Thanks." Mum replied with a smile

"Well here comes our food."

"Let's eat and then we must book in to a hotel... before we take that swim." Mum said

"Sounds like a plan!" Dad and I agreed

We checked in at the Stamford Plaza Hotel and booked a suite. It was a great room... I loved the designer artwork... and things such as a separate walk-in-wardrobe... a spa bath... tea and coffee making facilities... as well as bathrobes and slippers. It's going to be one fun night that we will make the most of... before we re-board the Ghan.

"We should put our valuables in the safety deposit facilities, so they don't get stolen!"

"We wouldn't want that to happen... would we?" I said

"We certainly wouldn't Cassie!"

"They will be safe there... we can collect them when we get back from the Aquatic Centre." Mum added

"Let's go swimming and cool ourselves." said Dad

The Aquatic Centre was full of families... we changed and headed to the main pool to swim some exercise laps.

"I bet I can swim more laps than you two!"

"I've been practicing in secret for five months now, without you finding out." I said, grinning

"Oh, have you?" Mum said, with a questioning tone to her voice

"You may have been practicing in secret... but I can swim more laps than you." said Mum, with a competitive statement

"I can do way more laps than you two... I have been treadmill walking for miles!" said Dad, proudly

We all laughed at that.

"Let's slide into our lanes… we'll do fifteen laps to see who is the best swimmer!"

"Let's go!" I said, fist pumping the air like 'Rocky'

Mum, Dad and I, slid into our lanes and proceeded to start our fifteen laps. At the fifth lap, I was just in front of Mum, with Dad who was not too far behind. I was thinking… *I'm doing well after lap five. Mum is almost catching up to me with Dad catching up to her as well. It's a close one between the three of us, but we'll see who is the best, in this Adelaide Pool!'*

After the tenth lap, I took a quick look to the left and saw Mum was getting really close, I glanced to my right and Dad was advancing too… *'It's getting close now, Mum is nearly beside me and Dad is not too far off the pace either. I can swim a little harder, I might just make it.'* I thought

It is a closely swum race between Mum, Dad and I… who is going to win?

I hope it will be me… but I don't mind if Mum or Dad beats me… it's not really about whoever wins or loses… it's about having fun with my family!

Mum, Dad and I swam towards the wall… it was closer than the swim final at the 2000 Olympic Games in Sydney!

I just touched my hand on the wall about 0.500 seconds before Mum touched the wall and about 0.725 seconds before Dad touched. I had won the fun swimming race… it was close but I outswam Mum and Dad in this one.

"I was just too good for you two!"

"You can't outswim me no matter how hard you swim." I teased

"Very funny Cassie!"

"You didn't 'cheat' did you?" Mum said, staring at me closely

"Err… NO, I didn't." I said, giggling as Mum looked for a reason to put in a protest

"I'm not sure about that!"

"I think you got a head start before I got to three." said Dad, joining in the debate

"I definitely did not!"

"You got a head start on us before Mum and I dived in." I laughed, turning the tables back on him

"Well you two started swimming… before I slid into my lane." giggled Mum

"We did not!" Dad and I chorused together

"Come on you two… let's stay for another half-hour before we return to the hotel." I said laughing

We picked up our valuables when we got back to the hotel lobby and when we returned to our rooms, I decided to have a nice spa bath. It was so warm and lovely, I relaxed for an hour and got dressed. After my relaxing spa I spent a couple of hours on my laptop, watching YouTube pop music videos.

I even watched some hilarious cat videos…they are always good for a laugh… my classmates watch similar videos and we upload and share them with each other… it's something we have in common… we love talking about the latest ones we've seen.

After I watched a pop music video of 'Quirky Service's hit 'Speedboat' taken from their 2000 album 'Secret Fantasy Island'… I checked the 'Bontel Family Band' website to see how our album is charting.

It's still going well in Australia… New Zealand… Asia… Europe… and North America… it is charting in the top ten of all those countries! I noticed that 'The Bontel Family' have started to chart higher than 'Quirky Service's latest album 'Blizzard Blast'… I giggled a little at that information.

"I can hear you laughing Cassie… what's so funny?" asked Mum

"Come and at look at this Mum."

"We're charting higher than Quirky Service." I sniggered

Mum came over to look at the music charts, she grinned.

"Oh My."

"We ARE charting higher than 'Quirky Service'.

"I hope they don't prank us after they see the chart!" says Dad joining in when he sees the chart positions

"I bet they will get a surprise when they take a look!"

"We can expect a ring any day now saying… 'Did you knock us off our music perch?'"

"To which our reply will be…Yes… Yes… I think we did!" I said, laughing out loud

"Cassie we're having dinner at the celebrity lounge this evening… won't that be great?" asked Mum

"It will." I replied, enthusiastically

"It is a lovely social evening… I'm sure you will enjoy it, Cassie."

"I'm looking forward to a good dinner… they have delicious combo meals and refreshing drinks." Dad added

"We'll put on some coloured clothes… add a little bit of bling… then hit the town!" I said, with gusto

Mum, Dad and I, walked to the celeb lounge… where the walls were lined with pictures of various celebrities… most of whom we recognised. I was surprised to see the three of us in a picture on the wall. There I was serving drinks as a barmaid! Dad was acting as the food waiter and Mum was resplendent in her yellow dress… lipstick applied… wearing a dazzling necklace… with a jewelled ring on her right hand. Mum was the 'guest' being waited on by Dad and I… it was an awesome picture and I was so happy to see it up on the wall with all those other celebrities.

"OMG!"

"That's us amongst all those famous celebrities!"

"It's awesome!"

"I never knew we were on this celebrity wall!" I said, excitedly

"We never knew either." said Mum and Dad together

"What an honour."

"Let's get to our table and order our food and drinks… I can tell we're going to have a nice time this evening." said Mum, happily

We sat at our table and looked over the menus… when the waitress came over to take our orders, she recognised us.

"Are you ready to order your… Oh, I thought I recognised you three."

"You're the Bontel Family."

"Nice picture on the wall of celebrities." said the waitress

"How did we get on the celeb portrait wall anyway?" asked Mum

"When you released your debut album earlier this year… we often played it in the celeb lounge… so we thought it would be a nice touch to add your picture as well… so the customers could see the performers as well as hear their music."

"The customers seem to love it." added the waitress

"We love it too… thank you for including us on your portrait wall." I said

"It's a pleasure Miss Bontel… keep up the excellent music." the waitress smiled

"Thank you." I replied

I ordered a soft tortilla wrap… with shredded chicken… Swiss cheese… bacon… roast capsicum… and basil and walnut pesto. Mum had a wholemeal baguette with grilled vegetables… herbed mushroom… and provolone cheese. Dad tried rye sourdough with smoked trout… beetroot… rocket… sprouts… and horseradish aioli.

They were all delicious!
Cassie, how do you think the road trip is going so far?" asked Dad

"It's going great!"

"I'm enjoying every minute of it... I have learnt a lot about Australia that I didn't know before we started." I said

"That's super Cassie!"

"Can you tell us three things you have liked about the road trip so far?" asked Mum

"I love performing at our concerts... learning to ski for the first time at Mt Buller was a blast... and I also love learning to drive!"

"There's plenty more things I love... but that's three major things." I said

"We're glad you're having fun, Cassie."

"Now, can you tell us about three things that made you feel anxious or upset during the trip so far?" asked Dad

"The memory of when I was four years old and got lost... the thunder and lightning storm on the Gold Coast... and the photo of when I was six years old at home."

"You helped me through those anxious moments and now I can be brave and talk openly about them... they don't make me feel upset or anxious anymore." I said, smiling

"We are amazed at the progress you have made and we know you can achieve so much more."

"We are very proud of you." said Mum

"I'm enjoying the 'Ghan' and I love the photos we have taken on it so far." I said

When we got back to the Stamford Plaza, I went to have a nice hot shower. As I lathered myself with the soap it slipped out of my fingers and dropped on to the shower floor.

"Oops! I've been dismissed for a duck!" I laughed

Mum and Dad laughed too. Their comedy pop music career which started as 'Dan and the Cheeky Babes' in the nineties... is hilarious to listen to and during this tour I've delivered a few pieces of humour which made our fans laugh too... I hope to do some more gags as the shows roll on.

As I bent down to pick up the soap, I notice my legs are looking a little hairier... I know what this means! It's time to shave my legs! I examined my leg hairs while still crouching down and thought... *'I feel a bit nervous about this, but it's time I learnt how to shave my legs so I can maintain smooth looking legs, like my Mum.'*

I never learnt to shave my legs when I was thirteen because I feared I would cut myself. Mum tried to teach me a couple of times how to do it... but I would resist and have a meltdown.

I realise I have to learn to shave especially as we plan to go into Western Australia... where the weather though a little less hot than the Northern Territory is still quite hot. It might be hard to learn to shave my legs... but if I don't... I might end up looking like my grandma and I don't want that to happen to me!

I turned off the shower went over to the door quietly opening it a little... I hid behind the door whilst poking my head around the edge... my hair dripping wet.

"Mum I want to learn how to shave my legs." I said, nervously

"That's good!"

"I'll help you with that in two minutes."

"I'll get my razor so you can learn how to do it without cutting yourself." Mum added

I didn't put on my pyjamas...because I don't want to get blood on my pyjamas if I cut myself... a couple of minutes later Mum comes in with the razor and also the Band-Aids! Just in case!

"Cassie this is a very important lesson in a girl's life if she wants smooth legs... to learn how to do it properly... so that you don't cut and scar yourself."

"I started shaving my legs when I was fourteen... it took a couple of practices... before I was proficient and learned how to do it without... 'nicking' my skin!"

"This is what you do."

"Take some shaving cream and spread it all along the areas you want to shave." Mum directed

I listened to all of the steps and sprayed the shaving cream onto my leg, it's best to do one at a time.

"Good."

"Take the razor and gently shave the areas of your legs that you spread the cream over...be very careful not to cut yourself... especially around the ankles."

"If you do 'nick' yourself... don't panic... keep calm... I've got Band-Aids just in case." Mum instructs me

"All right, Mum."

"I'll keep the razor steady." I said

I started slowly and took my time.

I nearly grazed my right leg at one point but managed not to.

When I was finished my legs had a smooth and silky look like Mums'... but much sexier looking... I thought... giggling to myself.

"You did a very good job, darling."

"You took your time and shaved your legs very well." Mum concluded

"Thanks Mum."

"It wasn't easy to do... but I'm very happy with my first effort."

"My legs will be much smoother now."

"Another skill learned... I will be pleased to help you until you are confident enough to do it without my assistance." Mum added

I checked the temperature on my iPhone... it was around twenty-four degrees... a little cooler than before. I sat on my bed to read 'Twilight Eclipse' it is one of the books in the 'Twilight' series that Nina gave to me when I was fourteen... I have loved it ever since.

We were about to have breakfast the next morning... before we went back to the station to board the Ghan again and return to Darwin.

Mum put her toast in the toaster before getting her cereal ready for breakfast... minutes later the toast popped up... black!

"Oh... for bleeps sakes!" said Mum, in a very cranky tone

"OMG... your toast is burnt."

"Not a good start to the day Mum." I said, trying to soothe her down

"No... it isn't." she said, huffily

"I love my toast."

"I think there is a major problem with this toaster... I'll have to check it out to make sure." Dad said to Mum

Mum tried to scrape the burnt bits off her toast... but the toast broke into pieces.

"Oh well looks like it will be bread and butter topped with Vegemite for me."

"It's a good 'Aussie' option anyway." Mum said

I got the milk jug out of the fridge and was carrying it to the table... when somehow it slipped out of my hands... it hit the floor and smashed... making the three of us jump.

"What the flaming...!"

Fortunately, no one was hurt.

"Well, there goes our milk for breakfast this morning." I added

"Looks like we'll have to have juice instead." I said, putting my hands up in an, 'I don't know gesture', and shrugging my shoulders

"I'll get the broom from the cupboard and sweep all the glass up and put it in the bin... be careful not to step on any of it." said Dad

Dad carefully stepped over the glass and went to the broom cupboard. He took out the broom and the handle fell off in his hand.

"Oh... for goodness sake!" Dad fumed

"What happened Dad?" I asked, tentatively

"The broom broke!"

"Looks like it was getting worn out with use." he added

"Are there any other brooms darling?" asked Mum

"That was the only one."

"We will have to let reception know... that our room needs a new broom!" said Dad, in an irritated voice

"What a way to start the day!"

"First Mums' burnt toast... then the milk jug shattering... now the broom handle breaking off in your hand!

"Is it Friday the thirteenth?"

"We won't forget 'this' morning!"

"We need to clean all this mess up... take care not to cut yourself." Mum said

Mum, Dad and I, picked up all the glass, taking care not to let it cut our hands and carefully put it in the bin. We managed to have breakfast, consisting of cereal, (without milk), juice and no toast. It wasn't our ideal breakfast, but we made the best of it. After we told reception what had happened, we walked to our car and drove to the station.

"We'll have lots of fun back on the 'Ghan' between Adelaide and Darwin."

"We might even see the Captain again...who knows?" I said, cheerily

"The Captain is a very nice man it was fun to have dinner with him in the Platinum Club." Mum agreed

"We can have fun despite the unfortunate start to the morning, what else could go wro..." I started

Bonk, before I finished that sentence, we bumped straight into a sign and staggered backwards, Whoops!

"Who put that sign there?"

"It wasn't there when we arrived yesterday." said Mum, rubbing her left eye

"Maybe it was a practical joker who put it there for a laugh." I said, rubbing my nose

"We play pranks on each other...this one is definitely not funny! said Dad, rubbing his forehead

We all moved closer to look at the sign. It read... 'Blind Area'.

"Blind Area!"

We then noticed a message on the bottom scrawled in texta... it read...

'Got you... Haha I got you!'

"That's not funny!"

"I knew it was a prank all along!"

"This sign is easily removed!" I said, pulling the sign out of the way

"Let's forget about it and get on the Ghan!" said Dad, firmly

We strode off to where the Ghan should be... but by this time...it had left!

"The Ghan has gone!"

"Looks like we might have to spend another night or two, in Adelaide!"

We turned hastily and tripped over our luggage behind us, which sprang open, spilling all our belongings on the ground!

"OOF!"
"OOF!"
"OOF!"
"For heaven's sake!" I shouted
"Are you three all right?
"I heard you landing on the ground." observed a train guard
"Yes, we're all right."
"A little embarrassed, but fine." I said, picking myself up
A couple of nearby passengers helped us gather our things, to put back into our suitcases.
"Thanks mate." said Mum
"No worries." said the passenger

Mum, Dad and I, went back to the Stamford Plaza where we had to book another room…one free from problems this time we hoped! We also got ourselves a hire car to use whilst we are in Adelaide, as our vehicle is back in Darwin waiting for us to return!

After settling in to our new room, (which the management assured us would not have any of the previous room's problems), we made our way to the Playford Restaurant for lunch, which was renowned for its world class cuisine. I was looking forward to this, after our meagre breakfast this morning!

As everyone was so hungry, we decided to have our main meal of the day for lunch, we definitely couldn't wait till the evening! I chose the free-range beef scotch fillet, it was delicious and it got my taste buds going, Mum loved the butternut pumpkin risotto, it was tasty and similar to one that Rebecca made in one of her cookbook recipes. Dad enjoyed pan seared barramundi, it reminded him of his holidays with Mum, Olivia and Rebecca, trying various fishes that they caught and cooked over an open fire.

We talked about possible music venues… now that we were going to be in Adelaide for another night. We decided to try and get something organised whilst we were here. As we didn't have time to organise a full concert venue… we chose 'The Gov'… an establishment with pub meals… including pizza nights… they put on different types of entertainment… such as Pub Scrabble and Open Mic nights.

We arranged with the management to just 'rock up' for their open mic session that evening…tell a few jokes… maybe play some songs… if we can borrow some instruments to play… during the evening.

We spent the afternoon in our hotel room practising our comedy routine and roughly sketching out what we would do in the evening's performance. It wasn't going to be a very long gig… each act had their allocated time of ten to fifteen minutes… the open mic nights were very popular with the locals and always plenty of acts wanting to take part.

When we arrived at the venue that evening, there were some people playing pub scrabble, others were eating meals, whilst a live band performed its last set.
"This is a great atmosphere to socialise, play scrabble and perform."
"Mum and I, were stand-up comedians in a comedy pop group called 'Dan and the Cheeky Babes' in the early nineties." said Dad
"We made our fans laugh with albums and TV comedy sketch series."
"We won an award for Best Comedy Group in 1991." said Dad, proudly
"I loved watching 'Dan and the Cheeky Babes' and the TV comedy sketch series."
"I also loved the 'Dan and the Cheeky Babes' story jokes." I said
"I might take my lead from you two tonight." I laughed

Later, when it was open mic time the MC made an introduction and announced our names. We walked through the curtain entrance, tripped and fell flat on our faces! Oops! That was not a good start...the audience fell about laughing...they thought it was part of the act.

"We're so sorry about that... I don't know what is wrong with us."

"We didn't drop in until seven this evening... from a pop music club."

"Me and Mum... in the front bar... in our shoes." I added

The audience cackled.

"It was a horrifying sight... I witnessed it all from my table...I was trying to eat my dinner!" quipped Dad

The audience chuckled with laughter, they are enjoying themselves and so are we!

"Hello, we are 'The Bontel Family'."

"We are a pop band from Melbourne in Victoria, you may have heard our debut album in the charts right now!"

"Are you all having a good time tonight!" I asked

"Yes!" the audience called back

"That's excellent."

'We would like to play you a few tunes from our album."

After our set, we watched the other performers in the evening's entertainment, everyone had fun and much later we went back to the hotel and to bed.

The next morning, after our late night the previous evening we were all running late... Mum, Dad and I grabbed our luggage and raced to the Adelaide Station.

"Excuse me... where is the 'Ghan'?" I asked, hesitantly

"It's gone."

"You might want to get here on time." the guard said, wagging his finger at me

"Oh."

"How long will it be until it returns here to Adelaide?" I asked

"It will return tomorrow."

"Thank you."

"We've missed it again!"

"We are not doing very well with our time keeping." muttered Mum, unhappily

Just then we all received text messages on our iPhones.

We read them and a smile of surprise spread across our faces at what we saw.

*To the Bontel Family, you are invited to the trial of a special event for autistic children in Adelaide at the Botanic Park. We would love you to perform at the event which starts at one. The children, their parents and carers would love to see you perform and get to meet you too.*

*If you can make it please dress in your best clothes, there will be food and drinks, if you want you can bring a dish to share. We hope to see you there the autistic kids are going to have a ball!'*

"Oh, Wow!"

"That's so exciting!"

"We can appear at a special event for autistic kids, perform for them and get to meet them afterwards as well!" I said

"That's wonderful Cassie."

"This will be a wonderful opportunity for us all!" Mum said

"Now we know why we kept getting delayed and missing our train connection on the Ghan!" said Dad

"We were all meant to be here for the autistic children's event in the Botanic Park!" we all shouted together, then burst into laughter at our voices in unison

"We'll help you to interact with the autistic kids... we're sure you can do this." said Mum, confidently

"We've been doing events such as this one for many years... so we're ready."

"It's going to be a special performance for all of us." said Dad

"If any of the autistic kids get anxious or meltdown... I will use the techniques that you have taught me to calm them down and make them feel safe."

"I will be ready." I said

## Chapter Thirty
## Adelaide Park Special Event

Mum, Dad and I, made our way to the Adelaide Park where the trial themed event is about to start. There are fifteen minutes until the autistic children arrive with their parents and we can't wait! They will be so excited and surprised to see us because we know they love our music.

There are two carers setting up the event with an underwater theme. There are fish... seahorses... manta rays... and a model shark... in the mountain of stage props. The two carers need some help... so we go over to lend them a hand.

"Hello Bontel Family."

"We're glad you can make it... I'm carer Nancy." said the first girl

"I'm carer Sophie." added the second

"We're so happy to see you here." Sophie smiled

"That's a wicked underwater theme!"

"Did the kids with autism from Adelaide Special School help you to make it?" I asked

"Yes, they did!"

"It's fantastic!"

"They used their creative and artistic skills to make these great sea creatures for our underwater theme." said Nancy, proudly

"Wow!"

"They did a good job!"

"We have helped autistic children with their art projects amongst other things... especially in our current work... as disability advocates."

"The children are such fun to work with and a pleasure to help." Mum added, smiling

We're very proud of our jobs it can be hard but we don't let that stop us... it's very rewarding." Dad said

"You're doing everything you can to change the way Australians think about disability!"

"Keep it up!"

"Thank you... Nancy."

"Cassie would like to follow in our footsteps."

"She would like to work with autistic children and those with disabilities...as she understands them... she helps out at the Melbourne Special School for girls with autism." said Mum

"She has two very positive role models to look up to." said Nancy, smiling at Mum and Dad

"They certainly are... and I most definitely DO... look up to them!" I agreed

"I'm ready to use the calming anxiety techniques that I've been shown...I use them for myself...so I can show the children what to do... if they experience anxiety... or become overwhelmed with a meltdown."

"Mum and Dad will supervise me and be ready to intervene... should I need any help." I explained
"That sounds like a good idea."
"We came over to help set up the underwater theme...it looks like it's coming together nicely." said Mum, nodding at the display area
"It sure is."
"Can you help us put these two models up?"
"The kids will be arriving in ten minutes time." Sophie added

We helped Nancy and Sophie set up the last two of the underwater props and then put out the food and drinks. When we finished, I could hear the children and their parents arriving. Most of them sound excited... that's a good sign.

However, two remain silent, I realise they have never been to this type of event before, I hope they acclimatise to it with gentle encouragement and help from their parents.

The autistic kids recognise us and run towards us. There are eleven autistic children, seven girls aged around nine to twelve years old and four autistic boys aged between nine and eleven.... a few of them were really excited flapping their hands and laughing. It made me smile with happiness to see the joy on their faces... I loved seeing that.

"Hello!"
"How are you today?" the kids called out
"We're good thanks, darlings."
"How have you all been?" asked Mum
"We're good thanks." said one autistic boy, aged about ten
"Cassie!"
"My sister loves your family's debut album and I love it too!"
"It's my favourite and you are my favourite member of the band." said an autistic girl of twelve
"Thank you!"
"That's a very nice thing to say." I said
"What do you think of the underwater theme?"
"Isn't it wonderful?" asked Dad
"It looks great!" said a ten-year-old autistic girl

An eleven-year-old autistic girl with long light brown hair seems a bit nervous. I think she's scared of a part of the underwater scene it might be the shark or the fish.

"It's all right Ava."
"The scenery is fun... it won't hurt you sweetie." said Ava's Mum
Ava calmed down a little... but still remained nervous.
"Ok, here's what's happening guys!"
"There are five game activities relating to the underwater theme... which will be supervised by Nancy... Daniel... Cassie... Mikayla... and myself." said Sophie
"Please take turns and don't forget to share."
"If it gets too much for you... one of us will take you to a quiet area in the Adelaide Park...where you can calm down and use your anxiety techniques...then you will feel relaxed again."
"There will be a performance from 'The Bontel Family' band later on where you can put your headphones on if you need to... if you don't have any headphones then your parents may take you to the quiet area.
"Please enjoy these couple of hours and stay safe and well." said Sophie

"There will be two autistic children to each game activity… you will have ten minutes each… and then swap to the next activity."

The children are:

- Ava (11),
- Billy (10)
- Sofia (10)
- Alex (10),
- Katie (10)
- Gracie (12),
- Nadia (9)
- Skyler (11)
- Harry (11)
- Caleb (9)
- Samantha (9)

I was supervising the fishing game… where you use a magnet with a string to fish for various aqua creatures… with different amounts of points on them. Whoever gets the most points when all the aqua creatures have been fished out… wins. A ten-year old autistic boy named Billy and a ten-year-old autistic girl named Sofia were the first players at my activity.

Mum was telling children's stories… with underwater sea related themes that she has published. She is a published children's author… her books have been world-wide best sellers on the children's reading list.

The two children, Alex nine and Katie ten, seem to be enjoying the stories playing along with the actions and guessing what's going to happen next.

Dad is dressed up as a pirate, a twelve-year-old autistic girl named Gracie and nine-year-old autistic girl named Nadia were his crewmates… they are acting out an adventure from an old pirate play… with a child friendly dialogue.

He is enjoying himself playing the role of Daniel 'Rickbeard'… Gracie and Nadia are playing the roles of… 'First Mate Gracie'… and 'First Mate Nadia'… they are having great fun.

"Ah-harr me hearties!"

"Are you enjoying having a pirate adventure?" asks 'Daniel Rickbeard'.

"Ah-harr, Captain Rickbeard, we are!" says First Mate Gracie and First Mate Nadia

Billy, Sofia and I, look across and laugh… Dad was hilarious playing the pirate!

"Mr Bontel is so funny playing Captain Daniel Rickbeard." said Billy, chuckling

"He sure is Billy."

"He sure is." I said, giggling too

"My dad worked on ships… I would like to do that one day." said Sofia

"I'm sure you will."

"Your Dad would be happy to hear that." I said

Nancy was doing a puppet show with lots of fish and a seahorse… Skyler and Harry were loving it. Sophie was teaching Caleb and Samantha about marine life… with interesting and fun things that they might not know about these sea creatures.

All was going well…I looked across and saw Ava sitting away from everyone… she seems to be interested in nature and is giggling which is good to see…I'm a bit concerned about her being by herself… she doesn't want to play with the other kids and prefers to be alone. I had been in that situation myself for many years... so I know what it is like.

Fifteen minutes later we all heard a shriek of pain that Mum, Dad and I... know all too well.

We looked over to see Ava having a meltdown near the shark prop. She was lying on her stomach... covering her ears... and she was screaming... as though the shark was about to eat her.

Nancy and Sophie ran over to calm her...Ava wouldn't calm down and struck them. Ava's Mum tried to calm her as well...Ava struck out at her too. She continued to shriek covering her ears at the same time. Nancy and Sophie gathered the other autistic students to a safe place... while Mum... Dad... Ava's Mum... and I... wondered what to do.

"Why don't I try to calm Ava down?"

"I will try to do my best for Ava." I said

"Are you sure Cassie?"

"Ava could hit you and hurt you." said Mum, concerned

"We don't want the problem getting worse and ruining the event for everyone else too." said Dad, with a worried look

"Hmm... you have a good point there."

"I know the techniques you two have taught me when I get upset or when I have a meltdown... I'll do my best to use those with Ava." I said

I went over to Ava quietly and crouched down to her level. Mum and Dad are supervising... ready to intervene if things get out of control...Ava's Mum is also close by.

"Ava."

"Ava... it's all right." I say, gently

"The shark won't hurt you... I am here to help you." I said, soothingly

Ava begins to calm down and looks at me. She takes my hand.

"Would you like me to take you to a quiet place away from the scary shark?" I asked

Ava nodded... so I led her to a quiet place with a bench and gently sat her down.

"Ava... take three deep breaths for me." I instructed, holding up three fingers

"You should start to feel relaxed."

Ava processed this for a few minutes and began to take three deep breaths... much to our amazement she became calmer... and her body began to relax.

"That is amazing Cassie." said Ava's Mum

"Does Ava communicate through sign language?" I asked her

"She definitely does." her Mum replied

"I hear that you're gifted with that skill."

"Are you able to use it to talk to Ava about what has upset her?" she asked

"I should be able to... I understand autistic children and enjoy communicating with them." I said

I got down to Ava's level again... looked her in the eyes... and we both communicated using AUSLAN.

I signed... "Ava are you all right now?"

Ava signed back... "Yes."

I signed again... "That's good... can you tell me what scared you?"

Ava signed back... "Shark scared me."

I signed... "Well done for telling me."

"Would you like to join us in the games?"

Ava signed... "No."

I replied... "Ok."

"Why don't you play with me for a while?"

"We'll have fun together."

Ava signed ... "Yes, fun together."

"I signed ... "Great... let's have fun!"

I was thinking that Ava and I could have fun with technology... she has an iPad but rarely uses it. Ava's Mum came up with a suggestion.

"Cassie... how about you and Ava play with her trains?"

"It's her obsession... she will lend you one of hers to play with."

"Thanks."

"We will have fun with trains then!" I said

Ava's Mum asked Ava if she would lend me one of her trains... Ava signed yes... and lent me her train. For the next half an hour we played trains, acting out stories from 'Thomas the Tank Engine', a children's show that we both love to watch.

Everyone was amazed at the calming effect I had on Ava... the conversations we had... and our interaction with the train game. Nancy and Sophie were impressed that I remained calm throughout the entire situation... and used my skills to turn the experience into a positive one for Ava.

Mum and Dad chatted to Ava's Mum... while we played with the trains.

"Isn't it nice?"

"Ava is playing with a friend for the first time?"

"Cassie has made another new friend which is wonderful." said Dad

"It certainly is... Ava did not have any friends before."

"Play dates were a disaster!"

"Ava did not like the other kids... she was scared of them... if they came near... she would strike out."

"She loves her trains... but she would not let anyone play with them."

"She would not go anywhere unless I was with her... as she was afraid of strangers."

"This is a big step!"

"Making a friend for the first time!" Ava's Mum said, happily

"That's wonderful."

"Like Ava... Cassie did not have any friends until she was fifteen."

"Cassie also had a fear of other kids...when we started this road trip... she began to make some new friends."

"When Cassie calmed Ava down just now... she was using techniques that we have taught her... it was amazing for us to see her use them with another autistic child." said Mum, impressed

"I didn't realise she was so good with autistic children." said Ava's Mum

"Neither did we!"

"It was great to see it happening in front of our eyes!" Dad added, enthusiastically

"Cassie could work as a disability worker... like you two one day."

"She seems to have the 'magic' touch when it comes to autistic children!" said Ava's Mum

"Yes... she could contribute to helping children with disabilities... to thrive and progress." Mum agreed

I signed to Ava... "Do you want to watch our music performance later?"

"No." signed Ava

"Do you want to stay here a little longer?" I signed

"No." signed Ava

"Do you want to go home with your Mum?" I signed

"Yes... home with Mummy." signed Ava

Just then, Ava's Mum came over to us both.

"Ava wants to go home with you now." I told her Mother

"I think it's the best idea if she does."

"I don't want her to have another meltdown after making great progress today." I added

"I think you're right."

"Ava... come to Mummy sweetie... let's go home now." said Ava's Mum

Ava came over and held her Mum's hand... before they left... Ava gave me a little gift with her Mums' encouragement. It was a home-made coaster with flowers on it.

"What a nice little gift... thanks Ava." I signed

Ava smiled and then she did an amazing thing! She walked over to me and hugged me... it was nice... and I hugged her back. Mum, Dad and Ava's Mum, took a photo of the moment... quietly and carefully.

Then Ava and her Mum left.

Later, we played at our performance... the concert went very well... the autistic kids had fun and so did Nancy and Sophie! Everyone loved to dance and singalong together to their favourite tunes. The afternoon had been a great success and after helping Sophie and Nancy to pack things up and clear away... we wished them well and set off back to our accommodation.

As we drove Mum said...

"Cassie, that was wonderful today."

"You remained relaxed through that tense situation with Ava and helped to calm her down... then had a lovely time playing with her... for her first time."

"You did very well!"

"I think Mum and I, could see you working with autistic children as a disability worker one day." Dad added, proudly

"Thanks... Mum and Dad."

"You inspire me."

"I might plan to work as a disability worker in the future... whilst keeping my pop star career intact as well." I said, with a wink

As it was now late in the afternoon Mum said...

"I think we should get some takeaway for an early tea"

Dad and I both agreed... all that playing and singing had made us both hungry!

We drove to McDonalds and Dad spoke our order into what he thought was the speaker phone intercom, but I noticed that Dad was actually talking into a 'fancy' rubbish bin that was next door to the speaker!

"Hmm... these speakers don't seem to be working properly." said Dad, puzzled

Mum tried not to laugh... I did too... but it was so funny.

"Um... Dad, you are talking into the... rubbish bin." I sniggered, before Mum and I both lost it and cracked up

Dad looked closer and found that he was in fact... talking into a rubbish bin!

"Oh."

"I thought that was the speaker!" said Dad sheepishly, shaking his head

"Dad is talking to the looney bin... what next the 'Crazy John' phone?" I said, cheekily

"Cassie, keep that cheekiness up and you will get a clip under the ear." said Dad peevishly, 'cranky' to have mistaken a bin for the intercom speaker

"That's hilarious… I have a husband who talks to rubbish bins!" laughed Mum, making matters worse
Ha..Ha..Ha.. very funny dear." said Dad, in a sarcastic tone
"Let's just get our takeaway!" he fumed, grumpily
"Yes dear." said Mum, trying to pour oil on troubled waters, but still giggling

We arrived back at our hotel and spent a quiet evening after our hectic day at the park. We turned in early…we did not want to miss the train a third time!

In the morning we made sure not to be late… we had a quick breakfast and straight off to the station to finally catch the 'Ghan'! We left the rental car to be picked up from the railway station by the car rental service… having settled our account before we left.

After another special trip onboard the 'Ghan' we arrived back in Darwin and picked up our vehicle ready to continue our road trip.

The next state we plan to go to is Western Australia.

We have to equip ourselves with plenty of provisions as Western Australia is a very big state.

It has lots of desert area… just like Queensland and Northern Territory… there are many, many miles between each town and the next. Sometimes, there is no habitation for days on end… so you need to make sure that you are well prepared when you travel across the Great Sandy Desert… the Gibson Desert… and the Nullarbor Plain!

# Chapter Thirty-One
# 'Dizzy' Darwin, Derby & 'Seashells' Broome

"It will take us forty hours to get from Darwin in the Northern Territory to Kununurra in Western Australia by car... it would only take one hour if we took a flight from Darwin." said Dad

I was terrified at the thought of going on a flight... it made me feel so dizzy... I held my left hand on my head and steadied myself against our car.

"Cassie, are you ok?" asked Mum

"I feel dizzy... I feel like collapsing on the ground." I said, swaying

"It's all right darling."

"Mum and I will hold you by your arms and sit you down." said Dad

I nodded, so Mum and Dad got my arms placed them around their shoulders and took me to a nearby seat and sat me down slowly and gently. They kept holding me until the dizziness had passed.

"Are you ok now Cassie?"

"You gave us a scare." Mum said

"I'm ok now Mum."

"I thought I was going to collapse." I added

"Can you tell us what terrified you?" asked Dad

"When you talked about going on a flight to Kununurra... I was terrified at the idea of flying."

"I have a fear of flying... if we went up in a plane... I think I would freak out!" I said, trembling

"It's all right Cassie."

"We won't go up in a plane until we can help you to overcome your fear of flying."

"Well done for speaking up about it." Mum added

I hugged Mum and Dad.

"We shall just have to continue our trip by car." she added

"The weather will be hot today... so we'll need plenty of water to keep us hydrated...we will need enough supplies of food and petrol to make the journey across Western Australia."

"It's going to be a long... long journey... through this state... but we can do it!"

"Right?" I said, to convince myself

"Right Cassie!"

"We can get through the huge state of Western Australia together."

"I will look up some West Australian towns we can stay in."

"Hmm." mused Dad

"Well… we won't even make it into Western Australia on our first day!"

"It will take us six hours to drive to Timber Creek… where we can stay at the Timber Creek Hotel for the night." Dad said

"We can stop halfway at Katherine… for lunch." Mum added

"There is a roadhouse there where we can get some food."

"The following day we will travel from Timber Creek in the Northern Territory… through to Halls Creek in Western Australia…we can stay at the Halls Creek Motel."

"The day after that we should be able to push on through to Broome." said Dad

"We could take a short detour on the way to Broome Dad… there's a very special tree I have been reading about… at Derby."

"It's apparently fifteen hundred years old… a giant… hollow… boab tree… used to house indigenous prisoners… on their journey through to Derby in the 1890's." I said

"That part is sad…but it must be an amazing tree…to have lived so long and to be so big!"

"That's true Cassie… it could be worth a visit." Mum agreed

"There's also an art and cultural centre in Derby." I added

"It's called the 'Mowanjum Aboriginal Art and Cultural Centre'."

"It says in this article I was reading… that it is the creative hub for the Worrorra… Ngaringin… and Wunumbal tribes… that make up the Mowanjum community…outside Derby."

"That could be an interesting place to explore." said Dad

"When we finally get to Broome… we will be staying in the luxury 'Seashells' Hotel."

"I can't wait for that!" Mum said

"Well let's get started then!" said Dad, as we piled into the car on our way to Timber Creek

The next day we passed through Kununurra on our way to Halls Creek… Kununurra means 'meeting of the big waters'… in aboriginal language.

We stopped at the Halls Creek Motel for the night and continued on our way the next morning after breakfast… we were making for Derby… another drive of five and a half hours. When we arrived in Derby… we booked into the Spinifex Hotel, Clarendon Street for a couple of nights… then got a table in the restaurant for some modern Australian cuisine.

The next morning after a hearty breakfast we ventured out for some sight-seeing, the famous boab tree was seven kilometres out of town so we decided to visit there first and take some photographs. Next stop back in town again, there were art galleries to see and then the art and cultural centre.

There is lots to see in the centre… with beautiful indigenous paintings and information about the three tribes that live in the community around Derby. We also found out that Derby is the main centre for the Royal Flying Doctor Service… in the Kimberley region of Western Australia.

After a full day of sight-seeing we returned back to the 'Spini'… as the locals call it… had a relaxing evening and went straight to sleep.

In the morning, we drove to Broome which only took us a couple of hours. We booked in to 'Seashells' Broome for a week's stay at their luxury resort at Cable Beach. Cable beach is a twenty-two kilometre stretch of white sandy beach on the eastern Indian Ocean.

"Broome is a lovely town… with an awesome beach!" I said

"It's an awesome beach indeed Cassie!"

"We'll have a great time here this week."

"Mum and I, had a lovely time when we visited before… and we know you will too." Dad added

"Hello weekend!" I carolled
"What a nice day in Broome this is going to be."
"The sun is shining in the blue sky and there are plenty of things to do... like swimming in the 'Seashells' pool... or walking along the white sandy beach... beside the beautiful sparkling crystal blue sea."
"Looks like we are going to have a fun week ahead of us." I said
"We certainly are Cassie!"
"You can choose what we do first." Dad said
"I vote we relax for a couple of hours by the swimming pool."
"We can have a swim afterwards."
"I'll relax in my bra and knickers like I always do at the beach on a towel... or beach chair... or at a hotel pool on an outdoor lounger... with my dark black sunglasses on like a sexy model... or I might parade around the pool like a stunning model... then all the boys will drool with excitement when they see me!" I said giggling

Dad snorted with laughter. He is amused by my 'flights of fancy'... but he doesn't know that I plan to put my cheeky ideas into practice!
"I'm sorry Cassie!"
"Did you say the word 'sexy?" asked Mum, trying not to smile
"Err... No." I said, giggling
"I think I heard you say that."
"I hope you didn't get that idea from me."
"I did a similar thing at beaches during my teens!"
"Mum, you were a stunning gorgeous sexy model in those days."
"A 'hit' with the local boys!"
"Dad must have loved it too." I smirked
Dad laughed
"Very funny Cassie."
"Mum could I be a model?"
"I feel confident... sexy and beautiful."
"I could parade around like one?" I said, hopefully
"No... Cassie!"
"Don't get any ideas!"
"You can't be a model until you turn eighteen." Mum said, firmly
"Well Mum... you were a model when you were sixteen years old!"
"You do one thing... but tell me another." I said, petulantly
"I have to admit to that!"
"Dad, Olivia and Rebecca... started then as well." said Mum
"Still Cassie... you have to remember that it was a different time then... the world has changed a lot since those days."
I went into the bathroom and admired myself in my bra and knickers in the mirror... like I did when I was ten years old.
'Ooh Cassie, you're looking so sexy and beautiful like your Mum. You're going to be one fine stunning model when you reach the outdoor pool. The local boys there will whistle at you and you will be the envy of all the local girls.' I thought

I did a little Bollywood dance with my arms out in a straight line in front of me and giggled... followed by a sexy move... a la 'Britney Spears.' I giggled again

"I've got some sunscreen to put on so we don't get sunburnt." said Mum

We all put sunscreen on and Mum put some on my back where I couldn't reach.

We made our way to the outdoor pool with all our stuff, wearing our dark sunglasses and carrying our beach bags. I got out my iPod, switched to 'Pop Songs for Summer' section and lay down on a pool lounger.

Ahh, so good to relax at the 'Seashells' in Broome, I reckon I could live here forever in my own private paradise! Dad was relaxing on his chair next to Mum, reading his Jo Nesbo novel. He does love his novels, Mum was between us, relaxing like she was in paradise too! After the 'Pop Songs for Summer' had finished I noticed Mum's bag on the ground beside her lounger, she had 'Cadbury' white chocolate bars sticking out of it.

I grinned and tried to pinch one out of the bag, but Mum saw me.

"Cassie!"

"Nice try but they're mine."

"Put it back or you'll get your ears boxed."

I put the chocolate bar back and lay down again. I switched my iPod to Eurodance songs and relaxed. This is so blissful it has to be the best resort in Western Australia! Even though to be truthful... it is the only resort I have been to in Western Australia so far!

One of the hotel waiters joined us at the pool deck.

"Would you like some drinks?"

We looked at the drinks, we can tell they are alcoholic.

"No thank you... we don't drink alcohol."

"Can we have some lemonade drinks please?" I asked the waiter

"No problem." replied the waiter

He went away and came back with a tray of drinks... which I noted were Solo... Fanta... and Sunkist... how lucky that those are our favourites!

"Thank you."

"Do we pay for them here?" asked Dad

"As it's your first visit to the 'Seashells' here in Broome... it's complimentary."

"Please enjoy." said the waiter

"We will... thank you." answered Mum

"Cheers!" we all said, clinking our glasses and downing our lemonades

At noon after we changed into our bathers, we had a nice swim in the outdoor pool. It was a lovely pool and the water was sparkling and cool on a hot day.

"Mum, Dad, this is a great resort we are staying in."

"Seashells is a brilliant name for it."

"I knew it was going to be excellent when we chose it... this is awesome!"

"The pool is great to swim in and it's wonderful weather!" I said, happily

"We are enjoying the resort too, Cassie."

"It's a great family pool to swim in... it reminds me of happy times spent with your Dad." said Mum

"I'm enjoying this holiday with you two...the hotel staff are very nice." I said

An hour later it is still hot... we are coping with the heat and drinking water to stay hydrated. Sometime later... my head begins to ache.

"What's the matter Cassie?" asked Mum

"I've got a headache." I said

"What does it feel like Cassie?" asked Dad

"Like someone is pressing my head down." I replied

"It must be the heat." I moaned

"Yes... it's probably heatstroke... too much time in the sun."

"It's best to lie down in a cool darkened room for that."

"Maybe take some headache tablets and rest for a couple of hours... hopefully the headache will go away." Mum advised

I took a couple of Panadol tablets which I washed down with a glass of water. I don't mind the taste of medicine anymore... I used to dislike the taste... including my behaviour medication but now I take medicine without resisting... because it helps me to get better.

When I woke up a couple of hours later... I was feeling fine... the headache was gone.

"How do you feel Cassie?" asked Mum

"I'm feeling much better Mum." I said

"We're glad your headache has gone." Dad said

We decided to go outside for some fresh air and a stroll. We walked along the brick path to the entertainment area... I looked around and saw several cabins and palm trees... I also saw a family playing in the pool... presumably getting a late afternoon swim before dinner. A couple were looking at a bush covered in flowers.

This fascinating view I see as I walk through the garden exterior of Seashells... is a private tropical oasis... I'm feeling the warmth of 'Broome Time" ... this is certainly a great start to our week in Broome!

"This is an awesome tropical oasis... and I am loving the warmth of it!"

"It's so bright and colourful... I'm keen to see all the activities that 'Seashells' has to offer." I said

"There are a lot of things we can do here!"

"Tomorrow... why don't we hire some bikes and ride around the bike track?" asked Dad

"I do enjoy a bike ride with you and Mum." I agreed

"It feels so good to ride in the sunshine and through the shady trees... with the wind blowing."

"We'll do that tomorrow... we can try a mango juice... that will be refreshing!" Mum added

"We can walk along Cable beach and soak up the shining sun... we can feel the sand between our toes." I said

"We might even chase each other across the sand for fun... just like Mum and I used to do when we were young." said Dad, remembering

We arrived at the entertainment area and ordered a nice meal then we proceeded to enjoy the beautiful evening.

Later, back in our suite Mum skyped her Dad. Darren had been to Broome once with Belinda in 1969 on their honeymoon, it was a year before they had Mum and Rebecca. Mum shares our Broome experiences so far with him.

'Hello, Dad. How are you doing this fine evening, my handsome, cheeky father?... I'm doing well thanks, my mischievous, pretty pop musician eldest twin daughter.... How are you?... I'm doing well, thanks, Dad. We're at a nice, relaxing and beautiful resort called the 'Seashells'....It's such a lovely resort and we're enjoying every minute of our stay so far...we are in Broome....it's a lovely town and Cassie is enjoying the experience with us....Yes, I am....The service is friendly and we had a delicious meal in the excellent spacious entertainment area, looking up at the evening sky.... Seems like you are having a great time Cassie....if you take some photos of Broome, show Belinda and I... if you can....I will take some awesome ones, we can have fun and laugh re-living the stories….We sure will….We are planning to go for a bike ride tomorrow, as we may take a long walk on Cable beach….It's going to be a fun-filled family day tomorrow….It sounds like a fun-filled exercise day for you three…have fun!…We will, Dad….we are going to try a mango juice too!…they are very refreshing…They are, last time Mum and I were in Broome for a few days, we stayed at 'Seashells', walked along Cable beach, tried the mango juice and had a massage, which was very relaxing….I remember that was in March 2008… I skyped you to see you how were, I told Cassie what you were up to and she enjoyed hearing all about it, she laughed at a couple of your funny stories….it was a good holiday for you and Mum.'

'It was darling, I still remember the time in 1989, I ordered four rocking chairs that I planned to use for decoration in the home, and Daniel, Olivia, Rebecca and you put the order in for me… but cheekily you ordered 'four rockers' instead! The day arrived for the 'rockers' to be delivered, you were in your cars and when the 'rockers' went into the Bontel-Macdonald mansion and started practising in the backyard, you drove off to the pub hysterically laughing all the way! I said…what's that awful noise? Who hired these rock musicians?!'

'We thought you four might be at the Melbourne Pub… when we got there you were hiding all over the place!…You hid behind the bar, Olivia was under a table, Daniel was behind the counter, and Rebecca was sitting at the counter….Then we heard muffled giggles, as you emerged from your hiding places, with guilty grins on your faces….Err… Hello, Dad….There are drinks on the house, you mumbled…. I replied… you will get you a clip under the ears when you get home…then Daniel emerged from behind the counter saying… err hello Darren…. there were plenty of drinks all around…. Olivia came out from under the table with…. Hi Darren I'm just cleaning under the table….I looked around for Rebecca saying… Rebecca I know you are around here somewhere….Come out from wherever you are….she tried to muffle her giggles but she never could successfully and came out with a sheepish grin saying…erm… Hi Dad….I've got a spare seat for you.'

'When we got home, you all finally confessed about the prank that you had pulled with the four rockers!… Oh, it was hilarious….This well-known band that you hired for me couldn't understand why they weren't expected!…It was a great laugh though after all!…That was the best prank that I ever pulled off!…We had a good laugh about it afterwards….You planned that prank very well and pulled it off perfectly….I'll tell you a Dad joke now!'

Mum laughed nervously… "Oh dear, I feared that might be coming."

Darren told his Dad joke and Mum thought it was hilarious, she laughed and Dad laughed too.

'You always get embarrassed by my Dad jokes, then you see the funny side…. I don't mind your Dad jokes, though they are sometimes embarrassing…I've published a few jokes books of my own Dad…Mikayla's Hilarious Jokes…Mikayla's Hilarious Jokes Two… Mikayla's Hilarious Jokes Three…Mikayla's Hilarious Compilation Bumper Edition Four and Mikayla's Hilarious Jokes Five'

'Compared with Daniel's Dad jokes they are much better than yours' Dad….Dad, Mum and I laugh loudly….Ha, ha, they are indeed much better than my Dad jokes….You better believe it Dad!…We've also got a concert in Broome on Tuesday, so we are going to have an excellent night….Have a good time at the concert, the fans will be happy to see you….They sure will….I'll log off now, we need some sleep before the bike ride tomorrow!… Bye, Dad…. Bye, darling have fun.'

The next day, we hired three bikes complete with helmets, then walked them to the starting point of the ride. It's a good day for a ride, Mum, Dad and I, are going to have fun.

"Bike riding is a popular family thing that we do together… due to my sensory issues before I was sixteen… we had to choose a quiet location with not many people or animals along the route… before we undertook the ride."

"We can take any route now without problems… we know the road rules for riding our bikes." I added

"That's right, Cassie."

"You have all the road rules covered!"

"We taught you to ride when you were five years old."

"It took practice and lots of encouragement each time you fell off...eventually you had no problems riding anywhere." said Dad

"When I had my training wheels taken off... I was scared to ride on my bike for a while...I managed to get back on and starting riding around the block... then a few years later we started having family bike rides."

"I learnt the road and bike safety rules before I had my training wheels taken off... I always obey them... regardless of what destination we are riding to." I said

"That's the right thing to do."

"Let's start riding around the assigned route... we can take in all the sights along the way." Mum added

We started riding along the route near 'Seashells' and saw a few lookout points. We took some photos of views along the way... we waved to some of the people who recognised us. It was a fun ride and I was loving it... Mum and Dad too.

"I can smell the ocean... it's a nice smell of salty sea and beaches."

"What great times." said Dad

"We're getting plenty of exercise and testing our leg muscles!"

"There are some more things to see on this route." said Mum

We stopped in town and went to a health food shop.

"It's got everything we need for our bike ride." Mum said

"Most of the visitors come here to get energy bars or water, particularly on a hot day like today." said the cashier

We looked at the stock before we decided on a water bottle each and a health food bar, we also got some apples and chocolate. I have never tried a health food bar before... this is the right time on our bike ride.

"Have fun on your bike ride... stay safe." said the cashier, as we left the shop

"We will... thank you." I waved goodbye

We ate the health food bars and drank some water, then we resumed our ride. It was a little hotter now, but we kept going. It was hard work but fun as well, as we returned to the start.

"I enjoyed that bike ride, despite the hot weather!"

"We enjoyed it too!"

"We were recognised by some visitors even in Broome."

"That water and those health food bars certainly kept us going." said Dad, smiling

"It's just as well we put sunscreen on... or we would be very sunburnt!"

"We'll have a little rest before we start the walk along Cable beach."

"Cassie, you love walking along beaches... don't you?" said Mum

"Yes, I do Mum."

After we had rested for a while, we made our way down to the beach.

We stepped on to the sand and started walking... it was my first time on Cable Beach.

"Mum, Dad, Cable beach feels lovely to walk along."

"The smells and sensations would have overwhelmed me when I was little... but when I turned four... I began to enjoy the sights and sounds and smells... every time I walk along a beach now."

"The salty sea air... the sound of the ocean crashing onto the shore... the feel of the yellow or white sand as you walk on it...the beach is one of my favourite places to be." I said, happily

"During summers we would take you to different beaches... you would love them."

"When Mum and I were thirteen... we went to the beach in Geelong and had a fun time there."

"At one point your Mum chased me around for five minutes... we were both laughing and your Mum tackled me to the ground... we both laughed and laughed... despite being covered in sand."

"Then we went in the water to wash the sand off and played in the waves... we went home soaking wet... it was good fun!" says Dad, remembering fondly

"Cassie you can play that game with us... if you would like to." said Mum

"I would love that... catch me if you can Mum." I laughed

Mum chased me around for ages before she caught me... then tackled me to the sand! We both laughed... it was fun! I brushed the sand off me... and then Dad started to chase me! We both laughed as we fell over in the sand... it was hilarious! It was fun playing this game with Mum and Dad... now that I am older and it doesn't frighten me anymore.

"There's sand all over our clothes... let's have a shower back at 'Seashells' and get into some fresh clothes."

"We've had such a good day together!" I said, happily

We booked an evening massage, we needed it after all our exercising on a hot and fun filled day. We made our way to the massage room, stripped down to our underwear, and lay down on three tables that were side by side. The three lady attendants have something new for us to try.

"Are those hot stones?" I asked, gingerly

"Yes, they are." replied the attendant

"These are designed to melt away tensions... ease stiffness in your muscles... and increase your blood flow circulation."

"If you have key points on your body that need relaxing just let us know... we'll place the massage stones there for you." said Tanya

"There's a point in my back that needs doing."

"It's been aching for the past two days... so those stones may be helpful." said Mum

"My shoulder needs relaxing it's been tight for days." moaned Dad

"My back needs relaxing too!"

"It's been tense... so it would be great if the massage stones can help me to relax it." I said

"No problems."

"The massage stones can be a little hot." said the second lady, named Linda

Tanya, Linda and Wendy got the massage stones ready... then Linda and Wendy applied them to Mum and Dad's tension points.

"OW!" yelled Mum

"Ouch!" grimaced Dad

"We have never experienced hot rock therapy before!" said Mum, screwing up her face

"I have never encountered hot rocks before either." I said

"That's all right... we will put them on very gently... so you will feel relaxed." said Tanya

The massage stones were a bit hot... but they relaxed not only our tight points... but also the rest of our bodies...making us able to unwind after our day of strenuous exercise. It feels so good to be totally relaxed all over.

We chatted to Tanya, Linda and Wendy... about our road trip so far.

"Our road trip is going very well... we've made a few discoveries... had a few adventures... and met and made new friends."

"There were a few moments where I got anxious and upset...I got through them with Mum's relaxation technique of rubbing her hands over mine to calm me." I said

"That's a good technique... there is healing in skin to skin contact."

It is calming and soothing to the mind."

"Your road trip sounds amazing... what a great time you must all be having together!" said Tanya

"Yes, we are!"

"Our music tour as 'The Bontel Family' is awesome...we're also gaining lots of fans."

"I enjoy seeing the smiles on the fan's faces...it's great to meet them." I said

"It's lovely to have a positive influence on your fans... performing your songs...brightening their day with your music." said Tanya

"Daniel and I, enjoy giving massages to our clients... especially those with special needs...they also enjoy the sensation and feeling of having relaxed muscles... especially after a tough day."

"We love seeing the relaxed and happy look on their faces." said Mum, smiling

"Some use the table and others use the sauna."

"We use a different colour setting depending on what body tissues need healing."

"The energy can be rebalanced in the body by applying the appropriate colour... that's where the colour healing properties come in." Dad adds

"It sounds like you are working wonders you two!"

"I agree, it is a rewarding job relaxing people... when their days have been tough." said Linda

"Some of our special needs clients feel more relaxed and do better... also with their parents help as well they have thanked us.... it is well worth the hard work." Dad said

"It certainly is." Wendy smiled

"Mum gave me a massage in our hotel room in Townsville... with classical music playing... it was very relaxing."

"It may be something I might do in the future." I mused

"We can teach her the skills we learnt during our Massage Therapy Courses at the University of Melbourne."

"Cassie is very good at relaxing children." said Mum

"That's a great start then." said Tanya

It is a couple of days later and Mum, Dad and I, are at our Broome Concert ready to go on stage. Around six thousand people are here waiting for us... it is thirty degrees... we have our water bottles ready to keep us hydrated between songs! A few minutes later our names are announced and we make our way to the stage. We introduce ourselves and get into position. I start things off with what I think is a hilarious joke... but I'm not sure Mum and Dad see it that way!

"Mum and Dad used to have a contest years ago in the early 90's!"

"That contest was to see who could pass wind the loudest." I laugh

Everyone else laughed too they thought it was hilarious! I collapsed laughing in a heap on the floor.

Mum put her hands on the drums and her head on them too...she was red with embarrassment! Dad face-palmed himself and cringed.

"Why did I get out of bed this morning?" mumbled Mum, her mouth still muffled by the drums

"What is happening to our concert!" said Dad, aghast under his breath

I tried to compose myself... I was still giggling.

"We will get you back for that!"

"Just you wait!" Dad threatened, ominously

"You are too rude Cassie!" said Mum, frowning

"All right let's get on with this Broome concert then!"

I high fived the air and Mum and Dad looked at each other and rolled their eyes at me!

During a break after our sixth song Mum and Dad sneaked Mum's iPhone into the left pocket of my spare pair of blue pants without me knowing. I changed into my spare blue pants during the interval and we walked back onstage ready to complete the second half of the show. This time we were about to start our first song when an iPhone started ringing, our fans can bring their iPhones or mobile phones to our concerts to take photos, but their call tones and ring tones are supposed to be switched off, or on silent, during showtime.

"Whose phone is ringing?" I ask, suspiciously

"It's not mine." said a fan from the front row

"Well we don't mind you taking photos of us... but if you're going to make a phone call please do it outside." I said, officiously

We went to start again... another phone call!

"Ok... whose phone is that!"

"Hand it over please." I said, holding my hand out

The audience didn't say anything... they were trying not to laugh.

We started again and sure enough off goes a phone.

I felt something this time in my left pocket... when I put my hand into the pocket out came an iPhone! What was that doing there? Who could have put that in there?

"Oh... for crying out loud!"

"Who did this?" I said red-faced, after making such a fuss to the audience

The audience were laughing out loud at me.

"Who would do that?" I muttered under my breath

Then I heard two people laughing behind me and the truth dawned... it was payback time for me from Mum and Dad after my bad joke on them at the beginning of the concert!

I saw some fans with water bombs... I had an idea of how to get Mum and Dad back for the iPhone prank. I needed to distract them so they wouldn't find out what I was planning.

"Hey Mum... Dad... look!"

"There is a plane flying over Broome."

"Look way up in the sky!" I said, pointing upwards

They turned to look, hoping to spot the plane flying over the Broome stage. Whilst they were craning their necks for a non-existent plane up in the sky, I walked to the front of the stage and asked a fan for two water bombs. I walked back a few metres, just the right distance from Mum and Dad, and threw them over my shoulder.

"Hey!" came the sound of two voices

I laughed and laughed clutching my sides. My counter-prank has worked perfectly. The audience are in stitches too!

"Oh, strewth!"

"That prank was hilarious Mum and Dad didn't expect that one."

"Thanks for helping me out!" I waved to the audience

The audience were grinning, the fan who handed me the two water bombs spoke.

"That's all right."

"You got them wet."

"Hee, hee!" I giggled

Mum and Dad come walking up behind me and stop.

"Erm... Mum and Dad are behind me... aren't they?" I say, facing the audience

The audience nod... I turn around and see Mum and Dad dripping all over the stage.

"Oh, dear."

"I'm going to cop it aren't I!" the audience nod again, loving every minute of it

"Cassie, you're about to get a clip under the ear from your Mother!" Mum threatened

"I bet you can't catch me." I giggled

"You got us back, all right!" Dad glowered

"Looks like you need a change of fresh clothes!"

"Yes... 'THANKS' to YOU... we do!" said Mum and Dad together very loudly

"Let's get changed so the concert can continue." said Dad

Mum and Dad went backstage to change, meanwhile I told a couple of jokes. When Mum and Dad came back on stage the concert resumed, it was wonderful!

"Broome was such a great place to stay!" I said days later, as we were packing

"Cable beach was a favourite highlight of mine." said Mum

"I enjoyed our bike riding."

"We certainly got plenty of exercise and saw some sights along the way." said Dad, happily

"The Broome concert was pretty amazing... except for the pranks we played on each other... though I suspect the fans enjoyed them...they thought they were very funny!" said Mum

"We have had a lovely time in Broome... I shall be sad to leave...there are still so many places left to explore though... on our great Australian road trip!" I added

"That's right Cassie... tomorrow we get 'back on the road again'... in the famous words of country singer Willie Nelson... and make our way to Port Headland... it will take us about six hours drive." smiled Dad, very pleased with his musical joke

"OK... here's another country gem for you...let's hit the hay!" said Mum, laughing as we made our way to bed

I groaned.

## *Chapter Thirty-Two*
## Markets, Music & Fishing Mayhem!

When we arrived at the Esplanade Hotel in Port Hedland, which we had booked by phone the day before, the receptionist gave us an envelope saying...

"This contains an event which is to be held in your honour... as special guests."

"Please open the envelope and see."

We went to our hotel room... excited to find out what the envelope contained!

"I can't wait to find out what this event is!" I said, excitedly

"Me too!" said Mum

"Me three!"

"Let's open it and see!" said Dad

What event could this be?

We opened the envelope and read...

To the Bontel Family,

*'We're so happy that you have arrived in Port Hedland. You are invited tomorrow to Port Hedland Community Day, which will be dedicated to the Bontel Family band.*

*You can explore our markets and see all the wares, such as textiles, artwork and jewellery, there are around fifty stall holders. You may perform in the shady gardens of the Courthouse Gallery if you wish, alongside our other street performers, and try an array of delicious food in the outdoor food court.*

*Check out the West End Markets off Edgar Street, you might like to eat at the Silver Café in the West End. It is housed inside a 1920s rail carriage used for travelling between Port Hedland and Newman by dignitaries and community members, travelling to the Mt Newman Mining Sites. You can try a great cup of coffee with delicious cake, or you may want to sample the tasty breakfast, lunch or dinner menu.*

*You might like a swim in the newly redeveloped South Hedland Aquatic Centre, it's an excellent way to cool off in this West Australian heat! There's also an exciting water theme park with a wave simulator that you may like to try.*

*We hope to see you out and about in our great community, if you can make it!*

From the Port Hedland Community.

"Wow!"

"How about that?"

"We get to participate... socialise... and have loads of fun... in a 'Bontel Family' Port Hedland Community Day!"

"This is wicked!" I said

"This is going to be so exciting!"

"We never had a festival day named after us before."
"There are plenty of activities for us to try… I would love to go on the 'Wave' simulator!" Mum grinned
"I would love to try the Wave simulator too!"
"That Silver Café sounds a nice place to eat."
"The 1920's rail carriage might be nice to dine!"
"You love your trains Mikayla."
"This one sounds great!" said Dad
"That 1920's rail carriage does sound a special place to have a meal… I do love my trains." Mum agreed
"That 'Wave' simulator sounds like fun."
"I'll try that too!"
We unpacked our things in our rooms and had an early night ready for all the fun in the morning!
Mum, Dad and I, walk through the market the next day and we are astonished to see all the local handmade items. I could buy them all… they are so well made and lovely to look at.
"The markets are full of great items to look at and to buy."
"I see a homemade jewellery stall just over there… Mikayla and Cassie!"
"I bet you can't keep your eyes off those shiny pieces!" grins Dad
Mum and I, made our way to the jewellery section, there were many pieces of homemade jewellery of various descriptions. Oh, wow! There are so many to choose from, I like one of the bracelets, and Mum likes one of the rings!
"This bracelet will look good on my left arm."
"It's a fashion statement that I'm about to make." I said
"Good choice young lady… it will look good on you!"
"We have the finest homemade jewellery… this is one of the most popular items that we sell to visitors who come to this market." the jewellery stall owner said
"This ring will look great on my index finger… next to the ring that I've always worn on my middle finger since 1990!"
"It will go well in my ring collection that I have collected and bought over the years." said Mum
"Er… I would like to buy a piece of jewellery." Dad said
"No… you can't!"
"It's for women only!" said Mum
"Well that's not very fair!" muttered Dad
"I would look great with an ear-ring!"
"Like a 'swashbuckling' pirate." Dad grinned
A few visitors nearby smiled at the idea of Dad with an ear-ring. It would be funny to see that!
"Okay ladies… you can wear the jewellery." said Dad, grinning again
Mum and I, bought a homemade bangle and ring, we tried them on and admired ourselves.
"You two look fantastic with your new purchases on." Dad said, admiringly
"I'll take a couple of photos of you both." he added
After we explored a little more it was lunchtime so we went to the West End where the Silver Café was located.
We went inside and made our way to a table to look at the lunch menu, the dishes sounded delicious! Which ones should we try?
"Welcome to the Silver Café!"
"You can have a great cup of coffee and enjoy the variety of delectable cakes and sweets."

"Or you can try something from the breakfast, lunch or dinner menu."

"You're the 'Bontel Family' aren't you?" asked the waiter

"Yes... we are."

"We've never been to this café before." I said

"It has a great history from the 1920s... I can guarantee that you will enjoy your lunch here!"

Mum, Dad and I, chose a burger each with chips, and a can of soft drink as well. We had a leisurely lunch before heading to the Courthouse Gallery... where we will be performing shortly.

The Courthouse Gallery looks like a good place, the shady gardens will be a cool place to play on a hot day like this. The audience is starting to gather... they can't wait to see us perform... we can't wait to perform for them either. We will have a great concert!

"Hello Port Hedland."

"We are having such a brilliant weekend at the 'Bontel Family-Port Hedland Festival', it was very nice of Port Hedland to do such a lovely thing for us."

"How are you all?" I asked the crowd

"We're good, thanks." the crowd called back

"Well let's get started then!"

"To all the visitors here for just a couple of hours... or staying a little longer... please enjoy the concert and make some happy memories with us."

"These shady gardens will keep you cool and there will be food stalls opening in fifteen minutes so you can get a bite to eat during the interval."

"Our music will have you dancing and singing... so let's see everybody up and having a good time!" I said

The performance was very successful, and one visitor came up and spoke to me.

"Cassie... I arrived for a bit of market browsing...then I heard the music!"

"You did brilliantly in the shady gardens with your singing... I'll never forget that ...you are one pretty pop star!"

I blushed and giggled.

"Thank you."

"I'm from nearby Dampier... I'm a regular visitor to Port Hedland." he added

"Thanks for coming to the concert." I said

"I really enjoyed it... my children love the 'Bontel Family'... they were delighted to hear your performance."

"Well, that was one cool concert!"

"The Bontel Family Port Hedland Festival, is awesome!"

"I found a new fan too!" I grinned at Mum and Dad

"Port Hedland loves us and the fans here appreciate our music."

"You seem to have made a big hit here with the locals, Cassie." said Mum, grinning back at me

"Maybe we can make a visit to a children's hospital whilst we are here... or take part in a charity sports event." said Dad, smiling

"I'm famished!"

Let's get something from the food stall... we need some food in us!" I stated, firmly

Mum and Dad looked at each other and laughed.

"You always need food Cassie!" they said, together

Later in the afternoon, we went to the South Hedland Aquatic Centre for some cooling down. It's a good swimming place, to get some exercise and also some relief from the heat! I will enjoy this... the pool soothes me although I wouldn't go in the deep end for years... because I feared I would drown... that is until I took swimming lessons when I was fourteen... which gave me the confidence to swim from one end of the pool to the other.

After we finished at the aquatic centre we walked back to the market for a little more fun. Then, an important looking figure walked up to us... Mum and Dad explained to me that it's the current mayor of Port Hedland... Bill Peters. I see some sort of award in his hand, I wonder what it is?

"Hello Bontel Family... it's nice to meet you in Port Hedland... having fun at your special festival day." said Mayor Bill

"It's nice to meet you too... Mr Peters."

"We're having an awesome day we have done plenty of 'wicked' things." I said, smiling

Mum, Dad and I, shook Mayor Bills' hand... he's very smart and professional... he has been the Mayor of Port Hedland since 2009.

"What fun things have you been experiencing today at the festival?" asked Bill

"We have been shopping at the market stalls, and performing in the shady gardens near the Courthouse Gallery."

"We had a fun time with our fans." I told him

"That's excellent!" Bill replied

"Thanks, Mayor Bill."

"I had my eyes set on some homemade jewellery... but Mikayla and Cassie wouldn't let me buy any!" Dad told him with a grin

"That's funny!"

"You bring humour and joy with your concerts... your music brings vibrance and positivity to Port Hedland!"

"Here in my hand are three awards... one for each of you." said Mayor Bill, cheerily

Mayor Bill handed us a sash each... my goodness... it's great to get an award like this. I'm so happy... so are Mum and Dad.

"Wow!"

"Thanks Mayor Bill."

"What are these sashes for?" I asked him

"They are for our honoured guests... the 'Bontel Family' band at the Port Hedland Festival."

"I hope you will wear them with pride... whilst you are here in our beautiful city of Port Headland." Mayor Bill said, as he presented us with our sashes

"Thanks Mayor Bill... it is an honour to receive them." Dad replied

"There is going to be a Port Hedland dinner tonight... you are invited as our honoured guests!" Mayor Bill added

"Why thank you Mayor Bill."

"That would be an honour." said Mum

"There will be my council colleagues and their partners... together with my wife Adriana and myself."

"It will be great if you can be there." Mayor Bill said

"Of course, we will be there Mayor Bill."

"We are staying in Port Hedland as part of our road trip... we are touring around Australia." I told him

"That's excellent!"

"Port Hedland loves listening to your music."

"We'll see you this evening... we would love to hear about your road trip." said Bill

"We'll see you tonight, Mayor Bill." Dad replied

"That's so nice of Mayor Bill to invite us to a special dinner function."

"It will be the first one we have attended as a family… how nice." said Mum

"We have been to many dinner functions over the years."

"We have even been to one with the royal family in 1992." remembers Dad

"You have been to some awesome dinner functions."

"You had great times, chatting, laughing and telling stories."

"I recall you telling me that." I said

"We sure did Cassie!" Mum agreed

"It will be such fun tonight." I said

Later in the evening we put on our best formal evening wear. Mum and I, have evening dresses in our favourite colours, mine is blue and Mum has a yellow gown, we are both wearing makeup and our hair has been styled at the salon in the hotel.

Dad is wearing a formal suit in his favourite colour of green, he is not wearing any make-up, but cheeky Dad has added a pirate ear-ring to his outfit, just to show Mum and I, that guys can wear jewellery too!

Mum and I burst out laughing… but we have to agree that Dad is pretty handsome as a pirate! We are definitely stylin' it tonight!

We made our way to the Port Hedland Dinner where Bill, Adriana, and six of Bills' work colleagues and their partners, are waiting for us.

"Hello Mr Mayor."

"We are looking forward to this dinner tonight." I said, happily

"Hello."

"This is my wife, Adriana."

"Adriana is also my assistant and helps me out with all the paperwork." said Bill, smiling

"Hello Adriana… it's nice to meet you." Mum said

"Hello Bontel Family."

"Bill tells me that you are touring Australia with your debut album, and it's doing very well for you."

"The 'Bontel Family' Port Hedland Festival is a great success I do hope you are having a good time?" Adriana asked

"We certainly are Adriana."

"It is great fun and we feel honoured to be in a festival like this… in a fantastic town like Port Hedland." added Dad

Port Hedland is such a vibrant place to come to here in Western Australia… you have contributed to the 'vibe' with your music… which we appreciate greatly." Bill added

"Thanks a lot!"

"We started this road trip so that Cassie could explore Australia, and we could show her the landmarks and places we have been to, on our travels over the years. We have been exploring and trying new adventures and activities along the way to encourage Cassie to be brave, and to help her overcome situations where she becomes overwhelmed, upset or anxious. Her progress has been immense, she has come such a long way since we began our journey together. In Adelaide she was even able to help calm an autistic child during a large event." said Mum, proudly

"You are taking an inspiring journey… that most of us only dream of doing!"

"Cassie must be enjoying every minute of her adventures with you both… embracing the wonderful beauty of the Australian landscape… and the fabulous flora and fauna across our vast continent." Adriana beamed

"Yes... it has been a beautiful blessing for us... to share it with her."

"Cassie has made so much progress that she is inspiring other children with disabilities to live a happy life... no matter how many obstacles there are to climb over... or to go around." Dad said

"That's wonderful!"

"I bet she will become an advocate for children with autism and other disabilities." said Bill

"We hope so Bill."

"She's using music to help them... and she's passionate about raising awareness."

"Our charity... 'Autism Angels'... which we formed in 2002 is doing brilliantly... she may work with us and help out in various autism charity events that we plan to do... once this road trip is over." Mum told him

"I hope she does... it will be good for her."

"Cassie, you're doing brilliantly appearing in the 'Bontel Family' band."

"We read a few news reports that you stepped onto the Sydney stage and sang brilliantly with 'The Sparkles' too." Adriana said

"Yes, I really embraced the experience!" I agreed, nodding to Adriana

"When I was about to step onto the Sydney stage, Mum and Dad were concerned that I might get stage fright and meltdown!"

"They didn't need to worry, I overcame my issues with crowds, loud noise, and bright lights, one by one, and broke through to sing my powerhouse songs... the crowd loved it!" I said

"Maybe Mum, Dad and I, will do a Christmas album together when it gets closer to December... possibly a Christmas concert too!"

"We would love to hear that and so would our children too!" Mayor Bill added

We are having so much fun... I'm enjoying the dinner... there have been many funny stories told around the table.

"I remember a funny story when Daniel and I were eighteen... it involves make-up and nail polish." said Mum, smiling

"Oh No!"

"Here we go again." muttered Dad, knowing just what story Mum is going to tell

"When Daniel, Olivia, Rebecca and I, were eighteen years old in the summer of 88/89 we were swimming in our pool at the Bontel-Macdonald mansion. We had a smashing time back then, swimming and throwing the beach ball to each other and splashing about."

"A little later Daniel had a rest and we decided to play a prank on him." Mum smiled

"Olivia, Rebecca and I, got our nail polish and decided to paint his nails blue!"

We shushed each other silently and giggled on the inside whilst we did it...thirty minutes later when he woke up, he was surprised to find his nails had turned blue."

"All right very funny... who painted my nails blue?" Daniel called out

"Olivia, Rebecca and I were hiding inside in the man cave trying not to laugh... it was no use... Daniel found us!"

"It was you three that painted my nails blue wasn't it!" he accused

"I replied 'Err...no'."

"Oh... I think you three did it all right!"

"You think it's funny... don't you?"

"Go on and laugh then!" but he wasn't really mad

"That was a little embarrassing for me...funny as well I guess." Dad recalls

"Speaking of funny... I have a story of my own to tell!" said Dad, giving Mum a mischievous look

"It was in 1983 at the Bontel-Macdonald mansion when we were thirteen."

"We were reading our books on a long winter's evening… whilst drinking our hot chocolate by the fireplace to keep warm."

"When Mikayla, Olivia and Rebecca were getting some food during a break… I decided to make the beds up for the night."

"Why don't I make the beds up?"

"We need extra blankets with this cold weather."

"They agreed, so I went to the bedrooms."

"However, I folded and adjusted the sheets in everyone's beds."

"When it was time to turn in for the night there were shouts all round!"

"Hey!"

"Who short-sheeted our beds?"

"We can't get in them our legs won't go down!"

"There's only one joker who would do this and I know his name!"

"How can we get him back?"

"I've got an idea."

Then…

"Mikayla, Olivia and Rebecca, got their cups of water and went into my room, they crept to the left side of my bed ready to throw it at me… but above them… rigged by me… was a cup full of glitter which emptied over them."

"Who did that?"

"We weren't expecting that!"

"Mikayla, Olivia and Rebecca, had to have a shower to get the glitter off them and then get changed into fresh pyjamas."

"I had filled the cup with glitter and hooked it up to the ceiling with a piece of string and positioned it ready to pull."

"Mikayla, Olivia and Rebecca came in and when they got near enough to my bed I pulled sharply on the string and the glitter came pouring down on top of them."

"That was a brilliant prank and I pulled it off perfectly… it was so funny!" said Dad, laughing all over again, as he remembered the way the others looked all covered in glitter from head to toe

We all chuckled! Dad can be a practical joker as well as Mum! He could be her prank assistant…they could open a joke shop together.

"Who knows what practical jokes you three will think of next?" said Adriana

We all laughed at that thought!

We said our goodbyes at the end of the evening and shook hands with Bill, Adriana and their colleagues, but not before Bill gave us a few words of encouragement to see us on our way.

"Keep making music to brighten up even the dreariest of days… no matter where you are… keep the humour to cheer your fans… they love that from you." he added

"Thank you for those kind words Bill."

"We'll remember them." Mum replied

A couple of days later, after an early tea, we made our way to the 'Staircase to the Moon' viewing area. When the full moon occurs in this region, dramatic tide changes happen throughout the entire day, so that pockets of water are caught in the sand and a 'rippled' effect, reflects the moon's natural rising colour.

If you view this area with a full moon on a still evening, you can see the light has created what looks like a 'golden staircase' that leads right up to the moon. We walked to the Cook Point Caravan Park, which has the best vantage point to view the staircase Moon. There is a viewing deck there, so we went and waited until the full Moon rose.

"It's a wonderful evening... it's very magical...I love seeing the moon on the water." I said

"I love seeing it too Cassie... it reminds me of my girlfriend days with your Dad." said Mum, fondly

"On some days when we were in our late teens Mum and I used to go to a place called Lover's Lane and sit on the bonnet of my Holden Barina... to watch the sunset until the sky went dark and the moon and stars came out."

"Then we would kiss... with our arms wrapped around each other."

"Good moments they were." said Dad, with a goofy grin on his face

"I love hearing those moments from you both."

"They make me feel good inside."

"We are going to see something phenomenal from this viewing deck."

"It's almost as good as you two on your Holden Barina... watching the sky like this!" I said, with a wink at Mum and Dad

The full Moon rose in all her glory and created something that I have never seen before in my entire life. It's a staircase, not just any staircase, a golden staircase leading to the moon! My goodness! I'll remember this always! What a wonderful story for us to tell future generations, and maybe if we are lucky, we can even show some of them this sight!

We took photos and so did other visitors, but I shall never forget it.

"A lovely sight, that will stay in my mind forever." I murmured, mesmerised by the beauty of the scene

"It will stay in our minds too... Mum and Dad would love to see the photos that I have taken, they will be amazed and so will our families and friends." Mum said

"This would make a great backdrop for a pop music album." said Dad, smiling

"It certainly would." I said, still mesmerised by the moon

We walked slowly back to our hotel lost in dreamy thoughts of moons and staircases.

The next morning when we were packing up the car again Mum said...

Cassie... would you like to try fishing?"

"I could give it a go I suppose Mum."

"Even though... I've never tried it before."

"I have only observed you two on previous occasions... I always thought the fish could bite me... or the hooks could cut me!" I said, warily

"Well, we'll teach you how to fish... how to avoid getting cut by the fish hooks... then you'll be able to enjoy it as a hobby." said Dad

"Ok Dad." I said, not very convinced

Mum and Dad told me about how to use a fishing rod... putting the fishing bait on the end and casting at the right distance away from your body... they also told me that fishers need to have lots of patience... when waiting for a fish to bite! I would need to look around me and observe the environment... until I felt a tug on my rod that signified a fish was biting.

"Cassie...Dad and I enjoy fishing... we chat to each other whilst we are waiting for the fish to bite."

"I remember a moment in the summer of 1986/87, when we were fishing at Portland in Victoria... Dad and I were fishing and Olivia and Rebecca were reading their books."

"Two hours passed and finally I felt a big tug on my fishing line."

"I called out excitedly...Dan!"

"I think I've hooked a big one!"

"Come and help me haul it in!"

"Dad, Olivia and Rebecca, ran over to help me and we reeled in a big fish that turned out to be an eleven-kilo silver Snapper."

"We were all delighted with my big catch... our parents and grandparents who were there as well... were thrilled too!"

I recall Dad saying...

"You did well 'hauling in' that big fish, sweetie."

"That's a big fish if ever I saw one!" Mum said

"You won that battle darling... with the help of Daniel, Olivia and Rebecca!"

"We took the fish home and ate it for dinner that night... it was a great moment that I still remember today!" Mum said, proudly

"That must've been a tense moment for you Mum... when you battled that fish and hauled it in."

"That great Silver Snapper took four people to bring it in... certainly demonstrated teamwork...your persistence paid off!"

"That's right Cassie."

All those qualities were demonstrated during that situation, we struggled until we got our fish in, I thought we might lose it but we didn't." Mum said, laughing at the memory

"Right, well we have a day's drive before we can get to the fishing at Exmouth." said Dad

"So, we had better get in the car and start driving... I will take the first couple of hours." He grinned

After booking in to the Ningaloo Beach Resort in Exmouth that evening, we planned our fishing trip for the next day.

"We all need a fishing rod and some bait, depending on what type of fish swim in the Exmouth fishing spots, at this time of the season." Dad informed me

"No matter if we don't catch any fish... we'll still have fun being together and trying to!" I said, (I'm still not sure I actually want to catch one)

"That's right Cassie."

"You'll still have plenty of fun fishing... whether we catch any or not." smiled Mum

The next morning, we went over to 'Tackle World' in Exmouth and browsed the range of fishing gear available... they also had bait and scuba equipment too.

"Hello."

"Keen to do some fishing are you?" said the owner

"We are keen." said Dad, answering the shop owner

"My wife and I have been fishing for many years."

"We love fishing." said Dad

"It's a great day for fishing."

"Is this your daughter?" he asked

"Are you excited to be going fishing?" the owner asked

I'm Cassie." I said, introducing myself

"I've never been fishing before, but I'll give it a try."

"Cassie would rather watch than fish, because she fears the fish could bite her." Mum added

"Use the fishing rod carefully, and you should avoid hooking yourself, that way you will stay safe."

"We have got the best range of fishing rods and baits here in 'Tackle World'."

"Choose a good brand rod and the best bait, then you are ready to fish!" said the owner

We chose a Game Type J rod each, and live fish bait...... we are set to catch a fish or two.

"The fishing rod you have chosen is the best one in the shop!"

"I hope you three have good luck, you might catch a big one, or some small ones." He added, laughing

"Thanks."

"We'll have fun, maybe we will catch some fish for our dinner!"

"When you are fishing, the old saying of 'patience is a virtue', is a really good one to remember!" I said, smiling

"That's certainly needed Cassie, when you go fishing." the fishing shop owner agreed

We decided to fish at Exmouth Beach. The sun was high in the sky shining down on the sparkly blue water, I hope that's a good sign. I have sneaked in an old boot, amongst our fishing gear and I plan to play a trick on Mum.

I wonder how I can do it without getting caught! This requires careful planning and sneakiness. Dad taught me how to cast the line and avoid snagging other things such as rocks and seaweed.

"When you cast your line and hear a little splash, you have cast your line right."

"You must be patient Cassie... no matter where you are fishing." Dad reminded me

I cast my fishing line into the water, sat in my chair and patiently waited for a nibble on my line. Whilst I waited, I looked around me, I saw the calm blue sea, with a couple of fishermen nearby on the rocks to my left. On my right, I could see little waves crashing ashore from a distance. It was an awesome environment to fish in, the sun and the brilliant weather makes this a really excellent day, the beach is such a great place to be!

Then I heard Mum shouting!

"Oh, I've got a bite, it's a medium-sized one I think."

Mum reeled in what she thought was a medium-sized whiting, but she had a look of amazement on her face when she hauled in... an old boot! Hee hee! Mum certainly got fooled there.

"All right, who's the hilarious joker who put a boot on the end my line!" Mum said, holding up the boot and her nose at the same time.

"Umm...Dad... did you do that?" I giggled, innocently

"Uh... I did not!" he said adamantly

"Cassie!" said Dad, pointing his finger accusingly at me

"Okay...I was the one that put the boot on your fishing rod." I said, grinning at Mum's frowning face

Before you went back to your sitting position where your rod was situated on the beach, I attached the old boot to the end of your line and threw it back out again.

"Then when you picked it up, it felt like you had a catch on the line and you reeled in your prize 'boot'!"

"Did you guess it was me Mum?" I asked, cheekily

"How shall we cook your 'catch' Mum." I added, rubbing salt in the wound

"Pan fried or coated in breadcrumbs?" I said, being very naughty as I winked to Dad, who was having nothing to do with this one

"I will give you 'pan fried' young lady!" said Mum, in her 'I am about to blow a fuse' voice

"You can just put that smelly boot in a plastic bag... and keep it away from my nose!" I knew I had better 'hop to it' or Mum was going to go from slightly pink to puce

"OK Mum... joke over...transporting one smelly boot away from your nose!" I said, beating a hasty retreat to the car to find a plastic bag to wrap it up in.

Half an hour passed, I looked out to sea waiting for the fish to nibble. This day is going well but we haven't caught any fish yet. Patience...patience... patience... is a virtue.

Another quarter of an hour passed and I felt a tug on my line… it's the start of something big… it could be a fish! Is it a fish?

"MUM!"

"DAD!"

"I think there is a fish on my line… it feels like a big one!" I shout, excitedly

"Ok Cassie!" said Mum

"Are you sure it's not an old boot?" she said sniggering, and Dad joined in

"Stop it you two, I'm being serious."

"Now she's being serious." said Mum and Dad smiling to each other

"C'mon you guys… it's heavy… I can't pull it in!" I looked at them both in exasperation

"All right… we'll give you hand to haul it in." Dad said at last

Mum and Dad held on to me and we all struggled to bring the fish in… the fish was determined to get away. I wonder what kind of fish it will be if we manage to land it?

It was a mighty struggle. Will we win against this fish? Fifteen minutes later we haul the big fish up the beach… with one last heave we all fall backwards on top of each other.

"Ooof!!!"

"Cassie can you get off me… you're squashing me!" said Mum, with a muffled voice

"Me too." said Dad, gasping

"Sorry about that." I said rolling off Mum and Dad with my 'catch'

"That's all right Cassie."

"That's quite a big catch you have!" said Dad, admiringly

"It's a Yellowfin Tuna… I think it weighs about twelve kilos!" I said, excitedly

"Strewth!"

"That's one big 'Yellowfin'!"

"I'll take a photo of it!"

"Everyone will be so excited to see this!" Mum yelled

Mum took out her camera and 'snapped' me holding the Yellowfin Tuna! It's my first fishing trip and look at my 'catch' what a haul!

I'll never forget this…how exciting!

"Where would be a good place to cook our catch?" asks Dad

"We could hire a BBQ and cook it here… that won't work."

"We can't take it to the restaurant… because they won't want to cook it for us."

"How about we put it in a plastic bag…not the one I put the old boot in… tie it up and take it back to our hotel with us."

"That's a good idea Cassie."

"We'll put the Yellowfin Tuna in a plastic bag, and we'll keep fishing." said Mum

"Ok." agreed Dad and I

Mum and Dad sat down in their chairs next to each other… cast their lines and waited patiently.

I had an idea and with a gleam in my eye I set about it. I got two containers of live worms and opened the lids… I crept up behind Mum and Dad's chairs… then dumped the first container of worms on Mum… and the second one on Dad. Nice one Cassie I said, mentally congratulating myself. Boy was that a surprise!

"Cassie!!!!" shrieked Mum

"Cassie!!!!" yelled Dad

"Err… yes." I said nervously, not sure I have done the right thing here

"One 'yucky' trick deserves another." growled Dad

"Mmmn... and I think I have the perfect one... smiled Mum, mysteriously

Uh! Oh! This is not sounding good. I'm starting to regret my rash decision with the worms! Mum and Dad put their 'wormy' heads together and began whispering and grinning to each other. I don't like the look of this at all!!!

"Mikayla dear would you like some worm bait?" said Dad snuggling up to Mum

"Ugh!"

"No thank you dear!" giggles Mum

"Daniel would you like some worm bait dear?" asks Mum, teasingly

"Ergh!"

"Get it away from me." says Dad, winking

Then they both laugh together. I wasn't laughing though... those two were up to something and I had no-one to blame but myself!

"Mum, Dad... I think you need a shower to wash all the bait smell off." I said, carefully

"We certainly do!"

"There's one nearby... we'll be right back." said Dad, too happily for my liking

"I'll keep an eye on the Yellowfin Tuna." I said, uneasily

I couldn't understand why they both burst out with uncontrolled laughter as they walked away to the showers.

Whilst Mum and Dad had their showers... I kept an eye on my 'Yellowfin'... I measured how long the tuna was. Mum and Dad came back with fresh clothes on and we took the Yellowfin and put it in a clean plastic bag.

We were about to drive back to our hotel when Mum and Dad said they had a surprise for me.

They both went to the back of the car... I'm starting to wonder what it is... when they both arrive at my door and open it.

"All right Cassie Annabelle Bontel it's payback time!" says Dad, ominously

"Yes!" Mum agrees

"We have decided that since you think it is funny to tip smelly worms all over us... you can hold on to your prize tuna during the drive... sat on your lap... all the way back to the hotel!"

"Look who is going to need a shower now when they get back!" they both giggled like teenagers, as I sat with the 'fishy' tuna in the backseat, holding my nose and thinking twice about pulling pranks for quite a while indeed

When we arrived back... I couldn't bolt to the showers quick enough... with Mum and Dad laughing all the way. When I got cleaned up... we cooked the fish and had a delicious meal together... Mum uploaded the photo of the fish and family and friends commented on our big 'catch'.

One family member commented... 'That's one big fish Cassie and it's your first one!'... 'Very proud of you'.

"Family and friends are amazed at my Yellowfin Tuna catch."

"I enjoyed that activity and I loved eating it for lunch!"

"I can't say I enjoyed riding with it in the backseat though!" Mum and Dad and I, all burst out laughing together.

It was my first fishing trip and I'll remember that 'catch' of a lifetime!" I said

"We're glad you gave it a go Cassie." said Mum and Dad

"Maybe next time we'll bring Caroline, Andrew and Jenna along with us... they would love a bit of fishing." I said

"They certainly would."

# Chapter Thirty-Three
# Monkey Mia, Geraldton & Mt Magnet

"Monkey Mia looks like a fun place to stay, but it will take us a day's drive to get there." I said the next morning

"They have some fun activities we can try when we get there...dolphins... camel rides... and great beaches."

"It would be great to see some more dolphins."

"The camel ride sounds great fun too." I said

"Camels are good to ride on... but they can be a bit stubborn sometimes."

"Dad and I, have ridden on camels before... twice in the United Arab Emirates with our UAE counterparts... Sarah and Ali Burhan." said Mum

"We had fun riding camels all over the desert landscape... although they spat at us the first time we met."

"We viewed the Arabian sun in the sky as we rode through the desert... we chatted to each other during the night... and had fun trying the Arabian food." said Dad

"Let's give this camel riding a try then!" I said, enthusiastically

A couple of days later when we had arrived at Monkey Mia and booked into our cabin, we went to the beach where the camel rides were taking place, we were surprised to see our guide wearing pants, but no top. What kind of camel ride is this?

"Hello."

"The camel ride is very popular at Monkey Mia visitors love riding along the sand when they come here for their holidays." said the guide

"Do you normally do this activity without a shirt on?" asked Mum, a little bewildered

Dad and I weren't sure either. I have never seen an activity guide with his shirt off before!

"Nothing to worry about."

"In the very hot weather we ride the camels along the beach... the sea water gets splashed all over us... especially if we race the camels."

"Oh, I see but I'm not sure we are up to racing... maybe a gentle walk perhaps." Dad said, hopefully

I'm Daniel." Dad introduced himself

"I'm Mikayla." said Mum

"Daniel and I, have ridden camels before a few years ago... it was fun." Mum added

"I'm Ed." our guide responded

"Who is this lovely young lady camel riding with you?" said Ed the young guide, winking at me

"I'm Cassie Bontel... lead singer of the 'Bontel Family' band."

"I would love to ride a camel... I've never tried before... but I'm keen." I added

"That's great."

"Your Mum and Dad and I... will help you be perfectly safe on your camel." said Ed

"Ed... our daughter Cassie has mild autism."

"Cassie has come a long way since we started this road trip... she has become more independent and confident... but needs a little assistance... especially with new activities that involve heights... insects... and animals." Mum explained to Ed

"Cassie has never ridden on a camel before, please get down to her level and look her in the eyes to let her know she will be safe when riding, as soon as you have taught her what to do." said Mum

"If she has an anxiety attack encourage her to take five minutes break... then she'll be ready to try again... we shouldn't have any problems Cassie is now able to tell us what makes her anxious."

"Cassie rarely gets anxious these days... so she should be fine." Dad said

"No problem... I have had special needs children riding the camels before... I choose my quietest and safest animals for them... they love interacting with the camels during their rides... there should be no trouble." said Ed, smiling

"Camels can be quite funny creatures at times... but unpredictable too."

"I'm ready to learn how to ride a camel Ed... I might be a little nervous but I'm sure I will be okay."

"That's good, Cassie."

"I will help you to get on the camel to start with."

Because camels are so tall when fully standing... when you are going to ride one... they start off in a kneeling position on the ground... so that you can climb aboard. Ed helped me up into the seating behind the second hump. When a camel stands up it goes backwards and forwards and if you don't hold on tight you can fall off... Ed gives me some advice. "There's a handbag strap like device, that you can hold on to during your camel ride... I recommend you hold on to it throughout the entire ride... so there is minimal risk of you falling off the camel." said Ed

I got both of my hands on the handbag strap holder, and held on tightly.

"Remember a camel is not like riding a horse... each leg moves independently... not together."

"It can be a little bumpy." grinned Ed

"You should be fine."

"I will be leading the camels at the front of the line... Cassie your camel is next in line... so hang on tight everybody... as we walk the assigned route slowly at a walking pace."

"Are you good to go?" asks Ed

"Yes Ed... we are good to go." We all chorused

Ed made a guttural sound in the back of his throat and the camels began to move forward.

We all rode along the assigned route... along the sandy beach... padding through the damp edged sand with Ed guiding the way. It's hot, but I'm having lots of fun riding a camel. As we ride along Ed chats to us about our journeys.

"So, what are you doing in Monkey Mia?" he asks

"We've been taking a family road trip around Australia for five months now... it's been fabulous."

"We've been climbing the Sydney Harbour Bridge... we visited Uluru in Alice Springs... and the Darwin Military Museum."

"They have been great places to visit and I've learnt so many things too!"

"Great!"

"You've been soaking up information in all those places and getting back to nature in between."

"You must be one smart young lady…with all that travelling."

"Thanks for the compliment Ed."

"She is smarter than you know Ed." laughs Mum

"Daniel and I have been to Monkey Mia before with my big sister Betty, my brother-in-law Glen and my cousin, Jacinta."

"We rode camels along this same route… and the girls bought jewellery…we also went on the Aboriginal cultural walk as well."

"We had loads of fun back then and took lots of photos which Cassie enjoys looking at and laughing at the funny stories we tell her about those times."

"We loved looking at Monkey Mia's stunning night sky… it was fantastic!"

"We might see the dolphins… Cassie loves dolphins."

"That would be fun."

"I swam with a dolphin on the Gold Coast in Queensland." I told Ed

"How long have you been taking the guided camel rides?"

"It's been two years and I love it!"

"The visitors all enjoy the camel rides… just like Cassie."

"I am enjoying the camel riding the camels seem friendly and what hilarious noises they make."

When we finished our ride Mum, Dad and I, climbed down from the camels. I went up to my camel and looked him in the eye.

"You have been such a lovely camel… I enjoyed our ride together."

"You are so funny with your noises… I won't forget our time together." I said stroking his chin

What a bad move that was! He looked right back at me and then he spat!

"Eurgh!"

"Yuck!"

"Hasn't your Mum told you not to spit in people's faces?" I screwed my face up in disgust, whilst wiping the spit off me with a towel

Mum, Dad and Ed lost it completely! It's lucky they had already got off their camels, or they would have fallen off them from laughing so much at my face when the camel spat at me!

"I'm sorry about that."

"Like I said… camels can be unpredictable." chuckled Ed

"What…" starts Mum, laughing as her camel did the same

"Manners." splutters Mum, as she wiped the spit off her face

Dad, Ed and I, began to laugh this time.

"Your camel got you a good one, dear."

"Mine has been well-behaved throughout the ride." says Dad smugly, but he spoke a little too soon

He was just finishing that sentence when 'splat'! His camel got him right between the eyes!

"Ugh!"

"Apparently not… got that one wrong." gasps Dad, scrubbing his face with a towel

Mum, Ed and I, lost it again!

"That's camels for you folks… never can tell exactly what they might do!" Ed grinned

We all laughed again.

We thanked Ed for giving us a great camel ride and headed off to our hotel for some lunch, before we decided on our next activity.

"Would you like to see the dolphins now Cassie?" asks Mum
"Yes, please Mum."
"I would love to." I said, excitedly
"Better get your bathers and put them on then."
"The viewing session starts in forty-five minutes." Dad added
"I can't wait to see them!"
"Another dolphin opportunity!"
We made our way to the Monkey Mia beach... I was wearing my bathers... so were Mum and Dad.
This is going to be my second dolphin encounter, my first being on the Gold Coast in Queensland. It's going to be awesome... I am so excited that I want to squeal with excitement!
"This dolphin is very friendly... who would like to meet her?"
"How about you, young lady?"
"Would you like to meet the dolphin?" asked the trainer
"Me."
"Oh yes please!"
"That would be wonderful!"
"Thank you." I said, excitedly
"What is the name of this beautiful dolphin?" I said
"Her name is Winnie."
"She is very friendly... she wants to meet you."
"Here Winnie."
I sat down gently at the water's edge, Winnie came up and nudged my feet affectionately.
That feels nice, but it's a bit ticklish."
"Ha, ha."
"That really tickles Winnie."
"Hee, hee." I giggled
"Winnie likes you... she's showing you affection by nudging your feet." said the trainer
He gave Winnie a fish as a reward.
I stroked Winnie a little... blew her a kiss and said...
"Everyone loves to see you Winnie."
The visitors laughed and clapped to see Winnie.
Later on, we decided to go to another beach...one that was especially for swimming.
"Cassie... did you enjoy seeing Winnie?" asked Dad
"Oh yes Dad."
"Winnie nudged my feet affectionately... I loved it."
"Dad and I, took a couple of photos so you can look at them and show them to our family and friends." Mum said
"That's great!"
"Now we have a record of it."
"I'm sure they will all love it." I said
The next day we drove to Geraldton, which took us several hours, we arrived and checked in to the Ocean Centre Hotel for a couple of days, as we have plenty to see whilst we are here.
The first thing we are going to do is visit the museum of Geraldton. It celebrates the rich heritage of the land, sea and people of the mid-west region... overlooking the Indian Ocean.

We decide to take a guided tour, where we learn about four major shipwrecks located in this area... the 'Batavia'... 'Gilt Dragon'... 'Zuytdorp'... and 'Zeewijk'.

European exploration and settlement developed the mid-west and started agriculture... fishing... mining... and science industries, in the region. Mum, Dad and I, ask questions and our guide tells us about Geraldton's history.

After the guided tour we explore the mid-west and shipwreck galleries. They were really interesting to see and to learn about the maritime history of Geraldton. Clay pipes... silver coins... cannons... and the original 'Batavia' stone portico... were articles recovered from those shipwrecks... all relics with a fascinating history.

We made our way back to our accommodation for some well needed refreshments before turning in for a good night's sleep... ready for our next day of exploration.

After breakfast the next morning, we made our way to the 'HMAS Sydney II' memorial. The rotary club started working on this project on the first of July, 1998. The City of Geraldton...the Shire of Greenough... the Batavia Coast Maritime Heritage Association... and the Midwest Development Commission... helped the rotary club with Joan-Walsh Smith and Charles Smith of 'Smith Sculptors'... to design the memorial.

On the eighteenth of November 2001, the memorial was dedicated... a day later, sixty years to the day, after the tragic loss of HMAS II... the eternal flame was lit on November the nineteenth 2001. It was declared a national memorial by the Australian Government on May the twenty-first 2009.

The 'Dome of Souls' was very moving to observe... we felt the pain and loss of the 'Waiting Woman'... frozen in time and bronze, looking out towards the sea seeking her young man and still hoping his ship would be found. The 'Waiting Woman' is near the 'Pool of Remembrance'... eternally at rest watching over her loved one and no longer 'alone'.

We walked along the Wall of Remembrance... representing the six hundred and forty-five men who lost their lives on the 'Sydney'. We also viewed the photos of the 'Sydney II' in action... everyday scenes from life onboard plus a group photo of the full crew of the ship.

When we reached the final panel there was a stone with the words...
'THE REST IS SILENCE'... engraved upon it. We will never forget these men and their remarkable journey... their ending is so well-told.

"It was an amazing experience to learn about this time and to view the HMAS Sydney II Memorial."

"It is a sombre reminder I will not forget." I said to Mum and Dad

"It is important to learn about our history and to honour those men."

"Why don't we go down to the Town Beach and relax now... maybe do a little shopping and check out some shady playgrounds... to have lunch in." said Dad

"Good idea dear." Mum said

We made our way to Geraldton Town beach and strolled along for half an hour... we did a little shopping, then found a nice shady spot to eat our lunch. It was very relaxing and it made me feel peaceful, I smiled to see families walking along the sand and kids playing on the playground equipment having lots of fun.

"This is a nice peaceful spot to eat with the sound of the waves and families having fun."

"I am enjoying this it makes me feel peaceful and relaxed."

"I love watching Geraldton and her people having good family times together, it reminds me of family times we have had together." I commented

"We have had such good family times at the beach... in playgrounds...even on mini-holidays over the years." said Mum, remembering

"Despite your sensory issues and fears... you still enjoyed those fun times." said Dad

"Occasionally, we would introduce one or two new things in to the mix... to keep your progress going in the right direction." Dad smiled

"I remember those fun times too!"

"We can have many more in the future as well!" Mum added

"We certainly can!"

"I will keep those memories and create more for future generations of our family to share." I said, laughing

The next day we drove to Mt Magnet and booked into the Mt Magnet Grand Hotel.

"I never knew Mount Magnet would be a nice place... but it's wicked!"

"There are a few things we can do here... there's also plenty of history to learn about." I said

"Mount Magnet history... Cassie."

"I'm sure you will find out several things." said Dad

"We'll make the most of our stay!"

"There are a couple of places we can eat too...Diggers Diner and there's also... the Swagman Restaurant!" I told Dad, grinning

After we had booked into our hotel, Dad asked...

"What activities would you like to do here Cassie?"

"I would like to go gold prospecting!" I said

"I've never tried that before... but I'm up for it."

"That's good Cassie."

"We can go to the Mount Magnet gold detector hire store... maybe hire a 'Minelab' metal detector each."

"We'll try our best to find some pieces of gold!" Dad laughed

"Yes... let's do that!" said Mum and I, together

We all went to the store and browsed the Minelab Metal Detectors.

"What excellent detectors!"

"I reckon they come with a few 'extras,'... don't they?" I asked the owner

"They certainly do!"

"They have a pick... scoop... external speaker... and even a GPS!"

"They can help you when you are searching for gold!" said the owner, proudly

"That's awesome!"

"Who knew those things would be on a metal detector?"

"They should make our gold finding a little easier." I said, hopefully

"When we went gold prospecting, before these things were invented...we mostly used pans...to find tiny pieces of gold in the river... sometimes we didn't find anything."

We chose a great metal detector and set off to a good mining area to do some prospecting.

With our detectors at the ready... Mum, Dad and I, walked to the field where there were still some gold traces left to discover. We might... or might not... find a gold nugget or two...still we will have fun being prospectors. Who knows what we will find?

"Are you ready Cassie?" asked Mum

"I am ready... Mum."

"Gold awaits me!" I said in a 'gold fever' rush

"Well let's go for it." shouts Dad

We all started searching in different areas of the field... hoping to find something gold and shiny.

"Any luck Mum?" I asked after a short while

"No... not yet Cassie." said Mum

"Dad?" I queried

"No... I haven't had any luck either Cassie." Dad answered

"Me neither!"

"Let's keep going." I said

We searched another area and Mums' detector beeped.

"I think there is something underneath this section."

"Can you pass me the shovel please Cassie?" she added

"Of course, Mum." I said, giving her the shovel

Mum dug the ground where the metal detector had reacted...all she found was a silver coin... a ten-cent piece.

"Well that's a find... just not the one we were hoping for."

"We'll keep trying." Mum said

We searched a few more areas and just as we were about to finish up my detector started beeping... I hope it's a good sign!

"Mum!"

"Dad!"

"I think I have found something!"

"Quick... pass me the shovel Mum." I said, excitedly

I used the shovel... digging hard... a few minutes later I hit something with a loud 'clunk'!

What could it be?

"There's something shining underneath that dirt... I can see a yellowish gleam." I shouted in excitement

I dug the dirt with my gloves... I think it's a nugget! A gold nugget! Wow! Awesome!

I have never seen one up close before.

"I've found a gold nugget... I need some help getting it out!" I said

"We'll help you Cassie."

"I can't wait to see how big that nugget is!" Mum chuckled

"We'll soon see!" said Dad, grinning

I picked up the nugget, it's not too heavy and I pass it carefully to Mum and Dad. When I removed it... I was amazed at how big the nugget was.

"That's a great nugget all right." said Dad

"Strewth!"

"That is a great nugget!" said Mum, admiringly

"What a wicked result!" I said, happily

"We'd better take it to the gold shop to find out how much it weighs... and see what it's worth." I said, eagerly

"We sure will!" agreed Dad

We arrived at the gold shop where I read the slogan... (gold = cash) ... and put our nugget down on the counter. The owner was amazed.

"Oh my!"

"That is a big nugget!"

"You three were very lucky to find that one!" said the owner of the gold mining exchange

"We are lucky indeed!"

"Our daughter was the one that found the nugget and dug it up." said Mum, explaining

"Well she is a very lucky young lady indeed!" said the owner

"Thank you." I said, giggling nervously
"Let me see how much it weighs and how much you are going to get for it."
He put the gold nugget on the scale and it weighed one and a half kilos. He looked at us with a smile on his face... I can tell he has good news for us.
"Well... you are going to earn big money...do you want to know how much?" he said, teasingly
"Yes!" we all shouted together
"The amount of money this nugget is worth is...sixty thousand dollars!" said the owner
"Strewth!"
"That's amazing!" said Dad, in disbelief
"What shall we do with the money?" I said, also 'blown away' at the amount
"That's one big find we won't forget!"
"It's quite incredible!" said Mum, totally flabbergasted
"It is certainly incredible... I've never seen a gold nugget quite as big as this one... in my twelve years of working at the gold exchange!" said the owner, scratching his head

The owner handed us a cheque for sixty thousand... he tells us that he certainly does not have that much cash on the premises... we plan to deposit it in Mum and Dad's bank accounts.

I haven't got a bank account yet, Mum and Dad will help me to open one sometime next year. We plan to spend at least five thousand in Tasmania when we get there. We took several photographs of the nugget we had found and sold... so that we could remember what it looked like... to show our friends and family in case they couldn't believe our 'lucky' find!

As we left the gold shop, news had travelled fast about our 'find'...there was a local news crew waiting outside to interview us all about the experience!

"That was a great nugget you found!" the reporter exclaimed
"Tell us what happened!"
"Well, we were searching the Mount Magnet gold field with our metal detectors... we nearly didn't find anything... until my detector beeped loudly."
"Mum passed me the shovel and I dug like I have never dug before... until I heard a clunk!"
"I hoped it was something good... when I brushed the dirt off... I saw a gold nugget!"
"We were all so excited by the find!"
"We took it to the gold exchange where it weighed in at exactly one and a half kilos!"
"It was worth sixty thousand dollars which is so wicked!"
"I'll never forget that find!"
"What are you going to do with the sixty thousand?"
"We will put most of it in our bank accounts, and possibly spend some on another part of our 'Australian Road Trip'."
"We also intend to donate a sum of money to an autism research charity as well."

After the interview we drove to the 'Swagman Roadhouse' for lunch, we were extremely hungry by this time.

There were a few people there when we walked in and up to the counter, the cashier had heard about our Brisbane radio interview and congratulated us on it.

"I heard about your radio interview from a visitor... well done for speaking up about autism and hyperthymesia... Cassie." said the cashier
"Thank you."
"I hope to continue raising awareness of both conditions through music... and autism charity events."

"Keep it up Bontel Family."

"Your music is doing brilliantly." said the cashier

"Thank you very much." said Dad

We ordered and made our way to a table. My iPhone rang. It was Aunt Rebecca ringing me about the radio interview

"I'm well thanks Aunt Rebecca." I replied, switching her to speakerphone so we could all hear... *'I listened to your radio interview and I loved it! You did very well and when you spoke about your autism and hyperthymesia, you were very brave and confident doing so. I'm very proud of you darling niece, you are raising a lot more awareness of both conditions'*

"I plan to work with Mum and Dad to organise more events... speaking about my autism and hyperthymesia... Aunt Rebecca."

*'Good luck with that, I'll contribute to those future planned events, just let me know what I can do to help Cassie'*

"That would be great... thank you Aunt Rebecca."

*'When you said you used to only tolerate smooth foods, did you tolerate the foods I made for you over the years, from my own cookbooks?* mused, Aunty Rebecca

"No... I could not tolerate anything that wasn't smooth in those days... they were not on my acceptable list."

"I would meltdown if they were served to me...my list inspired you to write your cookbook of smooth recipes... with smooth food ingredients titled 'Rebecca Macdonald: Smooth Food Recipes'...which you released in 2009."

"It was smooth food recipes for autistic kids and other kids with disabilities...those that only ate that type of food...Mum and Dad use them all the time now."

*'Well, you're doing well with it, and I hear you're starting to eat more food items that are on your 'not acceptable' list, that's great progress Cassie!'*

"Thanks... I've started eating Korean dishes and I'm still tolerating Italian dishes...I'm about to try other pizzas besides meat lovers too!"

"I still can't eat some foods that are on my 'not acceptable' list yet... but I may try them as this road trip goes on."

*'Well, let me know how they taste and if you like them, ok?'*

"Ok I will."

*'About your roast chicken, I know you would only eat it if it was roasted and smothered in BBQ sauce right? Not tomato?'*

"Right."

*'Well I always cook a roast chicken on occasions when you are about to visit me, and I always drizzle it with BBQ sauce just the way you like it, so whose roast chicken is better and tastier?'*

"Mum and Dads' are much better and tastier than yours." I say, giggling down the phone

*'What! I thought my roast chicken was much more delicious than Mikayla and Daniels'*

Mum and Dad start to snigger in the background

"We are at the 'Swagman Roadhouse' at Mount Magnet in Western Australia...we are about to have some lunch.

*'That sounds like a nice place to eat. I'm eating my lunch too, I'm having a dessert from my dessert cook book, Rebecca Macdonald: Dessert Princess (2007), which is White Chocolate Cake spread with whipped cream topped with strawberries'*

"That sounds delicious Aunt Rebecca... pity you can't send some of that down the phone line... I would like to try that sometime!"

'I'm sure you would! I'll whip it up for you when you are back in Melbourne. I've got a fun weekend ahead before I record the next episode of Rebecca. Anyway, I'll let you get on with your lunch, I'll call you again sometime. Bye, Cassie'

"Bye Aunty Rebecca."

"That was nice of Rebecca to call and congratulate you on your radio interview, wasn't it?"

"Yes, it was, Mum."

"She asked me about smooth foods...I told her that you and Dad make the best roast chicken... better than Rebecca's." I said

"Did you now?"

"Funny." smiled Dad

"It was funny."

"She is going to make me a nice white chocolate cake spread with whipped cream topped with strawberries when we are back in Melbourne... which is going to be delicious!" I licked my lips in anticipation

"Is she?"

"That was nice of her to offer to bake you a sweet dessert like that." said Mum, chuckling

"She is always making cakes...she sometimes puts nice little choc chips in it...it tastes awesome every time." I said

Our lunch arrived and we got stuck in!

After lunch we went for a stroll along the Heritage Walk, we had the feeling of days gone by as we walked along the wide road and saw the old shop fronts.

"This Heritage Walk is great... it's like walking through olden times... exploring the history of Mount Magnet."

"Gosh!" I said

"It reminds me of some of my holidays with Dad... Olivia... and Rebecca, exploring places like these." said Mum fondly, remembering

"We had great times learning about the history of places and notable buildings... we even had a picnic near here." Dad remembered

"Why don't we have another picnic sometime... along our road trip?"

"We had one with Jessica... Jason... Zara... and Melinda... which was fun."

"We'll need a bit more food and maybe a bottle of water each as well."

"I think I will try another brand of bottled water other than Mount Franklin, this time." I pondered

"That's a good idea Cassie."

"We have always enjoyed family picnics since you were four... we always chose a quiet spot away from the other kids and noises...prior to that the spots we chose had those nearby and it would always send you into a meltdown."

"Other meltdown factors were insects... including flies... bees... and ants... this would ruin our picnic."

"Mum and I were always preparing the food carefully according to your 'acceptable' and 'not acceptable' food list."

"I'm glad you've decided to try another brand of water to drink, besides Mount Franklin."

"That's progress." said Dad

"Thanks Dad."

"I'm exploring a little more at each destination." I said, cautiously

We went around the corner and saw the old 'School Masters House' and the 'Old School'…which were currently housing the 'Rural Transaction Centre'… after it was renovated when the old school closed down.

The first Police Station used to be there years ago… but it was destroyed by a fire. The Station Masters House… the original Bank of Western Australia… the Old Post Office and residence… were among other sights we saw during our walk.

With the help of the detailed map and guide, we learnt things at all of those interesting places and the history behind them… including the history of former Flight Lieutenant Bomber Pilot James "Bluey" Osmond… who worked as a paymaster at a Youanmite mine site before enlisting for World War Two in 1942.

He was in the thirty-fifth squadron and flew ninety-one flights in Lancaster and Halifax bombers… flying over Germany. A few months after he returned from the war… he was riding his motorbike in Mount Magnet at dusk near a dry creek crossing… when he hit a stalled truck which was in the middle of the dry creek bed… and he tragically passed away. He was just twenty-four years old.

In 1948, the Department of Civil Aviation (DCA), made a decision to call the new airport simply the Mount Magnet airport…the Mount Magnet citizens decided not to listen to them and put up a new plaque and a sign.

They named the airport… 'The Bluey Osmond Airport' as a tribute to Osmond… one of Mount Magnet's finest young men. Ever since that time the DCA have kept turning a blind eye… as the residents of Mt Magnet will never forget young 'Bluey' and his service.

Mum, Dad and I, thought it over and we all decided to do the Tourist Trail tomorrow… as we had already been walking for several hours today and needed a rest.

"That Heritage Walk was fascinating."

"We learnt heaps about Mount Magnet's history and got plenty of exercise too."

"The 'Bluey Osmond Airport was something new for me to learn about… it was brilliant!"

"I really enjoyed that walk."

"I hope you two loved it like me." I said, happily

"Mum and I really loved the Heritage Walk…we learnt more history about Western Australia than we have ever known before." said Dad

"Western Australia is a great state to explore… Dad and I have been here several times in the past." said Mum

"Western Australia sure is a great state!"

"The weather so far has been hot…still we're doing well with our water bottles and good food at hand." I said

"I bought another brand of bottled water for you to try Cassie."

"I hope you enjoy it." Mum said

Mum takes the water bottle out of the hotel fridge and places it on a coaster on the coffee table.

"It's a 'Cool Ridge' brand… it looks refreshing."

I picked it up… took the lid off and drink a mouthful…it is quite refreshing, indeed!

"I like the Cool Ridge water brand Mum."

"It tastes good." I said

"That's good Cassie… another trial done and dusted!"

"You're doing well…drinking six glasses of water a day… it's important, especially in the summer season!" Mum added

"Thanks Mum… I shall continue with that." I replied

"The Tourist Trail is going to be one wicked self-drive."

"Thirty-seven kilometres... sights we might see are the Amphitheatre... on the Boogardie-Lennonvile road... granite caves... and old mining settlements."

"It's really going to be fun."

"We might have a picnic near the Amphitheatre... on our first stop along the trail." I said

"We could Cassie."

"We have all our picnic gear we can use." Dad added

The next morning, we packed our picnic basket with food and drinks for the trip.

"We've got insect repellent in case of bugs!"

"We won't let insects ruin our drive!" Mum laughed

The first thing we saw on the Tourist Trail was an aboriginal grave, it was unidentified and heritage listed. We saw the Mia Mia house shaped in wood.

We learnt all about Poverty Flats.

In 1891 a bloke named Steadman was looking for a lost swag... when he came across alluvial gold. He and another bloke named Watson... of 'Yoweragabbie Station'... returned to the site and found over two hundred and fifty ounces of gold nuggets within hours of digging!

Wow, that was one very lucky spot! The men were digging up nuggets... like digging up potatoes!

People who were stricken by poverty... found some lucky fortunes there and managed to survive and become rich. The largest single nugget found at Poverty Hill... weighed in at over one hundred ounces. We had a good view at the Mount Warramboo tourist lookout, overlooking Mount Magnet town.

It was originally named West Mount Magnet by explorer Robert Austin in 1854... due to the rocks having magnetic qualities. The mountain is made of metamorphic rocks and desert sandstone... capped with a flat top. The surveyor general renamed the hill Mount Warramboo... its indigenous name... which means 'Camping Place'.

We skipped the Checker Mill as it was not open to the public... instead we looked at another grave... one of a mother and child who were unidentified... having perished in the typhoid plague of 1908.

We travelled on to Amphitheatre, where we had a nice picnic lunch. There was an ancient waterfall, surrounded by saltbush and mulga plains. It's a favourite spot for locals and visitors and a lovely place for a picnic site. As we ate our picnic lunch, we observed the spectacular scenery around us, it made us feel peaceful to appreciate the beauty of nature.

"This is really a great spot, not only to have a picnic but to observe all this magnificent scenery!"

"It brings us closer to nature...I like that."

"The sunny weather today makes it just right to picnic... relax... and enjoy this time together." I said

"You are right Cassie."

"This atmosphere certainly does bring us closer to nature."

"We have learnt some fascinating things on the 'Tourist Trail' so far." Dad mused

"Gosh... what a good day we are having."

"Cassie, we're so glad that you are enjoying this day as well." Mum smiled

"I sure am, Mum!"

"I remember that you told me once about a picnic you had on a hill in Melbourne in 1989... it was a funny story."

"It sure was Cassie, Mum... Olivia... Rebecca and I... drove to that Melbourne hill in my Holden Barina."

"We got the picnic blanket... picnic basket... food... drinks... and a couple of books each, and made our way to the top."

"We ate our food, read our books and absorbed the glorious sunshine and the beautiful blue sky."

"What a great day we were having."

"Then your Mum squirted us with tomato sauce and laughed herself silly!"

"We all tackled her and rolled her all the way down the hill and into the pond, at the bottom!"

"Splosh!"

"We all emerged from the water with lily pads on our heads."

"Didn't you realise that lily pad hats were not a fashionable trend that season?" I said, laughing again at the story

"I will agree... it was an embarrassing head-ware trend to set !" laughs Mum, remembering

"We packed up our picnic gear, drove back to the Bontel-Macdonald mansion and had hot showers to get rid of the duck pond smell!"

"Our parents had a chuckle about it later on when they heard the whole story." said Dad, grinning

Mum, Dad and I laughed.

"Thanks for telling me that story Dad... it's a funny one!" I said

After we had finished our picnic lunch, we viewed a cave that has not had any major upheaval since the pre-Cambrian period... the basis of the whole plain is formed from Archean rocks.

We decided to walk to the Lennonville railway platform... which takes visitors back to the days of yesteryear in Lennonville.

The contractors began extending the railway from Mullewa in 1895, the line was due to be completed in Cue by December 1897. Yalgoo was first in 1896... followed by Mount Magnet in 1897... it was finished in April 1897... eight months ahead of the deadline.

"That railway was interesting to learn about... I would like to ride another train one day... apart from the 'Ghan'." I added

"That's a good idea Cassie!" said Mum

We have an information booklet about the Lennonville town site which tells us that in November 1894, two men named Lennon and Parker made a gold find...known as the 'Rock of Ages' settlement. When other rich gold reefs were also found in the area, gold prospectors began to move in and the town site started to develop. It was a booming gold town from 1897 through to 1906.

"Cassie what did you think of the Tourist Trail?" asked Dad

"The Tourist Trail was awesome... we learnt so much history along the way!"

"The Amphitheatre was great to have our picnic lunch in and the 'Poverty Flats' was a highlight!"

"We're glad you enjoyed it Cassie, it was a great day for doing the walk."

"We have time to do some reading on our kindles... before we start getting dinner ready." said Mum

"Ok, Mum." I replied

# Chapter Thirty-Four
## William & Petunia

The next day we were soon on the road again, driving to Perth. Several hours later, I looked up from the book I had been reading and spotted the outskirts of the city.
"How about that... we have made it to Perth!"
"There are heaps of things we can do as we are staying here for two weeks...we also have our concerts to perform here as well!"
"We are going to have plenty of fun together!" I laughed
"We definitely are going to do that Cassie!"
"Our 'Bontel Family' concert will be performed in four days... later Mum and I are going to arrange for several children's bands to perform with you... that will be exciting on a big scale... won't it?" Dad said
"It sure will be exciting Dad!"
"I grew up watching and listening to those children's bands before I moved on to pop music...now I'm going to get the chance to perform with them!"
"It's so great!" I said, excitedly
"It will be good for you Cassie."
"We'll try as many activities as we can whilst we are in Perth."
"Choose the ones you want to do Cassie." Mum said
"Perth Zoo would be awesome!" I replied
"I knew you would go for that one, Cassie!"
"You have loved zoos since we went to the one in Emerald."
"I remember... we got squirted by elephants... and monkeys threw rotten fruit at us." I said, ruefully
"That was embarrassing... hopefully it won't happen again!" said Dad
"What animals might we see this time?"
"We'll find that out when we get up and go there tomorrow morning...right now we have to get booked into our accommodation for the first week!"
"It has been a long, hot drive to Perth, and I'm looking forward to some quality sleep time tonight... after a delicious evening meal." said Dad, licking his lips in anticipation
Well after that hot, dusty drive, I think we should treat ourselves to a premier resting place." grinned Mum
"Let's book in at the Parmelia Hilton in Mills Street... for our first week in Perth."
"It will be expensive... but we need to relax and get ready for those concerts." Mum added
The following morning after we had breakfasted at the Parmelia, we drove to the Perth Zoo. We paid our entrance fees and went to the 'Australian Animals' section. The Australian animals on show were emus... dingos... koalas... and quokkas. We viewed a koala fast asleep in a tree... it was cute.

"Isn't that sweet?"

"A koala taking a nice long snooze."

"He's probably tired after chewing leaves in the hot sunny weather." said Mum

"Years ago, ... we would find you sleeping in odd places... including the bath when you were seven once... and our bottom dresser drawer... when you were four. We would silently giggle to ourselves and carefully place your dark black sunglasses on and take a photo of you. We made sure not to disturb you... we showed the pictures to our family and friends who thought you were cute and adorable. We also found you asleep in the backyard when you were ten, you were in a chair after a couple of hours playing outside."

"They were good photos!" said Dad, grinning

"They certainly were good photos of me sleeping in odd places... I still laugh about them too."

"A koala sleeps in a tree mostly... I have never seen them sleep anywhere else... although it would be hilarious!" I giggled

The emus were up next... they were 'strutting' their stuff. They could be animal models for an animal magazine if they wanted to. We saw the male emu showing off in front of his female... who was very impressed by his moves. We went to the bilby enclosure where the keeper was watching over them.

"Hello."

"Are you enjoying the Perth Zoo?" asked the zookeeper

"Yes, we are... Perth Zoo is a great place to visit and see the animals." Mum said

"I'm glad you three are enjoying our wonderful Perth Zoo."

"What do you think of these two bilbies?" asked the zookeeper

"They are so cute and beautiful... they could fit in the palm of my hand." I said, with a joyful look on my face.

"They sure could."

"How would you like the opportunity to hold them?" asked the zookeeper

"Yes please!"

"We would love to hold the bilbies." said Dad

The zookeeper brought out two bilbies to us and they looked so sweet!

"What are their names?" I asked

"They are called William and Petunia."

"I knew you would be happy to see them."

"What are your names?" asked the zookeeper

"We're Daniel, Mikayla and Cassie... of the Bontel Family."

"We have a group called the 'Bontel Family' band... we are making our first Australian tour together." said Mum

"I thought you three looked familiar."

"Who would like to hold William and Petunia first?" asked the zookeeper.

"I would!" I said

The zookeeper placed William and Petunia gently in my left hand and tells me to stroke them softly so they won't be frightened.

"Aww!"

"They are so adorable."

"Their eyes are so cute and their fur feels velvety to stroke." I said, stroking William and Petunia with my right hand

William and Petunia looked at me sweetly... they like being stroked by a loving and gentle hand. It feels so nice to be close to small creatures like these and stroking them is very restful.

Mum stroked William and Petunia who were placed in her right hand... it brought a smile to her face when she remembered other animals she has known over the years.

"They remind me of two cats I looked after when I was twelve years old."

"I was with Daniel and I was looking after a neighbour's two cats... one was an orange tabby... and the other one was a Russian blue."

"The neighbour had to do a few errands to run and trusted us to look after the two cats... which were named Greg and Tabitha."

"We fed them and played with them... we stroked them and they would purr and rub their heads into our stomachs."

"When the neighbour came back... she said we could look after them anytime!"

"That was a lovely memory... I still remember those two cats."

Dad took his turn stroking William and Petunia they were so lovely with their eyes looking up at him, that he just had to smile back at them.

"These bilbies are so cute to hold and stroke."

"Mikayla and I did this when we visited Perth before... when we were both thirty-six... the bilbies were called Bert and Jackie then."

"They were probably the grandparents of William and Petunia!" said Dad, with a grin

That comment made us all laugh.

"Thanks for letting us hold William and Petunia."

"It was awesome and the experience will be engrained in our minds." I said

"It was my pleasure, I'm glad you three are doing well with animals great and small." The zookeeper smiled

"We love animals."

"Our parents taught us to respect animals... to look after them... and we're passing those lessons onto Cassie... who is learning those lessons well." Mum said, proudly

We handed William and Petunia back to the zookeeper and waved goodbye... then we made our way to the Perth Zoo café...we will have some lunch before deciding which exhibit to see next.

"Perth Zoo is a great zoo, the animals we have seen so far are wicked!"

"I will never forget William and Petunia." I said

"Neither will we."

"We have photos of each of us with the bilbies... I will upload them to my Facebook page...our family and friends will love them!" said Dad, happily

We checked out the Perth Zoo Guide and looked at the animal sections... thankfully there weren't any monkeys mentioned here!

"We can see the giraffes after lunch."

"They are awesome...such very tall animals."

"They may try to give you a kiss with their tongue... or steal your hat...which is funny too." I said

"They are indeed Cassie."

We went to wash our hands before preparing to eat our lunch.

With lunch over we went to see the Giraffes. There were three giraffes... two of them are close to the fence interacting with their baby... the third one is reaching up to a high branch eating leaves. These giraffes are so tall... we feel like we're shrinking... as we crane our necks up to see their faces high above us.

"Their baby is quite pretty... nuzzling close to its parents for affection." I commented

"This is great seeing giraffes up close."

"Let's take a few photos of them so we can look at them anytime." said Mum

We took a few photos each of the giraffes, as we turned to look at the other enclosure for a moment the father giraffe decides Mum's hat would look good on his baby!

"Hey!"

"Give me back my hat!" said Mum, with a surprised look on her face

However, the father giraffe had put the hat on the baby giraffe by then... Dad and I began to laugh... so too did a few other visitors

"You may think that's funny...it's a bit embarrassing for me though." said Mum, muttering under her breath

"Luckily... I have a spare one with me." said Mum

Then the mother giraffe decided to lick Dad on the right side of his face... giraffes have very long... blue tongues... Dad jumped back in amazement!

"Goodness me!"

Who licked me?"

"Cassie... did you do that?" asks Dad, suspiciously

"Nope...it wasn't me, Dad." I said, beginning to giggle

"Did you lick me dear?" Dad turns to Mum

"Of course, I didn't... darling." said Mum, with a twinkle in her eyes

"If it wasn't you two that licked me... then who did?" said Dad, in a puzzled voice

Mum and I pointed to the mother giraffe... just as Dad turned around in time to cop another lick from her!

"Ugh!"

"Awkward!" said Dad, scrunching up his face

We all burst out laughing. I took a photo of it, and so did Mum, we both plan to upload them to Mum's Facebook page.

"Ok, very funny you two." said Dad, wiping his face with a towel

"I reckon the mother giraffe thought you were one of her babies...you must have looked like you needed a good clean up!" I said, giggling

"You are right Cassie!"

"Mate... your face is a little dirty...let me give it a clean." said Mum, bursting into fits of laughter

"Righto you two... that's enough from the peanut gallery!" said Dad, with an embarrassed look on his face

Mum and I, had to make sure we didn't look at each other for a while after that... or else we both burst out laughing again... and Dad gave us a scowl.

Our last animals to view for the day, were the Asian elephants. Elephants sometimes like to squirt water from their trunks... that can be a nice way to cool down on a hot summer day! They may sometimes squirt water at visitors if they are in a playful mood.

We watched as three elephants played in the water with a mother elephant watching on... they were funny to watch. We took some photos and continued watching the elephants playing... suddenly one of the elephants raised its trunk full of water and squirted it straight at my face! Swoosh... splutter...choke...

"Blah." I gasped, as the water ran down my face and hair and into my mouth

Mum and Dad were crying with laughter at this point... so they didn't see another elephant aim his trunk at Dad and fire!

"Glug." said Dad, shocked

Mum and I, were busy laughing at Dad now, who was dripping and wet through... so we took no notice of a third elephant edging around the other two... with his sights set on Mum!

"Ugh"

"Yuck!" burbled Mum, through the torrent of water running down her neck and over her face

Dad and I point at Mum, while we all crack up laughing! All the other visitors were laughing too... but I notice that they have all moved back from the enclosure fence...they don't want to be the next victims of the playful elephant herd.

"Oh dear... you three got squirted."

"I'm sorry about that."

"These elephants can be cheeky... especially with water on a hot day like today." said the zookeeper apologetically, handing us three towels

"That's ok."

"They are definitely cheeky... when there's water about...there's mischief!" I said, grinning

Mum, Dad and I, wiped the water off with our towels, it was time to leave the Perth Zoo wetter and wiser, after having some fun times.

Dad decided to skype Zoe before tea.

'Hello Daniel, how are you doing. Hello Zoe I'm doing very well thanks. We are staying in Perth at the moment, we have been to the Perth Zoo today. Did you have a good time there? Yes, we did. While we were at the zoo, we got to hold a couple of bilbies named William and Petunia. Aw they must've been so cute to hold. I saw your photos of them and they are so pretty. They were indeed.'

'We then went to the giraffes where the father giraffe stole Mikayla's hat and gave it to his baby, then the mother giraffe licked my face clean, giving me a fright. Zoe laughs, the giraffes certainly gave you some cheekiness especially when the mother licked your face clean. Ha, ha, they sure did!

'At the elephant's enclosure, we saw them playing in the water, then three of them proceeded to squirt us! How embarrassing was that? Oh dear, those elephants that squirted you were in such a mischievous mood today. Yes, they were. We are the favourite people that elephants like to squirt water at apparently. We might have to bring umbrellas next time, even when it's summer! You sure might. It would be good to see.'

Can I speak to Cassie for a few minutes? I heard her on the radio when you were in Brisbane. Yes, you can. I'll get her for you.'

'Hello Zoe. Hello Cassie. I heard your radio interview in Brisbane, you spoke confidently about your autism and hyperthymesia issues. You did great. Thanks Zoe. It was my first radio interview of two that I did, it was a blast and I raised a little more awareness of both conditions. I'm sure you did Cassie! Peter, George, Ivy, Nina and I, are very proud of you for doing so. Thanks Zoe, it's nice of you tell me that.'

Zoe and I, chatted for a few more minutes before we said our goodbyes.

Then we got ready for dinner. We put on our best coloured clothes, and proceeded to Rambla on Swan restaurant. When we walked in it looked beautiful... several tables had good views of Perth and the Swan River... on the outside deck. We chose to sit on the outside decking area and ordered our meals. We talked while waiting and looked at the fabulous view of Perth under a glorious evening sunset.

"Cassie, we had such a fun day at the Perth Zoo today... didn't we?" mused Mum

"Yes, we certainly did Mum."

"Apart from the elephants squirting us...we both giggled again... including the bilbies we got to hold and stroke." I said

"That was such fun."

"We've been to beautiful restaurants, had some lovely meals, with another just on its way to enjoy." Dad smacked his lips

"It's going to be delicious Dad!"

"You have made great progress with trying new cuisines." added Mum, with a smile

"You've tried Korean and Italian cuisine, now you will enjoy modern Australian cuisine, I promise you that!" said Dad

Our meals arrived, they included 'Mt Barker Chicken Breast' as a main meal, 'Creamed Royal Blue Potato' with lemon and parsley and 'Dark Chocolate Delice' for dessert. It was one of the best dinners that I have had on this road trip... I tried something different and I loved it!

"Cassie, we've arranged an activity for you to try tomorrow... it involves gymnastics and includes a balance beam." said Dad

"You're going to try gymnastics at Active Gym... it will help you gain flexibility in your body... and provide benefits for your health... along with the right diet." said Mum

"I like the idea of trying gymnastics... I've never done it before." I said

"There is a nice gymnastics trainer named Lucille, who can help you with that."

"Lucille has worked with girls and boys in the gymnastics field, with disabilities, for ten years." said Dad

"Ok Dad."

The next morning, we went to Active Gym signed the 'visitors' book and went to the gymnastics room where Lucille was there to meet us.

"Hello Bontel Family."

"Welcome to Active Gym Perth." said Lucille

"It's nice to meet you Lucille."

"Our daughter Cassie is going to give gymnastics a try."

"It's her first time." Mum added

"I can certainly help her with that."

"I've never done any form of gymnastics before... but I'll do my best Lucille." I said

"That's the way, Cassie."

"Here's your leotard... which we all wear when taking part in gymnastics."

"The changing rooms are over there."

"I will talk to your parents whilst you are changing."

"Ok Lucille." I replied

I went to the changing room to get into my blue leotard, while Mum and Dad talked to Lucille.

"Lucille, Cassie has mild autism and a rare condition known as hyperthymesia."

"Cassie has no problems with her anxiety... but she gets a little nervous occasionally."

"If she gets nervous... especially on the balance beam... tell to use her anxiety techniques and when she needs a break give her five to ten minutes... and then she can try again." said Mum

"Mikayla and I have tried gymnastics before... which we included in our cover version of the Pointer Sister's 'Jump'... with the accompanying music video."

"That was back in the days with Quirky Service." explained Daniel

I came out of the changing rooms in my blue leotard ready to try the gymnastics exercises that Lucille sets for me.

"Cassie are you ready to begin our gymnastic warm up?" asked Lucille

"I'm ready Lucille!" I said

Lucille took me to the first gymnastic activity... it was the balance beam. I was thinking...*this is looking scary, but I can try.*

Lucille helped me on to the balance beam and I looked down at the ground and got nervous...*Oh dear It's frightening from up here!... I just can't do it.* I stood shaking, too frightened to take even one step.

"Cassie it's all right I'm here."

"Use your anxiety techniques that your Mum and Dad have taught you." called Lucille

I used my anxiety techniques and requested a five-minute break which I took.

"Lucille, I have taken my five-minute break and I'm ready to try the balance beam again." I said

"That's great, Cassie."

"Let's do it." said Lucille

Lucille helped me get onto the balance beam and called Mum over to help.

"Cassie your Mum and I, are going to help you walk across the balance beam two times."

"Then we'll see how you go on the balance with my help." said Lucille

"Right." I said

Mum and Lucile held my hands as they walked me across the balance beam and back twice. I didn't fall off at any point... I did well.

"Well done Cassie!"

"You did excellently."

"Now you do the same with my help." said Lucille

I walked across the balance beam two more times with Lucille holding my hand and that was all right too.

"Excellent job Cassie."

"Well done on the balance beam." said Lucille

"Thanks Lucille"

Lucille takes me to the next activity which requires flexibility.

"Cassie, we're going to do some gymnastic flexibility exercises."

"One is stretching your leg muscles... we'll do it on this beam that is designed for it." said Lucille

Lucille demonstrates the leg muscle stretch... I don't how she does that... but she does it well!

"Now Cassie... let's see if you can do it for fifteen seconds." said Lucille

I did the leg muscle stretch on the beam for fifteen seconds, then the same with the other leg.

"That's good Cassie!"

"Now the next flexibility exercise is lying on the gym mat and doing fifteen pull ups while holding a ball."

"You lie down on the mat and put your hands on both sides of the ball and do the fifteen pull ups.

"You got all that Cassie?" asks Lucille

"I got all that Lucille." I nodded

I did the fifteen pull-ups whilst holding the ball in my hands. I struggled a little bit, but I got through the exercise.

"Well done Cassie."

"It's good to see you putting in so much effort." Lucille smiled

"The last gymnastic flexibility exercise is push ups."

"Put your hands on one end of the mat and your feet on the other end... and let's see if you can do at least twenty for me." Lucille grinned

I put my hands on the front of the mat and my feet on the back of the mat... it was very hard work...but I did the twenty push-ups!

"Great job, Cassie!"

"There are about three more exercises to do… but let's take a fifteen-minute break first." said Lucille

"Will do Lucille." I puffed

"You're doing very well in your gymnastics session Cassie." Mum noted

"Cassie you look so good in your blue leotard."

"You can also do dancing in that."

"All you need now is a ribbon to complete your outfit and you could do 'Rhythmic Gymnastics'… like they do in the Olympics!" said Dad, enthusiastically

"I might add some gymnastic moves to my dance routines later on down the track…but we'll see." I said

"Mum… I've seen photos of you in a yellow leotard and they were beautiful."

"I would like to see you perform at one of our future concerts… while wearing that." I said, winking at Mum cheekily

Dad chuckled.

"Yes… right… that will not happen!"

"Another one of your cheeky ideas!"

"Yes." I giggled

"Very funny." Mum said

I then noticed some ribbon on the floor. It was going to be used in one of the last three gymnastic exercises that I'm about to do. A grin spreads across my face… I walk over and pick up the ribbon… I proceed to twirl it.

Mum and Dad tried not to laugh as they watched me twirl around with the ribbon… doing some gymnastic moves I have seen before… whilst watching gymnastic competitors on the television.

After the fifteen-minute break Lucille came in and saw me doing my moves.

"Cassie… what are you doing?" asked Lucille

"Erm… just practicing my gymnastic moves." I said, trying to keep my face straight

"So, I see."

"Nice moves… but you can't get out of your last session that easily!" says Lucille, chuckling.

"Let's get back to it."

"Well done Cassie you have completed all six exercises!" said Lucille, a little time later

"Thanks Lucille!"

"I really worked out hard… the sweat was pouring off my face…I got through them all!"

"Thanks for helping me Lucille." I said

"That's okay Cassie."

"I'm glad you enjoyed it."

"Cassie, we're proud of you for working so hard at another new challenge!"

"You can choose a reward for all that effort!" said Dad, grinning

"Thanks, Mum for helping me on that balance beam… and Dad thank you for encouraging me to keep trying." I said

"It was our pleasure Cassie." Mum replied

Mum, Dad and I, were going to the Galleria Shopping Centre to do some shopping for my 'chosen' reward. We went up to the revolving doors and tried them… but they wouldn't budge.

"These doors seem to be stuck."

"I don't know what's wrong with them."

"Maybe they need a spot of oil to get them moving." I said

"They might have something wedged in them." said Dad

"We'll give the doors one last big push and see if they budge."

We gave the revolving doors one last big push and they moved all right…they sent us flying through so fast… that we crashed into the clothes racks on the other side!

Ouch…how awkward.

"Are you three all right?"

"That was quite a crash!" said a familiar voice

It was Olivia… she had arrived for a week's stay and was doing some shopping like us.

"Yes, we are all right Olivia… it was quite a crash!" I said

Olivia and two staff members helped us up.

"That was a little embarrassing…we will be fine." Mum laughed, assuring the staff

"We are ok."

"That revolving door gave us quite a problem!" said Dad

"Hmmn… we will get the repairers on to that door right away sir." said the staff member

"Nice to see you again Aunt Olivia."

"Are you staying here this week?"

"I sure am Cassie!"

"Nice to see you all doing some shopping like me." said Olivia, with a wink

"We sure are!"

"Cassie chose it as her reward for giving gymnastics a try yesterday." Mum explained

"What gymnastic exercises did you try Cassie?" asks Olivia

"I walked across the balance beam… stretched my leg muscles and did fifteen-pull ups… whilst holding a ball in my hands."

"I worked out quite a lot!" I said

"Hope you keep your fitness up Cassie!"

"Keep a bottle of water at hand for re-hydration?"

"Yes, Aunt Olivia I will." I said

"Well let's go shopping together then and have a little lunch after we're done." said Mum

"Mikayla!" said Dad, a trifle worried

Mum's combat approach to shopping can be a little worrying for Dad… he still remembers when they didn't have much money to spend!

After we have finished shopping, we go to a café for sandwiches… tea… and cake… we have a chat about what we have done so far.

"Cassie, it's been weeks since I last saw you… what have you been doing?" asks Olivia

"We went to the Perth Zoo and saw some brilliant animals… there were a couple of funny moments too."

We showed Olivia some photos of our time at Perth Zoo.

"Haha, Daniel did get such a surprise when the giraffe licked him… didn't he?" Olivia chuckled

"He sure did Olivia!"

"The mother giraffe gave him a good clean up!" Mum said, chuckling

"She had to keep her baby clean!"

"I sure wasn't ready for that when it happened!" said Dad, screwing his face up at the thought again

"The father giraffe gave Mum a fright when he pinched her hat!"

"It sure was hilarious to see Mum 'freaking out'… I nearly split my sides laughing." I said

"The father giraffe thought my hat might be good headwear for his baby." admitted Mum

"I heard you found a one and a half kilo gold nugget in Mount Magnet!"

"That was an exciting find wasn't it?" asked Olivia

"It sure was!"

"It was worth…." I whispered in Olivia's ear.

"Strewth!"

"That's a gold-worthy amount!"

"What do you plan to spend it on?" asked Olivia

"We haven't planned anything yet…maybe a family makeover." I said, grinning

"That sounds very interesting."

"I'll be at your Perth Concert… I may guest star at your children's concert 'Cassie and Friends'… won't that be fun?" says Olivia, smiling

"It sure will be fun Olivia!"

"When all is arranged… it will be full of colours and joy."

"Well let's buy some clothes and accessories."

"Cassie you will love them… you may want to buy more blue clothes to add to your collection." said Mum

"I can't wait to see what clothes you will buy." Olivia added

Mum, Dad and I, went to a clothing shop to try on and buy new clothes… while Olivia sat on an outside bench reading her novel.

"Cassie what do you think of this sparkling yellow dress?" asked Mum, holding it up

"It's looks glowing… when you put it on it will make you feel like eighteen years old again." I said

"What Cassie?" says Mum, spluttering with laughter

"I said when you put it on it will make you feel like eighteen years old again…a fun time in your life." I laughed

"It was a fun age to be." Mum remembers

Then Mum and I laughed together.

"Don't mind my wife and daughter… they're having a 'mother and daughter' moment!" says Dad, gesturing to the change rooms where Mum and I are

"Are they?"

"They sound like they are having fun." said the cashier

"What are you two up to in there?"

"Not getting into any mischief, are you?" asks Dad, teasingly

"Nothing!" say Mum and I, in unison

"Show me the yellow dress again Mum."

"It seems lovely." I said

Mum holds up the yellow dress… it's sparkly with diamonds on it.

"Turn around." I said

Mum starts to turn around.

"Not you!"

"The yellow dress!" I laughed

Mum laughed too.

Mum bought the yellow dress. I bought myself a blue dress, and Dad bought himself a new green suit with an emerald tie pin.

"Certainly, suits you Mr Bontel." said the salesman

"A night on the town might happen… eh?" Dad smiled

We finished, then showed Olivia our purchases.

"They are very sparkly clothes!"

"Very nice purchases."

"While you three were trying things on... I bought a few purchases of my own." said Olivia triumphantly

Olivia then shows us her 'sparkly blue' clothing purchases! They are very nice indeed! That could be very handy having an Aunty with the same colour preference and size as me!

"Great purchases!"

"You'll be a hit with the Perth men tonight... they might be asking you on a date or two."

"You know Aunt Olivia I think it's time I checked out your wardrobe... you have great taste in clothes... and in just the right colour too!" I giggled

"Very funny Cassie... I might go on a date or two... but I'll remain single for life... I can tell you that!" said Olivia, happily

"Olivia, it's been great fun seeing you again."

"I hope to see you at your concert."

I'm off to my hotel room to rest up after all this serious shopping!" Aunt Olivia winked at me

"We'll see you Olivia."

"Bye." Dad waved

After we said goodbye to Olivia we headed to our hotel for some down time and showed our purchases to each other.

"We might be able to wear them at our concert...pop star clothes."

"They look 'fashionable' and our Perth fans will love them!" I said

"With this 'bling' we'll stand out like beacons on the stage!" said Mum

"We'll shine' bright like diamonds'... eat your heart out Rhianna!" says Dad, striking a pop star pose and then collapsing on the floor in a heap of laughter.

"Cassie we've got some brilliant news about your 'Cassie and Friends Concert." Mum said mysteriously, with a grin on her face

"It's brilliant news indeed!"

"You'll be surprised!" Dad added

What will Mum and Dad's brilliant news be?

How many children's bands will be performing at my 'Cassie and Friends' concert?

Which children's bands will be performing with me?

I can't wait to find out!

## Chapter Thirty-Five
## Perth, pranks & Christmas Concerts

"Cassie... there will be eight children's artists performing with you."
"They are Playground Kids...Children's Club...The Groove Kids...Liam de Vries...Gabby Sky...Melissa and Danielle Fairies...Max T...and the Doggies."
"They are all successful Australian children's performers... they are keen to join with you." said Mum, listing them off on her fingers excitedly
"That's so great!"
"That's brilliant news!"
"I own their albums...now I get a chance to perform with them all!"
"That's another item off my dream list!" I said
"We might have to extend our Perth stay... to let you record your debut children's album."
"It will be well worth it though!" exclaimed Dad
"It sure will be Dad!"
"It'll be best if we perform our concert today... then record my debut children's album next week... that will give us just enough time to rest in between." I said
"Great idea Cassie!"
"We can do that!"
"We'd better get ready... our Perth concert starts in two hours." Dad reminded us
Dad's phone started ringing... it's an Australian band called 'Mania' calling him. 'Mania' was formed in Brisbane consisting of six members...they include two sisters and a brother.
"Hello... how are you guys going?" Dad put his phone onto speakerphone, so we could all hear
"Cameron Ham here."
Cameron is the lead singer and keyboardist with 'Mania'.
"We are all doing well Mr Bontel."
"We just called to let you know that we are your opening act for your Perth concert today."
"That's great!"
"Where are you guys?"
"We have just arrived onstage at Subiaco Oval... we are rehearsing at the moment."
"You better be ready for two, the audience will be here by then."
"Ok."
"We will see you guys there."
"My daughter Cassie can't wait to meet you."
"OK, see you all soon."

"Bye."
"Bye."
Dad put his phone down and turned to speak to us
"We have got ourselves an opening act for the first time on our Australian tour!"
"Mania are rehearsing at Subiaco Oval... where they will be opening for us!" said Dad, excitedly
"Oh, wow!"
"That's just great!"
"What other band can do it... but Mania?"
"I love those guys!"
"They've released three singles... they are great!" I said excitedly, jumping up and down
"That's a brilliant piece of news!"
"Well, we'd better get down to Subiaco Oval and rehearse too!"
"We can't pass up a great opportunity like that!" said Mum, laughing
We drove to Subiaco Oval where we met 'Mania'... these guys are so lovely.
"Hello Mania."
"It's an honour to meet you guys." I said, shyly
"Hello Bontels!"
"It's an honour to meet you three." said Jessie
Jessie is Cameron's younger sister who shares lead vocals with her brother and plays harmonica too... she shook my hand as I admired her blue hair!
We all shake each other hands, star-struck at seeing each other for the first time... 'Mania' signed our autograph books and we signed theirs.
"What a moment this is!"
"We are both about to perform... with you guys as our first ever opening act!" said Mikayla
"We never performed with a family pop band before... we love listening to your album."
"Our parents' love listening to it too." said Lina
Lina is Cameron's second youngest sister and 'Manias' bass guitarist and backing vocalist.
"We plan to release an album in two, or three years' time."
"It will have a pop-rock sound to it." said Henry, the lead guitarist and backing vocalist
"We hope it will be a hit on radio or on a national music chart." said Matthew the rhythm guitarist and backing vocalist of the band
"Our debut album is charting in the top ten worldwide...listeners around the world are loving our music."
"Patience and persistence pay off... you can also do charity events in between." Peter the drummer and percussionist said
"We certainly can."
"Let's start rehearsing straight away!"
The time has arrived...Mania's opening performance is about to start... the crowds are in... and we are ready to bring the house down!
"Hello ladies and gentlemen welcome to Subiaco Oval."
"This will be one 'big' performance!"
"The opening act who have been playing together for two years now... will open the concert tonight with their single... 'Dream Door'!"
"Please welcome Mania!" the MC called out to the audience

'Mania' band members walked onstage and began to play 'Dream Door'… they are drawing cheers from the crowd as they finish.

"Ladies and Gentlemen the band you have all been waiting for… their debut album is a top ten worldwide smash."

"Ready to rock the house with a brilliant performance that will guarantee to bring the roof down… please welcome to the stage 'THE BONTEL FAMILY'!" screams the MC

Mum, Dad and I, walk onstage and wave to the audience… I walk up to the front of the stage and say…

"Hello Perth!"

"Thank you for making our debut album chart so well on the Australian music scene… your support is appreciated from us all… it's even charting well internationally!"

"We will perform all our songs from 'The Bontel Family' album…afterwards we will get together with our fans for a chat session…maybe sign some autographs for those that want them." The audience laughed and cheered!

"Let's get this concert underway… One…Two…Three…Four

The concert was on and we rocked the night away.

After the concert had finished and we met our fans, we thanked Mania for opening the concert for us and drove back to our hotel. The concert had made us ravenous so we had a tasty meal and then made our way to our hotel rooms. What an exhausting day it has been…but it was an awesome one too… we reflect, as our heads finally hit the pillows.

It's Thursday and I've finished recording my debut children's album… 'Cassie and Friends'! Here is the track list of 'Cassie and Friends'… released in November 2011… on Playground Records.

## Disc 1

| Tracks /Titles | Singer/s | Composer/s | Original Artist/s |
|---|---|---|---|
| Hello Mister Whiskers | Liam De Vries (Mr.Hat) | F.Henri | Franciscus Henri Netherlands/Australia |
| White Pyjamas | Liam DeVries | F.Henri | Franciscus Henri Netherlands/Australia |
| Dancing in the Kitchen | Liam De Vries (Mr Hat) | F.Henri | Franciscus Henri Netherlands/Australia |
| Move Your Body | Children's Club | Kellie Crawford | Hi-5 |
| Robot Number One | Children's Club | Leone Carey | Hi-5 |
| You're my Number One | Children's Club | Chris Phillips | Hi-5 |
| So Many Animals | Children's Club | Andrew Einspruch | Hi-5 |
| North South East and West | Children's Club | Leone Carey | Hi-5 |
| E.N.E.R.G.Y. | Children's Club | Chris Philips | Hi-5 |
| Come on and Party | Children's Club | Leone Carey | Hi-5 |
| Making Music | Children's Club | Leone Carey | Hi-5 |
| T- E- A- M | Children's Club | Lisa Hoppe | Hi-5 |
| Wow! | Children's Club | Duncan Fine | Hi-5 |

| Tracks /Titles | Singer/s | Composer/s | Original Artist/s |
|---|---|---|---|
| Rain, Rain | Children's Club | Leone Carey | Hi-5 |
| Snakes and Ladders | Children's Club | Leone Carey | Hi-5 |
| Party Street | Children's Club | Duncan Fine & Chris Philips | Hi-5 |
| Happy Monster Dance | Children's Club | Chris Philips | Hi-5 |
| I like to sing | Gabby Sky | Peter Dasent Garth Frost | Justine Clark |
| Dinosaur Roar | Gabby Sky | Justine Clark Peter Dasent | Justine Clark |
| Gumtree Family | Gabby Sky | Arthur Baysting Peter Dasent | Justine Clark |
| Painting a Picture | Gabby Sky | Peter Dasent | Justine Clark |
| Doin' it – Making the Garden Grow | Gabby Sky | Justine Clark Peter Dasent | Justine Clarke |
| Imagination | Gabby Sky | Justine Clark Peter Dasent | Justine Clarke |

## Disc 2

| Track No/Title | Singer/s | Composer/s | Original Artist/s |
|---|---|---|---|
| Hello | The Groove Kids | David Butts Bruce Thorburn Antoine Demarest | The Hooley Dooleys |
| Yumbo Jive | The Groove Kids | David Butts Bruce Thorburn Antoine Demarest | The Hooley Dooleys |
| Fire Truck Song | The Groove Kids | David Butts Bruce Thorburn Antoine Demarest | The Hooley Dooleys |
| Chicken Talk | The Groove Kids | David Butts Bruce Thorburn Antoine Demarest | The Hooley Dooleys |
| Pizza | The Groove Kids | David Butts Bruce Thorburn Antoine Demarest | The Hooley Dooleys |
| Ooga Chuga (In the Jungle) | The Groove Kids | David Butts Bruce Thorburn Antoine Demarest | The Hooley Dooleys |
| Aeroplane | The Groove Kids | David Butts Bruce Thorburn Antoine Demarest | The Hooley Dooleys |
| Fairy Dancing | Melissa and Danielle Fairies | Rob Pippan | The Fairies |
| Fairy Friends Forever | Melissa and Danielle Fairies | Rob Pippan | The Fairies |
| The Fairy Twist | Melissa and Danielle Fairies | Rob Pippan | The Fairies |
| Fairy Bootskooting | Melissa and Danielle Fairies | Rob Pippan | The Fairies |
| Raggs Kids Club Band Theme | The Doggies | N/A | RAGGS Kids Club Band |

| Track No/Title | Singer/s | Composer/s | Original Artist/s |
|---|---|---|---|
| Star Baby | The Doggies | Rebecca Kent | RAGGS Kids Club Band |
| Colors | The Doggies | N/A | RAGGS Kids Club Band |
| Wag & Wiggle | The Doggies | Dan Emmett (as Polly Wolly Doodle) | RAGGS Kids Club Band |
| You Gotta Move | The Doggies | N/A | RAGGS Kids Club Band |
| Spaghetti Bolognaise | Max T | Peter Combe | Peter Combe |
| Newspaper Mama | Max T | Peter Combe | Peter Combe |

## Disc 3

| Track No/Title | Singer/s | Composer/s | Original Artist/s |
|---|---|---|---|
| Joannie Works With One Hammer | Playground Kids | Traditional The Wiggles | The Wiggles |
| Toot, Toot, Chugga, Chugga, Big Red Car | Playground Kids | M.Cook. J.Fatt. A.Field. G.Page | The Wiggles |
| Can You (Point Your Fingers and Do the Twist?) | Playground Kids | M.Cook. J.Fatt. A.Field. G.Page | The Wiggles |
| Rock-A-Bye-Your Bear | Playground Kids | G.Page. A.Field | The Wiggles |
| Wake Up Gemma! | Playground Kids | M.Cook. J.Fatt. A.Field. G.Page | TheWiggles |
| Henry the Octopus (1998 Version) | Playground Kids | M.Cook. J.Fatt. A.Field | The Wiggles |
| Wiggly Party | Playground Kids | M.Cook. J.Fatt. A.Field. G.Page. J.Field. C.Abercrombie | The Wiggles |
| Look Both Ways | Playground Kids | M.Cook. J.Fatt. A.Field. G.Page | The Wiggles |
| Move Your Arms Like Henry | Playground Kids | P.Field | The Wiggles |
| We're Dancing With Wags the Dog | Playground Kids | M.Cook. J.Fatt. A.Field. G.Page | The Wiggles |
| Wave to Wags | Playground Kids | M.Cook. J.Fatt. A.Field. G.Page | The Wiggles |
| Dorothy the Dinosaur | Playground Kids | J.Field. M.Cook | The Wiggles |
| Dorothy (Would You Like to Dance?) | Playground Kids | M.Cook. J.Fatt. A.Field. G.Page | The Wiggles |
| Go, Captain Feathersword Ahoy! | Playground Kids | M.Cook. J.Fatt. A.Field. G.Page | The Wiggles |
| Captain's Magic Buttons | Playground Kids | The Wiggles | The Wiggles |
| Ooh, It's Captain Feathersword | Playground Kids | J.Field | The Wiggles |
| The Monkey Dance | Playground Kids | M.Cook. J.Fatt. A.Field. G.Page. J.Field | The Wiggles |
| Fruit Salad | Playground Kids | M.Cook. J.Fatt. A.Field. G.Page | The Wiggles |

| Track No/Title | Singer/s | Composer/s | Original Artist/s |
|---|---|---|---|
| D.O.R.O.T.H.Y (My Favourite Dinosaur) (1998 Version) | Playground Kids | M.Cook. J.Fatt. A.Field. G.Page | The Wiggles |
| Luna's Workshop | Playground Kids | M.Cook. J.Fatt. A.Field G.Page. J.Field. D Lindsay | The Wiggles |
| Here Comes a Bear | Playground Kids | A.Field. G.Page | The Wiggles |
| I Love It When It Rains | Playground Kids | M.Cook | The Wiggles |
| Lights, Camera, Action, Wiggles! | Playground Kids | M.Cook. J.Fatt. A.Field. G.Page. J.Field. D.Lindsay | The Wiggles |
| Dancing Ride | Playground Kids | A.Field. G.Page | The Wiggles |
| Dorothy's Birthday Party (1992 Version) | Playground Kids | M.Cook | The Wiggles |
| Henry's Underwater Big Band | Playground Kids | J.Field | The Wiggles |
| Play Your Guitar with Milly | Playground Kids | M.Cook. J.Field. A.Field. G.Page | The Wiggles |
| Romp Bomp a Stomp | Playground Kids | M.Cook. J.Fatt. A.Field. G.Page | The Wiggles |
| Dorothy's Dance Party | Playground Kids | J.Field | The Wiggles |
| Get Ready To Wiggle | Playground Kids and The Rest of the Cast | J.Field. M.Cook. J.Fatt. G.Page | The Wiggles |

I'm going to the Perth Entertainment Centre in three hours… to perform in front of lots of children… most of them have disabilities… such as Autism and Down's Syndrome…they will have their families with them too… it's my first time giving a performance like this…hopefully, I will entertain them all!

As well as singing I will do a little bit of magic… Playground Kids and Mum and Dad have helped me practice magic tricks… like the 'handkerchief' trick!

It doesn't take long till it's concert time and I am standing in front of the crowd ready to perform for the audience.

"Hello everyone… I am Cassie."

"I hope everyone will enjoy the concert today!"

"My friends and I… will be performing songs from our album of collaboration during the course of the show… we want you all to join in… sing… dance… and let's do all the actions!"

"We are all going to have a brilliant time and an awesome day!"

"Later on, some of you can come on stage and dance with us and have fun."

"Let's enjoy this our special concert!" I said

The concert was wonderful…one of the best projects I have ever done! The kids with disabilities loved every minute of it… a few of them danced with me and had fun. I signed all their autographs… then had photos taken with lots of them.

All the children's music artists that I performed with have been great, I thanked them all for making this children's concert a memorable one for all the children and their families, and for me too!

It has been a very big 'gig'... but so worthwhile... to see the happiness on the faces of the children.

"Cassie you were having a lovely time singing and dancing with all those performers and kids with disabilities... we're so happy and proud of you sweetie."

"Well done Cassie." said Mum, beaming

"That happy smile on your face was wonderful to see... you were interacting with all the kids...it was great, darling." said Dad, proudly

"Thanks Mum and Dad."

"It feels so natural interacting with them... this children's concert has proved it to me."

"It took a large effort from everyone to pull it all together...it was awesome!" I said, happily

"A great end to a great day!" I high fived the sky, Mum and Dad laughed to see me so 'pumped' and happy

We are now into the Christmas month of 2011...we're considering recording our first Christmas album in a week's time under the working title... 'Christmas with the Bontels'... it may include one or two songs written by us... plus several covers including...'I Love Jingle Bells' my Australian pop project Bubblegum Dance... for my Scandinavian fans.

'Bubblegum Land' and 'Christmas Magic' were originally recorded by Quirky Service in 1989, for their first Christmas album... 'Fun at Christmas'. We are certainly likely to tour to promote it... then later this month Mum, Dad and I intend to dress up as Santa... Mrs Claus... and Elf. We might do a special needs event with these costumes... a little differently to the normal autograph and photo sessions with Santa.

We will be not back home in Melbourne for Christmas... it will be the first time we are spending Christmas outside of Melbourne. We will celebrate in Perth this year... I heard on the grapevine that the Perth locals are planning a big surprise for us on Christmas Day! Teasingly, they won't reveal anything... I can't wait to see what the big surprise is...I'm getting excited now... I can't wait for it to be revealed! Calm down Cassie. Don't get too 'carried away'!

"Perth is a brilliant place to stay!

"We've been here for nearly a month now...there are so many things to do."

"The Swan Valley wine region is an interesting place to visit... we don't drink alcohol... but we can still go on a tour through the beautiful countryside." I commented

"Yes, we can Cassie."

"We'll get in the car and go for a drive." Dad said

When we arrived in the Swan Valley, we found several ways to explore the region. These included coach... horse-drawn carriage... limousine... bike... trike... or even a helicopter!

I don't want to go in a helicopter just yet... the height would scare me.

"We would like to explore the Swan Valley by coach please."

"It's a good way to see the Swan Valley." said Mum

"It certainly is... climb aboard and I'll take you on the tour." said the coach operator

We got onboard the coach and the tour started... all around us we saw the grape vines growing that produced the grapes for harvesting, that went into all the different wines in the area.

The guide told us the history of the Swan Valley and also about some of the wine making processes.

"After the tour you can indulge yourselves with gourmet cuisine... while enjoying the sweeping views of the vineyards. There are many great views here to relax and unwind with... whilst enjoying the local food and wine."

"Do you three like wine?" asked the operator

"No... we don't drink alcohol."

"I'm only sixteen...I'm not drinking alcohol... so I can stay healthy to the 'max'!" I said

"Daniel and I don't drink either... at parties and on overseas trips or holidays we have water or soft drinks instead." said Mum

"That's cool."

"The history here is great anyway...you will have learnt lots about the Swan Valley today." the operator replied

"We sure did."

"On this road trip we're taking we've been learning more about the Australian towns that we have visited along the way... than we ever knew before." said Dad, enthusiastically

"That's great!"

"Swan Valley will be a great memory for you all to remember."

"You can take some photos as well... to remind you of your visit!"

At the end of the tour we went to the Valencia Vineyard Restaurant... the dining room was in the federation style.

There were a few round poles trailed with delightful and historic glory vines... also a mixture of old and new brick paving, some of the older paving dated back to the early 1920s.

The Valencia Vineyard has a tranquil garden theme with a soothing, relaxing ambience. We look over the menu, the gourmet dishes sounded temping and delicious. I don't know which one to try first!

When our meals arrive, Dad makes another one of his embarrassing 'Dad' jokes.

"Well 'MY' dinner has arrived."

"I don't know what you two are having." chuckles Dad

I rolled my eyes up at the ceiling and muttered with embarrassment

"Very funny Dad." *not*... I mutter under my breath

Mum grinned as she looked at my face and said...

"Never mind dear... you know your Dad thinks he's a comedian... don't you?"

"What do you mean... 'THINKS'?" spluttered Dad, swallowing his water the wrong way

Then we all had a good laugh at that!

Dad decided to bring up some Christmas memories whilst we were waiting for our meals to arrive.

"For many years Cassie you had a fear of the Christmas tree."

"A few times when we put up the Christmas tree you would meltdown and hide... then Mum would have to take it down and put it back in the big storage cupboard."

"We didn't put up the Christmas tree again until you were fifteen years old... for fear of you melting down each time!"

"You were fine with the presents as long as the clothes we gave you were coloured blue and made of cotton... because you would have a meltdown if you were accidently given other colours or fabrics for your clothes!"

"For Christmas lunch and dinner... we made smooth meals for you."

"Christmas cake was out of the question!"

"We mostly celebrated by ourselves... occasionally with one or two family members... because we knew crowds would be too overwhelming for you."

"We would spend the afternoon either at home... or at the beach having family time together."

"We once tried to get a photo of Santa with you when you were nine... but you became overwhelmed and melted down because of the noise... the other kids... and the bright lights, so we went back home... that was the only attempt we ever made!"

Since 2010, we have been able to put up the Christmas tree...which you now love!"

"You can decorate it too these days…this year in Perth we will be putting up a big Christmas tree…with maybe some presents too!"

"We will be having chicken for Christmas dinner this year… with vegetables… and a custard dessert." Dad licked his lips in anticipation

"Of course, I will have a fun time for Christmas this year!"

"Maybe we could perform on Christmas Day in Perth… wouldn't that be fun?" I mused

"It would be amazing to have a 'Christmas' themed concert." said Mum

Mum's phone buzzed it was a text from the OZ Music Awards.

*Congratulations Bontel Family Band, you have won the following awards: Album of the Year, Best Group, Breakthrough Artist-Album, Highest-Selling Album, Single of the Year.*

*We are sorry you couldn't make it to the awards presentation, but when you are able please collect your awards. Well done.*

"You little beauty!"

"We have been nominated for seven… and won five awards!"

"We are gaining recognition as our Australian tour goes along!"

"These awards show that!" said Mum, excitedly

We are all proud of ourselves. We have won our first awards as 'The Bontel Family Band'! If we work very hard… we may be able to take our family band to the world stage!

A few days later Mum, Dad and I, have been to the Swan Valley again, this time to see how chocolate is made. We watched all the chocolate making processes, we even got to buy some chocolates. We all love chocolate! Who doesn't!

"Cassie, we are going to see a relative of ours who is currently staying in Perth looking after someone's house."

"He's your uncle and my big brother."

"Do you remember him?" asks Mum

"I remember him all right!"

"He's Uncle Mitchell Robertson."

"I recall that he wears glasses… has a white beard and moustache… he has two sons… my cousins Harry and Bill."

"He visited us once when I was eight years old… I amazed him by reading a chapter of a novel." I said

"That's right."

"I remember that too."

"We're going to spend Christmas day with him… and Nan Diane will be there too!"

"Come on let's go and see Mitchell!"

"We haven't seen him in a while… it'll be nice to catch up with him." said Mum, happily

We drove to the house where Mitchell was house-sitting… walked up to the door and I knocked on it. The door opened and Mitchell was delighted to see us.

"Cassie how are you my lovely?"

"It's nice to see you here in Perth." said Uncle Mitchell

"I'm always well Uncle Mitchell." I replied

"How are you?"

"I'm doing fine Cassie."

"Come and give me a big hug." he said

I went up to him and hugged him around the waist… he hugged me back.

His beard and moustache tickled my face which made me giggle... but I didn't mind that.

"Mikayla my little sister."

"It's good to see you."

"How are you?" Mitchell said

"I'm doing fine big brother!"

"You haven't changed a bit since I saw you last." said Mum, giving him a hug

"Daniel, how are 'ya mate?"

"A fellow Holden lover like me... twice you drove me to the Melbourne pub in your Holden if I remember rightly." said Mitchell

"That's right Mitchell!" Dad replied

"That Holden Barina I drove you to the Melbourne pub in... is still one of my favourite Holdens." Dad said, with a smile

"It's great to see you again." said Dad, grabbing Mitchell's hand and shaking it heartily

"Come inside and we'll have a good old chin-wag."

"Diane will be here in a couple of hours." Mitchell added

As I said, Mitchell is Mum's big brother and my uncle... Mum loves to spend time with her big brother when she can. Occasionally she plays pranks on him... she once put two smelly sardines in his shoes and never got found out for it at the time. They have a good bond and sometimes she spends time with Bill and Harry her two nephews as well.

They like to go fishing and play board games. On Bill's sixteenth birthday, Mum gave him a Play Station One console with a few games... which included soccer... because she knows he plays that game.

"So, how's the road trip going?" asked Mitchell

"It's going brilliantly."

"We've been on the 'Ghan' from Darwin to Adelaide and back... relaxed in Broome and viewed Uluru... in Alice Springs." I told him

"You seem to be having a good time!" he replied

"We are... we have taken lots of photos along the way... to show family and friends...some of them are hilarious." said Mum, laughing

"You're still quite the photographer then?" said Mitchell

"I am."

"One of my folders on my Facebook page is full of them... there is a video of Rebecca and I tricking Daniel... with our famous 'clothes switch' trick!"

"We fooled him into thinking he was talking to me...when he was really talking to Rebecca!"

"It was hilarious, it went viral around the world... Cassie's YouTube channel has accumulated over a hundred thousand hits on it!" Mum chuckled

"That was embarrassing... I was seeing double in front of my eyes!"

"Fooled yet again... but I will get Mikayla and Rebecca back somehow!" Dad vowed

"I bet you won't dear." chuckled Mum

"I bet he will." I said, laughing

"You are the naughtiest practical joker that I've ever known... that includes putting smelly sardines in my shoes when you were twelve years old!" said Mitchell

"Oh No!"

"What happened, Mum?"

"I can't wait to hear what happened." I said

"Well back in 1982, Mitchell was staying at the Bontel-Macdonald mansion and we were having sandwiches with chips on the side."

"I got a tin of sardines and after we had finished lunch Mitchell went to the bathroom to wash his hands and change his clothes."

"He was picking up his girlfriend for an evening out... so he wanted to look good in his suit.

"I was going to take him to my house to pick her up from there and drop them off at the movies... they planned to go to a restaurant for dinner."

"This provided me with the opportunity to put sardines in his best shoes whilst he was changing."

"Two or three hours later the smell was everywhere, including near the entrance door where he had taken off his shoes!"

Finally, Mitchell tracked down the smell to his offending footwear and said...

"What's in here?"

"Diving his hands into the smelly shoes... he ended up with two very fishy hands!"

"Who put these sardines in my shoes?" he yelled

"PHWOAR!"

"PEEUW!"

"Whoever it was they'll get a boot up the arse!"

"I was hiding behind the lounge room couch with my nose covered, trying not to giggle... I got away with that prank though."

"Poor Mitchell had to use Mum's shoes as a substitute... until the stench had cleared and he was able to wear them again." said Mum

"Yes, Mum's shoes were a temporary fill-in...the stench lasted for days!"

That was a good prank, I could hear you giggling somewhere... I couldn't find you anywhere, you were too good at hiding." Mitchell said, ruefully

"That's my cheeky Mum."

"I got that pranking side from her." I said, giggling

"Well young lady... no SARDINES from you... ok?" said Mitchell, wagging his finger

"Oh, I don't know if I can promise that Uncle Mitchell?" I said giggling

I went with Mum and Dad to pick up Nan Diane from her hotel, when we got there Nan Diane made her way towards our car and hugged all three of us.

"Hello, it is lovely to see you again." I said

"It's lovely to see you too sweetheart."

"Daniel and Mikayla... doing well... I hope?" Diane said

"Yes, we are doing well."

"Come with us... Mitchell is house-sitting and we are having a lovely chinwag with him." Mum told her

I spotted Diane's bag had Cadbury white chocolate, cheese flavoured Twisties and several chocolate bars in it. I grinned and reached into Diane's bag, but...

"Cassie!"

"Nice try...I saw you." chuckled Diane

I grinned sheepishly...caught out and busted! We all laughed.

"Cassie these are for when we are spending Christmas Day with Mitchell."

"You can have one chocolate bar only." Diane said, firmly

I chose one and ate it while we drove back to the house.

"Diane hello."

"Why don't you come in and have a 'natter'!"
"There are plenty of sandwiches to share." said Mitchell
"I love listening to your debut album." said Mitchell
"It's been selling very well around the world!"
"The world loves our music they can't get enough of it!"
"It's a chart-topper!" I said, grinning
"Well done you three!"
"We're about to record our first Christmas album tomorrow… it will consist of twelve songs… including one written by us four days ago… and eleven covers."
"It's very exciting." Mum added
"I can't wait to listen to it when it gets released!"
"It might make the Christmas Top Ten." said Mitchell
"It might."
"The recording will take two or three days… it should be released somewhere around the seventeenth or eighteenth of December."
"We'll have loads of fun making it!" Dad grinned
I've got more snacks in the fridge that the owner left for me…would you like some?" asked Mitchell
"Yes, please Uncle Mitchell."
"That would be yummy!" I said, and everybody laughed
Mum, Dad and I, are about to leave for our first ever Christmas concert!
Our first Christmas album entitled 'Christmas with the Bontels' was released on Saturday the seventeenth of December… I'm getting excited about performing those songs at the concert in Perth.
I found out that the surprise that Perth has arranged for us is the Christmas tree they have decorated… it's nearly finished! All it needs now is a star on the top… but who will be the person to put that star on the top?
Mum, Dad and I, have cooked our tea with Mitchell and Diane and it looks so good! We have chicken, vegies and salad, then custard and white chocolate pudding for dessert.
"Well we are in for one fantastic feast everybody!"
"Dig in and cheers!" I shout
After we had finished our delicious dinner, we got ready to drive to Subiaco Oval. Along the way we saw the Christmas tree… it was covered in many decorations with lots of brightly coloured lights. It looked absolutely amazing!
"Oh, my goodness!"
"This is wicked!"
"That Christmas tree is beautiful… look at all the presents underneath it!"
"Perth certainly have a splendid tree… the sign says 'Merry Christmas Bontel Family'!" I yelled, excitedly
"Mum and I, have been to Perth many times…this will be a memory for years to come!" said Dad
"This certainly will be a memorable Christmas… let's capture it and put it in our photo album!" said Mum, enthusiastically clicking away with her camera
The Mayor of Perth, Wallace Burke, came over to welcome us. He was holding a Christmas package in his hands.
"Hello Bontel Family."
"Are you enjoying yourselves?" asked Wallace
"We sure are, Mayor Burke."

"It may not be snowing... but the Christmas lights on this big tree certainly make up for that." Mum grinned

"I hear you three are going to perform your Christmas concert at Subiaco Oval?"

"That will be lots of fun!" Wallace added

"It sure will Mayor Burke!"

"Fans can come along and enjoy themselves... people who are spending Christmas alone will be able to have a happy time... smile... sing... dance and laugh...with Christmas cheer at our Christmas concert... and you never know who might be appearing!"

"We are grateful that you are bringing 'happy times'... to many people who may be lonely or on their own at this time of year, it will be a treat for us all!"

"I have a present for you in appreciation of your efforts."

"Open it on Christmas Day." said Wallace, handing the present over to me

"We will Mayor Burke."

"Mikayla and I have been dressing up as Mr and Mrs Claus since 1989...this year Cassie will be helping for the first time...it will be a little different." said Dad

"That's great... I know Cassie will do well in her role as the elf!" grinned Mayor Burke

"Thank you... Mayor Burke." I said, smiling back

"We will give out presents... interact with all the special needs children... and play with them...we shall be at the Perth Shopping Centre in the morning."

"It's now time for Mum, Dad and I, to perform our Christmas album."

Here are the tracks we will be playing for everyone at the Christmas Concert in Perth.

I can't wait to get started it will be so much fun!

| Tracks / Titles | Singer/s | Composer/s | Original Artist/s |
| --- | --- | --- | --- |
| Family Christmas | Cassie Bontel | C.Bontel. M.Bontel. D.Bontel | The Bontel Family |
| I Love Jingle Bells | Cassie Bontel | | Bubblegum Land |
| Christmas Magic | Cassie Bontel | D.Bontel. M.Bontel. O.Bontel. R.Macdonald | Quirky Service |
| Jingle Bell Rock | Cassie Bontel | Joe Beale, Jim Booth | Bobby Helms |
| Frosty the Snowman | Cassie Bontel | Walter Rollins & Steve Nelson | Gene Autry & The Cass Country Boys |
| Let it Snow Let it Snow Let it Snow | Cassie Bontel | Sammy Cahn | Bing Crosby |
| Rudolph The Red-Nosed Reindeer | Cassie Bontel | Gene Autry | Johnny Marks |
| Here Comes Santa Claus | Cassie Bontel | Gene Autry | Gene Autry |
| White Christmas | Cassie Bontel | Irving Berlin | Bing Crosby with Ken Darby |
| Ding Dong Merrily on High | Cassie Bontel | George Radcliffe Woodward | Traditional |
| Jingle Bells | Cassie Bontel | James Lord Pierpoint | Bing Crosby |

| Tracks / Titles | Singer/s | Composer/s | Original Artist/s |
|---|---|---|---|
| Santa Claus is Coming to Town | Cassie Bontel | John Frederick Coots and Haven Gillespie | Gene Autry |
| We Wish You a Merry Christmas | Cassie, Mikayla & Daniel Bontel. Santa & the Elves | | Traditional |

"I won't forget this Christmas concert!"
This could be the best Christmas ever!" I shouted to the crowd
"I think Santa may make an appearance during our Christmas concert." said Dad
The MC walked on stage and said...
"Welcome ladies and gentlemen to this very special Christmas concert in Perth!"
"Here to perform especially for you one night only... is a well-known family all the way from Melbourne... their just released Christmas album titled... Christmas with the Bontels."
"Please welcome this multi-talented band to the stage... 'The Bontel Family'!"
Mum and Dad walked on stage... I advanced to the microphone...
"Hello Perth!"
"Are you having a happy Christmas time so far?"
"Yes!" screamed back the audience
"Good, because your Christmas is going to get even better when we 'rock out' the songs from our new Christmas album... 'Christmas with the Bontels'... and there is more fun coming later with a surprise guest!"
"Won't that be exciting?"
"YAAY!" yelled the audience excitedly
"OK, let's light up the city of Perth with our 'take' on Christmas!"
"One... Two... Three... hit it!" I said, as Mum hit the drums
Later, after singing and playing the song, 'Santa Claus is Coming to Town', we heard sleigh bells ringing in the distance... we all know what that means... don't we?
"Listen... is that bells I hear?"
"That can mean only one thing!"
"Our special guest has arrived!"
"We turn around to see an enormous present on the stage with three ribbons flowing down from it!
"Mum... Dad...you grab a ribbon each and I'll grab the third!"
We all grasped the ribbons.
"Mum are you ready?"
"Yes... I am Cassie!"
"Dad are you ready?"
"I am definitely ready, Cassie!"
"Is everybody else ready?" I say, shouting to the audience
"Ready!" screamed the audience
"We will count up to three."
"On three we will all pull the ribbons together and hopefully see what's inside!"
"One... Two... Three!"

We pulled the ribbons which undid the bow... lifted the lid to the box... and out popped Santa Claus!
"It's Santa Claus everybody!" I called out to the children in the audience
"Ho... Ho... Ho!"
"Hello Perth... Merry Christmas!" said Santa
The crowd went wild, everybody cheered and clapped.
"Hello, Bontel Family."
"Are you having a 'jolly' good Christmas?" asked Santa
"We are Santa." said Dad, smiling
"Have you been good this year?" asked Santa
"Yes, we have been good all year." I said, trying not to grin
"That's good!"
"I have a gift for each of you."
"My three elves will distribute them."
"Elves!"
"Can you give the 'Bontel Family' their presents now please?" said Santa, with a big 'Ho' 'Ho' 'Ho'
The three elves came out and gave us our presents. My present had blue wrapping, Mum's present had yellow and Dad's was green. This Christmas is getting better by the minute!
"I've got a 'special' gift for you three."
"Here it comes!" said Santa
It had orange wrapping with pink bows, the elves towed it on stage... our jaws dropped!
What could be inside that huge parcel?
I'm getting very excited about this.
The audience are too!
Santa and the elves teamed up to open the giant present... it contained... a big bag full of lollies, of all varieties!
"Wow!"
"A big bag full of lollies!"
"It's got every sort of lolly that you can think of... including all the 'old favourites' that we grew up with!" I said, full of beans
"It's got my favourite butterscotch included!" said Mum, very excited
"Liquorice all-sorts!"
"Excellent!" said Dad, also very excited
"I thought that might hit the spot!
"Take them with you... but don't eat too much in one go!" said Santa, with a big belly laugh
"We won't Santa."
"Why don't you join us for the last song?"
"It's... 'We Wish You A Merry Christmas'... the elves can join in too?"
"The elves and I, would love that." said Santa
We all got ready to sing the final song of the concert together with, Santa, his Elves and all the Christmas concert goers... who were ready to join in enthusiastically!

## We Wish You a Merry Christmas

We wish you a Merry Christmas
We wish you a Merry Christmas
We Wish you a Merry Christmas and a Happy New Year (**Chorus**)

Now, bring us some figgy pudding (**Verse 1**)
Now, bring us some figgy pudding
Now, bring us some figgy pudding... and bring some out here

For, we all like figgy pudding (**Verse 2**)
We all like figgy pudding
We all like figgy pudding...so bring some out here!

Oh, we won't go until we've got some (**Verse 3**)
We won't go until we've got some
We won't go until we've got some... so bring some out here!
Good tidings we bring to you and your kin
Good tidings for Christmas and a Happy New Year

We wish you a Merry Christmas (**Chorus**)
We wish you a Merry Christmas
We wish you a Merry Christmas and a Happy New Year!

"We hope you enjoyed the Christmas Concert everyone?" I called out to the audience
"YES... WE DID!" the audience screamed back
"We did too...thank you all for coming and embracing the Christmas spirit."
"I hope you all have a very happy and safe Christmas and New Year...goodbye everyone, have a lovely Christmas!" I waved goodbye to the audience as we left the stage

# Chapter Thirty-Six
## 'special' Santa & Christmas Day

At our hotel Mum spoke to Dad in a concerned voice.

"For many years Cassie has believed in Santa... she still has the letter she received from him at age six!"

"She loves reading it... I'm worried that if we tell her that there is no Santa... she will get upset and never forgive us for years!" said Mum, with a worried look

"Hmm."

"She may not believe in the 'Tooth Fairy' anymore...but how are we going to tell her about Santa?"

"We will have to tell her...we need to do it very carefully and gently." said Dad

"All right dear." said Mum

I heard all of this whilst I was drying myself off after my shower. I don't believe in the tooth fairy anymore... and I had started to not believe in Santa either... so I'll be prepared for whatever Mum and Dad have to say to me about that.

"Um... Cassie...Dad and I have something to say to you."

"It's about Santa."

"For many years you have believed in Santa...we have to tell you that we don't believe in Santa anymore so..." Mum began, but she couldn't bear hearing herself say it and mumbled to a stop

"Your Mum and I, have discussed this and after careful thinking there is no..." Dad didn't get much farther than Mum, before he trickled out too

"Mum... Dad... I know what you are trying to say... and I understand that Santa must have retired... and asked you two to take over for him... from now on."

"He has been working extremely hard for years...he has earnt a well-deserved retirement and handed over to you." I said, smiling at them

Mum and Dad were relieved I didn't get upset or have a meltdown. I understand that Santa only exists in our imaginations... so I said something that I prepared... in case that 'Santa subject' came up.

"That's right, Cassie." said Mum and Dad together, obviously relieved that they don't have to explain any further

"When Santa asked Dad and I... to take over from him because he needed to spend more time looking after his house... we said..."

"Yes, we would love to Santa!"

"We won't let the children down... we'll make their Christmas magical." Mum added

"You two are going to do a good job at that!" I told them both

"I can help out as an elf... loading the presents onto the sleigh and seeing you off... I will look after the house until you two get back." I said, with a smile

"That would be so helpful Cassie!"

"Tomorrow... we are going to the Galleria Shopping Centre where we will dress up as Santa and Mrs Claus... you can be our elf helper named Cassandra."

"We bought the costumes earlier today!"

"Are you ready to play your part, Cassie?" asks Dad

"I sure am, Dad." I said, happily

It's seven-thirty in the morning and Mum, Dad and I, are at the Galleria Shopping Centre waiting for three special-needs children to come through the door. We are dressed in our costumes... as Santa Claus... Mrs Claus... and Cassandra the elf... we look very Christmassy!

"We know all the rules for the 'Special Santa'... I can't wait to see the children and talk to them." I said

"We can't wait either Cassie."

"This Christmas will be an improved encounter with Santa than their previous Christmas meetings." said Mum

"Usually, when special-needs children go to shopping centres to meet Santa, they become overwhelmed with sensory overload and melt down."

"It's often caused by other over excited or loud children... crying babies... loudspeaker noise and crowds."

"Photos with Santa are out of the question... under those, kind of conditions."

"It was a good idea to do this 'trial' 'special' Santa."

"Each child will have a ten-minute session... without all the loud noises.... bright lights and crowds of people around."

"It's my first time... I can't wait to get started!"

"When a special-needs child comes in Dad...you lay down on the floor at their eye-level... not too close... then interact with them... for example, if they are playing with their favourite toy you can join in with them... Mum and I will do the same, then give them their present...with no surprises!"

"You know autistic kids don't like surprises...especially at Christmas time...I know what it's like...I've been through that myself!"

"If they are verbal...we'll chat with them...we should have a fun time." I said

A few minutes later, the first special needs child came in. He was six years old and non- verbal... he has severe autism he is holding a toy car in his hand... maybe that's his obsession... he is with his Mum.

"Hello, my son Jack has never had his photo taken with Santa before because of his fear."

"We tried on three separate occasions...he melted down each time because of all the noise and bright lights."

"This may be our only opportunity to meet Santa without all the issues."

"I hope everything goes well today." said Jack's Mum

"We hope so too." Dad replied

Jack got down on the floor and started playing with his car. Dad got down to Jack's level but not too close and started to play along with him. I can tell that Jack is having a good time by his laughing and his mum is smiling too to see her son having fun with Santa.

It warms my heart to see Jack play with Santa... something he couldn't do in the past, I'm witnessing a lovely interaction between Dad and Jack... Mum is smiling too to see Jack and Dad at play together.

A short while later, Jack and his Mum leave, thanking us for making Jack's day better.

"Thank you all."

"It's our pleasure."
We're glad we have made Jack's visit with Santa, a happy one." I smiled at Jack and his Mum
The second child arrived... she is ten years old and uses an iPad to communicate... she is non-verbal too with classic autism...and she is carrying a toy train.
"Hello everyone, this is my daughter Kaylee... she has never liked Santa or the Christmas tree."
"She has meltdowns every time we put up the Christmas tree... so we have to take it down."
"Santa photos have been out of the question too!"
"When I heard about 'special' Santa it was the perfect opportunity to come and try again!"
"Kaylee's senses are all affected... going into stores and shops are 'no-go' zones... she gets overwhelmed and screams... covering her ears."
"Can you make her experience a great one without overwhelming her?" asks Kaylee's Mum
"We will certainly try our best to do that!" Mum said
"Does Kaylee use sign language to communicate?" asked Dad
"Yes...she does."
"Sometimes, if her iPad runs out of power... other times are on her own terms."
"The three of us are proficient in sign language... so that may help!"
"We'll interact with Kaylee...we will be careful not to overwhelm her." I added
"Kaylee started playing with her trains... it's Mums' turn to get down on the floor at her level at a distance and begin to interact via sign language. She is playing with her trains, which is good to see. Kaylee was giggling and flapping her hands a little... she was having fun and so was Mum. After a little while playing on the floor with Mrs Claus... Kaylee and her Mum leave... first thanking Mum for making Kaylee happy.
"Thank you." beamed Kaylee's Mum
"That's a great way to start Christmas... thanks to you three!"
"Kaylee may not remember you... but I will." said Kaylee's Mum, gratefully
"Well the first two were fun and went well... this 'special' Santa trial is fun."
"Great job everybody!" said Mum
"We are having a great Christmas... and the children are certainly going to have a better Christmas... now that they have met Santa and had some fun with him!" said Dad, happily
Then it was time for the last child to come in... she is fifteen years old and has mild autism. Jenny can speak fully, but mostly remains silent... too shy to speak to anyone other than her parents. I notice that she is holding a soft toy bear... I think that it comforts her when she is distressed.
"Jenny is shy... she will only speak to her Dad and I... she is timid around other people, including her family members."
"Her teddy bear is her comfort item... she is even shy with Santa...she won't go close enough to have a photo taken with him."
"If you can help her feel comfortable and give her a present... I would be grateful." said Jenny's Mum
"We will try our best." smiled Dad
I sat down and beckoned for Jenny to come over. She walked over and sat down although she was very nervous and shy. She has never met me before I'll try to make her feel comfortable without making her more nervous.
"That's a nice teddy bear you have got there."
"What's your teddy's name?" I asked, quietly
"His name is Oliver."
"I got him when I was seven years old... he has been my comfort ever since."

"I hug him when I get distressed… he used to sleep in my bed now he sits on my chest of drawers… keeping guard over me." Jenny said very softly

"That's a very nice name."

"I have a soft toy dolphin that I have had since I was five… she also used to sleep with me in my bed…she sits on my bedside table watching over me now." I smiled

"That's nice."

"Does she have a name?" asked Jenny

"She sure does."

"Her name is Heavenly." I said

"That's a pretty name."

"I love dolphins too… I have two posters of them on my bedroom wall… I also have a few dolphin books on my bookshelf." Jenny told me

Jenny is becoming less nervous and more cheerful. She is opening up a little more and that makes me smile. The others smile too.

"I loved dolphins since I was little." I said happily

"I went swimming with a dolphin on the Gold Coast in New South Wales and I had a blast!"

"Did you really?"

"Wow!"

"You must have had such a fun time there!"

"What was the dolphin's name?" asks Jenny, interested to know more

"Marlene…she was so beautiful."

"I did a couple of tricks with her…she even gave me a kiss!" I told Jenny

"That's great!"

"I would love to swim with a dolphin… it's been my dream since I watched a news segment about dolphins when I was eleven!"

I haven't had the confidence to try it…you have made me realise that I need to face my fears and be more confident."

"Talking with you is giving me confidence to follow those dreams… and to speak up." said Jenny, with a happy smile

"I'm glad you feel that way Jenny." I smiled back

"We are giving you a present that you can open' 'right away' instead of Christmas Day… that way you don't have to face the stress of the element of surprise!"

"I've been through that myself… so I know what it's like!" I said grinning

Mum and Dad passed me the present… which I in turn passed on to Jenny… when she opened it out fell three tickets to Dreamworld…. to swim with the dolphins! Jenny's face lit up with joy!

"Thank you"

"Oh, thank you."

"Santa Claus… Mrs Claus… Cassandra!"

"I now have the chance to see a real dolphin at Dreamworld."

"You have made my Christmas wishes come true." said Jenny, hugging me tightly

I hugged her back and said.

"That's so great Jenny!"

"I am so happy to help you."

Mum, Dad and Jenny's Mum, wiped tears of joy from their eyes. I will admit that I did wipe a tear or two, from my own eyes as well. Jenny, and her Mum, thanked us and we exchanged phone numbers and promised to keep in contact.

"That 'special Santa' was VERY special!" I said, elated

"It's so good to make those families Christmas time a little happier and more joyful... it feels great to have had a part in that!"

"We'll remember this Christmas for a very long time."

"Cassie, we're happy that you made another lovely new friend... and that now she gets to fulfil her dream as well!" said Dad

"You are becoming adept with children who have disabilities... making them feel comfortable and at ease when they are feeling nervous or shy... it helps that you know what it is like for them... drawing from your own experiences." Dad said, proudly

"Thanks, Mum and Dad."

"I owe it all to you."

The next morning, I wake up feeling joyful and happy it is Christmas Day! Hooray! This is going to be one big day, not only with Mum and Dad, but Nan Diane and Uncle Mitchell as well! There will be a few presents... there will be Christmas lunch of ham, chicken and vegetables...some chilling out... Christmas dinner...more ham, chicken and salad! Mum, Dad and I, may put on a special performance. Whatever happens it will be a great day filled with Christmas spirit! I'm getting very excited about this! I could squeal! This is going to be loads of awesome fun!

"Mum!"

"Dad!"

"I'm so excited... it's Christmas Day!!!"

"It's going to be an awesome day full of presents and food... a day where you can eat as much as you like... where you get to spend quality time with family and loved ones!" I said, jumping up and down

"You're on the right track Cassie, darling."

"There will be plenty of food for us to eat...still let's avoid getting sick from over-indulgence!"

"We will open lots of presents and spend time with loved ones... like Mitchell and Diane." Mum added

"We can help Mitchell and Diane prepare the lunch."

"Cassie, there will be crackers to pull... with a paper hat... some jokes and a trivia question... maybe even a little gift inside."

"We will have a good day!"

"Got all that, Cassie?" said Dad, grinning

"Yes Dad... I got all that!"

"I have helped prepared the Christmas lunch and dinner for three years now...I will be glad to help family with it again!"

"We will all work together to get the lunch and dinner made."

"Now let's open the presents that we bought for each other." said Mum

Mum handed me her present.

"Merry Christmas, Cassie!"

"I hope you enjoy your present." said Mum

I opened it and there was a butterfly brooch... I love it... a big grin spreads across my face.

"Thanks Mum!"

"You know I love butterflies… that was a great gift to give me." I said, giving Mum a kiss

"I knew you would love it Cassie." said Mum, beaming

"Dad here's my gift to you."

"I hope you love it." I said, handing Dad his gift

Dad opened it to find… an Australian travel humour book… he loves it!

"An Australian book full of humorous tales!"

"Thanks Cassie!"

"I'll enjoy getting a chuckle out of that!" says Dad, giving me a kiss

"Mum… I've got a present that I would like to give to you."

"I hope you will love it." I said.

Mum opened her present… it was a travel mug! I thought she might need one and she does!

"Thanks Cassie!"

"I can now put my lemonade drinks in this handy travel mug." Mum smiled

"We've all got great gifts from each other."

At ten-thirty we drove to where Mitchell and Diane were preparing the Christmas lunch. There are vegetables to be chopped… spices to be put on…chickens to be roasted.

We will work together to make a great Christmas lunch… it will taste delicious for everybody to eat!

"Hello Mitchell."

"Hello Diane."

"We've come to help prepare the Christmas lunch."

It's going to be battle-stations here now… everyone to their posts!" said Mum, like a military campaigner

"That's right!"

"We need 'all hands-on-deck', as they!"

"We are willing and able!"

"What tasks do you have for us to do?" asked Dad

"Mikayla you can help me chop the vegetables and put the spices on them…before we put them in the roasting pans to be cooked."

"Daniel you can prepare the ham and salads with Mitchell."

"Cassie you can prepare the chicken for roasting."

"Please be careful when you are handling the cutting knives." Diane said, giving us a safety warning

"Yes Diane."

"I can do it without cutting myself… I will be very careful." I replied

So, we all set to work. Mum and Diane chopping all the different vegetables…putting them in a big roaster dish…sprinkling a little spice on each one…before roasting them in the oven.

Dad and Mitchell slicing up the ham and placing the slices into a large silver foil container. Then they made the potato salad… cutting the cooked potatoes and tossing them through the creamy sauce and herbs. They prepared the bean salad and put all dishes in separate containers to keep them fresh. I cut the pre- roasted chickens into pieces and carefully placed them in a baking tins to re-crisp and heat through in the oven.

"How's everyone going?" I asked

"It's going well Cassie."

"The vegetables are roasting, the ham is cut, the salads are prepared and ready to be served when the hot vegetables and roast chickens are cooked."

"How long did you set the chicken for?" asked Mum

"I set the chicken for twenty minutes in a very hot oven so it should be thoroughly cooked and crispy by then...ready to complement the hot vegetables." I said, cheerfully

"I'll keep an eye on my watch... it's now five minutes past twelve... when it reaches twenty-five minutes past... I'll get the chickens out with this mitt being careful not to drop them!" I said, with a grin

Mum, Dad, Mitchell and Diane, put the salads and cold meats onto the bench and laid out tongs and serving spoons. We chatted outside on the patio with the overhead outdoor tent.

I looked at my watch after nineteen minutes and went inside to check the chicken pieces. I put my oven mitts on... opened the oven... then I took out the chicken... it looks well roasted and the skin is golden brown and crispy.

There were two extra chicken pieces besides the whole chickens that I had cut up... I didn't want to waste the meat so I quickly took the chicken off the bones... then I sneakily put the chicken bones into Mitchell's shoes!

He's going to be shocked when the chicken bones start to smell! Hee, hee! I placed all the chicken pieces and meat on a big plate and carried it out to the patio.

"Lunch is ready!" I called to everyone

We all helped ourselves to chicken, ham, salads and vegetables. We piled up our plates and sat down at the kitchen table... everyone 'tucked in' to their feast!

Boy... it was so delicious!

"Mmm."

"It's yummy!"

"I'm definitely embracing the Christmas spirit... great food enjoyed with my family." I said.

"We are too!"

"You did a good job helping us to prepare the Christmas lunch Cassie." said Mum

"We all did a great job and helped each other... and it has produced a great result!"

'It sure is a delicious 'result' at that." said Dad, helping himself to another mouthful with a grin

"It was so nice of you to come and spend some time with us... that's what Christmas is all about, spending time with family." said Mitchell

"Yes, it is and we are all having a good time!" said Diane, happily

"We are indeed!"

"Daniel, Cassie and I, exchanged lovely Christmas gifts with each other and loved them." Mum added

"That's fun." said Mitchell

"Yes, it's always fun to receive presents!" I said

"Let's pull our Christmas crackers!"

"Cassie, when we pull our crackers there may be a bang... it could be loud!" said Diane

"That's fine Nan."

"I have no problems with loud noises... since my Sydney performance." I said

Diane and I, pulled a cracker and out fell my little gift which turned out to be a photo frame in an oval shape.

"Here's the joke!"

"What do you get if you cross a kangaroo with a sheep?" I asked

"I don't know."

"What do you get if you cross a kangaroo with a sheep?" asked Mum, trying to keep a straight face

"You get a woolly jumper!" I laughed

We all laughed at that old familiar joke.

"Here's a trivia question for all of us."

"Which Australian Sports Stadium is the home of Cricket and Football?" I asked.

"That would be the MCG in Victoria." Dad replied

"You got that right Dad!"

"We might go there when it starts again in March next year." I said

"It would be my first time!"

"We might Cassie."

"Collingwood VS Richmond... Collingwood VS Carlton... or Richmond VS Carlton...they might have big crowds...you should have no problems with that now Cassie." Mum said

"We can still enjoy our meat pie and chips... like Mum and I have been doing since the late seventies!"

"You might try something else...still the meat pie is a very popular choice for football fans!" said Dad, getting all misty eyed just thinking about his lovely meat pie

Mum, Dad, Diane and Mitchell, opened their crackers and laughed at all the jokes. We answered all the trivia questions and Dad made another of his embarrassing Dad jokes... I cringed at that, still we all laughed out loud! Everybody was telling old family stories you never know where that is going to lead!

"When Cassie was eight years old on a cold winter's afternoon, she was playing her guitar and I was reading my novel... Daniel was reading the newspaper."

"She was playing a nice pop tune... then after about fifteen minutes it all went quiet."

"I heard a rustle coming from the kitchen so I went to see what it was and there was Cassie 'munching' cookies with the biscuit barrel in the middle of the floor!"

"Busted you little rascal!" I said, to which she replied...

"Uh, oh I'm in big trouble now!"

"Then we all laughed." said Mum

We shared some more stories... including Mum pranking Dad with a water gun when she and Dad were ten... then Mitchell trying to prank Mum when she was eleven, but ending up getting pranked by Mum via a rubber spider joke... and Dad teaming up with Mum to pinch Diane's ginger crunch! Much later, after we had finished eating and story-telling, it was time to chill out.

"What's that 'funky smell'? said Mitchell

"It seems to be coming from near the front entrance."

"I don't know Uncle Mitchell."

"Why don't you check it out." I said, innocently

"I will." Mitchell replied

Mitchell went out to check on the smell and Dad whispered to me.

"Quick, Cassie."

"Hide in the shed... so Mitchell can't find you!"

I dashed outside to the shed and hid behind the door, trying not to snigger.

"That Cassie is always cheeky... isn't she?" said Diane

"She is always cheeky... especially... when she plays pranks."

"Our rascal daughter is definitely mischievous!" said Dad, with a grin

"What are these chicken bones doing in my shoes?!"

"Whoever did this is going to get a kick up his or her behind!" said Mitchell, holding up the chicken bones that he had found placed in his shoes

"It wasn't me Mitchell... I didn't put them in your shoes." said Mum, sweetly

"It was not me... Mitchell."

"I had nothing to do with it!" said Dad, firmly

"Well, it certainly wasn't me… Mitchell!"

"I wouldn't do such a thing." said Diane, straight-faced

"Well who was it then?"

"I'll find out you know." said Mitchell crankily

I could hear Mitchell looking outside and did my best not to laugh…I couldn't stop myself!

"Ah Ha!"

"I know who that laughter belongs to."

"Cassie Annabelle Bontel!"

"Come out of that shed right now!" yelled Mitchell

I opened the shed door with a sheepish grin plastered all over my face. Unlike Mum in 1982 when she was twelve years old… I'd been found out for my prank… and there's nowhere to hide!

"Cassie!"

"Time for some straight talking!"

"Were you the one that put the chicken bones in my shoes?" said Mitchell, frowning

"Err…. it was Mum." I said, trying to shift the blame off me and pointing at Mum

"Hey!"

"Don't blame me!"

"You confess Cassie!" laughs Mum, pointing back at me

"It was Dad." I said, shifting the blame yet again

"It was not me!" said Dad, indignantly

"Cassie own up." chuckled Dad

"Diane was the one!" I said, desperate now to pin it on anybody but me

"Cassie… was certainly the one." Diane said firmly

I knew the game was up… I was the only one that did it… I would have to confess at last.

"All right!"

"I was the one that put the chicken bones in your shoes."

"I thought I would get could away with it… like Mum did in 1982."

"Problem is I can't stop myself from laughing… which gets me busted all the time!"

"It was hilarious though… the look on your face was priceless!" I giggled

"You think it's so funny… don't you, Cassie?"

"Would you like you a boot up the behind?" Mitchell said, showing me his 'smelly' boots

"No, Uncle Mitchell."

"I would not." I said, pinching my nose between my fingers as he threatened me with the boots

Everyone chuckled when they saw my face and Mitchells too!

"I see you're enjoying wearing the butterfly brooch Cassie… that Mikayla gave you."

"It could be part of your signature look." Mitchell grinned

"It might be 'ONE' of my looks Mitchell." I said, correcting him

"After all, I can't limit my fashion statements now… can I?" I said giggling

"I wish you three the best of luck on the rest of your tour of Australia."

"A Happy New Year too." said Diane, smiling at us all

It was now seven-thirty in the evening…Mum, Dad and I, went back to our hotel… waving goodbye to Mitchell and Diane.

A week has passed since we spent our happy Christmas Day with Mitchell and Diane... Mum, Dad and I are relaxing. In the early afternoon, Mum-received an email from the Perth Entertainment Centre, she had an excited look on her face.

"Daniel...Cassie...there's an email from the Perth Entertainment Centre!"

"Come and read it!" Mum said, excitedly

Dad and I, rushed over to see what the email said... it was an invitation to a New Year's Eve party event!

## Chapter Thirty-Seven
## Fireworks, Farmer's Market & a Humpback

To the Bontel Family,
'The Perth Entertainment Centre invites you to perform at a New Year's Eve Concert. There will be opportunities to socialise with the guests and play a game or two. At ten-thirty in the evening you are invited to perform songs from your new album to the Perth concertgoers who will be attending the NYE festivities. We hope you can attend, where fun times will be had by all!'
"This is so exciting!"
"We get to perform at the Perth Entertainment Centre again… this time for a New Year's Eve Concert!"
"This is too good an opportunity to pass up!"
"We'll have a great time there!" I said, very excited at the prospect
"We sure will Cassie."
"There will be food and drinks… and a game or two if you want to play."
"This will be a brilliant social event we won't forget." said Dad
"We can take a few photos… and chat with the guests."
"You're on your way to becoming a socialite Cassie!" Dad said, giving me a wink
"I hope you have fun at these special events as the Bontel Family." said Mum
"These social events will be good for me… to mingle with other patrons… and celebrities."
"There's plenty of time before the event… let's have a drive and some lunch… we can spend the afternoon relaxing before we need to get ready for tonight!" said Dad
We went for a little drive around Perth looking at the sights… we saw the WACA stadium where Australia played their third test of five in the 2010-11 Ashes series and won convincingly by two hundred and sixty-seven runs.
Australia were two hundred and sixty-eight first innings… England were one hundred and seventy-one first innings… Australia three hundred and nine for the second innings… and England one hundred and twenty-three for their second innings.
Mitchell Johnson took six for thirty-eight in the second innings… which included Alistair Cook on thirty-eight… Kevin Pietersen for a duck… Jonathan Trott for four… and Paul Collingwood for five… to earn himself Man-of-the-Match!
In the fourth test at the MCG England walloped us by an innings and one hundred and sixty-seven runs… England scored a big total of five hundred and thirteen and we could only manage ninety-eight in the first

innings... which became the lowest Ashes total scored at the MCG... then two hundred and fifty-eight in the second innings which was heart breaking for the three of us!

The fifth and last Ashes test was won by England by an innings and eighty-three runs...retaining the Ashes Trophy which they had won in the 2009 series... in England and Wales two to one!

"We could attend a cricket match in Melbourne when Australia play their next match which will be against South Africa for the best of three test series."

"Or against Sri Lanka in the best of three Tests... One Day Internationals...and Twenty-Over matches ."

"Or against the West Indies in the best of five One Day Internationals... or even against India in the best of four Tests in the Border-Gavaskar Trophy...which we won last time four to zero here." I said

"We could Cassie."

"It all on depends... on when our road trip finishes." Mum said

"You could be on to something there."

"It's fine if we don't get to attend any of those matches... we can watch them on television... or listen to them on the car radio." I said

"You're right there Cassie."

"When Mum and I... or Olivia and Rebecca... can't make it to a match... we listen to it on our car radios... or our portable radios when we're camping." Dad agreed

We chatted while we ate our café lunch... we talked about the upcoming New Year's Eve concert.

"Cassie the New Year's Eve concert may have fireworks too."

"You used to have a fear of fireworks for many years."

"You remember how you would wear your headphones to block the explosions out...we would have to watch it from our house... or a quiet spot away from the fireworks...if we were where the fireworks were being set off you would meltdown and hide...we would have to take you home to calm you down."

"Our friends and family didn't spring sparklers...you feared those as well... they understood that you didn't want to see any fireworks."

"I remember when you were thirteen... you hid under the bed because the fireworks startled you... despite our forewarning to get your headphones on."

"We had to coax you out of there...rubbing your hands...telling you it was safe to come out."

You couldn't find the words to explain to us that the fireworks had scared you... and why they did...over the past couple of years you have conquered that fear."

"You should be able to enjoy this year's fireworks... they will be colourful and make magical patterns in the sky...this time you will get to experience it with us." said Mum, hopefully

"I certainly will"

"When I was overwhelmed it was like an explosion right next to me... when I saw the fireworks... I became upset because I thought they were coming straight for me!"

"They were like 'exploding stars in the sky'...they certainly scared me then."

"With your encouragement and my anxiety techniques... I have learnt how to cope."

"I can enjoy the fireworks this time... and welcome in the New Year with you both." I said

"That would be great Cassie."

"You will be amazed by the colours and patterns that the fireworks make in the night sky!"

"Maybe you will be inspired to take a few photos of them too!" said Dad

When we arrived at the Perth Entertainment Centre at eight, there were several people arriving and the place was decorated with lots of New Year's Eve decorations... the food and drinks were prepared for the evening's entertainment. This is going to turn to be an awesome night!

"Hello, Bontel Family."
"Glad you could make it."
"Please help yourself to any food or drinks."
"Good luck with your performance this evening." said the doorman
"Thank you." I replied

We browsed the tables... tasting little cheese blocks and salami slices...sipping on a lemonade or two. A few fans asked for autographs and we happily signed.

"Bontel Family!"
"It's nice to meet you."
"I enjoy listening to your debut album... it's cool!" said one happy fan
"Thanks."
"We are glad you like it." Mum said, smiling
"I am looking forward to hearing you perform tonight."
"We are looking forward to performing for everyone too!" said Dad, cheerfully

We signed more autographs, mingling and socialising with the guests. One of them told me my singing voice was beautiful...that I have inspired several girls to start careers as musicians. I thanked her for the lovely compliment.

"I hope to inspire more young people as our family band takes off."
"How are you enjoying the New Year's Eve event so far, Cassie?" asked Mum
"I'm enjoying every minute of it Mum!"
"It's a great atmosphere and there are so many people turning up."
"The food and drinks taste good and the music playing at the moment sounds excellent."
"Yes... it is a lovely atmosphere." Mum agreed
"We are honoured to be invited to such a special event." Dad added

It was around ten when the first fireworks started. We went outside with the other guests to watch them. All sorts of fireworks exploded in the sky and burst into various colours and shapes... I am seeing this spectacular sight with my own eyes this time! I don't have a fear of fireworks anymore... I am just admiring them and enjoying them. I took out my iPhone and 'snapped' a few photos. Our family and friends back in Melbourne are probably taking a few photos of their own fireworks too!

"I got a few good ones here Mum and Dad"
"Aren't they fantastic?" I said, mesmerised by all the colours
"Yes... they are magnificent!"
"Mum and I have got a few photos of our own."
"Check them out." Dad says proudly, showing me his photos
"Wow!"
"These ones are cool"
"Let's upload them to show our family and friends... I'm sure they have got a few photos of their fireworks to show us as well."

When the fireworks had finished Mum, Dad and I went to get ready for the concert.
"This is going to be one wicked concert!"
"It will be an awesome way to bring in the New Year!" I said, grinning widely
"We'll have a little party after our performance... then we can face 2012 head-on together!"
"A sleep-in would be a bonus!" Mum said
I think that might be wishful thinking on her part... on NEW YEAR'S EVE!

Just then the MC made an announcement.

"Your New Year's Eve is about to hit the 'stratosphere' as this band performs from their charting debut album... some of their very special songs!"

"Please welcome to the stage.... 'The Bontel Family'!"

Mum, Dad and I, made our way to the stage

"Hello everybody!"

"Are you ready to rock in the New Year!" I asked the audience members

"YES, WE ARE!!!" they shouted back

"Then let's party!" I responded

We played all the numbers from our album and the patrons loved it all... they were up and dancing on the floor... till it was time for the traditional countdown to the New Year.

We began the count...

"Ten... Nine...Eight... Seven...Six... Five... Four...Three... Two... One!

"HAPPY NEW YEAR!" we all screamed

"Here's to 2012!"

"A good year ahead of us and a few more stops on our Australian tour." I added

"Happy New Year Cassie!" said Mum

"Happy New Year, Mum and Dad!" I said, excitedly

We partied with the guests afterwards... telling a few jokes... chatting and signing a few more autographs. This is so much fun, I'm having the best time ever in Perth!

We said a final 'Happy New Year' to everybody and waved goodbye...we drove to our hotel... ready for a well-earned rest. We are so tired we will probably have a long sleep in! Oh yeah! Our next destination will be Bunbury... *who knows I might even see a wild bottlenose dolphin near Koombana Bay if I'm lucky...* I think, as I drop off to sleep.

The next morning, we packed up all our things and drove to Bunbury... it was a couple of hours away and Mum decided to be the driver for this journey. As soon as we arrived, we booked in to the Hotel Lord Forrest and after checking out our rooms, we decided to take a look around.

We walked around Bunbury centre and discovered the Farmer's Market... where you can buy the freshest fruit and vegies in town.

"Hello."

"This is a great market!" I said to a stall holder

"It is young lady."

"You can buy the freshest fruit and vegies in Bunbury here."

"They sure are fresh!"

"We know a good buy or two when we see them!" said Mum

Mum, Dad and I, were checking out the fresh fruit and vegies available... there are so many varieties... we're tempted to buy them all! We select a few, including bananas and apples.

We haven't had an Italian meal for a while, so we look up a couple of eateries before settling on Nicola's Ristorante for lunch. Pizzas, pasta and grills are their speciality... with Italian artwork lining the walls. It was bustling and spacious, a very popular restaurant for visitors and Bunbury locals alike.

"Awesome!"

"The Italian artwork adds a nice authentic atmosphere."

"I can smell the Italian dishes being cooked." I said, sniffing the air

"Those smells are divine... I can almost taste the food." Mum licked her lips

"It's a great place to dine and a good space to eat." says Dad
We sat down at our table and ordered the best Italian pizzas and pastas.
"Boy that was delicious!"
"That's the best Italian meal I've eaten on this trip so far!"
"It certainly filled my stomach." I said, patting my round belly
"Me as well."
"The Italian desserts look delicious." said Mum
However, … we decide not to be little pigs…oink…oink!
"Now that we've eaten so much… let's go for a walk to burn it all off!"
"It will do us good to walk in this beautiful weather." I said

We all agreed on that, so we made our way to the beach. Ah… glorious sunny Bunbury back beach… is a great beach to visit. The sun is high up in the sky, shining down on the whole of Bunbury. There are a few clouds, it's a good sign that it's going to be an awesome day!

After strolling along the sandy beach for an hour or so we made our way back to our hotel and had a skype session with Rebecca, who wanted to catch up with what we had been up to on our latest leg of the trip.

'What have you been doing in Bunbury since you arrived?' 'We've been to the Farmer's Market and we plan to go to Koombana Bay for some relaxation and maybe a swim. It's a hot day…we've got plenty of water and sunscreen too.' 'That's good. I heard you performed at the New Year's Eve party in Perth. How did it go?' 'It was fantastic! All of Perth had an awesome time and so did we! We rocked the Perth Entertainment Centre with our hit songs and they loved it.' 'Wow, it must've been a brilliant performance.' 'It was. We signed heaps of autographs and chatted to many fans. It was a brilliant event overall.' 'What else did you do in Perth?' 'We performed as part of our Australian tour and also did a tribute to children's music… with several children's musical artists and performers. It was wicked doing that! We also went shopping we bought a few new articles to wear in our favourite colours.' 'I can't wait to see that. Send a photo if you can.' 'Will do. We also plan to see a whale. If we get lucky, we might take a photo or two of it.' 'I can't wait to see that… if you are lucky enough to get one!'

We chatted about our performances and things we have done so far.

'Cassie, I heard you coped with the fireworks in Perth. Well done to you.' 'I did cope with them and I enjoyed them.

We even stayed up for the midnight fireworks and what a spectacular sight that was.' 'That's great. I bet you three had a nice-long sleep in after that. I had a big night on New Year's Eve too. I watched the fireworks and I also had a big sleep in… then I had a late lunch and watched the New Year's Eve fireworks from Sydney in the afternoon.' 'We managed to watch a little bit of it… we've got some photos to send to you. All those colours and sparkles make such a great display, don't they?' 'They definitely do… it was the most spectacular evening to start the New Year!' 'It was special that Mum and Dad were there to witness it with me. Cassie really enjoyed the fireworks… we are happy for her that she has taken another big step. I am happy for myself that I did that too. Mum and Dad have thought up a reward for my bravery… with the fireworks.' 'Oh, what is that?' 'We are going to have a few days camping at Tuart Forest National Park in Busselton soon. It's a good spot with a self-guided trail… we might see a brushtail possum… or the western ringtail possum, which is rare. We may also see other wildlife and learn about local history.' 'I hope you have a fun time when you get there. I would love to hear about that, soon. Cassie, I loved your radio interview speaking about autism and related issues. I played the full audio to my audience during an episode of my show 'Rebecca'… they enjoyed listening to it very much. A couple of my audience members who have autistic children of their own… said it reminded people of sensory issues… also the funny things that can happen and be shared with everyone.' 'That's good. I want to bring positive change for those with autism, and their families too!' 'Cassie, I've got a letter from an autistic teen girl who listened to your radio interview and she loved it. I will read it out to you.'

*To Cassie Bontel, I am a sixteen-year-old with mild autism. I am a child prodigy in music, like you, and I've overcome my sensory issues, but I'm too shy to perform in public other than in my house. Since I listened to your radio interview and to The Bontel Family debut CD, it has given me the confidence to step out and face the crowd with my music.*

*In October 2011, I performed my debut in my hometown of Mildura and the crowd really loved it! I smiled and it was nice to see the smiles on the audience's faces, which made me feel good. Thanks for inspiring me to face the unknown, I am grateful to you for giving me the confidence to try. I hope to collaborate with you one day, maybe we can produce a great hit!'*

*From your great fan*
*Rachel Dorset.*
*P.S. I love your music. Keep it up and you will inspire more autistic musicians like me.'*

'That's an awesome letter. I feel really appreciated… it was so nice of Rachel to write that to me. Her path is similar to mine… she performed for the first time in her home town of Mildura… which is great for her.' 'It certainly is. I will send the letter to you… so that you can keep it to look at and inspire you… every time you read it… or when you are feeling down.' 'It's an inspirational letter that urges me to keep up my music. I've got another idea that I thought up for my music.' I said, cheekily

Mum, Dad and Rebecca snorted with laughter.

"Uh oh…what is your idea…Cassie?" asked Dad

"One of my future songs… a dance type song… Bubble-gum Dance… for my Scandinavian listeners!"

"I would be in a bath full of bubbles using a hairbrush as a microphone… with a male vocalist about the same age as me… singing his vocals off-screen… or in another room."

"The bathroom will be 'princess' themed with jewels all around me!"

"That's an interesting idea Cassie… hmmm?" muses Mum

"Yes… it's one of my 'fantasy dreams'…I plan to make it come true!" I said, firmly

"You got that idea from 'us'… didn't you?"

"We did a similar thing when we were seventeen."

"Our song 'Jewel Bath'… from our album 'Winter Snowflake'… featured us in the bath holding gems which were our birthstones… blowing bubbles through bubble blowers."

"We had such fun filming… it was a great song!"

"Fun times." grinned Dad

"We girls love our jewellery…we couldn't get enough jewels into the shot during the filming of that music video!" said Mum, laughing

'We would love to do it again!' Rebecca interjected

"Rebecca!"

"It would be a bit awkward if we did it now!" Mikayla squirmed

"We did it at seventeen and our fans loved it then…let's not do it again!" said Mum, looking at Rebecca like she has just lost her marbles

'You're right.'

'Better not.'

"Cassie… we'll help you film this music video when you want to…it will take some time to prepare… and put together properly.'

"I shall have lots of fun during the filming!" I giggled, as we signed off

Two weeks later… Mum and I are in the reception area of the Lord Forrest Hotel… discussing what fun things and gifts we are going to give to Dad. It is Dad's forty-second birthday… of course it's Olivia's forty-second birthday too… as they are twins! Whether Olivia will be here is yet to be seen…I'm sure Dad will have a big day with us!

"Cassie, it is Dad and Aunt Olivia's forty-second birthday today."

"We need to put the gifts we bought for him, in our hotel room cupboard so he won't find them!"

"I have made arrangements for a surprise dinner for Dad at a Bunbury restaurant."

"They are going to cook up a 'special dish' for him!"

"We shall dress formally… in our favourite colours for the occasion!"

"What an evening full of fun it will be." I said

Mum and I took the stairs back to our room and put the gifts in the cupboard.

Dad woke up.

"Morning you two."

"Whose birthday is it?" said Dad, with a cheeky grin

"Very funny Dad!"

"It's Aunty Olivia's!" I said, with the same cheeky grin

"Hey wait a minute!"

"It's mine too!"

"We are 'TWINS' you know!" Dad spluttered

"As if we could forget Dad… you wouldn't let us!"

"Happy forty-second birthday!!!"

"Mum and I have got some gifts for you." I said, taking the presents out of their hiding place in the cupboard

"I guarantee you will love what's inside." I added

"We thought about them carefully dear, when we chose them for you." said Mum

Dad opened my gift… it's 'The Leopard'… written by Jo Nesbo!

"That's a good book."

"It'll be a thrilling read… that Harry Hole detective is a real 'maverick'…just like me!" says Dad

We all laugh at that remark!

"I know you love your 'Jo Nesbo'…this book has plenty of thrilling scenes in there!"

"It had a great Norwegian title… 'Panserhjerte'… for its original Norwegian release!" I told Dad

I gave Dad a kiss on his left cheek and he gave me one back in return. It feels nice that he is always loved by me… even though I used to dislike affectionate contact…until last year.

Mum handed Dad his gift and said with a smile.

"I have chosen this gift especially for you dear on your birthday."

"I hope you will love it." she added

Dad's gift from Mum was…a Richmond Tigers mug!

"That's an excellent gift!"

"I can drink my lemonade or milk whenever I'm at home watching Richmond Tigers on the telly." said Dad, happily

"I knew you were a 'Richmond man' from the day I first met you in 1975." said Mum, stroking Dad's hair

"I always will be."

"I'll never forget when we walloped your Collingwood Magpies in the 1980 Grand Final by eighty-one... and Kevin "KB" Bartlett was the master goal kicker with seven." said Dad, his eyes going misty

"OK...OK." said Mum, good humouredly

"Our poor kicking resulted in the final score of 9.24 78... it didn't help our cause and the 'collywobbles' nickname...was 'VERY' embarrassing...Billy Picken was our best goal-kicker... if I remember correctly." Mum replied

"The third quarter was like a blooper reel... eight behinds were scored with only one goal!" said Mum, dejectedly

"I've watched that grand final replay online... I've spotted you two with your coloured clothes amongst the AFL gear!"

"What a crowd-standout you two were!" I said in awe

"It was a golden year for Richmond."

"It was."

"It was a wonderful premiership and we had a celebration back at the Bontel-Macdonald mansion!"

"Let's go to the Lord Forrest Hotel dining area and order you a nice birthday breakfast!" I said to Dad

Mum and I ordered Dad's breakfast... which included eggs benedict and bacon... with cold milk to drink. It was a great birthday breakfast and Dad enjoyed it very much.

"That was a delicious breakfast."

"Thanks, you two."

"It will be a brilliant day for Olivia and I!" said Dad

"It will be even more brilliant... when we take you out for some sight-seeing before lunch!"

"Let's get ourselves ready... we leave in fifteen minutes." Mum responded

We decide to visit Geographe Bay on a boat... we are hoping to spot a whale or two. I've got my binoculars ready, so have Mum and Dad. Terry the boat owner who is taking the tour has been taking visitors around the bay for the past five years, he is very a nice man. I told him it was going to be my first time seeing a whale up close... he told me that I would remember it for a very long time... if I am lucky enough to see one!

We had checked before we left on the trip... it is not official whale season now... it ended a month ago... still there is a one-off tour... to maybe see one of the four types of whale that sometimes appear here... in the summer season.

As the boat sailed, the wind blew through my hair, giving me the sensation of the elements onboard a ship at sea.

"Whales... like dolphins, are so beautiful."

"It must be amazing to see their size and the big splashes they make."

"I have enjoyed watching a few whale videos on YouTube and on DVD."

"It would be a dream to see a whale in Australia... perhaps Geographe Bay could be the place!" I said

"Dad and I will get our cameras out ready'... to take a photo if one appears... you can take one on your iPhone." Mum said

We waited for half an hour but no whales came. We looked at the beautiful views of Geographe Bay while we waited

Another twenty minutes had passed when we heard a big splash! We looked out quickly and just glimpsed the top of a humpback whale!

"Look at that!"

"That's a humpback whale!"

"I've never seen one before!" I said, excitedly

"Wow!"

"That whale is big indeed!"

"I'll get a photo if it comes up again!" said Mum, with her camera ready

The 'humpback 'emerged…Mum was able to take a good photo of it before it submerged once more

"That was amazing!"

"You can show me the photos after… I would love to see them."

"Only one species of whale comes out in summer." said Terry, with a smile

"This is quite wonderful… we'll never forget that." said Dad grinning

When the tour was finished, we showed Terry the humpback whale photo we took.

"You three were very lucky to see it." said Terry

"Here's a photo of Kate, Adam, Nicole and Amelia… with a whale they encountered in Portland." said Dad, showing me the photo

"That's a nice photo."

"They were at Nun's Beach in July 2006, reading on their beach chairs, when they noticed a humpback whale."

"They got out their binoculars and camera's and watched the whale for nine minutes before taking a couple of photos each."

"When they got back from their tour… they showed the photos to me… I enjoyed looking at them."

"This time we have photos to show them!" said Dad, smiling

"Yes!" I said, smiling back

I was reading a book back onshore… after a while Mum and I decided to play a little Frisbee…we had fifteen minutes of fun throwing the Frisbee to one another with Dad watching on smiling.

Next, Mum and I sat on our towels and played a game with one of my I-Spy books… which I loved… Dad joined in too.

We finished off with a swim in the ocean… having a good time splashing each other… and riding a few waves.

We all had so much fun watching the humpback whale that day.

I shall never forget seeing it…such a majestic sight.

# Chapter Thirty-Eight
## Birthday 'Mojo', Blue Nails & a Pink Lake

"Cape Naturaliste seems like a good place to check out... the lighthouse nearby is a fascinating building to learn about... before we wrap things up for this evening's entertainment." Mum winked at Dad
It was still a lovely sunny afternoon.
"The view here is awesome!"
"The cliffs are quite picturesque."
"I'm going to take a photo and send it to Olivia."
"She would love a picturesque photo like this!" Dad exclaimed
He took an awesome photo of the cliffs and sent it to Olivia's iPhone... she loved it and replied with a message.
'That is a beautiful picture of the Cape Naturaliste cliffs Daniel. What a great picture to send to me on my forty-second birthday. I'll put that in my photo album and send it to family members and friends so they can see it too!'
The headland scenery views were brilliant... with the ocean extending to the horizon... from the headland vantage point.
A French navigator named Nicolas Baudin explored this part of Australia arriving on the thirtieth of May in 1801. At that time the French were mapping the coast of Australia... which was then known as 'New Holland'. Baudin named Geographe Bay after his flagship...and the Cape was named after his expedition's second ship... called 'Naturaliste'!
Olivia rang through to wish her twin brother a Happy Birthday!
"Hello Olivia."
"I'm having such a great birthday so far."
"How about you?" Dad said to Olivia, as he switched her on to speakerphone so we could all hear
"Hello, Daniel."
"Yes, I'm having a good birthday so far."
"Mum and Dad called me this morning to wish me a Happy Birthday... I'm sure they will contact you later today... since we were 'born together' on January the sixteenth 1970!"
"How can I forget!" Dad grinned
"Did you receive a present from Mum and Dad?"
"Not yet...Mum and Dad are buying something to give to me when I get back home."
"Right... of course."
"Where are you at the moment?"
"I'm in Bunbury... holidaying for a few days."

"What!"
"Are you sure you are not taking a road trip like us?"
Olivia chuckled down the line.
"Umm... No."
"This is the last place I'm staying... before I fly back to Melbourne."
"I hope you're having a good time."
"Have you bought a present for me yet?"
"Yes, I have bought a couple...I'm not telling you what I got... you'll have to find out at dinner."
"Tell me."
"Nope."
"Not even..."
"No!"
Mum and I laugh.
"It's fine."
"I've got a couple to give to you...I won't reveal what they are either... until tea time!" Dad quipped back
"You mean you are keeping a secret from your twin sister?"
"Fess up!"
"Nope."
"Not...."
"No!"
Mum and I laugh again
"That's fine with me."
"I'll let you enjoy your time... until six o'clock when we meet up."
"Okay, we'll see you there."
"Don't get any cheeky ideas!"
"We could be as bad as 'Mikayla and Rebecca'!"
Everyone in the room laughed at that... as no one could be as bad as Mum and Aunty Rebecca!
"Bye, Livvie."
"Have a great birthday!"
"You too, Dan!"
"Bye."
"Dad, I'm sure Olivia is having a good birthday like you."
"We sometimes play pranks on each other...usually involving cake and whipped cream!"
"Those are always messy... but funny... moments." Dad grimaced
"Yes, they are!"

Later, back at the hotel... before we went to the restaurant that Mum and I had arranged for Dad and Olivia's birthday... Maria and Jim skyped to say 'Happy Birthday'.

'Hello son! Happy forty-second Birthday!' 'Thanks Mum and Dad. Much appreciated.' 'Are you having a great day so far?' 'Yes, I am. We're in Bunbury in Western Australia.' 'Great! Mum and I went there in 1968 on a holiday, we had fun.'

'What presents have you received so far?' 'A Richmond Tigers mug from Mikayla... and a 'Jo Nesbo' book from Cassie.' 'Those are lovely gifts from Mikayla and Cassie.' 'Olivia is having a great birthday too... she called me earlier.' 'Yes, she is having a lovely time in Bunbury on her holiday. She has a present for me but she won't tell me what it is... that cheeky twin sister of mine!' 'She can be cheeky, especially, when you two get together!'

'We're about to go out to dinner to a restaurant, where I'm going to be spoilt rotten with a lovely meal!' 'Oh, that sounds lovely... what is the name of the restaurant?' 'Mikayla and Cassie won't tell me so as not to spoil their surprise! All I know is that it's going to be one with a vibrant atmosphere... and a great view of Bunbury!' 'That sounds exciting! We have got you a gift for when you arrive back in Melbourne.' 'Thanks, I will be keen to see what it is. We'll be going to the restaurant in about ten minutes...so I'll sign off now! Bye Mum and Dad.' 'Bye son... Happy Birthday to you and Olivia. Bye son... have fun.'

When Mum, Dad and I went to the car... I tried to sneak in the front passenger seat...Dad was on to me.

"In the back cheeky!"

"Nice try... but no go." laughed Dad

"You got me Dad!" I said, putting my hands up in the air and laughing as I climbed into the back of the vehicle

Mum is driving us to the 'secret' restaurant destination for Dad and Olivia's forty second birthday dinner... I'm in the back and Dad is riding shotgun!

We pull into the carpark at 'Mojo's Restaurant.

Dad and Olivia are going to have a great forty-second birthday dinner... a cake will be bought out when it's time for dessert! We do not know what kind of cake or what flavour it is going to be... but we do know it's going to be a delicious one!!

"There will be a few people there Cassie." said Mum

"No problems Mum... I'll have fun!" I replied

We walked in.

SPLAT! Dad 'copped' a cream pie straight in the face!

Mum and I laughed.

"Ok... very funny"

"Who did that? ... as if I couldn't guess." said Dad, wiping cream out of his eyes

"I did that!" said a voice we all knew

It was Olivia... she was wearing her sparkly blue dress with a single ring on the middle finger on her left hand. She was wearing a single blue diamond ear ring in her right ear.

Doesn't she look lovely tonight?

Olivia walked up to Dad with a big grin on her face.

"Olivia that's a tricky thing to do to your twin brother...on our birthday!" moaned Dad

"It sure is!"

"I used a cream pie... I just couldn't resist."

"I got you good!" chuckled Olivia.

"Yes... you did get me good Olivia!"

"I haven't got a spare green suit with me at the moment." said Dad, trying to clean himself up as best he can

Dad and Olivia then hugged each other and kissed.

"We are forty-two Olivia!"

"We shall have fun...no matter what age we are!" Dad stated

"That is so right Daniel!" said Olivia, still grinning after her cream pie attack

"Special occasions bring the whole family together...or sometimes just a few...we always have a great time!" Olivia laughed

"Family bonds grow stronger with each journey." I said

"That's so true Cassie."

"You're doing well on this road trip… overcoming your barriers." Olivia added

"Thank you, Aunt Olivia…happy forty-second birthday to you and Dad." I said, hugging Olivia

"Thank you, Cassie."

"My lovely niece." said Olivia, hugging me back

We sat down at our table with another two guests… Narelle and Mark… who are Dad and Olivia's aunt and uncle. They are both dressed up for this special occasion.

"Hello Narelle."

"Hello Mark."

"Nice to see you two… it's been a long time." I said, hugging them

"Good to see you once again Cassie."

"You look so beautiful in that sparkling blue dress… just like your Mum and Olivia." said Narelle

"Thank you."

"Hello Mark."

"Hello Narelle."

"Lovely to see you again." said Dad, hugging them

"Happy forty-second Birthday!"

We've got a gift each for you both…not till after dinner though." said Mark, grinning

"Goodness me… Olivia and I are lucky." said Dad

We ordered our finger bites… chicken… ham… and… cheese fritters…then main course and side dishes… soon story telling time is on!

"I recall the time when Olivia and I were nine years old." began Dad

"We were in the backyard in the summer of 1979… we were in our bathers with our water pistols squirting each other!"

"Mikayla and Rebecca got into the padding pool in their bathers…then Olivia and I jumped out of the bushes and squirted them…we sure took them by surprise!"

"They got back us back though later on…squirting us when Olivia and I were relaxing on our garden loungers!"

"What summer fun we had back then." said Dad, reminiscing

We all laughed at that.

"I remember another funny time when we were seventeen… resting at home after returning from a world tour promoting our third album… 'Winter Snowflake'."

"We were doing some gardening at the Bontel-Macdonald mansion… digging and planting seeds… to grow vegetables."

"The garden looked so good when Mikayla decided to squirt us with the garden hose."

"She denied it was her…Daniel, Rebecca and I, knew exactly who it was!"

"We were soon all getting each other wet with hosepipes and our parents were laughing at us all…luckily the garden needed a drink." Mum said…

"Look at you four!"

"What fun!"

"You are all dripping wet!"

"Come on you lot…you need a shower after all that hard work!" Olivia chuckled, remembering

Everyone at the table laughed.

"Oh, the mischievous adventures that Mum, Dad, Olivia and Rebecca, got up to when they were young!"

"I could listen to them every day!"

"Dad...Olivia."

"I have written a forty-second birthday card for you both." I said

Dad and Olivia read the card.

*'To Dad and Olivia. I hope you have a brilliant forty-second birthday with lots of love and pop music all around, with your loving family. We will have loads of fun together and make some more memorable moments. From Cassie xoxoxo'*

"That's a lovely birthday card Cassie."

"Nice job... especially the three X's and the three O's." said Dad

"I loved the 'love heart symbol' in the card as well that adds a bit of love to our day." said Olivia

Dad, Olivia and I, hugged each other.... a big hug at that! It feels so good to give these birthday family members... a big birthday hug!

"Cassie, well done." said Mum

"Thanks Mum."

"I'm loving every minute of this party!"

"I'm so glad sweetie."

"I can see that you are having a good time."

Your Dad and Olivia are enjoying their gifts too!" said Mum

"They sure are Mum!"

Everyone had handed presents to Dad and Olivia.

They ranged from an Essendon Beanie... to Holden car magazines... and puzzle books... Dad and Olivia loved their gifts! They are having an excellent forty-second birthday.

The time has come for Dad and Olivia's cake to be revealed! It is brown and white chocolate... with blueberries and banana lollies on top!

"Wow!"

"What a tremendous looking cake!"

"It's full of chocolate... both brown and white." said Dad

"It's topped with blueberries... and banana lollies!"

"This will be one cake we can share with everybody... there is plenty to go around." Dad added

Instead of singing 'Happy Birthday'... I sang a birthday song I had written for the occasion...entitled 'Birthday Celebration'... in a dance-pop style... everyone enjoyed it.

"Well done Cassie... we love your song." said Dad

"Thanks Dad."

"Maybe you can record it on a future album Cassie." said Olivia

"I might Olivia." I replied

The cake was delicious and we all had a piece each... we chatted together for some time... then it was time to leave. Mum, Dad and I hugged Olivia and waved her goodbye then we went back to our hotel to sleep.

The next morning, we checked out early and went to the Bunbury Wildlife Park. We made our way to the kangaroo paddock where we saw a few kangaroos hopping about.

"Hello."

"These kangaroos love human company... especially when you have a big bag of animal feed." said the wildlife keeper

"What kinds of kangaroos do you have here?" I asked him

"We have Common Wallaroos... Red Kangaroos... and Western Greys."

"They are very friendly kangaroos."

"Would you like to take a seat and feed them?" asked the keeper

"Yes, we would."

"That should be fun."

The wildlife park keeper gave us a bag of feed and we sat down on the assigned seats... we watched the kangaroos hop around. Soon a Western Grey Kangaroo hopped over to us... I had the bag of animal feed... so I took out a handful... he ate it up making me giggle... I patted him while he munched away.

A Red Kangaroo and a Common Wallaroo hopped over... keen to share the animal feed.

"Guys one at a time please!"

"There is plenty to share." I said

The Red Kangaroo and the Common Wallaroo ate their handfuls while I patted them... and I handed the bag of animal feed to Dad.

"Olivia would love this too!" said Dad

"Cassie, are you are enjoying this?" Dad asked

"Yes, I am Dad!"

"Patting them makes me feel good... the sensation of their fur feels so soft." I said

"Here comes another Western Grey... he wants a feed and a pat as well." said Mum

Dad handed the Western Grey some feed with one hand and gave him a pat with the other.

"Hey mate... you're enjoying this feed, aren't you?"

The kangaroo nibbled the feed out of Dad's hand.

Dad fed a common Wallaroo before Mum took the bag of animal feed... another Red Kangaroo hopped over to us and Mum put her hand out with feed on it.

"You're a beautiful kangaroo... eat up there's plenty for you."

We thanked the wildlife keeper for the experience.

"That was great feeding those kangaroos!"

"They were keen to see us and very hungry too!"

"Cassie, well done for feeding the kangaroos... good on you darling." said Dad

"Thanks."

"I enjoyed feeding such cute kangaroos."

"We all had fun!"

"I think we'll take a look at the other animals now."

When we had finished looking at the animals in the wildlife park, we drove to the Tuart National Forest near Busselton, where we are going to camp for a couple of days.

That evening, we are walking on the self-guided trail in the Tuart Forest hoping to find a common or rare possum. We are carrying large torches to see the possums with... as they are nocturnal animals they only come out when it gets dark. The red reflectors show us the trail markers... the information signs are helping to guide us along the trail.

As we are walking, we hear a call... 'to-wit, to-woo'.

"That's an owl." I said, shining my torch

"It makes a lovely sound."

"We may often hear it at night... when we are camping." Dad said

"I'll be fine with that Dad." I smiled in the dark, showing my white teeth

As we walked the trail, we followed marker boards and signs with information... we shined our torches on them and learnt about the history of the area.

Before the Europeans came here... the Aborigines took advantage of grassland and there was plenty of water for them to live well in this area...then the Europeans came and the coastal forest areas made way for settlement... timber was used for fuel and building.

Grazing cattle was useful due to the wide variety of grasses and the open landscape... the poisonous heartleaf... Gastrolobium Bilobum... was eradicated from the undergrowth. Exotic species replaced the native grasses... which were unsuitable for grazing animals.

Throughout the 1800's...timber cutting operations were occurring...logs and timber products were transported by wooden-railed, horse-drawn trams... these ran the length of the forests... to the mills.

To service the timber industry... a one point eight kilometres jetty was built in Busselton...if you take a walk in the park... you can still see sleepers and other timber cutting relics there.

In 1920 at Wonnerup Beach... a sawmill was erected across the estuary ten kilometres east of Busselton... off that beach a small jetty was built... then timber was escorted to 'Geographe Bay'... via shallow draft boats to schooners.

The mill operated for ten years...wood was in strong demand again after World War II had ended...in 1955 a new mill was built in Ludlow which lasted until 1974... in 1987 a national park was declared.

"The history here is great!"

"That's another piece of Australian history that I've learnt about!"

"I might be known as 'Historian Cassie' by the end of this road trip... that's a nickname I'd be happy to receive!" I smiled

We continued walking along... so far... no possums!

"Find any possums Mum and Dad?" I asked

"No Cassie." said Mum

"Me neither Cassie." Dad added

"Looks like we might have to keep walking back to our tents... at least we got a bit of exercise." I grinned in the dark

"That's right Cassie." Mum agreed

We reached the end of the trail but still no possums. We walked back to our tents and were about to go in... when we heard a rustling noise in the bushes close by.

"That could be a possum!" I whispered

"Let's see if it comes out of the bushes... we will need to keep quiet so as not to scare it away."

We kept very quiet and waited. A few minutes later a possum emerged from the bushes. We look closer to see... a rare western ringtail possum! Oh my! I've seen it before in pictures when I looked it up online... this is an up close and personal encounter! It looked around and stared back at us as if we were visitors to its home...which we really were.

Then it scurried up the nearest tree and settled on a tree branch high up. Wow! I'm seeing a native animal in its natural habitat. I recorded it all with my iPhone... I got a few minutes of good footage to show Mum and Dad! Happy with our last-minute encounter we went to our tents. Dad had turned in for the night... but Mum and I were still awake. Mum whispered to me...

"Cassie Dad is sleeping... why don't we paint his fingernails blue?"

"He will sure get a shock when he wakes up tomorrow!"

"It will be hilarious seeing him with nail polish on." I whispered, giggling

When Dad started snoring... Mum and I crept over with a torch and quietly painted his fingernails blue. When it was done... I crept back to my tent and we both slept through the night. Hee, hee!

Dad woke up and unzipped the tent window... when the sun poured into the tent... he noticed his nails were blue! He was very surprised!

"What the...!"

"Who painted my nails blue?" said Dad, with a frown

"Whoever did it is going to get a flea in the ear!" said Dad, grouching

He walked out of the tent and heard Mum giggling.

"I should have known it was you Mikayla!"

"I can hear YOU...you know." he added

"Come out and confess!" he chuckled

Mum appeared looking sheepish.

"Mikayla dear." said Dad, sweetly

"Were you the one that painted my nails blue?"

"Maybe."

"I didn't do it all on my own." said Mum, dragging her accomplice into the conversation

"I had someone else helping me!"

"Exactly who was that 'someone'?" asked Dad, (knowing all the time)

I was peeking out of my tent... trying not to giggle... letting out a loud laugh instead at the sight of Dad's face!

"I knew it!" shouted Dad

"Come out right now!"

I emerged from the tent grinning all over my face.

"I was the one that helped Mum paint your nails blue." I said, giggling

"You think that's funny...do you?"

"Come here... I have a flea for you!" said Dad, flicking my ear with his two fingers

I ran away from him laughing.

"Now behave yourself Cassie." said Dad, pretending to be serious

"What about Mum?" I whinged

"It was her idea!"

"Oh... I gave up trying to get your Mother to behave... years ago Cassie!" Dad laughed heartily, and Mum had a scowl on her face now

That made me laugh so hard I nearly fell over!

A couple of days later as we packed up our tents... I was talking to Dad.

"As you want to visit Pink Lake... we will need to get on the road early!" Dad said

"It takes more than seven hours driving to get there...we will arrive in just about enough time to find ourselves some accommodation... have an evening meal... and go back to bed again!" Dad laughed

"I never realised how big Western Australia is!" I said, amazed

"I will take the first driving stint this morning." said Dad

"We can stop at Albany for an early lunch break and to refuel the car." he added

"It will take us almost four hours to reach Albany." said Mum, as she put her seatbelt on

"Yes... and it will take us almost another four... to reach Esperance." Dad concluded

"Well we had better get going then!" I said, with a laugh

After a very long day's driving we arrived that evening... we quickly booked in to the Pink Lake Tourist Park... had a quick barbeque tea before sorting all our things out... and then arranged our sleeping places in the cabin and promptly went to sleep.

The next morning at Pink Lake Lookout we were amazed at the size of the lake and the pink colour too! It was six hundred metres long... a rim of sand with dense woodland of paperbark trees surrounding it... eucalypts also grow there. A narrow strip of sand dunes covered by vegetation... separates the Pink Lake from the Blue Southern Ocean.

No-one knows why the lake is Pink...scientists suggest that the dye is created by bacteria... that live in the salt crust...which may cause the colour.

"Wow!"

"I've seen pictures of Pink Lake online... but strewth I never expected anything like this!" I exclaimed

"That's the first time we've seen a Pink lake!"

"It's very beautiful." said Dad

"Rebecca would have loved to see this!"

"Pink is her favourite colour!"

"I'm taking a few photos to send to her... she will love it!" raved Mum

Mum took a few photos and sent them to Rebecca's iPhone.

Rebecca loved them and texted her reply. *'These are lovely! I never knew such a unique lake as this existed! It really is in my favourite colour...PINK!'*

After we spent some time looking at the Pink Lake... we went to the kiosk to purchase ice creams and a Sunny Boy.

"Cassie this is one of the icy treats that Mum and I grew up with."

"A 'sunny boy' that is!" said Dad, proudly holding up a pyramid shaped package for me to marvel at

"Many times, during the summer... Mum... Olivia... Rebecca... and I... went to the general store and bought them... we would open one end and suck the triangular orange ice-block that was inside it."

"It used to last for ages and it was juicy and tasty."

"It's one of our happy memories growing up... that we still remember today." said Dad, with a faraway look in his eyes

"Looks like it might taste good."

"Maybe I will try one... next time."

I don't think Dad heard me... he had a goofy grin on his face as he sucked on his Sunny Boy!

Next, we decided to drive to Stonehenge.

"Wow!"

"It's closer than we thought!"

We all crack up laughing... because the real Stonehenge is in the United Kingdom... on the other side of the world!

The one in Esperance is a fully sized replica of the original... for people in Australia to visit.

It was interesting to learn all about the Esperance Stonehenge. It is five thousand years apart in age, and over fifteen thousand kilometres away in distance... from Stonehenge in England. The one hundred and thirty-seven stones of Esperance Pink Granite... were quarried locally for the 'Australian version' of Stonehenge... and transported from a kilometre away.

The horseshoe shape was formed by ten inner Trilithon stones...each one weighing between twenty-eight to fifty tonnes. Nineteen Bluestones make up another smaller horseshoe... inside the Trilithon Horseshoe.

The Altar Stone weighs nine tonnes and lies at the base of the tallest Trilithon Stone. The Bluestone Circle consists of a circle of forty smaller stones...thirty Sarsen Stones weigh twenty-eight tonnes each... with eight tonne lintels lining the top. Their total height is nearly five metres. Wow! That is tall!

I went over to the cow druid and looked at Stonehenge again, when I felt a sniff on my back and a nibble on my blue shirt.

"Hey?"

"Who's trying to eat my shirt?"

I turned around and saw a brown and white cow looking at me. I wonder why he thinks my blue shirt is so tasty? He then sniffed and licked me again.

"Eew!"

"Nice cow."

"Ermm...help." I said, nervously

Mum and Dad came over to assist me.

"It's all right Cassie."

"That cow is just checking you out affectionately." said Mum, reassuring me

The cow then decided to lick Mum.

"Yuck!" she screwed up her face

Dad and I laugh... Dad's laugh didn't last long when the cow plants a wet tongue on the side of his face too!

"Ergh!" he spluttered

This time Mum and I laugh... I decide to get out my camera and take a few quick pictures of our friendly visitors.

After viewing Stonehenge... we make our way to the esplanade in Esperance near the Taylor St café... for a round of mini-golf. It's the third time on this road trip we have played mini-golf and the competition is still on between the three of us! I've also got a rubber bouncy mini golf ball... that I plan to use to play a trick on Mum. I don't know which hole I'm going to use it on... but I'm up to mischief again!

We start the game and after the fifth hole the scores are close, I am on minus six... Dad is on minus five... Mum is on minus four. At the sixth hole, Mum places her golf ball on the starting point and whilst she is checking her scorecard and getting her golf club ready... I swiftly pinch the golf ball and put it in my pocket. Mum gets ready to hit the golf ball and realises it isn't there anymore. I try hard not to giggle... but Mum hears me.

"Ok Cassie where is the golf ball?"

"I don't know Mum."

"Hand it back please." said Mum, putting her hand out

"OK." I chuckled

I handed the ball back to Mum and we got on with the game.

By the thirteenth hole the scores have changed a little... it's still a close one... me on minus fourteen... Mum on minus twelve... and Dad on minus eleven.

It was at the fifteenth hole that I decide to put my prank in to play! Mum was near the hole and had hit four strokes... she lined the club up and hit the ball...the ball didn't go into the hole instead it bounced out... and stopped near Mum's feet.

She was a bit surprised.

"Eh?"

"There's a defect in this golf ball!" she said, picking it up

"That's not a golf ball!"

"It's a rubber ball!"

"Who did that?" glares Mum accusingly, looking around to see who could've done it

Everyone on the mini golf course were laughing... Dad and I tried not to give the game away!

"Very funny...very funny." fumed Mum

"I'll get whoever did this." muttered Mum under her breath.

Everyone laughed harder... including the staff.

After we had finished the eighteenth and final hole, we totalled up our scores... I had minus twenty... Mum had minus nineteen and Dad was on minus seventeen.

"It looks like I was too good for you two again...it was a fair game overall."

"Well played." I said, shaking Mum and Dad's hand

"Well played Cassie"

"You are too good today." said Mum

"You played well it was close...you came out on top though." said Dad

"This mini-golf game has given me an appetite...let's go to the foreshore near the Tanker Jetty...to get a smoothie from S'Juice and a burger from the Burger Barn van."

"We can view Esperance while we eat and drink." I said

We bought a smoothie and a burger each and sat at a table, we viewed the Tanker Jetty and along Esperance Beach.

"Mum... I was the one that replaced your golf ball with a rubber one... on the golf course earlier!" I said, giggling

"I might have known it was you!" said Mum, with a laugh

The smell of the ocean wafted through the air... it made me smile at the memories I have of many beaches over the years.

"I plan to recreate another childhood memory just like I did at the beach...only this time it won't be with sand or shells." I said

"What childhood memory is that, Cassie?" asked Mum

"Well... since I was four years old... I have loved bubbles."

"When I was having a bath... most times you would get the bubble mix out and blow them towards me or above me... I would laugh excitedly reaching out with my arms to catch them... or pop them when I touched them."

"Then you would put the bubble bath in... I would laugh with glee throwing the bubbles into the air... they were happy memories for me... that I would love to recreate." I said

"All you need is a hotel room with a spa and some bubble mixture!" said Dad

"Also, I have decided that I would like to try skateboarding... for my next big challenge!"

"Where would you like to skate?" asked Mum

"I would like to skate in Adelaide... since there are no skate parks in Esperance."

"It will give me a chance to learn a new skill." I added

"That's great Cassie."

"When we get to Adelaide... we'll all learn how to skate with some help from some veteran skateboarders."

"We'll have fun then...won't we?" said Dad, a little nervously

"We will Dad!" I high fived him

# Chapter Thirty-Nine
# Sausages, Skateboarding & Strudel

It is Australia Day tomorrow and Mum, Dad and I, are in Ceduna… South Australia.

"Cassie, do you want to go on an outback four wheeled adventure?" asked Dad

"Yes Dad… I would love that." I said

"Since we have our own four wheeled drive vehicle… we can visit the reserves… see the wildlife… such as kangaroos… wombats… and dingoes…we could also do some bird watching… at Goog's Track."

We can see the Transcontinental Line… when we are driving." said Mum

"We're going to have lots of fun doing it all!"

"There will be plenty of opportunities to take photos of the wildlife…maybe even a couple of rare birds!" I said

"That sounds great Cassie!"

We climbed into our Holden Colorado and started the two hundred kilometres round trip adventure… through the Yumbarra Conservation Reserve. We stopped at a good spot and took out our binoculars to see if there were any birds… we watched for a long time…we didn't catch a glimpse. We continued on… Dad taught me about the protruding rock that had given Yumbarra its name and the surrounding area.

"Cassie when it rains the rock hollow fills with water and the wildlife make their way here to use the temporary water hole."

"It is also not only an important site for birds… but for bird lovers… and bird watchers too!" Dad added

"Thanks for that great information Dad!"

"This is a beautiful reserve."

The next part of our journey took us through the Yellabinna Regional Reserve. There is a dingo fence on the outside of the reserve… on the east border is the only area where dingoes are tolerated.

It was getting a bit hotter at eleven in the morning… so we wound our windows down to get some fresh air.

"This four-wheeled drive adventure is wicked so far!"

"I'm embracing nature yet again… and I love it!"

"You are learning to respect nature… not to damage it." said Dad

As we were talking a blue… green… and red coloured… parrot… landed on my arm.

"Erm… I think a colourful parrot has just landed on my arm!" I whispered in amazement, not wanting to frighten it away

"Yes…it certainly has Cassie." Mum whispered back

I turned slowly to look at the colourful parrot... I notice that its chest is scarlet red and I recognise this parrot. It is a scarlet-chested parrot... it looks so amazing close up! I smiled at him... I'm sure he is looking right at me.

"Isn't that sweet?"

"The scarlet-chested parrot thinks your arm is a perch to sit on...he's looking at you like you're his new friend." said Dad, smiling

"He is."

"Look at his colours!"

"He's the brightest parrot that I've ever seen." I said

We both look at each other intently for several minutes... Mum quietly takes a photo of us together... before the male scarlet-chested parrot flies away back to his habitat.

"Goodbye scarlet-chested handsome parrot."

"I will definitely remember you." I said, with shining eyes

The next part of the adventure is Goog's Track! John 'Goog' Denton... envisioned a road that he planned to create from Ceduna... to Tarcoola. With the help of his family he constructed the track...it took him three years to make it... from 1976... to 1979.

We are at the beginning of the track which heads north to Malbooma... where the Transcontinental begins... and continues towards Tarcoola.

"Wow!"

"That's a long railway line!"

"It must've taken lots of hard labour even with help from your family...it certainly paid off for Mr Denton eventually".

"Look at all the material that has gone into making this line and the tools they must have used...it was well worth it." I said

"We looked to the left and the line stretched into the distance and when we looked to the right it was the same the other way. That is one heck of a long railway line!

"It's a pity there is no train to ride on... it would be fun!"

"Still... since there isn't one... I guess we can't." said Mum

"Let's just look at it for a little while." said Dad

The next day back in Ceduna we are getting ready to prepare our barbeque lunch on Australia Day... in two or three hours our Australia Day concert will follow.

We found a vacant barbecue site overlooking the sea... on the lawns near the Ceduna Foreshore Caravan Park. We purchased some sausages and hamburgers from the Streaky Bay and Ceduna Meat Service... then got onions and a few other items.

"These butchers love having a bit of a banter with the Ceduna locals... don't they?" grinned Mum

"Ceduna is such a great town!"

"The locals are friendly, some of them recognised us at the meat service shop... they wished us 'Happy Australia Day'!"

"Let's get the drinks now."

"I can imagine the smell of the 'barby' already!" said Dad, licking his lips

Whenever we have a barbeque at our house... we always have soft drink! Sausages are the honey beef flavoured ones... plus onions and hamburgers. Before... I would only eat sausage in white bread with no onions... no salad... and definitely... NO hamburgers... NO WAY!

I don't mind drinking any flavour of soft drink... I have been helping Mum and Dad out with the barbeque since I was thirteen.

Mum and Dad taught me how to do all the cooking without burning myself...using the safety rules. If family or friends have barbeques... they can ask me to help...I'm happy to oblige anytime! With all the ingredients we set to work. Dad put the sausages on and I turned them over carefully as they browned. Mum puts the onions on and I turned those carefully too.

"Cassie for many years we have always celebrated Australia Day with family and friends...mostly at our house... or with relatives and friends at their place... or in Melbourne Park."

"We had to help you through it... so you could cope with the busy day of celebrations."

"You wouldn't eat the salad... the onions or the hamburgers...we understood you only ate honey beef sausage in white bread.... drinking only lemon solo."

"Despite that... you managed to have fun with all of us and had a good day."

"This year will be better as you try new foods on the BBQ." said Mum

"When the food is cooked what would you like?" asked Dad

"I would like a sausage in white bread with onions... and two hamburgers."

"I'm keen to try the whole lot." I said

"No problems Cassie."

Keep turning the sausages... hamburgers... and onions... until they're cooked and brown enough."

"You're doing a good job, darling." said Mum

"Thanks for that Mum." I said

Soon the barbeque lunch is ready.

We loaded up our plates... grabbed a can of drink... and chose a nice spot to eat.

Everything tasted delicious... the lemonade was cool and refreshing...we chatted whilst we ate our Australia Day lunch.

"Cassie do you remember swimming in our backyard pool... or swimming at the Melbourne Pool?"

"You really enjoyed swimming as it would cool you down during the summer months and you would laugh and enjoy the sensation of the water." added Mum

"Whenever it was too hot to go outside, we would read... we taught you about Australia's history as well... we wrote a few stories about Australia and then read them to each other." said Mum, remembering

"Yes, we read Australia themed books and you composed your own stories... you certainly love writing stories... as well as writing songs!" said Dad

"I remember I did a little assignment at the special centre in 2011."

"One of the questions I answered was... 'What does Australia Day mean to your family'?"

"I answered with... 'it means we spend some time together... doing family activities like swimming... and having a barbeque'."

"We also did the Clean Up Australia Day in 2011."

"We did our bit cleaning up Australia...you taught me to put the rubbish in the right bins and recycle too!" I said

"You answered that Australia Day assignment question very well!" said Dad

"Cheers!" I said

"Cheers!" said Mum and Dad, as we clinked our cans together!

After we left Ceduna the next morning... we travelled eight hours to Port Adelaide... where we booked an apartment for two nights at Quest, Port Adelaide.

Today we are visiting historic Port Adelaide. We went to the tourist office to pick up a self-guided walking map... and then we walked to Lipson Street where the Maritime Museum is located.

"Hello and welcome to the Adelaide Maritime Museum."

"We have several collections here that you can view."

You can also find out what's happening behind the scenes... by reading our online blog." the curator informed us

"What collections are there in the Adelaide Maritime Museum?" I asked

"There are nautical instruments... ships model collection... and exploration collections."

"There is also a shipwreck collection."

"Have fun viewing... but be careful not to touch anything." he said

We went to the nautical instruments collection where there was a chronometer used on the 'SS Grace Darling'. It is an original time measure used to ascertain longitude. Englishman John Harrison, invented an accurate seagoing chronometer in the eighteenth century...that Captain James Cook would use on his voyages... when circumnavigating the globe.

It revolutionised the way we navigate at sea from that time on... during the first half of the twentieth century... the 'SS Grace Darling'... transported passengers and general cargo along the coast of South Australia.

Prior to that time, she was a workhorse along the South Australian coast as a schooner-rigged screw steamer. The current resting place is at the ships' graveyard in the port river. Many vessels that frequented Australian ports, had this fine-looking navigational instrument onboard... it was an expensive necessity until radio signals came in... much later a normal clock or watch could be used.

Next, we viewed the model of 'HMS Buffalo'... it was one of nine ships bringing migrants to South Australia in the year 1836. In 1813 James Bonner and James Horsbrough built 'HMAS Buffalo' in Calcutta... the Royal Navy purchased it as a store ship. It was in service during the Napoleonic wars... then it went to New Zealand to collect wood for spars... it took three voyages to collect enough wood.

In South Australia's centenary year... John Keynes Dawe built a working model when he was twelve years old...its plans were published in 'The Advertiser'. It was the overall winner of the Centenary Competition Junior Section... and the only model to successfully sail the Torrens River.

The 'HMS Buffalo' was one of the most significant ships in the history of South Australia...the museum have several models of the Buffalo... most notably made for the 1836 centenary of the original ships' landing at Holdfast Bay.

"That 'HMS Buffalo' is one wicked ship from the olden days!"

"It has awesome history and was very useful during the voyages it made."

"It has to be one of my favourite ships that I've learnt about on this road trip so far." I said

"Mum and I used to do a bit of modelling."

"Your mother built model trains and I built model ships."

"We helped each other and our parents helped us out too."

"We used paint and glue to add the finishing touches and we kept them in our rooms... we still have them at home."

"You used to enjoy looking at them Cassie...and on our birthdays you would leave a little lolly inside them." Dad chuckled

"That was a little gift from me!"

"I know what your favourite lollies are!"

We continued on to the exploration collection...there was a memorial tablet commemorating the voyage of English explorer and navigator... Matthew Flinders.

Lady Jane... the former wife of Sir John Franklin... fifth governor of Tasmania from 1827-1843... wanted the memorial tablet to serve as a monument to Flinders. Lady Jane went to the then Governor of South Australia... Colonel Gawler... who served from 1786-1847...to convince him to commission the tablet. Sir John was Matthew Flinders midshipman during his survey of the Australian coast... on the 'HMS Investigator'... from 1801-1803. During his 1847 expedition to the Arctic to find the north-west passage... Sir John Franklin disappeared.

The inscribed tablet reads... 'This place from which the Gulf and its shores were first surveyed on 26th Feb 1802, by Matthew Flinders R.N. Commander of H.M.S. Investigator... the discoverer of the country now called South Australia... was set apart on 12th Jan 1841.

With the sanction of Col. Gawler. K. H. then Governor of the Colony and in the first year of the government of Capt. G. Grey adorned with this Monument... to the perpetual Memory of the illustrious Navigator... his honored Commander by John Franklin Capt. R.N. K.C.H.K.R. Lt. Governor of Van Diemen's land.'

The significance of the tablet, is of the European explorer's discovery of South Australia. It also illustrates the relationship between the colonies. Besides being the fifth governor of Tasmania, Sir John was an explorer himself.

After we had finished looking at all the collections in the museum, it was time to find somewhere for dinner.

"I know a few good places." said Mum.

"Cliché Exhibition Restaurant is an awesome place to eat!"

"The menu is full of French dishes."

"I think I will try one."

"Oh...magnifique!"

"I think I'll go for the Duck Confit." I said

"I might go for the Basquaise Pork."

"I've tried it before and it was delicious." said Mum

"The Post-Modern Duck a L'Orange sounds great!"

"I think I'll try that." said Dad

When we ordered our dishes from the waiter, he said...

"Good choices!"

"They are very popular dishes with our customers!"

Our dishes arrived thirty minutes later and they were magnifique!

"They are very temping... I'm licking my lips just looking." said Mum

"I can't wait to try the sauce that goes with the duck dish!" Dad chimed

"Let's dig in." I said

Our dishes were delicious! Everything tasted so good that we decided to look at the dessert section of the menu as well. We all ordered a serve of the Gateaux au Chocolat and boy was it rich... but oh so yummy!

A couple of hours later we made our way back to our apartment and relaxed before bedtime.

When we arrived in Adelaide a couple of days later... we decided to try out a new central hotel close to all the different things we intended to explore... like the market... skate park...and the Adelaide Hills. We booked ourselves in to the sleek, modern Ibis Hotel in the central business district of Adelaide... with a great view of the Adelaide Hills.

Once we had unpacked and freshened up, we decided to walk to the Adelaide Central Market to take a look around. We had heard that there were local cheeses... fresh produce... and freshly baked pastries there.

"We'll be leaving in fifteen minutes so be ready please!" Mum called out to me

"All we need is a light snack and water...we'll go to the Central Adelaide Market for a gastronomic tour!"

"You're going to have a great day." said Dad, grinning as we walked along

"Welcome to the Adelaide Central Market."

"There are cheeses... pastries... and different honeys... for you to sample."

"Your taste buds will be delighted and so will you!"

"You will never forget the gastronomical experience... so enjoy!" said one of the stall owners as we approached

"Wow!"

"We get to walk through... and sample all of these wonderful foods!"

"Awesome!" I said, excitedly

"Mum and I have been on a couple of tours like this one... and now you will get to take one with us."

"I hope you enjoy it." Dad said

"I can't wait to try these foods!" said Mum

"Let's get into them!" I replied

We stopped at 'Dough' where we chose our pastries and they tasted yummy!

Then we went to 'Say Cheese' and sampled several cheeses, including cheddar and Swiss. We declined the samples of blue cheese!

"Eew!" I said, holding my nose... I thought they smelled off!

Everybody laughed.

When we stopped at 'Island Pure' there were stocks of flavoured oils... honey... and sticky figs. We sampled the honey it was sticky and good.

I declined to taste the figs as they were on my 'not acceptable' list of foods. We chatted to stall owners and learnt about their produce and the market too. I had a good time and I would love to do it again... maybe I will try more of the samples... including the figs... next time.

In the afternoon we went to the Adelaide Skate Park to learn how to use a skateboard. I felt a bit nervous about trying one as I'd never been on a skateboard before. I had a fear I might hurt myself... or fall off...or both! I'm ready to give it a go and Mum and Dad have said they are going to try it too! All we need is some safety gear and skateboards...then it will be all systems go!

There were three veteran skateboarders doing practice runs on several skate ramps when we got there. They look good...they are doing various tricks. They recognise us and come over to speak with us.

"Hello Bontels."

"How are you?" said Nathan, one of the experts

"We're good thanks Nathan."

"We have come for a skateboard lesson." said Mum

"We are complete beginners... it's our very first time!" added Dad

"We can teach you."

"Please remember it takes lots and lots of practice to become proficient on a skateboard!"

"We didn't get to become experts overnight you know."

"You'll need some safety gear and a skateboard each which you can pick up for hire at the skateboard shop over there." said Sean, the second skateboarder

"Thanks." said Dad

Mum, Dad and I, walked over and hired some safety gear in our favourite colours, plus a skateboard each. We put our skateboarding protection pads on our knees and elbows, then strapped our helmets on for head protection.

We went back to Nathan… Sean… and Grace… who were waiting to begin our instruction in the art of skateboarding.

"Don't worry we will take it slow… everyone must learn at their own pace."

"We will start with how to get on a skateboard."

"You stand next to the middle of the skateboard with your front foot slightly forward."

"Put your first foot placement to the front of the skateboard and put your foot down into position on the skateboard."

"Then put your other foot placement straight into position at the back of the board."

"Make sure the weight is equal between both feet." said Grace

I listen to all the steps Grace tells me and try them all… one at a time.

"Good job Cassie."

"Now for the next moves."

"Take your back foot off the board."

"When it's on the ground, shift your weight to your foot that's on the ground… then you lift your front foot off the board and place it on the ground as well." says Grace.

I went through the last few steps and it was not easy…I kept practising them with Grace's help… and became a little more proficient.

"That's great Cassie!"

"Now… I'm going to teach you a couple of basic moves."

"We will try learning the Manual… and the Tic-Tac."

"Listen to the instructions I'm about to tell you." said Grace, encouragingly

"Yes Grace."

I'm listening and will be ready to do what you have explained to me."

I listen carefully and I'm ready to try the two moves.

"Don't worry if you don't get them first time… you can practice whenever you want to… once you know the moves."

"If you fall off stay calm."

"We have a first-aid kit on hand in case of minor accidents." Grace said

"We have been practising our moves since we were young… gaining confidence over time."

"We've been skateboarding for more than seven years…that is why we are good at it."

"We also skate together in the summer months." said Nathan

"You've worked hard to get where you are!"

"I'm ready to try the Manual and the Tic-Tac moves now." I said, hopefully

I hopped on my skateboard feeling a bit scared.

"Cassie it's all right."

"Don't be afraid… take your time." said Sean, reassuringly

I felt calmer and proceeded with the moves one at a time, taking my time to do so. I almost fell off…I managed to steady myself and finish the moves… even if they were a little bit wobbly.

I think I like it…I would certainly need lots of practice to get to expert level.

Nathan and Sean taught Mum and Dad the same moves and they did well... considering they have never tried skateboarding before either!

"Well done Cassie... you can tell your friends that you have tried a new sport." said Sean

"I'm excited to tell our family and friends... thanks Nathan... Sean... and Grace... for showing us some moves on the skateboard."

"It's not easy...but it's fun to keep to practice." I said

"We're glad you had a good time."

"Hope your Adelaide stay goes well." said Grace

"Thanks."

"Bye."

The next morning, Dad said...

"Cassie we're going to visit the picturesque Adelaide Hills today."

"That's great!"

"We'll get to embrace that beautiful scenic environment and visit one of the three villages there... Hahndorf... Stirling.... or... Aldgate." I said

We chose to go to Hahndorf... which is Australia's oldest surviving German settlement. I look around when we arrive...I see fascinating buildings everywhere... and a beautiful leafy environment. It resembles a picturesque German village.

The first place we visit is 'The Cedars'... the original homestead of Australian artist Hans Heysen... who used to live there. It is one of the nation's most well-preserved historical homes today. We look around his studio and peruse his extensive collection of original artworks which are beautiful. His daughter... Nora Heysen's artworks are also magnificent.

It makes me think of my own artistic aspirations... as one of Hans' paintings reminds me of when I painted a meadow in Melbourne... and also the lighthouse at Port Fairy. I plan to paint more... now I shall probably paint Hahndorf!

"Cassie there is an art store here called the Paintbox."

"Would you like to go there and buy some art supplies?" asked Dad

"Yes, I would love to go to the Paintbox Dad."

"I'm planning to paint another picture."

There were various coloured chalks and lots of different art materials to see in the Paintbox.

"Welcome to the Paintbox."

"We have plenty of art supplies here to create your masterpieces!" said the owner, with a smile

"I've been creating pictures... drawing and painting."

"It's one of the ways I use to express myself and make my art come alive." I said

"Maybe you can draw or paint a picture of something in Hahndorf Cassie."

"Perhaps I will."

"To do what you love is good!"

"I love art!"

I bought a few brightly coloured chalks and paper... as well as some coloured pencils. We found an ideal spot and I drew Hahndorf in bright and positive colours... with a bit of Venice, Italy... added in for fun. It's a colourful and bright picture and when I finish... I show it to Mum and Dad.

"Mum, Dad, what do you think of my drawing?" I ask

"It's very colourful and bright."

"Hahndorf is well-drawn Cassie." said Mum

"It's very positive and I like that bit of Venice that you added in." says Dad, with a chuckle

"Thanks Mum and Dad... I appreciate it!"

"I'll keep it as a souvenir of our time in Hahndorf... on our trip... among the many drawings I have done over the years."

"It'll be good to keep... because I'm thinking maybe I can open an art exhibition with my paintings... called 'Colour Expression'." I said, thinking out loud

We purchased some chocolate and apple strudel to eat later on before we left Hahndorf...we just couldn't resist those scrumptious foods!

# Chapter Forty
# Kangaroo Island & 'Monicker' Madness

"Let's go to Kangaroo Island to visit my big brother Tim tomorrow." said Mum, later on back at the Ibis
"He's staying there at the moment working... he'll be delighted to see us." Mum added
"Yes, let's!"
"I still remember the snow globe he gave to me when I was ten years old." I said
"We'll give him a call before we leave in the morning... to let him know that we're coming." said Dad
Tim is another one of Mum's older brothers. Mum gets along well with him and sometimes plays pranks on him. She occasionally sneaks up and tickles his toes when he is reading in a chair. Whenever they chat on the phone Mum refers to him as 'my big bugger brother'!
He worked on a ship in Portland called 'Ragman' and fished for tuna. When Mum and Rebecca were seventeen, he taught them a trick... involving spring water tuna to make a rainbow in the water. I would love to learn that trick and see how it's done!
The next day on Kangaroo Island Mum greeted Uncle Tim.
"Hello Tim my big brother." said Mum hugging him, she is very happy to see her big brother
"Hello Mikayla... my mischievous little sis." said Tim, hugging her back
"I'm doing well Tim."
"How about you?" asked Mum
"I'm doing great Mikayla."
"Nice to you see again Daniel." said Tim
"It's nice to see you again, Tim!"
"Cassie, I haven't seen you in a long time."
"How are you?" asked Tim
"I'm doing well thanks... Uncle Tim."
"It's great to see you again." I said
I hugged him and he hugged me back... it's nice to catch up with my uncle again... his hug was strong... but I didn't mind that.
"I heard you are doing a road trip around Australia!"
"How has it been so far?" asked Tim
"It has been awesome!"
"We have tasted a bit of culture... lots of different food... fed some kangaroos in Bunbury...and performed an Australia Day Concert in Ceduna!"
"We are having loads of fun and making lots of memories too!" I said
"Sounds like you are having so much fun together."

"That is good." said Uncle Tim

"We have interacted with wildlife including kangaroos…there were some funny moments with them too!" said Mum

"Let me take you to a place on Kangaroo Island where there are even more kangaroos!" smiled Tim

Tim took us to a conservation area where there were not only, kangaroos… but also, koalas…and a couple of goannas as well! I watched as one goanna ran past it seemed like it was running to the other side of the conservation area to find a new friend. There were also a few echidnas… Tim had seen one yesterday and it might be here today… if we are lucky.

"The echidna was here yesterday… if we keep quiet and very still, we might see one today." whispered Tim

"We'll be very careful and quiet Tim."

"I like little creatures too… except mice, snakes and frogs."

"Cassie is the same."

"We're both cat lovers and we all love zoo animals!" said Mum

We walked to an area where there are lots of kangaroos. We watched as they 'hopped' about… one even stopped to look at us and say 'hello'… it was fun to see them on Kangaroo Island.

We took a couple of photos and then we walked through the conservation area and right near the exit we saw… an echidna with its babies… shuffling across the ground in front of us near the base of some gum trees.

We stopped and watched… crouching down…staying still from a distance. I smiled as I watched the echidna and her babies walk along the path to some shelter in the leaves.

I was thinking… *'Aw how cute is that, the mother echidna and her babies are beautiful, Echidnas are such amazing creatures.'*

When it was time for dinner Tim said…

"I've found a good restaurant for us to try."

"It's Sunset Food and Wine."

"It has tasty seafood dishes and good service." said Tim

"Mikayla and I love seafood…we're not sure if Cassie will try any."

"They are not on her 'acceptable' list because they are not smooth… she may have a meltdown if she is served them…the seafood aroma might also overwhelm her."

"She has never been into any seafood restaurants."

"Cassie is open to trying more new foods…we can see how she goes."

"Just be prepared to help out… in case things go wrong." Dad explains

"Ok… I'll be ready." said Tim

The smell of seafood wafted across my nostrils as we walked in and sat at the table. I would get overwhelmed by that smell years ago… this time it's not too bad. We ordered our dishes and while we were waiting… we chatted.

"What are some of the highlights of your road trip so far?" asked Tim

"We tried skiing at Mt Buller… viewed the Devil's Marbles in the Northern Territory… and we even rode on the 'Ghan'… from Darwin to Adelaide and back!"

"Those are three of my favourite highlights." I said

"Those sound great fun."

"Did you three try any unusual foods?" asked Tim

"Yes, we did!"

"Some of the unusual foods Daniel and I tried were delicious."

"Cassie tried some new foods that were not on her 'acceptable' list before and loved eating them!" Mum said

"We did a bit of bike riding and camping too."

"Our family bond is growing stronger every day and this road trip is the reason for that." said Dad, smiling

"I'm glad that you are spending more time together as a family... and doing more things than you thought you could." said Tim

"Cassie is becoming more confident... getting braver every day." said Mum

"Cassie... you're doing a grand job!"

"Last time you were very shy and quiet... even though you were happy to see me."

"Look at you now!"

"You're happier... calmer... confident... and so much braver...than before." said Uncle Tim, proudly

"I sure am Uncle Tim!"

"Thanks for the compliments." I grinned

"We are performing around Australia with our debut album... we're doing well with that... and I'm becoming braver by performing... in front of our fans." I said

"Good on you Cassie!"

"I am very proud of you all!"

"The Bontel Family band are doing well!" said Tim, grinning

"Yes... we are Uncle Tim!" I replied, with a big smile on my face

"It's been great fun seeing where you work and all the animals...we have to get back to Adelaide now... and start making preparations for our next concert."

Back in Adelaide a couple of days later... I am at the Norwood Concert Hall where I have been rehearsing... and waiting for Mum and Dad to arrive and join me. It is already one o'clock and nearly time to go onstage for our family concert. I'm raring to go... I have my guitar ready just waiting for them to arrive...they aren't here yet.

I wonder where they are?

They could be held up I suppose...why are they running so late?

I might have to do a solo concert if they don't get here soon!!!

My iPhone rings and I see on the screen that it's Mum calling.

"Hello Mum... is everything all right?"

"Cassie, Dad and I are all right...something has happened here."

"Oh no!"

"What has happened, Mum?"

"The car has broken down on the way to the hall, Cassie."

"Dad and I have called an auto repair man to fix the car...it's going to take him an hour or so."

"Oh dear."

"We are due on stage in five minutes!"

"I'll have to do a solo performance!"

"That makes me nervous."

"I've never gone on stage without you there before... I'm nervous just at the thought of it!"

"I don't know if I can do this!"

"I just can't bear to think about it!"

"You'll be fine Cassie."

"Use your anxiety techniques... just like we've taught you."

"All right Mum... I'll try."

"Remember the Sydney concert with your one-off band... The Sparkles?"

"Yes... I do."

"I remember it... I performed well... it was a milestone moment for me."

"That concert was a big milestone for you... sweetheart."

"You stepped onto that stage and overcame your fear of loud noises and crowds and performed brilliantly... we were so proud of you for doing so."

"If you could do it with 'The Sparkles'... then you can do it this time too!"

"Thanks for the reassurance Mum."

"I can do this...I know I can."

"I'll step out on to that stage and blow them away with my twelve bubble-gum... teen pop...dance style songs!"

"They're great songs that I have written... I'm sure the audience will love them!"

"I'm sure they will sweetie."

"Go and make Dad and I proud!"

"I will Mum... I won't let you down!"

"The show must go on... as they say!"

"I'm due on stage in two minutes... I'll have to go."

"Bye!"

"Bye, sweetheart."

"Ladies and Gentlemen due to a slight delay... the Bontel Family band will not perform as scheduled... one of its members will perform for you...I promise you she will blow you away with her music!"

"She is sixteen years old... and the lead singer and rhythm guitarist... of the Bontel Family band."

"This is her first ever solo performance... so please welcome to the stage... CASSIE BONTEL!" the announcer shouted out to the audience

I walked on to the stage waving to my fans...it feels different and a little scary without Mum and Dad...I have to do it and make them proud... as well as our fans.

I don't want to let them down... do I?

I've got my twelve songs ready to perform and I'm sure I can win the audience. I can do this... I know I can!

"Hello Adelaide."

"How are you? I ask, joyfully

"GREAT!" the audience shout back

"I apologise for the delay...it will be an hour or two before Mikayla and Daniel make it to the stage."

The audience groan a little.

"There is good news!"

"I will be giving my first ever solo performance for you all tonight!" I said

The audience cheered. I could feel the good vibes.

"I have twelve songs in my solo repertoire."

"They come from my perspective as an autistic teenage girl... they are styled in the teen pop, bubble-gum, dance genre... these songs are about... parties... family... life... friends and of course dancing"!

"I promise you will all have fun singing and dancing to them."

"Are you ready?" I call out to the audience

"YES!" they shout back

"Let's do this then!" I say, fist-pumping the air

**Song 1:** Show Me What You Got (Dance)
**Song 2:** Sunshine Beach (Bubble-gum Dance)
**Song 3:** Family is Your Heart (Teen-Pop)
**Song 4:** Party, Party! (Bubble-gum Dance)
**Song 5:** Dance Stage (Dance)
**Song 6:** Life's Opportunities (Teen-Pop)
**Song 7:** Best Friends (Teen-Pop)
**Song 8:** Cream Cake (Bubble-gum Dance)
**Song 9:** Tech Savvy (Dance)
**Song 10:** My Voice (Teen-Pop)
**Song 11:** Tropical Rainforest (Dance)
**Song 12:** Fitting in the World (Teen-Pop)

The audience cheered wildly as the performance began... my first solo was pretty awesome! I could tell the audience were loving the songs and having a great time when they jumped up and down... dancing to the beat!

I gave my pop star pose... pointing with my finger at the audience. The audience roared... this is going well... Mum and Dad will be proud of me if they ever get here to see it! I continued with all my songs till I got to the last one. Still no sign of Mum and Dad!

"Thank you so much for listening to my solo performance... this will be my last song in this set... before I take fifteen minutes break."

"It's a great pleasure to perform for you... I can see you're having an awesome time."

"Hopefully, after the break... Daniel and Mikayla will have arrived."

"If not... then I will perform some pop covers of songs from North America... Australia... and Europe."

When I went backstage for my break... I phoned Mum and Dad and pressed the speakerphone to hear what was happening.

"Hello Cassie." Mum's voice came out of the speaker

"How did your solo performance go?"

"It was brilliant Mum!"

"My songs were a hit with the Adelaide audience...they loved them!"

"I knew you could do it sweetheart."

"Dad and I are very proud of you."

"We'll have a big celebration with you... when our performance has finished."

"You have done very well in your solo debut."

"It might be uploaded on to YouTube, you could get lots of hits!"

"You could also upload it to your YouTube channel 'Butterfly Blue'!"

"Thanks"

"I might do that and who knows... I could develop a pop star following."

"We might end up being your band managers one day!" said Mum, with a laugh

"I would be happy to have you two as my band managers any day!"

"Anyway... how's our vehicle going!"

"Is it repaired yet?"

"It's just been finished... we are arriving at the hall."

"We'll be with you in five minutes."

"Meet you backstage!"

"That's great news, Dad."

"I'll see you and Mum in five!"

"See you soon darling."

Mum, Dad and I caught up backstage at the Norwood Concert Hall.

"Well done, sweetie!"

"We're so happy for you."

"Your solo performance was a triumph!" said Mum, hugging me close with tears in her eyes

"It went well... like the Adelaide leg of Kylie Minogue's 'On a Night Like This' tour... in 2001!" I said, laughing as I did my best Kylie Minogue 'walk'

"I'm glad I did it without you two there."

"It was very nerve-wracking on my own...but I did it!" I said, high fiving the air

"You certainly did darling!"

"Our family and friends will be so delighted for you."

"You have taken a tremendous step in your progress." said Dad, proudly squeezing me tight in a bear hug

"Thanks, you two!"

"You are my inspirational music angels... you give me lots of guidance... love... and support... not only, with my music... but also, in my unique life!"

"It makes me feel bright and happy... that I've got my two autistic popstar parents with me every step of the way... towards achieving my dreams." I said

"Give us a big hug... our popstar chick!" said Mum, grinning

I embraced Mum and Dad in a big hug and kissed them both on the cheeks. That's a great loving moment in my music career. Having Mum and Dad beside me whilst I work towards achieving my dream of becoming a popstar... means the world to me.

I'm overcoming my sensory issues and shyness to get out there... and I have my parents...carers... and support network... to thank for all of that. I'm climbing up the music ladder to superstardom and I'm getting closer to the 'big goal'...I'll tell you later what that is.

We performed in our family concert and the whole town of Adelaide really enjoyed it. I soaked up the atmosphere, and revelled in the cheers of the crowd. Gosh, it doesn't get any better than this!

Later, after the concert finished, we signed autographs for our fans and there was a funny moment... which initially I found embarrassing and annoying. It involved one of my fans and people's names. It was not funny at the time for me...for Mum and Dad it was!

"Hello Myra."

"Thanks for enjoying The Bontel Family concert."

"I enjoyed it as much as you did." I said

"It's Mandy by the way." said Mandy

"Dam!" I said, thumping my fist on the table annoyed

"Sorry about mispronouncing your name." I said

"That's all right Cassandra." said Mandy

That did not go down well with me! It's the one thing that you do not say to me...calling me Cassandra! Everyone laughed, including Mum and Dad! I don't find it funny! I dislike being called Cassandra... even though it is the full version of my name. How dare the fan call me Cassandra! It's not right and it's not (bleepin) hilarious! If you call me Cassandra... you'll cop it from me and I'll sure let you know about it! Humph!

I went red in the face. Mandy copped more than a glaring stare from me. I pouted at her and stuck my tongue out at her. That only made everyone laugh even louder!

"Well played mate!" (*not*) I said, to myself under my breath

What didn't help were a few fans recording the whole event and I put my head in my hands for a moment and groaned silently, thinking... 'This is really embarrassing big time...Bleep!... *my classmates will laugh at me, and my family will chuckle at that clip...it will go viral in not only Australia, but the world too... why on earth did I get out of bed this morning?... this concert was going so well until that comment from Mandy... never mind my solo performance, it was fine, but this?... this is more embarrassing than the mud slip at Echuca!*'

"Never mind Cassie."

"Mandy didn't mean to annoy you by using your full name."

"It's all right." said Mum, patting me on my shoulder

"Sorry about that Cassie."

"I didn't mean to make you mad."

"I thought it was Cassandra for a moment...I guess I was wrong." said Mandy

"That's... all right Mandy."

"You're forgiven."

"Just so you know... I dislike being called Cassandra... even though it's the full version of my name."

"I get mad when people do that...it upsets me."

"My own family said it once...I even got mad at them!"

"Anyway... hand me your autograph book please... and I'll sign it." I said, remorsefully

I signed Mandy's autograph and afterwards we headed back to our hotel for a rest.

"Cassie... it was hilarious hearing Mandy call you Cassandra." said Mum, chuckling

"It was a good concert and a great laugh from Mandy there." added Dad, grinning

"Oh, very funny, Ha Ha." I said, sarcastically

"So... you two think it was a good laugh... do you?"

"Well it wasn't!" I said, sticking my tongue out at them both

"Anyway...I'm off to have a nice hot shower!"

"I'll practice my singing whilst I'm in there and smooth my hair with Dove shampoo... like you do Mum." I said

"You do that Cassie... you do that." said Mum, sniggering behind her hand

I noticed that Dad was smirking too!

I took my iPhone with me... placed it on the bench... stripped... and stepped into the shower. Whilst I was showering, I wet my hair... took out my Dove shampoo... and lathered it into my hair. I sang and shampooed... shampooed and sang... it felt good to be relaxing in the hotel after the performance. I might even use my hairbrush as a microphone next!

Ring! My iPhone goes off signalling a message and video has come through...if that's the mispronounce name video going viral... I'm going to be very annoyed again! I turned off the shower, dried my hands on the towel and turned my iPhone on to check out the message, it's from Zara.

Cassie that fan's comment is so funny... the video is going viral... it's got around seventy thousand hits... you might want to check it out for yourself!

I selected the video and my jaw dropped as the video of me... glaring and sticking my tongue out at Mandy... appeared.

*Oh No I guess I'll see the funny side eventually...I may need some time for that!'* I thought, seething

Later, as I was drying off and getting dressed, I had to have a little chuckle to myself when I thought about it... after all I was the one who called Mandy by the wrong name to begin with and she didn't take offence... just told me the right name.

My iPhone rang... it was Aunt Kate calling.

"Hello, Aunt Kate."

"How are you?"

"I'm fine, thanks Cassie."

"Nicole, Adam, Amelia and I, have checked the Australian Charts and we've got a shock."

"Goodness!"

"What shock is that?"

"The Bontel Family have knocked 'Quirky Service' off the Australian charts with their debut album, 'The Bontel Family!"

"Do you know anything about that, hmm?"

"Err... no I don't."

"We think you do!"

"You reckon that's funny... do you?"

"We'll get you back for knocking us off the charts."

"Oh, will you now?"

"That's not going to happen... because we'll be better at that sort of game."

"Just you wait." said Aunt Kate, as she signed off

"Well, it looks like 'Quirky Service' are going to get us for being more popular than they are!" I explained to Mum and Dad

"They are going to the Mintaro Maze tomorrow morning...they suggest we meet them there to explore the maze together."

"How are we going to foil them?" I asked

"It will take some disguises to pull off a prank...so they don't recognise us." said Dad

"I've got an excellent idea for part one...you two can help out with it." I said

I whispered to Mum and Dad about my idea involving disguises.

"That's an excellent idea Cassie."

"I don't think 'Quirky Service' will expect that." chuckled Mum

"The disguises you've suggested are great... 'Quirky Service' won't know it's us." Dad added

"We will put part one into action tomorrow morning at Mintaro Maze!"

The next morning, Mum, Dad and I arrive at Mintaro Maze dressed in our park ranger disguises... complete with wigs! Kate, Nicole, Adam and Amelia, won't suspect a thing. This is going to be so funny! Here goes!

"Those Bontels' sure are becoming popular." muttered Nicole

"We've got our prank ready to go when we see them." said Adam, as he grinned

"They might be hiding in the Mintaro Maze...let's see if we can find them as we make our way through." added Amelia

"Yes, that's a good idea...these three rangers might be able to help us out." said Kate

"Excuse me... we're here to explore the Mintaro Maze."

Pretending to be park ranger Sandra I disguise my voice and reply to Kate.

"There are over eight hundred conifers... plenty of fountains... twist and turns."
"Even the most committed explorers can be tricked by the maze."
"Wow!"
"This going to be more challenging than we thought."
"Still we like a challenge!"
"Have you seen the Bontel Family?"
"They are wearing blue, yellow and green clothes."
Mum playing park ranger Nora replies.
"No, we haven't seen them."
"You might find them in the Mintaro Maze though."
"Thanks."
Dad disguised as park ranger Steve adds....
"Have fun...it's a tricky maze!"
"See if you can make your way through without getting lost."
Kate, Nicole, Adam, and Amelia, paid their twelve dollars each and went into the maze.
Mum, Dad and I took the opportunity to dash off... jump in the car... and drive back to Adelaide.
"It could take quite a while for Quirky Service to make their way through that maze... this is going to be so good." I giggled
"They will be bamboozled and confused!" said Mum, grinning
"I would love to see their reactions when they eventually find out they took directions from us...and not rangers Sandra, Nora and Steve!"
"I'd like a picture of that!" said Dad, gleefully
For the next two hours and fifteen minutes... Kate... Nicole... Adam... and Amelia... spend their time trying to find the right way out of Mintaro Maze. They keep taking wrong turns and getting lost again... whilst the staff who knew all about the prank watch on... some of them are filming with cameras located in the maze... so they can upload it later for us to share.
"I don't know where to go next."
"It's so puzzling." said Nicole, frowning
"This turn tricked me just as I was finding my way." said Adam, in a confused voice
"I don't even know where I am!"
"This maze has too many twists and turns!"
"You don't know where they are going!" said Amelia, who was becoming frustrated
"Let's all keep calm and not panic."
"I might have found the right path.... bugger!"
"Tricked again." said Kate, with a cranky expression on her face
Members of the public and staff, watching on the camera feed outside the maze all burst into laughter.
Meanwhile, back in Adelaide... we spent a lovely time window shopping. A couple of hours later I turn to Mum and say...
"We'd better get back to the Mintaro Maze Mum."
"We can't leave them in that maze all day, can we?" I said
"No, we can't, Cassie."
"It would not be good." said Mum, pretending to be serious
"Let's get in the car and drive back to the maze." said Dad
"It is time for us to confess to the prank we pulled on them."

"Yes, it is, Dad." I agreed

"It may be not the best prank we have played...let's just see when we look at the tape later on." I chuckle

We arrived back and found 'Quirky Service' waiting for us… they recognised us as we got out of the car. They weren't looking too amused… they were fuming in fact!

"Did you 'dump' us?!"

"We got totally lost in there!" said Kate, fuming

"We pulled the Mintaro Maze prank on you four!"

"It was so funny!" I laughed

"You think it was funny… eh? "

"We didn't even see you!" fumed Adam

"Oh… yes you did!" I laughed

"We were rangers… Sandra… Nora… and Steve… in disguise!"

"We got you!" said Mum, laughing loudly

"Oh, very funny!"

"That Mintaro Maze bamboozled us for hours… the twists and turns were really confusing!" said Nicole, muttering under her breath

"You must've got out of the maze though!"

"Yes… we did get out of the maze… eventually."

"You three are so sneaky!" said Amelia, annoyed

"We apologise for our prank."

"It was hilarious though!" I said

"We didn't even know it was you posing as rangers!"

"That was very sneaky Bontels!" said Kate

"Why don't we have a late picnic lunch together."

"We'll have a nice chat." said Mum

"All right." said Adam, grudgingly

"We came prepared… we have our picnic lunch with us."

"Let's go the park and have it there." said Nicole

We went to the park with our picnic lunches and settled down for a pleasant park picnic, with all the members of 'Quirky Service'.

"We heard that you performed solo for the first time. "

"You were very brave to do that in front of a big audience." said Kate

"I was a little bit nervous when Mum and Dad told me that their car broke down and I couldn't bear the thought of going on stage by myself...with Mum's encouragement and my anxiety techniques… I felt better and went on stage and blew the audience of Adelaide away… with my teen-pop, bubble-gum dance music."

"I felt proud of myself when I did that… Mum and Dad were proud of me too."

When we heard the news… I was thinking… *'You have done well, Cassie. I'm happy for you.'*

"We were a little nervous when we reformed in 1998...with help from our band manager Lisa Parkins… plus encouragement from the audience...we were able to step out on stage and perform!"

"We did the same for our overseas audiences and international adaptations of 'Quirky Service'." said Adam

"Cassie… we have something to give you to celebrate that brave moment." said Nicole

Nicole took something out of her bag and gave it to me. My eyes widened when I see that it is… 'Megalomania'… Aqua's newest album! It contains electropop… dance-rock… and pop rock tracks…the cover features the group on the shore… with a colourful background and island behind them. I love it!

"Thanks, Aunt Nicole."

"This will be a great album to listen to."

"They have changed their style for this album…I don't mind that at all."

"There will be some great electro tunes on it…it will be awesome!" I said

"In November 2011… we were staying in Copenhagen, Denmark… we were shopping and we came across this in a music store. I thought… *'Cassie will love this album, I know she loves European pop music, this will be a great present for her…she will be so excited when she gets it'*.

"You're doing so well with overcoming your issues and music certainly contributed to that!"

"Come and give me a big hug." said Nicole

I gave Nicole a big hug and she hugged me too. It feels loving when I receive a hug from family and relatives. I also gave Kate, Adam and Amelia a big hug as well.

Mum, Dad and I, received a message each on our iPhones.

"We have a video that features you in the Mintaro Maze."

"It's so funny… come and watch it for yourselves." I said

"Kate, Nicole, Adam and Amelia crowded around me and I tapped the video. I chuckled at the video… 'Quirky Service' members find it embarrassing… they don't want to look at one point!

"Oh, no!"

"How embarrassing is that."

"We've gone viral!" said Amelia, red-faced

"We didn't know that someone had sneakily recorded us and uploaded it to YouTube!" said Kate, blushing bright red

"The awkward meter has risen by ten notches." said Adam, cringing

"It might get in the top ten embarrassing and funny pop star moments… lots of viewers tune in to that!"

"Aargh!"

"Awkward." said Nicole, mumbling as she went from pink to red and back to pink again

"Ha-ha!"

"It's hilarious!"

"You four might be able to laugh about it later." said Mum, hopefully

"We'll see about that Aunt Mikayla!"

"We'll see."

"Anyway… keep up the good work with your fans."

"We may be able to collaborate on a single in the future… we'll probably spend a bit more time together then." said Amelia, extending an olive branch

"I'm sure Cassie might perform a song or two with you… she may also perform at a charity event… like the 'Autism Angels'." Mum added, as we waved goodbye to 'Quirky Service' and got back on the road

# Chapter Forty-One
## Blue Lake & Ye Olde Murtoa

We are enchanted by the bright blue cobalt colour of Blue Lake in Mount Gambier... near to the border between South Australia and Victoria.

"Isn't it an amazing blue!"

"It's shining like the ocean and very deep."

"This is a great highlight." I said

"It looks gorgeous!"

"This will make a good photo to upload to Facebook." said Mum

Mum takes a couple of photos of the Blue Lake...so did Dad and I.

We have arrived in Mt Gambier after driving down from Adelaide... we booked in to the Motel Mt Gambier in Penola Road... for a few days.

We found out that in the months of December to March... the Blue Lake turns cobalt blue...then during April to November, the colour changes to a colder steel grey. The cause of this phenomenon is not known, though it may be the warming of the surface layers around the lake to around twenty degrees during the summer time.

We read the commemorative obelisk marking the spot in July 1865 where Adam Lindsey Gordon... a famous Australian poet... performed a daring riding challenge on horseback. He was on a narrow ledge behind an old post and rail guard fence... which overlooks the blue lake... and then jumped back onto the roadway. It was a very risky stunt though he survived this daring feat. I wouldn't want to do that sort of stunt ever; it would give me a heart attack!

We wanted to visit Engelbrecht Caves, we thought it would be a very interesting place to see. It wasn't always a tourist attraction... it was originally used as a rubbish dump by its' private owners.

The Lions Club of Mount Gambier decided to restore and maintain the caves as part of a project in 1979. They had plans to beautify the area... after several months of hard work by the local council... they were handed the cave by the project owners...now tourists and cave divers from Australia and overseas... come here to explore the caves or to cave- dive in them.

We chose to take the exploration tour... to see where the cave divers swim through the water passages... under the streets and roads of Mount Gambier. Mum and Dad warned me not to touch the crystals... even though it was very tempting... I didn't touch them.

We first viewed the sinkhole which was very deep! Then we entered the Eastern Cavern Lake... which was a mixture of yellow and green colours. It was magic seeing that. We then viewed the Eastern Cave Walls which were rugged and fascinating to learn about.

"What is that Dave?" I asked

"I've never seen anything like this in a cave."

Dave Burchell is a well-known diver... who was in a team of four that made an exploratory dive...they discovered a small lake with a silty floor.... after going through a hundred years of accumulated rubbish... in a dark... muddy... passage!

"The team reported back to the council that it was not suitable for tourist development." he replied

A few days later... still in Mt Gambier...Dad and I were talking.

"What do you think about going for a bit of ten-pin bowling today, Cassie?"

"That sounds good Dad."

"I've done a bit of ten-pin bowling now and then."

"Gambier City Bowl is a good place to start."

"It's popular with families... especially during the school holidays."

We can play two games and have some family fun." said Mum

We arrived at Gambier City Bowl at eleven...we had to climb a long winding spiral path to get there... inside there were arcade machines... a couple of carnival type crane machines... and racing arcade games as well.

There were bowling balls... bowling shoes... twelve lanes... and even a jukebox on the left. Above the pins the graphics were futuristic themes... with colours of red... yellow... orange... and purple. I'm ready for some bowling action and a smashing good time!

We paid our fees and we're ready to bowl!

"All we need is a bowling ball each and the right size shoes and we can play."

"Let's check our sizes... we don't want to get the wrong shoes." I said

After we picked up our shoes, we chose a bowling ball each... then we made our way to lane three which was booked for us.

"Cassie do you want to use the bowling assistance ramp?" asked Mum

"No thanks, Mum."

"I haven't needed to use that since I was fourteen!"

"I'm fine without it."

"I can bowl well...since I moved on from that."

"Okay Cassie."

"Let's see who is the best ten-pin bowler!" Mum chuckled

"I'll bet I can knock you two over with my bowling skills!"

"I've been scoring well in most of the games I've played in Mount Gambier... Warrnambool... and Melbourne." Dad bragged

"We'll see who is 'REALLY' the best Dad!"

"Bring it on!" I fist pumped the air

At the end of game one I emerged the winner in a close game between Dad and I. There was one 'gutter-ball' from Mum in her fourth turn... it was so close to knocking a few pins but just missed out. We had a quick drink and snack break before we started game two.

"Dad and I love cricket and golf and since 1993 we have been playing ten-pin bowling too...especially during the school holidays." Mum said, smiling

"I remember you taught me to play when I was nine... by using cardboard tubes as the pins...and a tennis ball as the bowling ball, then later with plastic bowling pins... and a plastic bowling ball, when I was eleven."

"Then when I turned twelve, we moved on to real bowling balls and pins at Kingpin Bowling Crown."

"I had to wear my headphones then so I could cope with the loud noises, also there were bright coloured lights and many people to get used to."

"I used the bowling assistance ramp for two years…we always had fun regardless of who won."

"If a family tournament were to occur would you like to participate in it?" asked Dad

"Yes, I would love to play in a family tournament."

"We could compete against a few other families and see who comes out on top." I said

We started game two and this time Mum won… just beating Dad and I. At one point I got two strikes in a row… I missed out on a 'turkey'… which means three strikes in a row!

"We have played two brilliant games and the three of us have had fun putting our bowling skills to the test." I said

"You played well Cassie."

"We were surprised when you got two strikes in a row." said Dad

"I was surprised too!"

"I was that close to getting a 'turkey'…it was great fun." I laughed

"It was a good contest and now we have worked up an appetite!"

"I know a great takeaway placed called 'Chicken Boss'."

"Why don't we go there for a spot of lunch." said Mum

"Sounds great!"

"I'm starving after all that exercise!"

"Let's get a delicious meal or two."

Mum and Dad laughed at my eagerness.

There were lots of choices when we arrived at Chicken Boss. Not only, meals… but also, drinks on the right-hand side…and ice-cream on the left. Oh boy, my mouth is watering! Eventually, we chose a meal deal that included chicken… chips… and salad… plus drinks, then we drove to a nearby park to eat it.

It was sunny and a young couple were eating lunch at another table. We were under a tree for shade with the sunlight dappling through the leaves. What a good day it has been so far.

"Cassie, do you like Mount Gambier?" asked Dad

"I sure do!"

"It's a great city with good shops and interesting activities to do."

"Visiting the Engelbrecht Caves has to be a highlight." I said

"Definitely!"

"Now we're going to talk about a life lesson with you."

"If we were sitting with an elderly family member… having lunch here in the park…if they were to sit on the grass… they wouldn't be able to get up again… unless we helped them."

"To prevent that problem from happening… if you were to let them sit on the bench and you sit on the grass… they could easily get up when it's time to go." said Mum

"I'll have no problems remembering that Mum… in fact I've been practising it a few times already…thanks for the life lesson." I said, happily

"That's great Cassie." Dad smiled

When we got back to our room at the motel, we packed up our things and loaded the car ready to leave early next morning.

After breakfast the next day, Dad jumped in the driver's seat and we drove to Casterton.

"Cassie… we have arrived in Casterton." Dad called from the front of the car

"There is a lookout called the Mickle Lookout, where we can look at panoramic views along the main street." said Dad

"There's the Casterton Railway Station."

"It's a good site to visit and learn about."

"You could take a few photos to send to Mia if you like." said Mum

"They both sound like good things to do."

"I choose to go to the Mickle Lookout first."

"It's a good photo opportunity... to capture the panoramic views of Casterton's main street."

"Good choice Cassie."

"Years ago, Mum and I went to a similar lookout... I'll tell you a story about it once we get there." said Dad

We got our binoculars out as soon as we arrived at the lookout. The main street of Casterton looks splendid from here. People are walking on the footpaths and cars are driving down the road. People stop to chat to each other as it is a fine day to be out and about.

"I am happy to be spending some time in Casterton on a lovely day like today... enjoying the sights and sounds... the flora and the scenery." I remarked

"Years ago, in 1986, Dad and I went to a Ballarat scenic lookout during a holiday."

"We went to the top and lay down on the grass looking up at the beautiful blue sky and the fluffy white clouds passing by."

"We were holding hands whilst the sun shone down on us... it was one of our boyfriend/girlfriend ... moments."

"We turned to each other and whispered loving words... and then we kissed."

"It is one of my favourite moments to remember." Mum said, with a sigh

"I like hearing that story Mum...even if it is a bit mushy!"

"I don't want to get a boyfriend for at least another two years yet!"

"When I do get one...I'll take him to a lovely romantic spot... like you two did."

"Maybe... I will even kiss him on the lips!" I stated

Mum and Dad smiled at each other fondly.

They know that I'm starting to speak a little about having a boyfriend... they will support me... whether I choose to have a boyfriend... or not. Maybe... I will meet someone during our future world tour... or somewhere in Australia.

Right now, I feel too young for any of that!

"There is plenty of time Cassie... you can stay my little girl for a bit longer." said Dad, giving me a bear hug

"Oh Dad...I will be your little girl even when I am fully grown up." I said, hugging him back

"Hey... what about me!"

"Don't I get any hugs!" Mum said, joining in

We got our lunch at Entwined Café and Restaurant which has a Maori flavour to the cuisine... that's another international cuisine I have tried now... and I haven't even toured overseas yet!

We chose to go to the Casterton Railway Station for our next historical building.

In September 1884 the railway line was constructed, work started on the station in 1886. A.C. Findley was the builder and Robert Watson was the designer and architect... during the Victorian period from 1851-1901... 'Gothic' revival was the architectural style in use at that time. The opening ceremony started with a banquet... the principal guest being the Honourable. W. Shields, a representative of Normanby.

Until 1949 a mixed passenger-goods train rode on the Casterton line...it was withdrawn and replaced with a goods service run. On the fifteenth of March 1954 they trialled a rail-car service... which ran from

Branxholme and Casterton…it was removed only four months and sixteen days later… as it didn't work out. Goods trains used the line until the third of March 1977, with the closing of the railway station.

The old railway bridge spanned the Glenelg River just to the south of the railway station. In 1986 a little over one hundred years after it was built, it was sold for removal. The railway building had a 'Casterton' style… using Gothic and Tudor detailing… instead of classical 'Italianate' design. The station master's plaque shows each Station Master from 1925-1977 who have served at the Casterton Station.

We are driving to Murtoa next.

"I'll look up a few places!" I said

"Murtoa may have some history we can check out… there are cabins that we can stay in." I say to Mum and Dad whilst checking out the map

Mum pre-booked a cabin for us… for when we arrive in Murtoa.

"The water tower museum might be worth checking out… there is a little restaurant called Ye Olde Murtoa that we can eat in… it has some great paintings some of them are for sale." I read out of my travel book

"One of our family members was born in Murtoa in 1931."

"Do you know who that is?" asked Mum, as we drove along

"It's Nan Diane!" I said

"That's right Cassie."

"Diane was born in Murtoa in 1931 and lived there for several years before she moved to Melbourne."

"She played the piano when she was young… she is still a talented pianist today." said Mum

"Rebecca was taught to play the piano, though she rarely plays it today… except at retirement homes… or occasionally at her home."

"One day, I might ask her to teach me how to play the piano." I mused

"Rebecca could certainly do that."

"I'll give her a call sometime… then you can go to her house for a lesson." said Dad

"I'll be more than happy to take lessons with Rebecca."

As we arrived in Murtoa, Dad said…

"Let's check in to our cabin and then find a place to get a nice hearty lunch somewhere."

The cabin Mum had booked didn't turn out to be quite what we imagined.

The loungeroom and kitchen areas were ok… the bathroom was sort of ok…the bedrooms were a lot smaller than we expected. Oh My!

"Hmm."

"There's a bunk bed and there's a double bed near the bathroom… with a single bed to the right of the double bed."

"It looks like we will have to make the most of it." said Mum, resigned to our circumstances

"If I sleep in either of the bunk beds… I will have a hard time getting in and out of them!"

"I might sleep in the single bed next door to you and Dad." I decided

"We can still have fun staying here."

"We'll help each other cook the meals."

"Cassie… this will be a good time for you to practice making a meal… independently." said Dad

"No problems Dad!"

"Although… I have never cooked in a cabin before!"

"I will try and make a nice delicious meal for the three of us."

"You two can supervise… to make sure nothing goes wrong!"

"We can supervise...but we reckon you will make a brilliant job of cooking a tasty dinner tonight!" said Mum

"I think so too." I said, confidently

The Water Tower Museum turned out to be an old four-storey, thirteen-metre high water storage tank. It was built in 1886 by the railways so that steam engines could be supplied with water.

We also saw Concordia College with a taxidermy collection of five hundred birds... which dated back a hundred years!

"Ew!"

"This is not my thing at all." I shuddered

"It grosses me out!"

"We know Cassie."

"It makes us feel grossed out too!" said Mum, scrunching up her nose

"Perhaps the photographs and artefacts can distract us!" said Dad

"Good idea Dad!" I said, very relieved to move away from those 'birds'

There were cuttings... photographs... and artefacts... relating to Murtoa's history... as well as the local German... Irish... and English... farming communities. I've never been to a farm I'm interested in visiting one and seeing the animals there. Maybe... I will get to play in the hay... if I'm lucky.

"The farming communities really contributed a lot to Murtoa's history."

"They worked hard." I said

"They sure did."

"We visited a farm Dad and I...once when we were sixteen...we had to round up some pigs."

"Every time we got near a pig... it would dart away...we ended up getting muddier and dirtier each time."

"Olivia and Rebecca helped us too."

"We eventually rounded them all up... we needed a shower to wash off all the mud!"

"We mischievously hid from the farmer in the hay and emerged twenty minutes later covered in straw."

"It took a lot of picking to get it all off our clothes...it was fun just the same." said Mum, smiling

"That's a funny story, Mum."

"I would love to try that." I said

"We can one day... it will be a whole lot of fun." Dad agreed

There were local community archives... including local family history... schools... churches...organisations... transport records... and photos. There was information about blacksmithing and hand farming tools... house implements... and toys. All part of Murtoa's history... viewing them gave us a sense of the town that stayed with us.

"I am liking this town and learning heaps about its' history...these archives make Murtoa come alive in my mind."

"It's clear the locals love their community."

"It's good to support them too!"

"We can contribute by playing our music." said Mum

"We can do something special for our fans." said Dad

"There's a nearby restaurant to have a great lunch!"

"You know how much I always need food." I reminded Mum and Dad

"We sure do!!" said Mum and Dad in unison

The counter reminded me of a similar one I've seen in a chef's kitchen in a high-class restaurant. We ordered our lunch and sat at a vacant table. It was a vibrant atmosphere and a good environment to eat it in.

"Cassie, you know we all love sheep… so we're going to a farm."

"We are going to help Nan Diane's friends to shear their sheep." said Dad

"I remember when we tried shearing sheep in Blackall."

"It was a new thing for me to do and I was a little bit nervous… but you helped me to shear one."

"There is a tour group from the USA… coming to learn all about 'aussie' shearing."

"We'll be dressed in shearer's clothes… to give the tourists a show." said Mum, winking

Diane's friends and family were there when we arrived… they were happy to see us.

"Welcome to our farm!"

"How are you all?" asked Elena

"We got your message…so we're here to help out." I said

"That's good… you're just in time!"

"The American tourists will be arriving in twenty minutes."

"Here are your sheep shearing clothes."

"Then you are good to go!" said Nathan

We got changed into the shearing 'gear' just as bus full of American tourists arrived… they climbed down from the bus… walked to the shearing area and got ready for the 'show'!

"Hello, everybody."

"We have the 'Bontel' family here… they are going to show you how to shear a sheep 'Aussie' style."

"Our sheep are sometimes mischievous… so we hope they will be on their best behaviour!" said Nathan, with a wink to the crowd

"Are you ready Bontel family?" asked Elena

"We're ready!" we say together

Mum and Dad started their sheep were behaving well… the American tourists loved it.

Then I started with my sheep…. all was going smoothly with the American tourists enjoying themselves greatly.

We did a few more sheep… then the last one came out and I volunteered. I went to grab him, he dodged me and escaped back out to the field. The American tourists started to chuckle.

"Err…sorry about that."

"This particular sheep seems a little naughty… just like me when I play pranks on Mum and Dad!"

"We'll try and catch him." I said, trying not to grin.

Mum, Dad and I ran out to the field.

"There here is!"

"Let's try to sneak up behind him and catch him… then drag him back to the shearing shed to be shorn." I said

"Let's hope this plan works Cassie." said Mum

"That sheep needs a well-deserved haircut!"

"We'll catch him as quick as we can." said Dad

I entered the field first and crept up behind him, I was about to make a grab for him, when he ran off and I fell over in the mud.

"OOF!"

The American tourists burst out laughing…they thought it was hilarious.

"Let me try… I won't let him escape!" said Dad

He sidled up to the sheep and spread his arms out in an… 'I'm about to catch you' gesture…the sheep charged through and Dad fell into the mud too.

Hahahaha! the American tourists were bent over laughing at Dad in the mud

"I'll teach that 'bleeping sheep' who's boss!" said Mum, threateningly

Mum pretended to be going in the opposite direction...then at the last minute she turned and made a charge for the sheep!

Unfortunately, the sheep was getting pretty used to this by now and dodged out of the way...leaving Mum to slip up in the wet mud and land face down.

Mum came up spluttering with a mouthful of mud.

The American tourists were now nearly wetting themselves...Mum didn't look too happy at all!

"He's getting too 'cagey' for us to catch him!"

"We'll try and catch him together... that could work." I said

Mum and Dad agreed wiping the mud off their faces and looking very determined indeed!

The sheep was in the middle of the field... so Mum, Dad and I took up positions in different corners... we moved in until we were close enough to dive on him...except he torpedoed straight through the middle... causing Mum, Dad and I, to collide head first into each other and end up down in the mud again!

The American tourists had given up standing by now and were sitting down holding their bellies as they rolled from side to side with laughter.

"Oh shoot!" said one tourist, wiping tears from his eyes

"That sheep is really too fast for us!" I said

"We look like pigs in mud... red-faced pigs... from embarrassment!" muttered Mum

Mum, Dad and I stood up... rubbing our heads...with scarlet cheeks.

"That'll be a nice bruise tomorrow!" Dad grimaced

"The embarrassment meter is certainly rising a few notches."

"Just like the Echuca horse ride!"

We've made a fool of ourselves." I said, embarrassed

"The American tourists might think it's hilarious...we don't." Mum mutters under her breath

"How embarrassing!" Dad agreed

We finally managed to catch the runaway sheep with some assistance... then Dad and Mum held him while I gave him a 'close shave'!

"Do you have a shower that we can use?" I asked

'Yes...you will need some fresh clothes as well." said Nathan, trying not to smile

We had a shower each to wash off all the mud... got changed into fresh clothes and waved goodbye to Elena and Nathan... as we headed back to our hotel.

Ye Old Murtoa had turned out to be a pub... where we wound down after our very strenuous afternoon!

"We've got some 'olde worlde' costumes that we can change into so that we blend in with Ye Old Murtoa pub...we will look the part." said Mum

"These will look fantastic... the locals will get a surprise when they see us in them."

We got changed into the costumes... they are lovely.

"Mum you look beautiful in your costume." I said

"Daniel your costume looks magnificent!"

"You look like a nineteenth century English gentleman." Mum admired

"Thank you... Mikayla."

"I feel very aristocratic and snazzy."

"Cassie you look wonderful in your costume."

"Just like a Scottish lass." said Dad

"Thanks Dad."

At 'Ye Old Murtoa' the locals turned their heads to see our costumes. We've only spent two days here and Murtoa seems to love us...I enjoy it!

Next to Ye Old Murtoa was a little art gallery... it was closed for renovation. The patrons in the pub turned to look at us... I could tell they admired the costumes we were wearing.

"Hello... you all look fantastic in your costumes." said the barman

"Thank you." I said, doing a little twirl

"You are the 'Bontel' family... aren't you?"

"Are you planning to play a concert during your stay?" asked the barman

"Yes, there will be a one-off concert in a couple of days." said Mum

"That's great."

"We hope you have a lovely dinner here at Ye Old Murtoa"

"In the room on your right you will see several paintings... most of them are available for purchase." said the barman

"Thank you." Dad replied

We walked into the dining room and there were paintings lining most of the walls, there was a big painting over the fireplace.

What a nice painting it is, we may buy a painting or two if we get time to choose during our stay. We sat at a circular table near a cabinet full of antiques and looked at the menu.

"Kangaroo meat looks tasty."

"I think I might try that!"

"Mum, you have tried kangaroo before... including on the Ghan, haven't you?"

"I wouldn't try it for several years because it's not a smooth food, I'm going to try tonight."

"That sounds adventurous, Cassie."

"That dish looks good to me." said Mum, pointing to an item on the menu

"I'll try that dish." said Dad

Our dishes smell so good when they arrive at the table. The kangaroo meat is cooked just right, so are Mum and Dad's dishes too.

"Dig in, Mum and Dad!"

"Cheers to our road trip journey and the 'Bontel Family' tour." I said, raising my glass

"Cheers!" said Mum and Dad, 'clinking' our glasses together

The dishes were indeed delicious. Whilst we were dining, Mum showed me a photo from 1987, which featured Mum... Dad... Olivia... and Rebecca... in 'Quirky Service', eating in their favourite family pub in Melbourne.

The meals we were tasting there... were chicken schnitzel with bacon for Olivia... kangaroo for me... lamb for Rebecca... and seared fish for Daniel." said Mum

"I bet they were tasty meals!"

"It's a great photo... I can see you were having fun." I said

"We were!"

"It was after our 1987 'Winter Snow' world tour."

"These paintings are lovely... such brilliant colours in them."

"These colours remind me of the fun times we had painting... even the Wodonga art class we did." I said

"I was the most prolific artist during Quirky Service... Playground Kids... and the Bontel-Macdonald mansion years!"

"We would all paint pictures together... then hang them on our bedroom walls."

"We all had art smocks in our favourite colours... we would wear berets like the 'French' painters and paint away in the back yard." said Mum smiling broadly, at the memory

"Our parents were very proud of our artwork... we even created a few pieces which were used as 'cover artworks'...for our albums!"

"Whenever we toured France during our Quirky Service world tours... we would take art classes and continue painting artworks there."

"A few mischievous moments occurred... mixing up each other's colours and swapping each other's artworks...we had creative times painting and learnt a lot about art that way." said Dad, smiling as he remembered

"I have fun creating artworks too!" I said, enthusiastically

"Maybe... I could create an artwork cover for my solo album... or upcoming single soon."

"We can't wait to see what your artwork cover might look like." said Mum, enthusiastically

We took some time to choose a couple of paintings that we all liked, which we bought and took with us. We will love looking at them for many years to come, and who knows they might just give me a little inspiration to paint one of my own!

A couple of days later, we are ready for our Murtoa concert! A small crowd is expected, we will give our best performance for them. When our names were announced we walked on to the stage waving to everyone as we went to our positions. The crowd cheered, and when Dad made his entrance the cheers got noticeably louder!

"That's right ladies!"

"Dad's a man who likes to look after himself." I pointed out

Everyone in the audience laughed... except Dad... who went red in the face.

"Cassie you're in big trouble... you wait till the end of the concert." hissed Dad, out of the side of his mouth

Mum was giggling like a little girl... that made the audience and I laugh even louder... whilst Dad was still glowering at me.

Dad decided he had something to say to me right now!

"Did you say that I'm a man who likes to look after himself." asked Dad, squirming as the audience finds this even funnier

"Err... maybe Dad." I giggled

"You know Dad... somebody else might take that as a compliment!" I tried, soothing him

"Well I'm not somebody else young lady... I'm your father!" said Dad, in his huffiest parent voice

Well that brought the house down... everyone in the audience were now giving Dad wolf whistles. He quickly realised he was outnumbered on this topic... so even though he was still embarrassed by the attention to his physique... he decided the best thing to do was to get on with the music... ASAP! This proved to be a little bit difficult... because by this time Mum and I were crying with laughter and almost not fit to play our instruments... or to sing.

Looks like Dad might have to do a solo!

"Oh... my ribs are hurting from so much laughter." I groaned

"Oh... my tummy is sore." said Mum, clutching her belly with another laugh

Then we all burst out laughing together, including Dad.

"OK... Okay!" said Dad, with a bashful look

"Enough about my 'body beautiful'... let's get this music show on the road!"

Everybody clapped, we all pulled ourselves together and the music began!

Later that night when we got back, Mum skyped Belinda to tell her what we had been doing, and where we have been. I always love the banter between those two, Mum sometimes makes Belinda cringe, with her rude jokes. I hope she tells another one!

"Hi Mum."

'Hi darling.'

'How are you today?'

"I'm well thanks Mum."

"How about you?"

'I am well thanks.'

'I hope you're not getting up to mischief.'

Mum sniggered at that.

"I hope not."

'I think your sniggering tells me that you are!'

'Your laughter always brightens up a room, and Cassie's laughter does the same.'

"Hello Belinda Bonkers." I chime in, giggling

'Very funny Cassie.'

I burped loudly in the background.

'Cassie!'

'What should you say when you burp?'

"Mum did it." I said giggling

"I did not Cassie!"

"Ladies do not burp!"

'How un-lady like from you… young lady!'

'Mikayla… you have taught Cassie another bad habit I see!' said Belinda

"Blame my older siblings!"

"You don't know what I have to put up with!"

'You might have me there… you're still very cheeky, darling.'

"I sure am!"

"I'll tell you a rude joke if you like?"

'No… I would not like that… Mikayla you are incorrigible!'

We all laughed at that… because we know that Mum IS incorrigible!

"In my defence… my older siblings have taught me everything I know… they make me laugh." said Mum, looking a bit guilty

"Anyway, we're staying in Murtoa and we've performed our concert here and the fans enjoyed themselves and so did we."

'You're making fans everywhere you go.'

"We are."

"Earlier in the week we were shearing sheep…we had a lot of trouble catching the last one…we ended up getting very muddy."

'Oh dear… I saw a bruise on your forehead.'

'Did you get that trying to catch the sheep?'

"Yes, I did."

"The video of us has gone viral on YouTube."

"We can laugh at it now...initially... it was very embarrassing and awkward."

"Anyway, moving right along from that unfortunate episode...we explained to Cassie that Diane was born here...we also went to the water tower museum to learn more about Murtoa.'

'You sound like you had a fun time.'

'I'd better log off and go to bed.'

'If you see Diane or call her... tell her that you discovered her birthplace.'

"We will, Mum bye."

'Bye, darling.'

# Chapter Forty-Two
## 'Budj Bim' Landscapes

"I would like to see 'MacKenzie Falls'."
 "Good choice Cassie."
"Dad and I have enjoyed looking at many waterfalls and we have even swum in a couple." said Mum
"There's a walking track down to the falls viewing area... so we'll get plenty of exercise...we may even spot some flora and fauna along the way."
"We will need a water bottle each and some snacks to eat."
We drove to the MacKenzie Falls carpark in Halls Gap and parked our car. We got out and made our way on foot to the bushwalking trail. When we got to the falls it was a magnificent sight!
Water was flowing down to the pool of water below and the noise of the waterfall was amazing. With our snacks and a water bottle each, we walked up the track to the top of McKenzie Falls. We got our hats and put on sunscreen before we started, so that hopefully, we will all make it back sunburn free! Along the way, we saw a lizard soaking up the sun it was a highlight of our walk.
We continued on our way our muscles got a workout... it was a long walk up the steep hill...we were puffed by the time we reached the top. We can't leave without taking a photo or two though! We sat down and ate our snacks and had a long drink of water. It is autumn now, still we must not neglect our hydration after such a long and at times strenuous, climb.
"This is a wonderful waterfall."
"Seeing all the water flowing into the pool below is stunning!"
"All this water reminds me of swimming in outdoor pools with you two." I said
"When Dad and I were nineteen we went to Millaa Millaa Falls in Innisfail, near Cairns."
"We swam at the base of the falls surrounded by tropical ferns and vibrantly coloured flowers."
"We swam for hours splashing each other into the late afternoon, when we spotted a platypus and took a couple of photos of it."
"Then we relaxed on our towels in the warm sun."
"It was a great holiday for Dad and I during our teenage years." says Mum, going all misty eyed
"Did you two get up to any mischief?" I asked, suspiciously
"Oh yes... we did Cassie!"
"We did... and we got away with it!" laughed Dad
"I think that's enough of that... DEAR!" said Mum, snapping out of her misty memories and wagging her finger at Dad
"Time for a little censorship I think!" said Mum, laughing at Dad
Dad just grinned mysteriously.

Later, back in Hamilton, we checked out the Sir Reginald Ansett Transport Museum...which was full of historical transport... including a car that Sir Reginald had driven in 1931!

On December the fifth, 1931 a Studebaker car was driven from Hamilton to Ballarat by a young Reginald Ansett...that identical car is in the museum.

That was the beginning of the Ansett empire... eleven years later it had become the biggest road passenger service in the Commonwealth. The road wasn't always a smooth one...as the Victorian Government took steps to curb the development of the Ansett company...because the state-owned railways were losing popularity to Ansett.

Reginald Ansett wasn't going to let that stop him...he flew his Moth aircraft to Sydney using a road map to help him... and he bought a Fokker universal passenger plane...the Fokker universal flew between Hamilton and Melbourne and the rest as they say... is history!

Ansett then developed an international airline...operating one of the world's most modern fleets... Reginald Ansett was an aviation pioneer in Australia... and also made history in the vehicle industry. The memorabilia we saw included a Fokker universal aircraft similar to the one operated during the 1936 Ansett Flight...the 1928 Studebaker... and documents from the early days of the Ansett Empire.

The company's first prospectus set out the capital and the proposed development. There was also a Boeing 727 wheel...which signified the advances that flight and road transport operations have made... other items included in the museum were flight attendant uniforms... and an array of smaller items.

I own a Studebaker toy car in my car collection, which I rarely play with but enjoy owning. The Studebaker car is fascinating to look at, I'm discovering more vintage cars every time we visit museums that feature cars. I own a few similar ones in my collection of toy cars... I used to enjoy playing with them when I was younger.

At first, I wouldn't let anyone play with them... I would strike out and meltdown...these days I don't mind when my young relatives play with them... I like to teach them the history behind each one.

"I could keep my collection and talk about it on TV one day." I said

"You could do that... you've always loved cars... like your Dad."

"You always played with them...you used to examine their wheels closely... that was before you were diagnosed at age two." Mum added

"You're a Holden mad person like me." said Dad, proudly

"I am definitely a Holden mad person like you Dad!"

"I enjoy watching the V8 supercar races with you...Craig Lowndes is my favourite driver!"

"I know that your favourite driver is Mark Winterbottom."

"Someday, I want to go to a V8 event in Bathurst Dad... I can take you there!"

"Mum you can come too if you like."

"We could experience the thrills and excitement... as the V8 cars race around the Bathurst track!"

"It would be a great event to attend sometime." Mum agreed, smiling at my enthusiasm

Tyrendarra is a small country town in south west Victoria... I don't know how long we will be staying here we have one or two things to do. We're meeting some local indigenous band community members... who are like us. They will be taking us on a tour through the Budj Bim National Heritage landscape...we want to show respect for their culture and our environment... we are going to learn about their history.

"Hello Lynette."

"Nice to see you again." said Mum

"Hello Mikayla."

"Nice to see you too." said Lynette

"Hello Joseph."
"It's great to see you again." said Dad
"Hello Daniel."
"It's great to see you again." Joseph replied
"Hello Cassie."
"I love your music and I've heard so much about you." said Charlotte
"Hello Charlotte."
"Thank you."
"It's nice to meet you." I said, shyly

Lynette Orkins is the keyboardist and vocalist with the indigenous band 'Nature'. Joseph, Katherine and Patricia, were counterparts in their indigenous band… to Rebecca and Olivia in their band… when they attended Melbourne University from 1989 to 1993.

Lynette currently works as a Tafe teacher at the Hamilton Campus in the disabilities section since 2010… teaching students with disabilities… she is an advocate for them and she was also the cook… before teaching Charlotte that role.

Joseph Orkins plays drums and sings vocals in 'Nature'… he currently works alongside Lynette as a Tafe teacher in the disabilities section… he is also an advocate like his wife Lynette.

Charlotte helps her parents Lynette and Joseph with the Budj Bim tours, she cooks the meals for the family. Unlike me, she doesn't have any sensory issues, although she is shy when around new people, particularly the visitors. For the past two years, she has overcome her shyness with help from Lynette and Joseph and has been a singer/songwriter since she was ten. Charlotte helps the young visitors on the tours… since 2010 she has been working as a young aide assistant at Hamilton Tafe campus… in the disabilities section.

Charlotte supports students with disabilities and helps them with their work… encouraging them so that they don't feel alone… or afraid to follow their dreams. The Orkins family formed a band called the 'Orkins Family' in 2011… they have written several songs but are yet to record an album. Maybe we can collaborate on a song with them and feature on each other's albums…as guest artists.

"We're here for the Budj Bim tour."
"Do you normally have plenty of visitors on the tours?" I asked
"We normally do…today there's not many visitors."
"We've got plenty to show you so we'll walk some of the way and drive our cars the rest of the way." said Lynette
"Firstly, we'll give you some introductory information about Gundjitmara culture and country… then we will watch a ten-minute video."
"That sounds like fun."
"We are keen to hear what you have to say…we wish to gain knowledge." said Dad, respectfully
"Gundjitmara people were traditionally river and lake people."
"They benefitted economically and spiritually from the Framlingham forest… Lake Condah… and the surrounding river systems."
"They practised aquaculture and eel farming…where they created stone dwellings."
"The purpose for building dams was to hold the water… thus creating ponds and growing Short-Finned Eels and other fish in the wetlands… and the channels."
"Women made large woven baskets to harvest the mature eels… they were taken from the channels… which contained weirs." Joseph explained

"That's very interesting."
"We have learnt something new about Australia's culture that we didn't know before." I said
"That's amazing." said Mum
We listened to some more information about Gundjitmara culture from Lynette... Joseph... and Charlotte... then we watched the video. After that, we drove to the Tyrendarra Indigenous Protected Area... where the unique stone dwellings and remnant house sites are situated. They were fascinating... as we walked along the trail we learnt about Australia's earliest and largest stone aquaculture systems... including the fish and eel traps.

Lynette and Joseph explained the dreaming story about the creation of the magnificent landscape with Charlotte drawing examples from geographical formations such as Tumuli. I took all that information in... I was amazed at the history behind it all.

It was a two-hour guided tour... it made me hungry so we sat down at a nice spot to talk while we ate our rolls... salads... and meats... that the 'Orkins' had provided for us.

"You are helping many students with your jobs as teachers and assistants at the Hamilton Tafe campus".
"What inspired you to take on those roles?" I asked, thoughtfully
"We were inspired after Lynette and I worked with children and teens with disabilities for many years."
"We had been fill-in substitute teaching at a couple of special schools... before we applied for the positions available at Hamilton."
"Charlotte has been working as a young assistant at Hamilton Tafe since 2010... helping the students with disabilities...she is doing a really great job."
"She may become a disability worker like us one day." said Joseph, proudly
"I might."
"I enjoy what I do... and although it's hard work... it's very rewarding too."
"The students love me and I love helping them."
"A disability worker might be a good job for me." said Charlotte
"I'm inspired to follow Mum and Dad in their footsteps as disability workers... whilst pursuing my music as well."
"I'm becoming very good with autistic children... calming them down... like I had to in Adelaide." I told Charlotte
"That's great work Cassie."
"You must have a knack for it!"
"We use similar techniques to calm Charlotte when she gets shy around new people...or when she gets anxious." said Lynette
"Cassie has come a long way... she is more confident around new people... also when talking to them as well." said Mum
"You're taking some sort of road trip... aren't you?" asked Joseph
"Yes, we are doing a road trip around Australia."
"We're making our way through Victoria now... staying at towns... trying new things... creating memories along the way." said Dad
"Wow!"
"You must be having loads of fun." smiled Charlotte
"We are doing lots of fun things!"
"You are keeping this protected area intact... making good use of it with the foods you gather here." I said
"This protected area that we're keeping safe... is for visitors... and for us." said Lynette

"We get by together through our music... working hard... studying among other things... then at the end of the day we always have a laugh and some fun... no matter what obstacles occur." said Mum

"That's what describes us as a family...the family that plays together... stays together!" laughed Joseph

"I plan to do another solo concert and a meet and greet on Thursday, before the 'Bontel Family' concert on the first of March."

"I performed my first one in Adelaide."

"Would you like to come?" I asked

"Let us check our dairies and see if we are available." said Lynette

They checked their diaries and luckily Thursday was available!

"Cassie we are available."

"You are doing so well... we would love to see you perform." said Charlotte

"Thanks Charlotte!"

"I would love to see you all there."

"We haven't got any visitors on Friday either... so we would love to be your opening act." said Joseph, with a cheeky grin

"You are welcome to be our opening act!"

"What songs will you perform?" asked Dad

"We will perform two songs... both in the pop rock genre... 'Pop On' and 'Lively'."

"These are two great 'catchy' songs that will get the Tyrendarra crowd going!" Lynette said, smiling

"My concert will be tomorrow afternoon around two." I said

"Good luck with your solo performance."

"Your songs will amaze your fans... just like the 'Bontel Family' concerts have done." said Charlotte

My solo performance at Tyrendarra was 'choc full' when I arrived the next day.

The fans are excited to see me perform and so am I to be here! I've got my party pop star clothes on, (blue of course), and my make-up too...so I'm ready to go! Wish me the best of luck! When the announcer said my name, I walked in to the sounds of cheering and clapping. I smiled and waved, and went to my position. I see the excited looks on my fans faces and I feel joyful that I will be singing my songs for the whole of Tyrendarra! Here I go!

"Hello Tyrendarra... how is everyone?" I ask the crowd happily

"We're good thanks Cassie!" the audience replies

"Did you see the Herald Sun?"

"I just had my first solo performance in Adelaide!"

"It was scary at first...since then I have gained more confidence."

"I hope Tyrendarra enjoys my Scandinavian inspired pop tunes like the Adelaide audiences did!"

"There will be a meet and greet afterwards and some autograph signing."

"Are you ready to sing and dance along with me?"

"YES!" the crowd screams

"Awesome!"

"Let's do it!"

When my concert had finished, I signed some autographs then went backstage to meet two lucky fans who had been chosen for a 'meet n greet'! They were two autistic sisters, who were fans of my music and also the 'Bontel Family' band. As I entered backstage, the excited sisters ran over to me and hugged me tight. Wow! They are excited!

"Whoa!

"You seem very excited to see me."
"How are you two?" I asked
"We're great thanks Cassie!"
"I'm Renee."
"Your songs are wonderful." said Renee
"I'm Marissa."
"We love what you do...your music inspires us." said Marissa
"That's much appreciated."
"Are you musicians too." I said
"We are."
"I play guitar and Marissa plays keyboards."
"We formed a pop duo named 'Cherry', we have started to perform in our home town and your songs have given us extra confidence to perform." said Renee
"I'm glad about that."
"Mum and Dad have inspired me with their music."
"I have been performing onstage since last year in Sydney."
"I have also been performing at destinations along the road trip that we have been taking around Australia."
"That's wicked!"
"I love 'Party Party'!"
"It takes us back to all our parties with family and friends!"
"We played fun games... performed our music... and ate cream cake with your song 'Cream Cake'." smiled Marissa
"Your songs... 'My Voice'... 'Fitting in the World'... and 'Tech-Savvy', are excellent...they
describe life with autism spectrum conditions so well."
"It makes us realise we are not on our own in this journey... that we have support... encouragement... and love... no matter where we are... or what we do." said Renee, smiling
"I couldn't have said it any better myself!"
"I love performing my songs...I feel a sense of confidence and happiness when I sing."
"Music gives bravery to reach for the skies!" I said
"We plan to become music teachers at a special school after we have studied at university."
"Maybe we can inspire others too." said Marissa
"You can."
"Chase your dreams... if you work hard enough you can achieve anything you want to."
"That's what I believe...I plan to achieve more." I said, resolutely
"Thank you for the advice." said Renee

The meet and greet was such a fun experience...Marissa and Renee were such fun to talk to. I took a 'selfie' with them so we would all remember our meeting. I wished them the best of luck for their futures, they thanked me and told me to keep going with my popstar career! I said goodbye to the girls and went to catch up with Mum and Dad. Who knows what the next meet and greet might hold?

"How did you go Cassie?" asked Dad
"It was wicked Dad!"
"Renee and Marissa turned out to be musicians just like me!"
"They loved my songs and I inspired them to become more confident."

"They want to work as music teachers." I said, excitedly
"That's great!"
"Sounds like you had a lot of fun at your meet and greet!"
"Maybe my next solo project could be a tribute to eighties music."
"I love eighties music and I would like to perform some… as well as my own songs." I mused
"After the road trip we can help you to choose some eighties songs and places to perform them."
"I'm getting the picture…. 'Cassie's Smashing Eighties Tribute Night'!"
"That will be a great solo project… complete with eighties party pop star clothes." said Dad
"Ooh… I can imagine it now!"
"You and Mum were the eighties superstar idols performing your smash hits… black sunglasses on… very 'hot' you guys!"
"Cassie Annabelle Bontel brings the eighties all back… in 2012!"
"Now that will BE smashing!" I grinned, as we drove along the road

We are on our way to Heywood… where it will soon be time for the Wood, Wine and Roses Festival!

When we arrive in Heywood, I see it's a small town with a few shops… including one that makes pizza. It has a tennis court and an archery range… I'm going to have a nice couple of days and maybe try a new sport whilst I'm here.

The township called Second River was razed by fires in 1851, it has historical significance for settlers and gold seekers who made their way from Portland and then further inland, for settlements.

In the 1840's a bridge was built across the Fitzroy River and it is said to be Victoria's first bridge. Heywood was born out of the ashes… isn't it amazing that a small town like this was burnt to the ground by fire…yet it was rebuilt into a new town!

On the last Saturday of February… the Wood… Wine… and Roses festival… is held in Heywood. There is local food and wine tasting… wood chopping… parades… carnival rides… market stalls… floral art… photography… painting… live bands… and family entertainment.

Mum, Dad and I will be able to attend… as it's the last Saturday in February… which is in two days!

We bought our lunch at 'Hollyrock' which is a nice shop. We noticed a poster on the wall featuring legendary American actors… Elvis Presley… Marylin Monroe… James Dean… and Marlon Brando. It's a good poster to look at, Mum and Dad have at least two of their movies… Mum also has an Elvis Presley CD.

"Dad… I would like to give archery a try… I've never tried it…I've seen you practice archery a couple of times though."
"We'll go to the Heywood archery range where I can teach you all about archery."
"You may want to learn with a group… like I have in the past."

We drove to the Heywood Archery Club and range, where there is a shed that Dad and his archery group get ready for their archery shooting in. They always have a BBQ lunch after they finish their archery practice. The practice area is nearby, where they shoot at the targets with their bow and arrows. I'm a bit nervous about trying archery…being with Dad gives me confidence.

We met up with Dad's archery group which include Damien… Jonathan… Josh… Ed… and Andrea. They are very friendly and I shake hands with them all.

"Hello Cassie."
"We hear that you are in the 'Bontel Family' band and performing brilliantly…inspiring others to chase their dreams." said Damien, with a smile on his face
"Thanks."
"My inspiration is Nikki Webster… I love to sing and play music."

"We are charting in Australia and around the world...helping to inspire our fans and people with disabilities." I told him

"You're doing a fine job with that, Cassie!"

"Our children love your music... we do too!" said Jonathan

"Thank you."

"I'm here to learn archery."

"Dad is going to teach me." I said

"He's a very good teacher... always encouraging and helping you." said Josh

"He sure is."

"I'm a bit nervous...though I'm willing to give it a go!" I said

"That's the spirit, Cassie"

"We are taking a break after our first session... so you'll have plenty of time to practice."

"The targets are over there for our first-timers." said Ed

"It will take time...you will feel confident eventually." said Andrea

"I sure hope so." I said

Dad took me to the practice targets and taught me how to hold an archery bow correctly and fire the arrow at the targets.

"When you first handle the bow... you hold it perpendicular to the ground... whilst the bow is in a horizontal position."

"You grasp the bow with your non-dominant hand." said Dad

I listened carefully to his instructions and gave them a try.

"Good Cassie!"

"Bend your fingers around the grip and keep your hand relaxed but steady." Dad continued

I managed the last two steps without any problems.

"Good job Cassie."

"You have now learnt how to hold an archery bow."

"Now we can have some practice shots at the targets and see how you do." said Dad

I aimed my bow at the targets...a couple of the arrows missed the target completely...a couple hit the target... I did okay.

"Cassie with practice you will be able to hit the centre of the target...that's not bad for your first try." Dad smiled

"I'll practice some more with you next time." I said

"Cassie... in five minutes we'll start our afternoon session."

"Would you like to be our scorer?" asked Damien

"Yes please... Damien."

"I would love to be the scorer."

"We'll give you a score card... keep well back at a safe distance when we fire the arrows."

"When we all have had our turn, we'll tell you the points we scored one at a time... you can write them down in the correct sections with a pencil."

"Use a rubber if you make a mistake." said Jonathon

"Ok, I got all that covered." I grinned

There are eighteen targets, with numbers for each one. We followed along the route that was set up... and when Dad and his archery group fired their arrows at their targets, they would tell me their score... and I would write it down. It was fun watching Dad and his archery group... maybe after lots of practice... I could be firing at targets with them one day! It would be fun competing with Dad! When I went into the Heywood forest where the targets were set up it was an exploration of nature too.

When the afternoon session was over, we had a BBQ consisting of sausages... bread... and onions... it was very tasty after all our exercise... the weather was fine and we sat in the shed and talked together.

"Cassie did you know your Dad joined our group in 2007?"

"Every now and then, we come to this range and shoot at the targets."

"He's good!" said Jonathon

"He certainly is!"

"I learnt by watching you all...the instructions Dad gave me improved my confidence." I said

"I've played a few sports...cricket and basketball are the two main ones I'm good at."

"Mum and Dad were cricketers back in their teens... they gave some cricketing comments for the 1994-1995 Ashes series in Australia." I said

"It was great to hear them live."

"We heard you three are doing a road trip."

"Going well is it?" asked Andrea

"It is going well."

"That's great." Ed nodded

We said goodbye to Damien... Jonathon... Ed... Josh... and Andrea... then headed back to the Heywood Motor Inn to wind down for a few hours before we went out for dinner.

We went down to the pool for a swim. I swam for an hour, then got out and relaxed on my towel with my sunglasses on, soaking up the sun. Later, we went back inside our hotel room, and I had a nice warm shower.

"Scotty's Pizza seems like a good place to get our tea."

"Would you like to have tea there?" asked Mum

"Sure... sounds good Mum."

"Let's try some pizza!" I agreed

We arrived at Scotty Pizza's... I noticed the DVD's when we walked in, we might be able to rent one overnight to watch. We walked up to the counter and ordered our pizzas and sat down at a vacant table.

Mum showed me some photos of Kate and Adam at the Warrnambool Ten-Pin Bowling Centre.

"Cassie, this is Kate when she got her name in the girl's section in 1997 when she was fifteen years old."

"She couldn't stop smiling for ages... she had an ice-cream afternoon tea it was such a fun time." said Mum

"Kate looks delighted with her score of 286."

"This is Adam when he became the new champion in the boy's section in 1999, when he was sixteen."

"He scored 275...he was very happy!"

"Kate... Nicole... Amelia... and Adam... went out for pizza to celebrate afterwards... they had a great time!" said Mum, smiling

"He looks very happy."

Our pizzas arrive and they smell good! We poured ourselves some water and ate a few slices. We drank our water but it didn't taste right.

"Eeew!"

"This water tastes awful!"

"It's worse than our Melbourne water." said Mum in disgust, wiping the water from her mouth

"I agree Mum."

"We can't drink that!" I grimaced

"We'll get soft drinks instead." said Dad, drying his mouth with a napkin

We got a soft drink each and after dinner we hired a family movie overnight to watch at our hotel.

In the morning, Mum, Dad and I put on our pop star coloured clothes ready to go to the 'Wood Wine and Roses' festival.

"I've never been to a festival like this before... I'm going to enjoy it... taste the delicious food and have a great time!"

"We certainly are going to enjoy ourselves... lots of people will be here... it's a great social event." said Mum

"We could try a couple of activities." said Dad

"We're going to have loads of awesome fun." I replied

Then one of the organising committee handed us a note, I read it out loud.

'The local Heywood band will not be performing at the Wood, Wine and Roses Festival.'

I continued to read the rest of the note...

*'We're sorry to inform you that we will not be able to perform at the Heywood Wood Wine and Roses Festival due to the illness of our keyboardist/singer. We cannot perform without him, so hopefully another band will be able to perform in our place. Our apologies for this bad news.*

"One of the members of 'Grass' has an illness... they can't perform today."

"Looks like we might be needed to perform at the 'Wood Wine and Roses' festival today."

"We still can have lots of fun." said Mum

"I can smell the food already!" said Dad, with a grin

We entered the festival grounds I can see lots of activities and lots of people having fun. It's my first time at the festival, I'm sure I will have an awesome time too!

"Hello Bontel Family."

"Welcome to the Heywood Wood Wine and Roses' festival."

"How do you like all these activities and food?" asked one of the show workers

"It all looks great!"

"My nose is leading me to the food." said Dad, with a guilty grin on his face

"You're in luck then."

"You three get to be food tasters!"

"Go over to the food area and enjoy."

"That will get your taste buds really singing!" said the organiser

"Thank you... sounds good to me!" said Mum

We made our way over to the food area...there are many foods to try... including cheeses of every description. Mmm, they sure look delicious... I can't wait to try them. I'm not sure about the blue cheese though... it looks awful and smells disgusting! Eurgh! Yuck!

The foods are tasty our taste buds do love them! We tried the cheeses. I was a bit hesitant to try the blue cheese...I managed to eat it.... despite a disgusted look on my face as I chewed.

"Among those wares were a couple of new foods... the cheeses were tasty as well." I said to Mum and Dad

"We enjoyed them too Cassie."

"How did you go with the blue cheese?" asked Mum, with a glint in her eye

"It was.... okay."

"It initially tasted funny...I managed to eat it though." I said

"Well done for eating it."

"Now let's try a couple of activities."
"Painting seems to be good choice." said Dad
"Photography would be good too!" said Mum
"I'll do a bit of painting."
"I still chuckle at the Wodonga art class where we painted each other across the forehead and I painted down the front of your face, Mum." I laughed, remembering
"I shall keep an eye on you so you won't be tempted to do that again!" said Mum, pointing at me Dad and I had fun painting, whilst Mum was into the photography. It was nearly time to set up for performing, so we went to prepare...
"Ladies and Gentlemen... are you enjoying the Wood Wine and Roses Festival?" asked the announcer with his microphone
"Well... it's going get more exciting!"
"We have a family band here from Melbourne to perform songs from their hit debut album."
"Please welcome the 'Bontel Family' band!"
"Hello Heywood."
"We hope that you are all having a good time at the 'Wood Wine and Roses' festival?"
"We are going to perform some of our tracks from our current album charting right now in Australia and overseas."
"After our performance is finished, we will be happy to sign autographs for you and have a chat too!"
"Are you ready to have some fun?" I asked the crowd
"YES!" the crowd responded loudly
We played our set and the crowd were involved, dancing and having fun to the music. Some of the people knew some of the songs and sang along with us, which made for a happy party atmosphere!
"Well that was fun wasn't it?" I asked, at the end of our performance
"Yes!" shouted the crowd, clapping
"Before we get to the autographs... I see Mum and Dad have something they want to give me."
Mum and Dad walk over to me and hand me a can...before walking back to their instruments...I open the can and out springs a coiled rubber snake.
"Aah!"
"Bleep bleep bleep!" I shriek, as the audience bursts into laughter
Mum and Dad are giggling in the corner like a couple of naughty school kids, they emerge from the corner with big grins on their faces. They have finally got me back after all the counter-pranks I've played on them... I really didn't see that one coming!
"You got me with that one!"
"After all the pranks I've played on you two lately... I should have expected that!"
"Well done." I said, with a grimace
"We sure did Cassie!"
"Your reaction was priceless!"
"The look on your face was hilarious!" said Dad, wiping the tears from the corner of his eyes
Everyone else was laughing at me too!
"I shall have to get you two back for that!" I threaten
"That's how you got into this in the first place... remember!" said Mum, shaking her finger at me
"Let's go sign some autographs." laughs Mum

# Chapter Forty-Three
## 'Tubing' at Bridgewater Lakes

"Come on... we are going to Bridgewater Lakes today!"
It's going to be such a great spot...I can tell it is going to be a hot day today! We are going to have an awesome and thrilling time... I am feeling excited that I'm going to be trying a new activity! I am less nervous and more confident these days...I'm ready to give it a go! Today we are going to use a rubber round tube... pulled behind a boat... to bounce along on top of the water. We're going to call Zoe and her family to see if they can meet us there for some wicked fun!

'Hello Mikayla.' said Zoe, on the speakerphone
'It is a lovely day isn't it?'
"Hello Zoe." Mum replied
"Yes, it is."
"Would you like to meet us at Bridgewater Lakes today...for some boat... rubber tubes... and water fun!"
'Yes... we would that!'
'Our boat is ready and Ivy and Nina are blowing air into the tubes.'
'George is about to help Peter put the boat onto the boat trailer and attach it to the back of George's car.'
'We will bring some food and meet you in a couple of hours.'
"Great."
"We'll see you then."
"Cassie we're going to have a blast at Bridgewater Lakes... having a go on the round rubber tube is so much fun!" laughed Mum
"I'm ready to have a go... you may hear me laugh out loud... as I bounce up and down." I grinned
"That would be good to hear!"
"Today is going to be loads of fun!" said Dad
We arrived at Bridgewater Lakes just as Zoe and her family were pulling up too.
"Hi."
"We've got the boat and the tubes ready for some water thrills." laughs Zoe
"Hello."
"We are keen to get started... especially Cassie." Mum smiled
"I sure am!"
"I'm no longer frightened...I'm ready to have a blast... riding along the water!" I said, in a sing-song voice
"Good on you Cassie."

"Zoe and I, are going to tow the boat into the water, then Nina, Ivy and George are going to tie the rubber tube to the boat with the rope and it will be ready for us to begin." said Peter

"Can I help out with the rope?"

"I've been taught to tie various things and I'm good at knots." I said

"Of course, Cassie."

"An extra pair of hands would be a great help." said Nina

"We'll bring the tube to the water and you can help us tie the rope to it and then onto the boat." said Ivy

"I'll help you with it, Cassie." George said

After we all got changed into our bathers... Zoe and Peter towed the boat into the water... then Ivy and Nina brought the round rubber tube to the water... and George and I tied one end to the tube... and the other end to the boat.

"Great job, Cassie!"

"Your rope skills are very good." said George

"Thanks George."

"Now that's all done... who's going first?" asked Zoe

"I would like to go first Zoe."

"I'm ready for it!" I said, eagerly

"Good Cassie."

"Hop into the tube and hold on tight."

"It's all right if you fall off... it's all part of the fun...just be safe." said Peter

I sat in the round rubber tube and put my hands out on either side of it and gripped tightly.

"Are you ready Cassie?" asked Zoe

"I am ready for a bouncing... Zoe!" I said, excitedly

Zoe turned the ignition on and revved the engine up... then away sped the boat with me bouncing behind in the rubber tube! I was laughing out loud and trying to hang on the whole time... I was speeding along on top of the water. Zoe and Peter knew I was enjoying myself and so did Mum... Dad... Ivy... Nina... and George... when they heard me squealing with delight!

I managed not to fall off and Mum was up next. I boarded the boat and Zoe and Peter showed me the controls. I would need to get a boat driver's licence before I would be allowed to take control of the boat. Maybe that could be a goal in a few years' time! I shouted to Mum above the noise of the boat engine

"I've had a blast!"

"You look like you are having a great time too!"

"I am!"

"You feel the adrenaline pumping with the speed of the boat!" Mum shouts back excitedly

Everyone had a go and we rolled around with laughter when Ivy and Nina fell off the tubing. It was brilliant having a go, I enjoyed the rush of speeding on the water so much. This is definitely not going to be the last time I try this... now I know how much fun it is! We had certainly used up lots of adrenaline and energy with that activity.... now comes the food!

"How was your ride on the tube Cassie?"

"Did you enjoy it?" asked Dad

"Did I ever!"

"It was brilliant Dad!"

"It's of the best activities I've ever done!"

"I enjoyed it with everyone."

"I felt the sensation of the boat and the water speeding by... I imagined myself going over a waterfall... then landing in the bottom of it." I said, cheerfully

"That's great Cassie!"

"Now you will be able to do it each time we go."

"I can't wait and maybe I can learn how to drive the boat in a few years and get my boat driver's licence!"

"I could wear a boat captain's cap and steer through the water on a sunny day with the seagulls flying around up above." I said

"I bet you would."

"One of us can be your first mate!"

"All you need is a parrot on your shoulder... it would be a great look for you." Ivy smiled

"Captain Cassie ahoy!" I joked

We all started chatting about our trip, getting caught up with what everybody has been doing lately.

"At the recent concert in Adelaide, we were to perform as the 'Bontel Family' but the car broke down on our way to the hall... leaving Cassie on her own to hold down the fort... until we could get there after our car was repaired." Mum said

"Oh dear."

"What happened?" said George

"Cassie was all ready to go on stage when it happened... she was a little nervous as she had never done a solo performance before...she held the fort and everything went brilliantly for her." said Dad, proudly

"I wowed the audience with my Scandinavian inspired tunes... they loved them."

"I wrote all the songs myself... I loved performing them for the audience." I told them

"That must've been a wicked performance Cassie!"

"You could release them for your debut album in Australia... Europe... Scandinavia... and Asia." said Nina

"I might do that one day... it's a long way off yet though."

"I'll give you a copy each when it gets released." I said, cheekily

"We had a ten-pin bowling contest against each other in Mount Gambier, we played two games."

"Cassie won the first game and I won the second."

"We got active and had fun together as a family as we often do." said Mum

"We hear that Cassie is becoming very good at bowling."

"What is your secret?" Peter asked me

"It just takes practice and persistence... with Mum and Dad's help...using all my skills to play the game well."

"That's what paid off for me!" I said

"It certainly did!" said Dad

"You are having an adventurous time also gaining more fans along the way!" laughed Zoe

"We've started charting higher than 'Quirky Service' in most of the countries!"

"Our self-titled debut album has been knocking them off the top of some music charts."

"It surprised them all right." said Mum, giggling

"I bet they're planning to get you three back for that!" said George, with a smile

"You can bet they are!"

"We don't know what they had planned for us...we had a counter plan and foiled them!"

"They weren't expecting that." I chuckled

"We got them lost in the Adelaide Maze." Dad said, winking

We relaxed on our towels in the sun Nina... Ivy... George... and I reading our books... whilst Mum... Dad... Zoe... and Peter...were resting. It was a great view of the big lake stretching out in front of us as far as we could see, the weather was sunny and bright.

What a great day for relaxing after all that thrilling excitement out on the lake before.

"Cassie, I remember how much you loved the 'Twilight' books that I gave you on your fourteenth birthday!"

"I got my first one when I was fourteen... and over the next three years I received another on each of my fifteenth... sixteenth... and seventeenth birthdays."

"I enjoyed reading them after a long day of work or during our family summer vacations when we went to relaxing locations like this one."

"Ivy enjoyed reading them as much as me." Nina laughed

"You two do love your 'Twilight' as much as I do... that's for sure."

"I was delighted when you gave them to me...I get lost in their fantasy world every time I read them."

"I haven't seen the films yet... because they would likely frighten and overwhelm me."

"I usually take one or two books along with me... whenever we go on holiday."

"You also loved the albums we gave you on your sixteenth birthday too... 'Twilight to Twilight Eclipse'."

"What do you visualise when you listen to them?" Nina asked

"Every time I listen to the music... I visualise myself in a bright light forest... walking through it and listening to the lovely sounds of the beautiful creatures."

"Then when I leave the forest... I walk in to a small, quiet American coastal town...make my way to the beach... where I relax on a towel on the sand... with all of the forest creatures gathered around me watching the waves."

"Nina and I imagine similar places when we listen to the music as well."

"We know your seventeenth birthday is a couple of months off yet... but would you like the first three 'Twilight' CD's for your birthday?" asked Ivy

"Oh, Yes please!"

"That will be something delightful to look forward to."

Later, Ivy, Nina and George were busy...I took the opportunity to play yet another prank on those three! With a mischievous twinkle in my eyes I found their bags and switched all their iPhones over! I put Ivy's in George's bag... George's in Nina's bag... and Nina's in Ivy's bag... trying hard not to giggle out loud. Zoe... Peter... Mum... and Dad... saw me do it but they kept quiet. When I put Nina's iPhone in Ivy's bag... I saw Nina, Ivy and George coming so I hid behind the bushes.

Nina, Ivy and George decided to listen to music on their iPhones. George noticed something was up when he got out Ivy's iPhone instead of his.

"Ivy... how come your iPhone is in my bag?" George asked

"I don't know George."

"I didn't put it there!" said Ivy, shrugging her shoulders

"George... your iPhone is in my bag!" said Nina, looking puzzled

"I didn't put it there!"

"I don't know how it got there." said George, in an exasperated voice

"Nina... what is your iPhone doing in my bag?" asked Ivy, frowning

"I don't know!"

"Someone must've done it while we were away from our bags."

"Who could that be?" said Nina, suspiciously

They heard a muffled giggle but as I was well camouflaged, they couldn't work out where I was hidden.

"We know that giggle!"

"Where is it coming from?" Ivy asked

"Girls... I've got a plan to get her back."

"We'll go somewhere else for now and when she comes out to lie on her towel... Ivy... you and I will tickle her toes... and Nina you tickle her under the arms."

"We'll need some long feathers for this one!" said George

"Great idea... George!"

"We will make the 'giggler' pay... soon enough." chuckled Nina, with a sneaky grin

Nina, Ivy and George left, I emerged from the bushes and lay down on my towel. I put on my black sunglasses, and set out to kick back and chill for the afternoon. Ivy and George crept up to my feet without me knowing, feathers in hand, ready. They crawled on their hands and knees till they were in position and then began tickling my feet all over with the feathers.

Hee hee hee hee

"Who's tickling my feet?"

"That really tickles!"

"Stop it!"

"Ha ha ha ha." I laughed

I couldn't get my feet away because I was laughing hysterically by this time... then Nina dived in... and began tickling me under the arms.

Ha ha ha

"Who's that?"

Hee hee hee hee

"Uncle."

"I give up!"

I curled up into a ball so that Nina couldn't get any more access to my armpits! A couple of minutes went by before I was sufficiently recovered enough to sit up, take off my sunglasses and find out the culprits!

"I should've known it was you THREE all along!" I said, glaring at Nina, George and Ivy

"You got me that time!"

Hey... is that feathers you two were using to tickle me?" I asked

"Err...."

"What feathers." said George

"The feathers you are trying to hide behind your back!"

"Hand them over!" I held out my hand

Ivy and George handed over their feathers and I put them in a pocket in my bag.

"I confess it was me that switched your iPhones." I smiled, naughtily

"Well... we are even now!" laughed George, Ivy and Nina together

After our pranking, we climbed up a steep slope fifty metres to the Tarragal Limestone Caves, which overlook the Bridgewater Lakes. It took us some time but the view across Discovery Bay was excellent once we reached the top. The views were so good that we took several photographs to send to our family.

Views like this relax and soothe me. When I daydream, I can visualise myself relaxing on a luxury boat in blue bathers and black sunglasses... holding a lemonade glass in my right hand... being tended to by butlers in white shirts and black pants... sailing around European waters winking at the locals... viewing brilliant scenes of European cities and the countryside.

"It's a fantasy dream of mine and one I plan to make come true, eventually!" I said

We all chuckled at my fantasy dream... even me.

"Cassie, that fantasy dream of yours is so funny." Mum, laughed

"We can imagine you doing those things." said Dad, chuckling

"That's hilarious... a fantasy cruise around Europe... with two butlers!"

"You are a scream Cassie." laughed Nina, as we waved goodbye after a great day

"Portland is going to be a fun place to stay for a week."

"The city is the oldest European settlement and its most noted resident was a whaler named William Dutton." I said, reading my book as we drove to Portland

"It was around the time the Henty clan arrived and Dutton provided seed potatoes for their gardens."

"We can learn more about that whilst we are there."

"We sure can."

"You have been learning lots about Australia on this road trip."

"You are excelling at the Australian Trivia questions...you know the answers without needing to look them up on the Internet."

"You're doing so well... with two more states to go." Mum said, proudly

"Our family has been to Portland many times."

"You're going to enjoy Portland... Cassie."

"The locals are friendly and will help us if we need some information." said Dad

We looked at the accommodation listings for Portland and there were quite a few. These included Quality Hotel Bentinck... Clifftop Accommodation Portland... Seascape Accommodation... and the Whalers Rest Motor Inn.

After looking at the options, we decided to have a few days at Quality Hotel Bentinck and also Seascape Accommodation. We might also stay for a couple of days at Victoria House as well.

Quality Hotel Bentinck is a Victorian-styled hotel dating from 1855... it is situated twelve kilometres from Cape Nelson Lighthouse... and fifteen kilometres from Bridgewater Bay.

"Good morning Bontel Family."

"Welcome to the Quality Hotel Bentinck."

"We've got Wi-Fi... flat-screen TV's... and minibars."

"Most of our rooms here offer ocean views of Portland... and since you upgraded your room options... you get a sitting area and a whirlpool bath... which you can relax in."

"There is an exercise and fitness room... plus a second room for playing pool in."

"I hope you enjoy your stay." the receptionist said, as she handed us the keys to our rooms

"Thank you." Mum replied, as she took the keys

Our room has a seaside feel...just like Portland! The fitness room looks ideal for a bit of exercise whilst we are here, and maybe we can play a game of pool tonight after dinner.

"This is a great room."

"I have the 'beachy' feel that you get when you are in your favourite seaside town... or getting close to the sea in your car... on the way to your summer vacation... or a day at the beach!"

"That's a great description Cassie."

"Mum and I know the feeling you mean."

"The restaurant will be a good place to eat, and then we can have a game of pool afterwards before we turn in for the night." said Dad

The next day dawns bright and clear. Today is going to be such a hot day... a day like today is a... 'going to the beach' kind of day... relaxing on the sand... or in the sea. All we need is sunscreen and nice big hats and we will be set!

Mum calls Jessica to see if she is available to meet us at Nun's Beach for a few hours of kayaking and swimming. We have done that several times with Zoe and her family... now it's Jessica's turn!

'Hello Mikayla.' Jessica's voice floats over the speakerphone

'It's such a hot day already where we are.'

"Hello Jessica." Mum replies

"It is a hot day in Portland too!"

"Where are you staying?" I heard Mum ask

'We are on holiday in Port Fairy for six days...we're trying a few fun activities.'

'We're having a good time here.' answered Jessica

"We're also having a good time in Portland!"

"We're planning to go to Nun's Beach to do some swimming and probably some kayaking if you are available to meet up with us?" Mum said

'That sounds like a good place to spend a few hours...we've got our kayaks, oars and bathers... so we can come to meet you.' Jessica said, enthusiastically

"We'll get fish and chips for us all for lunch when you get here." Mum said

"I know what I am going to have...two fish cakes...chips...and two calamari rings."

"I'm going to have...two crab sticks...chips... and three dim sims." said Dad

"I'm having a hamburger with the lot... two fish cakes... two calamari rings...and chips." I piped up

"You must be very hungry!" laughed Jessica

'I'm always hungry!' I said, laughing too

"See you soon."

'See you.'

"Bye."

We changed into our bathers got our books and drove to the beach near the Maritime Museum. We didn't take any beach chairs with us we had big towels to sit on. After we had been there a while... Mum took the car to the local fish and chip shop and ordered up the family feast fish and chip lunch... it would take some time for the order to be cooked and wrapped!

The Smith family arrived a while later, they too had their bathers on. Jessica's siblings... were Jacinta and Joseph... Jason's siblings were Oliver and Felicity... who both had Savant Syndrome. Jessica's parents Josephine and John... were joined by Jason's parents Ruth and Paul... they arrived with their kayaks... oars... and beach chairs.

Then a cheer went up as Mum arrived back with the fish and chips lunch!

We all helped to set up an area for the lunch to be spread out and the hot 'fishy' parcels to be opened up. Everyone descended upon the parcels of hot food like a flock of 'scavenging seagulls' at the beach! There was lots of laughter as we all tried to eat 'too hot' chips and chase it down with cold lemonade to soothe our burnt tongues!

This is going to be an afternoon full of fun.

"Portland looks like a nice place."

"How are you three enjoying it?" asked Jessica

"We've tried a few activities... the restaurant at Quality Bentinck Hotel is a good place to eat too." said Mum

"We recommend the Fern Restaurant at Port Fairy if you go there."

"It's got great modern Australian family fare...the venue is vintage style."

"We like to have a surf every now and then in the hot weather... as well as kayaking." said Jason

"We went surfing on Fitzroy Island... it was my first time." I responded
"Mum and Dad taught me the basics... I had a good time... despite falling off several times!"
"That's great!"
"Mum and Dad taught us when we were ten and eight."
"We practiced once a week at a Melbourne Beach, eventually we got good at it."
"You might become as good as us if you practice hard enough." said Zara
"I tried kayaking for the first time too!"
"It was good seeing Echuca's landscape as I paddled my kayak with Mum and Dad."
"It was embarrassing when we fell out of the kayak...it was caused by the waves made by a Polycraft Centre Console boat...we laugh about it now." I smiled
"We tried kayaking at Queenscliff one time... when Zara and I were fifteen and thirteen... we were paddling along when a big wave caused us to fall in to the water... fortunately we had our life jackets on."
Mum and Dad laughed at us... initially it was embarrassing...we saw the funny side later on." said Melinda
"There will be no boats to cause waves here and the ocean looks calm enough to kayak." I said
"Jessica loves kayaking... whenever we go camping, we pack our kayak... we kayak with her and we always wear our life jackets and observe the sights around us... whilst teaching her all about the history and nature of the places we camp at." said Josephine
"We do the same with Jason."
"He kayaks occasionally with Oliver and Felicity... we can hear them talking and laughing...it's good for them to try different activities." said Ruth
"Cassie, we heard you gave kayaking a try for the first time... while camping in Echuca."
"That's great!"
"You can observe nature and have fun at the same time." said Jacinta
"You sure can, Jacinta."
"We fell out when the Polycraft Console Boat sped past us... it was a bit embarrassing... but nobody hurt themselves so it was ok." I finished
"It was funny when we heard that."
"Similar things have happened to us a few times...we just laugh it off."
"I can see you're enjoying Portland."
"It's a lovely town with plenty to do." said Oliver
"It is."
"I am loving it already."
"The beach is our favourite place too."
"We go there each summer... we play volleyball and beach cricket... it's fun playing together as a family." said John
"Occasionally we surf... we fall off sometimes but we always get back on again!"
"We wear wetsuits in the surf... and we 'LOVE' having fish and chips afterwards!"
"Who doesn't!" said Zara, grinning
"Let's try some kayaking and swimming right now!" said Melinda
Melinda and Jessica went in one kayak and Dad and Jason went in the other.
Zara got on her paddleboard and moved the board through the water, with the oar. She looks like a real professional... looking good Zara!

# Chapter Forty-Four
## Cooling Down & Cat Rescue

Then my iPhone rang, it was Jim. I switched him to speakerphone mode so that it was easier to speak to him.

"Hello Jim."

'Hello Cassie.'

'I'm keeping cool with Maria inside our house.'

'It is a hot day today... we've got the fan on to cool us down.'

"That sounds good."

"Well we are having fun in Portland... kayaking and swimming!"

"It's a great way to cool down... I'm relaxing on a big towel like a model does!"

Jim chuckled.

'Your Mum must have given you that cheeky idea, did she?'

'Your Mum's a cheeky bugger!'

Mum laughed.

"I heard that!"

"Mum is always a good role model, but she's a funny one as well."

'She sure is!'

'I heard you have been learning to surf on Fitzroy Island.'

'Well done for trying something new.'

'I'm happy for you.'

"Thanks."

"I might become good at it if I keep trying."

"Maybe I might become the next Layne Beachley!" I said, laughing

'You're becoming quite the pop star grand-daughter from what I've heard.'

'You might be able to record one of my favourite classic songs.'

"Maybe... but I'll add my own dance-pop twist to it as well." I said

'I can't wait to hear that!'

"I'll have to go now."

"I'm due to have a paddle on the board."

"Zara, one of my friends will teach me how to do it."

"The local boys might give me a wolf-whistle!"

'Even though I wolf-whistled Maria when I first met her when she was swimming at

Melbourne Beach… I thought she was what 'you, young people' call 'hot' these days… I would not be happy with my granddaughter of sixteen… being wolf whistled at by a bunch of boys… Cassie!'

"Eew!"

"Not in front of Mum with the 'hot' reference to grandmother please!"

"Grandad how come it was all right for you to wolf whistle grandmother all those years ago…but it's not all right for the guys to whistle at me on the beach today?"

Mum laughed.

"I think she has you there Jim!"

"This might be a topic of discussion for another time Cassie."

'Sorry about the Nan story Cassie… I think I will leave all further explanations to your Mother.' said Jim, hastily

"Err…OK Grandad."

"Moving right along, I'm off to get a board and have a paddle."

"Bye."

'Bye Cassie.'

Ten minutes later Mum and Dad got in the kayak… I went over to the board where Zara was going to teach me to paddle with an oar.

"Cassie this is how you do it."

"You get an oar and stand up on the surfboard."

"You put the oar out like this and paddle just like you were paddling in a kayak." said Zara, demonstrating

I tried to copy the steps as Zara had showed me…I was nervous… it wasn't easy to do what she had demonstrated.

"It's okay Cassie."

"It takes some practice…you can do it."

"I'll help you." said Zara

I stood up on the paddleboard and Zara handed me the oar carefully, I shook a little but I steadied myself and used the oar to paddle a couple of metres.

"That's the way Cassie."

"You're doing great."

"Daniel and Mikayla have started paddling out… so see if you can catch up to them as close as you can… don't go too far out…be careful not to crash into anything." said Zara

"I will be careful Zara."

"I'll try to keep steady as I go." I said

I started paddling out, taking my time to look around Portland. I saw the Maritime Museum and the Portland Pier, I glanced at the fisheries hauling their load of silver fish on to a table, and looked to my right to see a couple of families going into the Maritime Museum. I have a great view of this area of Portland on my paddleboard, and the environment is lovely. Everyone was amazed at how well I was doing paddling on the paddleboard and happy to see me giving it a go.

"You're doing so well with that Cassie"

"Zara must've taught you well." said John

"She certainly did."

"I've seen her doing it before… but I was too shy to try it."

"Now I am enjoying it."

Mum and Dad were coming towards me and I began to plan a trick on them with a big grin on my face....
'*When they come near, I can tip them out of the kayak with my paddle, it's going to take a bit of strength but I'll put a bit of muscle into it...*' I was thinking.

When Mum and Dad came close enough, I put the tip of my oar in the kayak and flipped them over 'splosh' I laughed and paddled away. Jessica... Zara... Melinda... and Jason... were also laughing... so were Jacinta... Josephine... John... Oliver... Felicity... Ruth... and Paul. In fact, everyone was laughing... except Mum and Dad who came up spluttering!

"Did you have a nice swim!" I shouted, cheekily

"Glub." said Mum

"Phew." said Dad

"You are going to get it now." laughed everyone

I paddled for several more minutes, while Mum and Dad got back in the kayak. They planned to get me back for my prank...they came up beside me... slipped out quietly on the other side and started swimming to my right side. I heard them swimming and carefully stepped into their kayak...I took one of their oars and paddled back to shore. When Mum and Dad arrived at the right side of the paddleboard... (where I should have been) ... and tipped the board over saying...

"Ah, ha... got you... Cassie!"

I wasn't there.

"Huh?"

"Where is she?"

"She was there a moment ago." said Dad, puzzled

"Hey!"

"Where's our kayak?"

"It was here two minutes ago." said Mum

Mum and Dad turned and saw me paddling off towards the shore. They were very surprised to say the least!

"Cassie Annabelle Bontel!"

"Come back here with our kayak!" said Mum

"Nope!"

"It's already booked five minutes ago... and it's full to the brim!"

"See you... suckers!" I laughed, sticking my tongue out and blowing a raspberry

"She got us again!"

"How does she do that?" Dad mumbled

"Because... she is a little devil!"

"She may look like an angel... but underneath that smile... she is naughty!" Mum muttered

I parked the kayak on the shore and pulled it up on the sand... so that it doesn't float out to sea again... I walked back to my towel.

"That was hilarious Cassie!"

"You were very sneaky there." said Melinda, impressed

"Very funny." said Zara

"It sure was!"

"Mum and Dad tried to prank me...I foiled them once again!"

"They didn't expect the double round I pulled on them." I said, high-fiving Zara and Melinda

"Daniel and Mikayla have taught you well...they were out-pranked with that one!" laughed Jessica

"You are quite the practical joker!" said Jason, admiringly
"I'm too fast for them." I bragged
"You may be the practical joker Cassie... but you had better watch out now!"
"If I know Daniel and Mikayla... they are not going to let you get away with that for too long!" said Oliver
Mum and Dad came up to us... they were dripping sea water everywhere.
"Cassie you just wait." said Mum, growling
I just laughed.
"So... you think that's funny... do you?"
"We'll see who is laughing soon." said Dad, ominously
I sniggered out loud.

After kayaking and paddle boarding, we were all getting peckish we decided to get some snacks. We went to Portland IGA and chose Doritos... Cadbury white chocolate... Shapes... and Sunkist...then we all sat down and chatted.

"Since we saw you last when we helped to put the tyre back on your car, how's your road trip been progressing?" asked Jason
"Very well."
"We've just travelled back from South Australia into Victoria... Portland is the one of several stops we plan to make."
"We've got lots of activities planned... and several performances as well." said Dad
"Do you have a performance planned for Portland?"
"We were planning to go back to Port Fairy sometime tomorrow... but we can go later in the day... if you do." said Jessica
"We do have one planned for tomorrow."
"You can come along if you would like to."
"Friends are always welcome at our concerts."
"We would appreciate that." said Mum
"Cassie... you are a star and your voice sounds lovely."
"You are becoming popular as a favourite female artist!" said Melinda
"I have gained more recognition since we formed the 'Bontel Family' band."
"I love to sign autograph books for my fans after the concerts... it's fun to chat with them too."
"You might get do to more solo performances."
"We heard you did very well in Adelaide." said Zara
"I haven't released a solo album yet...I shall sometime." I replied
"We'll buy that when it gets released!"
"We love hearing your voice... it brightens up the day." said Joseph
"Thanks Joseph."
"I'm quite proud of how our album is doing on the music charts." I said, as we waved goodbye

Back at our accommodation I volunteered to make Mum and Dad a cup of tea. I filled the kettle with cold water. Whilst I was waiting for the kettle to boil, a big grin slowly spread across my face. I'm up to mischief again. This prank involves Mum... Dad... salt... and tea! It's going to be so funny when they try their tea. When the kettle had boiled... I poured the water in the cups... added the salt... and handed them to Mum and Dad.

"Thanks darling."
"We'll enjoy our tea." Dad said, as he took the cup

"I'll be in the bathroom brushing my hair if you need me." I said, beating a hasty retreat
Mum and Dad sipped their tea and both spat it out together!"
"PFFT! EW!
"There is salt in this tea!" said Mum disgusted
"Yuck!"
"This tea tastes awful!!" Dad yells
I let out a loud laugh.
"Cassie Annabelle Bontel!"
"Come out right now!" Mum ordered
I knew I was in trouble so I exited the bathroom wearing a 'sheepish' grin.
"Cassie you put salt in our tea instead of sugar." Dad stated
"Err...I... did not." I said, faintly
"You're telling us a 'porky' Cassie!"
"Anyone can tell by the look on your face!" said Mum, glaring at me crossly
"Surely... I can get away with it... Dad." I said, grinning and giving him my cutest look
"Don't you play cute with me... Cassie!"
"I'm not falling for it!" said Dad crossly, though I noticed he was struggling to keep a straight face
"OK."
"I did put salt in your tea instead of sugar."
"You were my inspiration for that trick Mum!"
"You played it on your family... for many years." I said
"Yes... I tried that trick with Rebecca... when I was five."
"Most of the time we got away with it."
"Right!" said Dad, in a firm voice
"It's now time for you to go and make a proper cup of tea for your Mother and I... with sugar... not salt... Cassie!"
"Yes... Dad." I said, as I made my way to the kitchen and put the kettle back on to boil.

After an hour of watching the comedy channel, I went for a bath in the whirlpool bathtub. It feels good when I'm in the water, I love relaxing in the bath. I practice my singing, taking care not to overdo it. We've got an upcoming performance so I'd better save my voice for the concert.

In the morning I was talking to Dad.

"Why don't we sit out on the private balcony... whilst we wait for our gourmet breakfast to arrive?"

"We might see a whale or dolphin if we are lucky... it'll be a delight to see one if it emerges from under the water." I commented

"Good idea Cassie." said Dad

"We've got a performance this afternoon at one...let's do some things this morning before we need to get ready for the concert."

"Let's go and see the Maritime Museum... before we have a light lunch."

We had our breakfast, which included pancakes and watched the views and the sun rising over Portland bay. It was a magnificent sunrise and I was feeling happy seeing the ocean. What a picturesque scene, it would make a great picture for me to draw.

A short time later, we made our way to the Portland Maritime Museum. Built in 1998 it has a Visitor Information Centre and a Maritime Museum.

There are permanent displays everywhere we look, documenting Portland's rich maritime history... including whaling... ship wrecks... rescue... navigation... and the local fishing industry.

The centrepiece of the Maritime Museum is the 1858 Portland Lifeboat... in 1859 it became famous for rescuing the 'Admella'... it is one of the oldest remaining unrestored intact vessels in Australia... and possibly the world!

We looked over the photographs... technical instruments... diving equipment... and maritime tools... and we found out much more about Portland's history.

The 'Admella' was a steam ship travelling from Adelaide to Melbourne...it struck Carpenter Rocks off the South Australian coastline... altogether eighty-nine people perished... including many children.

The vessel was two kilometres from shore with people clinging to the wreckage for their lives... no vessel could reach them because of the treacherous reef... horrendous weather... and high seas. Despite being pummelled by massive waves for eight days... a handful of people managed to survive. The Portland lifeboat was eventually towed to the scene where the Captain and his crew rescued the final nineteen Admella survivors... in heroic circumstances.

Fawthrop and his men navigated their boat through the reef and waves... during the rescue they sustained injuries...losing many oars and the boat's rudder...somehow, they managed to push on. For their bravery... each lifeboat crew member was presented with an 'Admella' Commission Medal... a Board of Trade medal... and cash bonuses... their names were etched onto to a brass plaque that is next to the lifeboat.

What brave men they were and what a heroic rescue effort indeed!

We asked a couple of volunteers about Portland's maritime history and they were more than happy to tell us about it. We finished off our visit by looking at the skeleton of a fourteen-metre sperm whale! It looked a bit 'creepy' to Mum and I.

We picked up some brochures at the Visitor Information Centre of different destinations in Victoria... that we are going to visit.

We went to the Harbour Lights café for a light lunch before we walked to the hill near the Portland Foreshore where we have a truck set up as a music stage... it has all our instruments arranged and ready for us to perform. I can't wait to see how the Portland audiences react to our music I hope it goes well! It may be a small audience...we don't mind that...we just love performing!

The MC introduces us as we walk onto the stage area... there are several people sitting on the grass and some market stalls dotted around... with jewellery... books... and snacks... there is a van selling flavoured liquorice.

"Hello Portland!"

"What a lovely day to be out and about in the sunshine... enjoying yourselves on the foreshore."

"We hope to add to your enjoyment now with our musical performance!"

"We will be playing songs for you from our self-titled debut album."

"Are you ready to sing along and have a dance?" I asked

"YES!" said the audience

"Let's go then!" I called out happily

Much later that afternoon... we were strolling along the sandy beach as we made our way back to our car when a young man came up to us... by the 'panicked' look on his face... he was in some sort of trouble.

"Can you help me please?" asked the man

"Of course, we can."

"What do you want us to help you with?" I asked

"My cat is stuck up a nearby tree in Bentinck Street it's too tall for me to climb up."

"If you three can help me to get him down I would be so glad." said the man

"We can try." said Dad

We followed him to where he was now standing underneath a large tree. We looked up at the tree and I was thinking... *'Wow, that's one tall tree for a cat to climb up...I wonder how it got stuck?'*

"My cat's name is Jared he is quite high up."

"I can't climb up there because I get dizzy at that height!" he said

"We'll get Jared down if we can." said Mum

We quickly discussed who was going first.

"I'll go up the tree first."

I've climbed trees to get cats before... I will bring Jared down safely." said Dad, confidently

Dad climbed up the branches and reached out his hand to Jared... but Jared backed away.

"I'm sorry... Jared is too scared to come to me... so I couldn't get him down." said Dad, unhappily

"I'll go up."

"I'm a cat person... I should have no trouble getting Jared down quickly." said Mum

Mum climbed up but when she reached out her hand to Jared... he hissed at her.

"Jared was frightened of me too... I couldn't get him to come down." said Mum, dolefully

"I'll have a go!"

"I'm fit and nimble...I should be able to climb up and get Jared down safely." I said

Mum and Dad didn't look too sure about that. I had never climbed up a tree that high before and they were concerned that I would get hurt. Mum put her hands on my shoulders with a worried look on her face.

"Are you sure you can do it Cassie?"

"We don't want you falling out of the tree and hurting yourself."

"It would be dreadful if that were to happen." Mum said, in a squeaky voice

"You might get scared, and be too frightened to move up there."

"We might have to call the fire brigade and get the two of you down!"

"It could be an anxious time for you darling!" said Dad, who was secretly thinking it would definitely be an anxious time for him and Mum on the ground watching!

"Mum!"

"Dad!"

"There's no need to call the fire brigade just yet!"

"I won't fall out of the tree and injure myself."

"I promise I'll be very careful, and I will get Jared down safely without him scratching me." I said

"I can't watch!" said Mum, letting go of my shoulders

I began to climb carefully up the tree... one branch at a time... I was nervously thinking... *'Ooh, it's a long way up and to tell the truth I feel a bit shaky, but I want to rescue poor Jared, he must be scared too, if I can't manage it then we will have to call the fire brigade in.'*

I managed to reach the branch were Jared is hanging on, I hold out my hand and gently talk to Jared in a soft, soothing voice, trying to coax him towards me. I do hope he doesn't fall off!

"Puss, puss, puss." I say softly, with my fingers outstretched towards him

"Here Jared."

"Here kitty, kitty."

"Come on don't be afraid."

"I am here to rescue you... you'll be alright and safe with me." I say sweetly

Jared hesitated for a few seconds, before steadily walking towards me. I gently tuck him inside my clothing, so that I can use my hands for climbing down the tree again. Getting down with the cat tucked inside my clothing as well... is much more difficult than climbing up the tree freely.

I gingerly begin the climb down... navigating every branch and avoiding the pesky twigs that are sticking out... Jared is wriggling inside my jumper... I don't want him to drop out now! That would be dreadful! Mum still can't watch, and Dad is peeking through his fingers! It seems to take me forever till I finally reach the ground again. Jared didn't really seem to appreciate that he was on 'terra firma' once more... he was obviously only interested in getting out of the confinement of my jumper... as he squirmed and wriggled to make his escape!

"Thank you so much Cassie... for saving Jared."

"Here is Jared... safe in your loving arms again." I said, as I extracted him from under my jumper and handed him to his anxious owner

"What's your name?" I asked

"Jonathon." he replied

"I'm guessing he was chased by a dog... based on how high he travelled up the tree?" Mum mused

"He was."

"I was tending to my garden when my neighbour's dog came in and scared Jared... he chased him up that tree."

"We're glad Jared is back with you... safe and sound." said Dad

"I must feed Jared after his scare... then let him get some rest on his pet bed after all that excitement!"

"Goodbye and thank you so much."

"Goodbye." we waved

The 'Portland Observer' got to hear of the cat rescue and called us up for an interview. We spoke to the news reporter from the paper, whose name was Mick.

"Bontel Family what a great rescue effort!"

"Cassie what you were thinking when you climbed that tree to rescue Jared?"

"I was thinking that the tree was very tall and I was quite scared...I wanted to save Jared and get him safely back to Jonathon."

"Mikayla... what were you feeling when Cassie was climbing up the tree?"

"I was feeling worried!"

"I couldn't bear to watch the whole event."

"I thought Cassie might fall and injure herself... but she is safe... and I'm happy for her that she saved Jared."

"Daniel, when Cassie made it up the tree to Jared were you hoping that they would get down safely?"

"I was hoping that she would get down intact without hurting herself."

"I couldn't bring myself to watch much either...I peeked out a little through my fingers... I saw Jared move towards Cassie on the branch... I felt relieved when she came down safely.

"Cassie that was an excellent rescue!"

"Dad and I, were worried that you might injure yourself, we're so proud of you for making a brave rescue effort like that." said Mum, hugging me

"You were a little scared...still you managed to remain calm... and we're glad you made it back to the ground safe and sound!" said Dad, happily

"I did what I had to do."

"I would gladly do the same... for any animal in trouble."

"You deserve a reward for your bravery today, Cassie."
"What would you like?" asked Mum
I thought about it for several minutes.
"I choose to have some fun ten-pin bowling when we go to Warrnambool."
"I enjoyed it in Mount Gambier and I would love to do it again!" I said
"That's a good choice Cassie."
"Mum and I, have been bowling champions before, we'll you show you our 'moves' when we go to Warrnambool!" said Dad, grinning

# Chapter Forty-Five
## Adventures in Portland

I woke up to the sound of waves breaking as I rose from my queen-sized bed… it's a good sound to hear in the morning. I drew back the blinds and the sun's rays shone in on me as I took in the panoramic views of Portland Bay. A few early morning risers were up and about walking along the sand… three of them were heading towards Nun's Beach for an early morning swim.

"Morning Mum and Dad."

"I had a good sleep last night and what a great way to wake up in the morning… with the sound of the waves breaking on the sands at Portland."

It's a lovely soothing sound on a summer morning." I said

"We had a good sleep last night too Cassie."

"It feels good with the sun shining on you and the sound of the waves breaking on the shore when you wake up." Dad grinned

"Seeing the beach views when you open the blinds adds delight to your day…especially when you're on holiday." said Mum

Seascape Accommodation Portland gave us panoramic sea views of Portland Bay and its surrounds. We were able to look out on the ocean, ships, and boats in Portland Harbour and at night there was the magnificent Portland night sky and lovely sunsets to see.

We had booked a Queen suite and were making good use of the many features, including modern cooking facilities that we could use whilst we are here.

During our Portland stay, we have been asked to appear at the Portland TAFE campus, to demonstrate to a group of 'Life on Line' students, who are preparing to start Tafe in three weeks' time.

"Hello Bontel Family."

"Welcome to Portland TAFE campus."

"You will be demonstrating how to wash a car for the 'Life on Line' students…they will be arriving in fifteen minutes time."

"Their teacher for the year will be giving instructions to the students on how to wash a car… as you demonstrate for them."

"They will gain new skills as part of their course."

"I hope you have a good time instructing." Said the Tafe receptionist, smiling

"We certainly will."

"Mum and Dad have been working with students with disabilities for many years." I said

We walked to the area where the cars are in the Tafe carpark...one of two Tafe cars are on the lawn nearby. Near the basketball court the cars are ready waiting to be washed. A lady who will be one of the two aides for the 'Life on Line students'... greets us.

"Hello, I am Lisa."

"I am one of aides at Tafe this year... it's nice to see you here Bontel Family." said Lisa

"Hello Lisa."

"Tafe has great courses for students to learn and help them get ready for work." said Mum

"Yes, it's handy place to have."

"Most of the students haven't washed a car before... so you will be their instructors for this session." said Lisa

"We can certainly show them what to do...so they know when they practice on their own later."

"Cassie has been washing our car since she was fourteen... she's become very good at it after we taught her the skills." said Dad

Ten minutes later... the 'Life on Line' students which included two autistic females and two autistic males... arrived. They recognised our faces through our music, they were very happy to see us.

"Hello Bontel Family."

"Welcome to Portland TAFE."

"How are you?" asked the students

"We're very well thank you." said Mum

"Hello Bontel Family."

"I'm Ann, the teacher."

"I am looking forward to the students learning some new skills today." Ann said

"So are we Ann."

"It will be a pleasure to help them do just that!" said Dad

"The Bontel Family will now demonstrate step by step... how to wash a car."

"Listen very carefully... pay attention so you don't miss out on crucial steps you will need to remember."

"I know this task is new to most of you...Daniel, Mikayla and Cassie... will help you out if you have any questions or concerns." said Ann

"This is Daniel, Mikayla and Cassie." she said, introducing us to her class

Mum, Dad and I started following the procedure for washing a car.

I filled the bucket up with the hosepipe.

Then I put the car wash liquid in the bucket to make the soapy liquid to wash the car with.

Mum dipped her sponge into the soapy water and cleaned the left side of the TAFE car.

Dad dipped his sponge in and cleaned the right side, I did the same to the back of the car.

We all cleaned the front of the car together... including the bonnet and the roof...the car was almost done. There was one more thing to do... I took the hose and cleaned all the soap off including the tyres and the car was looking spick and span.

"That is how you wash a car."

"All shiny and new again!" I said

The students were now keen to try...for the next car we had the students working on it... and were pleased to see how much they remembered from the practice lesson.

The 'Life on Line' students will practice on Monday mornings...they will be doing this task during Term One...maybe they will even get to wash the TAFE bus next." said their teacher Ann smiling as we left

Dad and I, are outside our hotel room, whispering to each other. It's Mum's forty-second birthday as well as Rebecca's, (they are twins of course). Dad and I purchased our gifts for Mum in secret.

That way she should have a nice surprise when she wakes up. Rebecca may appear, (she's due to film the twelfth season of her talk show in a few days), this will be a fun day for her and Mum.

"Cassie, we've got Mum's gifts ready to give to her and we've arranged a surprise for her later on in the day."

"It will be a fun day she won't forget." said Dad

"She'll love her surprise and the gifts that we are about to give her."

"We've bought her favourite cake…we won't let her know until dinner tonight."

"That will make another great surprise."

"She will love them all."

"Let's wake her up." I said, excitedly

We went back inside and woke up Mum.

"Do you know whose birthday it is!" I said, with a big grin

"Umm… no."

"Whose is it?" asked Mum

"It's Aunty Rebecca's forty-second birthday today." I said, trying not to giggle

"Aren't you forgetting someone Cassie?" spluttered Mum

"Err… no, I haven't forgotten anyone Mum." I said, giggling

"It's my forty-second birthday too… I think I know when I was born!"

"Nice try sweetie!"

"We are twins remember!" said Mum

"Mum we've got a couple of gifts for you that we thought you might love."

"We hope you do." I said

Mum opened my gift.

"Lovely!"

"A brooch!"

"Thanks for that birthday gift, sweetheart." said Mum

"I'm glad you love it." I said, giving Mum a hug and a kiss

Mum then opened her present from Dad.

"It's Forty-Four Charles Street by Danielle Steele."

"Nice gift!"

"I might spend a few hours reading it on the beach… at home…or on the train."

"Thanks, dear." said Mum

"Enjoy reading it dear… I know you are a Danielle Steele fan!" said Dad, giving Mum a hug and a kiss

"We've planned a surprise for you later in the day, we promise you're going to enjoy it." I said

"I can't wait to see what the surprise is!"

"Cassie and I will cook a delicious birthday breakfast for you." smiled Dad

"Thank you dear… I can't wait." said Mum

Mum settled down to read '44 Charles Street', whilst Dad and I cooked her breakfast of eggs on toast, with bacon on the side. I cook the eggs and Dad starts the bacon. Mum is sure to love her breakfast!

"We need a tray for the breakfast."

"I'll see if I can find one in this kitchen." I said

I looked for a tray in the kitchen of our hotel room…so far I am having no luck.

"Where's a tray when you need one?"
"There doesn't seem to be any trays in these cupboards... ah!"
"I've found one!" I said, pulling a tray from the back of the cupboard
"Good job Cassie!"
"I'll put the breakfast on it and you can carry it to your Mum."
"Be careful though not to drop anything." said Dad
I carried the tray of breakfast and Dad carried the tea.
"Here's your birthday breakfast, Mum."
"Thank you, sweetheart."
"You did a great job of cooking." said Mum
"Here's your morning breakfast tea... darling." said Dad
"Thanks, dear."
"I'll enjoy that... tea always tastes good!"
"Join me for my birthday breakfast?" said Mum
"We would love to Mum!"
We all enjoyed eating eggs on toast with bacon.
When breakfast was finished, we took Mum to the Portland Cable Tram Depot Museum for her surprise.
"Here is your surprise!"
"We are going to ride on a cable tram... across Portland's spectacular foreshore for over seven kilometres... learning about Portland's history along the way." I said
"That will be wonderful!"
"I've never been on a tram before... I'm sure it will be an excellent ride." said Mum, happily
"We've arranged this with the Portland Cable Tram Depot Museum...we can all enjoy our first tram ride together." said Dad
"That's lovely." said Mum
"Hello Mrs Bontel." said the owner
"Daniel and Cassie have arranged this tram ride for you."
"Is it your first time on a tram?"
"Yes... it is."
"I'm keen to try it out...how exciting."
"The views of Portland will be unique from the tram." said Mum, happily
"Well the tram has just pulled up so all aboard and enjoy your ride Mrs Bontel." said the owner, smiling at Mum
Thank you... I will!" Mum replied
Mum, Dad and I, boarded the tram where the tram driver greeted us with a friendly handshake. He looked very nice and the tram has been lovingly restored. The saloon is modified and the grip cars are too. I love it, as it gives me the feeling of being taken back to the days of tram travel... before everyone owned a motor car in Australia.
"Hello and welcome aboard the Portland Tram!"
"Happy birthday Mrs Bontel... my name is Ian." said the tram driver
"Thank you, Ian."
"This is such a lovely tram."
"It takes me back to lovely memories of my young days... such fun." says Mum, reminiscing

"We are going to be exploring Portland's foreshore and learning about Portland's history today... I hope you enjoy the ride." said Ian

"I'm sure I will... it will be fun." Mum smiled

We had a blast riding the Portland Tram! I could see Mum enjoying herself...Dad and I are too...we took a few photos to remember this lovely day... and to show our family and friends what a great tram ride we had.

After our tram experience we went to Harbour Lights to pick up some lunch and took it to eat on the foreshore. Mum's iPhone rang, it was Rebecca ringing to wish her twin a happy forty-second birthday!

"Hello Rebecca... Happy forty-second Birthday to you on this magnificent sunny day!"

'Hello Mikayla, Happy forty-second birthday to you too!'

'I'm having a lovely day.'

'How about you?'

"Yes, I am too."

"We're having lunch in Portland on the foreshore... fish and chips from Harbour Lights!"

"This morning Mum and Dad rang me to wish me a happy birthday just as the sun was shining through my Port Fairy Central Motel bedroom curtains!"

'That's good.'

"Daniel and Cassie had arranged a tram ride on the Portland Cable Tram which was a nice surprise for me!"

"I enjoyed myself and took a few photos... which you might enjoy seeing."

'I know I will.'

'I can't wait to see them.'

'I've bought of a couple of presents for you but I'm keeping my lips sealed until dinner tonight.'

"Can I guess what they are?"

'Nice try cheeky twin sister but I won't tell!'

"Not even..." Mum wheedled down the phone line

'No!'

Dad and I laughed.

'Oh well, two can play at that game dear sister.'

'I've got a couple of presents that I bought for you... but I'm not revealing them either... until we meet up for dinner!'

"Oh ho... I guess I asked for that!"

'Yes, my lips are sealed.'

'I'll let you enjoy your day until we see each other later.'

'It's going to be one fun birthday evening.'

"Daniel and Cassie won't tell me what restaurant they have chosen...except it will be a great place with excellent service."

'I'll see you later then.'

'Bye Kayla.'

"You too Becky...Bye."

"We used to make cakes for each other on our birthdays... they usually included chocolate and lollies... Rebecca included a couple of our 'creations' in her cookbooks." said Mum, laughing

"We enjoyed eating them!"

"We've asked the restaurant that Cassie and I have chosen to make a cake for you and Rebecca."

"We promise you will both love it." said Dad

"I'm very tempted to find out what kind of cake it will be." said Mum, licking her lips in anticipation.

Later that evening, we were getting ready for Mum's birthday dinner. I was ready in my blue dress and bangle… Dad was also ready in his green suit and tie… when Mum entered the room… Wowee! Mum looks beautiful in her sparkly yellow dress…her diamond ring… and shiny necklace… she could be a model in a celebrity magazine!

"Wow!"

"Mum!"

"You look like a hot model in a celeb mag." I said

"That's me!" said Mum, with a big grin

"Dear… you look beautiful… just like you were when we got married in 1990!"

"You are still as pretty today." said Dad

"Thank you dear." said Mum, smiling at Dad

"Look at us!"

"We are all 'blinged' up… ready for your birthday dinner Mum!"

"You can choose any tasty meal you want… plus a fancy dessert." I said

"The menu should be good!" said Dad

"Mum… do you mind if I brush your hair?" I asked

"Of course not, Cassie."

"I brushed it when I showered earlier… but it can always have an extra brush." said Mum

Mum sat down on the bed and I sat down on my knees behind her and proceeded to brush her hair. I wouldn't tolerate brushing for many years, (it hurt like someone scratching my head), I would meltdown if Mum or Dad tried to brush my hair. I would knock the hairbrush out of their hands and then I would hide. I brush my own hair now and Mum and Dad don't need to try and brush my hair anymore. I took great care to brush Mum's hair gently and smoothly and a couple of minutes later Mum's hair was looking 'smooth'!

"All done Mum!"

"You are totally smooth now!" We both laughed together at that

"Thank you, Cassie." said Mum

"Now that we are in our 'fancy pants'… let's go to dinner!" said Dad, hungrily

"I second that motion!" Mum cheered

We arrived at our surprise rendezvous.

"How nice… the Gordon Hotel."

"What a great place to have my birthday dinner." said Mum

We went inside and sat at the table we had reserved for the evening. We were joined by Rebecca… Mia… Aunt Sally… and Uncle Tom. They had driven to meet us with presents for Mum and Rebecca. They were all dressed up for this special occasion and very

smart they looked too!

"Hello Mikayla…Happy forty-second birthday… my beautiful cousin." said Sally, hugging Mum

"Hello Sally… Thank you." said Mum, hugging Sally back

"Hello Mikayla… Happy forty-second birthday… you look beautiful tonight." said Tom, hugging Mum

"Hello Tom… thanks for that nice compliment." said Mum, hugging Tom

"Hello Aunt Mikayla… Happy Birthday to you."

"What a nice necklace you have got on." said Mia, hugging Mum

"Thanks Mia."

"This is a favourite necklace of mine." said Mum, hugging Mia back

Mum then went over to Rebecca and they hugged each other.

"We're turning Forty-Two!"

"There is going to be some fun tonight and a delicious cake later on!" said Rebecca

"I can't wait for that!"

"I do love cake!"

"These meals on the menu all sound so tasty."

"We're going to have a hard time deciding which ones to choose." said Mum

"Before we choose our meals… let's get our presents for Mum and Rebecca."

"They're going to love what we have bought them." I said

"We thought about these gifts that we have chosen for you."

We all sat down and then began to hand out gifts to Mum and Rebecca. They included a Collingwood scarf from me for Mum, a Carlton scarf for Rebecca from Dad, a jar of White Raspberry Bullets from Sally, 'My Spin on Cricket' by Richie Benaud OBE from Tom, and 'Original Me' by German pop group 'Cascada' from Mia. Mum and Rebecca love all their gifts.

"These are all excellent presents!"

"Thanks everyone!"

"How thoughtful." said Mum

"We're proud to wear the colours of Carlton and Collingwood!"

"Thank you." said Rebecca

"Let's order our meals and a dessert if anyone can fit it in!" laughed Dad

As everyone began to peruse their menu… Mum and Aunt Rebecca began to reminisce and tell old stories… of when they were children.

"I remember the time when Rebecca and I were ten years old… we were making an art project together… painting a lovely picture of the Bontel-Macdonald mansion with some collage work."

"It dawned on us that it was going to be Mother's Day the next day."

"We said to each other… why don't we give this picture to Mum on Mother's Day?" Mum recalled

"We had to hide it in our room so she wouldn't find it."

"On Mother's Day we gave it to her with some chocolates and she loved it!"

"She gave us both a kiss and said…that's a lovely picture, darlings you've put lovely colours into your collage… what a good job!"

"I recall when Mikayla and I were seventeen years old and it was our former special centre teacher, Mrs Natalie's birthday."

"Mikayla and I, as well as Olivia and Daniel, were asked to make a cake… because Mrs Natalie and her husband James… had been invited to the Bontel-Macdonald mansion for tea."

"I put in the chocolate…I remembered Mrs Natalie loves chocolate as much as Mikayla and I do."

"Daniel put in the other ingredients… Mikayla did the stirring… and Olivia put it in the oven to cook."

"I iced the cake with milk chocolate icing and added strawberries on top!"

"When Mrs Natalie and her husband arrived, we gave her a present each and she loved them."

"The cake was a great success and we had a fun time on her birthday." said Rebecca

"Those were happy times." Mum added

"With great cakes!" she said laughing

"Who doesn't love desserts and cake and chocolate!" exclaimed Sally

Tom, Sally and Mia, wanted to ask me about my radio interview.

"Cassie, we heard your Brisbane radio interview… you were very brave to talk on air."

"Your Melbourne Secondary College years must have been scary... because the students were not like you... but positive too... because you worked hard to get A's in every subject you took."

"What about winning the UNO tournament against your teachers?"

"What was that like?"

"When I attended the college for three years, my thoughts on the other students in my year were...*these people are from planet 'Stranger', they are frightening!...they are not like me, I don't trust them and they don't trust me!...I'm not letting them near me and I don't want them to find out about my life...ever!*"

"I worked hard in every subject to get A's... I felt delighted about that!"

"I thought to myself... *'despite all the other scary students, I've worked hard to earn these A's, I'm happy and proud of myself for doing so!'*"

"When I won the UNO tournament against Mrs Petunia, I thought... *'I have done it! It was very close, but I managed to win a UNO tournament against Mrs Petunia! I'm very happy to get this far and I deserve the win! Yes! Yippee! Well done Cassie!'*"

"My feelings were mixed... I was scared... frightened... delighted... happy... and ecstatic."

"Overall, I managed to get through the three years... then I attended a special centre for girls with autism the next year."

"You did very well to get to where you are now!"

"When you talked about your sensitivity to touch... wearing gloves to touch things... did the gloves give you comfort?"

"They certainly did give me comfort... that way I could touch things...without having a meltdown."

"It was also one of the ways I could show affection to Mum and Dad."

"I stroked their skin...I didn't say 'I love you Mum'... or 'I love you Dad'."

"I wore mittens until I was nine... when I overcame my fear of being touched."

"Mum and Dad didn't mind...some of the time they longed for me to say... 'I love you'...but I didn't say it."

"I can say it to them now... when I kiss and hug them."

When the chocolate cake was brought out to our table Mum and Rebecca were amazed to see that it was white chocolate with blueberries. They were both delighted, as everyone sang 'Happy Birthday' to them before cutting the cake!

"This cake is some really good 'tucker'! said Mum and Rebecca together

Everybody laughed as they 'tucked in' to the delicious birthday cake.

When we got back to the hotel, Mum skyped Belinda and Darren for her birthday, despite it being late in the evening.

"Hello Mikayla."

"Did you have a fun time on your birthday?"

"Hello Mum."

"I did have a fun time!"

"A few of the family members were there for it too."

"Hello Mikayla."

"Did you behave yourself there?"

"Hello Dad."

"Yes... I did behave myself."

"That's good!"

Dad and I laughed.

"You're usually cheeky when you and Rebecca get together for a party!"

"What did you get for your birthday?"

"We both received a 'Collingwood' and a 'Carlton' scarf, a music CD and a jar of white chocolate raspberry bullets."

"We loved all our gifts… we're going to have fun with them."

"You are always proud to wear the black and white of Collingwood, and Rebecca is always proud to wear the blue and white of Carlton."

"We've been staying at Portland for the past week… it's a lovely seaside town."

"You're having a good time there, then?"

"We are indeed."

"Cassie learnt how to paddle on a paddleboard for the very first time."

"I was proud of her… despite her playing a trick on us… when she tipped Daniel and I, out of our kayak with her oar!"

"Good on her."

"I bet you weren't ready for that one!" said Darren, chuckling

"No… we weren't!"

"Daniel and I plan to get her back!"

"Mum… you do realise that I'm standing right here listening…don't you?"

"Ahh…."

"She is cheeky just like you Mikayla."

"Dad and I are about to watch a romantic comedy movie."

"I do love romantic comedies!"

"We're off now… so bye darling."

"Bye, Mum."

"Bye Dad."

The next morning, we went to Portland Strawberries… where they stock strawberries… chocolates… jams… and sauces. This was one place we did not want to miss out on!

This family owned business was originally called Bolwarra Berries in the 1990's when it started… now its name has changed to Portland Strawberries. The thought of all those strawberries is making me hungry! The aroma of fresh strawberries made our mouths water with anticipation as we walked through the gate.

The owners greeted us and showed us into the store full of strawberries… strawberry products… and much more. Everything looks so tempting, I want to buy it all!! The strawberry fields are growing out the back.

"Our business here at Portland Strawberries has been running since the 1990's."

"We've got plenty of products that you will love… and some tempting items to try."

"We also have recipes that you can take home and recreate."

"Have a good look around, there's plenty to choose from!" said the lady in the strawberry shop

We looked at several products before Mum spotted the Glenelg Chocolates… she has tasted them before and is delighted to have found them.

"I've tried these Glenelg chocolates before and they are so tempting."

"I am a bit of a naughty girl when it comes to chocolate!"

"I can't resist the temptation!" said Mum, guiltily

We all chuckled at that! Mum is such a fiend when it comes to chocolate! Sometimes she tries to hide it so Dad and I can't find it! Most of the time I manage to find it and eat a row or two before Mum finds out. Dad rarely gets away with it!

"We can see you love your chocolate you two!"
"I was six years old when Mum first gave me a row of white chocolate."
"I was delighted when I received it… I've had a sweet tooth ever since." I admitted
"I have a sweet tooth on occasion."
"Mikayla has plenty of chocolate at our house… she is a bit of a chocoholic!" Dad grinned
"I understand…it's very tempting!" said the lady
"My twin sister Rebecca, has used these jams in a couple of her cookbook recipes, they were so tasty. She sold some on her market stall just like my grandmother and Diane did…Diane still does today." said Mum
"Cassie has been to several markets… and helped Diane in Melbourne… Port Fairy and Warrnambool."
"Yes… I love helping Nan Diane on her market stall!"
We bought a punnet of strawberries each… some Glenelg chocolates… a few jams and recipes… plus icy poles… dips and sauces! We thanked the owners for their time and drove back to our hotel to store the strawberries for later use.
"We can do some shopping… we could have a swim at the YCMA pool… or take a walk on Nun's Beach… maybe even practice a little lawn bowls at the Portland RSL."
"They are giving lessons to visitors at the moment." said Mum, who was busy checking out the local information brochures
"I would like to give lawn bowls a try, Mum."
"I've watched you play and I'm inspired to give it a go."
"I have seen Belinda and Georgina playing, and admired the trophies that they have won, too."
"It looks like a fun sport to play." I said
"That's a great idea Cassie, trying another sport!"
"It will be fun!"
Georgina and Mum have previously represented Australia in lawn bowls."
"They were very good in their playing days and although I played occasionally for fun with Dad… I didn't take up lawn bowls until 2010."
"I play on occasion at the RSL but due to our busy lifestyle I haven't played enough games to be eligible to be selected to play for Australia." Mum added
"That would be a fun thing to try, Cassie."
"In the meantime, … I hear that the Portland Returned Servicemen's League have some great meals!" I say, with a big grin
"Oh Cassie!" laugh Mum and Dad together
"You are always hungry!"
"I can't wait to decide which meal to eat… although I have never tried one before… I might try a lemon squash too!"
I looked at Mum and Dad and shrugged my shoulders with a grin on my face.
"I'm a growing teenager guys… what can I say?"
They both burst out laughing and rolled their eyes at me
"We'd better get you to the RSL bistro then before you expire from hunger." said Dad, still grinning
"Sounds good Dad." I say, giving him the 'thumbs up' sign
There were quite a few people at the RSL but there were still a couple of vacant tables. There was an honours board on the wall with the names of previous Lawn Bowls Champions… and the year in which they

had won their matches... also game machines and two television sets. We ordered our lemon squash with ice to drink and sat down to look over the lunch section of the menu.

"What are you going to have, Cassie?"

"Some of the options Mum and I have tried before, are delicious." said Dad

"I've looked and decided on Chicken Parma."

"It's an Aussie favourite that I'd like to try."

"That's an excellent choice, Cassie."

"I'll have the Beef and Bacon Meatballs."

"It's a great dish and I remember that my grandma would cook a similar dish... I still have the recipe that she passed on to Mum and I."

"I still love to cook and eat it." said Mum

"What is the secret to that yummy dish... Mum?" I asked

Mum looked around to see if anybody was listening then whispered the secret to me. I won't reveal the secret to you... readers. It's a famous family recipe on my Mum's side of the family... and I'm not telling!

"I'll try the lasagne."

"It's a favourite dish of mine for many years!" said Dad, licking his lips

The meals were ordered and arrived a short time later... we took them to the Bain Marie where all the vegetables were kept hot to add to your main dish... using serving spoons and tongs... and ladles for the gravy. I chose peas and carrots to add to my Chicken Parma meal and it's looking delicious. Our meals went down a treat! We are full up! The drinks were cool and refreshing on a hot day.

Afterwards, we sat outside near the bowling green, we were watching two lawn bowlers practicing. I've seen Mum practicing, I was never interested in giving it a go before, I'm very keen to learn about it now. After a while we asked a veteran bowler named Penny about lessons... for visitors who want to learn how to play lawn bowls.

"Our daughter Cassie has never tried lawn bowls before... but she is very keen to have a try."

"Can you teach her all the basic moves...then she will feel confident to have a go." said Dad

"I can help her with that."

"I can see she's keen to try." said Penny

"Yes... I am Penny."

"I was inspired by Mum practicing in our loungeroom... I'd love to learn and practice too."

"Good on you Cassie!"

"Come over to where the lawn bowls equipment is and I'll teach you the basic moves." said Penny

"Cassie, these are the basic moves of lawn bowling."

"Stand with your feet together on the mat... bend your knees and waist slightly...not too much."

"Choose your right or left hand to bowl the ball."

"Step out the with your left foot if you're bowling with your right hand... or step out with your right foot if you're bowling with your left hand."

"Take a small back swing with your arm... bend down and roll the bowl along the playing area to get the right speed."

"If you roll it along the ground at the right angle the bowl can curve towards the jack."

"Please avoid damaging the green... make sure not to drop or bounce the bowl on it." said Penny

"Right... I've got that Penny." I said

Penny also taught me the draw shot... and the drive shot...I listened to the steps and also watched what Penny did. I was taught the scoring and the main basic lawn bowls terms. Finally, ... I was ready to practice on my own while Penny observed and guided me.

"I'm ready Penny."

"I'm putting all the steps you taught me in to practice." I said

"Good Cassie."

"Show me what you can do." encouraged Penny

I walked up to the beginning position on the mat. I was a little nervous and scared to bowl.

"It's okay to be nervous on your first go Cassie."

"When I took up lawn bowls for the first time... I was a little scared but with practice and confidence... I became very good at it."

"Take your time... I know you can do it." Penny reassured me

With that reassurance I bowled... it curled around a bit and it went towards the jack... it touched the jack... making it roll a little.

"Not bad for a first try." I said

"Let's practice for thirty minutes and have a bit of fun." said Penny

"I've played alongside Mikayla for several years...I may be a little rusty as I haven't played lately." said Dad

We all chuckled.

"Come on dear."

"You can play alongside me."

"It's fun." wheedled Mum

"All right Mikayla."

"I'll do it."

"Let's practice." said Dad

I had fun playing lawn bowls... a few of my shots were off target...I still enjoyed myself.

I've got a long way to go if I want to become good at lawn bowls like Mum.

"Thanks Penny... for teaching me about lawn bowls moves."

"That's ok, Cassie."

"You've done well." said Penny

"Does the Portland RSL sometimes get musicians here for entertainment nights?" asked Dad. "We sometimes do."

"They usually entertain the lawn bowlers and the guests."

"We also have bingo games." said Penny

"We would love to try that one night!"

"We're the 'Bontel Family' band... we are touring around Australia promoting our self-titled debut album and we wonder if we can perform our songs for you with the RSL's permission... this weekend?" asked Mum

"Just let me check with the manager." said Penny

Penny checked with the RSL manager and came back to us with a smile.

"I've checked with the manager and you're lucky."

"There is an entertainment night on Saturdays... which is tonight!"

"The RSL would be very happy for you to perform."

It's at eight in the evening...you can come back at six-thirty...have some dinner and get ready afterwards." said Penny

"We sure will Penny!"

"We'll be back to perform our hit songs later."

"We'll see you tonight."

"We'll have a fun music night then."

"Cassie you gave lawn bowls a try and you did very well."

"That's another new activity you've tried." said Mum, proudly

"What activity would you like to do as a family now." said Dad

"The family activity I choose is swimming… at the Portland YMCA."

"It will be nice to swim in this weather." Mum agreed

We had a lovely swim at the Portland YMCA. There were at least five lanes in the outdoor pool, Mum, Dad and I, had a nice cool swim. We spent a leisurely hour in the outdoor pool… there was also a waterslide nearby…we tried it out and loved it! I wouldn't try it for many years…this time I had no fear… and slid down laughing all the way.

The afternoon sped by quickly, soon it was time to go and get ready for our evening at the RSL. We arrived looking pretty smart in our best gear! We went inside and saw the stage set up for us with our instruments ready to go. The bowling team and other diners were in the audience…I hope we amaze them with our music.

"Welcome to entertainment night Bontel Family…you are our guest performers tonight!"

"The dinner menu has some delicious meals to try… they are a big hit with our diners!"

"There may also be bingo later…enjoy the night!" the manager said

"Thanks very much."

"We promise your patrons they will have a fun entertaining night." I said

"Yes… we all will." said Dad

We chose Chicken Schnitzel… Porterhouse Steak… and Pork Belly… for dinner, it was devoured by us all.

A couple of hours later a little before eight…it was time for us to prepare for our performance. We tuned our instruments… changed into our stage clothes… and went to the performing area.

"Hello Portland RSL!"

"Entertainment night is about to kick off with a bang!"

"We are the Bontel Family band… here to perform some songs from our self-titled debut album!"

"We hope you are really going to enjoy yourselves… please join in."

"One…Two…Three!" Mikayla boomed in with the drums and we were off

Everyone had a great time at the Portland RSL. We signed some autographs and had a few photos taken with some diners. It was the first RSL performance we have done…it won't be our last! After our musical set, we played a little bit of bingo before we headed back to our hotel for a good night's rest.

# Chapter Forty-Six
## A Ghostly Fright!

We are at Cape Nelson today to look at the lighthouse, it will be an interesting place to learn about. In the 1800's the lighthouse witnessed many high-sea dramas... the lighthouse is one place I'm keen to tour!

We did some whale watching first up at the Cape Nelson Lighthouse Viewpoint... we tried to see if we could spot any blue whales. During the summer months the Blue Whales come to feed on millions of krill... the 'Bonnie Upswelling' brings them to the ocean's surface. During the winter months off the coast near the cliffs of the precinct... Southern Right and Humpback Whales can be spotted. In fact, they come so close you might be able to hear them sing...which is a sweet sound that I love to hear.

Fifteen minutes pass... but no Blue Whales.

"It doesn't matter if they come or not... it's still a great view of the Portland Ocean!" I said

"That's right Cassie."

"You were so joyful when we saw a whale in Western Australia."

"It was great to see that excited look on your face!" Mum smiled, remembering

"We took a photo of that lovely moment... so you can tell family and friends about your whale encounter." Dad added

We went for our tour of the Cape Nelson Lighthouse starting with the maritime room.

We walked up the stairs with port hole circles in the walls... as well as a machine that presumably operates the lighthouse... there was brass work everywhere, it was fascinating.

There was a warning sign above a door way that said... Low Headroom! We kept our heads low and went in... it was a tight spot but we enjoyed the view. We toured the rest of this room in the lighthouse which included the kitchen and fireplace, it was fun. It had good facilities and seemed like a nice place to stay for a night or two... but when we looked at the rates for one or two bedrooms... we decided to give it a miss!

After touring the lighthouse, we went to Isabella's café... which was named after the (barque) ship 'Isabella'... that ran aground on the South West Coast and was wrecked. The good news about this wreck... was none of the people on board lost their lives!

We ordered a meal and some cakes. We viewed the artworks on the walls, there was a movie poster, which featured 'Paris'. On the counter were some jars of lollies, we bought some to take with us before we left.

We decided to visit the Portland Botanical Gardens next which were very colourful and full of beautiful flowers.

William Allitt, established the gardens in 1857, with staff from Melbourne assisting him...Portland has Victoria's second oldest botanical gardens... they have a croquet lawn...plus native and exotic plants.

The flowers peak in Summer and Autumn...I can smell the perfumes and see the vibrant colours of all the flowers...this makes me smile and brightens up my day.

"Oh... it smells so good in here!" I laugh with pleasure

"It brings back memories of Valentine Days!" said Mum, happily

"1987 was a good one!"

"I was helping my Mum cook a roast chicken dish with vegetables... Daniel was busy with something in the garden."

"When we had finished preparing the roast lunch... he came in with a red rose and said..."

"Mikayla this red rose represents our love on this Valentine's Day... we will always love each other no matter what happens."

"I thought that was lovely of him... I gave him a kiss on his left cheek... he gave me one on my right and we hugged each other."

"My Mum thought it was sweet of him."

"In the afternoon in my old room at the Bontel-Macdonald mansion... we sat on my old bed stroking each other affectionately and saying romantic things to each other... that evening he took me out for a dinner date to our favourite Italian restaurant... where we ate spaghetti to end a perfect day." said Mum dreamily, with a faraway look in her eyes

"I still remember that Valentine's Day... I had a good green thumb back then!"

"I knew how much you loved red roses... so on that day I picked one especially for you."

"You loved that rose... our relationship grew a little stronger that day." Dad remembered

"That's a great Valentine's Day memory for you both to keep Mum and Dad!" I said, looking at some of the roses in the gardens

We walked along a gravel path, noticing the shady trees as we passed beneath them.

This is a beautiful day, relaxing and colourful. We sat on one of the park benches and took in the panorama... flowers... trees... lawns...pathways. We continued our walk, looking at a group of flowers.

Then... I spotted something shiny underneath one of the flowers... it looked like a twenty-cent coin. There were thorns on the plant so I had to be careful not to prick my fingers on any of them. I knelt down and reached out carefully to get the coin... I still pricked my finger on a thorn.

"OW!" I yelled

Mum and Dad ran over to see what was wrong.

"What's wrong Cassie?"

"Did an insect bite you?" asked Dad

"No Dad... an insect did not bite me!"

"It was a thorn!" I said, pulling a face

"Lucky... I am always prepared!" said Mum, triumphantly holding up a small box

"I have plenty of Band-Aids... I'll get one out and put it on your finger."

"You'll be 'as right as rain' in a jiffy!" said Mum, cheerily

We went back to the bench and sat down. Mum took a band aid out of the little box and Dad held my other hand stroking it gently to relax me. I remained calm while Mum put the band aid on my finger.

"There... all done Cassie." said Mum, soothingly

"I'll live Mum." I said, flexing my 'band aided' finger

"That's the way Cassie."

"Good find too!"

"That's twenty cents to pop in your pocket ready to spend." grinned Dad

"Sure is Dad...I didn't even need a metal detector!" I said, laughing

"The Botanical gardens are beautiful to visit and all the flowers and trees were great to learn about."

"I love visiting botanical gardens and beaches... they are fun places to be and very relaxing."

"Botanical gardens are very therapeutic places to visit... that's why I like to visit them regularly... the beach is also a great location in Summer... for swimming... water activities...and fun in the sand... I really enjoy spending time there." I added

Before, when I hurt myself... I would not let Mum or Dad touch me... as I was sensitive to touch. I would tend to my wounds alone...Mum and Dad would have to somehow help me to put a Band-Aid on... without making me more upset. I learnt first-aid skills by observing, during my special centre years.

I took out my sketchbook and drew a row of red and purple flowers. I added red and purple colours to the sketch... then sun and sky... and coloured them in as well. After I had finished, I showed my drawing to Mum and Dad... who were amazed at the details.

"Cassie that is brilliant." said Dad

"Thanks Dad."

"Maybe you can design our upcoming album."

"Maybe."

"It depends on my inspiration." I replied

We made our way back to our hotel, ready to pack all our things up and move to the next destination tomorrow.

Early next day we booked in to Victoria House... we plan to spend a quiet relaxing day after all our recent activities. Victoria House looked gorgeous when we arrived... it is a bluestone residence built in 1853... and restored as a guest house.

There are antiques lining the halls and the walls. There is a lounge room where we can sit and next to the couch, there are DVD's. In another room... there is a fireplace with chairs nearby to sit in the warm firelight glow. There are family rooms in the 'Georgian' style... we can a have a hot breakfast and a buffet in the morning.

"Victoria House is unique...the rooms are awesome...it takes you back to the Georgian era."

"We'll be glad we chose to stay here!" I said, excitedly

"We shall, Cassie."

"There are so many antiques here... Jessica would love to stay here for a few days."

"It's a little cooler at the moment... this fireplace will certainly warm us up." said Mum

"It's got a great garden out the back...we can walk along the paths and through the garden... to admire it all." said Dad

The owner with an eccentric flair greets us... and tells us about the history of the house... with a few ghost stories thrown in as well.

"I hope you sleep well tonight." said the owner, with a mischievous grin

"We hope so too."

We had a walk before dinner along the garden paths and admired the flowers along the way. Olivia would love this... she loves gardening... Olivia and I admire gardens like these for hours. It was time for dinner so we went to the dining room... there was no menu...the owner had kindly cooked a tasty meal for us which was delicious.

"Mum, Dad."

"I love Victoria House!"

"The rooms make me feel like I am back in the olden days of Victoria."

"The paintings are so beautiful and everywhere you look the designs mesmerise."
"A few of the rooms remind me of times spent at Nan's house... having fun and lots of laughs." I said
"We were thinking the same thing Cassie."
"The Victoria House fireplace takes us back to our years at the Bontel-Macdonald mansion."
"In the loungeroom we would read books... discuss our ideas... watch movies... and play the occasional board or card game."
"Those were fun memories... we had lots of happy times together." said Mum, reminiscing
"I love it when you tell me those stories!"
"I would love to pass on those memories to my own children one day." I said
"We hope you have the chance to do that someday too, Cassie."
"Would you like to stay at the Bontel-Macdonald mansion for a few days?" asked Dad
"Oh yes please... Dad!"
"I would love to do that!"
"I have never stayed there before"
"I can't wait to see it with you two!"
In the evening we put on our robes and sat down by the open fire to watch a classic old movie.
It felt very relaxing in the warmth of the fire and reminded me of when I was ten years old and going through a phase of wearing my cotton blue robe in winter!
It was in 2005 and I had been watching 'kids' movies and family comedy movies with Mum and Dad and holding my dolphin soft toy. They were good times for me, the memory is being recreated here in Victoria House.
Later that night, when we were sleeping in our rooms...Mum and Dad's room was next door to mine... I felt a chill go through the room. I sat up startled thinking.... *'What is that?... I don't think that is the wind blowing.'* I looked around but I didn't see anything.
I was a little anxious wondering what had caused the chill. Then I looked up and saw something that made me a lot more frightened! I looked up to see a ghost! It was a young woman who had perished in the hotel many years ago... she is staring at me like she knows me! I grabbed the sheets in front of me and pulled them up to my chin.
I was shivering and shaking and thinking... *'Go away!... don't scare me!... get away from me... freaky young ghost woman!'*
The young ghost woman came a little closer and I totally freaked out!
"M-m-m-Mum!"
"D-d-d-Dad"
"A..g..g..Ghost...w..w..Woman!"
"Help!!!! I shrieked
Jumping out of bed I ran to Mum and Dad's room... hurled myself on their bed and wrapped my arms around Mum's head... shaking all over.
"Hey!... What!... Who's that!"
"Cassie! Get off me!... I can't breathe!"
"Get off!!!" comes a series of muffled yells
I unwrapped my arms from around Mum's head.
"Cassie you almost strangled me...what's the matter sweetheart?"
"Did you have a bad dream." said Mum, holding my hands and rubbing them

"Firstly... I felt a weird chill creep across my room like an ice-cold vibe... sweeping over me...then the apparition of a young woman just mysteriously appeared in front of me... she was just staring at me."

"I felt frightened...for a moment I couldn't find the words to speak because I was too afraid."

I shivered again

"It's all right Cassie... I'm here."

"Thank you for telling me about what happened."

"Well done."

"That young woman ghost won't scare you agai.... Whaat!!!"

"It's the young W-W-Woman... she followed you!" said Mum, shaking in the bed

"What's going on here!"

"H-H-holy ghosts!!!" said Dad, starting to shake too

Mum, Dad and I, huddled together hoping the ghost would go away... she looked at us for a few more terrifying minutes... then thankfully she disappeared. We did not sleep well at all after that encounter and I certainly hope we don't meet any more ghosts on our road trip!

We are attempting to get ourselves some cereal for breakfast... too terrified to speak to each other about last night's 'ghostly' encounter. It was one 'scary' night that I won't forget in a hurry... and I bet Mum and Dad won't either!

"Hello how was last night... did you sleep well?" asked the owner

Mum, Dad and I turned 'ashen'... at the thought of last night's encounter.

"Come and sit in the lounge chairs... you three don't look so well." said the owner

"I can see by your faces that something happened during the night." said the owner, in a concerned voice

"Yes... we had an unwelcome visitor!" I squeaked

"It was a ghostly young woman!"

"I'm sorry that the ghost scared you." said the owner

"Never mind...though it was one experience we'd rather not repeat... thank you."

"It was shocking!" said Mum

"It frightened the wits out of the three of us...we got very little sleep after that!" said Dad

"I have never encountered a ghost before... I don't even watch horror movies... neither does Mum." I said

"You're the first guests that have been 'visited' by the legendary ghost that resides here." said the owner

"Thanks...I think." said Dad, not really impressed with that 'dubious' honour

"Hopefully... other visitors that come here won't be 'visited' by the 'resident ghost'!" said Mum

"I hope so too!"

"I can certainly commiserate with them if they do get a visit!" I said, shakily

Mum, Dad and I managed to finish our breakfast... packed up our stuff with the greatest of speed... and dashed out of Victoria House! We jumped into the car and sped off to the Comfort Inn Richmond Henty... which we hoped would be non-eventful and ghost free!

The Comfort Inn had nice rooms... and a pool which we could swim in... there was also a restaurant for dining. We heard of a place called the Iron Bar... it's open seven days a week and serves lunch and dinner. We all agreed to go there for dinner as it sounded like it might be a very interesting place to have a meal.

There were three pool tables...a jukebox...a bar...and a restaurant next door...as we walked through. Lining the walls were pictures of celebrities such as Johnny Cash...Jim Morrison...and the rock band, Queen. There were two pictures of 'Quirky Service', one from the 1985-1994 line-up... blowing bubbles in a big bath tub... and another of the 1998 to current line-up, in their pop star party clothes playing their instruments.

I can tell it's going to be one fun night I can feel it in my bones!

After we ordered our meals and a raspberry lemonade drink each, we decided to play a game of pool. Mum and I are up first…I was too good for Mum in the end…I even tried a couple of pool techniques that Mum and Dad use when they play.

"Mum and I used to play a bit of pool during our Quirky Services years at various pubs."

"Whenever we had breaks in performing, we played pool… the competitions were even every time."

"Mum and I were quite good… we occasionally played for money… we participated in a couple of tournaments too."

"We still play sometimes at Jessica's house for fun." said Dad

"The Iron Bar is a fun place." I smiled

Dad and I were playing our second game when a member of the staff came over.

"Would you like to participate in tonight's pub quiz?"

"Sure… we would love to."

"Daniel and I have played in pub quizzes before."

"I hope you have fun playing!"

"You need to come up with a name for your group…you will be provided with a sheet of twenty-five questions…you will definitely need a pencil as well." he said

We came up with the name, 'Cassie & the Quiz Gods'…which made us sound like a rock group…we picked up our pencils… grabbed our sheet… and we were ready to rock and roll!

We agreed on a system… I would answer the first five… Mum the next… Dad after that and then all of us together… for the last ten questions. It's going to be fun. It doesn't really matter what score we get.

"Ok everyone."

"Welcome to tonight's pub quiz!"

"You will answer twenty-five questions using the pencils provided."

"No cheating… if anyone is caught using a mobile phone they will be disqualified!"

"You may whisper to your teammates if you know the answer."

"When everyone has answered the twenty-five questions… I'll collect the quiz sheets and announce the winners."

"The third placed team will get fifty dollars."

"The second placed team will get one hundred dollars."

"The team in first place will get two hundred and fifty dollars!"

"Everybody got that?" said the staff member

We all nodded to show we understood the rules.

"Great… let's get started."

Some questions went like this:

"What type of fruit is a Pink Lady?"

"Who was the captain in the Original Star Trek series?"

"What type of animal appears on a Kellogg's corn flakes packet?"

There were lots of laughs in between, as we wrote all our answers down and handed the completed sheets back to the staff. A staff member announced the third and second placed quiz group winners and then we got a real surprise when we were announced as the winning quiz group. Mum, Dad and I, high-fived each other, as the staff member handed us first prize of two hundred and fifty dollars! Everybody in the room clapped and cheered, it was my first pub quiz and I won't forget it in a hurry.

"That was wicked… we did well." I said

"We sure did Cassie."

"It was fun playing together." said Mum

"It's another highlight to add to our Australian road trip." said Dad

"I also won't forget that one and only night at Victoria House... but for completely different reasons!" I grimaced

## Chapter Forty-Seven
## Port Fairy Payback

There are many places to visit in Victoria, we looked at the map and decided to visit Port Fairy next. It is a pretty seaside fishing village with lots of history and things to do there.

We drove to Port Fairy and chose to book in at Oscars Waterfront Boutique Hotel. It turned out to be a spacious hotel... with a fireplace... a spa bath... several comfortable rooms... and a good view of Port Fairy Harbour. We can view the boats in the harbour whilst dining. I had never been to Port Fairy before I plan to make the most of our four day stay here and have plenty of fun!

There was a petrol station with a little shop attached, so we went in and bought a Herald Sun newspaper. When I picked up the paper what did I see on the front page? It was a picture of me performing in Adelaide, with the fans dancing and singing along. The headline above the photo read:

'Autistic pop star 'Cassie Bontel' wows Adelaide during her solo concert!'

"OMG!"

"That's me!"

"How awesome is that!" I said, excitedly

"We are so proud of you."

"You held down the fort for us when we were delayed then did your solo concert brilliantly." Dad said, admiringly

"I won't forget that experience!"

"I hope I get the chance to try a few more solo projects during the tour of our last two states."

"I shall be better prepared next time... now that I know what to expect." I said, grinning

The article read:

'16-Year Old Cassie Bontel who is on the Autism Spectrum and has a rare condition called Hyperthymesia, performed a solo concert for the first time, which blew Adelaide away with her musical performance! Reported to be a bit nervous during a phone call with her Mother Mikayla beforehand, she nevertheless went onstage reassured and confident, performing all twelve pop tunes which amazed the audience.'

This direct quote comes from Cassie... "When Mum called me to tell me she and Dad were delayed because of car troubles on route to the performance, I got a little nervous and feared I wouldn't be able to go onstage without them."

"Mum reassured me... gave me encouragement... and 'WOW' Adelaide you were great!"

"I'm proud of myself for achieving one of my dreams."

'Cassie went on to tell me that she plans to do more solo performances in the future. There may also be a few 'meet and greets' with her too, so look out for those future dates folks!' There were a few photos of me signing autographs... performing... taking 'selfies' with fans... and talking to the interviewer.

In Port Fairy... at Railway Place, they hold markets... sometimes community markets are also held on every second and fourth Saturday of the month at the wharf... and sometimes on the village green.

We wondered, if there was a market being held today...we drove around the village and saw several people that we know very well!

There is Maria and Belinda... Josephine, who is Jessica's Mum... Julie, Zoe's Mum... Carol, Caroline's Mum... Ruth who is Jason's Mum... Jacqueline, Peter's Mum... Gwen, Andrew's Mum... Julie, Sally's Mum... and Celia, Tom's Mum.

We could see they had a stall where they were selling all sorts of sweet treats... from chocolate hedgehog...to vanilla slice...apple slice...and even ginger crunch. They also had home-made pies and pasties for sale too.

We want to try some...how are we going to sneak some away without the Mums busting us?

"Here's the plan and this is how we do it."

"When the 'Mums' take a break to get a coffee... we sneak in and grab some of their sweet and savoury treats... maybe eat a few and drive to our hotel... to eat the rest!" suggests Mum

"That's a brilliant plan Mum!"

"It's sure to be a success... if we put it into action." I said

"We've got the bags here...when the 'Mums' go for their break we'll put some treats in them." agreed Dad

When the Mums left for the coffee shop... we got out of the car with our bags... carefully put the treats in... and drove back to our hotel... planning to eat them.

"Was that Daniel, Mikayla and Cassie, I just saw driving past?" asked Josephine

"Yes... they are probably staying here and came to the market for a visit." said Maria

When the 'Mums' went back to the market they were shocked to see many of their wares had disappeared!

"What!"

"Somebody has stolen our produce!"

"I bet I know who would do that!"

"They've tried similar pranks before." said Jacqueline

"It was Mikayla... Daniel... and Cassie... I'd bet my wares on that!"

"Let's get into our cars and see if we can find them."

"We'll try the Port Fairy harbour first." said Belinda

Mum, Dad and I, were sitting at the table overlooking the Port Fairy Harbour... eating our 'ill gotten' gains.

"These are so delicious!"

"I've tried most of them... the apple slice is the only slice I wouldn't eat...until now."

"The pies we got are so tasty true-blue... we've got a feast right in front of us!" I said

"We've got a feast here all right."

"My plan worked really well...I hope the 'Mums' don't suspect it was us that swiped their produce." said Mum

We drank our glasses of milk... but then we saw the 'Mums' cars in the distance.

"Oh, dear!"

"I think the Mums are on to us... they are on their way!"

"Quick let's get the bags of treats and hide with them in our hotel room!" I said

We grabbed the bags and 'scooted' to our hotel room... locking the door... hoping the 'Mums' haven't spotted us.

They didn't find us at the Port Fairy Wharf... so they tried Oscars Waterfront Boutique Hotel where we were staying. They looked in many rooms and just as they were walking past our hotel room door... Mum burped loudly... and gave the game away!

"Ha ha!"

"I knew it!"

"Daniel Fred Bontel!"

"Mikayla Natalie Bontel!"

"Cassie Annabelle Bontel!"

"I know you are in there... come out and show yourselves!" said Maria

"We are busted." I said, whispering to Mum and Dad

I emerged from the room with hedgehog crumbs around my mouth and a guilty grin. I'm in big trouble now! Gulp!

"Cassie!"

"What a naughty girl!"

"Did you eat the treats we were selling?" asked Maria

"Err.... it wasn't me that ate them."

"It was Belinda." I said sheepishly, pointing at her

"It was not me Cassie!"

"I can see the crumbs around your mouth!"

"What a cheeky girl you are!" Belinda said

Mum and Dad then slunk out of the room with pie and pastry crumbs around their mouths and guilty grins all over their faces.

"Daniel and Mikayla!" Belinda said, sternly

"Erm... it wasn't us that ate them."

"It was him!"

"It was her!" said Mum and Dad together pointing their fingers and trying to pin the blame on each other

"We knew it was you three all along." said Carol

"It is very lucky that we have some extra produce that we made to sell... and as you three culprits have eaten our stock... you can help to sell the rest... in payment for what you consumed!" said Belinda, very firmly

"Do we have to?" said Mum, with a grimace

"You most certainly do!" said Maria, with a glint in her eye that meant business

That's how the three culprits...ended up selling slices... pies... and pastries... for the next hour. A few customers laughed when they heard about our 'crime' and the punishment...but we weren't laughing! A few times we tried to sneak off... but one of the Mums' were always on to us saying...

"Not so fast... back to work please."

After the hour ended, most of the other Mums left to go back to their hotel... ready to pack for Melbourne...Maria and Belinda went with us to a café.

"Now that you're back in Victoria how is the road trip proceeding?" asked Belinda

"There are several towns in Victoria that we mean to visit on this road trip, we will take them one town at a time." I said

"That's great."

"Your trip is going well and you are becoming more confident." said Maria

"Yes, that's right."

"We've seen more independence from Cassie... she has made even more progress since we saw you last." said Mum

"That's so good to hear."

"We bought the Herald Sun earlier... we read about your excellent performance in Adelaide!"

"We saw about that on the news several days ago." said Belinda, holding up the Herald Sun and pointing to the front page

"I was a bit nervous to start with...but I couldn't let our fans down."

"The show must go on as they say!"

"Our fans really enjoyed the experience too!" I said

"We were so proud of our beautiful grand-daughter."

"We're happy that you had a chance to perform solo... even if it wasn't planned."

"Before we got here, we stayed at Victoria House in Portland for one night."

"The ghost of a young woman came into the room where we were sleeping and scared the wits out of us!"

"We packed up and fled to another hotel the next morning!"

"We're sorry to hear about your experience with the ghost...we're glad that you're safe that's what really matters." said Belinda

"Port Fairy is such is a vibrant town we plan to go Blarney Books and Art."

"Cassie will love that." said Mum

"I definitely will!"

"I looked it up... they have a great range of books and fabulous artworks there... it sounds like a great place to visit." I said

I took out my sketchbook and showed Maria and Belinda the artwork I have sketched on our road trip so far.

"You have been doing well with your sketching and artwork Cassie!"

"Some lovely colours there."

"We have a very artistic grand-daughter!"

"Maybe you can put a couple of your art pieces into an art section."

"Take a photo of them and send it to us if you can." said Maria

"My artistic side has come alive even more on this trip my pictures have helped to build my confidence too."

"I plan to explore my art further... hopefully raise some money for autism awareness with them." I said

"We will come to the art events when you display your artwork!"

"You could also promote your pop music as well." said Belinda

"I could do."

"I could write a song about autism in the next few months in Melbourne... during autism-related events... then perform it to raise money and awareness."

"I am becoming more open about these issues... since I gave my talk." I told them

"We would love to hear you perform your song it will be like shining stars in the dark sky." said Maria, poetically

"It certainly will!"

"The autistic audiences will enjoy and appreciate for they will understand and realise they are not alone."

"That they are loved... supported... and understood."

"One more step on the road to autistic superstardom status!" I said, with a wink

"That's our cute… talented… autistic… prodigy musician!" said Dad, grinning back at me

"Thanks Dad." I said, blushing a little

Meanwhile… 'Quirky Service' were back in Port Fairy having dinner at the 'Royal Oak'… and reading the Herald Sun!

"Wow!"

"Cassie performed well on her own in Adelaide."

"We're proud of her… even if she is stealing our thunder… with the help of Uncle Daniel and Aunt Mikayla!" said Kate

"She's on her way to becoming a pop star!" said Adam, impressed

"We love her…we're a bit jealous though… that the 'Bontel Family' is gaining more fans than us!" said Nicole, screwing up her nose

"Cassie is doing really well."

"She always looks lovely and loves performing on stage…ever since Sydney."

"We love hearing her angelic voice… it lights up the darkest of places." said Amelia

"Hey… Cassie has made a mischievous quote about my height."

It says…

"Kate's popularity is close…a little more height should just about do it!"

"That little monkey."

She goes on to say…

"Kate is freakishly short… it's like she's a shrinking violet."

All the diners laughed when she read that out… most of them had seen the article in the Herald Sun and thought it was funny.

"You think that's funny… do you?" said Kate, glaring and blushing as she tried to stand up as tall as she could in the circumstances

The other diners laughed louder, even the staff had a little chuckle.

"We have inspired her as well as Daniel and Mikayla…now she may be outselling her favourite popstars soon!"

"Let's drink to Cassie's success."

"Cheers!" said Kate

"Cheers!" said Adam, Nicole and Amelia together

Meanwhile Mum is looking for interesting places in the region…

"Flagstaff Hill in Warrnambool has interesting maritime history… the village overlooking Lady Bay… transports people back to the 1870s."

"We can soak up the maritime history and put some photos on our Facebook pages." said Mum

"Yes, our Dads love history so they will enjoy seeing photos of seafaring in the 1870's." said Dad

"We've tried ten-pin bowling in Mount Gambier… so how about in Warrnambool…it sounds like a good family activity for us."

"I read in the Warrnambool Community Newsletter, that Ten-Pin Bowling Warrnambool is having a spooky-themed disco, with pop music playing in the background."

"I like the idea they decorate the Ten-Pin bowling centre very nicely and our music is going to be included too!"

"It's going to be one awesome, brilliant, ten-pin bowling session, we won't forget!" I said excitedly

"It definitely sounds like fun Cassie!" Mum agreed

"Mum and I have bowled there before." said Dad

Sometime later…we walked through the Warrnambool Ten Pin Bowling Centre entrance, there were a few games being played, I saw some families bowling together.

The lanes were decorated with spooky themed backgrounds… above the lanes in blue… yellow… and purple colours… making up the sky. There were ten-pin bowling computers where players enter their names and scores and pop music videos were playing.

In the area where the players change into their bowling shoes, there were arcade games which included racing car games which we might play if we get a few minutes. This is a wicked environment I am going to have fun here!

Years ago, this sort of environment would overwhelm me, I would have a meltdown because of all the loud noises and people everywhere, it doesn't bother me anymore and I love it!

We went up to the counter, where we got our bowling shoes.

Now this presented another challenge that I have had to overcome! For many years I wore non-laced blue shoes only. A few times Mum and Dad had tried to get me to practice tying shoelaces but I would resist, throwing the laced shoes across the room and having a meltdown. This would also happen in shoe shops. Mum and Dad ended up having to throw out my laced shoes… replacing them with Velcro shoes… which I found acceptable.

This time I'm feeling more confident at lacing my ten-pin bowling shoes. If I can master these today… then I can consider buying laced shoes in different colours!

At the area where we put on our bowling shoes, Mum shows me again how to tie my laces after putting the shoes on my feet.

"Cassie… this is how you tie your laces up."

"It's an important skill for you to learn."

"You fold each end of the lace into a shape of a bunny's ear."

"Cross the bunny ears into an X shape like so."

"Loop the bottom bunny ear over and through the top bunny ear."

"Lastly… pull the bunny ears out to the side away from the shoe." said Mum

I listened to all the steps and had a go. I was a little nervous and Mum put her hand on my shoulder reassuringly.

"You can do it Cassie."

"Keep trying."

"I know you can get there." Mum smiled

"I took my time to tie the laces on the bowling shoes…finally it worked out right."

"Good job Cassie."

"That's great progress made!"

"You tied the laces on your bowling shoes really well." said Mum

"We might go to a shoe shop and buy a couple of pairs of laced shoes for you later."

"You should have no problems with them now." said Dad

"I tied my shoes really well!" I said, very pleased with myself

Mum then showed me something special… we were at lanes five and six… I looked up and there were several champion boards… for Men…Women…Girls… and Boys. I looked at lane five the lane that we were using and written on the board it said:

| Section / Name / Year / Age | Score |
|---|---|
| Men's Champion: Daniel Bontel<br>Year 2003 Age 33 | 300 |
| Women's Champion: Mikayla Bontel<br>Year 2001 Age 31 | 300 |
| Girls Champion: Kate White<br>Year 1997 Age 15 | 286 |
| Boys Champion: Adam Hunter<br>Year 1999 Age 16 | 275 |

"Our family were ten-pin bowling champions in those years in this particular lane…Dad and I got perfect scores in 2001 and 2003."

"We got a trophy for our scores I have some photos to show you of that soon." Mum told me

"Aunt Kate and Uncle Adam were great ten-pin bowlers at that age… they were powerhouses in the sport!"

"They had loads of fun… their parents encouraged them to try bowling when they were around eleven and ten."

"I would love to see photos of them… family stories say they were quite the party playful, mischievous teens… during the early years of 'Quirky Service' from 1998-2000."

"They sure are great ten-pin bowlers!"

"They once participated in a tournament in Warrnambool in 1998, with Amelia and Nicole representing the 'Party Animals'… against another group named 'Pop Kids'… and beat them in a great contest."

"They had a little party afterwards back in Geelong, Kate and Nicole's hometown, with their friends from the Geelong High School of International Autistics… which Kate…Adam…Nicole… and Amelia attended."

"At the time, 'Quirky Service' had just reformed and were busy recording their 1998 album 'Rainbow Party Teens'… so it was a nice time for them… before they went on a world tour." Dad remembered

"It was party time back in that year!"

"I admire them and their great bowling skills!"

"I'll do my best to get a good score…I'll have a fun time no matter what score I get." I decided

"That's a great attitude Cassie." Mum smiled

"We're all 'kitted out'… so let's go bowling!" Mum raised her arm in a salute

The scores were progressing after five bowls each…

**Cassie    150    Dad    135    Mum    130**

"Cassie, you are doing well… at this rate you may be able to reach 280-300." Dad beamed

"I might get there, Dad!"

"Who knows what can happen with the bowling ball."

"I might just 'bowl' you two over with my superb bowling skills." I kidded

"Well we shall have to see about that Cassie!"

"I've got my brilliant bowling skills at the ready." chuckled Mum, pretending to polish the ball

"Don't forget me!" said Dad, flexing the muscles in his bowling arm

We looked at the scores at the end of the game, and something amazing has happened!

| **Cassie** | **300** | **Dad** | **272** | **Mum** | **264** |

"Sorry Mum and Dad… I was just too good for you at the end."
"Good game." I said
"Yes Cassie, it was a good game."
"A brilliant family game, well worth the result." said Dad, proudly
"You have set a new record darling." Mum said
"Oh, I have too!"
"Wow!"
"I've taken over Kate's status as reigning champion for the girl's section by bowling three hundred!"
"Ha ha, I bet Kate will get a surprise when she finds out." I giggled with glee
"Yes, I imagine she will!"
"Let's go to the counter and inform the owner of your winning score." said Dad
"Our daughter Cassie has set a new record for the girl's section with three hundred."
"We're so proud of her." said Mum
"Well done to you, Miss Bontel."
"Your name will replace Kate's in the girl's section."
"You will receive a special trophy… which we will send away to be engraved with your name… and winning score on the front."
"Your name will also be added to the champions board, so you will be able to read it up on the board, next time you come back to bowl again."
"Congratulations young lady." said the owner, shaking my hand as he showed me a replica trophy from his collection.
"When your trophy comes back from the engravers it will look just like this one… except it will have your name and score on it…won't that be exciting?" he smiled
I look at his trophy and imagined my name on it… 'Cassie Bontel'… 'Girls Champion 2012'… 'Score 300'. It felt awesome to imagine, I just can't wait to see it! I shall be so honoured to take the trophy home with me when it's done.
"I can't wait for my trophy to come I can't wait to tell my classmates at the special centre all about it!" I exclaim, excitedly
"This calls for a celebration Cassie…let's get some takeaway for lunch…how about KFC?"
"KFC it is Dad!"
"I'll order a burger and maybe a cheesecake as a dessert if they have any." I said, grinning
We left the bowling centre… me with my head in the clouds… dreaming of trophies… lace up shoes… and fast bowling lanes!

# Chapter Forty-Eight
## Maritime Village & International Mini-Golf

The first item we saw in Warrnambool's maritime village was a golden pocket watch dating back to 1814... 'Carmichael's watch' is a fascinating piece of old gold jewellery... a McCabe watch.

'Loch Ard' was Victoria's greatest maritime disaster... fifty-two lives were lost... only two people managed to survive. Dr Carmichael was both a passenger and the ship's surgeon onboard.

The Loch Ard left Gravesend on the second of March 1878... with three thousand tons of cargo... both luxury... and household, items. These items included pianos... perfumes... clocks... confectionary... railway ties... cement... lead... and copper.

Eighteen passengers and thirty-six crew were on board... by the end of May it had made its way to the coast of Victoria... before the ship could land there was a disaster on the first of June 1878... the 'Loch Ard' ran aground on a reef and within fifteen minutes it sank to the bottom of the ocean...the captain had sailed too close to the cliffs of the 'Shipwreck Coast'.

The captain had been unable to see ahead because of the heavy fog and the ships compasses proved inaccurate...possibly due to magnetic interference from the load of railway iron they were carrying onboard ship... apprentice sailor Tom Pearce aged eighteen... and doctor's daughter Eva Carmichael from Dublin... also aged eighteen... were the only two survivors.

Eva lost both of her parents and four siblings, in the wreck.

Capt. Gibb asked Eva to tell his wife... 'That I stood with my ship to the last... and went down with her like a sailor'...one of the sentimental anecdotes, told about the shipwreck.

The real heroes of the story were Eva and Tom.

Tom saved himself by clinging to an upturned lifeboat through the treacherous surf.

Hearing Eva's cries for help he swam out to rescue her... she was floating on a hen-coop and spar.

Tom revived her with brandy that was salvaged from the shipwreck... before making her a bed of grass in a sea cave and resting her there. He then climbed fifty metres up the cliffs to find help...when he and the search party got back to the beach... they found that Eva had strayed. She was found 'in a mass of sandy brushwood'...

"I'm dying... where's Thomas Pearce." she moaned

Eva recuperated at 'Glenample Station'... Tom and Eva went their separate ways... never to meet each other again.

The Carmichael watch worth one hundred guineas... was originally intended as a gift from the Corporation of the City of Dublin... to mark a visit to the city by Dr. Evory Carmichael Eva's father.

Mrs Carmichael snatched it up when the ship sank... it was found secreted in the waistband of her dress when her body was washed ashore. Eva got the watch back and gave it to her husband Thomas Townsend... whom she married in 1884. His name can be seen on the rear movement cover.

Tom Pearce was the man of the hour and the 'darling' of the colonies. Everywhere he went he was mobbed he was forced to travel in the guard's van. He was awarded the first medal of the Victorian Humane Society.

Charles Hilder a Warrnambool photographer... who dabbled in the portrait postcard trade took his photograph... Coleman Jacobs composed 'The Young Hero Schottische' in his honour... over one thousand pounds was raised via public subscriptions in New South Wales and Victoria.

Tom was presented with an award on behalf of the Government... by His Excellency the Governor Sir George Bowen... 'a slight token of the respect and admiration in which your noble conduct is held by all the classes in this colony.' Ironically, the 'slight token' was a gold watch!

We had a look at the Flagstaff Hill collections... including the collection of two thousand, five hundred books... and learnt about the Lady Bay Lighthouses. It was an interesting experience to visit Flagstaff Hill and to learn about its history. I came away with lots of information, we also came away with quite a few photos too.

We booked in to our accommodation in Warrnambool that afternoon and the next day we received some texts inviting us to Warrnambool Mini-Golf by the Sea... for an International Tournament between celebrity autistic families.

The text read:

*'To the Bontel Family,*

*You are invited to Mini-Golf by the sea for an International Tournament. You will compete against fifteen countries, Argentina, Japan, Greece, England, France, Brazil, USA, Ireland, Spain, Germany, Italy, New Zealand, Denmark, Canada and Sweden.*

*Whichever team has the lowest overall score will win five thousand dollars. We hope you can make it and the best of luck!'*

"That's really awesome!"

"We get to do another round of mini-golf...this time we are competing against other autistic families for a chance to win five thousand dollars!"

"How good is that?" I said

"We won a trophy each and broke a record the first time we played mini-golf on this road trip... who knows what we might do in this game." said Dad, grinning

"Who knows ...we'll just have to wait and see." said Mum

We drove to Mini-Golf-by-the-Sea, where we met the other fifteen families who were going to be competing. Spectrum Key: HFA = High Functioning Autism MA = Mild Autism SS = Savant Syndrome A = Asperger's

| Country | Family Members & Spectrum |
|---|---|
| Argentina | Valentina Alvarez - Mother (HFA)<br>Santino Alvarez - Father (HFA)<br>Sofia Alvarez - Daughter (HFA) |
| Japan | Hinata Yoshida - Mother (MA)<br>Saki Yoshida - Father (MA)<br>Misaki Yoshida - Daughter (MA) |
| Greece | Meliza Petridis - Mother (MA)<br>Thanos Petridis - Father (MA)<br>Cora Petridis - Daughter (MA) |
| England | Sophie Robinson - Mother (SS)<br>Harry Robinson - Father (SS)<br>Ruby Robinson - Daughter (SS) |
| France | Emma Fournier - Mother (MA)<br>Nolan Fournier - Father (MA)<br>Camille Fournier - Daughter (MA) |
| Brazil | Leticia Melo - Mother (MA)<br>Gabriel Melo - Father (MA)<br>Larissa Melo - Daughter (MA) |
| USA | Kaitlyn Reed – Mother (MA)<br>Brent Reed – Father (MA)<br>Crystal Reed – Daughter (MA) |
| Canada | Sophia Stewart – Mother (A)<br>Owen Stewart - Father (A)<br>Madison Stewart – Daughter (A) |
| Spain | Claudia Delgado - Mother (HFA)<br>Sergio Delgado - Father (HFA)<br>Marta Delgado - Daughter (HFA) |
| Germany | Johanna Muller - Mother (SS)<br>Felix Muller - Father (SS)<br>Charlotte Muller - Daughter (SS) |
| Italy | Chiara Russo - Mother (HFA)<br>Luca Russo - Father (HFA)<br>Alessia Russo - HFA) |
| New Zealand | Isabella Thomas - Mother (MA)<br>Joshua Thomas - Father (MA)<br>Hannah Thomas - Daughter (MA) |
| Denmark | Karen Petersen - Mother (A)<br>Henrik Petersen - Father (A)<br>Kirsten Petersen - Daughter (A) |

| Ireland | Sarah O'Neil - Mother (MA)<br>Adam O'Neil - Father (MA)<br>Katie O'Neil - Daughter (MA) |
|---|---|
| Sweden | Linnea Jansson - Mother (MA)<br>Elias Jansson - Father (MA)<br>Ebba Jansson - Daughter (MA) |

    These families are golf and mini-golf champions of the past… so Mum Dad and I face some stiff competition…we'll have loads of fun regardless of the result. The tournament organiser who also happens to be the owner… gives us all a welcoming address.
    "Welcome to the Warrnambool Mini-Golf International Tournament."
    "You will be divided into two groups of eight."
    "Group One will play their eighteen holes and then Group Two will follow."
    "The top two finishers of each group will progress to the semi-finals."
    The winners of the semi-finals will progress to the grand-final."
    "The grand final winner will take home five thousand dollars in cash!"
    "Ladies and Gentlemen think of what you can spend five thousand dollars on!" he chortled
    "Some new golf clubs perhaps?" everyone laughs at that
    "Group One can you go to the first hole please."
    "Australia you can putt first."
    "I wish you the best of luck"
    After eighteen holes have been played, our scores look like this:

| Australia | 203 | USA | 204 | Ireland | 213 | New Zealand | 216 |
|---|---|---|---|---|---|---|---|
| Canada | 218 | England | 219 | France | 223 | Germany | 231 |

    "After Group One has played Team Australia is on top with two hundred and three points, just one point in front of Team USA on two hundred and four."
    "Team Australia and Team USA will advance to the first of the two semi-finals and two more top two finishers from Group Two will advance to the second semi-final."
    "Group Two, would you please begin."
    "Team Sweden you will go first."
    "The best of luck to you."
    After round two the scores were:

| Japan | 207 | Sweden | 210 | Denmark | 212 | Argentina | 213 |
|---|---|---|---|---|---|---|---|
| Brazil | 218 | Italy | 220 | Greece | 223 | Spain | 228 |

    "Round two is over and advancing to the second semi-final are Team Japan and Team Sweden!"
    "The semi-finals will begin shortly, the first two teams to play are Team Australia and Team USA."
    "We'll have ten minutes break, then we will resume." the owner announced
    "The first semi-final is between Team Australia and Team USA."
    "They are both well matched… so we are expecting to see a close contest." he announced
    "It sounds like a bit of 'sledging' going on out there… Ladies and Gentlemen!"

"We've played more mini-golf than you three together."
"I've won a few titles so we're going to beat you!"
"That's what you 'Ossies' think."
"We won a few titles between us too!"
"Plus, we played golf and mini golf for years!"
"Not a chance you can beat us!"
"There's a little banter going on between Team Australia and Team USA...that's so funny."
"Let the first semi-final begin!"
Sometime... later.
The scores after the first semi-final are:

| Australia | 214 |
|---|---|
| USA | 224 |

"Team Australia have won over Team USA 214 to 224 and will play the winner of semi-final two between Team Japan and Team Sweden."
"We'll get ready for that in five minutes."
"We're in the Grand Final!"
"We are doing so well to get this far."
"I'm so excited I could burst with joy." I said
"We are close to taking out the title."
"We proved to Team USA that practice makes perfect!"
"Whoever we play in the Grand Final, we will need to work hard to defeat them." said Mum
"Let's work hard for a good end result!" said Dad, enthusiastically
After the second semi-final the scores looked like this:

| Team Japan | 209 |
|---|---|
| Team Sweden | 206 |

"Team Sweden are the winners in this close second semi-final, they will play Team Australia in the Grand-Final!"
"We'll be ready in ten minutes time so don't go anywhere."
"It will be a tight one." said the owner
"We get to play against Team Sweden in the Grand Final!"
"I hear they are champion golfers in their native country of Sweden... they've won several titles between them."
"They are a force to be reckoned with...we'll need to play our best!" I said
"That's right Cassie."
"We are up to the task of playing against them."
"We'll soon get to see who wins!" said Mum
"We are ready for the challenge we have been practicing and playing well." said Dad
"Are you ready for this?"
"It's the Grand-Final of the Warrnambool International Mini-Golf Tournament between Team Australia and Team Sweden."

"These two countries have been playing mini-golf for many years and have a few titles under their belts... this will be a close contest!"

"Can Team Australia putt their way to victory?"

"Will Team Sweden come out on top?"

"We'll find out in less than an hour!"

"The best of luck to these two countries." the owner smiled, encouragingly

After the seventeenth hole the scores were even with:

| | |
|---|---|
| **Australia** | **212** |
| **Sweden** | **212** |

Team Sweden has just finished the eighteenth hole and now it is our turn. I was assigned to putt the ball up the steep hill, through the middle between the two hills and into the hole, where the golf ball returns to the counter. I was thinking... *'This hole looks quite difficult. I had a hard time getting the golf ball up these hills, the past few times I've been to Warrnambool, this time, I've practiced so hard... I will get this golf ball up the hill... I can do it!'*

I lined my golf club in front of my feet ready to hit the ball. All eyes are on me hoping that I will hit the ball up these steep hills and into the hole... except for Team Sweden... who are hoping I miss!

I hit the golf ball hard and it races up the first steep hill... through the middle hits the wall of the second steep hill... rolls slowly towards the hole slowly... slowly... I hope it makes it to the hole and hands us the victory!

I've had a lot of fun at Lake Pertobe Mini-Golf.

The golf ball stops on the edge of the hole and everyone gasps. We all thought it was not going to go in the hole! Then an amazing thing happens... the ball rolls over the edge and into the hole!

Everyone cheers and they are very happy for us... even Team Sweden!

Mum and Dad hug me tightly saying...

"You did brilliantly sweetie!"

"You handed us the victory!"

"Thanks Mum and Dad for teaching me how to play mini-golf!"

"I love playing it!"

"Team Australia... congratulations!"

"You've played brilliantly and won through!"

"Here is your trophy... and your cash prize of five thousand dollars!"

"Well done!" said the owner, beaming at us

The other international teams clapped. We all got together for a chat, to socialise and play at Lake Pertobe. The girls played in the maze... and on the playground equipment... whilst the adults were talking together in groups. Many of the contestants were multi lingual.

"Why don't I get us some ice-creams."

"It's the near the end of summer here in Australia...I'll buy some for everyone to try." I said

"Great idea Cassie!"

"We have never tried the ice-creams in Australia before."

"I can't wait to try one!" said Hannah

"I'll be back in ten minutes." I said

I went to a nearby shop which sold ice-creams and explained to the cashier that I needed lots of ice creams!

"There are fifteen of my new friends and myself."

"We have been playing in a mini-golf tournament which was very hot and now I plan to buy sixteen ice-creams for us all!" I said

The cashier looked surprised.

"I think you will need a big bag to carry all those ice-creams in... so they don't melt in the heat."

"I'll get a big cool bag to put them in after you choose the ice-creams you want."

There are plenty of types of ice-creams...I chose sixteen different ones which I think they will like... pay for them... and then the cashier carefully puts them into a big cool bag for me... so the ice-creams won't melt.

I walk back to the girls whose eyes light up when they see the bag full of assorted ice-creams!

"I can see you're all quite keen to try one so let's get started!"

I handed the ice-creams out to my new friends and they tasted them and...boy did they enjoy them too!

We chatted a little more and they were amazed that I was doing a road trip... and also performing in the Bontel Family band.

"Your pop tunes remind me of Winter and Summer times... in Stockholm."

"I can't wait to hear your solo album, when it gets released." said Ebba

"I plan to release one in a couple of years... I also plan to release a 'Bubblegum Dance' album... under the stage name Miss-Tique... mysterious and amazing like me."

Before we leave, we exchange phone numbers on our iPhones and promise to keep in contact with each other. They are good friends... I will see them again someday... maybe in their own countries... when I travel the world.

A day later, Mum was talking to me.

"Cassie we're visiting Warrnambool TAFE for a tour and then lunch at the cafeteria today."

"That will be fantastic." I replied

"It's a big building, I can find out where all the rooms are when we visit."

"There will be lots of classrooms... I think they have a pool table there." I mused

"They sure have!"

"This is a good time to go on a tour and check out their facilities." said Dad

"I'm keen to do that!" I said, enthusiastically

When we arrived at the Warrnambool TAFE campus, we went to the main reception desk where we were greeted by the reception staff. One of them kindly gave us a tour around the buildings. I never expected a TAFE campus to be this big, I can't believe how many rooms there are. There are many facilities to check out, I may consider going to one instead of university in the future. Lots of big decisions to make after this tour!

"This is the Verde Beauty Room, where the students who are studying beauty courses, learn to put into practice what they are being taught in their classes." said Karen, one of the receptionists

"What an excellent room... I think I could get a makeover in here and look very stylish... like Mum." I said

"I bet you could Cassie...maybe I could get a refresh and go back to my younger days." said Mum, dreamily

"Err... I might try and look handsome... just like when I was a lad." said Dad, grinning

Mum and I chuckled at that, so did the receptionist! It would be hilarious to see Dad being pampered with treatments at the hands of the students who study in the Verde Beauty Room. I reckon he might still look stylish like he was during his 'popstar' days!

"I'll let you ladies get stylish whilst I consider my options." Dad winked at Mum and I

"This is the pool table where the students play during their breaks."

"They enjoy a relaxing game of pool it gives them a break from their studies for an hour." the receptionist explained

"Here is the Library, where the students' study... use computers... or play the occasional game when not studying... there is also the student learning centre and bookshop."

We also explored the arts department and several other buildings. Warrnambool TAFE Campus is indeed a big place to study. I've decided to study at university in the future, TAFE looks interesting...I don't intend to study there... it was fun to check it all out though!

"I hope you enjoyed Warrnambool TAFE Campus." said the receptionist

"We sure did, it has plenty of courses for students to get a job in the future, it is very spacious with lots of friendly staff to help the students out when they need it."

"It's a very good facility." said Mum

"Have a nice lunch at the cafeteria."

"Bye"

"Bye." we all said

Mum, Dad and I, ordered our lunch and paid for it, we sat down at a vacant table.

"Cassie, what do you think of Warrnambool?"

"Are you enjoying yourself?" asked Dad

"Warrnambool is a great place."

"I am enjoying myself and having loads of fun."

"The mini-golf tournament at Lake Pertobe was great fun, and a definite highlight!"

"My mini-golf skills were put to good use against Team Sweden."

"The Ten-Pin Bowling was also a good activity to do as a family."

"We're having more fun and making more memories in each place we visit."

"I'm enjoying this special trip with you two and loving it more and more." I said.

"Let's enjoy the food and make the most of our last day in Warrnambool... before we leave tomorrow." said Mum

## Chapter Forty-Nine
## Camperdown Poets & Castlemaine Capers

"We've got a few days before we go to Tasmania... so let's get planning!" said Mum
"We can drive to Port Campbell to view Gibson's Steps and the Grotto."
"We can visit Port Campbell and Timboon... before we go inland to Camperdown... and then to Castlemaine... and the goldfields." I said, laying out the plan
"That sounds like a good plan, Cassie."
"Gibson's Steps looks like an interesting attraction in Port Campbell." said Dad, checking his phone
Gibson's Steps proved to be a spectacular sight... we were dwarfed by the cliff-line and offshore stack's enormity... locally the two offshore stacks were given the names of 'Gog' and 'Magog'. They are not considered to be part of the Twelve Apostles.
Local settler Hugh Gibson carved the steps into the cliff... when he was working on traditional access... used by the original Kirrae Whurrong inhabitants.
"Woah!"
"Wicked!"
"Look at the sheer scale of sculpting!"
"It is quite a landmark!" Mum agreed
"It's quite a feat!" Dad admired
"I could explore the nearby caves or run along the beach twirling and singing!"
"I could write a pop song about it called 'Golden Sun'... it could be a hit!" I laughed
"Those will be golden memories for you, Cassie!" smiled Mum and Dad
I took a few photos of Gibson's Steps and got Mum to record me dancing and twirling on the sand, which Mum uploaded later.
Later as we drove along, I asked Mum...
"How about we stay a night in Timboon?"
"It's only sixteen kilometres away from Port Campbell... there are a couple of things we can do there."
"That sounds like a good idea Cassie." Mum replied
When we arrived in Timboon... we learnt all about their special historical bridge. The 'trestle' railway bridge crosses the Curdies river... it was first built in 1872... and closed ninety-five years later.
It was restored in 2009 and reopened in November 2010 after the railway track was established. It was constructed of twenty trestles of large diameter bush timber poles... bolted together with a sawn timber superstructure... and a footway. It is a traditional utilitarian bridge... using wharf building techniques.

The bridge is one of the few surviving railway structures of this type in Victoria... it illustrates vernacular bridge building traditions... of the late nineteenth century... according to Heritage Australia!

After our historical sightseeing we decided to take a stroll to another of Timboon's favourite places... called 'Timboon Fine Ice Cream'... where they have twenty-four natural flavours of ice cream... and five sorbet flavours, to choose from!

There were a few flavours that I have never tried before... I chose Maple and Cinnamon.

I was not the only one to try a new flavour... Mum chose apple pie... to remind her of the apple pies cooked by Belinda and Grandma Georgina!

Dad selected Milk and Cream... all of the flavours we chose were delicious!

"I hope you enjoy your ice-creams... have you been here before?" asked the shop attendant

"No, we all love our ice-creams... you're doing a good job!" I said

"Thank you I've been here for several years... I enjoy seeing everyone's faces... particularly the children."

"They can't get enough I hear their delighted laughter every time they come in to choose their ice creams." she added

"We are ice-cream lovers too." smiled Dad, as Mum and I agreed

"I won't forget it!"

"I would love to come back again and try another flavour."

"Our friends and family would go crazy for this place." I said

"Timboon may be a small town... but I'm sure the locals love living here." said Dad

"I bet they do!" I agreed

Timboon's name comes from the local Aboriginal word 'Timboun'... which describe the pieces of rock they used in this area to open mussels.

We stayed the night and then the next morning got back on the road on our way to Camperdown.

Camperdown is situated on the world's third largest volcanic plain... with dormant volcano cones... craters... and waterways...these amazing natural features were created from lava flows that happened thousands of years ago, in the history and formation of this land.

You can climb Mt Sugarloaf or Mt Leura and check out the town's views...I don't think I would want to climb either of them just yet... because I might get lost!

Gnotuk Lake Lookout is an amazing lookout that we decided to go to, we need to stock up on some biscuits and chocolate first!

We went to the Camperdown IGA shop, I remember Nina and Ivy telling me about their work experience in IGA last year. I might consider doing a bit of work experience...I would like to work on the checkouts or the shelf-stacking...not the cleaning of the bathrooms though...Yuck!

That's one job that I would not like to do!

At the cereal aisle we noticed an old man struggling to reach the boxes on the top shelf. He looked like he could use some assistance!

"Excuse me... would you like some help?" I asked

"Thank you... I can't quite reach." he said

I reached up as far as I could... despite being taller than the old man...I couldn't reach the cereal either.

"Dad, can you give me a boost to the top shelf?" I asked

"Ok Cassie."

I grabbed the Weet-Bix, Dad put me down and I handed it to the man.

"Here you are." I said

"Thanks for your help young lady." said the old man

"No worries." I replied

After the shopping was done, we went to the Gnotuk Lake Lookout... it had an excellent view of the lake. The hills were very picturesque...the surroundings reminded me of all the fun picnics Mum, Dad and I, have had.

"This look out is really awesome!"

"The lake is so sparkly in the sunshine."

"It would make a great landscape picture... I could frame it and put it on my wall!"

"Yes, it's a really great view Cassie!" Dad agreed

"I want to teach my children about the beauty of nature too... someday." I said

"That's certainly a great thing to teach children!" smiled Dad

"Mum, Dad, we can have really big family picnics then!" I laughed

"We sure could... it would be lots of fun." Mum agreed

"Camperdown is a very sporting town too... Scott Lucas of Essendon... and Paul Broderick of Fitzroy and Richmond... were both born here!"

"Olivia and I enjoyed seeing them both play in Melbourne... at the MCG." Dad said, as we drove back into town

We were strolling down the main street of Camperdown now, when I spotted something interesting in the civic centre.

"Look, Mum, Dad... there's a statue of Robert Burns!"

We went inside to take a closer look.

"My Scottish relatives have enjoyed reading his work...so do I."

"He is a famous Scot!" said Mum, in her best Scottish accent making us chuckle

"He is indeed a famous Scotsman!"

"There have been functions to honour this famous bard... since of the arrival of the first Scots people in 1836... with poetry... music... songs... and writing." said Dad

"That's a fact Dad!"

"I have written a few pieces at Melbourne Secondary College... plus many songs...I've never written poetry before!"

"I was never interested...after seeing this statue... I feel inspired to try my hand at some poetry pieces." I said

"Well that's good to hear, Cassie."

"You can write rhyming poetry, verse or prose."

"There are many types of poetry... even Japanese Haiku... which only has five lines!" said Mum

"We would love to read your poetry darling." she added

"Maybe I could write one about Camperdown." I said

"If you want to...you could send them to a poetry magazine... or read them at a social event." Dad mused

"I'll just write for fun for now...I'll let you know when I'm finished." I added

Here are some things that I found out about Robert Burns.

He was born in the tiny village of Alloway, near Ayr. He wrote many literary works and greatly influenced Scotland's poetry... and Scottish culture. His father was a peasant farmer and he grew up in poverty... he didn't have much formal schooling... his father and a local teacher John Murdoch... became his tutors. Robert learnt reading... writing... arithmetic... Latin... French... and Mathematics.

He was a gifted scholar from a young age... 'Poems Chiefly'... was his first ever published book in 1786... in the Scottish dialect. The Scottish public loved reading his work and it was one of the most famous books that Burns wrote.

He published several more during his lifetime including... 'A Red, Red Rose'... 'To a Mouse'... 'Tam O'Shanter'... and 'Ae Fond Kiss'... but his most notable work was... 'Auld Lang Syne'... which is sung at Hogmanay on the last day of the Scottish year... also known as New Year's Eve!

Despite all of these works... he fell into poverty as his health failed... he developed rheumatic fever and passed away from that fever at the age of thirty-seven... he was eventually buried at the Burns' mausoleum, in September 1817.

His widow Jean Armour's body was buried with him in 1834... at the time of his passing he had twelve children! If I ever visit Scotland, I should like to write a poem... about its scenery and cities. Maybe, I could turn a couple of them into songs... like Robbie Burns did!

"I'm getting peckish Mum!"

"There's a bakery nearby... I'm keen to get an apple slice and a pie!"

"Mum, would you like to try a 'snot-block'?" I asked sneakily, waiting for the response

"Yuck!"

"That's gross Cassie!" cringed Mum

"Just kidding, Mum... I got you there...I mean vanilla slice." I giggled

"Good one, Cassie!"

"Let's go to the bakery." said Dad, grinning too

Mum just rolled her eyes at both of us.

"I love Camperdown." I laughed as we entered the bakery

We are on our way to Castlemaine today it's a lovely place, with interesting things to see and do. When we arrived, it was still early morning... we chose to visit Buda Historic Home and Gardens... an authentic house and garden surviving in Castlemaine since the Victorian gold rush times!

The house was named after Ernest Leviny's homeland in Budapest... the Hungarian Leviny family were its owners... and lived there for one hundred and eighteen years.

Inside, it contains family collections of furniture... art works... and significant belongings. It also has an historic garden of 1.2 hectares...being an important piece of goldfield history... this home and garden has many treasures on display.

Ernest and his wife Bertha who was born in Greenwich England... had ten children between the years of 1865 and 1883. Louis... Alfred... Ernest... and Francis... Mary... Ilma... Beatrice... Gertrude... Bertha... and Hilda... making four sons and six daughters in all!

Mary the eldest, helped to run the household... and contributed to clothes-making... and embroidery. Hilda was excellent at embroidery... Kate in photography... Gertrude did wood-carving... and Bertha worked in metal and enamel.

The eldest son Louis served in the Boer War... and for a time lived in South Africa... Ernest Junior worked in Western Australia as a surveyor... on projects such as the Kalgoorlie Pipeline... early railway works... and similar projects.

The other two sons passed away under the age of five.

Ilma married Dr. Jim Thompson and lived in Castlemaine near Buda... having five daughters... who spent most of their time with their aunts at Buda.

Buda was originally known as Delhi Villa...built by Reverend James Smith... a retired Baptist missionary. It was a six-roomed brick house with an encircling veranda... it was put up for auction two years later.

Ernest Leviny purchased the property in 1863. Between the years of 1890-1900... many changes and alterations were made to the house... it was renamed Buda after the capital of Hungary in Budapest. The house still has its 'parsley green' trims and shutters characteristic of Ernest Leviny's Hungarian origins.

We went inside the house and learnt about the domestic items that were used in those times and saw many items of silver... original artworks... and decorative arts... on view. The artworks amazed me... especially the rose painting.

I imagined myself for a moment in the rose-garden dancing and exploring... smelling the beautiful perfume. Mum has a red rose perfume, which she created and released in 1991...I would like to try it out soon.

"Cassie what do you think of the house?" asked Mum

"It feels like I've stepped back into the 1800's."

"I love the paintings and domestic items."

"For a moment I imagined myself in the rose garden, playing amongst the roses and smelling their perfume."

"The domestic items remind me of the some of the ones you used to use in our house." I said

"It reminds me of similar items I used... as well as Mum's domestic items... which she passed on to me... which I then in turn, used for some time." said Mum

After lunch, we decided to cool down at the Castlemaine outdoor pool which is open from December to March. Mum and Dad got changed into their bathers... while I stripped down to my bra and knickers. I'm about to put my cheeky idea into practice...I've noticed several boys here... I'm going to make their eyes pop when they see me parade near the pool! Hee, hee! Hope Mum and Dad don't notice!

We found a nice vacant spot on the grass and put down our beach towels. Mum was relaxing in her black sunglasses... whilst Dad was reading his book. While they were busy doing that I stood up and put on my dark black sunglasses. I thought... *'Here I come boys!... Sexy looking...drop-dead gorgeous... stunning pop star Cassie...is coming your way!'*

I paraded around the Castlemaine outdoor pool like a sexy gorgeous model... I see the local boys turn their heads... jaws dropping. This is starting to look good... cue the sexy music... I make a couple of model moves... and the local boys are mind-boggled! I pull down my sunglasses... and give a cheeky wink... giggling with excitement.

Dad looks up from his book and notices me making my 'model 'moves. His jaw drops!

"Err... Mikayla"

"You had better see what your daughter is doing!"

"I think she is being a sexy lingerie model in her underwear!" said Dad, with a gurgling noise in his throat

Mum sits up and can't believe her eyes! She is speechless!

I continue parading around the pool... making my moves... and giggling... I pull down my sunglasses and give the boys a final wink, saying...

"Sexy Cassie is leaving the area!"

I walk back to my towel...where Mum and Dad are in disbelief and shock. Uh Oh... by the looks on their faces... I am in big trouble! The smile drops from my face... it's not looking good for me at the moment!

"Cassie!... what the hell were you thinking?"

"Showing off your underwear... to those boys like that!"

"You have embarrassed us and yourself... with your actions!" Dad yelled

"That was very silly and very immature Cassie!"

"You have embarrassed us... that was a totally inappropriate thing to do!"

"You know that you will get into trouble if you go too far with your behaviour." said Mum, sternly

"But...Mum... Dad..."
"I was only having a good time... showing the boys... my lovely model moves."
"They loved it."
"Mum... how come you got away with modelling years ago... and never got into trouble... not even once?"
"It's very harmless and it's only fun!" I protested loudly
"Cassie Annabel Bontel... it may seem like fun to you... but it is not fun for us to see... and it is not appropriate for you to do... either!"
"It is obviously another topic that you and I need to discuss!" said Mum, firmly
"All right... all right." I scowled
"I don't want to talk about it here." I said, grumpily

I went back to the change rooms and got into my bathers... then I went for a lovely swim to cool off. At one point I cheekily winked at one of the boys and pointed my finger at him with a big grin. The local boy laughed...Mum and Dad noticed which made me sigh... thinking about the lecture I was going to get from them both... when we got back to our rooms!

Meanwhile, Mum and Dad were thinking... *'We have definitely got to discuss this topic with her, she needs to understand what is socially appropriate and safe behaviour especially if she chooses to go on a date in the future!'* After we had finished swimming, we went to the kiosk for an ice-cream... then made our way back to the hotel.

In our hotel Mum Dad and I, sat down for the 'talk'!

I've been dreading it whilst having my shower...I'm prepared to listen to what Mum and Dad have to say to me...I will have my say without any of us getting into an argument...I hope!

"Cassie, we know you love to relax in your bra and knickers or bathers whenever we are at the beach... and we know you also love to model...Mum and I are concerned about you modelling in front of boys." said Dad
"What concerns do you have about me showing my modelling 'moves' to the boys?" I asked, confused
"We have a few concerns."
"The boys may get the wrong impression or idea... about what you are doing."
"They might tease you...or hurt you...or do something that you wouldn't like them to." said Mum
"If that were to happen you could be embarrassed, upset or shocked... the humiliation might cause you to lose all the confidence that you have built up...and make you want to stay inside."
"We don't want that to happen...so we must teach you the 'social steps'... as well as the appropriate things... to prevent this from happening again." said Mum, firmly
"Right."
"It's another lesson I need to learn about."
"I'm starting to see a bit of what you are saying...you may have a point!"
"I've done the wrong thing here...I apologise for it."
"Good Cassie... now listen carefully... there is nothing wrong with celebrating your body... but it belongs to 'YOU'... it's not meant for the 'entertainment' of others."
"I don't want the boys to do something that upsets or humiliates me...I'm prepared to do something about it." I said
"That's good Cassie."
"It's fine if you model in the privacy of your bedroom...just not in a public place like a pool." Dad told me
"We'll teach you the places where to model and not to model...hopefully you won't slip up again... now that you understand a little better." Mum said
"Also, Cassie...now that you are growing from a teenager into a young woman...it might be best if you only wear your 'bathers' when you are outside at the beach or swimming...instead of your underwear."

"Of course, Mum."

"I'll try my best not to embarrass myself... or you and Dad." I said

"Good girl Cassie."

"We know you want to be more independent...and you are gaining confidence every day...just let us assist you a little more... that's all." Dad added

"Yes, Mum and Dad I promise I will." I said

"You know...I've got another modelling idea!" I piped up

Mum and Dad looked at each other, with a... 'Oh here we go again'... look!

I just got into trouble with my latest modelling foray, so they weren't too sure about more modelling in public, since that... err, shall we say 'slip up'.

"I would have an unusual 'bath of my dreams'."

"It would contain melted white chocolate... maple syrup... ice-cream... and condensed milk."

"I would strip... hop in right up to my shoulders and bathe peacefully... blissfully content... dreaming of delightful things... like cats... performing pop music... winter... and horses."

"It's just a dream bath... for me in my fantasy world... that I sometimes go to."

"I would eat some afterwards...what a delicious bath that would be." I said, dreaming of white chocolate and imagining myself in a bath of it

Mum and Dad's jaws dropped! Oops! That didn't go down too well either!

"Cassie Annabelle Bontel!"

"Whatever made you think of that!?" asked Mum, in a horrified voice

"Erm... it's just another fantasy of mine."

"I'm sorry... if I shocked you." I said, sheepishly

"Good!"

"Because you will do no such modelling!" Mum said, with a disapproving look on her face

"It's not a good idea."

"Definitely not before you turn eighteen... it would not be a good look at all!"

"It would damage your reputation and give people the wrong idea about you...especially impressionable young men!" said Dad, in a very serious voice

"Imagine how sticky it would be in the bath... when the chocolate got cold it would set... making a terrible mess everywhere!"

"The drains would become clogged up...it would be very unsafe trying to get in or out of the bath...it is not practical at all Cassie!"

"You can't do that, sweetheart." said Mum, firmly

"Ok... ok... it's not a very good idea."

"When is the best time and place to do it then...can you tell me." I groaned, theatrically

"If you really want to try something like that... do it at home in your own bathroom...when you are an adult...and only use milk!" Mum said, in an exasperated voice

"Still, it would take loads and loads of milk to fill a bath!"

"You can enjoy it then...we will not take any photos... that would not be right." said Mum

"All right?"

"I might take a selfie and put it in a private folder or photo album...I won't upload it to YouTube."

"Then I'll decide whether to show it to the family at my twenty-first birthday... or not!" I said

"Good, Cassie... promise?" said Dad

"Yes, Dad... I promise." I replied

# Chapter Fifty
## Victorian Goldfields

"Cassie, we're going on the Victorian Goldfields railway train today... we will be travelling through the central goldfields."
"Isn't this going to be fun?" said Mum
"It will be wicked!"
"I've been on the 'Ghan'... I'll have lots of fun on this Goldfields railway train too!"
"I have another dream on my list."
"What's that Cassie?" Dad asked
"To ride on a steam train!" I replied
"I'm so going to enjoy this awesome dream experience!" I said, very excitedly

We went into the ticket section and paid for a first-class fare which was one hundred and twenty-five dollars... I can't wait to see what the first-class compartments look like on the 'Goldfields' train... compared to the 'Ghan'!

"Enjoy your journey to Maldon."
"It will be a great journey." Mum agreed

We felt like we were transported to an era of elegance and sophistication when we stepped onboard the train. We made our way to the parlour car and embraced the Edwardian decoration, as we looked around.

"Wow!"
"I'm in another era with this Edwardian decor from 1919... it's so very beautiful."
"I feel like I could live in this world for a long time." I said, smiling
"Look at all of this... the art nouveau fittings are stunning." said Dad
"The large lounge and cane chairs add a nice homely feeling to this parlour car." said Mum
"The views will be good from the end viewing platform." I commented

We went to the end viewing platform... it is quite lovely to see the trees and buildings pass by... we took a few photos to record our journey. I sent a picture of the train and some views to Mia. She will love them, I'm sure this train will be one her favourites.

We sat down in our cane chairs and the stewards served us lunch. For our premium gift certificate, we received a cheese platter, plus lemonade at our request it was tasty and refreshing.

I phoned Jenna to tell her about the fun times we are having on this magnificent train. Jenna was relaxing in her garden with Caroline and Andrew, when she received the phone call.

"Hello, Jenna."
"How are you?"
"Yes, that is a train that you can hear in the background."

"It's the Victorian Goldfields railway train... we're in the parlour car enjoying the lovey views and enjoying the refreshments."

"Yes, you would love to travel on it!"

"I'm having a blast!"

"I've sent Mia a picture of it, she will love it!"

"This train would be her ultimate ride!"

"It runs from Castlemaine to Maldon."

"We are planning to stay for two to four days we might visit Kerrie Michele's jewellery shop."

"Who doesn't look beautiful with some 'bling' on!" I laughed

"I might have to raid a lolly shop there too!" Jenna laughed at that one

"We're nearing Maldon so I have to go now."

"I'll send you a couple of photos."

"Bye."

The train stopped at Maldon which is a small historic town in Victoria... we checked in to the Maldon Eaglehawk Motel...then headed to the Maldon Lolly Shop.

Inside were old fashioned and traditional confectionery such as... liquorice... boiled sweets... lollipops... jujubes and jellies... delicious chocolates... and old English lollies... sherbet favourites... and every sweet treat and lolly you could possibly imagine!

We were so excited just like the proverbial 'kids in the candy shop'... we were so tempted to buy everything we saw! There was local honey... Murray Brewery Cordials... and an array of beautiful tins... gifts... and novelties.

Oh, my goodness! I'm drooling at the thought of all those yummy treats! I want to buy 'boatloads' of them! Calm yourself Cassie... just calm down...take your time... only buy a couple. Problem is... which ones do I choose?

We bought some lollies to eat at the hotel and on the way back to Castlemaine. They look very tasty. We spent the afternoon visiting a couple of bookstores... a teddy bear store... and a newsagent. We bought a local paper to read and made our way back to our hotel.

"Mmm... these lollies are so delicious."

"I will definitely remember that shop!" I said, appreciatively

"That reminds me of a sweet memory with your Dad." said Mum

"In 1985, Dad and I went down the street to do some shopping for our parents at Safeway."

"We got all the groceries and paid for them... we had some money left over so we decided to spend it on a couple of lollies each... at the lolly shop."

"We ate them like naughty kids... while watching an AFL match in the evening."

"It was a 'sweet' memory in more ways than one that I still recall today." said Mum, fondly

"It's a sweet story Mum."

"I felt like a naughty kid myself today in the lolly shop... I didn't know which ones to choose... I wanted them all!" I giggled

When we returned to Castlemaine the next day... we picked up our vehicle and drove to Bendigo, which used to be Belinda and Darren's hometown. They were originally neighbours from the age of six and five respectively... until they were seventeen and sixteen.

They became boyfriend and girlfriend at the ages of eighteen and seventeen they were married a year later... they became parents to Mum and Rebecca the following year. We are meeting Ken and Wanda... Darren's older brother and sister as we're planning to do a few things with them.

Like visiting the Golden Dragon Museum... the Discovery Science and Technology Centre... and Chancery Lane.

We're going to have a fun wicked time this week... full of activities... we also will also give a concert performance here as well.

We booked a spa suite at the 'All Seasons' quality resort. I might try a bit of roller-skating... maybe relax and swim in the indoor heated pool... chill in the sauna or spa... and take part in a personal training session. It's a quality hotel...it says it in the name! I'll have an awesome time staying here... there are historic sites to visit as well.

We met Ken and Wanda at Rosalind Park. I haven't seen them in a long time... so there's some catching up to be done.

"Hello, Ken and Wanda."

"It's nice to see you after such a long time." I said, hugging them tight

"Hello Cassie."

"It's good to see you too!" said Ken, hugging me

"Hello Cassie."

"I haven't seen you for a long time... it's so lovely to see you." said Wanda, hugging me

"Nice to see you both."

"We haven't seen you for ages." said Dad, hugging them

"No, we haven't seen each other for ages Daniel." agreed Ken, hugging him back

"How are you doing on this fine day Wanda... my precious aunt?" said Mum, hugging Wanda

"I'm doing fine Mikayla... my pretty popstar niece." smiled Wanda

"We've got plenty of catching up to do... let's go to the 'Rocks on Rosalind' and have a good chin-wag."

We ordered our lunch at 'Rocks on Rosalind' and the chatter began!

"How is our adorable Cassie going?" asked Ken

"I'm awesome thanks Uncle Ken... even though it's a little embarrassing being called 'adorable' in front of Mum and Dad... now that I'm sixteen years old!" I said, blushing

"You are taking a road trip I hear?"

"How's that going?" asked Wanda

"It's going great guns!"

"We have returned to Victoria to explore some more towns before we make our way to Tasmania... which is the last state on our Australian road trip."

"We've been to Maldon via the Goldfields railway train we had a blast on it!"

"We went to Castlemaine and learnt some history... bought some jewellery... and some yummy lollies... now we are here in Bendigo planning to have some more fun!" I said

"It all sounds great!"

"We heard that you performed at the 'Wood, Wine and Roses' festival in Heywood."

"How was that?"

"What was the experience like?" asked Ken

"It went really well."

"It was our first time performing at a festival as the 'Bontel Family' band!

"Our fans that attended had a great time at the festival... which made it memorable for us." Dad added

"Great to hear you had fun in Heywood." Wanda smiled

"When we went to Warrnambool... Cassie mastered a new skill."

"We went bowling and Cassie tied up her shoe laces for the first time on her own." Mum told them

"Well done Cassie… that's progress!" Ken grinned

"What activities have you got planned for us to do together?" asked Wanda

"Well there is the Golden Dragon Museum."

"It's dedicated to the history and culture of the Chinese people who came to Australia in the great gold rush times… they worked on the goldfields in Ballarat and Bendigo." I said

"You're very smart for a pop star."

"You know lots about Australia, don't you?" said Ken

"I sure do!"

"I've learnt even more since we started on this road trip!"

Ken and Wanda… Dad and Mum… all laughed out loud at that statement.

We had lots of fun at the Golden Dragon Museum… we chose the general guided tour… learning about the highlights of the collection… as well as learning about the history of Chinese settlement in Bendigo.

The collections included dragon banners and lion dance drums, which were very interesting items to view. The guide was able to answer our questions about all the things we saw.

After lunch we headed to Chancery Lane with an eclectic mix of food… fashion… and art. It was originally known as Dispensary Lane after the busy pharmacy that used to be located in the lane… where for decades, locals had remedies and medications dispensed to them.

'Foodies Haven' was a sensation to the senses!

Global wines… boutique beers… coffee aromas… and inspired food… were featured there. We had food at the European-style hub… a good little nook to explore.

Next, we found some of Australia's emerging brands in both fashion and cosmetics… we delved into the salons and boutiques… the ladies couldn't resist trying on a 'few things'…or as Dad would put it…several hundred!

We bought a couple of items and left to go back to our hotel. Ken and Wanda went back home, they still live in another area of Bendigo. That lane was unique and fascinating, I will recommend it to our family and friends. It's a nook not to be missed!

As we drove back to our hotel, I couldn't resist trying to turn down the volume of Mum's Madonna CD… Mum was on to me like a hawk!

"I saw that Cassie."

"Don't touch it!" Mum said

I just giggled. I tried again, reaching my hand towards the volume dial, Mum playfully slapped my hand away.

"Cassie!"

"Get out of it!"

"Hands off!" laughed Mum

That evening after my dinner I took my bubble mixture and bubble wand with me into the bathroom… I poured bubble bath mixture in to the spa…there were bubbles everywhere! I decided to be cheeky and pour lots more mixture in… the bubbles cascaded all over the edge and onto the floor.

I laughed happily, reclining amongst the bubbles… blowing more and more! This is awesome! There are bubbles all around me… so many that I get lost in them. The bubbles float around for a while… I pop most of them giggling all the time. This is so much fun I don't want to stop!

A short time later Mum came in and saw the scene…she does not look happy!

"Cassie!"

"What a mess!"

"What Mum."
"I didn't do it."
"Of course, ... you didn't."
"It must have been the fairies then." Mum said, sarcastically
"We both know who made this mess!"
"Someone has to clean it up afterwards." said Mum, with a knowing look
I laughed even louder.
"You think that's funny do you Cassie?"
"I'll show you how funny it is... when you get out of the spa bath." said Mum
"Mum... I'm having loads of fun in the spa bath." I moaned
"I don't want to stop." I added
"I know Cassie... I know."
"You don't have to stop your fun right now...when the water turns cold... you must get out and put your nightclothes on."
"Ok Mum." I replied
When I got out and dried myself off later Mum handed me my pyjamas to put on.
Mum went out and came back with... Oh no... a scrubbing brush... a bucket and a big cleaning towel!
My face dropped!
Guess who gets to clean up the mess I made readers?
"Cassie... since you made the mess... you can clean it up!"
"Here is the cleaning equipment." Mum hands me the gear, with a smirk on her face
"Aw Mum!"
"You can clean it up... can't you?" I pleaded
"I could... but I'm not going to!" she replied
"You can clean up your own mess from now on... you are not a little child anymore... it's not up to Dad and I... to clean your mess." said Mum, firmly
"Can't 'HE' do it... instead of me?" I asked sullenly, pointing to Dad
"No... I'm too busy doing other things." said Dad, with a grin on his face
"It's called responsibility!" he added
"You made it...you clean it!" Mum stated
"M-u-u-u-m... but I don't want to!" I whined
"No buts!" said Mum, starting to sound cranky
"But... but..."
"But Nothing!" Mum said, with a final note in her voice
"FINE!"
I grabbed the bucket... the scrubbing brush... the big cleaning towel... and stomped around the bathroom... cleaning up the floor.
Mum was watching me to make sure I did it properly.
Initially, I grumbled silently with a grumpy look on my face... giving Mum a 'dirty look' which said... *'you're the one that's meant to be scrubbing the floor clean not me. I don't know why you're not cleaning up after me this time... like you usually do.*
Grumble... grumble! Bleep... bleep!
"There is no need to grumble and mumble under your breath Cassie!"
"The job is not hard."

"Make sure you do a good job!" Mum added

"Sure... Mum... sure." I mumbled grudgingly, under my breath

Yeah, yeah, I can hear you sniggering to yourselves as you're reading this.

You may think it's funny...but to me... it's not!

You may think that I'm like Cinderella, scrubbing the floors while her sisters go to the ball without her, with Mum playing the role of the stepmother supervising!

It's a little different though! There is no fireplace here and instead of Cinderella in her ragged clothes, there's me scrubbing and cleaning the floors in my nightclothes!

I can still hear you laughing! It's not funny OK! Ha, ha! Cassie gets to scrub the floors while we only have to read about it.

As I scrubbed and cleaned... the job wasn't as bad as I thought. I am independent in most of the chores Mum and Dad have taught me.

Whenever I used to take a bath... I always made a mess with the bubbles and the water...then Mum and Dad... or a carer... would have to clean it up.

I always keep my room neat and tidy and other areas of the house... except the bathroom!

I also occasionally made a mess in the shower with water and shampoo, then Mum and Dad or a carer would have to clean that up too.

I know Mum and Dad are not my slaves...so this is another area where I can become more independent... and enjoy doing things for myself.

I finally finished the bathroom floor, it looked so shiny and clean. It was a lot of work, but I put in the effort and got the job done! The floor looks so sparkly I can see my reflection in it.

"Well Cassie, did you clean the bathroom floor properly?" asked Mum, coming back in to check my work

"Yes... I did Mum."

"I scrubbed and cleaned and worked hard."

"Let me see Cassie if you really did a great job... otherwise." said Mum, ominously

Mum looked around the bathroom to check if it was really clean. She inspected it carefully... looking around all the areas... she is happy that I have done the job properly!

"Cassie this floor is very clean!"

"You did a great job!"

"I hope you can keep up the good work from now on darling!"

"I shall be watching to make sure." Mum added

"Yes Mum."

"I promise I will keep the floors clean from now on." I said, as I made my way to bed

The next morning, I was checking out the local attractions in the hotel brochures.

"Mum, Dad, I've looked over a few more activities... the Central Deborah Gold Mine sounds like a fun and interesting activity... for us as a family."

"We think so too, Cassie!"

"We'll do the underground adventure tour."

"We get to dress up in miner's clothes...overalls... boots... miner's hat... and lamp... then we descend eighty-five metres underground... and explore tunnels... drifts... and slopes." Dad explained

"We will also get a taste of what life was like working and eating underground... in the underground function room where we will be served a traditional miner's lunch!" he added

"Then we'll explore the surface of the mine with vintage mining machinery... gold panning... and interpretive museums."

"I've never been in an underground mine before, I think I'll be fine." I said

"That's good Cassie."

"If you get anxious use your techniques...and we can continue the tour from there."

"I'm sure you will be fine though." said Mum

Ken and Wanda came with us on our mine expedition.

We all dressed in miner's clothes and went to level two via an industrial lift... we climbed six sets of four metre ladders down to level three...there's medium fitness and ladder climbing involved... then back up to level two.

In between all that climbing we ate our 'Miner's lunch' and had a drink as well.

We learnt about what life was like working underground.

The Central Deborah Gold Mine operated from 1939-1954... their three hundred and fifty-seven male miners... successfully extracted almost one ton of gold from underground... which in today's money is worth forty-six million dollars!

The mine is four hundred and twelve metres deep... it has seventeen separate levels...with fifteen kilometres of drives... and cross cut tunnels. Most of the back-breaking work was done by hand... the conditions would be considered appalling, by today's standards!

The men were lowered underground in a cage with only two sides... often working in ankle to knee deep water... filling up to thirty-two ore trucks a shift by hand. These trucks were then pushed a mile or more along rails in the drives... using only carbide lamps as a light source... whilst breathing in fumes and rock dust... with bells being their only source of communication.

I can't imagine how they got through it every day... but they were tough men who did those jobs!

Back then the working conditions were considered to be among the best at Central Deborah mine... it was one of the only mines to have hot showers!

When the Central Deborah Gold Mine closed, the Bendigo skyline started changing. Poppet heads... engine rooms... service quarters... battery houses... and chimneys... steadily disappeared. Bendigo City purchased the Central Deborah Gold Mine for the mere sum of six thousand dollars, after intense lobbying in 1970... it was still intact at the time.

It was purchased to ensure that a vital link to Bendigo's historic golden past was secured.

The Bendigo Trust was formed so it could oversee the operations of the Central Deborah Gold Mine... the surface of the mine was opened to the public in 1971. It was originally opened for twelve hours a week, then increased as a part of Bendigo's history.

It was gazetted as a Public Historical Purposes Reserve in 1974, and H.R.H. Prince Charles was one of the visitors. The underground workings had become flooded... so no one could view them.

The community became involved in a monumental effort and on June 20th 1986... the Honourable John Cain, then Premier of Victoria... officially opened it to the public... with a long-standing dream brought to fruition.

In 1998 the underground adventure tour on level three was launched, and thirteen years later... the Central Deborah Gold Mine became Australia's deepest underground mine tour... the 'Nine Levels of Darkness' tour was launched... allowing visitors access two hundred and twenty-eight metres underground... to level nine.

We also explored the surface of the mine... the vintage mining machinery was fascinating... we didn't find any gold in the gold panning section. In the interpretive museums we learnt about gold's place in the history of Bendigo... 'the gold rush'... and Australia's history and fortune.

Back at the hotel... Mum, Dad and I, relaxed by the indoor pool lying on pool loungers. It was an excellent day on the gold mine tour...it proved to be very energetic at times...it was good to be relaxing and unwinding by the pool, at the end of the day.

"That gold mine tour was brilliant!"

"It was a little scary at first...I didn't let the dark and depths bother me... I enjoyed the whole tour and learning about the history."

"The climbing was hard work... but it was worth it." I added

"It was hard work climbing down all those stairs...at least we got plenty of exercise as well!" smiled Dad

"I would like to do that sort of thing again."

"It was awesome, we've got a couple of good photos to look at too!" I said

I relaxed for half an hour watching all the other people swim in the indoor pool, having loads of fun. I like watching everyone have fun together as a family, when they are away on holidays.

I decided to chat to Mia on my iPhone, telling her about the mine experience, she told me that she loved the photos of the Victorian Goldfields Train and the views I sent her.

She tells me that her Mum and Dad loved the photos too and they send their love. It's great to chat to loved ones, whilst we are taking this trip!

# Chapter Fifty-One
## A Carousel, 'Cats' and Cricket

We have travelled back to the coast for the last day or so… before we return to Melbourne and prepare for our last state to visit on our road trip… which will be Tasmania!

I smelt the fresh sea air when we arrived in the evening at Lorne and booked into our hotel for the night. After breakfast in the morning, we pack up our things to spend the day by the sea, I love the beach and intend to make the most of it!

There are lots of things that we could try… such as visit the great Otway… experience nature like misty and ancient waterfalls… discover Erskine Falls… or see the rich ochre cliffs at Bells Beach via the surf coast walk…as we don't have enough time to do all of those…we decide to go to Lorne surf beach and cool ourselves down instead.

After changing into our bathers and sun-screening ourselves, we go straight to the beach. Mum and I get out the Frisbee and spent twenty minutes throwing it to each other, back and forth, Dad joined in and we all had fun.

"That was so much fun with the Frisbee!"

"We stretched our muscles and got lots of exercise running about… catching… throwing… and diving for it!"

"This is so much fun… now we get to cool off in the water!"

"Let's have a little rest first though… I'm a bit puffed after all that running around!" I said

"It's great to see you enjoying yourself." said Mum

"You've always been a beach girl!" Dad smiled

"You are so right, Dad!"

"Mum, when I sit on my towel can you massage my shoulders?"

"Ok." Mum replied

We spread our towels on the sand… I got out my MP3 player and chose some relaxing music. I rested for a while imagining myself on a tropical island… swimming in the ocean…relaxing on the beach. Sometime later I sat up… Mum massaged my shoulders it was very relaxing… I enjoyed the sensation of Mum's gentle hands… after a while I was ready to hit the waves!

We swam in the waves doing all the things we love… kicking… and splashing… bobbing under… and having fun.

Later, we got out… dried ourselves off and went to get changed back into our clothes… then we went to a sidewalk café for lunch. We had given ourselves appetites with all the exercise at the beach… we were hungry and ready to eat! The Lorne view was wicked from where we were sitting, the food was delicious!

"Hey Mum, Dad, I'm enjoying Lorne a lot!"

"The water is very cool and clear to swim in."

"Let's enjoy the Lorne view and soak in the fantastic environment together." said Dad, smiling at me

'I sure will Dad!" I said, grinning back at him and Mum

Later that morning, we got back on the road, leaving Lorne behind.

We are now arriving in the big city of Geelong.

"It's great to be in Geelong!"

"Look at all these buildings to see and activities to do!"

"There's plenty."

"I don't know where to start!" I said

"How about we start with the carousel?"

"Dad and I have been on one before and really enjoyed it." said Mum

"The carousel sounds like it will be fun to ride on." I said, happily

We went over to the carousel…we bought a ticket each and had a blast riding on it!

It has taken three years… and thousands of hours of painstaking research… and hard work to restore it to its former glory. I notice that the carousel boards which adorn the carousel have forty-eight original artworks… about the King Arthur Legend.

I love to listen to the carnival-style music provided by the organ whilst riding round and round. It is such fun I would love to stay on here all day long!

We got off and started walking away when a lady approached us.

"Will you help me with something?" she asked

"If we can."

"What do you need help with?" Dad said

"My four-year old daughter is too scared to go on the carousel… I can't convince her to get on."

"Can you help?" she asked me

"I can try."

"I'll do my best to help your daughter on to the carousel." I said

"That would be great if you could."

I walked over to where the little girl was sitting… she seemed nervous and I felt I could help her feel better.

"Hello."

"Do you feel ok?" I asked

The girl shook her head from side to side.

"Are you too scared to go on the carousel?" I asked her

This time the little girl shook her head up and down.

I thought about it for a couple of minutes. How can I get the girl onto the carousel without making her more scared? I then got an idea. I hope it works.

"How about you go on the carousel with me?"

"We'll have a fun ride together." I said

The girl looked up at me and took my hand, we both walked to the carousel. We got our tickets and sat side by side on a bench seat ride …where we both had a fun time.

"Thank you… young lady."

"My daughter will be more confident next time… because of you." the little girl's mother smiled at me

"I'm glad that I could help."

"That's good of you."

"We had better go now."
"Come on darling time to go home."
The girl and her mum left.
Cassie, well done for helping that young girl on the carousel." Mum said
"We heard you laughing... you two had a fun time together."
"Well done Cassie." said Dad, proudly
"Thanks Mum and Dad."
"I think you deserve a lovely ice-cream." Mum decided

As we ate our ice creams, we had a good look at Simonds Stadium... which is also known as Kardinia Park... it is the home of the Geelong Cats Football Club!

Geelong have won nine premierships... including the most recent one in 2011... where they beat Collingwood by thirty-eight points!

Oops, sorry Mum... bad luck!

It was formerly called Simonds Stadium, but due to naming rights as a public park it was re-named as Kardinia Park. From August the twenty-sixth, 2007... to August the twenty-seventh, 2011... Geelong won every match here!

It's one of the few clubs that not only practices on the field but also plays there too... according to Jimmy Bartel from the Geelong club... the Geelong supporters call it...'The Cattery'!

Kate and Nicole both barrack for Geelong... whenever they can they attend their home games... usually with Adam and Amelia.

They had a celebration party in 2011 at their home when Geelong won their ninth premiership and they have been to the 2007 Grand Final when Geelong thrashed Port Adelaide, by one hundred and nineteen points which was the AFL's biggest winning margin, in a VFL/AFL Grand Final!

These two grand finals were the most memorable for the Geelong Football Club.

"Eastern Beach might be good to walk on." I said to Mum, as I munched on my cereal the next morning

When I woke up this morning the sun was shining through the windows of our bayside hotel. It feels a little cool, it's still all right for a couple of hours at the beach!

This is the day that I intend to put my cheeky idea into practice... the one that involves me wearing my bathers and parading around on the Eastern Beach... making the boys jaws drop with amazement!

We got changed into our bathers before we left for the beach.

Mum and Dad put down their towels... Mum takes out her 'Centre Stage' book by Judy Nunn to read... while Dad has a relaxing sleep. I have noted that Mum has a copy of 'Fifty Shades of Grey 'in her bag.

Ooo! Cheeky Mum! I plan on busting her reading it!

I sat on my towel and watched the local boys play cricket. I can see they are playing a very good game. I'll see if I can make their jaws drop!

I got my black sunglasses out of my bag... put them on... stood up and was about to start walking towards them in a sexy model way... but Mum was on to me quick smart!

"Cassie Annabelle Bontel!"
"What do you think you're planning to do?" asked Mum, fixing me with a steely glare
"I'm just about to join the boys for cricket Mum." I say, with an innocent air
"I don't think so!"
"You're about to do your sexy model moves in front of those boys."
"Well that's not going to happen Cassie!"
"Remember what we talked about in Castlemaine?" Mum said

"Yes Mum."

"I remember."

"The boys might get the wrong idea about me if I do my sexy model moves in front of them...and might do or say things... which I don't like."

"I'm not doing them again I promise... I'll limit my modelling to at home." I said, grudgingly

"Good Cassie."

"One more thing... can you please promise Dad and I... that you will not continue to keep doing immature things like this again?"

"It would be a good thing if you can keep your promise." Mum said, seriously

"I promise Mum that I won't do immature things like that again." I mumbled

I sat back down on my towel with my arms folded on my knees looking into the distance... I was a little bit peeved that Mum had spoilt my fun... I was thinking... *'trust Mum to spoil the fun even before any got started! What a spoilsport...blah blah... moan moan... etc!*

I kept dwelling on what Mum had said... eventually... when I was thinking straighter... I realised that Mum and Dad only want me to be safe... to understand what is socially 'acceptable' behaviour.

I decided to make a real effort to understand all that Mum and Dad have been trying to teach me about those things... then maybe I can go on a date and eventually get married one day...somewhere in my future.

Not long after that, a tourist agent with a camera crew in tow appeared. It seems they are filming a tourist promotion for Geelong and the agent has spotted me on the beach.

"Hello young lady."

"What is your name?" asked the agent

"I am Cassie Bontel."

"Are you shooting a tourism promotion?"

"That's right Cassie."

"We're shooting a tourism promotion for the city of Geelong... you would be perfect for it!" the agent replied

What a nice opportunity...Mum and Dad would have to check it out with the agent and crew first.

"You would need to run it past my Mum and Dad first."

"I am only sixteen... so I would need their permission."

"No worries Cassie."

We'll check it out with your Mum and Dad."

Mum and Rebecca had a role in a tourism promotion ad for Geelong when they were eleven years old in 1981... during a family holiday.

"Mikayla!"

"It's good to see you again!"

"I remember you took part in a similar advertisement in 1981 when you were eleven."

"It was a good tourism ad for our beaches back then." said the agent

"It was a good ad!"

"Rebecca and I, were playing in the water... throwing a beach ball to each other... playing cricket... and relaxing on our towels."

"I remember we said... *'Come on down to Geelong. You'll have plenty of fun and smashing times there, we promise you that!'*

"I still remember it... I've converted it to a DVD... it's also on YouTube." said Mum

"It was a popular Australian holiday ad!" he nodded

"Cassie has mild autism... you will need to explain to her how the process works... then teach her the basics." said Dad

"She'll be fine once you teach her the processes of how you go about shooting an advertisement." Mum said

"We have done a few shoots with people with different abilities in the past... so that should be no problem."

"Cassie... this is how we are going to shoot the tourism advertisement."

The tourist agent and his crew explained to me that I was to play and swim in the water... dance... throw a beach ball to a local boy... then hit a cricket ball for six.

I liked these ideas and they asked me if I had any suggestions. I suggested I pull down my sunglasses and wink at the local boy. The crew agreed with that... but Mum and Dad were hesitant and decided not to go with the idea... I reluctantly agreed with them.

It took several takes to get the required shots, but the finished product was well worth the effort. Mum and Dad were proud that I had achieved a stepping stone on my way to confidence and maturity.

The ad went something like this:

**Me** (hitting the cricket ball for six)
"What a nice shot that is."
"It's gone in to the water for six!"

**Me** (swimming in the water):
"The water is nice and cool to swim in."
"I enjoy it."

**Me** (emerging from the water):
"That was a nice swim."
"Now I'm going for a delicious ice-cream."

**Me** (relaxing on my towel with a boom box playing pop music):
"Isn't it nice, relaxing on a fine day... listening to your favourite summer music?" Music plays
"Cassie you did really well with that tourism advertisement."
"Wait till it airs on TV and gets uploaded onto YouTube!" said Mum
"You will be seen by lots of people then."
"I sure will be."
"I might become famous."
"You might." Dad smiled, at my excitement
"Rebecca may see your ad... she might call you about it."
"Maybe she might even show it in her segment 'Popular Ads/Viral Ads'!"
"How exciting would that be?!" I said, jumping up and down laughing with joy
"All right, enough excitement!" smiled Mum
"Let's go and have a nice lunch together."
"'Sailors Rest' is a great place to eat."
"I hear they have a global menu."

I've arranged for my third solo performance at one this afternoon... before the 'Bontel Family Band 'concert in the evening.

Just before I am ready to go onstage... I receive a call from Mum and Dad to tell me that they are experiencing traffic hold ups... and to wish me good luck for my performance and meet and greet sessions afterwards... in case they don't arrive in time to see it all.

After my performance had successfully concluded... I made myself ready to meet three female fans who had been picked to come backstage and have a conversation with me.

"Cassie your songs were amazing!"

"I love pop music like you do!"

"Thank you."

"I wrote those songs myself... inspired by my life... and the things I enjoy!"

"You're very good at what you do... I bet Lady Gaga... Nicki Minaj... and Katy Perry... would be jealous of those songs!"

"Maybe."

"Thank you for the compliment... I've got their albums too."

"I've been using my music to help children and teenagers with disabilities."

"If an autism charity asks me to perform for an event to raise awareness... I will be right there!"

"You'd make a great performer at birthday parties too!"

"You could entertain all the kids."

"I could... I might even do a few magic tricks here and there!"

"'The Great Cassio' would be my name!" I laugh

"Dad can teach me as he has done magic tricks during his time as a member of the 'Playground Kids' band."

The girls all laughed together with me... as I pretended to be a magician

After we had finished our shows in Geelong, it was time to get back on the road and drive home to Melbourne.

We are back in our hometown of Melbourne contemplating the last leg of our road trip!

We still have Tasmania to explore! I would love to go to Tasmania... but I am terrified of flying and I am fearful at the idea of going on a boat or ship as well! I'm determined to complete our road trip... no matter how long it takes!

"Cassie the last leg of our road trip is Tasmania."

"We've booked a cabin on the 'Spirit of Tasmania'."

"Won't that be a fun family adventure for us to share?" said Dad, hopefully

"It will be fun."

"I like the idea...I have to admit I've never been on a ship before and I'm feeling a bit nervous about this." I said shakily

"We can help you through this process Cassie."

"Step by step."

"Once you feel calmer and more confident, you will be able to enjoy travelling on the 'Spirit of Tasmania' with us."

"You can enjoy many things onboard... maybe we can give an impromptu performance for the crew members." said Mum, cheerfully

"Ok Mum."

"I'm feeling a little less nervous."

"It's okay."

"I'm ready to go on the 'Spirit of Tasmania' with you two... to enjoy the fun and games that might lie ahead." I said with a smile... to make Mum less worried

We got in the car and drove towards the terminal. I saw the 'Spirit of Tasmania' and thought...

*'Oh Wow! It's huge! The Spirit of Tasmania is a big ship indeed! It's scary! Oh dear. Help me!'*

"Cassie, are you all right? said Dad, looking at my pale face

"No... I'm not all right."

"Can we pull over for a few minutes?" I said, shakily

Luckily, there was a car park where we could stop...so we pulled into a vacant spot and Mum got out of the passenger side and sat next to me.

"Cassie... can you tell me what's making you anxious?" Mum said, holding my hands

"Mum, Dad... when I saw the 'Spirit of Tasmania'... I was afraid that I might fall off the side and drown!"

"I was also scared that I might get lost amongst all the cabins and rooms."

"It has made me feel very anxious." I added

"Well done Cassie... for telling us what's wrong."

"Dad and I are so proud of you for expressing yourself."

"That's big progress!" said Mum, patting my back

I hugged her and cried a little I was glad to be breaking through and speaking up about my issues.

"It's all right Cassie... I am here for you."

"Let it all out." said Mum, gently smoothing my hair with soft touches

I let out a few sobs and when I calmed down, I felt a whole lot better. It feels good to have Mum calming me down when I get upset, anxious or overwhelmed. I always feel happier, calmer and better afterwards. I feel that Mum and Dad are like my guardian angels... protecting me... and making me feel safe... from the things that scare and upset me.

For the last two years... I have been able tell Mum and Dad what upsets me... or makes me anxious and scared... and they help me to overcome that fear. It's a great feeling! I now feel ready to conquer my fears and go onboard the 'Spirit of Tasmania'. Let's do this.

"Thanks Mum!"

"You're a great help to me!"

"I think I'm ready to board the 'Spirit of Tasmania' now."

"I can do it." I said

"You are so welcome Cassie... I love to help my daughter."

"You are doing brilliantly sweetheart." said Mum, giving me a big squeeze

"Well what are we waiting for... let's go!" said Dad, giving me a high five in the air

We were provided with a boarding pass... cabin key... and ship's directory.

"The gates for boarding open at six... always follow the blue line and board via the bow...or the sky bridge." instructed the ship's marshal

"We won't forget... we'll follow your directions." Dad replied

# Chapter Fifty-Two
## Spirit of Tasmania and Family

The crew directed us on board the ship at six and Dad parked the car, he placed it in park and engaged the park brake. We noted the deck and position of our vehicle, so that when we dock, we will have no problem finding our car.

We made our way to our private porthole cabin it was a little small but we are on board a ship so we must acclimatise ourselves to that. Although I was enjoying the new experiences, I was still feeling nervous about being on a ship for the first time. I sat down near the porthole it didn't take long before the tears were streaming down my face again. I looked out at the ocean, it reminded me of a therapeutic place that I regularly visit. Mum and Dad came over and Mum held my hand.

"Cassie, you can tell us what's making you sad." said Mum, softly stroking my hand

"Mum, I feel a bit nervous about being on the Spirit of Tasmania."

"I know you calmed me before we got on…I still need a little bit more help before I can enjoy being here." I sniffed

"We can get someone to take us on a little tour… to encourage you to have fun… and enjoy the journey to Tasmania."

"Would you like that Cassie?" asked Dad

"Yes, I would like that Dad."

"It would be a great help to me." I said, wiping away my tears with my handkerchief

I felt calmer and gave Mum and Dad a big hug and a kiss each. I feel a little better, but I need more encouragement to enjoy this overnight trip. Dad proceeded to make a phone call.

"Hello?"

"Is this the ship's guided tours section?"

"Yes sir, this is the 'Spirit of Tasmania' guided tours?" we heard, as Dad had put his phone onto speaker mode

"My daughter is a bit nervous about being on the 'Spirit of Tasmania' for the first time… so my wife and I would like a staff member to show her around… so she can feel safe and confident on the ship."

"No problems, Mr Bontel."

"We have had guided tours with special-needs clients since 2006… we'll send a staff member right over to help your daughter."

"He's excellent with special-needs clients… he'll be a great help to you all."

"Thank you, I am most grateful."

"Bye."

The staff member arrived at our cabin. I noted that he is probably in his thirties wearing a smart 'Spirit of Tasmania' uniform. He has a badge on his lapel that says Tony... he is a very nice man. I hope he can help me feel braver and give me some confidence.

"Hello Mr and Mrs Bontel."

"I am Tony your tour guide."

"I hear your daughter Cassie is feeling a bit nervous on the 'Spirit of Tasmania'... I have come to show her around our wonderful ship." said Tony, with a broad smile

"Hello Tony."

"Cassie is a little better... but still nervous... we would be happy if you can help her." Mum explained

"No problems... Mrs Bontel."

"I'll show her all the facilities we have on board I guarantee you she will enjoy herself and have a pleasant journey." smiled Tony

"We do hope so."

"We shall come along just in case she gets upset again." said Dad

Tony began to show me around the ship and where to locate all its facilities.

First, he showed me the tourism hub... and a reading room where we can choose reading material... and get away to a quiet corner whilst at sea. There were dining rooms and bars... like the Tasmanian Market Kitchen... where we could choose family favourites... delicious desserts... and a selection of Tasmanian cheeses and beverages... to add a touch to your meals. There was also the pantry... which offered 'grab and go' sandwiches... snacks... and breakfast foods.

We saw shops that sold a range of souvenirs and Tasmanian wines... that we might purchase and take with us as we travel around Tasmania... or back to Melbourne with us on our return journey. This is a ship that I will never forget...my first ever ship journey!

Let me tell you a few things that I found out about the 'Spirit of Tasmania'!

On July the first 1985... the Trans-Tasman line introduced passenger and vehicle transport on the German-built 'Abel Tasman'... it did regular and reliable service until 1993, ...when the larger and original 'Spirit of Tasmania'... was its replacement.

When the 'Devil Cat' was introduced in 1997... things went up a gear! It was a Tasmanian built catamaran... which travelled from Georgetown to Station Pier in Port Melbourne... via Tasmania's north... in six hours. During its peak season... the original 'Spirit of Tasmania' operated with the Devil Cat until 2002.

In 1998, Mark one and two were constructed in Finland... they operated between Greece and Italy... for four years. They were 'Spirit of Tasmania's replacements... making September the first 2002... the first ever dual maiden journey across the Bass Strait.

The weight of that craft was twenty-eight thousand tonnes...it measured one hundred and ninety-four point three metres... it was twenty metres longer than the inside of the MCG! That's pretty amazing!

In 2004, the 'Strait' was introduced and it operated between Sydney and Tasmania... Spirit of Tasmania three... took overnight sailing between Darling Harbour and Devonport. That route was discontinued in 2006, despite the passengers enjoying it.

"Thanks Tony... for helping me and showing me all the rooms and facilities."

"I feel braver and less anxious than before."

"I am going to enjoy this trip."

"You're doing a good job working with clients on tours and helping them."

"Keep up the great work." I said, happily

"Thank you, Cassie."

"I'm glad you enjoyed your tour of the ship."
"Well... I'd better get back to work."
"I've got another group coming up in thirty minutes"
"Bye"
"Bye Tony."
"Thank you for your help." Mum added
"What an awesome... magnificent ship she is!"
"We're enjoying the journey to Devonport along the smooth waters...enjoying the wicked views as the ship sails along."
"That is so right Cassie!"
"It is good to see that you are enjoying yourself now."
"You have done well to face your fears."

Mum reaches into her bag and pulls out a box of Cheddar Shapes! It's one of my favourite shape flavours... that cheddar cheese is so good!

"You can share some... you deserve it!" said Mum
"Thanks Mum!"
"They taste delicious!"
"Let's enjoy the journey together."
"We could participate in some trivia bingo, perhaps?" Dad said

We walked out on the deck and heard a familiar song... 'Ice World'.

We peeked around the corner and saw... Kate... Adam... Nicole... and Amelia... performing their hits from 'Blizzard Blast'!

How did they get onboard the 'Spirit of Tasmania' before us?

I don't know why...it puzzles me.

"That's 'Quirky Service'!"
"What are they doing here on the 'Spirit of Tasmania'?"
"They must have known we were going to travel on the Spirit of Tasmania and got here first."
"They are 'stirring' us up!" said Dad
"They are probably 'pranking' us for knocking them off the music charts!"
"We can play a prank on them!"
"I've got an idea for a big prank!" Mum said
"We'll go back to our cabin... then I can tell you all about it."

We went back to our cabin and closed the door...we don't want any chance of 'Quirky Service' getting wind of our plans!

"My idea... is... we disguise ourselves as Italian waiters... we can start off by serving 'Quirky Service' their meals."

"When we come to serving them their dessert... we will 'accidently' pour cream all over them... and maybe add some fruit for decoration!"

"When they jump up in horror to yell at the 'waiters'... we signal for the other diners and staff to take photos of the results!"

"That should cause some laughs!" said Mum, sniggering
"I like that idea Mum!"
"We'll let the staff and diners know what is going to happen... so they are in on the prank." I said, chuckling
"Let's get our disguises and get ready!" whispers Dad

We silently 'shushed' each other as we got changed into our Italian costumes and went to the kitchen. We alerted the staff and diners... who agreed to go along with the prank.

"Here comes 'Quirky Service'!"

"Let's start putting our prank into action!" I said, grinning widely

"The 'Spirit of Tasmania' is a great ship!"

"Our cabin looks comfortable and the bar is great!"

"I wonder what the 'Bontels' are doing?" we heard Kate say

"I think they're having a good time back in Melbourne... taking a break before resuming their road trip."

"They probably don't know where we are." Adam replied

"They have knocked us off the music charts in most countries now... we need to sort them out!"

"Mmmn... but how?" Nicole added

"We'll think of something!" Amelia was heard to say

We walked up to the table where 'Quirky Service' was sitting and prepared to take their orders in our Italian waiting disguises.

Kate said hello to Mum who answered in an Italian accent.

"Bonjourno... welcome aboard the 'Spirit of Tasmania'."

"I'm Signora Chiara."

"I move from Italy to work on this magnifico ship!"

"I am Signore Ricardo."

"I too move from Italy with Chiara and help her in the kitchen!" said Dad, waving his hands about

Now it's my turn to try out the accent!

"I am Signorina Aurora."

"I work with Chiara and Ricardo since four weeks."

"The meals will be 'stupendo' tonight!"

"Crikey!" said Kate

"That sounds authentic... what foods are you cooking up?"

"We have pasta, lasagne, spaghetti with meatballs, pizza all kinds!"

"They all sound delicious!" Adam licked his lips

"We're very thirsty... what drinks do you have?"

"We have water... lemonade... wine... champagne!" said 'Senor Ricardo', with a flourish

"Wow!"

"That's a great selection of drinks." said Nicole

"What desserts are you serving up?" asked Amelia

"We have ice-cream... Bombe Alaska... Banana Split... Macaroon Tower... Apple Pie... all sorts of thing... you can only dream of!" tempted, 'Signorina Aurora'

"My word!"

"It all sounds so tempting... that I may order a couple of desserts and pour cream all over them!" said Amelia, drooling at the thought

Mum Dad and I had to quickly turn our heads away from the table when she said that...so she wouldn't see us having a giggle.

"What do you like for dinner?" said 'Signora Chiara'

"I would like pasta with mushrooms." Kate replied

"I choose spaghetti with meatballs." said Adam

"I'll have lasagne with a side of vegetables." said Nicole, smacking her lips

"I'm having spaghetti bolognaise with shredded cheese." chortled Amelia

"Coming right up." 'Signore Ricardo' bowed and exited

We went back to the kitchen where the staff finished cooking the dishes... when they were ready to be served... we took them to the members of 'Quirky Service' to enjoy.

"This meal is delicious." Amelia sighed

"This is the best meal I've tasted since our Scandinavian cruise in 2003!" Adam agreed

"That was great!" said Nicole

"Can we fit any dessert in?"

"I think we just might be able to." grinned Amelia

"Let's order dessert and some drinks."

"Are you ready to order your desserts?" I asked

"Yes...we are ready."

"I'll have a banana split." said Kate

"Mine's apple pie." Adam jumped in

"I'll have Bombe Alaska." said Nicole

"I choose triple sorbet with raspberry topping." Amelia said grinning

"You will be delighted when you taste them." said Mum

"We'll bring cream to pour on top." offered Dad

The real staff made the desserts... we took them and put them in front of each member of 'Quirky Service'...then returned a few moments later with jugs of cream for pouring. However, instead of pouring them over their desserts we poured them straight over their heads!

'Quirky Service' sat like 'stunned mullets'! All the diners and staff burst out laughing. Mum, Dad and I, were 'corpsing' holding our bellies tight as we shuddered with laughter! Finally, Kate managed to speak through the cream dripping down her face.

"Look at us!" she shrieked

"There is cream all over our best clothes!"

"We're so sorry." Mum mumbled, trying hard to keep a straight face

"We'll get some towels to get the cream off."

By this time, Kate has had enough and tries to stand up saying..."

"These are our best clothes!!!"

"You must be held responsible for replacing..."

...before Kate can finish her sentence... she steps in a puddle of wet greasy cream that has collected on the floor underneath her chair and goes sliding across the polished wood floor on her bottom... landing upside down in a tangle at the foot of the nearest diners at the next table!

"Aaaah!" yelled Kate, as she shot across the floor

The others were still sitting 'dumbly' round the table in disbelief... they jerked their bedraggled heads round at the sound of Kate's scream to see what was happening to her. They all jumped up from their chairs in a hurry to help rescue Kate...it was not a good move!

Everybody started slipping and sliding on the same wet cream pools... which had gathered around the chairs... by their feet! Adam went shooting past Nicole... clutching at thin air to try and stop himself as he hurtled across the room...at least he was still standing at this point. Amelia grabbed Nicole's arm to steady herself and ended up pulling them both over in a heap underneath the table! Kate was still trying to untangle herself whilst the diners at the tables were wetting themselves with laughter.

Mum, Dad and I, reached the exit door and tried to signal for everyone to start taking photos...but as we looked around it was just pandemonium everywhere! Nobody could stop laughing long enough to take a picture... and our 'little prank' seemed to have snowballed to gigantic proportions... with nearly the whole dining room looking like a disaster area!

Uh!... Oh!... Think it might be time to beat a hasty retreat to our cabin!

We got back to our cabin as quickly as we could, still laughing when we thought about it all.

"That was brilliant!"

"Our prank went off thanks to you Mum!"

"Quirky Service' did not see that one coming!" I said, excitedly

"Thanks." said Mum, still chuckling

"Still... I think there may be some repercussions... things worked out in a much 'bigger' way than I intended them to!"

"They sure did Makayla!" said Dad, grinning

"I have a feeling we are going to be 'paying' for far more than just a new set of clothes each!"

"Tomorrow... we shall have to face the music... and reveal Ricardo, Chiara and Aurora!"

"It will be hilarious!" I chortled

"I'm not so sure that 'Quirky Service' is going to see it that way Cassie." said Dad, with a wry smile

"We'll keep a low profile until then." I said, still sniggering

There was trivia-bingo after dinner... we dressed up in our best...then went to the room where it was being held. We 'scouted' round for 'Quirky Service', fortunately they weren't there. We had fun and ended up winning, we were given a little prize each. It was my first bingo game I would like to try it again sometime, at the Melbourne RSL... maybe I could 'dabble' at being a bingo caller!

"Cassie, we see you are having a great time."

"Thanks."

"This ship is no longer a fear for me."

"It is a pleasure."

"The views are lovely from the portholes and the sounds of the ocean are relaxing and peaceful... I feel like I am taking a cruise."

"Tony was a very nice staff member to show me around."

"I enjoyed the trivia-bingo very much... thank you for helping me overcome my fear of the ship." I said

"That's all right, Cassie."

"We're glad you're making happy memories with us... that way we can come again!" said Dad, cheerfully

As we slept throughout the night... the gentle soothing sound of the blue water outside relaxed me...I had a great dream. I dreamt I was the captain of a cruise ship... navigating around the world... picking up and dropping off tourists... spotting creatures in the ocean... and taking photographs of it all.

We'll arrive in Tasmania tomorrow and there will be plenty of things that we plan to do once we arrive. We've booked at Quality Hotel Gateway in Devonport, so we'll be driving there once we have docked.

It's morning, we have arrived at our destination! We are beginning the docking process, there is just time to have breakfast before we disembark. During breakfast, Mum and Dad tells me what is going to happen, so that I can be prepared.

"Cassie... straight after breakfast... we are going to pack up all our things... someone will announce our deck number... then we will collect our car."

"Once we get into our car... we'll wait till instructed to start our engine... the ship staff and security will direct us off the ship."

"Once we have dis-embarked, we'll make our way to the hotel we have booked in Devonport."

"OK, Mum and Dad I got all that."

"I shall be fine... I can't wait to do the things we have planned in Devonport." I said

When the announcer called our deck number, we walked to the car carrying our cases and got in, several minutes passed before the announcer told us to start our engines, the ship staff and security quickly directed us off the ship. We made our way through the carpark and drove to the Quality Hotel Gateway.

I am looking out the window of our hotel room... the sun is shining in the morning sky...it is a beautiful sight to see... it makes me smile. We all took some photos.

"Mum, Dad... it's great to see the sun shining." I said, cheerfully

"The sun's rays are a tonic on a winter's day!" said Dad, happily

I got out my iPhone and clicked, I'll add that one to my photo collection! I have been taking photos since I was fifteen years old... when I first received my iPhone.

"Last's night trivia-bingo was good fun... it's lucky that 'Quirky Service' weren't there!"

"When we've unpacked and settled in, we can get some lunch... later this afternoon we can reveal ourselves to 'Quirky Service'!" I said, grinning

"That will be funny." said Dad, laughing out loud

We were getting hungry...we haven't had fish and chips for a while... so 'Strait off the Boat'... is the best place in Devonport to get this family favourite!

It's a name that makes me chuckle as well.

On the menu board outside there are several types of fresh fish from Bass Strait, such as...Gummy...Pink Ling...and Flathead... they also have potato cakes and a burger or two, we know what we love eating twice a week... fish and chips!!!

While we waited for our fish and chips, I looked out the window. There are fine views of the city and shops. Locals are walking around possibly shopping, I remember the times when I couldn't go into shopping centres without my headphones on or I would get overwhelmed and meltdown...now I love shopping like other girls instead of dreading the sensory overload!

I'm going to enjoy being in Tasmania!

At two o'clock in the afternoon we went out to the Mersey Bluff Reserve where 'Quirky Service' were relaxing on the beach. They have spread out their towels and are lounging and reading on them.

"Hi... it's us!" I called out

Kate looked up, amazed to see us.

"We have something to confess." said Dad

Dad then proceeded to tell them all about the Italian waiter costumes... the whole prank dreamed up by Mum... with the ensuing pandemonium that followed! He promised to replace their clothes... also that the clean-up bill for the dining room had already been settled by him and Mum.

"Go away... I'm not in the mood to talk to you at the moment!" muttered Kate

"I might've known it was you three... all along!" she added

"We understand why you are 'cranky' with us...our prank went a little bit 'larger' than we expected it to!" Mum said, with a guilty look on her face

Adam, Nicole and Amelia looked up with their jaws dropped!

"You mean you were the three Italian waiters on the 'Spirit of Tasmania'?" Adam said, incredulously

"Yes... we were." Mum said, with a shame faced grin

"We thought you were new staff!"

"You fooled us big time." said Nicole

"Did you enjoy the 'pouring cream' on your desserts?" asked Dad, with a wicked grin

"Ha... ha... very funny!"

"You three are such practical jokers!" growled Amelia, sarcastically

Later... when everyone was not quite as cranky with us... they began to ask questions about our trip.

"Well how is your tour around Australia going?"

"It's going brilliantly."

"Tasmania is the last leg of our tour... before we return home to Melbourne." I said

"We saw in the paper that you played a solo performance in Adelaide, Cassie!"

"Well done."

"You did really well... we're proud of you." said Adam

"Thanks, Uncle Adam."

"I was nervous and thought... 'I'm a bit scared... I can't do this', then I spoke to Mum and Dad when they were delayed in the traffic...they reassured me that I could do it!"

"You keep inspiring more fans and musicians as you go...which is amazing." said Nicole

"It's amazing for me too, Aunt Nicole."

"A few female fans want to become musicians too... 'Sunshine Sky'... have recorded their self-titled debut album... they are planning their tour of Australia and New Zealand at the moment."

"We might be the opening act on their Melbourne leg for them." I said

"You can inspire more fans to chase their dreams, Cassie!"

"What have you been doing and seeing on your trip recently?" asked Amelia

"We had a ride on the Victorian Goldfields railway train... caught up with relatives in Bendigo... and Cassie starred in a Geelong tourism advertisement."

"She had a fun time during the whole process." said Dad

We watched that advert a few days ago...Cassie was amazing in it."

"Maybe Cassie could star in a follow-up ad overseas." said Kate

"Maybe."

"When I saw the 'Spirit of Tasmania', I got nervous and nearly had an anxiety attack."

"I was still nervous when we got on board... with help from a guide named Tony I felt braver and more confident... I was able to enjoy the overnight journey."

"Good on you Cassie!"

"You're growing up to become a talented... musical... comedic... woman!"

"We admire your progress... you continue to amaze us." Adam smiled

"I hope so." I replied, giving Kate, Nicole, Adam and Amelia a hug each

Their hugs made me feel happy and relaxed.

"Mum, Dad and I, might get a tour bus someday...we can call it the 'Bontel Family Party Tour Bus'!"

"We'll tour many countries in it and have loads of parties with our fellow musicians."

"We can sing, dance and party away in between 'gigs'... on our musical transporter!"

"It will be one heck of a party when we eventually get one!" I laughed

"It sounds like loads of fun!"

"Count us in!"

"We would love to go on your tour bus." said Kate, excitedly

"You four might need to get booster seats." I said, with a mischievous grin

Adam, Nicole and Amelia face-palmed themselves and Kate glare-stared me. That suggestion did not go down well with her. Gulp! Oops!

Kate looked down for several seconds and then looked at me and said...

"So, what... if Adam... Nicole... Amelia... and I... need to sit on A-Z phone books on your tour bus?"

"SO... WHAT!" she said, huffily

"You can come on our tour bus anytime... we'll make room for you." I said, trying to smooth things over

"We'll be there when it happens."

"It will be a party full of pop music." said Nicole

"Kate... since you're shorter than me... you'd have to sit in the lower deck." I said, giggling

Everyone laughed again, except Kate.

"A sledge... straight at me again!"

"Yes... I may be shorter than you...remember sometimes things you say can come back to bite you on the backside!" said Kate, pointing her finger at me

"We've got a concert later... so why don't you three perform with us?" said Adam, quickly changing the subject

"We'll have a great time rocking the house together." Adam said

"Yes, that sounds like fun."

"We'll get ourselves ready and see you in an hour." said Mum

Before the concert started... I was still making jokes about Kate...she still wasn't seeing the funny side.

"Kate... besides Mum... Dad... Olivia... and Rebecca... I idolise you."

"Singing and jumping all over the loungeroom!" I giggled

"That is not what I do!"

"I'm a smooth operator... a woman that operates on many different musical levels." said Kate

"Why does my being short seem so funny to you... Cassie?" Kate, wondered

"I don't know why Kate." I laughed

"I'm not short... I'm fun-sized." said Kate, wagging her finger at me

"You just keep telling yourself that." I replied

Everyone laughed louder...except Kate...who went red in the face.

"Kate you're shorter than me... I would be towering over you and taking anything that you had in your hand...you would be begging me to give it back." I chuckled

Everyone laughed louder than before...Kate was not laughing... she just went even redder in the face.

"It is true that I am shorter than you... but 'YOU' Cassie are being unkind." Aunt Kate said, quietly

Suddenly... no-one in the room is laughing... and I am the one with the very red face! I have no jokes...no smart remarks to say... as I look at the ground shamefacedly and reply.

"Yes... Aunt Kate."

"Sorry... Aunt Kate." I apologise

"That's all right Cassie... I know you meant no harm... you just got a bit too carried away with yourself!"

"Just remember that what might seems like a joke to you... can sometimes be hurtful to others, Cassie."

"I will Aunt Kate."

"Good girl Cassie."

"Now let's get on with this concert and play some music!" she smiled

Both groups got together and performed at the Devonport Entertainment Centre... which is also known as the Paranaple Arts Centre...we thoroughly enjoyed ourselves. It was the first time that the 'Bontel Family' had performed in Tasmania and we had a brilliant time!

After the concert we went to Pioneer Park for a chat.

Kate, Nicole, Adam and Amelia have some news to tell us. I wonder what it is?

"Our news is that the members of 'Quirky Service' are going on a 'hiatus'."

"We are taking a break from the music scene for about a year... because of upcoming commitments."

Mum, Dad and I are shocked to hear their news! What a surprise. What could be the reason for such a long break?

"That is startling news... what's the reason?" I asked

"Kate and I have got a job hosting... 'Game of Prices Australia'." said Adam

"Kate has been hired as the new host...I am the new announcer."

"It's very exciting for us to get these parts on such a successful show."

"That's wonderful!" said Mum

"Thanks, Mikayla!"

"We'll be going to Eveleigh, NSW in a few days... we start on the seventh of May 2012."

"We hope you can tune in to watch us."

"We hope so too Kate!"

"It would be nice to see you on TV becoming a TV Presenter!" Dad, grinned

"Thanks Daniel."

"Nicole and Amelia... what are you two going to be do doing during Quirky Service's hiatus?"

"I'll be having some downtime... tending to my house....the loungeroom needs a makeover...garden needs some landscaping... working with children with disabilities and occasionally making music...to keep my hand in." Nicole smiled

"I have been hired as the new host of a reality show called... 'Isolated Houses Australia'... for its' upcoming ninth series on the Gold Coast."

"I'll also be taking some downtime too!" Amelia said happily

"Resting...sprucing up my garden... painting...working with children with disabilities... if I have any time left after that... I may make a little music too." she laughed

"I've also been asked to present... 'Comedy Word Teams'... I shall be starting that in May."

"It sounds like you four are going to be having an incredibly busy 'hiatus'!" I laughed out loud

"I might write a song or two for 'Quirky Service'."

"Just call us anytime and we'll be right there." I said

"We'll be more than happy to do it." said Kate

"We might collaborate together on some singles and do some charity work with 'Autism Awareness' and other groups."

"That would be great fun."

"It's true, we may not see much of you...we'll call you to see how things are going."

"We'll take plenty of pictures...especially Mikayla will...to send to your iPhones." Dad chuckled

"We will love to see your photos and chat on the phone."

"Cassie... I heard you got a trophy for bowling a perfect three hundred in Warrnambool."

"Congratulations for putting in a fantastic effort."

"I got a surprise!"

"Did you knock my name off the girls champion section of lane five to get that score?"

"Who me?" I said, with an innocent face but spoiling it with a giggle

"You think that's funny?"

"I'll give you funny when we choose to do a ten-pin bowling game next time we go to Warrnambool!"

"Whilst I was there... I overcame another challenge!"

"That's great Cassie, what was that?"

"I learnt to tie my shoelaces for the first time!"

"I was a little nervous, with Mum's reassurance and remembering a similar technique that I used to tie the garbage bin bags, I took my time and tied my laces perfectly!"

"Well done Cassie."

"You'll be able to wear laces comfortably and in style now."

"Yes."

"I will be able to buy lots of shoes… in many different colours and styles… just like other girls do!"

"Dad looked horrified at that prospect!"

"He reckons I might buy too many and cost him lots of money!"

Everybody laughed at that comment.

"Oh No Cassie!"

"It will be…you bought another pair of coloured shoes… didn't you?"

"This will cost me a fortune!" Dad said in his 'horrified' voice

"I shall say blah…blah…blah… Dad you can never have too many shoes… no matter what colour… style… or bling… they have on them."

"I'm a very stylish popstar daughter you now have… who can tie as many shoelaces as she needs to!"

Everyone chuckled at that one… except Dad… who groaned at the thought of all those expensive shoes!

# Chapter Fifty-Three
## Speaking Up

"Cassie... the autism talk date is getting closer." said Mum, the next morning

"It's getting exciting... my daughter opening up about her autism to an audience for the first time... taking another big step." said Mum, imaging the scene

"Yes, it is exciting...a little bit nerve-wracking too!"

"I'm sure I can do it...talk about it...so that the others will gain understanding and support in their journeys... whether they have autism... or care for a loved one with autism."

"There's one more thing we need to organise... I'm yet to book a venue for my talk!"

"The question is which venue will be best?"

"Let's look up to see if there are any halls that we can hire." I added

I couldn't find any that were suitable... apart from an Entertainment & Convention Centre...which I decided not to book.

"Any lucky finding a hall... Cassie?" asked Dad

"No luck Dad."

"None of the halls were suitable."

"Let's try Devonport Primary School...if that's not available... we can try Devonport High."

"Otherwise... I will have to give it on radio and the audience will be radio listeners." I decided

We checked our iPhones to see if Devonport Primary had a suitable room...unfortunately...none of the areas or classrooms had the required space.

We looked up Devonport High and fortunately they had a couple of big inside areas that would be suitable. It was a school day, so Mum decided to wait until lunch break to contact the principal.

"Hello... is this the Devonport High School?"

"This is Mikayla Bontel, calling to see if we can use your school on Saturday night."

"My daughter wishes to give a talk on Autism... we were wondering if the space is available for hire... and if you would approve it for use that night... for her talk?"

"We can use the space from seven in the evening...that's wonderful to hear Principle."

"Thank you so much... my daughter will be delighted!" Mum said, happily

"Yes, I look forward to seeing you too Principle on Saturday evening."

"Bye."

Mum had a delighted look on her face when she put down her iPhone. I know what that means and I get excited too!

"Cassie, I've called Devonport High... they have agreed to let us use their school for your autism talk." said Mum

"That's great, Mum."

"We have got the location… then there's the setting up to do… power point… slides…then I'm all set to go." I said, happily

"We'll be there for support and encouragement…we're sure that you can talk openly about your autism… to an audience of parents and their autistic children, Cassie."

"We know you can do this…you have our full support." said Dad

On Saturday evening at seven the parents and their autistic teenagers arrived. There were four girls and two boys sat in their seats ready to hear me speak. Two of the autistic teenagers are twins…a brother and a sister… the girl has mild autism and the brother has savant syndrome. I was surprised to find they both have hyperthymesia like me. I don't know how the talk will go…I hope I can do this bravely and confidently… speaking openly about my condition.

"Hello everyone."

"Welcome to my talk… my name is Cassie Bontel."

"I am here to talk about two conditions which I have… called mild autism and hyperthymesia."

"I hope to raise a little more awareness through this talk… and let you know that you're not alone… in this autistic journey that we share."

"I will start by talking about my life with autism first of all… I've got some slides to show you as well."

"The first one is of my early years."

"Mum and Dad brought me home after several days to twenty-three Henry Street… it had blue… green… and yellow… wallpaper."

"At the time I was too young to remember much of it… Mum would hold me in her arms and feed me."

"I was mostly a quiet baby… Mum and Dad would have no problems taking me out anywhere… even on date nights and visiting their friends."

Their friends would say…

"Cassie seems very calm and content."

"She's a very good baby."

Mum and Dad would say…

"She sure is."

"When I was about eighteen months old autism symptoms started to show… I still wasn't talking… I resisted all forms of physical contact or affection."

"I would kick… scream… shriek… hit… and bite… like a wild animal…whenever I was touched, or didn't get my way."

"It was like a stranger was touching me…I would do all those things…to get away from those strangers."

I felt like…

"Who are you?"

"Go away!"

Later more symptoms emerged…

Mum said to Dad…

"Something's not quite right here, Daniel." Dad agreed

"They thought I might have autism…so they made an appointment with a doctor to find out what was happening."

"They made an appointment with a Dr Hannah when I was two… they filled out a form answering ten questions… based on my behaviour… symptoms… and preferences."

"It was then that I was officially diagnosed with mild autism."

"I did not have high-functioning autism or Asperger's."

"Mum and Dad knew then… they finally had the answer to what was wrong… they were numb when it sank in."

"Their lives were changed…they knew that I was different from the other kids…they would need to look after me…teach me different skills to survive… in this 'puzzling and scary' world!"

"They were gifted with AUSLAN sign language and used this tool to communicate with me and help me express myself until I became fully verbal at four years old."

"My first word then was Mummy."

"Mum and Dad were so happy and relieved when I said that word… I squealed and 'flapped' my hands with excitement."

"I had broken through the barrier of non-verbal!!!"

"I started interacting with my parents and communicating with them… I began socialising." "During that time… Mum and Dad taught me life skills such as empathy… I picked up on them quickly."

"I tried a little scripting from age five to six…I gave that up as I preferred to use my own words instead."

"Now… moving on to my schooling years." I said, as I clicked on the next slide which was entitled Primary-Secondary Years

"When I was five years old Mum and Dad looked for a suitable school that would help my needs and gain me valuable skills for life."

"They looked all over Melbourne and eventually they found a special centre for girls with autism, (MSC). At the time they thought to themselves…

*Ah this is definitely the right for school for Cassie…it has one classroom, various subjects being taught, nice facilities and trained staff…what more could you want?'*

"They met with Mrs Joelle who would become my teacher and my aide Helen… then enrolled me."

"I was a little shy when I was dropped off the first day but with Mum and Dad's help, as well as Mrs Joelle and aide Helen, I settled in."

"I didn't make any close friends during the original seven years I was there…I was more than happy to play with everyone… gain lots of vital skills….and study Maths, Art, English and life skills."

"The one classroom had a blue velvet carpet… butterflies lined the green walls… the desk had ten seats because there were ten students…there was a fish tank on Mrs Joelle's desk."

"Artwork by the previous autistic girl students was pinned on the green walls."

"The cupboards were full of sensory materials…these were used by the students to aid us with sensory issues…they helped a little."

"Most of us were shy and going through the same challenges as one another… sensory issues… and anxiety."

"Whenever one of us got upset or had a meltdown… we would be taken to the quiet area in the corner… there we could calm down… and practice the techniques our parents and Mrs Joelle had taught us."

"We also did swimming lessons and music…many of us were child prodigies in music… the Melbourne Special Centre was a fun place to learn…I never complained about going there."

"At twelve years old I made the transition to Melbourne Secondary College."

"I studied hard at my subjects…including studying at lunchtimes in the library…I had an aide named Dina, to help me with my work."

"It was a good place to go and I did three years there…throughout the entire time… I refused to socialise with the other students."

"They were not like me… they were pretty frightening and scary."

"Mum and Dad were dismayed that I refused to socialise... they tried to help me make a friend... Dina tried to do the same... my social skills worker and the Melbourne Secondary College tried...I still refused."

"I even spoke to Dina in a sarcastic tone when I was fifteen and in Year 9... about enjoying being by myself!"

"I did not do any team sports... and refused to attend the social skills classes they were running."

"The social skills worker and the counsellor eventually gave up trying... they didn't come near me... for the rest of Year 9!"

"They would hide in their offices whenever they saw me coming!"

"There were lots of strangers there... I had a difficult time adjusting to them."

"I didn't trust the other students...they didn't trust me... not wanting to work with me...thinking I was a 'freaky weirdo chick'... or a 'princess dumb arse'!"

"The names hurt me...I was too scared to speak up about that."

"I knew all the answers to the questions that my teachers asked...I was too afraid to put my hand up... fearing I would look stupid... and then freak out in front of the class...or Dina would have to answer them for me instead!"

"In the second half of year nine a fire drill occurred and I had a huge meltdown!"

"I was taken to a special room... as I was the only autistic student at Melbourne Secondary College."

"I lay down on my side still distressed... curled up in a ball... whilst my Mum was called to pick me up."

"I didn't notice she was there at first...I held her hands and managed to tell her with some encouragement... that the fire drill had frightened me."

"That's where I began to make a little bit of progress."

"Mum praised me for talking about my fear...then took me home."

"I would not return to that particular classroom again... because it once was a good place to learn in at Melbourne Secondary...now it held a horrible memory for me."

"I'll probably need help to return there in the future... I can't that let that memory get the better of me."

During those years there were a couple of positive events.

"I got A's in every subject for all of the three years I was there... I also entered a UNO tournament competing against the teachers and won the final... against my year nine teacher Mrs Petunia."

"At the end of year nine... I had a graduation in the integration office with Mum... Dad... and the integration office ladies...with no other students."

"The Melbourne Secondary College was frightening... but I got through it"

"Part three of my talk will be covering my sensory issues."

"Let me tell you about a few sensory experiences at different ages."

"One issue was clothing...when I was five years old... Mum and Dad took me clothes shopping to buy a new shirt and pants."

"At the time... clothing shops were the worst nightmare for me!"

"I thought I was getting a new blue shirt and pants...my favourite colour."

"Unknown to me... Mum and Dad had decided it might be a good time to try out a new colour and fabric with me!"

"Mum chose a green shirt and pants and took me to a vacant changing cubicle."

When she asked me to try them on, I resisted...

"Come on, Cassie." she coaxed

"Try them on for me and see if it fits you."

I resisted even more. Mum managed to get the new clothes on me...they were green and made of silk...they didn't feel right to me. It was not my style of clothing...I was itchy and it felt like I was on fire! I screamed... ripped the new clothes off... and had a meltdown in my birthday suit. I thumped my fists and kicked my legs and shrieked!

Mum tried to calm me by saying...

"It's all right, Cassie... it's all right... it won't take long."

"You can still wear your blue clothes if you want to."

"Just try these please."

She reached out her hand to touch me on the shoulder...I lashed out and struck her... then I ran out of the cubicle and past Dad... squealing and crying... and flapping my hands. Dad said to Mum...

"What happened?"

"Cassie had a meltdown when I was trying to get her to try a new shirt and pants on...they were green."

"Apparently... she didn't like the feel of them."

"Hmm...apparently not."

"Let's have a look for Cassie."

"I think I saw her running towards the 'jumpers' section."

Mum and Dad found me in the 'jumper section' curled up in a ball crying loudly. They also noticed a small yellow puddle on the floor next to me...where I had an accident.

Mum and Dad apologised to the shop assistant for any embarrassment I caused...put the green clothes back... cleaned me up in the nearby bathroom... put my blue clothes back on...then took me home!

Mum decided that maybe it wasn't the right time to buy me new coloured clothes in other fabrics!

"We'll try them when she is a little older." Mum said to Dad

"I think we'll do that then." said Dad, happy to leave that shopping experience to a time in the future

Mum probably thought she had left a long enough interval till her next clothing attempt with me...as I was ten years old this time. I was at home reading my maths book when Mum came in with some new clothes for me to try. They were a pink dress and pink shirt and pants. I was nervous and reluctant because they were not blue...with the promise of a food reward... I agreed to try them on.

First came the dress... I managed to put it on but it was made of satin not cotton...it felt uncomfortable on me like it was squeezing me...I lasted five minutes and ripped it off shrieking!

Mum managed to calm me down and I reluctantly put on the pink shirt and pants. Even though they were cotton...they were the wrong colour...so I took them off as well and had a meltdown.

I lay down on my back and shrieked like a banshee and sobbed. Mum had to lie down next to me and say soothing words...staying with me until I calmed down. It was a sensory issue overload... it overwhelmed me...I wasn't ready to try different clothes yet... not for a few more years, anyway.

When I was eleven years old... I was out at an Italian restaurant with Mum and Dad...my aunt Olivia was with us also. It was a bit noisy but not too crowded, so I put my headphones on. My favourite meal...spaghetti bolognaise...was on the menu and at the time it was the only Italian meal I could tolerate.

When the waiter came to take our orders Mum and Dad decided it was time to choose a non-smooth food. I didn't want to...Mum and Dad assured me that it would be tasty when it arrived.

I reluctantly agreed though I was not convinced. When the waiter put down our meals, I was horrified to see that my meal consisted of lasagne with vegetables in it and even more vegetables on the side! What made it worse...it was not smooth in any way whatsoever...it was on my not acceptable list of foods! I flatly refused to eat it with a...

"NO!"
Dad tried to reassure me with...
"It's okay, Cassie."
"It's just lasagne."
"It will be good for you." Mum added
"I love my lasagne and I hope you love it too... when you eat it will be delicious." Olivia said

I was upset and agitated by now...I picked it up threw it across the room, narrowly missing a lady and her husband who were eating their meal...I then had a meltdown. I sobbed and shrieked... stamped my feet...and flapped my hands. Mum and Dad were so embarrassed and tried to calm me down... so did Olivia...I was too far into my meltdown to calm.

The other customers looked at us...they were disturbed by my meltdown... so Mum, Dad and Olivia managed to use soothing voices to lead me to the car... where they encouraged me to use my anxiety techniques...where I finally calmed down.

Mum said...
"Cassie... do you feel better now?" I nodded

I couldn't find the words to tell Mum, Dad and Olivia what had upset me. They let me wait to recover for half an hour before Dad asked me...
"Do you want to come back inside and order your usual meal?" I nodded quietly

We went back inside and I ordered my spaghetti bolognaise telling the waiter how I liked it.
Dad spoke to Mum...
"She's not ready to try lasagne yet."
"When she is a little older...we'll try again and see how it goes then."
Mum agreed...
"Yes... we'll try another time."

There was a time when I was nine years old... Mum, Dad and I, were walking through a park in Geelong. It was a fine day... I had my headphones on... I was very shy at that time, if any people said hello to us I would either hide... or look down and ignore them.

We looked around us and talked while we walked... then we stopped at a bridge and looked over. It was walkable but I could tell it was a long way down and I had a fear of heights back then. I freaked out and ran away screaming and shrieking...looking distressed.

Mum and Dad had to catch up and look for me.

They found me five minutes later...sitting down in front of a tree with my hands on my knees and my head on my hands... sobbing and crying.

Mum and Dad tried to put their hands on my shoulders to try and calm me...I struck out at them and continued crying. Mum and Dad had to sit down near me and stay with me until I calmed down...which was forty-five minutes later. I didn't want to talk...I could not find the words... so another fifteen minutes passed before Mum said...
"Do you want to go back to the hotel now Cassie?"
"Yes." I whispered

We went back to our hotel, where Mum and Dad gave me some space to decompress for an hour.

Sometimes, I would get dizzy with heights... or I would become overwhelmed and have to sit...or lie down. Mum and Dad would be careful not to touch me...just stay close by until the dizziness had passed.

Another sensory experience was in the bath... I was seven years old and playing with my toys...a ship and a submarine. I would pretend to drive the ship across the waves and dive the submarine down into the water. I would throw the bubbles up in the air, laughing and splashing in the water. On this particular night I was making ship noises and laughing when Mum came to check me.

"You're loving playing with your toy ship... aren't you... Cassie?" she said

I replied giggling...

"Yes, Mummy."

Then Mum said...

"That's lovely Cassie... now it's time to wash your hair."

I freaked out at that! Back then, I disliked getting my hair wet! Mum tried to reassure me saying...

"It's all right Cassie... don't panic."

"I will be quick...it won't take too long."

I wasn't sure about it and I remained nervous and flapping... as Mum filled up the water jug.

With each step that Mum got closer to the bath with the jug of water... I got more anxious and upset. Then when Mum produced the jug and said...

"Time to pour the water on your hair now Cassie."

I jumped out of the bath and ran around the house... screaming and flapping my hands... as Mum tried to catch me.

"Come back, Cassie."

"The water won't hurt you."

Mum couldn't catch me though... I ran to the loungeroom... lay down curled up and had a meltdown... tears running down my face...crying very loudly. Mum tried to reach out to me saying...

"Cassie... Cassie... it's all right... Mummy's here."

I kicked out at her and lashed out... I struck her as well as crying and shrieking all the time. Dad tried to calm me...he got the same response! They were pretty sure the neighbours were thinking... 'What the heck is going on in the Bontel family household?'

Mum and Dad looked at each other, wondering what to do next. They lay down near me, taking care not to touch me, and stayed there until I calmed down after about an hour. We were all absolutely exhausted, Mum said to me...

"Sorry if I frightened you Cassie."

"Can you tell us what part frightens you?"

I just couldn't speak...I couldn't express my upset.

Dad said...

"We won't wash your hair Cassie."

"You're safe with us."

"Come on... dry yourself off and put your pyjamas on."

"I'll bring you your milk and biscuits." he said

I thought, but couldn't say... 'It was like nearly falling into a whirlpool...I thought I was going to pass away.'

"The textile world and I have had a chequered past... sometimes it is just not for me!" I grimaced

Everyone smiled when I said that... no doubt thinking of their own problems in that area.

From the ages of five to nine I would do the total-strip down to my birthday suit and do strange... quirky... funny and weird things... like dancing... playing with the toilet paper...running around the garden... rolling around in the mud or on a blanket... playing in the dirt... pretending to be different animals at play, with the exception of dogs, or running through the sprinklers.

Mum and Dad were fine with it then... I would also do the same at the beach. At that age it's not unusual for little children to run around naked and strip off their clothes.

However, when I turned ten and blundered into the loungeroom naked... where Mum and Dad where chatting with my former carer Isabelle... Mum and Dad decided!

*'This needs to stop right here! We've got to teach Cassie when to be in her 'birthday suit' in the right place and also when to cover up! That way she won't be embarrassed or cause embarrassment, get into trouble or bring judgement or criticism on herself.'*

Mum and Dad taught me about wearing clothes to fit into the unwritten 'social rules' of society... how to cover up when outside your own home. Starting with underwear and working outwards from there. They helped me to understand... that some areas of our bodies are very personal and more private than others... these areas are different for men and women.

Mum took me to choose my first bra when I was twelve... that is one of those private areas for a girl... when her body starts changing and growing... through childhood to puberty and then into adulthood...when she becomes a woman.

Since turning thirteen I would only be in what I call my 'free state'(naked)... at night during the hot summer weather or inside my room... if the heat was unbearable during the day.

I must say that I have had the occasional slip-up along the way! My natural preference is to be without clothes at all...it's a tactile sensory thing!

I would forget to put on my clothes or pyjamas... such as whenever we are going out...or staying at a hotel...usually after I had a shower. Fortunately, Mum and Dad were able to stop me before I ventured too far... then I would run back to my room...blushing and covering myself up. I still need to be reminded sometimes... even now at sixteen!

The parents nodded, their children encountered similar sensory experiences...and the autistic teenagers understood...because they struggle with these issues in their day-to-day life.

"Then there is the problem of sound." I said to my audience

"I was very sensitive to loud noises."

"It was like someone screaming at me very loud... I would lash out and hit the person that caused the noise."

"Whenever I went out to public places... cafes... and restaurants... I would wear my noise-reduction headphones to block out the loud noises."

"Once when I was fifteen, I did the shopping at Safeway by myself without headphones, it was one of the rare times I didn't get overwhelmed."

"Bright lights were also a pain to me... like the sun shining too fiercely and blinding me."

"I had to wear dark black sunglasses to block the harsh light out...I always wear them at home... and in public."

"Even when there was only one bright light in a room...I would refuse to take my sunglasses off."

"I was sensitive to camera flashes so I always wore my sunglasses for photographs."

"I had skin sensitivity to touch or skin contact."

"Whenever someone touched me... even someone I knew... I would get frightened or overwhelmed... then I would become angry and upset and strike out at the person...including Mum and Dad."

"It was very hard for them... when they were trying to show their love and affection to me."

"Even when I hurt myself... I would not let them touch me...they had to work out how to comfort me without making me feel worse."

"There were some things I didn't like to touch... like rubbish bins... or my parent's skin...because they felt so disgusting to my touch...so I would wear gloves to touch them."

"It was an unusual way of showing affection to Mum and Dad... I stroked their skin with my gloves on... I did not say... 'I love you Mum'... or... 'I love you Dad'... for several years... until I was sixteen."

"I rejected all forms of affection... the only touch I could tolerate was Mum and Dad rubbing my hands to calm me down... it always helped me to feel calmer... it's a very important technique... and it still works well."

# Chapter Fifty-Four
## Routines and Rituals

"Certain smells would upset me... like my Mum's perfume... or cooking aromas."

"I would become overwhelmed by the smell...sometimes I would throw up... which would make me angry or upset with the creator of the smells!"

"From age fifteen to sixteen whenever I took the bins out... I always wore a surgeon's mask as the rubbish smell would overwhelm me!"

"I would wear a mask in any environment where there would be overwhelming smells."

"Food was always bothersome to me for many years."

"I could only tolerate smooth foods... I would refuse those with texture... including fruit and vegetables."

"The texture in my mouth would overwhelm me and make me gag."

"Mum and Dad had to draw up a long food list...with what was 'acceptable' and what was 'not'...that the whole family and support network could follow."

"It was very hard for Mum and Dad to find a restaurant that had smooth foods...I would not eat anything that was not smooth!"

"My Aunt Rebecca, was inspired to write a cook book full of smooth food recipes after getting to know my long list...which Mum and Dad use all the time."

"Also, if the foods I did like were not cooked in a certain way... I could not eat them either."

"I would meltdown if 'non-acceptable' foods were served to me."

"I would use tricks...stealth... and sneakiness...to fool Mum and Dad."

"Very similar to the tricks they used... to try and make me eat my fruit and vegetables... like sneaking weird things into the salad!"

Some of the teenagers grinned at me and looked at their parents...who shrugged their shoulders as if to say...*well we had to try something!*

"When I returned to the Melbourne Special Centre... where the other students were glad to have me back... I soon made my first 'official' friend... named Jenna Williams, who has Asperger's."

"Since that time, we do girly things together and always have a laugh...as well as helping each other out."

"Also, that year I did 'Meals on Wheels' again... before Mum and Dad announced to me that we were going on a road trip around Australia!"

"Which is the trip that we are on right now!"

"I had a special graduation at the MSC in early June."

"The students at MSC and I have known each other for several years... we remain friends today ...I plan to help out at the MSC."

Whilst we were in Wodonga during our road trip, we went to the Shopping Plaza Centre for some clothes for an evening dinner with our friends. I looked over all the coloured dresses before I eventually decided on a light blue lace dress.

It was the start of several progresses that I have made during our journey so far. I went into the dressing room and tried the dress on… I felt the sensation of the lace on my body…for the first time I felt really comfortable in another fabric.

Mum praised me for trying something new…I was proud of myself for persevering.

I have since bought a couple of other fabrics…both in blue…soon I hope I will not only buy other fabrics, but also try colours other than blue…to get myself used to the idea of other colours hanging in my wardrobe!

The autistic teenagers understood my talk and the different circumstances I was describing to them… many had been through similar experiences of their own.

"I'm eating more and more different foods these days since I started the road trip…I'm more open and willing to try new foods now."

When we arrived in Mount Buller, I tried the Spaghetti Saltati… I was hesitant at first…with encouragement from Mum and Dad… I tried it and loved it!

I made more progress with my food choices when I ate vegetables… nuts and chicken… in my dish of San Choi Bow!

I even tried a Hawaiian pizza with pineapple on it at the Wodonga Pizza Place!

Everyone laughed at that statement, even me.

Since then… I have enjoyed eating many new foods that I couldn't tolerate… or wouldn't try before… and I have found them enjoyable.

I've still got a long way to go…when I travel overseas… I hope I will be able to enjoy the national dishes and foods of other countries.

"Now I want to talk to you about routines and rituals.

"One of my routines is that when I am tidying up my room… I must do it in a certain order."

"First, I clean up my books and put them on my bookshelf…then my toys into the toy box…then my guitar."

"When I complete that routine not only does my room become tidier…also I feel a lot calmer."

"However, if someone came into my room and cleaned it in the wrong order…then I would get upset and melt down!"

"I also have a particular order that I sort… my books… DVD's… and videos into… one that only I understand… I would become distraught and upset if somebody accidently changed the order of any of my objects."

"Once I overcame my fear of showers…I also developed a shower routine."

"I turn the hot tap on first… then the cold… wet my hair… lather myself up with soap… wash the soap off… put the Dove conditioner in… wait for three minutes… wash the Dove conditioner out… put the shampoo in… and wash the Dove shampoo out."

"Whilst I am doing that, I sing… Mum, Dad and carers… are not allowed in!"

"I only use Dove shampoo and conditioner for this routine…if I run out then I refuse to get in the shower!"

"I have had a routine for several years that whenever we have visitors or family over…the table must be set in a certain way… MY WAY!"

"This involved setting the cutlery with a fork on the right of the plates… and a knife on the left of the plates… seats had to be equal to the number of guests… and the fruit bowl must be placed in the middle of the table."

"Depending on the food… it had to be served on the table rather than the bench…I always insisted that I must be head of the table."

"If anything in that routine went a different way than the way I had set it I would get upset and meltdown."

"That routine is no longer in place and I don't mind where I sit now." I smiled, and I could see the parents in the audience, nodding hopefully

"Another one of my former fears… was thunder and lightning!"

"Since I was four, I had been afraid of thunderstorms…I would scream and meltdown…Mum and Dad would have to calm and reassure me that I was safe and protected from the storm."

"I would hide under the bed…blankets…or table…I would refuse to come out until the storm was over."

"I had therapy over the years to try and help me to overcome this fear…wearing my headphones…playing games to distract me from the noise…it still scared me for many years."

"I made some progress when I was fifteen…then I overcame my fear entirely at sixteen on this trip at the Gold Coast…telling Mum and Dad that it was the sight of the thunder and lightning that scared me… not the noise anymore."

"Another fear I have are insects."

"I would shriek and hide whenever I saw one."

"I would only go into the backyard with gloves on every time, even to do gardening…or jump on my trampoline."

"Pictures of an insect would even frighten me!"

"If I saw an insect I would meltdown and ruin our family picnics."

"I need a bit more assistance in activities involving insects…with help I can overcome those fears one at a time."

"I used to fear other kids for many years too!"

"I was scared of them and I would strike out at them whenever they came near me…or else I would hide from them."

"Playdates did not go well."

I could see the Mums and Dads nodding in commiseration with each other at that revelation.

"I wouldn't socialise as they were strangers to me…. so, because of this they seemed frightening."

"I did not go to birthday parties…I only played in playgrounds when there were no kids around."

"We always had family activities away from the other kids…Mum and Dad feared I would meltdown if our chosen spot was nearby to other children."

"From my perspective… it felt like a deer being trapped by a tiger!"

"Ooh…it felt so scary back then!"

"Since I have had Jenna as my first friend, and going on this road trip, I have made several new friends as well…I'm no longer scared of other kids."

"I was even able to calm an autistic child during a special event in Adelaide."

"I used to have a fear of crowds…Mum and Dad would plan on how to escape… if it got too much for me."

"They would always give me forewarning of any plans… and how to manage any issues I might encounter."

"When I overcame that fear at my debut concert in the Metro Theatre, Sydney…it was a joyous occasion for me!"

"There were other fears like the 'Christmas tree' and 'heights'…I overcame them…I'm proud of myself for every fear that I have conquered so far…with the help, support and encouragement of my family and friends."

"Now, I want to talk to you about the positive aspects…gifts that having autism and hyperthymesia brings."

"I am a musical child prodigy… I have been singing since I was five… and playing the guitar since I was six years old."

"I can see things that others miss... like finding vital clues in a mystery."

"I have knowledge of almost every subject...also a ninety-nine point-five percentage when answering quiz questions."

"After I hear song lyrics and music once...I can sing them and play the notes on my guitar."

"My IQ is one hundred and ninety-seven...which classifies me as a universal genius."

"My hyperthymesia... means that I remember almost everything about my life... except my birth."

"If anybody asks me about what I did on a particular day or date... I can use experiences...words... language... emotions... and visualisations... to describe that day in detail."

"I may become a professional quiz player someday." I said laughing

The audience laughed with me.

"These are some of the positive gifts my autism gives me... that go towards making me the unique person that I am."

I played a couple of autism news videos for the audience... including one of Mum, Dad and I from 2010.

"In 2010, Mum, Dad and I, formed a pop music band called 'The Bontel Family'...we recorded our self-titled debut album and released it in March 2011."

"It has charted top ten in over fifteen countries... including Australia and New Zealand."

"We're currently touring Australia to promote it and gaining lots of new fans!"

"Our single, 'A Family United' is selling well since we released it as our debut single in February... it has become a 'special needs' anthem... in the vein of 'Understand Us'...by 'Quirky Service', which charted way back in 1986!"

"We plan to write some songs... for autism related events that we will be hosting...to raise awareness of special needs groups."

"Sometimes we have good, bright days... and sometimes we have bad, dark days...we need to be positive to get us through...through to the bright days again!"

"Some days I would be happy... bright... positive... laughing and talking...other days I would be upset... anxious...worse when sensory issues got in the way... even on the happy days... angry and filled with fear."

"During my early to mid-teens when I had bad moods days... I refused to talk to anyone...I didn't use any words... locked myself in my room...and refused to come out for hours!"

"Mum and Dad would give me space to calm down...and when the bad mood had passed...I would emerge from my room."

"It was a safe place... with a sign on it which said...Cassie's Room...Keep Out...Ask Permission First!"

"It doesn't happen anymore...when I have bad days... I don't let it get the better of me... I can tell Mum and Dad what I'm going through...then they can help me through it."

"I do the things that I do...forget the bad mood... put it behind me!"

"During my mid-teens... I would sit in my backyard on a chair wearing my sunglasses and looking at the bright blue sky... it would calm me and let me reflect on all the good times I've had... forgetting the bad."

"Once I went to the rocks near the beach and sat looking at the sky... Mum and Dad gave me space to reflect."

"I was shy and too scared to talk when we walked there...then when I sat on the rocks looking at the sky...I relaxed and enjoyed the view."

"Overall...I have worked hard to navigate my way through the world with help from family and friends... and to overcome barriers... making breakthroughs...to get to where I am today."

"I overcame my sensory issues... made new friends...learnt lots of new skills too."

"The road trip that Mum, Dad and I have been taking... is changing my life for the better...I am becoming more independent... confident... braver...than ever before."

"Without the help of my family and friends... I wouldn't be confident... brave... and able to appreciate the unique gifts that make me the young woman you see before you."

"Thank you all for coming and listening... remember you are not alone in this autism journey."

"You can live a happy and wonderful life... no matter what obstacles you may face."

"Your autistic children love you in their own way... as you love them... life can be a positive experience for you both."

Everybody clapped. They seemed to enjoy my talk very much and hopefully learnt more about life with autism! Now for Q&A time.

"If anyone has any questions...I will answer them to the best of my ability." I said

I answered the questions the audience asked me...including one that an autistic teen girl asked.

"What's the difference between High-Functioning Autism and Asperger's Syndrome?"

Another question I was asked is...

"Did you have any stimming behaviours?"

I responded with...

"I used to have a stimming behaviour for many years."

"Sometimes, I would flap my hands accompanied by a loud squeal...whenever I got excited or distressed."

"Mum and Dad would cringe at that... especially when I did it in public...they would have to take me to a quiet place or home!"

"It helped to distract me from the stress...I would block it out by using the stimming behaviour."

"My other stimming behaviour was rocking back and forth when distressed... moaning and groaning, usually accompanied it."

"I used my grandma's rocking chair for a few years until I was eleven."

The autistic brother and sister thanked me for reassuring them that they weren't alone.

"Thank you for talking to us tonight."

"When I found out I was different at thirteen I felt upset and unsure about myself."

"I shut myself in my room for several hours sobbing my heart out."

"I was thinking at the time... *'I feel frightened about being different. I'm afraid I will be alone and no one will understand me or what I'm going through. I'm jealous of my peers because they can do some of the things that I can't do.*

*It's a puzzling and frightening world that I'm living in. I'm scared and terrified... of the things that scare and terrify me... Autism is a frightening word to hear...ARRRGH!'*

"I allowed Mum and Dad to comfort me...they had a conversation with me about my autism...the strengths... and the challenges... that come with it."

"I gained a bit more confidence then and this talk has given me more." said Sarah, another autistic teenager

"Your talk was inspiring for me as well."

"When I was thirteen...I found out I was different."

"I was upset for a while thinking... *'It's awful to be different from my peers. No one can understand me and what I am battling through. My peers can do so many things that I am unable to do yet. I'm scared that I will be alone and no one can help me through. This world is scary and puzzling to live in. Autism is such a scary word.'*

"Mum and Dad had the talk with me about my autism and comforted me."

"They understood what I was going through... they are helping me... like my sister... so I can feel safe and be myself." said Sean, Sarah's twin, also aged fifteen

"I'm glad to be giving inspiration and confidence with my talk."

"It shows us that we are not alone in this journey... with understanding... love... support and encouragement... we can become confident and be braver... if we just start to step outside our comfort zones... and try new things!"

"The world might seem a frightening and scary place to live in... but we can find a way to fit in that suits us... we can be ourselves... no matter what our differences and strengths are." I said

Sarah and Sean then hugged me tight and I hugged them back.

I'm glad I could reassure these two that they can survive and do well in the world. I'm making a difference... one step at a time... through music and sharing my autistic experiences.

I hope I can give similar talks in other countries overseas... inspiring more autistic teenagers and their families.

"Thank you all for coming tonight and listening to my talk on autism... I hope you have enjoyed it and it has given you a little more confidence to follow your dreams... try new experiences... and keep learning... and growing every day!"

Everyone clapped and congratulated me on my talk as we left the school and they made their way back to their homes and we returned to our hotel for a good night's sleep.

# *Chapter Fifty-Five*
## 'Berry' nice

"Hey, Mum and Dad." I called out from the back of the car the next morning as we were driving "There's a place called the Turners Berry Patch... where there are a variety of berries such as Strawberries... Blackberries...Raspberries... and a berry that I have never heard of...Tayberries."

"I can't wait to try some of those." I said

"That sounds a fun place to explore...I do love my berries." said Mum

"I admit that I'm a berry lover too!" said Dad, smacking his lips

We arrived to find lots of berries growing in many rows, there were so many to choose from that we didn't know where to start! Hmm... so many tempting berries...which ones to pick? First, I need a basket to carry them in!

"Welcome to the Turners Beach Berry Patch." said the owner

"I loved eating berries during my childhood."

"I would put them on my Kellogg's Corn Flakes for breakfast in the mornings"

"I would also put them on my ice-cream for a sweet treat."

"I love to put them on cakes... they taste so good...juicy and sweet!" said Mum, getting carried away with berry fever!

"I recall when my wife and I would visit berry patches...particularly my grandmother's...we would pick berries and put them in our basket...then carry them back to her house and help her to make delicious desserts."

"I loved those times...I want to continue the tradition with our family." said Dad, smiling at his 'berry' memories

"I have to confess... I never liked berries growing up."

"They were on my 'not acceptable' food list!"

"I never liked the taste and the texture of them."

"If I was asked to eat one... I would have a meltdown!"

"However, ...I'm starting to eat more new foods...and I'm keen to try these berries." I said

"Get a basket each and pick as many as you like."

"If you want to... why not try our food and drink menus after you finish berry-picking." said the owner

"Right...we've got our baskets...let's get berry-picking!" I said, dashing to the berry patches

"Wait for us, Cassie."

"We're coming too." said Mum and Dad, running after me

There were many rows of berries lining the patch. You can see them for miles around when you walk through them with your basket. I start to daydream about walking through the rows... picking berries for my grandma... as many as I can...sneakily eating some and making a couple of pies with her... topped with whipped cream and ice-cream of the vanilla flavour then eating them with her.

That was a great daydream...I would love to take some berries to grandma and make a variety berry pie with her and get cream and ice-cream on top of it! Mmm! That would make a great dessert to make!

Mum, Dad and I start picking berries.

I go for the strawberries to start with... Dad goes for the blueberries... and Mum chooses raspberries. Our baskets are half full, we decide to pick some more. I had a big sneaky grin on my face, I decided to pinch a few of Mum's berries.

I crept quietly on tiptoe up to where she was bending over picking and took some of her berries out of her basket while she wasn't looking. Then, I did the same with Dad's berries while his back was turned. I crept towards the tayberries, trying not give myself away by chuckling out loud. Mum picked up her basket and noticed that her basket seemed a lot lighter.

"Hey!"

"Whose been pinching my berries?" Mum called out

Dad's reaction was similar when he noticed his berries.

"Oy!"

"Whose taken my berries!" Dad yelled

I could hear them as they walked around... muttering and mumbling about the berry thief. I decided to eat a few while they were searching. I couldn't resist laughing out loud.

"Where's that coming from?" said Mum, suspiciously

"We know that laugh!"

"We'll find her soon enough!" said Dad

They look around for the berry thief searching through the rows... as they get closer... I let out a loud sneeze which gives me away.

"We definitely know who the culprit is now!" said Mum

"Cassie!"

"Did you eat our berries?" asked Dad, suspiciously

"Erm... it wasn't me."

"It must have been you... Dad." I said, innocently

"It wasn't me... I didn't eat them." said Dad, huffily

"Then maybe it was Mum." I said, pointing to her

"You know how much she likes berries... Dad." I said, craftily

"It was not me... Cassie!"

"You... cheeky girl!"

"Look at you!"

"I can see berry stains all around your mouth!"

"You are busted!"

"Own up!" Mum said, indignantly

"Oh... all right."

"It was me that pinched your berries."

"You didn't suspect... did you?" I said grinning

"You were very sneaky!"

"Come on clean the mess off your face and let's pick some more."

"No more pinching!" said Dad, looking at me

I just laughed.

"Oh... Cassie."

"You're just as bad as me." said Mum, with a sigh

"Who do you think I learnt from Mum? I said, giving her a wink

We picked more berries and our baskets were soon full to the brim. No berry picking trip would be complete without photos, so we took a few of each other.

We took our baskets back to the farm shop and paid for them... then we sat down at a table and checked out the menus. There were some foods that I had never tried before... I decided to try... the 'Wood-fired Beef Risotto'.

Mum and Dad chose 'Wood-fired Roasted Pork Kofta' and 'Berry-cured Tasmanian Salmon.

We chatted while we waited for our lunch to arrive.

"I'm really enjoying the Tasmanian leg of our road trip... I love picking berries... and I love eating them even more!" I say enthusiastically

"I particularly liked the tayberries...I couldn't get enough of them!"

"We love picking berries too!"

"These berries are going to taste great, especially in pies."

"I reckon our grandmothers would be so proud of us continuing that fun activity... they do love their berries." said Mum, smiling

"That's another fun filled family activity that we have tried together and some funny memories and pictures created for everyone to laugh at too!" said Dad, laughing

"I reckon I could do something with the berries... I could put them in a big bucket along with grapes... and squash them with my feet... in the summertime in my bathers."

"I reckon that might be fun!" I said, sniggering like a naughty child

Mum and Dad burst out laughing at that image of me.

"Cassie...I think we know where you're going with that!"

"That's another idea you have come up with...you could have fun making the fruit into juice." Mum said

"I'm not sure I would want to drink that juice... after your feet were in it though... Cassie!" said Dad, laughing at me and wrinkling his nose up at the thought

"Funny Dad... very funny." I said, sarcastically

"I would wash my feet first Dad!!!" I said pulling a face

"Mum, Dad, would you like to do it with me?" I asked, cheekily

"No." said Mum and Dad together

"Come on it might be fun." I said, teasingly

"No thank you Cassie!"

A couple of people nearby giggled at the idea of Mum and Dad stomping on strawberries!

Ok, fair enough." I said, giving up

We decided to have some dessert...we looked at the dessert pizza menu.

"I have never tried a dessert pizza before... I would like to see what they are like!"

"I might have to go for the 'Strawberry Lovers'."

"My taste buds would love that!" I said, licking my lips at the thought of it.

When the dessert pizzas we have chosen arrive...we are drooling at the sight of them! Just like little kids discovering ice-cream topped with sprinkles for the first time! We got stuck in to them...they went down very well.

"They taste so good that I would like to make my own dessert pizza when we get back home."

"We can put on any dessert topping we like." I said, gleefully

"We certainly could." agreed Mum

"Olivia and Rebecca will be jealous and probably want one each." said Dad, as we drove off to our next destination

Our petrol tank was nearly empty...we needed to fill up at the next petrol station.

Why don't I get us some drinks for the journey...whilst you put petrol in the fuel tank?" Mum said

"Good idea, dear." Dad replied

Dad filled up the tank with petrol...when he got back in the car, he had a gleam in his eye.

"Cassie...we're going to play a prank on Mum."

"You can help me out by recording it with your video camera." said Dad, sniggering

"Ok Dad."

"It's going to be hilarious it might even go viral on YouTube."

"I can't wait to see Mum's face when she finds out she's been tricked." I chuckled

"Neither can I."

"It will be so funny." said Dad, grinning

Dad moved our car to another spot at the petrol station...just as another four wheeled drive vehicle the same make and colour as ours... pulled onto the forecourt. This was the cue for me to start recording... Mum's going to be fooled and she's likely to get a bit cranky...but it will be fun for Dad and I.

Let's hope we can pull this prank off. Hee, hee!

Mum came out of the store and walked over to what she thought was our vehicle at the petrol pumps area...just as she was getting close to the vehicle and preparing to get in...it started pulling away.

"Hey!"

"Wait for me!" yelled Mum, in an exasperated voice

Mum raced up to the passenger side and jumped in the back...behind the front passenger seat. She began searching in her handbag...when a boy of about ten years old turned around in the front seat and said...

"How are you?"

It dawned on Mum that she was in the wrong car! What a blunder! Mum went red in the face with embarrassment and managed to mumble...

"Good... thanks."

...before she bolted out of the stranger's car and beat a hasty retreat to our four wheeled drive! I managed to stop recording before Dad and I collapsed in our seats laughing hysterically...tears streaming down our faces.

Mum went even redder.

"Oh...dear."

"I'm so sorry."

"I must've got in the wrong car"

"It's not that !!!! funny... ok!"

"You two are behind this... aren't you!" asked Mum, seething

Dad and I just laughed even harder.

"I thought so!"

"You two are in big trouble now!" Mum threatened

"Mum, I'm going to upload this video to 'YouTube', on my YouTube channel 'Butterfly Blue'...it will go viral, probably receiving more than one million views!"

"Our friends and family will see it many times...they won't stop laughing for some time."

"You'll be on a blooper TV show Mum... I'll tune in to watch it and so will Dad." I said

"Oh... no." she groaned

"How embarrassing."

"Everyone will laugh at me... including Mum and Dad and Rebecca!"

"You two are as bad as one another when you play pranks like these!" said Mum, woefully

We drove on to our next destination.

We had heard about the Vietnam Veterans Memorial Avenue, we decided to pay our respects to those who sacrificed their lives in the Vietnam War.

There were seventeen plaques on plinths showing the names of seventeen Vietnam serviceman from Tasmania who perished during the Vietnam War.

The Australian Army training team arrived in South Vietnam during the months of July and August 1962... that was the start of Australia's involvement in the Vietnam war. It continued for nearly eleven years until January eleventh 1973... when the Governor-General issued a proclamation putting an end to the war which claimed sixty thousand Australian lives...including the seventeen men from Tasmania.

A new date of April twenty-ninth 1975 is now accepted as the end date after Australia's further involvement during the 1975 fall of Saigon... recognised by the Department of Veteran Affairs and the Australian War Memorial. Mum, Dad and I took off our hats and looked down at the graves...solemnly thinking of the men who perished in service to their country.

I visualise the Vietnam war in my mind... see our soldiers fighting... the U.S combat operations... the civilians fleeing the 1972 Battle of Quang Tri. I imagine myself as the daughter of one of the soldiers... receiving bad news from her mother that her 'soldier father' has perished in action...and will not be coming home.

I held Mum and Dad's hands.

"I sense the grief of the families of these soldiers who lost their loved ones during the Vietnam War."

"I imagined what it was like going through the bloody battle... dodging bullets...and fighting for your country... it made me feel sombre and sad." I told them

"We feel it too Cassie."

"These soldiers gave their all."

"All wars come at a cost." Dad said, quietly

"We visited Vietnam in the early nineties to meet our Vietnamese counterparts, Thanh and Minh Tran."

Thanh and Minh work in the same areas of disability and entertainment in Vietnam...that Mum and Dad do in Australia.

"We listened to the stories of their family members...we respect them...and offer them sympathy and empathy."

"We played sport with them... to help make some happy memories between us."

"When we visit them... we hope you will do the same... listen to their stories and always show respect... so we may continue to have a good friendship with them." said Mum

"Yes, Mum and Dad."

"I can do that."

"I've gained an understanding from visiting these graves... I would like to help where I can."

"I hope I can apply the lessons you have taught me when we go to Vietnam." I promised

After our sombre visit to the memorial... we decided to have a change of pace... and take a fun visit to a chocolate house next!

"The 'House of Anvers' chocolate... sounds a very delicious place to visit!"

"I've always loved chocolate... since I was very young...you know that I am a confirmed chocoholic!" said Mum, grinning

"I think I might be taking after you Mum!" I said, laughing

I've never tried Belgian chocolate before, but if we are allowed to 'taste test' I should like to!"

"Imagine if there's white chocolate there as well...my taste buds will be going berserk...I will be jumping for joy." I said, happily

"You two do love your chocolate!" Dad grinned at us both

"I have to admit...I like it occasionally."

"I might not have a sweet tooth like you two... but I find it tempting sometimes."

We found out that the property was originally known as 'Wyndarra Lodge'...it was a stylish Californian house which was built in 1931...it featured trees from around the world in the gardens. I have visited a chocolate shop before... but none quite like Wyndarra Lodge!

We could see the staff...tempering...moulding... and enrobing the fine chocolate... adding truffles... pralines...and fudge. We were told by a staff member that if we were to see the secret recipes...we wouldn't be allowed to leave the premises! That sounds frightening! I think they were only joking...but we promised the staff that we wouldn't peek!

Before we can taste or buy any chocolate there's the museum to explore! In the museum we go on the journey of... CHOCOLATE...which all started with the Aztec Indians!

In the 1700's chocolate was consumed as a liquid...it was a drink made from crushed cacao beans. In 1875... Henry Nestle, a Swiss confectioner...combined milk with the cacao...to make the type of chocolate that we buy in blocks today.

We watched the DVD and looked at the interactive displays...we came away with lots of new information about our favourite sweet treat.

After all that learning... we were ready for some sampling... so off to the tasting centre! There were so many chocolates and Tasmanian products to choose from.

Mum and I were delighted to see it all. I wanted to buy as many as I could...Dad chuckled at the sight of us... like little kids running up and down trying to see them all. The big problem is... which ones do I choose? I can't decide on any...they all look so tempting!

Eventually, we choose a few...then we make our way to the cake section! There are whole cakes and wedding cakes, to be purchased.

"We could try one but look at the prices for the round and square ones."

"They are meant to serve twelve to fifteen people... there are only three of us!"

"Still, it's fun to look at them...there's no harm in that." I said, grinning as I licked my lips

"That's right, Cassie!"

"We ladies love our window shopping!" said Mum

"I may not like window shopping as much as you two... I might if there were 'manly' products to look at." said Dad, grinning

I silently laughed at the thought of Dad window shopping with Mum's friends.

That would be hilarious to see...imagine the look on his face if he got dragged into a salon for a makeover with them!

After our chocolate trip we moved on to Mersey Bluff, at the mouth of the Mersey River...the Mersey Bluff Lighthouse is located there... it's very unusual, with a distinctive red striped day mark.

Let me tell you a few facts about this unusual lighthouse... if I may.

The Mersey Bluff Lighthouse was built in 1889...it was made of bricks with a stone base underneath... in 1920 it was de-manned when its light was converted to DC electric operation...it wasn't until 1978 that mains power was connected.

No more ships were wrecked there once the lighthouse was built!

Another unusual feature of this lighthouse was its' connection to the town water supply in 1901...I have never seen a lighthouse quite like it before...the red striped day mark adds a decorative touch.

"Another photo opportunity coming up!" I said, taking my iPhone out

"I will send one of them to George...he likes seeing landmark buildings on his holidays."

We looked around and there were more red striped day marks...it looks like a barber's pole... with red and white stripes...as I look closer at the lighthouse... it really resembles a red and white striped big top circus tent! I would like to attend a circus one day... to see the clowns... gymnasts... and tightrope walkers. George sent me a message about the lighthouse photo... *'That's one unique lighthouse. I'll show it to Ivy and Nina, they will be impressed by that. Thanks for the photo, Cassie. I love viewing landmark buildings!'*

It was soon time after a big day of sight-seeing to find a place for dinner... we headed to 'Drift' restaurant for some hearty fare.

"Turners' Berry Patch Farm was fun... especially when I tried to get away with eating your berries!" I grinned

"Cassie, are you enjoying Tasmania?" Dad asked

"Yes... I am enjoying Tasmania Dad...it's been so much fun in the second smallest state...I loved the 'House of Anvers' chocolate museum... seeing all those chocolates!"

"We have had many meals together... played on lots of beaches... made music in such varied places."

"You two have had to help me to adjust and work through my former sensory issues...now we are able more and more... to have such happy times together."

I reflect as I look out of the window... *'I have an understanding, caring and supportive family, the scenery is majestic and beautiful, I love going to these places. I'm so lucky to experience this and all the wonderful memories that we are making together.'*

I want to express to my parents how I feel about this trip and our lives together.

"I'm very lucky to have you two by my side every step of the way since we started... I can't help but be grateful that you have helped me to embrace this journey... to make many beautiful memories that we can look back on with future generations of our family... I love my unique life... I wouldn't change it for anything." I told Mum and Dad

"We wouldn't change our lives either Cassie... we have enjoyed this journey with you and we love the many memories we have made... our bond as a family has grown stronger... we have helped each other and braved new experiences together."

"This wouldn't have been possible before...but now here we are... spending quality time...embracing challenges... together...let's make the most of our time in Tasmania." Mum said, smiling

"Yes let's!" said Dad and I, together

We high-fived our palms in the air and got down to some serious eating!

# Chapter Fifty-Six
## Antiques and Radios

We've decided to start off today by visiting The Antique Emporium... Tasmania's largest antique and collectables emporium! There's an amazing display of awesome treasures...new and old. Antiques and collectables... old books... and French style furniture...you name it and it's probably here somewhere! We will have fun exploring...but we must take care not to break anything!

As we go through the archway on level one, there are treasures of yesteryear. A huge collection of model cars... records...football cards... 'Star Wars' memorabilia...dolls and teddies...Coca-Cola marketing... furniture and giftware. I am so excited about it all!

"These model cars are similar to ones that I have played with Cassie."

"Grandad Lucas had these ones in his collection!"

"What a find!"

"I'm going to take a photo of this and show it to him."

"He will be surprised." said Dad, happily

"These teddies are so adorable."

"I used to have some...including all the Beanie Kids!"

"Mum you got them through Grandma Georgina...they used to be my calming tools when I hugged them years ago." I said

"We're never too old for toys...it's a good find in this wonderful shop."

"These dolls are nearly life-like."

"They used to be my favourite toys...before trains came into my life!"

"Barbies were my all-time favourite dolls...Rebecca and I used to brush their hair and do their make-up... as little girls like to do." said Mum, fondly

We entered level two to find Captain Jack Sparrow and his pirates...alongside a large range of French wrought iron...& giftware! 'The shed' is where men can buy things to furnish their man cave! Like old tools... architectural pieces...taxidermy... 'garagenalia'...and junk for re-purposing. This is a mecca for blokes and Dad was no exception!

We have a man cave at our house where Dad spends time on the weekends. When there is AFL or cricket...he takes a lemonade and a bag of chips and watches the game. Sometimes, Dad watches the game with Jason...Peter...Andrew...and the husbands of Mum and Dad's female classmates...from the special centre.

I occasionally go in there when Dad is on his own...I enjoy being in there with Dad for some father-daughter time. Mum helped Dad build his man cave with Darren...Jim...Jason...and Andrew's help...it looks fantastic!

There is one thing Mum won't allow in there though… and that's eating cake! If she finds cake crumbs everywhere…he'll be in trouble. I wouldn't mind seeing that…it hasn't happened yet!

When Mum and Dad used to live in the Bontel-Macdonald mansion…a man cave was in the backyard… Darren and Jim used to watch sports matches with their mates.

Dad and the husbands took over in 1988 watching AFL… cricket…and sports movies. Dad…Mum…Olivia and Rebecca… occasionally played pool or snooker for practice…when they played on their world tours with 'Quirky Service'. I might play a game or two with Mum and Dad sometime…in Tasmania.

"My man cave is great…I might need to upgrade it though… these old tools could look good…and these pieces of 'garagenalia'…would look perfect on the walls!" Dad mused, stroking his chin and thinking out loud

"They would." I said

"I hope you don't buy taxidermy!" Mum shuddered

"That would look awful in my opinion!"

"Yuck!" said Mum, holding her nose in disgust as if she smelt something really bad

"I won't dear."

"I think they would smell awful too." said Dad, smiling at Mums' look of distaste

Next… in the 'Emporium'… was 'Shelia's Kitchen' which had vintage magazines…plus retro…& vintage kitchen items. Mum was in heaven, with a delighted look on her face now!

"I used to read similar magazines like these, I can still recall Mum and Dad using these kitchen items passed down from generations."

"I could do with a catch up from the past… I might buy a few." said Mum

"I've seen you buying home and garden magazines before."

"Those magazines had tips for both the kitchen and the garden…you put them to good use." Dad, commented

"I would like to read them as well."

"Ok Cassie, we'll get some for us." Mum, smiled

We climbed up the stairs to level three and saw items from yesteryear again. This time, there were antiques…collectable items…interesting and quirky things…everywhere. There was fine china…old toys… coins… medals and stamps…antique furniture…clocks…and postcards. There were dolls…kitchenware… ephemera…and too much to mention!

"Some of the coins we have are rare…we keep them in a special box…containing all the coins that we have collected over the years."

"We told you all about them and the stories behind each one… you loved hearing them." said Dad

"I sure did."

"It was just like a history lesson…hearing about where they came from on your tours."

"These postcards remind me of our family postcards from Sydney… Hobart… Paris… Rome…and Perth."

"Cassie, you loved reading them and chuckling at the funny stories." Mum, reminded me

"I still have them in my special treasures memory box."

"Although…I've never sent a postcard myself."

"I would love to send one to our family and friends." I said

"We can do that!"

"We just need to find a shop with some postcards…you can write on them…and we can send them off… to anyone you would like to receive them!

"Everyone likes receiving a postcard!" said Dad

"I find the antique furniture very interesting to look at...an antique couch looks nice in any home including ours...this antique rocking chair reminds me of when I used to use one as a calming tool...rocking it back and forth when I felt distressed.

"This antique coffee table looks similar to ours... I would put my magazines and puzzle books on it... sometimes even cheekily rest my feet on it!"

"Then you would say..."

"Cassie get your feet off the coffee table please." Mum supplied

"I would smirk and get my feet off."

"This antique furniture is lovely to look at... Grandma and Grandad have a few antiques in their home... I've always loved looking at them." I remarked, as we looked around

Lastly, we went up to level four where there were books of every genre you could imagine!

"I've loved reading throughout my whole life... especially 'Jo Nesbo' novels!" said Dad, enthusiastically

"They are thrilling... I would read them for hours... especially on the train."

"I've always owned many books I love reading them." said Dad, smiling broadly at the thought

"Besides novels...I enjoy reading comics...particularly 'Andy Capp'."

"He's hilarious that character...especially when he plays pool or soccer!"

"I read 'Wonder Woman' comic books...I still have a costume that I dressed up in for the 1988 Superhero concert special...I like classic novels too!"

"I have read stories that my Mum read... and she read stories that her Mum did too...classic novels never go out of fashion." Mum added

I grew up reading children's books...travel books...maths books...books on geography...and sport. I used to take a maths book with me so I could solve problems and sums without using a calculator...I learnt a lot about geography...which is one of the many subjects I really enjoy. I learnt about Australia from travel books... also other places in the world.

"I guess I can say I am a bit of a bookworm like you Dad."

"You passed that on to me." I said, grinning at Dad

"Thanks Cassie!"

"I think that's a great trait to pass on to anyone!"

"Since you were thirteen...most nights you would read an encyclopedia...absorbing the information."

"We called you our 'genius professor daughter'...you loved that term."

"Our shelves are full of books and your shelves are full of books... our house is like a library!"

"We would sometimes find you reading upside down on our bed... or on the trampoline."

"I used to sort my books in an order that only I understood."

"I sorted them by genres in a particular order."

"When I finished reading the book... I would put it back in the right spot... I would become very agitated if the order was messed up!"

"You two called it my... 'Don't mess with the system' or... 'All things in the right order' technique."

"We all have our own way of doing things...and autistic people are no different in that respect."

"Autistic people like doing things in a 'particular way' ...the way that suits us." I said

Tonight, we are dining at Dannebrog Café, I observed a group of teenagers walking by, doing normal teenage things without their parents assisting them and I thought...

'Those teenagers are independent, without their parents help, they have completed their routines and are walking down the street safely without any problems. I am becoming more independent and confident, but I'm still embarrassed that Mum and Dad keep telling me to stay at a close distance so they can see me... they don't' want me to go too far in case I get lost somewhere...in case the paparazzi might pounce on me! I think it's the right time to tell Mum and Dad that I need a bit more independence...but I can't tell them here...somewhere quiet would be the right place.'

I looked Mum and Dad in the eyes with a serious face and said...

"Mum, Dad, I've got something that I want to have a talk to you about...but not here."

Mum and Dad look at each other with worried faces and they think...

*We knew this was coming. She wants to be more independent... but we're concerned about her safety and her future. We'll listen to what she has to say... and hopefully... she'll listen to what we are saying too... without arguing or resisting too much...then the outcome will be a happy one for the three of us.'*

"We'll talk back at our hotel."

"Not here, the other diners might hear us." I said

"All right Cassie...we'll do that."

Later, at our hotel I sat down on my bed facing Mum and Dad so they could listen to what I had to say about more independence. It's time for me to make my points clear...so I screw up my courage...and begin to talk to them.

"Mum... Dad... I've been more independent since this road trip began...I would like even more independence...so I can begin to make my own way in life down the track...and still be with you sometimes."

"Even though I'm sixteen years old... you embarrass me when you tell me not to go too far... so that you can still see me...I won't get lost!"

"Even when we are just with family or by ourselves!"

"I know you are trying to keep me safe from the paparazzi... I know that's a good thing."

"Still... I feel the need to venture out a little more... to take my own path in life whilst still practising our music careers... combined and solo."

"I understand that I may need a little more assistance with activities that involve heights... insects...or animals...but I can do other things without help."

"In the future I might have an autistic boyfriend... maybe marry one day...and have kids of my own."

"I could move into the Bontel-Macdonald mansion and still make more music...while attending the University of Melbourne...and raising my kids at the same time...the possibilities are endless!"

"I know you are concerned about what will happen to me when I get older and gain more independence...I am speaking up and talking to you about all of that."

"That's what I want to say to you about it all." I finished with a big rush, glad to get it out

"We are listening...Dad and I understand how you feel." Mum said, in a sympathetic tone of voice

"However."

*'Oops here it comes.'* I think to myself

"You must realise Cassie that we are just the same as any parent... it is our duty and our loving right...to ensure the safety and well-being of our child always...especially until they have reached adulthood and can fend for themselves." Mum said, in her very best 'Mother' voice

I can tell that Mum is getting wound up now...I am in for the full lecture mode...I hope there is going to be some room for negotiation...I can feel a sweat breaking out on my brow at the thought of it! *'Uh Oh, looks like it's Dad's turn now!' 'They are bringing out the big guns!'*

"We need to protect you and keep you safe from the paparazzi... to protect our privacy as a family...also to avoid tarnishing our professional image." Dad reiterated

"That's why we need to know where you are and what you are doing... we fear the paparazzi might spot you and take unwanted photos!" said Dad, grimly

"We understand that you get embarrassed when we tell you all these things… we apologise for that… we still need to protect you and do what's best for you sweetheart… after all you are still under eighteen!"

"We don't want you to be humiliated or get depressed by all the unnecessary attention…that's all."

"We will let you have more independence…but we will also help you when it is required."

"One day you will have children of your own… move into the Bontel-Macdonald mansion and attend the University of Melbourne whilst making more music… if that is what you want to do."

"We can help you with some of those things…we are also sure that you will be able to do them by yourself… if you choose to." said Mum, with a worried smile at the thought of her daughter growing up

I listened to what Mum and Dad had to say.

I thought about it all… I wasn't sure I agreed with everything they had to say…I know they always care about me and worry…so I will just have to show them that I am capable of so much more than they can see.

I know I will make mistakes…everybody does…that is how we learn things…there is a big wide world out there and I am keen to see it all!

"I understand where you are coming from Mum and Dad."

"Any independence you can give me would be great!"

"I understand how difficult it is to let go of your 'little girl'…maybe you need to look just a little closer, guys… I'm nearly all grown up!" I threw back my head and laughed out loud at the expressions on Mum and Dad's faces

I don't think they can believe what they are hearing!

"Well Cassie… you have certainly given your Mother and I lots to think about… that's for sure!"

Dad coughed and cleared his throat several times.

Mum on the other hand was priceless! I don't think I have ever seen a situation where Mum was ever lost for words until now! She kept opening and closing her mouth as if she was going to talk…but nothing came out. Her face was flushed and she was gripping on to the edge of the bed as if she was about to fall off.

"Are you all right Mum?" I said, concerned with Mum's appearance

Mum indicated she was by nodding her head up and down and patting my hands in a distracted way… Dad handed her a glass of water which she drank deeply.

"I'm so glad we had this talk about my independence… thanks for telling me about the paparazzi!"

"I think we could all do with a hug after that." I laughed

I went over to Mum and Dad and hugged them and patted their shoulders. They still seemed quite stunned and very quiet…I think it was because they had a lot of information to digest!

"That was a good talk and now I think I will take a rest in my bedroom before we start our next adventure." I waved to Mum and Dad as I left the room, they both seemed pre-occupied with their own thoughts

After I had rested for an hour or so I joined Mum and Dad in the living area.

"Now, we've still got a few places to see in Tasmania."

"There's plenty of fun to be had!" Mum said

"I plan to write a couple of autism songs under the working titles of… 'I Am Unique'… and… 'Anxious Minds'…then in two or three weeks I hope to perform them."

"I plan to release the songs as singles after we return to Melbourne."

"It's going to be very busy…I like variety…it's fun to do different things!" I commented

"I may include a few songs about autism in my debut album… it may even be autism-themed."

"I would like to do an Australian and New Zealand tour… or a world tour alongside our family world tour with our second album."

"It will be a big step…I know I can achieve these goals if I put my mind to them!" I grinned

"We will have loads of fun with our fans in different countries."

"Anyway, that's in the future...for now we will need to rest up after our road trip is finished...before we start recording our second album...to be released in early 2013." said Mum, with a tired smile

The next day we decided to take advantage of the good weather and make our way to the Tamar River for a picnic lunch. We bought the ingredients for our picnic at the IGA shop in Georgetown...we made our lunch and drove through vineyards, where we chose a pretty spot to lay out our lunch...and take in the views of the Tamar.

We found out that in December 1804, the river was named after Colonel William Paterson a Scottish soldier and explorer. On the east side of the mouth of the Tamar River you can see Low Head Lighthouse... Batman Bridge is the only way you can drive over a full crossing located in the relatively remote area of Sidmouth...which is halfway up the Tamar River.

I take some photos to send to Zara, Nina, Ivy and George.

We spent a lovely couple of hours... I'm enjoying Tasmania...it's a beautiful state to explore...with plenty of things to see and do. I've taken some lovely photographs my collection is growing. Thanks Mum, for getting me into it! You passed that on to me. I have many photographs to show family and friends when we return to Melbourne...there are always more opportunities for great shots...I'll make an Australian family road trip photo album out of them all!

We drive on a little further to Launceston where I have found an interesting place for us to discover.

"It's called City Park Radio Museum in Launceston." I say eagerly to Mum and Dad

"It's got over fifty radios dating back to the 1930s." I said excitedly, as we arrived in Launceston

"Our family used to have old radios... let's see if they have the same ones that we used to." Dad exclaims as we enter the museum

"Here's another photo opportunity... our parents and grandparents would love to see photos of these old radios... it will bring back the nostalgia of the 'radio age' for them." said Mum

It felt like we were in radio land as we made our way round the museum. The radio makes included... Astor...Mickey Astor...Storm Burg Carlson... Chrysler... Philips... AWA... HMV...and Hot Point.

We looked at them all...appreciating the history and the role that radio played in every household...long before television was ever invented! I still remember the times I visited Grandma Georgina and Grandad Lucas' house...they would listen to the radio with me...to classical music that used to play...that became part of my life. Mum and Dad often play classical music during their massage work...to help their clients feel relaxed.

It relaxes me too when I get upset or anxious. When Mum and Dad were out, I would listen to the radio in their bedroom.

"Look at all these radios!" I said, in radio heaven

"Grandma Georgina and Grandad Lucas still have one of these in their house... I remember Mrs Petunia talking to me about it...during our one-on-one conversations."

"During my anxiety run in the summer of 2010/2011 I listened to relaxation CD's and instrumental classical music which helped."

"I also listened to the cricket and AFL... I enjoyed listening in on the action as much as watching it on TV!"

"These radios are great I've found more of them from back in the days when TV wasn't invented."

"Our 'Quirky Service' hits were on radios around Australia and the world!"

"My grandmother and grandad listened to cricket and radio serials, with Mum and Dad."

"During our Bontel-Macdonald days Dad, Olivia, Rebecca and I, would listen to news and sports results... we even did radio interviews as 'Quirky Service'." said Mum, proudly

"One of our hits 'Pop Radio' was released in 1987...it represented the music on radio... pop music style." grinned Dad

I groaned at Dad's 'DAD' joke!

"I love listening to 'Quirky Service' on the radio...the European popstar style voices shining through... even if they are 'golden oldies' now." I said slyly, shooting a mischievous grin at Dad

Dad turned bright red and pointed his finger at me.

"That's enough from you... young lady... about golden oldies!"

"I'll have you know I'm in my prime... just ask your Mother!" he spluttered

"Bit of a problem there, Dad... Mum's right behind you and she's laughing her head off!"

Dad turned around to find Mum with her hands tightly over her mouth trying not to laugh.

Think I shall move on to another radio... this could get ugly! Looks like Dad has decided to turn the tables back on Mum.

"Well...I recall a hilarious radio story from 1988." said Dad, sniggering

"Oh...No!"

"You wouldn't bring that up... would you?" pleads Mum

"It was so embarrassing for me!" says Mum, knowing that Dad is going to tell

Dad is not listening...he launches into his story...with Mum cringing in the background... looking sheepish.

"In 1988 during the Australian leg of our world tour to promote our fourth album 'Fantasy Paradise'... we were doing a radio interview in Port Fairy... talking about our upcoming plans for the rest of the tour... the themes and inspiration that went into making it."

"We spoke about the activities we had planned for the 'Fantasy Paradise' tour and our special events."

"Mikayla was asked to throw to a commercial with the phrase... 'We'll be right back after the break... so don't go away!'

"However, what came out was... 'We'll be right away after the break...so don't go back!'"

"Having realised it wasn't right she then blurted out still on air... 'What on earth did I just say?'"

"Everyone was laughing with tears streaming down their faces... the radio interviewer was almost wetting himself and the only one not having fun was your Mum."

"Mikayla went red in the face with embarrassment... she later saw the funny side of it... just not right at that moment!"

"It was included in radio's funniest gaffes and reported on TV and in the local newspaper."

"It still makes me laugh today when I retell it." says Dad

"I turned to you to help me out of it...you were too busy laughing to do anything!" Mum groaned

"Our family had a good hoot when they heard my 'blooper' line...they will never let me forget it!"

"It was embarrassing when it happened...I'm over it now!" said Mum, grinning ruefully

We made our way outside of the radio museum and found ourselves viewing the

oldest wisteria tree in Australia! This tree is one hundred and sixty-five years old!

Wow!

I took a couple of photos of it and so did Mum.

After our long day I needed a nice warm shower...the weather had turned colder and was getting a little chilly.

We are booked in to an apartment at the Quest Savoy in Launceston...I am glad to be hopping into a nice hot shower after our day's sightseeing.

Whilst I am showering...I hear the phone ring.

It's Maria ringing Dad to see how our trip is doing.

"Hello Mum... how are you?" I hear Dad say

"We're in Tasmania Mum... the last state on our road trip before we come back to Melbourne."

"We sailed over on the Spirit of Tasmania and played a prank on Quirky Service who were on board as well."

"Well it was like this Mum... we disguised ourselves as Italian waiters serving them their dinner."

"When we served them their desserts... we poured cream all over them and when Kate stood up to tell us that we would be held responsible for replacing their clothes... she stepped in some cream on the floor and landed in a tangle."

"Adam, Nicole and Amelia tried to rescue her they slid in cream too, Adam to the other side of the room, Amelia tried to hold on to Nicole's arm to stop her from falling, they ended up in a heap under the table."

"Chaos was all around with most of the dining room covered in cream, it went bigger than Mikayla expected it to."

"There were repercussions afterwards."

"Yes Mum... I know we went too far."

"We replaced their clothes with new ones...we also settled the bill for the mess in the dining room."

"They were cranky with us for a while...we had a long talk with them about our trip so far... they came around eventually."

"Yes Mum... I will behave myself." I heard Dad sheepishly say, from the bathroom

"When we stayed in Devonport, we visited the antique emporium and found lots of things that we grew up with...we even bought a few!"

"Yes, we were surprised I've never visited an emporium quite like it."

"We discovered a hidden gem in Launceston today...we found a radio museum with radios from the thirties to the present day."

"Uh let me check... she is in the shower."

"Who is it Dad?"

"It's Maria... can you talk with her?"

"Yes, I'll just finish my shower, get dressed...and then I'll talk to her... give me five minutes." I said

As soon as I was dressed, Dad handed me his iPhone and I sat on my bed.

"Hello, Maria."

"Yes, I am having fun in Tasmania."

"I got a bit anxious when I saw the 'Spirit of Tasmania' and got on it...Mum and Dad calmed me and we had a fun time on the sea journey."

"Yes, I'm glad this road trip is changing my life... it may be the best thing I've ever done so far!"

"Earlier today we visited the Tamar River...it was a spectacular view!"

"The nature is fabulous... our fans are loving our music...we are discovering hidden gems along the way... it all goes to make up so many wonderful memories on this amazing trip!"

"During our stay in Devonport I gave a talk... about my life with autism."

"I did it to raise awareness...and inspire other autistic children and their families...to know that they're not alone in their journey."

"We found a venue at Devonport High School and arranged my talk complete with PowerPoint slideshows and clips of Mum, Dad and I."

"The audience were really appreciative and I had a great time speaking up about the issues of Autism and Hyperthymesia."

"Thanks Maria... yes I was very proud of myself."

"I have been unwinding in the shower."
"Singing in the shower still relaxes me… I have done it since I was fifteen!"
"It soothes me and the practice before each concert is good for my voice too!"
"Like all shower singers… I feel like I'm a hot and sexy singer whilst doing so!"
I hear Maria chuckling down the line and imagine her smiling at the other end of the phone.
"I'd better go… I'm about to put my pyjamas on and watch a movie!"
"Bye."
"Wow, what a phone call that was!"
"I think I lost ten years of my life during that phone call!" chuckled Dad
I turned and gave Dad one of my 'withering' 'Yeah right Dad' looks…as Mum laughed at his comment.
"That was great banter between you and Maria… when she told you to behave yourself."
"Funny as!" said Mum giggling, as Dad's chuckle turned to a scowl
"You two think you are SO funny."
"I told Maria that when I sing in the shower that I look and feel like a hot, sexy singer." I said, sniggering
Boy… what a way to wipe those smiles off Mum and Dad's faces… quicker than lightning!

## *Chapter Fifty-Seven*
# Milkshakes, Hobart & Sandy Bay

"I feel like a milkshake... and I know the best place to find one!" said Mum the next day as we were walking in Launceston
"Swirlz Milkshake and Lolly Shop!"
"As well as normal milkshake flavours they've got unusual ones."
"I'm keen to try a new flavour and make my tastebuds go really wild!" I said
"I do love my milkshakes!"
"I still remember having my first one when I was seven... chocolate is still my favourite all-time flavour." said Mum, licking her lips in anticipation
"Banana is my favourite flavour of all-time!"
"It tastes good when you drink it... the flavour hits you!" said Dad, smacking his lips together
"Vanilla is always my favourite milkshake flavour!"
"It tastes awesome!"
"Especially... when it's got white chocolate in it... made by you Mum...it's awesome!"
"Several years ago, between the ages of thirteen to twenty-four...Dad...Olivia...Rebecca and I...used to go to 'Monica's Milkshake' shop...for our weekly milkshake!"
"We tried unusual flavours and sometimes added extras to them."
"We could take you there Cassie, it's still open... it is now called Marvellous Milkshakes." Mum said
"I would like that."
"Let's go to 'Swirlz'!"
"I wonder what unusual milkshake flavours they have?"
We went inside 'Swirlz'... Mum was right they had lots of unusual milkshake flavours.
"Hello."
"Welcome to 'Swirlz Milkshake and Lolly Shop'."
"What flavour milkshakes do you have on the unusual side?" I asked
"We've got 'Tiger's Blood'... 'Chuck Norris'... 'Monkey Mayhem'...and much more!"
"They are guaranteed to tickle your taste buds!" said the lady, smiling
"Strewth!"
"Those are certainly unusual names."
"How do you make them...what are the flavours that go into them?" asked Mum, with a worried look
"We like to keep them top secret... so we can't tell you that." she replied
"I think we have to buy them to find out for ourselves?" said Dad
"That's exactly right."

"Take your time to choose." she smiled

Mum chose the 'Chuck Norris' flavour...Dad chose the 'Tiger's Blood'...and I chose the 'Monkey Mayhem'. Guess what?

We enjoyed them!

Our taste buds went wild it opened up our choices of milkshake flavours, I recommend it to our family and friends. They might like to visit 'Swirlz' and try out these flavours for themselves when they are in Tasmania!

I woke up this morning in Hobart feeling excited and I know why.

Today, it's my seventeenth Birthday!

Oh wow! I can't believe it! Hobart is the best place to celebrate in, I'm really excited and there will be presents! Yay for presents!

We also have two performances today. What a great birthday this is going to be...I've written a song called... 'Birthday Party Time'...I will perform it this afternoon and again tonight at my birthday dinner!

Before this trip, my family would drop my presents off at our house every year...they knew I didn't like crowds...and loud noises...that come with birthday parties!

That song... 'Happy Birthday'...was terrifying! It upset me for years...so it was banned in our house! I used to spend a quiet day with Mum and Dad...presents...and a cake. The cake was usually white chocolate... my favourite...then we played a few games. Sometimes we would spend a couple of hours at a beach...or a quiet place...spending quality family time together...without all the noise and sensory stimulation.

I love my family, so I apologise to them now...for leaving them out of my birthdays...due to my former sensory issues... this time Aunt Betty...Uncle Glenn...and cousin Jacinta...will be joining my celebrations.

I can even tolerate the 'Happy Birthday' song...if I have to...bring on the headphones!

I will give them all a debut of my birthday song in return...which I may possibly release as a single or on an EP later on.

I am reminded of a prank I played on my tenth birthday...I took my birthday cake out of the fridge and spirited it away to my room... then I ate it! It was so good. Mum and Dad noticed that the cake and I were missing...they didn't find me as I hid so well.

Mum said...

"That Cassie is a little devil."

"She has swiped the birthday cake!"

"Lucky we have a back-up cake!" Dad grumbled

Sometime later I made a noise and gave the game away. Mum pointed a stern finger at me and said

"Cassie did you eat the cake I baked?"

I said with an innocent air

"No...I didn't Mum... Dad was the one that ate it."

"I don't think he did it, Cassie."

"You ate it Mum!"

"Didn't you?"

"It was not me."

"Look at the chocolate around your mouth."

"You are busted Cassie."

"You...naughty little rascal!"

"Let's clean up."

I still laugh at that funny memory today.

I am going to play a little prank on Mum today...it will involve an inflatable cake...that I've managed to buy in secret.

Sandy Bay is where I shall probably spend a couple of hours before my birthday lunch.

Mum and Dad have arranged with a limo hire company in Hobart to take me to my birthday dinner at a Hobart restaurant this evening...I wonder which one it will be? I shall have to wait to find out as it's all part of my birthday surprise! It's going to be an awesome... wicked...and brilliant...seventeenth birthday for me! I know I am going to have loads of fun!

I shook Mum and Dad awake

"Mum! Dad!"

"A special day is happening for me today!"

"I wonder what that could possibly be?" says Mum, pretending she doesn't know

"It's my seventeenth birthday!" I yell, excitedly

"Oh gosh...it's exciting." I clap my hands with glee

"Are you sure about that?" says Dad, winking at Mum

"Well if you two don't remember... we are all in trouble!" I say, looking sternly at them both

"Happy birthday sweetheart." said Mum and Dad laughing at me together

"Thanks Mum and Dad."

"You had me worried there for a minute... I thought you two were getting 'old-timers' brain." I said, grinning wickedly at them both

"Hey young lady... that's enough from you!"

"Lucky it's your birthday Cassie." said Dad, with a smile

"You can have your presents after we have had our showers and breakfast...Cassie." Dad said

"We hope you love them!" added Mum

"May I try to guess what my presents are?" I asked

"Nope." Mum replied

"Come on... let me have a guess." I wheedled

"No sorry."

"You'll find out after shower and breakfast."

"No peeking...or I'll give you a 'flea in your ear' if I catch you." said Dad with a grin, flicking his fingers

"Yeah right."

"As if that could ever happen Dad."

"You know I am way too fast for you to catch me!" I giggled

We had our showers...I practiced my singing as usual...we all want to look good and smell nice on my special day. After we are all dressed, we go to the Grand Hotel Chancellor dining room for my birthday breakfast!

It was a breakfast buffet which I enjoy.

"Thanks for my birthday breakfast."

"You did a really good job creating such a lovely spread...it was delicious." I said

"That's all right Miss Cassie."

"We are happy to do it for you."

"We hope you will enjoy the rest of your special day." said the staff, as we left the dining area

I have got radar!

Sometimes, when Mum and Dad have presents to give to me...I will mischievously sneak into their room when they are not looking and quietly search for them...whilst trying not to giggle and give myself away.

That same radar applies to my favourite munchies!
I will check every cupboard or fridge to see where Mum had hidden them after shopping!
Every time I am found out Mum and Dad say...
"Out of there Cassie!"
"Those munchies are for later."
"Get out of there Cassie!"
"The presents are to open later."
Shall I try to get away with it again?... I think I should give it a 'red-hot' try!
Whilst Mum and Dad are busy, I creep over to the cupboard and quietly look inside for my presents. My jaw drops open in excitement, I'm thinking...
*'Ooo I wonder what's inside my presents? They may be wrapped, but I'm still very excited to see their shapes. I can't wait, whatever could they be?*
I have thirty minutes to wait until it is present time!
Oh, boy I wonder what I will receive?
I can't wait!
At last the wait is over and it is time to open my presents.
"Cassie I've brought you a present that is music-related." said Mum
"Oh, goody!" I said excitedly rubbing my hands together
I opened the present which had star wrapping and inside was 'Love'...the latest album by American singer and actress Jennifer Lopez. The cover is sparkly and it contains... 'On the Floor'... which features guest vocals...by American rapper Pitbull...whose real name is Armando Christian Perez. I'm going to have lots of fun listening to that album.
"Love by Jennifer Lopez!"
"I'll have awesome fun listening... dancing... and singing to it."
"It's an awesome present Mum...I love it!" I said, giving her a big kiss
"I bought that for our popstar daughter."
"This one will make you dance to the pop and Latin beats of J-Lo!" said Mum, kissing me back
"Cassie here's your birthday present from me."
"I hope you like what I bought for you." said Dad
"Ooh boy!" I said getting very excited.
I opened the blue moon wrapping and the 2011 AFL almanac was inside. It contains all the matches from the 2011 AFL season...including Geelong's premiership win over Collingwood. The cover features Gold Coast Suns player Gary Ablett, trying to outrun two Geelong players who are trying to tackle him. It will be a good read seeing the re-caps of every 2011 AFL match written by the people known as the 'Almanackers'!
"What a great book Dad!"
"Every match of the 2011 AFL season in re-caps whether they're at home...at the ground... or, if the match was played somewhere else...like a pub!"
"Thanks for that great gift Dad."
"I'll enjoy reading it." I said, hugging him tightly and giving him a big kiss too
"I'm sure you will Cassie."
"You're a great Carlton supporter...even though Mum and I support Collingwood and Richmond."
"There's always rivalry in our house whenever two of our teams play live on TV!" said Dad, grinning
"We all love it when we are wearing our AFL team scarves and beanies!"

"Dad... you and I have a bet on whose team is going to win."

"Then the winner gets to choose the takeaway of their choice for the whole family."

"It is such fun and we are doing it again for the 2012 AFL season!" I said, fist pumping the air

"Of course, we will Cassie."

"Richmond may have been beaten by Carlton...we can beat you next time!" said Dad, determinedly

"That's what you think."

"Carlton may be in the top four... they beat Collingwood last round by sixty points...one hundred and twenty-two... to sixty-three...they can defeat Richmond and Collingwood again by fifty to sixty points... I reckon." I stated

"Hang on...what about Collingwood?"

"They can bounce back after their sixty-point loss to Carlton last round...they won convincingly against Richmond by twenty-one points... they will wallop both Carlton and Richmond this time!" says Mum, getting' fired up'

Then we all laughed together. We all love our 'footy'...it's nice to have a bit of football rivalry between the three of us... our family and friends get involved too! We all have a laugh and barrack for our teams hard and loud!

"Just one question Cassie... you didn't peek at your presents...did you?" asked Dad, craftily

How did Mum and Dad know that I had peeked at my presents? I knew I did peek and I grinned sheepishly...

"Err... I might have... guilty your honour." I said, turning red

"I'll let you off seeing as it's your birthday Cassie." said Dad, winking at me

"Getting back to footy." I say, clearing my throat loudly

"Carlton is playing against Essendon...Olivia's team, today at the MCG...and Olivia will be at the game today...it doesn't matter if Carlton wins or not...they will be performing their best on my seventeenth birthday!" I stated firmly

To which Mum and Dad both laughed together.

"Let's get our bathers and hit Sandy Bay." said Dad

We got changed into our bathers...put sunscreen on...and laid down our towels with our beach gear beside us. It is relaxing at Sandy Bay despite a small breeze...I put my sunglasses on and lay down on my towel, looking up at the sky. The weather is a little cool.

"Sandy Bay is an alternative location for what you and Dad used to get up to under the Melbourne Pier." I chuckled

Mum and Dad burst into coughing fits of laughter.

"Oh Cassie." said Mum, wiping tears away from the corners of her eyes

"You are such a comedian." Dad smiled

I started to receive birthday messages on my phone, I settled back to read them. There were messages from Jenna...Caroline and Andrew...Mia...Tom and Sally...Jessica...Jason... Melinda and Zara...and one from Zoe...Peter...Nina...Ivy...and George.

Jenna, Caroline and Andrew sent... *Happy Seventeenth Birthday to you Cassie. Hope you have a great day full of fun and music. The Williams Family.*

Mia, Tom and Sally said... *Have a Happy Seventeenth Birthday, Cassie. We hope you have an awesome day. Barrack hard for Carlton today. The Wilson Family.*

Jessica, Jason, Melinda and Zara sent... *Cassie, have a wonderful seventeenth birthday today in Hobart. Don't eat too much cake. The Smith Family.*

Zoe, Peter, Nina, Ivy and George wrote... *Happy Birthday to you, Cassie. Seventeen years old! Wow! Have an excellent, musical and fun birthday. Send us a photo of your performance today, if you can. The Jones Family.*

After reading all the great messages I thought.... 'Awesome! *These are great birthday messages. How nice of them!*'

They told me I would receive a late gift from them when I returned to Melbourne. I can't wait to see what it will be! I showed Mum and Dad the messages, they thought they were lovely messages too.

"It's a great start to my seventeenth!" I said, happily

"Can I guess what my cake is going to be?" I asked

"Nope."

"Not until later."

"We'll reveal the cake then." said Mum

"Come on fess up."

"Tell me the flavour of that special cake." I whined in a sing-song voice

"Nope." said Dad

"Not even a teensy weensy...."

"No!" Mum and Dad said loudly together

"Plus, no peeking or eating of the cake!!!" Mum concluded

"OK! OK!"

"I get it!" I muttered

It was eleven in the morning when I received a call from Rebecca... she has made a few cakes for my birthdays in the past and dropped them off at my house. I wonder if she knows anything about this one?

"Hello Rebecca." I switched to speakerphone, so that I had my hands free

'Hello Cassie.'

'Happy Seventeenth Birthday...darling.'

'How are enjoying your stay in Hobart?'

"I'm enjoying every minute of it."

"I'm just relaxing at Sandy Bay... like a gorgeous model soaking up the early Autumn sun." I giggled

'You're my gorgeous model niece...I'm glad you're having a brilliant time.'

'I'm sorry I couldn't be there for your seventeenth... my talk show commitments have clashed with it...I'm sending you a text message later on behalf of the crew at 'Rebecca.'

"That's so nice."

"I got some lovely presents this morning from Mum and Dad...we had a buffet birthday breakfast."

"Are you spoilt rotten yet?"

"No...I will be later this evening though!" I laughed

"I've asked them what cake they will be serving...they won't tell me!"

"Hmm...that's disappointing!"

"You don't happen to know anything about it...do you?" I asked, suspiciously

'Not me.'

'Even if I did... my lips would be sealed.' Rebecca said, annoyingly

'What else are you doing on your birthday?'

"I'm performing in two concerts... one solo one in the afternoon...and the second one in the evening is our family band performance."

"It will be a magical musical day for me on my seventeenth birthday!"

"You have a great day… send me a few photos… I would love to see them!"

'I'm just off to record my talk show so have a wonderful seventeenth…I can't wait to hear your stories back in Melbourne.'

'I plan to bake a cake for you then as well…I won't tell you what flavour it's going to be.'

"Not another secret cake." I groaned

"I will have to wait even longer to find out about that cake!"

"Can I try to guess what flavour it will be."

'Nice try…no!'

'Cassie I've watched that Geelong Tourism ad and you looked like you had such a fun time in it.'

'Tell me a couple of things that you did.'

"I sure did have fun Aunt Rebecca."

"I hit a cricket ball for six and I did some dancing."

"It took several takes…I had a great time shooting it."

"It was also another new thing that I tried…since being on our road trip."

'Good on you…Cassie!'

'That's great to hear.'

'I might even show it on my 'Popular Ads-Viral Ads' segment of my talk show… I'm sure the audience and viewers will love it.'

"Friends and family have loved seeing it…I might do an overseas tourist ad possibly in Europe or Asia."

"Who knows where it might lead me."

'Have a great birthday…bye.'

"I will… bye Rebecca."

I sat up and preened my hair like a model. I am feeling gorgeous and sexy! I decided to do a couple of stretching exercises…being careful not to strain my leg and arm muscles. Then I leant forward…reached out and touched my toes…taking care not to strain my back. When I finished my exercises, I rubbed my legs with my hands to relax them…now it's time for a nice swim to finish off.

# Chapter Fifty-Eight
## 'Limos' & Laughs

It was almost lunchtime so we headed to Cascade Gardens...I was wearing my blue party clothes.

"Some family and friends may not be here with us for my seventeenth birthday...still we're going to have a lovely time celebrating." I said, happily

"We are going to have a lovely time indeed."

"We've got a few presents for you from...Kate...Nicole...Adam...and Amelia... which they bought and left with us...to give to you on your birthday before they left, we know you're going to love them." said Dad

"We know you have never liked loud noises...bright lights...and crowds of people at birthday parties before... this time we're going to have lots of fun...maybe sing 'Happy Birthday' later on."

"You have always loved the cake part...we have bought a nice white chocolate one for you...we know it's your favourite chocolate flavour... the bakery kindly made a 'Cadbury' version of it."

"I see the silky white chocolate it looks so delicious."

"I'm in chocolate heaven just looking at it!"

"I just want to eat it all!" I said, in a rush

"We've bought some cupcakes and party pies and lollies too."

"You're going to be spoilt rotten... like a princess!" said Mum

"I will be!"

"That cake is so tempting."

"Mum... why don't you cut it after I open my presents?" I said, eagerly

"I can do that for you Cassie" said Mum

I opened the presents from...Kate...Nicole...Adam...and...Amelia. Kate got me a pop music CD...a story joke book came from Adam...some puzzle books from Nicole...and a bangle to wear on my wrist from Amelia. I love all the presents that they have chosen for me!

"How kind of them to buy me all these lovely gifts."

"It gives me great joy and I love them all."

"I love birthdays now!"

"I get to enjoy them with family and friends...it's another big step that I am taking...with celebrations to come."

"Thanks a lot!" I said

I hugged Mum and Dad and they hugged me back. Birthday parties no longer upset me...I feel brightness and happiness when I celebrate them...my seventeenth birthday is going to be the best one ever! It will be a happy memory for me to look back on.

"Right then let's cut your cake Cassie." said Mum, with a tear in her eye

She is going all 'mushy' on me!

She gets out the sharp knife and cuts into the cake...it deflates like a tyre. Dad and I are laughing, but Mum isn't!

A couple nearby are chuckling as well.

"Very funny!" said Mum, in a sarcastic tone

"Who swapped the cake?!" she said, with a thunderous look on her face, pointing to the now flat cake

I threw a cupcake, it landed in Mum's hair. Splat!

"Cassie Annabelle Bontel!" Mum shrieked

"Wait till I get my hands on you!"

Oh dear! Whatever possessed me to do that? I'm up that creek without a paddle this time!

I started running and Mum chased me... around Cascade Gardens... with Dad laughing loudly in the background. I was too fast for Mum to catch and we both ended up back at the table where Dad was collapsed holding his tummy. Mum was gasping and wheezing like she had run a marathon and didn't have enough air left to say anything to me.

"Sorry Mum."

"I'm having lots of fun and the cupcakes are delicious!"

"Mmm...good." I said, munching away

I could tell that Mum really wanted to say something...all she could do was glare at me as her cheeks went crimson...and her chest pumped up and down like a pair of bellows!

Dad wasn't much help to her either...as he must have laughed so much that he gave himself a stomach ache... he was clutching at his sides moaning and groaning...something about the funniest thing he had ever seen in his life... Mum charging after me round the park like a wounded bull...and now he had stitches everywhere.

It took them both quite a while to recover from that and I was getting restless for the birthday cake!

Finally, Mum was able to string a few words together.

"Let's have the birthday cake." Mum mumbled, while still giving Dad the... 'Well you were no help at all' look

"It's Cadbury's white chocolate cake!"

"Yummo!"

"I feel like eight years old again... I'm in chocolate seventh heaven!"

This is such a great cake that Mum ordered. I shared the cake with Mum and Dad...we cut it into equal pieces... then afterwards Mum and Dad handed me a card from Kate...Nicole... Adam...and Amelia.

It said... *'To Cassie, we can't believe how far you have come since we last saw you. You're making more progress which is so wonderful to hear from Uncle Daniel and Aunt Mikayla. We love you for what you are and hope you can amaze us even more and probably record one of your solo albums with us. From Kate, Nicole, Adam and Amelia of Quirky Service.'*

"That is a lovely card from 'Quirky Service'...I'd like to thank them for it."

"I may record a solo album featuring them... I have made progress since I last saw them... before our road trip started."

"Nice little pictures and the message makes me feel happy inside and out."

"That's lovely." I said

"They're glad they can contribute to your birthday." said Dad

"I love you two."

"You're great guardian angels!"

"Someone said… 'it takes a village to raise a child'…and that village, is all of my family!"

"I'm glad I enjoy birthdays now…it's great to be spoilt rotten like a princess for a day!" I grinned

The three of us chuckled, we ate our food and drank our drinks, it was an awesome birthday lunch. I wonder what the afternoon and evening will bring? It's so exciting and will be even more so, when I create my solo performance this afternoon.

The time has come, the MC is announcing me as I stand waiting to stride onstage.

"Please welcome to the stage for her solo performance on this her seventeenth birthday… Cassie Bontel!" boomed the MC, through his microphone

As I walk onstage, I see many fans wearing party clothes this is so good! The fans wish me a happy seventeenth birthday and I thank them… I feel very appreciated. I am ready to bring the house down to shine on my birthday and my fans!

"Hello Hobart!"

"I thank you all for making it to this very special and wicked seventeenth birthday concert!"

"This will be a special concert with memories to keep for a long…long…time!"

"Please dance and sing along to the tunes… be happy and bright on this wonderful day!"

"That's what I plan to do!"

"Now, are you all ready to sing and dance!" I shout out to the crowd

"YES, WE ARE!" the audience screams back at me

"Let's get this party started!"

I performed the same songs as in Adelaide with four additional cover songs… one of them was 'Strawberry Kisses' made popular by Nikki Webster…I sang 'Fireflies' by Owl City…

'Viva La Radio' by British pop singer Lolly…which 'Quirky Service' covered for their 2003 album 'Party on the Beach'… and two more songs made famous by Australian singer Vanessa Amorosi… 'Aliens and UFOs' and 'Absolutely Everybody'.

The fans loved it all… Mum and Dad watched the performance too. I signed autographs and chuckled when I saw Mum and Dad lining up to get autographs as well! It was awesome… wicked…fun!

"Cassie it was a brilliant performance!"

"You will remember that one for a lifetime!" Dad fist pumped the air

"You amazed us all with that performance!"

"You are indeed our popstar daughter!" Mum exclaimed

Mum received a skype call from Kate…Nicole…Adam…and Amelia. They are wearing their party colour clothes and wising me a happy birthday. I sat down on the chair and Mum placed her laptop in front of me.

"Happy Seventeenth Birthday Cassie!" there were 'whoops' and 'cheers' from the gang!

"Aw!"

"Thank you… beautiful relatives of mine!"

"My day is getting more exciting by the minute!"

"You four are lovely and I love you to bits."

'We love you to bits too, Cassie." said Kate

"We're sorry we couldn't be there today…due to our TV commitments…we are sending our love and wishes to you on your special day."

"That's all right."

"I'm enjoying the presents I've received from you all…I love the cake Mum bought me."

"I bet it tasted delicious and silky like Cadbury white chocolate." Adam winked

"Ooh…Uncle Adam." I said, laughing

"How did you know it was Cadbury's white chocolate?"
"The bakery was kind enough to make it with Mum and Dad's request."
"I played a trick on Mum when she bought out the cake!"
Nicole giggled.
'What trick did you play on Aunt Mikayla, Cassie?'
"Before she carried the cake out... I swapped the real one for an inflatable replica!"
"Then when Mum cut into the 'cake' it just deflated and went flat on the plate!"
"Then for some strange reason I decided to throw a cupcake...which landed in Mum's hair!"
"You should've seen the look on her face when the cupcake hit her!"
"It was on then!!!"
"She chased after me all round Cascade Gardens...I was too fast for her."
"It was so funny...Dad was too busy laughing to take any pictures of it."
"It was a blast on my birthday!"
"I'm pretty sure Mum didn't share my view though." I said, with a wicked grin
Everybody laughed.
"I wasn't expecting it at all!"
"Cassie was sneaky and fast!"
Amelia laughed.
"All I can say is it is lucky that Mikayla didn't catch up to you...it doesn't sound as though Daniel was of much help in the chase... that's for sure!"
"You're definitely a sneaky monkey Cassie."
"Who can tell what you are going to do next?"
"You're unpredictable... but we love you."
"I love you all too."
"I'll enjoy the presents you have given me...especially the bangle and puzzle books."
"Birthday parties have been quiet in previous years... heck I couldn't even tolerate the 'Happy Birthday' song... until Dad and Olivia's party last year."
"I apologise for leaving you out before....as you can see my birthdays are changing!"
"That's okay Cassie...we understood."
"Birthdays no longer scare me... I love them!"
"I might even be able to go to Mia's and Jenna's next... I've never been before."
"I'm sure they would love me to celebrate with them."
'I'm sure they would!'
"We always had big parties whenever we were on our world tours and if any of our birthdays occurred... whichever country we were in we would celebrate there...sometimes having a birthday concert in the evening."
"We had lots of fun and we hope you have fun at your birthday concert if you have one planned!"
"I have performed my solo concert this afternoon...there will be a second family one tonight."
"The fans wished me a happy birthday... there were lots of autographs to sign... I can't wait for the next one tonight!"
"You will have lots of fun at your birthday concert we would love to see how it goes."
"Your Mum and Dad need to take photos and send them to us!"
"Ha, ha."
"They likely will."

"Your music making is excellent!"

"We don't mind so much if we get knocked off the music charts by you… we just love making music and touring the world performing."

"Every time we listen to your songs, we feel you're contributing to changing Australia for the better."

"Having a fun time since music became part of your life in 1997."

"We love to hear you sing and play your songs for us on your guitar."

"I appreciate all your compliments… I've always loved music it brings out my emotions… which flow into the lyrics that I write."

"I have songs that mention your names… I plan to write a few more for a special event."

"We'll sign off now."

"Happy seventeenth birthday Cassie from 'Quirky Service'!"

"Bye."

At five minutes past six I am decked out in my shiny blue dress…my butterfly bangle…blue shoes…and blue headband. Mum and Dad have arranged a birthday surprise for me…I'm getting really excited about it! I can't wait!

A long vehicle comes into view…I know what vehicle that is…it's my Limousine ride!

I've never been in a limo before…today I will get to ride in one… it's going to be taking me to the restaurant where my family will be meeting me for my birthday dinner. It's a wicked ride that I won't forget!

"Cassie, your limo from Hobart Limo Hire is here…it will take you to the Astor Grill restaurant… where we will all be meeting for your birthday dinner." Mum said

"Isn't it exciting getting to ride in a limo for the first time in your life?" Mum said, smiling at me

"It definitely is exciting Mum!"

"You and Dad have been in limos many times before… but for me it's a first!"

"Thank you…Mum and Dad!"

I hugged Mum and Dad tight as I could.

"You will have so much fun riding in the limousine… we'll take a photo before you get in."

"You have come on in leaps and bounds… this moment on your seventeenth birthday is definitely worth capturing with a memorable photograph!" Dad beamed, as he clicked

"This is a moment I will cherish forever."

"You have done the nicest thing for me… it's awesome!" I said, admiring the shiny limo

"Okay…I'd better go."

"My chariot awaits!"

"See you later Mum and Dad."

We all laugh together.

"Chariot?"

"You are funny, Cassie." said Mum, laughing

I stepped into the back of the limo… the driver turned and said…

"Hello Miss Cassie Bontel… Happy Seventeenth Birthday!"

"Thank you… I'm having a lovely day so far and look forward to a beautiful evening." I replied

"I will be driving you to the Astor Grill Restaurant…so sit back and enjoy your ride Miss Bontel." the driver nodded his head

The limo started and I looked out of the windows…on my right I saw several people walking down the street…a few of them were wearing fancy clothes for a night out on the town like me. Through the window on my left I saw the beaches of Hobart…with more people walking and talking to each other…the sun was going down and there was a beautiful sunset…this would make a lovely photo…but I capture it with my eyes…and my memory instead.

When we arrive at the Astor Grill the driver assists me from the vehicle…a couple of my fans are there and ask me to sign autographs which I do…one of them wishes me a 'Happy Seventeenth Birthday'…I thank them and giggle.

I don't know how they knew it was birthday…it was nice of them to acknowledge it.

I went inside and pretended to blow kisses to my left and right as I passed, chuckling.

I made my way confidently, if cheekily, to the table where Mum and Dad are sitting. Aunt Betty…Uncle Glenn…and cousin Jacinta are also at the table…they have come all the way from Sydney. They are all wearing fancy clothes in different styles and colours…this is going to be one excellent evening, I can tell!

"Hello Cassie…you look very pretty."

"Thanks." I said, doing a twirl

"Your shiny blue dress matches your blue shoes and headband!"

You're drop-dead gorgeous!" said Dad, proudly

"Thanks Dad." I said, blushing

"Cassie, how nice to see you again."

"You look lovely…we can tell you're having a wonderful birthday!" said Betty

"Nice you to see you again Aunt Betty… Uncle Glen… Jacinta."

"I am indeed having a great birthday!" I said, excitedly

"Last time we saw you in Sydney, you had lots of fun with us, having a laugh or two and overcoming some fears!"

"You saw our new house and helped us cooked the BBQ." Glenn reminded me

"That was the first time I'd been to Sydney."

"I enjoyed visiting your new home, I had a great time."

"I did overcome my fear of dogs by helping you to feed them."

"I would like to visit again… I might even enjoy swimming in the pool Betty… I might pull you in." I said

"Don't get any cheeky ideas Cassie!"

"Your aunts and uncles are just as bad as you!" chuckled Betty

"We're all dressed up and you have your favourite colour blue on." said Mum, happily

"You will be a hit with the Hobart boys!" said Dad, giving me a wink

"I do love blue…it's my favourite colour."

"Yes Dad… the Hobart boys were excited when they saw me in the limo!" I said, winking back at Dad, who stopped smiling instantly at my quip

"I was imaging I was a Hollywood superstar… riding in my limo to my movie premiere!" I said

"You're going to be spoilt rotten like a princess… even more when we get the cake out later!"

"There's plenty to choose from on the menu… so pick whatever you would like." said Dad

"These look good, Dad."

"I might give one of them a try." I said

We ordered our main dishes… whilst they were being cooked…Mum and Dad gave me their card, it had butterflies of many different colours all over it.

"It's a beautiful card."

"I love the butterflies on it." I said

I opened the card and read the message inside…

*'To our darling popstar daughter. We can't believe how far you have come since we started our road trip journey together. We also can't believe how much you have grown up! We have had funny times together, spent quality family time, made music and so much progress since we started. We're very proud of you sweetheart, and who knows what you will amaze us with next. We will always support and encourage you with every new venture that you try. You are our princess and always will be. From Mum and Dad.'*

"That is a really awesome message...Mum and Dad!"

"Thank you."

"I'll add it to my treasure box back home and read it whenever I need inspiration." I said

I then gave Mum and Dad a big group hug. It was nice to be able to give and receive a hug like that these days!

"Cassie...here are our presents."

"We thought about them carefully...we hope you like them." said Glenn

I opened Aunt Betty's present first it was...a 'Best of Kevin Wilson' CD containing all of his most hilarious and rude songs.

Mum blushed with embarrassment, she loves Kevin Wilson...she used to listen to him in secret with Dad years ago... they hid it in her room in 1986 when they were both sixteen... before Belinda found out and they eventually got busted! Belinda was giving her room a clean one day when she came across it!

"Thanks Aunt Betty."

"I'll enjoy listening to it as much as Mum did for many years." I said, sneaking a look at Mum's red face out of the corner of my eye

"Yes...she will!"

"I got away with it I thought...then I received a phone call from Mum when I was twenty-one...telling me she had found it whilst cleaning out my old room!"

"I was busted big time... I gave Daniel a 'dead arm' for stashing it there and forgetting about it...then Mum told me she listened to it and laughed!"

"I was very relieved... I thought she might not approve of it at all!"

"I was her partner in crime helping her to hide the CD 'Kev's Back... (The Return of the Yobbo)!"

"It was an innocent time...trying not to laugh whilst hiding it so that Mikayla's Mum wouldn't find it." chuckled Dad, recalling the memory

"We all love Kevin Wilson regardless of the rude and naughty lyrics!"

"We have never been to his concerts...he is hilarious to listen to on CD."

Uncle Glenn gives me his present which is a Carlton mug.

"You can drink your drinks in this mug while watching Carlton on the telly."

"I sure can."

"Aunt Rebecca has got one herself and it takes pride of place."

"We can watch a Carlton game at her house if we visit." I said

Jacinta, with help from Betty gives me her present which is...a newly released maths book

"We know you're an expert in maths like Mikayla... so this maths book will give you some new problems to solve."

"It's amazing that you can work them out without using a calculator or writing them down." said Jacinta

"I got my maths talent from Mum!"

"Thanks for all the presents you have given me... I love them Betty... Glenn... Jacinta."

"I'm delighted that you three could make it for my party!"

"I am enjoying this evening with my family."

"I love my presents and the cakes you have made for me."

"I've written a couple of birthday songs I've performed one of them at Dad and Olivia's forty-second birthday... I'm set to prepare the other one tonight...called 'Birthday Party Time'."

I went up to the bar to order my lemonade squash and the barman wished me a happy birthday, which was very nice of him.

"Thank you."

"I'm having a great time." I said

"Have you heard about what happened earlier today." I said to everyone at the table when I returned with my drink

"I played a prank on Mum!"

"I bought an inflatable cake and before Mum could cut the real white chocolate cake I swapped it."

"When Mum cut into the cake you could hear a hissing noise as the cake deflated... Mum had a thunderous look on her face... then I playfully threw a cupcake and it landed in her hair!"

"Oh boy...I was in big trouble!"

"I started running and Mum chased after me like an angry bull chasing after a bullfighter!"

"All the time Dad was laughing his head off... 'cos it was the funniest thing he had ever seen!"

"No matter how fast Mum ran I was too fast for her...eventually we ended up back at the table."

"Mum was exhausted by then she couldn't say anything to me until she recovered... she could only glare at me!"

"Dad had a sore stomach from laughing too much and Mum eventually managed to say,

"Let's have the birthday cake."

"It was very funny... I've laughed at many pranks before but never quite as much as the sight of Mikayla charging around the gardens behind Cassie!" Dad said, beginning to laugh again until he caught sight of Mikayla glaring 'daggers' at him and quickly wiped the smile from his face

"That's our niece... always cheeky!"

"Wait till the rest of the family hears about this...they will love it!" said Glenn, grinning

"Oh No." groaned Mum, putting her face in her hands as everyone started laughing again

# Chapter Fifty-Nine
## 'Daddy Long Legs' & Dragon-Slayers

Our main meals arrived and we all tucked in! Everything tasted great. I'm having a lovely birthday dinner...but I'm saving room for when the dessert comes out!

Dad said...

"I remember when you were ten years old...we were walking down the street...you had your headphones on... and we were going to the shops."

"We had almost got to the shops when you got down on all fours and started meowing like a cat... doing the paws action and licking your hands."

"We chuckled and said... 'Get up Cassie you're being a mischievous cat there'."

"You got up and giggled."

"We still laugh about it." said Dad

"I was channelling my inner cat in that moment!"

"You know that I love cats...I felt like I was in cat land... acting out a kitten washing itself with its paws... like they do."

"You are so funny always the comedian... loving childhood memories too." said Betty

"Cassie loves hearing the history of each place... she has learnt lots of things about each place along the way." said Mum, smiling at me

"I enjoy making memories with Mum and Dad as we travel together."

"We discovered some old radios in Launceston... that was a gem of a place we found!"

"I loved visiting there, we've sent some photos to everyone back home to see." I said

The dessert came out...it was chocolate mud cake!

I'm licking my lips already. It is so rich and tempting. Mum... Dad... Betty... Glenn... and Jacinta, all sing 'Happy Birthday', I enjoy it...I still put my headphones on... just in case!

I cut the cake into equal pieces and put a dollop of cream on each piece. It went down a treat!

"I would like to thank you all for coming to my seventeenth birthday dinner... it is fabulous and awesome!" I said

"The gifts everyone gave me are wicked and I love them!"

"The cake is 'delish'!"

"So... was that trick I played on you Mum...the best prank ever involving cake!?"

"Thanks to my family who sent birthday messages... to 'Quirky Service' for skyping and sending their birthday messages...to Rebecca who gave me a birthday call."

"I hope to celebrate my birthday with you all for many years to come."

"Cheers!" I said

"Cheers!" everyone replied, clinking their glasses together in response to my thank you speech

It's time for Mum, Dad and I to leave for our Hobart concert scheduled to begin at eight fifteen this evening.

Later, onstage the audience wish me a happy seventeenth birthday. Betty, Glenn and Jacinta are watching in the audience at tonight's performance.

I told a story joke which made Mum and Dad cringe, Mum told a Mum joke which embarrassed me, so I guess we were even...sort of!

The audience were laughing madly...Dad was too... he was probably trying to get back into Mum's 'good books' after the gardens' incident! It did not go down so well with me...I covered my red face. It's a family concert, not an embarrassing story show! I wanted the ground to swallow me up!

"Who are you people?" I said, pretending not to be related

Mum then made a joke about me which I didn't find funny at all!

"Mum!"

"Stop it!"

That wasn't the worst thing though.

Dad decided to tell a lovey-dovey story about when he and Mum met.

I think I'm going to vomit!

For your sake I'll leave out the story that he tells to the audience.

Now Dad is getting wolf whistles and 'whoo hoos', after his mushy story!

"You bad boy!" I say, sternly pointing my finger at him

The audience is laughing and then Dad decides to tell them a funny story about me

"Stop it Dad...and the embarrassment meter rises to eleven!"

"Mum are you hiding any mischievous and naughty secrets?" I say, hoping to divert attention away from Dad's story about me

"Anything you would like to tell us?"

"Cassie!" Mum says, with a red face

"Ah yes... I recall a story going back to your 'first kiss' with Dad... when you were sixteen years old... on a fine afternoon in the Melbourne Botanical Gardens?"

"What's redder than this fan's shirt over here?" I say, enjoying myself immensely

"It's pink, Cassie." hissed Mum, through gritted teeth

"It's not pink, Mum!"

"It's more like electro fairy floss!" I smirk

The audience screamed with laughter at that comment and Mum's outraged expression. Then suddenly... streamers cascaded down all over me from above.

"Whoa!"

"Where did that come from!" I said, freaking out

Everybody laughed then... including the stage guy way up in the rafters... who was bombarding me with streamers!

"OK. OK"

"Funny mate."

"That was definitely a birthday surprise!" I said

"Cassie you look hilarious with all those streamers on you."

"More like a Christmas tree than a girl!" chuckled Mum, getting her own back

"Ha, ha very funny Mum." I muttered under my breath, though I had to smile too

It was a fun surprise and our concert performance went down a treat, Mum and Dad were pleased that I enjoyed myself ...laughing and singing on my birthday.

When we were back at the hotel and about to get ready to go to bed, Dad spoke to me.

"Cassie you had a fantastic time enjoying your seventeenth birthday."

"We're happy that you had a great time performing in your solo concert."

"You sang the birthday song that you wrote... had loads of fun with our family and enjoyed your birthday in a way that wasn't possible before... it was a delight to witness." said Mum

"Thanks Mum and Dad...except for the awkward story you told at our concert...I had a really wicked time!"

"I'll never forget today... I will look back on it often."

"It has been one of the best moments on our road trip!"

"What more could I want on my birthday!"

I gave Mum and Dad a big hug and kiss and headed off to have my shower. We all got into our PJ's ...we were exhausted after a big day celebrating... socialising and performing. We slept very well all night.

The next day, we were having lunch at Caldew Park taking in the views and watching the kids playing.

I've had an idea and this one involves modelling... and a tutu!

"Mum...Dad...why don't I dress up as a ballerina in a tutu... sit on a bench in the gardens... then you can take some photos of me." I said

Mum and Dad were a little doubtful about that idea.

"Are you sure you want to do that, Cassie?" said Dad

"It may be a good photo to take...I'm just not sure how we're going to do it in this playground." said Mum

"I have an idea." I replied

I told Mum and Dad my idea and they agreed to it. I got changed into a blue ballerina's costume complete with tutu and we went back to Caldew Park. There were no other people around...I sat down on the bench with a ring on my hand and held it out like I was admiring it... Mum took a photo.

Then Dad took one of me displaying my butterfly bangle on one wrist whilst holding a 'Cadbury' white chocolate bar in my other hand. I was enjoying myself as a jewellery model!

For the two final photos I used a ballerina wand that I used to play with when I was younger... I had lots of fun making model poses with it... whilst Mum took snaps.

"Mum... Dad... I had lots of fun being a model in a ballerina costume."

"The photos are hilarious."

"Our family and friends will think I look just like a ballerina." I said, giggling

"They might at that...we're glad that you enjoyed it Cassie."

"You looked beautiful." said Mum

"You could be the cutest model your Mum and I... have ever raised." said Dad, winking at me

"I might just be at that!" I said, winking at back at him

"I plan to show my modelling skills to the world once I am ready."

The weather was getting a little cold so we decided to head back to our hotel for a while. I sat down on the balcony of our room and viewed the whole of Hobart. As I was sitting still a little butterfly flew by and landed on my finger. I smiled and whispered in a soft voice...

"Hello little butterfly."

"Your wings are so pretty!"

"How lovely of you to come and visit me."

I looked at the butterfly for several minutes and whispered to Mum...

*"Mum, a butterfly has come to visit me, this would make a good photo."*

*"I'll get the camera out and try not to scare it away."* said Mum.

She took out her camera and carefully shot a photo of me with the butterfly...then it flew away.

*"Fly away butterfly... join your butterfly friends."*

"Thanks for dropping by!" I laughed

Fifteen minutes later a bird flew up and landed on the balcony rail. He was brown coloured with a red chest. I thought he was cute. I was munching on a white chocolate cookie at the time, so I offered...

"Do you want a few crumbs?"

He seemed to agree... so I broke a piece of the biscuit into crumbs and he gobbled it up! He ate a few more crumbs then flew off.

"Nice of you to visit me." I said, waving him goodbye

Mum uploaded the photo of the butterfly to her Facebook page with the caption...

'A butterfly came to visit Cassie today'.

Our family and friends thought the photo was lovely and they sent comments like, 'You sure do love butterflies Cassie!' 'That's a cute photo.' 'Aw, how beautiful.' 'What a nice moment for Cassie... a butterfly visiting and making her smile with delight.' 'Very lovely.'

Those two pretty creatures had brightened up the sky and made me smile. When I see nature's creatures... I love to look at them and communicate with them... sometimes I even chat to my fish at home. Nature can be a source of inspiration for my music... providing me with a song idea or two!

Unfortunately, ...I don't do so well with creepy crawly creatures!

Later in the evening when I got undressed to get in the shower, I noticed something moving inside, I slowly peeked around and saw...a 'daddy long legs'! It looked very creepy and scary... and frightening and terrifying to me! I got scared by a spider in Mount Buller...until I worked out it was a rubber spider...I have never seen this type of 'creepy crawly' before and it freaks me out!

Are you getting the picture that I don't like spiders?!

"MUM!"

"DAD!"

"THERE'S A DADDY LONG LEGS SPIDER IN THE SHOWER!"

"HELP ME!" I shrieked, hiding behind the curtain in the bath

Mum and Dad came running into the bathroom and saw the daddy long legs. Mum screwed up her face in disgust...she doesn't want to go near it either.

"It's all right Cassie."

"Daddy long legs are quite harmless." said Dad, trying to reassure me

"It may be harmless...JUST GET RID OF IT!"

"IT'S FREAKING ME OUT!" I shouted, shaking all over

"Ok, Cassie!" Dad soothed

He grabbed a tissue and squished the daddy long legs...oh the bravery of my Dad!

He then put the tissue in the bin and said...

"Cassie, it's gone now."

I emerged from behind the bath curtain and got out of the bath.

"Thank you, Dad."

"You are my hero and guardian angel... all rolled into one!"

Dad went a bit red and coughed.

"That's all right Cassie...it wasn't a dragon or anything."

"Just a little Daddy Long Legs."

"To me it was a dragon Dad... and you are my hero!"

"That's a lovely thing to say Cassie...I think we must work on this fear of spiders... Mum is not too keen on them either!" Dad smiled

"Thanks Dad."

"I'll need a lot of help to overcome THAT fear!"

"Now I'm going to have my shower!" I said, with a relieved sigh

"Enjoy your shower Cassie."

"Don't make a mess with the shampoo and soap... or you will have to clean it up!" Mum reminded me

"OK Mum." I replied

Even though the shampoo was tempting I decided to shower and sing instead! I don't want to be on bathroom cleaning duties again!

When I finished my shower... I put on my knickers... my gloves... and slippers. I went to the wardrobe got a blanket out spread it out on my bed...then I sat in the middle of it despite the weather being chilly.

"Cassie... what on earth are you doing?" asked Mum

"I'm about to reflect on summer times I have had... from when I was thirteen trying to keep myself cool in the hot weather." I said

"I see."

"Well don't get too cold, sweetheart." Mum added

"We don't want you catching a cold." said Dad

"Mum... Dad...I'm not getting cold!"

"I'm revisiting a phase in summertime of things that I loved to do." I explained

"Ok sweetheart."

"If it gets colder then you will need to put your pyjamas on." Mum said, firmly

"Yes, Mum." I replied

Even though we are into the autumn months now... I am reflecting on the summer months... which is something I have done since I was thirteen. In the summer months in the evenings... I would either wear my bra and knickers... or knickers... gloves... mittens...slippers...and headband. I was frightened by sweat on my pyjamas in the middle of the night or when I woke up in the morning.

Let me explain clearly... why I wore these items during that time.

I would wear the gloves... because I didn't want to touch gross things! I imagined touching those things during the night and I would have a meltdown! Who knows what gross things are around during those times?

The slippers...I would wear them to make a fashion statement...not sure who I thought would see this fashion statement sleeping in bed at night. It reminded me of my grandad's cotton slippers, in my room I would parade in them and relax.

My bra and knickers...I felt much cooler and freer that way... like a beach babe model...keep that one quiet from Mum...a few times I would relax lying on my bed listening to pop music... sometimes with a drink in my hand. I would model them in the privacy of my bedroom... before I took off my bra, headband and slippers when I went to bed.

I felt cooler from the heat that way...of course there is the total strip down when the heat is just too unbearable...let's keep this PG for now!

Once when I was thirteen, I came down in the middle of the night to get a glass of water. I was wearing knickers, gloves, slippers and my headband. Mum came into the kitchen and said

"Cassie, are you all right?"

"Yes, Mum."

"I woke up and I felt a bit thirsty because of the heat... so I came down to get a glass of water to refresh me."

"Cassie, here is something to help you during the night if you get thirsty."

She took a water bottle from the fridge and handed it to me.

"This will help you feel refreshed on hot nights."

"Whenever you run out... fill it up at the kitchen sink."

Since that time... I always have a cold bottle of water on my bedside table whenever I need a drink in the heat of a summer night.

Mum, Dad and I are still in Hobart... planning more activities.

There's a couple of things I want to try! One of them is experimenting with rock music and forming a one-off rock band to perform a concert in Hobart! I'm going to have a blast doing that and I think Mum and Dad will have fun doing it also. We'll have to think up a rocking name! We will need to find a good venue to perform our songs in.

This will need to be a rocking performance, so that we blow the audience away! I'm going to give it my best and just see what happens!

"Mum... Dad... we have thought of some names... and a couple were not great!"

"I have decided on 'Rock Star Family'."

"I like 'Granite'!" said Dad

"That's like 'a real heavy' rock band!" he laughed

Mum and I groaned together.

"We'll look up a recording studio in Hobart... to record our one-off rock album." Mum said

"We own a few rock albums ourselves... we have a few favourites like Survivor... The Rolling Stones and Crowded House."

"We can really rock the house with rock tunes!"

"We may do one of 'The Police' songs." said Dad

"We need to think of some rock songs that we would like to record and then get some studio airtime for recording." I replied

Over lunch we chose the rock songs we wanted to record for our one-off rock album!

"How about 'The Cockroaches'... She's the One'... from their self-titled debut album?"

"It's one of my favourite rock songs."

"Paul Field was such a heartthrob in his days with that band." said Mum, dreamily

"I've got a good one!"

"Split Enz was a wicked New Zealand rock group why don't we include their best hit... 'I Got You'... from their 1980 album 'True Colours'?" said Dad, with enthusiasm

"I've got an awesome song!" Mum exclaimed

"True Colours'... by Cyndi Lauper from her album released in 1986... 'True Colours'."

The lyrics in that song describe our true selves... our fans may relate to that theme." I said

"That's three songs so far... we will need a lot more than that for an album!" Mum states

A man sitting nearby who looked to be in his fifties, overheard us talking... he came up to where we were sitting. I noted that he was wearing a badge that said Rock Star Legend! From the type of clothing he was wearing... I think he may have been in a rock band he smiled and said...

"Hello, did I hear right... you want to be a rock band for a change?" he asked

"That's right!"

"We're the Bontel family."

"We plan to experiment with some rock songs and maybe record some tracks… for a one-off rock album." I said

"What's your name?" I asked

"My name is Darryl I was in a rock band from the late seventies to the early nineties called 'Rock Gods'… I was the lead guitarist and vocalist."

"We had hits in… Australia… New Zealand… and North America… we recorded seven studio albums… and two live albums."

"Since we dis-banded I have been living in Hobart and managing a recording studio called 'Red Planet Recording'." Darryl told us

"It sounds like you really lived the rock star life!"

"We have some of your albums." said Dad

"I'm glad you enjoyed our music." said Darryl

"We decided we would like to record some rock songs for a change and challenge ourselves to make a one-off rock album." Mum explained, to Darryl

"You can certainly do that!"

"Come to the 'Red Planet Recording' studio tomorrow at two and we can help you record your album."

"Have you thought of a name for your one-off rock band?" Darryl asked

"We like 'Rock Star Family'!"

"We threw several other names into the mix…in the end… Rock Star Family was the perfect name." I said

"That should do it all right." Darryl laughed

"I'll see you tomorrow at two to record some rock 'n' roll magic!" Darryl laughed again, this time we laughed with him

"We'll see you there, Darryl." beamed Dad, already imagining himself as a 'rock star'

# Chapter Sixty
## 'Rock Stars'

We walked to the 'Red Planet Recording Studio' the next day, to begin recording our album. We are going to title it 'Rock Star Family'. We've chosen fourteen rock songs...it will take us over two weeks to record the album. It will take hard work and lots of laughs along the way...we know the final result will be well worth our efforts. Here we go!

"Hello guys!"

"Have you got your songs ready?" asked Darryl

"Sure have, Darryl."

"Majority of the songs we chose are Australian...we do have some from other countries." I said

"We are mostly a pop music band...with this album we are ready to challenge ourselves...rock out some heavier tunes." Mum explained to Darryl

"We love music... no matter what the genre... pop... country... rock."

"We will surprise our fans with our versatility...maybe gain some more!" said Dad

"Good for you Bontel Family!"

"Let's make sweet music."

"That's sweet 'rockin' music!" Darryl laughed

We all laughed together as we went into the studio.

Here are the rock tracks that we laid down during the next two weeks.

| Track No/Title | Singer/s | Original Artist | Composer/s | Genre |
|---|---|---|---|---|
| Living in a Dream | Cassie Bontel | Pseudo Echo | Brian Canham | Pop Rock, Synth-Pop |
| Hip to be Square | Cassie Bontel | Huey Lewis and the News | Bill Gibson, Sean Hopper, Huey Lewis | Rock |
| Eye of the Tiger | Cassie Bontel | Survivor | Frankie Sullivan Jim Peterik | Rock |
| Who Can it be Now? | Cassie Bontel | Men at Work | Colin Hay | Pop Rock, New Wave |
| Cool World | Cassie Bontel | Mondo Rock | Ross Wilson | Rock |
| Blue Sky Mine | Cassie Bontel | Midnight Oil | Rob Hirst, Jim Moginie, Peter Garrett, Martin Rotsey, Bones Hilman | Alternative Rock |

| Track No/Title | Singer/s | Original Artist | Composer/s | Genre |
|---|---|---|---|---|
| In the Summertime | Cassie Bontel | Thirsty Merc | Rai Thistlethwayte | Rock |
| Howzat! | Cassie Bontel | Sherbet | Garth Porter, Tony Mitchell | Rock |
| It's Only the Beginning | Cassie Bontel | Deborah Conway | Deborah Conway and Scott Cutler | Pop/Rock |
| Planets | Cassie Bontel | Short Stack | Shaun Diviney, Short Stack | Pop Punk, Alternative Rock |
| She's the One | Cassie Bontel | The Cockroaches | John Field | Pop Rock |
| I Got You | Cassie Bontel | Split Enz | Neil Finn | New Wave |
| To the Moon and Back | Cassie Bontel | Savage Garden | Darren Haynes, Daniel Jones | Pop Rock, Electronic Rock |
| True Colours | Cassie Bontel | Cyndi Lauper | Tom Kelly, Billy Steinberg | Pop Rock |

 Mum… Dad… and I… have chosen our stage names for our one-off rock concert…we've chosen rock style clothes for our concert so we fit the part…no tattoos! Our album has been recorded on the Rockstar Records Label…our concert is scheduled for this evening.
 "Mum… Dad… I'm getting excited about this!"
"I've never experimented with rock music before… this will be an exciting concert for me and the fans!"
"We're excited too Cassie."
"It's our first time as a rock band together… we look awesome in these rock star outfits!"
"Our parents may not be sure…but we'll win them over!" Dad laughs
"Whatever happens we will make great memories and have awesome fun playing at this rock concert!"
"We've been to rock concerts and they were so much fun."
We came to rock tonight and raise the roof…so let's do it!" said Mum
The announcer took to the stage speaking into his microphone to the audience, with the words…
"Ladies and Gentlemen."
"Let me introduce you to this mysterious rock band."
"They are about to raise the roof and rock the house down!"
"They are familiar…not as rockers… tonight they are quite the super three!"
"Here's a clue."
"QUIRKY and hilarious… please make some noise and welcome onstage tonight… 'Rock Star Family'!" screamed the MC
 We walked on to the stage at the Wrest Entertainment Centre and 'WOW' there are lots of people in the audience! We started things off by introducing ourselves.
"Hello Hobart."
"We are 'Rock Star Family'."
"I'm rock star Cassie"

"I grew up listening to rock music...pretending to be my favourite rock star idol...singing in my bedroom."

"I was lead singer of all-female band in high school...we performed at two festivals."

"When I'm not making rock music... I like to write stories... cook...exercise at the gym twice a week." I said, grinning

"Hello... I'm rock star Kayla."

"I was born into a rock-star family...I would practice in the shower singing my favourite rock star songs... wearing a rock star chain around my neck!"

"I performed with one rock band which recorded one album... I became the drummer and singer in a worldwide rock band...we achieved success performing in several countries."

"When I'm not performing rock music...I read books... garden...and swim at the beach." said Mum, giving the rock star salute

"Hello... I'm rock star Dan."

"My parents were former rock stars and I followed in their footsteps when I was fifteen."

"I practiced my singing in the bedroom too!"

"I later became a well-known rock star in a worldwide hit band."

"I wore an earring in my left ear...I was a big hit with the girls!" Dad grinned, and everyone in the audience laughed

"We recorded a few albums and achieved rock star legend status."

"When I'm not playing rock music...I work in my garage... play cricket...relax in my man cave." Dad chuckled

The audience crack up... they are having fun! We can feel the excitement building.

"Now it's time to get you rocking!"

"Make sure you all rock out!"

"Ready... One... Two... Three... let's rock Hobart!" I said, fist-pumping the air

**Song 1:** Living in a Dream (Pseudo Echo)
**Song 2:** Hip to Be Square (Huey Lewis and the News)
**Song 3:** Eye of the Tiger (Survivor)
**Song 4:** Who Can It Be Now? (Men at Work)
**Song 5:** Cool World (Mondo Rock)
**Song 6:** Blue Sky Mine (Midnight Oil)
**Song 7:** In the Summertime (Thirsty Merc)
**Song 8:** Howzat! (Sherbet)
**Song 9:** It's Only the Beginning (Deborah Conway)
**Song 10:** Planets (Short Stack)
**Song 11:** She's the One (The Cockroaches)
**Song 12:** I Got You (Spilt Enz)
**Song 13:** To the Moon and Back (Savage Garden)
**Song 14:** True Colours (Cyndi Lauper)

We had a brilliant time at the concert...when we finally finished... Mum... Dad... and I...definitely needed some time to wind down afterwards... we were buzzing from the electric atmosphere that a fabulous rock concert creates.

"That was a wicked... awesome... concert!"

"The fans loved it!"

"We definitely brought the house down with our rocking songs."

"That was exhausting...totally rad!" I said, jumping up and down still 'wired' from the experience

"The Wrest Entertainment Centre was a great venue the whole place was smokin'!" Dad cheered

"We are going to need a good night's sleep to recover from all that... when we come down off our performance 'high'!"

A new day dawns and today we are going to Battery Point! It is named after the battery of guns established in 1818 as part of the Hobart coastal defences...thankfully an invasion did not happen. On ceremonial occasions... the guns were used for firing salutes... a review of Hobart's defences in 1878... found that the enemy would fire into the surrounding residential neighbourhood... and it was decided it would best if the guns were decommissioned.

The Hobart City Council was given the site and turned it into a place of recreation and amusement... whilst beautifying the park in 1934...underground tunnels were discovered which served as the magazine to the original battery.

We looked at the weatherboard houses and were amazed at their age...they had grey roofs grey window frames and white walls... Arthur Circus had lovely cottages with beautiful gardens, which I loved looking at. They reminded Mum and Dad of a relative who currently lives in a cottage, that they have visited a few times... they recall chatting and sharing a cheese pie and vegetables together.

We spent a few hours at Sandy Bay before we went to the Hope and Anchor Tavern for a meal. There is a museum nearby that is full of maritime history...wartime decorations... memorabilia...and historic tools.

"This is Australia's oldest pub that we are sitting in." I said

"It has a lovely atmosphere... with great memorabilia items... including a model ship... there is even a pool table, so we can play pool!" I said, impressed

"We could play a game or two." said Mum

"I was too good for you last time we played... I bet you still can't beat me." she winked

"I bet I can Mum!"

"This game will test our pool skills for our first game in Tasmania... it's game on!" I said, grinning

"Oy!"

"What about me?"

"I'm pretty good at pool...I think I can beat the two of you in this historical pub!" said Dad, smirking

"Well... we'll see who is the best out of the three of us, after dinner." I said, with my 'game-on' face

There was a deer head at the back of the room which made Mum and I cringe...we won't let that get in the way of our pool playing!

Mum was too good for Dad...I was too good for Mum...and Dad had beaten me in a close game. At one point during my game against Mum I accidently sneezed and Mum missed her shot.

"Sorry, Mum."

"That helped me a little... with you missing that shot though." I said, smirking

"Ha, ha, very funny Cassie."

"I'll catch up to you sooner or later." muttered Mum

"When we are staying in Swansea... let's visit the Spiky Bridge."

"I'm keen to learn about its history."

"We can do that Cassie."

"It seems like a great bridge to walk on as well." said Mum

"We could get an awesome view of Great Oyster Bay too." I said, enthusiastically

The next day we were doing just that in Swansea!

Spiky Bridge is just a bridge… but it's an awesome one!

The convicts built the bridge in 1843…it baffles those passing by…with its odd design that blends into the landscape. No mortar or cement went into the making of this bridge…field stones were used…causing the spiky appearance… made by the stones being laid vertically along the parapet. A claim was made that the spikes on the side of the bridge were designed to prevent cattle from falling over the sides… though we doubt that is true.

Mum and Dad… did you walk on bridges in your boyfriend-girlfriend years? I asked

"We did a few times when we were teenagers."

"Dad and I would go out to the Melbourne Bridge… when there was no risk of traffic."

"We would spend a lovely hour or so… looking at the water and city views… appreciating the city skyline."

"Now here we are as a family walking along this bridge… checking out the views." I laughed

"Sometimes we would take our fish and chips to sit at a nice spot near the bridge." Dad remembered fondly

"The Sydney Harbour Bridge climb was the best bridge I've been on!"

"That bridge climb was amazing… even the locals love climbing it as well!" I said

"They sure do Cassie!" said Mum

Mum and Dad kissed each other on the bridge and then we left.

A new day dawns and guess what day it is?

Today is Mother's Day!

Dad and I are making Mum a Mother's Day breakfast… before we give her our gifts. We plan to do one or two things and take her to a local restaurant for Mother's Day lunch. It will be a fun time for her…it will be an excellent day!

"Cassie, how's the bacon going?" asks Dad

"It's cooking very well Dad."

"How's the eggs?" I asked

"They're going along nicely, Cassie."

"I'm going to add the baked beans on toast topped with an egg, to make a lovely breakfast." Dad grinned

"I'll get the milk."

"Mum is going to enjoy this." I said.

When breakfast was ready…Dad and I woke up Mum.

"Happy Mother's Day… Mum."

"I hope you enjoy your breakfast." I said

"Thank you, darling."

"You did a great job of making breakfast." said Mum

"We did really well!"

"We'll join you if you like." said Dad

"Of course, I would be happy for you to join me." said Mum, smiling

"We thought long and hard and we've got a gift each… Cassie has also drawn a picture to give to you." Dad said

Dad and I handed Mum our gifts… which were a Collingwood Beanie… and 'MDNA' Madonna's recent album. Mum loved them all!

"Thank you for my lovely gifts."

"I was born to be a die-hard Collingwood supporter!"

"I'll have fun listening to MDNA by Madonna… how lovely." said Mum

"I've drawn a lovely picture for you Mum... that you can hang up on the wall in our house."

"I hope you like it." I said

I handed Mum my drawing of us singing on stage at a pop concert... complete with our popstar clothes... in our special colours. She looks at it and smiles.

"That is a really perfectly drawn picture of you and I singing onstage at our concert...with our popstar clothes on!"

"That's really thoughtful of you sweetie." said Mum

"I love it."

I have put a lot of effort into drawing this picture... the colours certainly make it look beautiful and bright.

"It's one of the best pictures I have ever done... it will look good on your wall." I said, giving Mum a big hug and kiss

She deserves it after all the nice things she has done for me over the years.

"Later, we are going to take you to a restaurant for lunch...no guessing allowed before lunchtime!" said Dad, grinning at Mum

"Can't I just have one guess?" pleads Mum

"No."

"At lunchtime... all will be revealed!" I said

"It might have good views of Swansea." said Mum, trying to get information

"That's the only thing you can be sure of." I winked at Mum

Sometime later we were preparing to take Mum out for her birthday lunch. Unfortunately, just as we were about to leave Mum accidently spilt milk on her best dress.

She was not happy!

"Bother!"

"My favourite dress spoilt by milk!"

"That is not good... my very best dress." said Mum, mournfully

"It's all right Mum."

"There's no need to be unhappy about it."

"Why don't you look and see if there's any more of your best dresses left." I said

"All right, I'll look and see." said Mum

Mum looked in her suitcase... she sees a few of her best dresses...some are not suitable... and the rest need washing!

"Bother... bother... (bleep)!"

"These dresses need washing I don't know what I'm going to wear now." Mum moaned

"I'll look up to see if there are any clothing shops nearby... I hope." says Dad, looking flustered

He looks up 'clothing stores in Swansea' and finds two of them.

"There's a children's clothing store...that will never do!" wails Mum

"The Lair might be our only hope to find a suitable dress for you Mum."

"There are a few styles." I said, hopefully

"That sounds great... I hope I can find a suitable dress for this special occasion."

"Otherwise we're just going to have to think of somewhere else to have lunch!" said Mum

We drove to The Lair... it had clothes galore... from dresses... to shorts... to pants...thank goodness! Mother's Day is saved!

Clothing shops used to be an absolute nightmare for me. I would only buy blue cotton clothes... I would resist trying on any other colours or fabrics...otherwise I would have a meltdown. My wardrobe was full of blue cotton...now I can buy different colours and fabrics! Clothing shops are dreamland for me now...like most fashion conscious...teenage girls...instead of being a nightmare!

"Hello...have you got a yellow dress in satin... silk...or cotton."

"I need a new dress for Mother's Day... to go out for lunch." said Mum

"We've got several dresses in those fabrics... come this way." said the sales assistant

We were escorted to the dress section... where thankfully there were dresses... in silk... satin... cotton... and various other fabrics.

"Oh... so many dresses."

"Which one do I choose?" said Mum in 'dress heaven'

She chose a yellow silk dress to try on and it fitted perfectly. Mum is looking more beautiful than ever in this dress. Heads will turn when she walks down the street!

"Seeing how good you look Mum...I think I will get a blue satin dress myself." I mused

"Hmm."

"I could get a handsome suit in green silk."

"I wonder what the ladies would think of that?" said Dad, winking at me

We all sniggered. Oh Dad. That would be funny you turning lady's heads with your green silk suit! Hahahaha

We took Mum to a restaurant that was named after a household dinner item.

"Mum...this is 'Saltshaker Restaurant'...where we are going to have Mother's Day lunch!"

"It has great food and there are stunning views from our table...it's a fine day, if a little cold." I said

"That sounds excellent!"

"This is a lovely restaurant I will enjoy myself."

"I can't wait to taste the food!" said Mum, excitedly

"We thought this might be the perfect place."

"You might even be able to fit in dessert!" says Dad, grinning at Mum

"The smells are filling my nostrils already!" says Mum smiling back at him

Many of the menu options were so tempting that Mum had trouble deciding which ones to order.

"There are so many choices I can't decide which one." said Mum

"Well why don't we choose a nice 'surprise' lunch for you?" I said

"You can do that!"

"I'll just go and powder my nose." said Mum

While Mum is 'powdering her nose' we decide on her delicious lunch. Her mouth will water when she sees what we have ordered for her. I guarantee it!

Mum came back to our table and smelt a delicious aroma. Her eyes were bright as she spotted the 'Salt and Pepper Calamari' with 'Vietnamese Rocket Salad' in front of her. Placed at the side was some dip and a bowl of chips.

"Gosh that smells great." said Mum

"Thank you for choosing it."

"Enjoy dear, it's a filling meal." Dad said

"Bon Appetit!"

"Cheers!" I said

"Cheers!"

"That was a great Mothers' day lunch."

"I thank you two for making it a special one." said Mum

"You have done nice things for me over seventeen years and I appreciate them."

"I recall the things we have done as Mother and Daughter... art, reading, watching movies, making music together."

"You're a very special and unique Mum to me...I can't help but feel happy and safe that I got a nice Mum who is supportive... understanding... positive... and always there to help me when I need it." I told Mum

"Thank you, Cassie."

"That's a lovely thing to say to me and I appreciate it." Mum smiled at me

"Hey I want to get in on this too!" said Dad

"Dear... remember when you were eighteen and sick with the flu?"

"I gave you some chicken soup...made with Belinda's help...then I played you Lionel Richie's 'Hello'... to cheer you up and make you smile."

"I recall the fun autumn times when we played in the leaves and toasted marshmallows around the campfire at campgrounds."

"You're my beautiful Mikayla... Mother to our pretty Cassie...I would never leave your side."

"Let's make many more beautiful memories together...and share laughter and joy always." "That was sweet of you to say all that darling."

"It's just like when we were boyfriend and girlfriend all these years ago... you are still the same loving person to this day." Mum said, her eyes brimming with 'happy' tears

She then hugged and kissed both of us, what a lovely moment.

It was too cold to go to the beach today...so we decided that Freycinet National Park was the place to spend the afternoon. We encountered possums...kangaroos...and echidnas...we saw flora of all types and geology... especially Devonian Granite. I took a couple of photos as it was such a unique geological specimen. The echidnas were delightful...I crouched down and watched them as they ambled by.

When we got back to Swansea Waterloo Inn where we were staying Mum received a skype call from Belinda... to see what fun she was having on Mother's Day.

"Hello Mum... Happy Mother's Day!"

"I'm having a fun Mother's Day so far in Swansea, Tasmania!"

'Thanks, dear.'

'Are you?'

'Yes...I can see that you are!'

"I received a Collingwood Beanie and a Madonna album from Daniel and Cassie."

"Cassie also drew a picture of us performing onstage in our party clothes."

'Those were nice gifts.'

"Daniel and Cassie also took me to 'Saltshaker' restaurant...where they ordered a nice lunch for me...Salt and Pepper Calamari."

"I was spoilt for choice."

'You're one very lucky woman with your handsome husband...and darling daughter, to celebrate with you.'

"I am indeed, Mum."

"Daniel and Cassie are planning for us to have a quiet dinner at the Swansea Waterloo Inn restaurant this evening."

'I knew you two were made for each other when you were sweethearts.' said Belinda, thinking back

'I would see you lying on the couch... your head on Daniel's stomach and one hand on his stomach also... him stroking your hair and saying romantic things...I would smile to myself.'

"Those were romantic moments for Daniel and I."
"I'll buy a late Mother's Day gift to bring back for you… when we return from Hobart."
'I hope you have fun for the rest of Mother's Day.'
"I will Mum."
"Bye"
'Bye darling.'
Dad received a skype call from Maria.
"Hello, Mum."
"Happy Mother's Day to you!"
'Hello, son.'
'Thanks.'
'What have you been up to this Mother's Day with Mikayla?'
"We made Mikayla a Mother's Day breakfast of eggs…baked beans…toast and milk."
"We gave her gifts and took her to lunch at 'Saltshakers'…where she enjoyed a delicious lunch."
'Sounds like she was spoilt rotten!'
"Yes, she was!"
"She had a fun time, despite having no Mothers' day cards…we couldn't find a store open that sold them…we gave her love and spoke about the joyous times we have had over the years as a family."
'She's very lucky to have a loving husband…and a beautiful daughter…to help her celebrate a special occasion like Mother's Day.'
"Cassie and I are lucky too… to have Mikayla."
"We are planning to take her out for Mother's Day dinner this evening."
"I'll get your Mother's Day gift while we are here!"
'You are a very good role model for autistic boys…and autistic men… everywhere!'
'You're a handsome son…Mikayla was always the one for you!'
'Ah…the memory of the Melbourne Town Hall reception… with you in that green suit.' she said, taking a trip down memory lane
'I still remember that special day… Mikayla was very pretty in the dress that Belinda passed on to her.'
"It was a memorable day I shall never forget."
"I've got to sign off now… we need to make plans for this evening."
'Have fun…I'm sure Mikayla will enjoy everything.'
'Bye, son.'
"Bye, Mum."
Mum did enjoy everything at her Mother's Day dinner in the Swansea Waterloo Restaurant.
She had a fun time all day on Mothers' Day, so did Dad and I.
Who knows where we will be for next Mothers' Day!
Who knows what we will be doing?
Mother's Day 2013 seems so far away…

# Chapter Sixty-One
## Huonville Jet Boat Ride

A few days later after booking into our rooms at Cambridge Bed and Breakfast in Geeveston, I was checking out the attractions in the surrounding areas.
"Mum... Dad...while we are staying in Geeveston...why don't we try the Tahune Airwalk?"
"The tranquil forest will be good for our minds...bodies...and souls."
"It's quite peaceful and it's a nice day for seeing it...despite the cold." I said
"That's a great choice, Cassie!"
"Mum and I have been to this walk before."
"It has a few places to stop and rest... and you get the best views of the forest." Dad said, enthusiastically
"There's about one hundred and twelve concrete steps to the top of the airwalk...so there will be lots of climbing involved Cassie."
"You have climbed the Sydney Harbour Bridge...you shouldn't have any problems with this."
"I climbed the Sydney Harbour Bridge...so I can climb one hundred and twelve concrete steps." I said, psyching myself up

We went to the Tahune Airwalk centre and paid twenty-nine dollars each for our visit. If I get anxious during the walk...I can let Mum and Dad know and we can stop for five minutes...it will be fine. I gazed all around me at the luxuriant forest growth and tranquil scenery.

It is so beautiful to see and walk through...I feel the sense of calmness...and my mind relaxes...my body relaxes...and so too does my soul. We stopped at different spots along the way... sitting and resting...taking several photos as well.
"Cassie, how are you doing on this climb?"
"Are you having fun?" asks Dad, at one of the rest stops
"I'm having fun climbing Dad."
"The stairs are a little tiring...but I'm doing very well."
"The rest stops have helped and the views are fantastic...even though we're not quite to the top yet."
"I'm not feeling anxious...just enjoying myself with you two." I said
"We're glad Cassie."
"We've taken several great photos!"
"Perhaps you might use one as a screen on your phone." said Mum
"I might do that Mum!"
"It would look good." I said

We walked up more concrete steps it was well worth the effort when we reached the top. Oh, wow! The view is... just.... spectacular! I took a couple of photos of it and sent one to Jenna...she's going to love that scenery shot.

"Cassie, did you enjoy the Tahune Airwalk? asked Dad
"I had a blast Dad!"
"It was well worth the climb."
"We also got our exercise for the day too!"
"I enjoyed every minute of it!"
"We've taken some magnificent photos that will go in our road trip family album, for everyone to see."
"They will love them!"
"You've taken a few good photos too Cassie."
"You're becoming quite the photographer... just like me!" said Mum, proudly
"You have taught me well, Mum." I said grinning at her
"I have taken quite a lot of photos."
"We may have to buy a second photo album for them all." I laughed and so did Dad
A few days later...
"I want to try a couple of adventurous activities, so since we're in Huonville today... I have decided to explore Tasmania's wild rivers and stunning scenery... by taking the Huon jet boat ride!" I said, excitedly
"That sounds like quite an adventurous choice, Cassie!"
"We will have lots of fun taking a ride on the jet boat and seeing the beautiful scenery as we pass by...or should I say 'roar' by?"
"That will be very exciting for us all!" said Dad
"Let's go!" said Mum
"I've got the departure times, by my watch it's about ten thirty-five...the next jet boat departure time is at eleven o'clock...so we need to hurry up!" I said, pulling Mum and Dad along
Five minutes before we need to get on the jet boat and Dad is giving me the 'Cassie' talk!
"Cassie, the jet boat will be going fast."
"Hopefully you won't get sick because that could ruin the jet boat ride."
"The guide will take us on a thirty-five-minute ride...we will go over exciting rapids...and make three hundred-and sixty-degree spins...in the water." warned Dad
"At various points along the way the jet boat will stop for a few minutes to view the magnificent Huon pine trees...or spot the local wildlife...like white-bellied sea eagles...and platypus." Mum said
"I got all that covered."
"I'm ready to do this!"
"If I have any questions...I'll ask the driver." I added
Just before eleven... we put our life jackets on and climb into the jet boat.
"You are going to experience a thrilling ride across an everchanging landscape."
"I hope you are ready to have awesome fun." the driver shouted back to us
"We certainly are!"
"This will be brilliant... let's do this!" I said, excitedly
We started along the river...weaving in and out of the forest canopy...during the ride, our guide provided commentary.
"I've never seen a sea eagle before."
"Their average weight is between two...and two point seven kilos...the largest is nine kilograms."
"Their diet consists of birds...reptiles...fish...mammals...crustaceans...and carrion."
"They are located near the Indian Ocean...where four tropical species are found...resulting from the first initial sea eagle divergence."

"There is a platypus over there." I shout, excitedly

"Isn't it a beauty?"

"Look at it watching us go by."

"They swim very well and their bill is a great searching tool for finding food."

"It's an amazing creature all right... did you know that Australia has the only two monotremes in the world... the platypus is one of them." said Mum, proudly

"Wow, that's awesome Mum!"

"It is a very shy creature we are lucky to have seen one!" said Dad, laughing

The landscape was stunning and the three hundred-and sixty-degree spins were thrilling...the rapids were scary...but exciting...all at the same time!

All of my senses are buzzing... I've enjoyed it all...I would like to experience it all again!

Awesome! Awesome! Awesome!

"Thank you so much!"

"It was wicked riding on a jet boat along the riverbank and experiencing all those spins... rapids...learning new things about wildlife that live here near Huonville." I said, shaking the driver's hand up and down... till I think he thought his hand would fall off

"My pleasure."

"It's great to hear the laughter...and see the joy on our customer's faces...when they experience these thrills."

"I'm glad you've enjoyed the experience." he added

"After all those thrills...I need a feed!" I said

"We've got plenty of picnic food with us...let's go to the picnic grounds and find a nice table to sit and eat." Mum said

"Cassie, what are two of your Tasmanian highlights so far?" Dad asked

"They would have to be...visiting the Antique Emporium in Devonport...and seeing the majestic views of the Tamar River."

"I loved visiting those two places."

"I won't forget them, they had the 'WOW' factor all the way!" I added, happily

"You were enchanted by the Tamar...it's great that you tried a couple of new foods too!"

"Now we have all had fun on the Huon Jet Boat ride too!" Mum smiled

"You tried an unusual flavour of milkshake from 'Swirlz'...then performed on your seventeenth birthday in Hobart...and finally coped with a birthday celebration party as well!"

"We are very proud of all you have achieved so far... now if you can overcome a couple more of your fears... that would be fantastic." Dad smiled, encouragingly

"I have a few more fears to conquer...before we can travel overseas on our world tour though."

"What fears are those...Cassie?" asked Dad

"Don't be scared to tell us." he added

"Well...there are needles... dentists... doctors... and hospitals!"

"For many years...I have been fearful of needles."

"I would become anxious in the waiting room...you would hold my hand to calm me down...still when I sat in the chair you would have to hold me down...because I would kick...scream and bite...as the doctor would try to get the needle in!"

"It was very frightening to me because of the office...the bright lights...smells...and the change to my routine."

"I thought I would never escape…though I managed to bolt from there a few times!"

"The dentist was equally as terrifying."

"Sitting in the waiting room…I would feel anxious and shake…you would hold my hand and reassure me that the dentist wouldn't hurt me…and that I would be safe with you."

"Still, the minute that I sat in the dentist's chair…felt the glare of the bright lights…smelt the unfamiliar odours…and heard the noisy equipment…it would overwhelm me completely… and I would fight…kick…scream…and struggle."

"Then you two would have to hold me down…sometimes with a couple of reinforcements… whilst the dental staff tried to examine my teeth with the equipment."

"Many times, you would promise me that if I could get through this ordeal…I would earn myself a reward."

"I remember that once you promised me that if I could remain still for ten to fifteen seconds…I would get to listen to fifteen seconds of my iPod… and another time… a new blue cotton dress."

"It was no use… I still fought…a few times I bolted from the dentist's office and you would have to search for me… ending up with yet another cancelled appointment!"

"Once… when I was fifteen…I screamed so loudly that I scared off two other patients… and you were given a bill for sixty dollars… instead of the usual twenty dollars fee!"

"You were both very unhappy about that!"

"I heard you say angrily…what's with this sixty-dollars bill?!'

"Hospitals tell a similar story."

"Whenever I had to go there for whatever reasons…you would have to be with me and sleep in beds on either side of the hospital bed… just so I could feel safe and comfortable enough to get through it."

"I still recall when I was going through my anxiety run at age fifteen during the 2010-11 summer."

"It was the week in January before we went to the doctors."

"I was upset and crying…having a meltdown…you tried to calm me down but it didn't work… so you had to call an ambulance."

"When I heard it arrive…I fled through the house…jumped over the fence…then continued running…into the centre of Melbourne!"

"The 'ambos' had to wait while you two searched for me…calling my name and things like… 'Cassie, don't be afraid…come to us we'll help you'…eventually you found me shivering and shaking under a table at the K-Mart entrance."

"I refused to come out…with gentle encouragement and soothing voices…I finally emerged and we drove home."

"When I saw the ambulance again…I freaked out!"

"Mum you kept me calm while Dad talked to the Ambos. "

"The idea was that I lie down on the ambulance bed… whilst Mum rubbed my hands and reassured me… Dad put the breathing apparatus on my face to relax and calm me."

"No anaesthetic or sedation was used…because they would make me feel worse!"

"Once that was accomplished…you would take me to the hospital in our car…instead of the ambulance."

We finally arrived at the hospital and the nurse said…

"Mum and Dad…the doctors and the nurses…are here to help you feel safe and to get you better…we can help you and so can your Mum and Dad… it's all right Cassie you are safe."

"I got through it with everyone's help… and medication!"

"But…. and it's a 'BIG' but!"

"Things cannot go on like this!"

"I have to overcome these fears...otherwise we cannot tour the world as the 'Bontel Family' band'!" I said, vehemently

"Great job for speaking up about this Cassie!"

"It takes a lot of courage to name and face your fears." said Dad, proudly

"When the time comes for you to need the dentist or doctor again... we will help you through with our support...also with research for your best options." said Mum, smiling at me

"We have a special needs doctor now... so that is good progress." Mum said, happily

"Yes, we can do the same by finding a special needs dentist too!" said Dad, encouragingly

"We will visit the doctor many times before our overseas tour is going ahead...to give you more confidence and familiarity with visiting doctors... making appointments... meeting new people...and having medical procedures such as injections, for travelling to other countries... and getting prescriptions for medications." Mum explained

"Yes." Dad nodded

"We will all have to do that...to prepare for our trip...not just you Cassie!" Dad grinned

"Remember, we are all going on this journey together!" Mum said, happily

"Next thing to work on after that is your fear of flying!" said Mum, with a grimace

"Thanks Mum and Dad...you're the best!"

"I know I can do this!"

"I can do this!" I said

Next on our list of places to visit is Strahan... it is such an awesome little town!

Long Bay or Regatta Point, was Strahan's original name up until 1877... the colony's governor at that time Sir George Cumine Strahan... gave his name to the town. It was originally developed as a port of access for mining settlements in the area.

Fishing is very popular in Strahan and a favourite pastime among the locals. There used to be a railway line called the Strahan to Zeehan Railway... it operated from February eighteen hundred and ninety-two... to June nineteen hundred and sixty. The railway which operated for sixty-eight years...had several stations and stopping places along the way... such as Ocean Junction and Professor.

It's going to be awesome staying in this place for a few days... there's even the Bonnet Island experience that I might try with Mum and Dad.

"The Bonnet Island Experience looks like a great activity for us to do, Mum and Dad!" I said, eagerly

"We might see little penguins walking back to their burrows...and get the opportunity to photograph them using the light of the red torches...no camera flashes."

"Not only that we get to see inside their burrows!"

"How exciting will that be!?" I said, happily

"That sounds like a good idea Cassie."

"We'll have a fun time cruising on the way to getting there and then we'll be able to see the adorable little penguins!" Mum added

"That's another great cruise for us to take!" said Dad

"Yes, the cruise will be fun for us all."

"The twilight sky will make us feel mesmerised by its brightness and beauty."

A couple of days later at twilight we boarded the 'MV Sophia'...we set off to Bonnet Island... the sky was beautiful.

"This twilight sky is enchanting and such a relaxing canvas."

"Cassie, do you mind if I take a photo of you against the twilight sky?"

"It would make a good photo cover on my iPhone." Mum added

"No, of course not Mum."

"I might use a similar cover for my next solo album." I grinned, watching the twilight sky all around us

Mum took the photo and changed her iPhone cover.

We arrived at Bonnet Island... exploring the remote and isolated island where the lighthouse keepers and their families once worked. It was amazing to see how they got by working in Strahan's unpredictable weather...with all the challenges of working on an island.

Then we saw the cutest sight!

The little penguins were making their way back to their burrows.

Aww...they are so cute!

We used the red light of the torches to photograph them and got some nice shots.

"This is a great place to visit...I'm having the time of my life experiencing Bonnet Island... and seeing the adorable little penguins."

"It's wicked watching them walk back to their burrows!" I chuckled

"I adore cute animals they brighten me up... I love interacting with them." I smiled

As the evening drew on, we were treated to Tasmanian cheeses...soft drinks...and hot chocolate. We chose cheese and hot chocolate! It was so cold that evening that hot chocolate seemed the way to go! The cheese tasted ok.

"I had a fun time on the cruise and seeing the penguins walk."

"The sky was beautiful... I would love to do that sort of activity again and maybe bring Jessica...Jason...Zara...and Melinda...along with us." I said

"I bet they would be happy to do that." said Mum

"Maybe you could write a song about the lighthouse, or some poetry...it would make a beautiful painting too." Mum said

"Yes, it's a really beautiful place for doing creative things and inspiring people." I agreed

"Mum...Dad...I'm enjoying our Tasmania adventure...I'm a bit sad that we're finishing our road trip soon... even though it will be great to get back home and share our trip...with our family and friends."

"The towns have been so interesting... the people here are friendly...the food is great!"

"Thanks for taking me on this journey."

"I could not have done this on my own... that would be too scary...I've gained a lot of confidence since we first started out...tried new things...eaten new foods...met new people and made friends along the way... and had such an awesome time discovering Australia!" I said, hugging them both

"That's great Cassie!"

"You've learnt lots about our history...discovered hidden gems...tried new activities that you would not have tried before...and faced and conquered many fears...and issues...along the way."

"We're so glad you took this trip with us...we couldn't be prouder of you...for how you have faced all the challenges and triumphed." Mum said, with tears in her eyes hugging me back

"Cassie, you have made big progress with every mile that we have covered and every barrier that you have overcome."

"We're glad to see that you have caught the travel bug from Mum and I." said Dad, laughing and squeezing me tight

It was time to complete our journey back to Devonport ready to sail across to Victoria again.

We booked in to our accommodation for our last night's stay in Devonport...we will be boarding the Spirit of Tasmania tomorrow.

"It was so much fun in Tasmania...it will be sad to leave and go back to Melbourne." I said, realising that our awesome family trip around Australia... is almost at an end

"Let's make the most of our last day here." I said wistfully, as we all went to bed

The next morning, after we had packed all our things up and paid our hotel bill...we decided to have a stroll around and see some of the lovely attractions nearby. We had several hours to kill...as our sailing time was not till early evening.

There were plenty of things to see...the Devonport Regional Gallery...Tasmanian Arboretum...and of course, lovely ocean views.

The time passed all too quickly, we decided to have our last feast of 'Tasmanian fish and chips'...before we left 'Tassie' shores.

Ah...I see our fish and chips are ready!"

"Here's to our last night in Tasmania...dig in!" I laughed

"We shall!" Mum and Dad agreed

I decided to give Nina a call.

"Hello, Nina."

'Hello, Cassie.'

"We're making the most of our final tea in Devonport before we return to Melbourne."

'That's great... it's a nice town.'

'What fun activities have you three been doing together?'

"We visited the Turner Berry Patch and picked lots of berries."

"We also visited the House of Anvers Chocolate and learnt how chocolate was made...we bought heaps of chocolate too... Mum and I couldn't get enough of it!"

'Wow!'

'That sounds lots of fun... Ivy loves her chocolate and I do too.'

"We've had a lovely tea of fish and chips and I put honey on mine."

'Honey on your fish and chips!'

'Yuck!'

'Is that one of your 'weird' food combinations?'

"I got you there Nina... Ha, ha!"

'You got me Cassie... nice one.'

"I love pulling pranks on family and friends."

'Cassie...I'm having my boyfriend over for the night... he's autistic too.'

"You've got an autistic boyfriend!"

"Wow."

"Who is he?"

'His name is David... he was born in Chicago...USA.'

'He rides a motorbike and works at a motorbike shop with his parents.'

"I would like to meet him when we get back Nina."

'Let me check with him.'

'Are you available for the next few days?'

'I see.'

'I'll tell her.'

'Sorry, Cassie.'

'He can't meet you because he's got work.'

'He said he would love to meet you when he's got some time off.'
"Ok, I'll meet him then."
"I've got to go and get ready to board the ferry now."
'I'm getting ready for bed.'
'I'm getting excited about snuggling up!'
'I'll see you when you arrive back in Melbourne.'
"Bye, Nina."
'Bye, Cassie.'

We are back on board and sailing to Melbourne overnight... I have no fear as we're sailing along and looking at the spectacular views of the ocean. I would like to draw a picture of it to frame and put on my bedroom wall. The sight of the ocean relaxes me...the waves are gentle and hopefully the rain will hold off long enough till we get back and dock... though the sky is looking grey.

Suddenly, I begin to feel sick... it isn't a good feeling.

"Mum... Dad... I feel seasick... help me." I murmur, feeling queasy

Dad gets a bucket quickly and puts it between my legs where I throw up immediately!

I hope the other passengers did not see that happening... I would be embarrassed if they did.

After I finish being sick, Mum gets a nearby chair and she and Dad help me to take my shirt and pants off, leaving me in my underwear they help me to a chair. Mum puts a blanket over me and Dad gently wipes my face.

I am in distress I try to use my anxiety techniques to manage my discomfort. Mum gets me a glass of water which I sip, it helps to calm my stomach. I feel guilty that I may have ruined our last journey.

"Mum...Dad...I'm very sorry I've ruined our last journey...I feel sad and embarrassed this has happened."
"Our trip has been going so well...this has spoilt it for me." I said, in tears
"Don't be sorry Cassie...it's all right."
"It happens to many people when they travel on a boat or ship."
"Don't cry."
"It probably wasn't the best idea to have a heavy meal just before we sailed." Mum said sympathetically
"Yes...too much excitement also." added Dad, nodding
"We're glad you told us and we could help you out." said Mum, gently stroking my hair
"I don't like being seasick... it's horribly embarrassing!"
"What if the other passengers saw me?"
"I would be even more embarrassed!" I sniffed
"They haven't seen you Cassie." reassured Dad
"You were a brave girl for telling us you were going to be sick."
"You rest for a while in our cabin... then we'll see how you feel." said Dad
"All right Dad."
"Don't leave me on my own... I need you two to stick close by." I said, tearfully
"We won't leave you Cassie." Mum reassured me
"We'll take turns to hold and stroke your hands and smooth your hair." Mum added
"Thanks."
"It will be a great help to me." I replied

Back at the cabin I rested on the bunk, while Mum and Dad took turns to hold my hands and stroke them, smoothing my hair with gentle touches.

These sensations helped to relax me and make me feel peaceful.

"You've done so well to overcome your fears during this trip Cassie." said Mum softly

After a long rest I felt a lot better.

"Do you feel a bit better sweetheart?" asked Mum

"I do Mum."

"Thank you both...I feel a lot better now."

"I'm glad I told you that I was going to be sick."

"I'm also relieved that I feel better."

"We're glad we could help you, Cassie."

"You coped well...you can take it easy for the rest of the journey." said Dad

"I don't want to eat anything." I said, cringing at the thought

I am feeling happier now that I don't feel seasick! We decided to go to the reading hub for a relaxing read in the quiet area. I grabbed some books to read...fiction...English literature... and fantasy. It's the first ship's library I've ever seen...I have to say it does look peaceful.

One of the cabin crew tells us that after a bout of sea sickness...it is best to ease back into eating again... with just a little dry toast...or grated apple to start with...if you don't want to end up being sick again!

I certainly don't want to be seasick again...so I am going to watch what I eat this evening... and take it easy!

"Mum...Dad...I admit I'm a little sad...now our road trip is coming to an end."

"I don't want it to stop."

"We have had so much fun together...creating memories...making new friends at each destination." I said.

"That's so true Cassie."

"We were just thinking the same thing."

"We're so glad you came with us... you definitely have come a long... long way... on this trip... and I don't mean the distance we travelled!" smiled Mum

"You were very shy at the start... having never travelled interstate before... fearing the unknown... a few teary moments...you made big...big...progress...and broke through barriers... to enjoy this once in a lifetime experience with us!" stated Dad, proudly

"You learnt more about the history of Australia...made and helped new friends...tried new activities that you feared before...and triumphed!"

"Best of all we made new family memories together...to share with friends and relatives back in Melbourne...when we return." Mum added

"I'm glad I did... I'll never forget my first road trip...it turned out to be a big one!"

"We've performed in various towns... discovered hidden gems... I even spoke up about my autistic issues to an audience!"

"You both helped me through and I feel as though I've found my voice!"

"I love you two and I always will." I grabbed Mum and Dad in a group hug

"We love you too Cassie." said Mum and Dad, in the middle of a big bear hug

Later that evening... due to my earlier seasickness we decided to take things easy for the rest of the crossing. Mum and Dad ordered a light meal for themselves in our cabin and I kept things sensible with some lemonade, toast and apple.

We turned in for an early night...so that we would be 'bright eyed and bushy tailed' as they say... for when we dock in the early morning!

# Chapter Sixty-Two
## A Letter & a Mystery package

We docked at Port Melbourne and disembarked from the 'Spirit of Tasmania' on Friday June fifteenth, 2012... our road trip around Australia has ended!

It may be over but I have so many new memories to cherish...I overcame lots of my fears...I tried many new things...I ate lots of foods that were not on my 'acceptable list'...and now are! I have performed all over Australia including capital cities... making music and also lots of new friends and fans...along the way. I have made tremendous progress since I started on this road trip...I have inspired lots of kids with disabilities to live a happy life...no matter what obstacles get in their way. I hope I can continue to do this when I travel the world soon... though I don't know when that will be...yet!

"Mum...Dad...thanks for taking me on this road trip."

"I have had loads of fun."

"I will remember this trip for the rest of my life!"

"I will tell stories to future generations of our family and friends... to inspire them to start a road trip of their own!"

"We've got lots of photos and funny stories to share with them all."

"We have stories that involve...heights...insects...animals...and a great one about Mum running 'round the park on my seventeenth birthday!" I said, winking at Mum as she gave me 'the look'

"I've become more confident and independent than before we started this trip!" I stated firmly

"We know!" said Mum and Dad together... giving each other a worried look

"We're very proud of you for making this special once-in-a-lifetime journey with us Cassie."

"You've made several new friends...assisted others...performed brilliantly in our spin-off bands."

"We hope you can take more journeys with us... regardless of our music careers." said Dad

"I sure hope so Mum and Dad."

I gave Mum and Dad another big hug and kiss...before we bundled up our things...and drove home.

We pulled into our driveway and stepped out at the box to collect our mail...a car pulled up and drove straight through a large puddle near the mailbox...splashing us all with water!

Swoosh!

"Splutter...all right, who did that!"

"We are soaked!" I yelled

The driver got out...it was Rebecca. It had rained earlier and she hadn't seen the large pool of water near us when she pulled up.

"Rebecca what an unusual way to greet your family."

"What a surprise you gave us with that drenching!" Mum said, wiping the water from her face

"Sorry guys."
"I didn't look where I was going...must have driven right through the middle of that puddle." she said
"Anyway...welcome back to Melbourne!" she continued, cheerily
"Thanks...we've had a brilliant road trip!" said Dad
"I'm glad to hear it."
"What have you been doing in Tasmania? she asked
"We visited the Spiky Bridge in Swansea."
"We learnt lots about its history and saw the remains of the Governor's Cottage nearby."
"It was fascinating to learn about and I soaked up lots of information." I said
"Did you?" said Rebecca, smiling
"You have been learning lots."
"We sure did." said Mum

Rebecca moved her car to park it properly... we made sure to stand clear this time!
We checked the mailbox and there was a letter inside addressed to all of us.
'I wonder what that can be.' I thought
We opened the letter which said...To the Bontel Family,

'We've been following your road trip around Australia, all the amazing things you have been doing and seeing, as well as your concert performances as the 'Bontel Family' band.

We have watched your videos, viewed your Facebook posts and loved it all! You are an inspiration to us all, we love hearing your stories. Join us at the Bontel-Macdonald mansion on June sixteenth, there will be a party starting at three o'clock. Dress in your fancy clothes, put on some 'bling', come share some afternoon tea, fun and frivolity! We can't wait to see you and hear all of those stories in person!

Your loving family and friends.
P.S.
There is a special package for you at Bontel-Macdonald mansion...open it and you can put it in the loungeroom when you arrive!

"Well, that is very nice of our family and friends to throw a party for us at the Bontel-Macdonald mansion."
"It's going to be a celebration by the sounds of it!"
"We'll need our fancy coloured clothes." I said
"We'll need some 'bling'!" said Mum, smiling
"Lucky we bought some on our road trip!"
"We can certainly get 'blinged' right up!" said Dad, smiling
"Wow!"
"You have bought lots of stuff on your road trip!"
"I'll help you to unpack it all." said Rebecca

We started unpacking our stuff...then Olivia arrived too...and started to help as well.
"Hello, guys!"
"Many hands make light work!" I smiled

Olivia and Rebecca helped us unpack our things. Our house is looking snazzier than ever... the pantry is filled with food...fruit...vegetables...and drinks...thanks to Tom...Sally...and Mia. They shopped while Mum, Dad and I, were on our road trip and were kind enough to restock our pantry.

"Good to be home, eh?"
"The house is looking nice and the pantry has been restocked."

"It's definitely good to be back home, Cassie." said Mum

"We've recorded lots of videos and uploaded lots of photos on to Facebook."

"They are going viral on YouTube and lots of views are coming in." said Dad

"We loved watching them, some of your videos are hilarious."

"You're quite the comedians...especially you Cassie." said Olivia

"Your autism talk in Devonport was fantastic, Cassie!"

"You have inspired autistic individuals to live life to the full... including some of my regular viewers."

"You might like to perform your autism song on my show 'Rebecca'...when Daniel and Mikayla drive you there." said Rebecca

"I might just do that!"

"It is an exciting and awesome opportunity." I said, laughing

"Cassie loved the road trip... she'll never forget it."

"It's the best trip she has ever taken." Mum added

"We all had loads of fun!"

"You three get yourselves ready for tomorrow's festivities...we'll see you there at three o'clock."

"We will have everything ready." said Olivia

"It's going to be a big celebration from afternoon till late at night!"

"We'll see you soon." said Rebecca

"See you there...we shall all have plenty of fun!" I said, excitedly

The next day, Mum, Dad and I, were getting ready to put on our fancy clothes. Mum and I did our make-up and put on our jewellery 'bling'! We met in the loungeroom and admired ourselves, and each other.

"Don't we look fabulous and beautiful...we are looking fancy." I said

"We sure do!"

"It's like a night out on the town... we are sure to turn heads in this garb!" said Mum, giggling excitedly

"The jewellery suits us all... including that 'pirate' ear-ring of mine!"

"It is funny to wear it since Port Hedland!" said Dad, preening in the mirror

"The party will be a smash!"

"Our family and friends will have such fun." I added

"Right, it's almost three so if we've done everything that we need to do... let's 'hop it' quick smart to the car and drive to the Bontel-Macdonald mansion!" I cheered

"Yes... let's 'hop it'!" said Mum and Dad in unison, laughing

We pulled up at the Bontel-Macdonald mansion... as we were walking past a bench in the gardens... we saw a package on it addressed to us.

"I wonder what's inside that package?"

"It must be something wonderful." I said

"Does it contain a special message?

"Is it something exciting... like an award?

We picked up the package fascinated about what might be inside. I opened the parcel it contained... a 'throwback' photo of us and a special message! The photo was taken when I was sixteen... just two weeks before we started our road trip! We look nice in our coloured clothes... I am looking fashionable in my black sunglasses. We read the message to find out who the package is from and why they have left it for us to find today!

'To Daniel, Mikayla and Cassie,

*We've been following your road trip through your blog, your photos and funny stories...it's been a success story for you! We were amazed when Cassie tried new things... inspired when she took on challenges like calming an autistic child down in Adelaide and saving a young girl's life in Brisbane!*

*We laughed at your funny stories... watched your performances as the 'Bontel Family Band'... and Cassie's solo performances too!*

*We were happy that you helped each other through all sorts of situations... breaking down barriers along the way... it was so wonderful to watch and hear! You have inspired many people, and amazed your fans and family along the journey. We hope you enjoy this photo to remind you of the very beginning of your trip together.*

*We are waiting at the Bontel-Macdonald mansion to celebrate with you!*

*From your loving family and friends. xoxo*

"That's a lovely message from our family and friends."

"It's nice to have encouragement and support...we have had skyping...phone calls...catch-ups...and messages... during our road trip!" I said, happily remembering

"Yes, we have loved talking to them during our famous road trip!" smiled Mum

"They have been our support crew when the challenges were tough!"

"We had many laughs together and learnt so many things about Australia...that we didn't know before this trip!" exclaimed Dad

"I think it may be the best trip we have ever taken as a family!"

"Despite a few anxiety-ridden, teary moments...I have managed to complete it all... with you two helping me through!"

"I have had an awesome and wicked time... I can't wait to tell our family and friends our many stories."

"Let's go inside the Bontel-Macdonald mansion and do just that!" I said, joyfully

We walked up the long driveway and went inside the mansion to be greeted by our friends and family. The lounge room looks changed... the walls are coloured brightly and so too are the carpets and curtains. I place the photograph next to other family photos on the sideboard.

Mum, Dad, Olivia and Rebecca's bedrooms... are exactly the same as they have always been.

The bathroom looks snazzy...so too do Maria...Jim...Belinda...and Darren's...former bedrooms.

"Hello Daniel...Mikayla...Cassie."

"Did you enjoy your road trip?" asked Belinda

"We certainly did!"

"We had such an awesome time together as a family."

"The Bontel-Macdonald mansion looks lovely and right up to date!" I said

"We're glad that you had a fun time."

"We've painted and updated the mansion... it is indeed lovely."

"We helped to decorate it too!" said Tom

"Thank you all for doing that."

"It adds that family touch to the rooms."

"Especially with our portraits on the loungeroom wall." said Mum

"We have plenty of photos to show you!" she added

"We also have plenty of stories to tell you!"

"Some are hilarious...some are inspiring...and a couple of them are amazing!" Dad grinned

We all went into the kitchen and sat down...I sat down at the head of the table... I like it here!

Mum put a princess tiara on my head.

Then the story telling began...I was the first to speak.

"The first destination we stopped at was the Melbourne Zoo."

"We had fun viewing the elephants...which were quite funny!"

"They did a mischievous thing by squirting us and giving us a soaking!"

"It was a bit embarrassing...but very funny."

"We got to hold a koala named George...which was a definite highlight."

"Cassie was reluctant to hold him at first...she soon loved holding him!" smiled Dad

"Then we viewed the lions...Cassie got a bit emotional...I told her to use her anxiety techniques...she soon felt better."

"Next, came the funniest and most embarrassing part!"

"As we left the zoo...the monkeys decided to throw rotten fruit at us!"

"We had to dry ourselves off with wet towels." said Dad, with a rueful grin

"Sounds like you had a great time there!"

"The elephants and the monkeys must've been in a cheeky mood that day!" said Caroline

"Our next stop was Emerald... where we visited the Emerald Lake Model Railway."

"We viewed several trains...such as the Orient Express...the Flying Scotsman...the Super Chief...and the Amtrak."

"They were good trains to look at and I learnt lots about them...such as the purposes and the different carriages."

"My favourite was the Flying Scotsman!" I said

"Those trains must have been fascinating."

"I would have loved to see them."

"It would be paradise for me to look around and learn about them!" said Mia, excitedly

"One day...we can take you there."

"Maybe Cassie can talk to you about them." said Mum

"Mia would love to go there...she definitely loves her trains and the Emerald Lake Model Railway sounds like a good place to visit!" Sally agreed

"At Traralgon we visited the Railway Reserve...we got out our binoculars to view the colourful birds which matched our clothes...we also fed the ducks."

"We saw some swamp hens...which I was nervous of at first...I soon calmed down and loved them."

"The music from the birds was lovely to hear and it made us happy."

"We spent the afternoon at Woodside beach where I collected several shells to add to my collection...Mum and I then built a sandcastle together."

"I did most of the building and she put the shells on when I had finished."

"I filled up a bucket of water and threw it at Mum and Dad soaking them...they planned to get me back for that trick!"

"When an eight-year old girl named Lucy, came to look at my sandcastle... I thought she was scary and frightening...I hid behind Mum's beach chair."

"I thought she was going to stand on the sandcastle and ruin it...thankfully she didn't!"

"When she asked me to show her how to build a sandcastle like mine...I agreed and made my first new friend on our road trip!

"That was a good thing to do Cassie!"

"Making new friends and having fun times together." said Maria

"I certainly did."

"I showed her how to build a sand-castle and while we did that...we talked to each other about our favourite things...and had a giggle as well." I smiled

"We're glad you did that."

"We were concerned that you might not make friends...good on you!" said Jason

"We were so happy when that special moment occurred."

"Cassie did well and had fun with Lucy."

"At our hotel after a shower to get the sand off us and some dinner via room service...we watched the Sydney and Collingwood match."

"It was a very close game but we all fell asleep wearing our clothes...before the final result occurred!"

"The next day, we tried to find out via the radio what had happened... but the batteries had run out... then we tried the television...it was on the blink...we tried the newsagents for a paper...only it was Sunday and they were shut!"

"Lastly, I checked my iPhone and thankfully got the result!"

"Collingwood had won by six points and I was very happy for them!"

"What a start to the day that was!" Mum crowed

"You did great searching through all the possible options...I'm happy too that Collingwood won on the night!" said Georgina, grinning at Mum

"The next place we arrived at was Bairnsdale."

"We went straight to an antiques shop...we browsed and bought a few things...such as classic videos...dolls...and novels...that we grew up with in the seventies and eighties!"

"Cassie enjoys reading novels too, she is a bookworm...must have got that from me." Dad said

"We then decided to play mini golf at the archery and mini golf course."

"We all scored a hole-in-one on the fifth hole!"

"Mikayla and Cassie bet me five dollars that I couldn't get a hole-in-one!"

"My ball hit the walls in a zig-zag style...rolling closer to the hole...and in it plopped!"

"I made ten dollars out of that hole!" Dad chuckled loudly

"Six holes later at the eleventh hole...somebody cheekily pinched my golf ball... I didn't know who had taken it."

"I asked Mikayla and Cassie...they denied it."

"Turned out later to be Cassie...when she put the pinched golf ball into the hole...just as my spare golf ball rolled up to take the shot!"

"That rascal Cassie played a trick on me!" Dad grumbled

Everybody laughed at that...including me.

"Cassie got a bit frustrated at one point during the game...when she missed some easy shots...Mikayla and I gave her a bit of advice...which she put to good use."

"Cassie ended up scoring thirty-seven...I scored thirty-nine...and Mikayla scored forty-two!"

"When we told the owner Mike our scores...he announced to us that we had broken the record for the Melbourne section...the world section...and the family section...which was exciting news."

"The score we set was one hundred and eighteen...beating the Anderson Family's record of one hundred and twenty-three...achieving a new record."

"We got a small trophy each and a special trophy...with our names engraved on it."

"That was an excellent round of golf...all round!" said Dad, proudly

"Brilliant mini-golf Daniel...Mikayla...and Cassie!"

"We saw a photo of it and you look like winners are grinners!" Nina laughed

"I want to tell you about Falls Creek." I said, eagerly

"It was the place where I tried skiing for the first time!"

"Last Hoot Café-Bar and Pizzeria was a great place to eat and warm up!"

"We tripped over in the snow two times before we got in the door!"

"I had my headphones on as it was a bit noisy…with lots of people there."

"I chose the 'Spaghetti Saltati'…when it arrived at the table, I was scared to eat it…the creamy cheese sauce seemed unfamiliar to me…it looked like it had gone off!"

"Mum and Dad supported me…I took my time eating it and I ended up loving it."

"That's now on my acceptable food list!" I said, fist pumping the air with delight, as everyone did the same and laughed together

"Well done Cassie."

"You might be able to eat my cream cheese pasta now…that I cook for special occasions!" said Lucas, smiling at me

"I might at that." I said, returning his smile

"After our bellies were filled…we went to Falls Creek Alpine Resort for some skiing."

"As it was my first time…I took the beginners class with my instructor Shelia…starting out on the nursery slopes."

"I kept practising on the nursery slopes with Sheila…it takes a long time to learn all the skills needed to be a proficient skier!"

"Mum and Dad have been skiing before…so they took the veterans refresher class…with their instructor Barry."

"I heard Mum and Dad having fun and acting like teenagers not grown-ups… which made Shelia and I laugh."

"Mum and Dad skied down the mountain, laughing all the way enjoying themselves."

"When Sheila and I we were about to ski… I had an anxiety attack telling Shelia… 'I can't do it… I just can't!"

"Sheila told me to use my anxiety techniques…which I did."

"It was one of many new activities I've tried and I am sure I will try it again if I have the chance to." I added

"We had fun in Falls Creek…I enjoyed the whole snow experience!" I said, laughing

"You did really well Cassie…you've had a blast in the snow and embraced the cold with your skiing."

"Good on you sweetheart." said Olivia

"Thanks Olivia…I did have a blast!"

"I'd never experienced snow up close before…I was so excited and ecstatic when I arrived."

"I saw snow everywhere we went in Falls Creek…I'll never forget my time in the snow!" I said, enthusiastically

"I skyped Mum and told her what we were up to in Falls Creek…I tried to ask her what the Dads' were doing on their months' holiday…she wouldn't tell me!" said Mikayla

"She spoke to me about a family member that I hadn't seen for almost twenty-two years…her clue was that the family member was a man!"

"When I tried to ask her for a little more information she said."

"We are not skyping every day."

"I said 'Blah… blah… blah… I shall find out somehow… no matter what it takes'!"

"You are always cheeky to me whenever we skype…a cheeky little bugger that's what you are, Mikayla!" piped up Belinda

Everyone tried not to snigger at that comment!

"Echuca was the first destination we camped at." said Dad, moving on to the next yarn

"We set up our tents and gear and were reading our books...then we saw Cassie sobbing... tears rolling down her face."

"Mikayla and I went over... to ask what had made her upset... she could not find the words to tell us... so we rubbed her hands, and let her cry a little."

"When she calmed down...we sat on a log and she told us that it reminded her of a horrible memory from June 1999."

"The memory involved the time when she wandered off into bushland...when she was four years old."

"Most of us remember the news coverage...it was terrifying and we were so relieved when Cassie made her own way back safe and well...despite being wet and dirty."

"Cassie opened up to us and made progress...she became a little braver after telling us all about it." said Dad

"Well done for opening up to your Mum and Dad about that memory, Cassie." said Zoe

"That event terrified me for years...it often upset me and I didn't want to talk about it...so I stayed away from camping... we always stayed in hotels... no camping grounds!"

"I'm glad I opened up to Mum and Dad about that frightening event...otherwise I would have been tortured by it for years."

"We're very proud of you for doing so." stated Mum

"We started off a fresh new camping experience by swimming in the river." I told everyone

"Mum and Dad made 'wussy' excuses for not going in the water...I told them that the water was warm... okay to swim in."

"Mum jumped in to find that the water was in fact... very cold...I tricked her good!"

"Dad jumped in twenty minutes later...it was a nice swim despite the cool weather."

"Later, Dad and I tricked Mum...she didn't know there was only cold running water at the camping grounds...then she went to have a hot shower after swimming in the cold creek!"

"She shrieked like a wuss when she turned the tap on and icy cold water hit her body!"

"Dad and I thought it was hilarious...I'm not sure Mum thought the same."

Everybody cracked up looking at Mum, who was giving Dad and I the death stare!

I quickly moved on to the next story.

"At night Mum and Dad told me a couple of camping stories from their past...which were very funny."

"Then the next day we went shopping in Shepparton...we bought a few music CD's... including 'The Wolverines'...and 'Kylie Minogue'."

"Cassie found a remastered 'Shyness' CD which was released originally in 1983...when Daniel...Olivia... Rebecca...and I...were thirteen." said Mikayla

"It had eight songs on it...plus four more which didn't make the final recording...Shy... Star...Paradise...and Saturday."

"We bought a copy of it...we loved listening to it...it was nice hearing our younger voices once again...it was a precursor to our teen-pop super stardom." she added

"The title certainly describes your personalities at the time." said Jessica

"We went to lunch at a Chinese restaurant...where Cassie made big progress!"

"She tried the San Choi Bow...including nuts...and chicken!" said Dad

"I'll be happy to serve her stir-fry on any night of the week!" said Jim

"A couple of days later we met up with Caroline...Andrew...and Jenna...for horse riding... which I had never tried before!"

"The horses we rode had sky-themed names and lovely flowing manes."

"I fed one of them a carrot...his name was Sun...I placed my hands on both sides of his mouth and kissed him on his nose...when we first met."

"Everybody laughed... including me!"

"Then 'Sun' let a 'big one' go...which made everyone laugh even harder...and we ran away to avoid the pong!"

The party room which we had all moved into when everyone arrived, erupted in laughter!

"We all did the Goulburn-Murray ride...which took three hours...we talked while we rode through the wet and rainy weather."

"We had a good ride...the most embarrassing moment was when we all slipped and landed on our bums in the mud...after we got off our horses!"

"We kept falling over...every time we tried to stand up again!"

"Caroline...Andrew...and Jenna...filmed it all with their iPhones...a French tourist from a European tourist group...filmed it all with his video camera...which made it even more embarrassing for the three of us!" we groaned

"We've watched the recording and viewed the photos...they are very funny...even Mrs Joelle and Helen thought they were hilarious to watch."

"Cassie you could do a live show as a comedian!" Jenna grinned

"I'll think about it." I replied, with a wry grin

"The next day we put on our lifejackets to go paddling our kayak down the river!"

"I told Mum and Dad I had never tried anything like that before...because I feared I would fall into the water and drown."

"They assured me that I would be safer with a lifejacket on...then if I did fall in...the jacket would help me to float."

"We loved paddling our kayak...just as we were returning to the riverbank later in the afternoon...a power jetboat sped past us...causing the backwater to overturn us and we ended up in the water!"

"We suffered nothing more than wet clothes and red faces...we carried our kayak back to the tents...dried off and got changed...into nice dry clothes." I told everyone

"We sometimes fall out when we go kayaking too...we always climb back in and continue paddling...regardless of how wet we get." said Zara

"As we were leaving Echuca the next morning...something landed on our car roof...it turned out to be a magpie that had injured its wing."

"Cassie carefully climbed up to get it down...then we showed her how to put a small splint on the injured wing with the first-aid kit...to keep it stable."

"The Shepparton Clinic was closed for relocation and the Wangaratta Vet Clinic was under repairs...so we searched for help elsewhere, for the magpie we had named Margaret.

"We took Margaret to the Wodonga Family Vet Centre...where we left her in the capable hands of Dr. John Parr overnight...the next day we collected Margaret and took her to 'The Caring Bird'...owned by a lady named Valerie, Margaret could fully recover there before being released back into the wild again."

"It was a great effort by Cassie to look after a small creature and learn about birds." Mum added

"Your Grandma Margaret would've been proud of you for doing a good deed like that." said Belinda

"By now she will be flying free in the sky...as free as she can be." I said

"As we were walking back to our car in Wodonga a familiar voice called out to us...Mikayla went off to see who it was."

"We walked into a house and that's where the trick started."

"Mikayla served us green tea and iced biscuits...we talked about the house and our road trip so far...then when Rebecca walked in...the penny dropped!"

"Throughout the entire two hours...I thought I was talking to Mikayla when I was actually talking to Rebecca...Mikayla gave the green tea and iced biscuits to Rebecca in the kitchen... who in turn served them up to us!"

"I spat out my tea and went red in the face with embarrassment... big time!" said Dad, turning pink at the thought once again

"Cassie recorded the whole two hours with her video camera!" said Dad, squirming

"It was the funniest trick I've ever recorded and witnessed."

"I was laughing so hard tears were running down my face."

"I thought I would nearly wet myself."

"Mum and Rebecca were laughing hysterically too."

"Mikayla and I have loved playing that trick since we were young girls...we still do today!"

Everyone in the room shouted out...

"WE KNOW!"

"You'll never know when we're going to do it next." said Rebecca, cheekily

We all chuckled at that remark...poor Dad...just groaned.

# Chapter Sixty-Three
## Reunions

"Beechworth was a beautiful place to visit."

"The Beechworth Sweet Company was a delight to us all."

"We went crazy!"

"There was so much to see and so many types of sweets and chocolates to choose from!"

"We carried on to Beechworth Honey…to learn about bees…and how they make their delicious tasting honey."

"Prior to our visit I had a fear of bees…I would only go into the backyard when there were none around."

"I overcame my fear of bees with this interesting experience…I learnt a lot more about bees and honey."

"Then we looked at GIGS art gallery and the Army Museum…which had lots of military stuff."

"When we got our tea from Red Rooster…Cassie told the server that her order was wrong in a calm and positive voice…the social worker's helpful advice had paid off!"

"We did a half day tour at Chelbec Tours and Charter with the Jones Family in Wodonga… we all learnt about our relatives who lived there and contributed to Australian history… including Mum's grandad…Percy Macdonald…Edith Jones… Zoe's Grandmother…and Harold Jones…Peter's Grandad."

"We viewed the Hume Dam and Tribute Wall on this tour, it was fun and I soaked up some more information." I said

"We had fun learning about our families too!"

"I'm part of a Richmond footballing family…I've continued the tradition from Dad…our house is decorated with Richmond memorabilia."

"Every time we attend a game as a family… we barrack hard!"

"Zoe's grandmother was a really good cook in the hospitality industry…we still make her dishes…honouring her tradition in the family on Zoe's side."

"Boy, do those dishes taste good too!" said Peter, smacking his lips

"I might consider working at the Collingwood Football Club one day!"

"I skyped Mum and talked to her about our grandads and great-grandads service…in World War II…about wearing their Anzac medals…and marching in the Anzac Day Parade for them…since 1996."

"Then I asked her for the second clue about my long-lost relative… she told me he is one hundred and seventy-six centimetres tall!"

"I tried to ask her can we skype every day and she told me 'NO' we can't!"

Everybody giggled.

"We purchased some fancy clothes at the Wodonga Plaza Shopping Centre…then Cassie and I went to have a makeover at the beauty room."

"After that we headed to the Wodonga Pizza Place to have our dinner with the Jones'."

"Cassie ordered a tropical pineapple pizza...aka Hawaiian Pizza...she loved eating it!"

"Next day, we headed to Wodonga GIGS where we took an art class with three others."

"Our art teacher was Hilary, she instructed us to paint something Australian."

"I painted a lamington...Daniel painted the Sydney Harbour Bridge...and Cassie painted the city of Melbourne...a butterfly...a diamond...and the sun!"

"I admit I was standing back smugly admiring my painting...when that cheeky Cassie painted a line right down my face!"

"The cheek of her!"

"I got her back by painting a line across her forehead."

"Everyone was chuckling...including Daniel."

"Hilary asked Cassie and I who had started it and we tried to blame each other...Daniel dobbed us in... and we got the rap for our tricks!"

"There was a real face-painting event afterwards... so we were able to get our faces painted properly... as a tiger...a fairy...and a butterfly!" said Mum

"Wodonga sounds a fun place to stay."

"That GIGS art class must have been inspiring...you and Cassie were a bit naughty painting each other... we don't often know about what you two get up to with Daniel!" said George smiling

"Ha, ha, that's true!

"We then moved on to Canberra...where we had to help an MP Darryl Samson...to find his briefcase full of personal papers...he had lost it just before he was about to go for a meeting, with the Prime Minister... Sophie Lewis!"

"We searched through hedges and eventually found his briefcase...we got Darryl to his meeting on time... which saved him from a lot of trouble."

"We even met Prime Minister Sophie and her partner George Robertson...we had a small chat with them before heading to Lake Burley Griffin."

"We viewed the Captain Cook Memorial Jet, which sprayed water three metres into the air...it was awesome!" I said, very impressed

"After that we visited the Australian National Botanical Gardens...we learnt about the many flowers there."

"In the evening we attended a concert at the Llewelyn Hall...to hear the Canberra Symphony Orchestra perform."

"I chose Sydney as our next destination, when it came time to leave the car wasn't working properly."

"I volunteered to fix it...but after I looked it over carefully...we all decided to take it to the City Car Care Braddon...as the crankshaft needed repairing."

"We stayed another day and night...then we left for Sydney the following day, when our car was repaired."

"When we arrived at the bridge... (I said speaking to the rest of the family) ...we bumped into Tom...Sally... and Mia, who were also going to do the climb...so we joined forces."

Everyone laughed when I said that.

"We did a health and safety assessment which we all passed, then headed to the pre-climb up area and put our gear on."

"We started through the dark purpose-built tunnel and began climbing the side of the bridge."

"At the halfway point Cassie got dizzy...we gave her the choice of whether to continue the climb or not... she thought about it for a few minutes before she decided to continue...with a determined look on her face."

"We finally reached the top of the bridge where we had a group photograph taken and received a certificate of achievement!"

"We also received a bridge climb cap...and free entry to the Pylon Lookout."

"Cassie overcame her fear of heights...it is one of her greatest achievements on our trip." said Dad

"We are very proud of her for overcoming her fear of heights...she was very proud of herself too and so happy...she'll never forget that climb and neither will we!" said Dad, proudly

"That was very brave of you Cassie!"

"We were delighted when you achieved your goal and joyful to see that delighted look on your face!"

"We all hugged which felt good...I felt closer to you after that shared experience together." said Mia, smiling happily

"We booked backing dancers from a dance school called 'Pop Dance Music School', for rehearsals the next afternoon...for my upcoming solo performance at the Metro Theatre.

"Then we went to visit Aunt Betty...Uncle Glenn...and cousin Jacinta...for tea."

"I helped them with the BBQ and whilst we ate tea, we talked about our road trip and Glenn busted Mum for teasing him about his team Sydney Swans...being beaten by Collingwood!"

"I overcame my fear of dogs by feeding Betty and Glen's dogs...Max and Smoochums...I laughed when they jumped up and licked my face." I said, reminiscing

"The next day we went back to the 'Pop Dance Music School', to practise my routines with the five backing dancers...Sarah...Petunia...Prunella...Macy...and Dina...to the music of Nikki Webster's, 'Strawberry Kisses'."

"When I said to Mum and Dad that I didn't need my headphones anymore...they were concerned that I would get stage fright...and meltdown in front of the entire Metro Theatre audience!"

"Luckily...that didn't happen!"

"Their concerns disappeared when I sang like an angel and wowed the entire audience!" I said, with a big grin across my face

All the family laughed when I said that...and my cousins rolled their eyes and bowed and curtseyed in front of me...like they were in front of a princess...which cracked me up and we laughed all over again.

"We performed our first 'Bontel Family' concert and rocked the house...we signed autographs and there was a little rivalry beginning to show between...Mum...Dad...and I when my popularity started to grow with the fans." I winked to my family, as they watched Mum and Dad's faces closely...for a reaction

"Mum's eyebrows raised a little at my speech...Dad tried to do his best 'rock star' look... neither of them said anything...I wondered how long they could keep quiet." I said sneakily, with a wink to everyone listening

That made everyone chuckle.

"Mum and Dad were proud of me for coping with the crowds...bright lights...and loud noises...throughout the entire night."

"We had a breakthrough at the end of the concert evening...when everything had gone so well...and we were all excited with the success of our first Bontel Family band performance together!"

"Mum and Dad wanted to hug and kiss me to celebrate."

"Initially, I wouldn't let Dad kiss me...because I thought I might hit out at him... and have a meltdown."

"Mum and Dad reassured me that it was just another way to show affection...care...and love...to those who mean the most to you in your life."

"I let Dad kiss me and I kissed him back...then Mum kissed me affectionately...and I did the same to her!"

"That was such a big step for me...now I can kiss them anytime!" I said, grinning

"I remember you couldn't even hug or kiss me when we came to visit…you used your gloves to touch." said Kate

"You never said I love you to anyone…so it's wonderful that you are finally able to show your affection to your Mum and Dad."

"You sure had a fun time in Sydney!"

"We enjoyed watching your performances on television and loved both of the albums."

"Thank you…we sure did have a blast there Kate!"

I continued with more stories about our trip…

"When we got to Newcastle, we had a great hotel overlooking the beach."

"We changed into our bathers…then I pulled my famous 'deodorant' trick on Mum… swapping her deodorant for shaving cream!"

"Mum worked out it was me by the time I came back from the kiosk, where I bought ice creams for Mum, Dad and Olivia…who had just arrived to join us."

"We talked and played in the surf…we had lots of fun there…then we went to Newcastle's Domino Pizza shop…where we participated in the 'Domino's Pizza Experience'…learning how to make pizzas which was great fun."

"I enjoyed my time and the memories we made in Newcastle…I still enjoy surfing!" said Olivia, enthusiastically

"Cassie has always loved the beach…it's her favourite place to visit…it relaxes her and she loves the sights and smells of it." Mum smiles

"When we got back to our hotel, I skyped Mum for the third and final clue about the mystery family member…the clue was…he has a comb-over!"

"Mum wouldn't reveal anything else after that….so cheekily I stuck my fingers in my ears and my tongue out at Mum!"

"Mum was baking scones and chocolate cake at the time and she wouldn't keep any for me!" said Mikayla, in an offended voice

"You were always trouble Mikayla and that hasn't changed now that you have turned forty-two years old!" said Belinda wagging her finger at Mum, whilst Mum just grinned back at her and everyone else in the room laughed

"Then we stayed in Tamworth…where we viewed the sights and found a parcel containing cowboy-cowgirl costumes for us to wear…then we formed a one-off country music band… called 'The Outback Family'."

"We released a self-titled album of twenty songs…which the Tamworth crowd loved."

"What fun times we had there!" said Dad, smiling

"You had a 'boot skootin' time in Tamworth." somebody piped up

"We loved listening to that album…it really sounds like you were having a country party on it!"

"Maria…Belinda…Darren…and Jim…loved it!" said Adam, grinning

"We stopped in Stanthorpe to look up some family history."

"I have a bit of New Zealand heritage on Mum's side through Nan Diane's sister…I've got a grandad and eight relatives…born in New Zealand."

"I've also got Irish heritage through Nan Diane's parents…who were born in Ireland."

"Then Mum remembered something significant about the long-lost family member!"

"It was a dove badge which said 'peace' on it…another special clue!"

"Armed with that information…we then headed to the Gold Coast for two weeks."

"Paradise Playground was fun...we drank tea and watched the kids play on the play equipment...indoor jumping castle...and the PlayStation."

"Then a Mum asked for our help...her three-year-old son was too scared to come down the slide."

"I was the only one out of the three of us small enough to fit through the playground equipment."

"I clambered up to where the boy was stuck...then with gentle talk and encouragement...I used a soothing voice to convince him to slide down with me...he was laughing all the way down." I told everyone

"That was great Cassie...you used your calming skills and action...to get that boy down the slide...well done!" said Nicole

"As we were getting ready for bed that evening, after dinner at Mario's Italian Restaurant...a thunderstorm occurred which frightened me."

"I sat on Mum's bed and she rubbed my hands to calm me...I told her it was the sight of the storm and lightning that was scaring me...not the noise."

"After she hugged me and stroked my hands gently, I felt a lot better."

"I am not so scared of thunder and lightning now...I like watching the sky...seeing the rain that usually accompanies a big storm."

"That's another fear faced!" said Amelia, with a smile

"Next, we went to Robinson Lane in Coolangatta where we found my long-lost family member...Steve Roberts!" said Mum, triumphantly

"Steve is our cousin he is five years older than Rebecca and I!" Mum said, proudly

"We had a lovely time catching up with him...while eating sandwiches and drinking lemonade!"

"He was impressed with our OAM medals...he told us we could be working as university professors one day!" said Mum, grinning

"We're glad you found him after all those years and had a great time having a 'chinwag'!"

"Most of us remember him...we plan to catch up soon." said Jim

"I took a photo of him... I had fun seeing him again... I remember we had good times together... before we lost contact in 1999." said Mum, fondly reminiscing

"After our visit we had to go and get ready for our Gold Coast concert."

"Mikayla and I prepared a prank involving the use of wigs and disguises...what we didn't know...was that Cassie had been listening outside the door...and had planned a counter-attack of her own!"

"Whilst she was on stage waiting for us...Mikayla and I put on John Farnham and Madonna disguises... then we successfully lured fans over to our signing lines...while Cassie's line was empty!" chuckled Dad

"Cassie went backstage and disguised herself as Nikki Webster...then she weaved in and out of the throng of fans...crept up behind us and ripped our wigs and masks off... busting us!"

"We thought it was Nikki Webster...it was really Cassie all along!"

"To add to our embarrassment...she threw cream pies at us... which she thought was hilarious!"

"We were interviewed by the camera crew and featured on the news...we're getting used to it lately!" Dad grimaced, as he glowered at me

"It was a hilarious concert that will remain in my memory...I'll remind Mum and Dad about it every now and then like... *remember that Gold Coast concert, blah, blah, blah*... and Mum and Dad will never live it down!" I chuckled

Everyone laughed and Mum and Dad said...

"We'll never live it down." with a rueful look on their faces

"We hired a metal detector one day and found a brown coloured chest with silver edges and a couple of shells on top."

"We also found a key… when we opened up the chest… inside was a piece of paper with a message in code… I worked it out in five seconds!"

"It said… 'Gold Coast is a sunny place to visit in Australia and make some special memories there'… I'm very good at code-cracking and that was one of the easiest codes I had to work out!"

"The Egyptians would be so jealous of me I was thinking… 'She is so much better at cracking codes than us, we might lose our treasure because of her'! I said, cracking up

We all laughed at my very cheeky statement.

"Cassie loves puzzles and code-cracking…she even does our puzzles when we can't solve them." Mum said

"While we were at the Gold Coast…Daniel and I arranged for Cassie to swim with Marlene…a dolphin at SeaWorld." said Dad

"You definitely had a good time there Cassie."

"Aunt Mikayla and Uncle Daniel showed us photographs of you with a delighted look on your face." Kate added

"Then we stayed in Brisbane."

"Whilst we were there, we followed up the location of the Dads 'holiday stay…at the Brisbane Holiday Village…which Aunt Mabel had told us about when we caught up with her earlier in our trip!"

"A prank involving 'soft drinks and shaking' was the key!"

"When the 'Dads' left to get food…we shook their soft drink cans…then hid to watch the fun!"

"The Dads got soaked!"

"It was awesome!!!" I said, which made everybody at the party laugh out loud

"Along our way down Kensington Parade…discussing what to have for lunch…we had to hide in the bushes from Maria and Belinda…who had found out about our prank."

"At our hotel, we thought up another plan!"

"It involved dressing up as a barmaid…casino dealer…a teen champion pool player…and waiters…to trick Maria and Belinda."

"It all went pretty smoothly…we put salt in their tea instead of sugar…disguised as waiters."

"We fooled them big time and you should've seen the look on their faces!"

"It was so funny to see and we all chuckled and smirked…we talked with them afterwards and Mum tried not to grin whilst saying it was Aunt Mabel that gave us the location…she did anyway." I commented

"You planned that prank very carefully."

"We did not suspect it was you three…the entire time."

"Cheeky buggers that's what you are!" said Belinda crossly, but with an admiring tone

"The Brisbane family pub helped us out too…it was priceless!" I said, very pleased with myself

"The weather was cold but we decided to walk along the Brisbane River…when a young Mum needed our help."

"Her daughter who was four years old…had fallen into the Brisbane River…she was in the water struggling to keep her head above water."

"Cassie ran to the riverbank and took her shirt off to use as a rescue aid."

"When Daniel and I reached the riverbank…he went to assist Cassie with the rescue…and I called Triple 000 for an ambulance."

"You worked really well together…to help save that young girls life!"

"You remained calm in an emergency situation…it was a happy ending for that little girl and her mother." said Amelia, impressed

"When we went to the YMCA in Brisbane...I opened up to Mum about a girl issue of mine...and probably lots of teenage girls, growing up...which was about my small breasts!"

At this point in my story all the 'guys' in the family decided it was time to go and have some 'men' talk together somewhere else! They quickly shuffled off to another area...did I say shuffled...more like ran...you couldn't see them for dust! All the girls and ladies laughed so hard they nearly cried.

"Way to clear a room Cassie!" laughed Zoe, admiringly

"I guess the men in the family don't want to hear our 'boob' stories." I grinned, mischievously

"Anyway...I was previously too scared to bring up the subject...now I'm glad I spoke to Mum about it."

"We exercised together and talked about strengthening my muscles...of taking care of my body as I grow...about changes that are still happening... as I grow and develop into a young woman."

"I had fun exercising...I'm going to use my twelve weeks pass with a personal trainer soon... to exercise at the YMCA." I said

All the young girls and ladies at the celebration, were eager to share their stories about the changes in their bodies when they were growing up...how 'boobs' come in all shapes and sizes...and that is perfectly natural! All us 'ladies' chin-wagged for ages about female issues...having quality time together...until Dad poked his head into the room gingerly and said.

"Is it safe for us men to come back in yet?"

"Yes Dad...we have put the 'boobs' away now." I said naughtily, which made Dad blush like a beetroot and all the ladies start laughing again

"Good let's get back to the trip!" said Dad, firmly

"OK Dad."

Mum began to speak

"We received a note asking us to do a radio interview at Brisbane Triple M FM."

"Cassie chose to speak about her mild autism and hyperthymesia...she did really well... speaking clearly and confidently...as she always does."

"Daniel and I were very proud of her...she is going to do more talks...autism will be one of her topics."

"We loved listening to the two radio interviews you did...well done Cassie for being brave enough to speak up...we can't wait to hear your second album too."

"Your music interview may have inspired your fans to follow their dreams...the autistic listeners understood that they're not alone in chasing their dreams of music and living happy lives...no matter what barriers are in their way." Andrew said

"We went to a historical museum in Charleville...where we saw various vehicles including a replica Cobb and Co coach...and a Denis Fire Engine...then we visited Blackall where we learnt how to shear a sheep!"

"It was Cassie's first time shearing a sheep so Mikayla had to help her...she did really well."

"At Longreach we rested at a hotel and Cassie chatted to Nan Diane."

"During that call, Cassie asked Diane whether she thought she was weird... Mikayla and I were shocked to hear Cassie say that!"

"We knew it was time for the 'Autism talk'...we couldn't say anything for a moment in case it might upset Cassie...she seemed pretty calm and she didn't mind."

"We talked to her about her diagnosis of mild autism and hyperthymesia... and all the... strengths... challenges...and behaviours...that can come with those conditions."

"She remembered the best and worst moments...the milestones she has achieved... her 'anxiety run'... and the progress she has made."

"She showed us her drawing of the 'Autism Spectrum Rainbow'...which was lovely and well-drawn...we read the letter that she had written to us when she was fifteen."

"We talked about a couple of her funny moments...we also told her a story of a crossroads situation in our lives...initially it was difficult, but the talk became easier as we went along." said Dad

"You were preparing for the autism talk...but it seems like Cassie realised she was different from the other kids long before you had the talk." said Jason

"Yes, she did realise before we talked about it with her."

"She had looked up her mild autism on the internet...and also on our blog... Celeb Autism Life Bontel... and knew that she was definitely different."

"She is fine with it and we're glad that we had a good long discussion with her about it."

Mikayla and I are currently writing a book...called 'Cassie Bontel: our Universal Genius Daughter...she will become the voice of that book." Dad said

"It will be a joy to read about Cassie, and how much progress she has made in her life so far." Lucas commented

"I may give some more talks on autism...I'm more open to talking about it now...and I want to help others to understand." I said

"We stayed at Blackall Caravan Park where we saw our friends the Smith family...we decided to play a prank on them, by pinching their cake with a fishing rod with a mechanical hand attachment...unfortunately for us...it backfired when they poured water all over us!"

"We did not expect that!"

"They also planted whoopee cushions on our seats and left us red-faced!"

"A double prank played on us!"

"I guess if you dish it out you have to be prepared to take it... as they say!"

"Too right you do!" came mutterings from the 'party crowd'

*I guess there are a lot of our prank victims in this home party crowd!* I thought, as I looked around the room at a sea of grumbling relatives

We all had a picnic together which consisted of...fairy bread...cupcakes...scones...fruit... and white chocolate."

It was the most delicious picnic and we told funny stories." I grinned

"As we were heading to Townsville the left back tyre of our car blew out...we needed the spare tyre... which Daniel had forgot to check and pack!"

"We found out that 'Tyreplus' in Townsville was closed when we tried to call them!"

"Fortunately, Cassie thought of an idea and suggested we call up the Smith family who might bring a spare tyre to replace our blown one...so that our road trip could continue."

"We called them and waited for them to catch up with us...we chatted...read...and listened to music...to pass the time away."

"The Smith Family arrived with two spare tyres...they fixed one and put the other one in the back for emergencies...they even bought us some food supplies to keep us going!" said Mum

"We're glad we could help you out when you needed it."

"You might have had to spend the night in your car...thankfully, we were able to help you continue on your way."

"That's what friends are for...to help each other." smiled Melinda

Everyone cheered and clapped, they were all having a good time at this reunion party!

# Chapter Sixty-Four
## Storytelling

Dad carried on with the story telling or as somebody else said more 'yarn' telling time...with a wink!

"We arrived on Magnetic Island via the ferry."

"We changed into our coloured wetsuits...we had underwater cameras...and a glass-bottomed boat...we were ready to go!"

"Cassie photographed the corals...Mikayla viewed the fishes and saw a magnificent turtle... which she took a selfie with."

"I saw a rare dugong and grabbed a nice photo."

"We explored other areas taking photos as we went, the skipper loved our photos and we were mesmerised by the life under the sea."

"Back at the Arcadia Village Motel where we were staying Mikayla gave Cassie a practice massage... before we booked in for one at the 'Massage on Magnetic'.

Mikayla massaged Cassie's head...back...and...arms."

"She also tried to massage Cassie's feet...Cassie found it so ticklish...that she wriggled and giggled too much for Mikayla to continue with that!"

"Overall it was relaxing for her and she was happy."

"We loved looking at the photos of you in the Great Barrier Reef."

"The aquatic animals must've been lovely to see and photograph."

"We've been swimming there before and thoroughly enjoyed ourselves...we're glad you did too." Darren said

"Yes, we had a grand time indeed!"

"We played our Townsville concert and had another meet and greet...this time for four autistic teenagers who formed a band called... 'Sunshine Sky'."

"We agreed to be a contact for them if they choose to tour Australia and New Zealand."

"Dad and I played a prank on Mum the next morning by switching her Madonna 'Like a Virgin' CD...for Skyhooks 'Horror Movie' CD!" I laughed remembering, as I explained to the others

"Mum suspected it was us...Dad and I tried not to laugh...we couldn't hold it in and got busted!"

Everyone laughed, when Mum starting pointing and wagging her finger at us

"We walked the 'Mamu Tropical Skywalk' in Innisfail...I took a few photos then afterwards we searched for lunch places on our iPhones...I cracked up at one that was called the 'Cock and Bull'!" I said, sniggering like a naughty schoolgirl laughing at a rude joke

Everyone else started laughing when I mentioned that...which set me off laughing all over again!

"Sounds like you had a fun time in Townsville!"

"You sometimes find the rudest place names Cassie!" Diane said

"What can I say…it's another talent of mine." I grinned broadly at Diane, who laughed back at me

"We had lunch at 'P.J. O'Brien's' Irish pub and chatted about doing a world tour in the future…also about celebrating Maria and Jim's upcoming forty-fifth wedding anniversary there, in a couple of years." Mum said

"We went to Fitzroy Island for the walking and hiking trails…we got plenty of exercise!"

"At one point a rotten mango fell on Dad and he looked very fruity!"

Everyone laughed at the image of Dad with a rotten mango splattered all over his head…Dad just looked sheepish…which made everybody laugh even harder.

"We finished day one by chilling on Fitzroy Island beach, it was very relaxing." I said

"What else did you do on Fitzroy Island?" asked Caroline

"We shopped at the general store… then later I recreated a memory of when I was five years old."

"I buried Dad in the sand up to his neck and put shells all over him whilst he was asleep."

"We were going to leave him there whilst Mum and I went surfing!"

"When he woke up, I denied burying him in the sand…I admitted it was me that pranked him later on." I grinned

"I learnt to surf for the first time with Mum and Dad's help…it was hard to learn the moves at first…but I became better at it."

Dad took up the story next

"We then went on to Winton…where we tried the musical fence…and played the drums."

"We recorded some great footage there."

"That footage of you playing the musical fence and drums was great to watch." said Sally

"Cassie played a prank by placing a rubber mouse near Mikayla's feet nearly giving her a heart attack…I got a fright as well!"

"Mikayla and I placed a rubber snake near Cassie's right hand whilst she was sleeping…in order to get her back for the rubber mouse prank… but then when we exited the tent, she was right behind us…nearly giving us a heart attack again!"

"She asked if we wanted to sleep with the rubber snake which she named Rob…we both declined…who wants to sleep with that creepy rubber snake!" shuddered Dad, making us all laugh

"We walked along the 'Jump-Up' on top of the plateau near Winton."

"We went on to visit the Combo Waterhole…checking out the unique flagstone 'overshots'… and having a picnic at the waterhole."

"At Alice Springs…Cassie and I tried to overcome our fear of frogs…with the help of Oliver Dermot the weatherman of 'Rise and Shine'…and Vincent…of the Reptile Centre staff."

"Vincent brought out a frog named Freddie and placed it in my hands…since Oliver chose me to go first!"

"I was terrified when I held him and shook a little…I think I did well."

"Cassie was up next…she stiffened up a bit when Freddie was placed in her hands…she did well too, holding on to him gently."

"Cassie and I then crept up behind Oliver with Freddie and placed him inside his shirt."

"He was hopping around trying to get Freddie out…Cassie…Daniel…and I…ran like hell and back to our hotel!" said Mum, with a grin

"It was the first live TV prank you've pulled off…we nearly split our sides laughing!"

"Looks like Oliver might have to be careful next time you see him."

"The way he was hopping about like mad…Freddie seemed to be attracted to him…he didn't want to let go." chuckled Zara

"We stayed at West MacDonnell National Park for a few days...we visited Simpsons Gap... the towering cliffs at the Simpsons Ranges means you can see for many miles...overlooking the permanent waterhole."

"We took some great photos!"

"On day two we hired airbeds and floated through Redbank Gorge...looking up at the lovely clear blue sky."

"We also took some photos of the flowers as we walked along section twelve of the Larapinta Trail." Dad remembered

"You have taken some great photos...wouldn't we all love to float on airbeds through Redbank Gorge looking up at the sky...it would be an awesome thing to do." said Mia

"We can certainly recommend it!"

"Darwin was the next stop!"

"The Museum and Art Gallery of the Northern Territory was awesome."

"We viewed several specimens including butterflies...we saw indigenous art... and Northern Territory rock art... and of course Australian art!"

"Then we went to the Northern Territory Library... there were lots of books...magazines... and newspapers."

"If we had several years, we could've read all of them!" I said, laughing

"That would be ultimate library heaven in the Northern Territory!" said Maria

"Also, in Darwin, Mikayla and I started teaching Cassie how to drive."

"We taught her all the basics of driving and all about the car parts."

"To gain confidence, she practised driving to a quiet area where Georgina and Lucas were staying."

"We had a little catch-up, talking to them about our road trip and Cassie's first driving lesson."

"It was nice to see them again as they were holidaying in Darwin." said Dad

"That's great Cassie, learning to drive is a big step towards your independence."

"You can drive yourself to a nice place for a holiday...or drive friends to different locations...or drive to the shops...or pick up a family member." winked Tom

"I might just do that when I am good enough to pass my driving test!" I winked back

"We went on the Ghan...it was fun riding on a train like that...even though it was my very first time!"

"When we were in Adelaide, we had a cool swim at the Adelaide Aquatic Centre."

"At the hotel I spent an hour or so on my laptop...checking the 'Bontel Family' website...I sniggered to find our debut album had charted higher in most countries...than 'Blizzard Blast', 'Quirky Service's' latest album!"

"Later that evening, I tried another 'girly thing!"

All the men started to look uncomfortable again...probably still traumatised from the 'boob' talk earlier! Dad was giving me the... 'do we need to leave the room again look?'

"It's all right Dad...it was shaving my legs for the first time!" Dad only looked slightly less uncomfortable with that statement

"I was a bit nervous and nearly cut my right leg...then I took my time and managed it." I said, proudly

Everybody smiled and the men looked very relieved.

"We hit a sticky patch there in Adelaide for a while." Mum remembers

"I got up to make my breakfast in the morning...first the toast burnt after only a few minutes in the toaster."

"I tried to scrape it and the toast broke into pieces...so I had to settle for bread spread with butter and Vegemite."

"Then Cassie got the milk jug out of the fridge and somehow it slipped through her fingers... and smashed to pieces when it hit the floor...scaring the heck out of us!"

"So, we had to have juice instead and cereal without milk!"

"Then Daniel tried to sweep the mess up with the broom...and the handle broke off in his hand!"

"That morning turned out to be the worst day on our road trip!" Mum moaned

"We were careful not to let the glass cut our hands as we picked the pieces up and put them in the bin."

"Next, we walked to the station to catch the Ghan and missed the train...then we tripped over our luggage and fell in a heap on the platform!"

"Luckily our electronic equipment didn't break...so we picked ourselves up and put our belongings back in our luggage." Mum said shaking her head at the memory

Everyone was laughing out loud by this time, as Mum told of our 'disastrous' patch...and started sharing stories of similar days...and situations...that they had encountered on holiday...or at work...when things had not gone to plan!

"Sorry to hear about your 'sticky patch' where everything went hilariously wrong!"

"We have all had similar situations at some point...it's good if you can laugh about it afterwards!" Kate said, smiling

"We had a great dinner at the Playford Restaurant then headed to The Gov to perform."

"We were running onto the stage for a big entrance, when someone tripped and we all fell over!"

"We made a joke of it which the audience loved before we started playing."

"We could not believe it when we missed the Ghan in the morning again... before we received a text inviting us to a special event for autistic children... that was going to have its' trial run at the Botanic Gardens."

"We made our way to where two carers Nancy and Sophie, were setting up the underwater theme for the event and helped them to complete it."

"Eleven autistic kids arrived and they were pretty excited to see us."

"There were five game activities...a fishing game...storytelling...pirate play...puppet show...and...learning about marine life."

"The activities were supervised by...Cassie...Mikayla...Nancy...Sophie...and I...we were having so much fun with the autistic kids."

"One little girl Ava seemed interested in nature...we could see her giggling and having fun by herself...she had a meltdown when she came across the shark model prop."

"We were concerned for her...thankfully Cassie stepped in and calmed her down."

"She had a conversation with her using AUSLAN...then played the train game with her... which was amazing to see."

"Ava then gave Cassie a homemade coaster before she left... later we performed a concert for the rest of the autistic children which they thoroughly enjoyed." Dad said, happily

"Those autistic kids seemed to be having a ball at the event and concert."

"Cassie did well in calming Ava down and interacting with her...we were amazed at the skills she used to calm Ava and have fun with her."

"She turned it into a positive outcome and everybody had a good time!" Olivia beamed

Everyone told me how proud they were of me... now it was my turn to blush!

"I spoke up about my fear of flying...after I nearly gave Mum and Dad a scare." I said

"I was so terrified at the idea of going on a plane I got dizzy...and Mum and Dad had to help me to a nearby bench...and hold me until the dizziness passed."

"At Broome, we stayed in a hotel called the Seashells Broome…we relaxed in our bathers at the outdoor pool…reading…and listening to music."

"We drank our favourite lemonade…swam laps in the outdoor pool…it may be one of the best hotels I've ever stayed at…I would definitely stay there again!"

"In the afternoon we had a walk and Mum skyped Darren."

"We went on a bike ride the next day… we also walked on Cable Beach…and played games on the sand."

"After a day filled with hot sun and exercise…we tried a hot stones massage…ooo…it was good."

"Our Broome concert that night was a success…with jokes…pranks…waterbombs…and music!" I said

"Sounds like you had a great time in Broome!" laughed Rebecca

"In Port Hedland they held a community day in our honour…we had lots of fun with various activities…the 'Golden Staircase' at the Cook Point caravan park…shopping at Port Hedland market…performing our concert at the Courthouse…then cooling down at the South Hedland Aquatic Centre."

"We were invited to the Port Hedland Dinner with Mayor Bill Peters…his wife Adriana… and six of Bill's colleagues…and their partners."

"It was a lovely honour and we talked about our road trip with them."

"Daniel and I taught Cassie how to fish in Exmouth."

"Cassie played a prank…placing an old boot on my line and dropping it underwater."

"Then Cassie hooked a big one…Daniel and I had to help her haul it in…it was trying to get away…we managed to pull it in and landed on top of each other!"

The fish Cassie had caught was a twelve-kilogram Yellowfin Tuna…we took a photo of it… we were so proud of that fish!"

"Cassie cheekily decided to play another prank by dumping two containers of worms on us!"

"So…we put the Yellowfin Tuna on the backseat and told Cassie she had ride in there holding the 'fishy' tuna on her lap…the entire ride back to the hotel!"

"It was hilarious for Daniel and I to watch…not so funny as far as Cassie was concerned!"

"She bolted for the showers as soon as we got back!" chuckled Mum

Everyone else chuckled too…not me…I was holding my nose…thinking about that 'stinky' fish!

"Then we travelled on to Monkey Mia…for some camel riding."

"Cassie had never tried camel riding before…so Ed our guide taught her how get on the camel…and to ride it without falling off."

"At the end of the ride…the camels spat at us which was very embarrassing."

"Cassie also got the opportunity to feed a dolphin named Winnie which she really enjoyed."

"Winnie showed her affection by nudging Cassie's feet making her giggle, she had a fun time." Dad added with a smile

"What a fun time you had at Monkey Mia." said Olivia

"We viewed the HMAS Sydney II Memorial in Geraldton…and found out about the Dome of Souls…including the Wall of Remembrance." I said

"We searched for gold in Mount Magnet."

"We searched and searched until I found a nugget which weighed one point five kilos…when we took it to the gold shop…it turned out to be worth sixty thousand dollars!"

"We saw about that Mount Magnet gold find on TV you must be delighted with what you found…who wouldn't be!" said Rebecca, enviously

"We put the money into Mum and Dad's bank accounts…they will help me to open my own account soon."

"I'll never forget that find!"

"We also went on the Heritage Walk and Tourist Trail...where we learnt more Australian history about Flight Lieutenant bomber pilot James "Bluey" Osmond."

"When we arrived in Perth, we visited the zoo...there were emus...dingos...koalas...we also got to hold and stroke two bilbies...named William and Petunia."

"That was amazing, they looked up at us with their lovely eyes and we smiled at them."

"Then the giraffes were up next, the father giraffe was cheeky, pinched my hat and put it on his baby's head."

"The mother giraffe licked Daniel's face twice to give it a clean, he was embarrassed but Cassie and I laughed." Mum retold the story smiling

"Lastly, we viewed the elephants, took some photos, then they decided to squirt water at us with their trunks!"

"We were soaking wet and had to dry ourselves down with towels." said Mum, ruefully

"You had a 'zoo full' of fun there!"

"We loved those photos!" said Zoe, grinning

"Whilst we were still in Perth, Cassie did gymnastics for the first time." said Dad

"Another first!" said Jason, admiringly

"Yes, it was fun to learn new things...but all that exercising sure gives you an appetite!" I said, to which everyone started giggling

"We went shopping at the Galleria Shopping Centre...Olivia was shopping there too...we purchased clothes in our special colours, we also chatted to Olivia in the café where we had lunch."

"Those special clothes you bought, would be good for a night on the town Cassie!"

"Are you sure the local boys in Perth didn't whistle at you and say things like 'hello gorgeous'?"

"You could go on a date with a local in that shiny blue dress of yours!" said Caroline, teasing me

"Ha ha... maybe I could!"

"I might do that in the future...who knows?" I said, winking back at her

"I'll stick to being single for now!" I said, trying not to blush and giggle

"We performed a concert at Subiaco Oval with a Perth band called 'Mania'...as our opening act."

"Cassie recorded her debut children's album called 'Cassie and Friends'...she performed all seventy-one songs during the day...with nine different children's bands and artists...for children with disabilities, such as Autism and Downs Syndrome."

"She had a marvellous time... all the children with disabilities had a blast!"

"They sang...danced...did all the actions...and a few of them even danced with her...which was very special to see."

"Cassie had photos taken with lots of the children and signed autographs...to see the happy looks on all their faces was wonderful." Mikayla said, proudly

"Cassie you gave the kids with disabilities a day they will certainly remember!"

"Maybe you can record further children's albums and perform at special schools...and children's hospitals, on disability days." suggested Maria

"I hope so Maria."

"Children with disabilities grew up watching these artists... it makes them feel very excited to meet them in person."

"They certainly loved the 'Cassie & Friends' album...I hope to do some more."

"Special schools would be good places to perform... having fun with the kids during 'interactive' concerts."

"In December 2011…we recorded our first Christmas album… 'Christmas with the Bontels', and we performed it in Perth.'

"We received a gift from Mayor Wallace Burke, which we opened on Christmas Day… during our concert."

"We received a present from the three elves… and a big bag of lollies from Santa!"

"Santa and the elves joined us for the final song… 'We Wish You a Merry Christmas'…we all had a fun time at the Christmas concert." Dad smiled, remembering

"We listened to your concert on Christmas Day…we loved it." said George

"You helped to bring Christmas joy to Perth… gave them a Christmas they'll never forget! he smiled

"We had a 'special needs' Santa segment that we tried out."

"Mum, Dad and I dressed up as Santa…Mrs Claus…and…Cassandra the elf…we did Santa for three special needs children… a six-year-old boy named Jack with severe autism…a ten-year-old girl named Kaylee who has classic autism…and a fifteen-year-old girl named Jenny with mild autism."

"The first two were fun to interact with… they were both non-verbal but they enjoyed themselves with Mum and Dad… and joined in the fun Christmas games."

"When Jenny came in, she was nervous and shy like I used to be…she gained confidence and started to open up and become cheerful…which made me smile and feel good too."

"When we gave her a present straight away instead of waiting till Christmas Day to open it, she was delighted and hugged me tightly."

"It contained three tickets to Dreamworld to swim with the dolphins!"

"Seeing the joy on her face was awesome…she had a lovely Christmas!" I beamed

"It was great to do special Santa we would love to do it again next year if we can!" I said, so happy at the recollection

"You did a great job… they had a lovely Christmas… and you made a new friend in Jenny… which is good to hear." said Maria, proudly

"Thank you Maria I used to be like Jenny always nervous and shy…only speaking to family and some adults."

"I'm glad I could help her to feel comfortable and happy, she may visit me sometime soon."

"I got a picture from her… she was doing tricks with Marlene the dolphin she had a big smile on her face."

"There was a message underneath the photo which said… 'having a lovely time with Marlene doing tricks…I'm loving every minute thanks to you and Christmas 2011… I'm living my dream… can't wait to see you in Melbourne, when I visit very soon!' Jenny"

"Isn't that nice, Cassie?" Mum commented

"It makes my day… it's great!" I said, happily

"Cassie, Daniel and I, exchanged gifts with each other on Christmas morning, then we spent Christmas Day with Mitchell and Diane."

"We all pitched in to help cook lunch…Diane and I doing the vegetables…Daniel and Mitchell doing the ham and potato salad."

"Cassie cut up the pre-roasted chickens and placed them on the baking dishes, to get hot and 'crisp up' in the oven."

"When everything was ready, we had our golden-brown roasted chicken in the middle, with all of the vegetables and salads arranged around, the final result was delicious!"

"We all did an excellent job with the Christmas lunch!" said Mum, pleased as punch

"That Christmas lunch sounded delicious!" said Jason, licking his lips

"We celebrated New Year's Eve in Perth and mingled with the locals at the Perth Entertainment Centre… we performed before the midnight fireworks started."

"We got some photos of the fireworks it was well worth it." stated Dad

"We got some firework photos of our own when we celebrated New Year's Eve, plus the added bonus of a sleep in!" said Zoe, laughing

"We visited a Farmer's Market in Bunbury…then had a nice Italian lunch at Nicola's Ristorante."

"Then we heard a familiar voice calling out to Mum."

"Dad and I knew who that voice was, so we teamed up to play a prank involving the telephone."

"Dad put on an excellent Italian accent telling Mum that her pizzas had arrived…I put on a Spanish accent telling Rebecca that her boxes of Spanish doughnuts had been delivered."

"However, when they went to the door there was nothing to be found!"

"After they went back to the kitchen scratching their heads… we crept in and busted them big time!"

"Mum spat her coffee over Rebecca which was so funny to see!"

"We had to confess that Dad and I, were the ones on the telephone!" I smirked

"That was a bit embarrassing for Mikayla and I…Daniel had a partner-in-crime, Cassie…helping him out!"

"Cassie is just as mischievous as Mikayla and I!" said Rebecca, shaking her head as though she couldn't believe it

"I've recorded it all and uploaded it to YouTube… it's gone viral with fifty thousand hits!" I laughed

"It was so funny…you're the prankster princess Cassie!" said Jenna, giggling

"Ha Ha…I sure am!"

"I received a letter from an autistic teen music prodigy… named Rachel Dorset." I added

"Rachel said that our 'Bontel Family' self-titled debut album had given her confidence to step out and perform in public for the first time in her hometown of Mildura… where she amazed everyone with her musical prowess."

"We may collaborate together on some singles or albums… so watch this space!" I grinned

# Chapter Sixty-Five
## Pranks and more Pranks

"Moving on from that… at Geographe Bay we got to see a Humpback Whale in the summer season… even though Whale season officially finishes in December."

"We got some great shots… we'll remember that for a long time!" said Dad

"We gave Dad a birthday breakfast at the Hotel Lord Forrest restaurant, then we visited Cape Naturaliste and looked at the awesome views."

"We celebrated Dad and Aunt Olivia's forty-second birthday at Mojo's restaurant."

"When we arrived at Mojo's, Dad copped a cream pie in the face from Olivia!"

"Dad and Aunt Olivia are still making mischief… no matter how old they are!"

"Dad and Olivia received their presents… next came cake… brown and white chocolate with blueberries and banana lollies on top… it was delicious!"

"I finished off by singing a song called 'Birthday Celebration'."

"Next morning, we went to the Wildlife Park where we fed a red kangaroo… a common wallaroo… and a western grey kangaroo.

"When we arrived at Tuart Forest, we used our torches to search for possums."

"We looked but we didn't find one."

"Then, back at our tents we heard a rustling in the bushes… keeping quiet we saw a rare western ringtail emerge from the bushes…Cassie got some great footage of it looking at us… and climbing up a tree!"

"Later, whilst Daniel slept and snored, Cassie and I crept in and quietly painted his nails blue!"

"He found out the next day when he woke up!"

"Daniel gave Cassie a flick of the ear and told her to behave herself…she had the nerve to blame me… he said he gave up trying to get me to behave years ago!"

"What a cheek!" Mum spluttered

All the partygoers grinned at Dad's statement.

"Sounds like you had a good time camping at Tuart Forest, we loved the footage of the rare western ringtail possum."

"Daniel blue nails really suit you Cassie and Mikayla must've had trouble not to laugh whilst doing your manicure!" Zara said, playfully

"Mmmn." said Daniel, trying to look stern and failing

"I've had my nails painted blue before… I can't believe they got me again!"

"I can't get them back because they like having their nails painted!"

"We started our Esperance stay by visiting the Pink Lake."

"I took a few photos and sent them to Rebecca… she was delighted because we all know it's her favourite colour!" Everybody laughed at that comment

"Well it is!" Rebecca answered, loudly

Next, we viewed Esperance Stonehenge… the real Stonehenge is in the UK across the globe…so we had a good chuckle at that comparison."

"Esperance sounds great."

We all loved the photos." Tom said

"We hope to visit the real Stonehenge in the UK… sometime in the future!"

"Then we played some mini-golf where Cassie played a prank on me!"

"At the fifteenth hole she put her plan into action."

"She replaced my golf ball with a rubber bouncy one, which I found out when I hit it into the hole only to have it bounce back out and land at my feet!"

"Eventually she confessed, later on… it was very cheeky of her!" said Mum, with a frown

"On Australia Day in Ceduna we visited four nature reserves and saw some rare birds… including some Mallee fowl… and a scarlet-chested parrot."

"We went to 'Goog's Track' and saw the railway line, which stretched for many miles on either side, we then looked at the Transcontinental railway line, and had a BBQ lunch back at Ceduna."

"We visited Port Adelaide and went to the Maritime Museum to learn about the collections… see the model of HMS Buffalo… and learn the history behind it all."

"We went to the Adelaide Central Market on a 'gastronomical tour…we sampled honey… cheeses… and figs… it was a fun tour and Cassie enjoyed trying the samples…although she didn't try the figs!"

"We learnt how to skate at an Adelaide skate park, with help of three veteran skateboarders called Nathan, Sean and Grace."

"First the basics of the skateboard, then two moves called the Manual and the Tic-Tac."

"We were all nervous… especially Cassie…with reassurance from Grace and Sean she managed the moves… if a little wobbly, Mikayla and I did too."

"The following day we visited the picturesque Adelaide hills… Hahndorf village… and Hans Heysen's original home… 'The Cedars'."

"We viewed the historic home and various artworks including those painted by Hans's daughter… Nora."

"We visited 'The PaintBox' shop for art supplies… bought some chocolate… and apple strudel."

"We went to Kangaroo Island where we caught up with my big brother, Tim."

"He took us to a conservation area where we saw various creatures like a goanna and an echidna with her babies… which were so cute."

"We had seafood at 'Sunset Food and Wine'… Cassie loved it… which was amazing." said Mum grinning

"Back in Adelaide, Cassie was preparing for our 'Bontel Family' concert… when Mikayla and I called to tell her the car had broken down…and we were not going to get there on time!"

"She was nervous having never performed on her own before…she stepped onto the stage with encouragement and did brilliantly… performing all of her twelve dance songs!"

"We were so proud of her for accomplishing that!" said Dad beaming at me

"Well done Cassie!"

"That's another milestone you achieved!"

"The video of you was amazing to watch."

"You were brave and happy… dancing and singing on the Adelaide stage… we're all so proud of you!" Jason high fived me

"Thank you everyone."

"I enjoyed myself a lot... I wouldn't have tried anything like that before this trip... it has given me more confidence... every time I try something new and succeed!" I smiled

"There was a funny moment after the Adelaide concert... I mixed up a fan's name as Myra, when it was Mandy."

"That made me cranky... then Mandy called me Cassandra and I went red in the face... glared at her, and stuck out my tongue!"

"I eventually forgave her...I needed a little time to get over it."

"Whilst I was having my shower Zara messaged me to look at a video... it was footage of me sticking my tongue out at Mandy!"

"I was seething, eventually I had to chuckle." I grimaced, remembering

"When we all saw the footage... we laughed too... that look on your face was priceless, Cassie!"

"That fan didn't mean to call you by your full name...it was so funny to watch... Hahaha!" George laughed heartily

"It wasn't funny for me, at first it was embarrassing...I can laugh about it now."

"I'll never live it down though... my classmates will remind me of it forever." I groaned

Everyone sniggered at that.

"I chatted to Kate on the phone, before I posed like a model in the spa bath that night."

"I recreated a childhood memory, it involved the use of bubbles, bubble bath mixture and a bubble wand."

"My memory involved blowing big bubbles and popping them all!"

"I ran the idea past Mum... involving model poses in the spa bath... with bubbles... wand... and bubble maker."

"Mum was initially not confident about doing the photography...I told her that I trusted her to take lovely shots... and bin any 'awful' ones!" I laughed... and so did everyone else

"Mum and I filled the spa with fresh water and lots of bubble mixture... so much that the bubbles were frothing over the edges of the bath!"

"Mum eventually settled into the role of photographer taking shots... some under the bubbles... holding my bubble wand... poking my toes out at the other end of the bath like a 'Loch Ness Monster'... emerging from the bubbles...it was great fun!" I told them all

"We looked at the photos, I suggested sending them to a modelling agency when I turned eighteen to see what they thought."

"Cassie sure had fun with that childhood memory and photo shoot, it made me chuckle." said Mum

"Quirky Service' called us, they had found out our popularity was outstripping theirs, so they planned to pull a prank on us."

"However, they didn't expect us to counter-prank them using ranger disguises at the 'Mintaro Maze'!"

"Quirky Service were lost for quite a while... pipped at every turn... as they tried to find their way out."

"Eventually we picked them up... they were so surprised that we had counter-pranked them."

"We got together for a picnic lunch and Cassie showed them the footage from the Mintaro Maze hidden cameras, they were very embarrassed, but they had to laugh!" Mum grinned

"We certainly weren't prepared for that counter-prank!"

"We like a challenge... it was very tricky!"

"We got frustrated and cranky trying to find the way out, the staff and visitors weren't helping us at all... they were too busy laughing!"

"When we eventually got out, we were shocked to see Daniel, Mikayla and Cassie reveal their true identities!"

"We were fuming…we all laughed later."

"The taped footage from the hidden camera was embarrassing… that was of the best pranks you have pulled on us…we fell for it… hook… line… and sinker!"

"It went viral and our fans have been laughing about it and enjoying it ever since!" said Nicole, with a wry smile on her face

"Next stop, we played ten pin bowling in Mount Gambier… and had lunch at a place called 'Chicken Boss.'"

"Our next stop was Casterton where we went to 'Mickle Lookout' and scanned the main street of Casterton with our binoculars."

"We told Cassie a story about one of our sweet boyfriend-girlfriend moments… which she enjoyed even if it was a bit 'mushy' for her." Dad said, looking at me and winking as I rolled my eyes to the heavens

"Then we visited the Casterton Railway Station, it was fun and full of history too." said Dad

"Our next destination was the birthplace of Diane…you guessed it… Murtoa."

"We booked our cabin in advance, but when we arrived it was not quite what we expected it to be."

"Most of the rooms were all right, the bedrooms were much smaller than we originally imagined."

"We had to accept the circumstances… Cassie chose to sleep in the room next to us… instead of the bunk beds."

"She cooked a lovely meal for us with Daniel and I supervising, she did an excellent job."

"We started our explorations with the Water Tower Museum… and Concordia Cottage."

"The taxidermy collection of five hundred birds grossed us out… thankfully the photographs… and artefacts… distracted us from the birds."

"Cuttings… photographs… and artefacts of Murtoa's history… amazed us and the local community archives… fascinated all three of us."

"Then it was off to visit a farm where Diane's friends, Elena and Nathan lived… to help them 'shear' some sheep."

"We got changed into 'working gear' just in time for a bus full of American tourists to watch our shearing demonstration… about 'how to shear' an Aussie sheep!"

"It was going so well…then the last sheep was not in the right mood to be shorn…it dodged Cassie when she tried to grab it… and ran out to the paddock."

"He needed a shave so Cassie volunteered to catch him, he ran off and Cassie fell over."

"Daniel tried next, the sheep charged him and he fell over too getting very muddy at that point."

"The American tourists were by now bent over laughing like mad."

"I decided to show the sheep who was the boss… I pretended to go in the opposite direction and then turned around at the last minute to catch it…somehow the sheep avoided my 'grab'… causing me to slip… and fall face down in the mud!"

"The tourist group had completely lost it by now…I didn't think it was very funny!"

"Daniel, Cassie and I, were so determined to catch that 'bloody' sheep… we went to different corners of the paddock and started moving towards him…he torpedoed right through us and we all collided head on together…each one of us ended in the mud with some pretty spectacular bruises to show for it!" said Mum, in a very cranky tone of voice

The sheep shearing scene set everyone in the room into uproarious laughter... there were people everywhere wiping tears from the corners of their eyes...all except Mum, Dad and I...who looked on in stony silence...which seemed to make it all the more fun for everyone else!

"Don't laugh!"

"It's not that funny!" said Mum, red-faced

"It wasn't that hilarious!" said Dad, embarrassed

"It happens sometimes on farms all right!"

"It was even more embarrassing than the horse ride we did in Echuca!" I said, turning bright pink

It took a while for the room to settle down again after that, so Mum suggested that someone put the kettle on for a 'cuppa' and we all agreed it was time for a tea break! We stopped for afternoon tea and 'revived' ourselves before continuing on.

"Two days later we had played our Murtoa concert."

"Before we got started, Cassie made a cheeky remark highlighting my physique, when she said..."

"Dad's a man who likes to look after himself!"

"Everybody laughed and the audience gave me wolf-whistles."

"I was mortified... I wanted to get on with the concert ASAP...Cassie and Mikayla were too busy crying with laughter...they weren't able to play their instruments or sing!"

"That could have been my cue for a solo career!"

"Eventually they pulled themselves together and got the concert going... I eventually found my sense of humour... and had a chuckle about it later on!"

"When we arrived in Halls Gap... I decided I wanted to see 'MacKenzie Falls'."

"We put on our hats... not forgetting our sun screen... picked up some snacks... and a bottle of water each."

"We spotted a lizard along the way... viewed the flowing water to the pool... and walked up to the top of McKenzie Falls."

"When we reached the top we sat down, had something to eat and drink and looked at the amazing waterfall and beautiful scenery all around us."

"This reminded Dad of a memory of him and Mum when they were nineteen, visiting Millaa Millaa Falls, in Innisfail near Cairns."

"He was just about to tell me the X- rated part of the story when Mum stopped him quick smart and told him it was time for a censorship cut!"

"That sure was a very good 'save' by Mum...it was a very funny moment too!"

I winked at Dad, who was pretending not to see me...looking in the opposite direction!

Everybody at the party started giggling and one 'smart alec' in the crowd shouted out...

"Would you like to tell us that whole story right now Daniel?"

...to which everyone cracked up... Dad went bright red and mumbled something about... 'getting some fresh air in the garden'... and bolted.

He returned sometime later with a tall glass of iced water that he kept sipping on.

I continued with our trip recollections... as everyone ate... drank... and had a good time 'yarning'... with each other.

"When we drove back to Hamilton, we checked out the Sir Reginald Ansett Transport Museum." I told them all

"It was full of transport including aircraft and cars... I learnt about the history of each one."

"The cars reminded me of similar ones I used to play with when I was younger, I enjoyed looking at them and learning about the history behind them."

"MacKenzie Falls must've been a spectacular sight to see, we would love to see some photos of that!"

"The 'Sir Reginald Ansett Transport Museum' must've been excellent to check out, if we get time, we might be able to visit there." Nina added

"Our next stop was Tyrendarra...where we met our Indigenous counterparts... Lynette... Joseph... and... Charlotte Orkins."

We learnt about Gundjitmara culture and country... we watched a video... and gained knowledge about Australia's indigenous culture in that area."

"We learnt about the 'Dreamtime'... the magnificent landscapes... and the geographical features, such as the Tumuli."

"The 'Orkins' provided us with meats... rolls... and salads... for lunch, which were very tasty."

"Charlotte did the cooking... Lynette taught her all the skills needed."

"Lynette and Joseph are doing a grand job working at the Hamilton TAFE Campus as disability teachers... Charlotte is doing very well as a young aide assistant at the campus... helping in the disabilities section."

We had a nice chat with them and they supported our road trip, we may even collaborate with them on one of their songs... it may be a 'featured artist' spot... on one of our albums." said Dad

"You three had such a fun time with the 'Orkins' family... going on their Budj Bim tour... eating... sharing stories and knowledge...together."

"They must've been awesome people to talk with?" said Caroline, enthusiastically

"Yes, they were."

"They're doing a great job at Hamilton Tafe campus... working with students with disabilities."

"Charlotte will make a great disability worker, like Lynette and Joseph she is good with students who have disabilities."

"I performed my second solo concert in Tyrendarra and had my first meet and greet with two autistic sisters... named Renee and Marissa."

"They were very interesting to talk to they had formed a band called 'Cherry' and performed in Tyrendarra."

"We can't wait to hear when 'Cherry' will release their debut album."

"They told me my songs inspired them and they plan to become music teachers after finishing university."

"I'm sure they will inspire other students too!"

"Heywood was our next destination as Cassie wanted to give archery a try."

"Daniel took her to his archery group in Heywood."

"We met up with the other members of Dad's archery group... Damien... Jonathon... Josh... Ed... and Andrea."

"Dad taught me to how to hold an archery bow in the right way and to shoot the arrow at the targets... as close as possible to the centre."

"Despite two of my arrows not hitting the target... two struck near the middle... so I did okay for my first practice session."

"I was the scorer for the afternoon session... I enjoyed being located in nature at the Heywood forest."

"When we were finished, we had a BBQ and chatted together... if I practice enough, I could shoot targets with Dad... Damien... Jonathon... Josh... Ed... and...Andrea one day."

"In February we went to the Heywood Wood Wine and Roses Festival."

"There were many different foods and activities at the festival!"

"Daniel and Cassie did a painting activity...whilst I tried photography which was lots of fun." said Mikayla

"We also performed at the festival!"

"A local band named Grass was due to play until one of its members became ill... so we were asked to perform instead."

"Afterwards, Daniel and I handed Cassie a can... when she opened it a coiled rubber snake sprang out... making Cassie shriek with fright and drop the can... along with a few swear bombs along the way!"

"Daniel and I chuckled at that one... we finally got her back after all the pranks she has played on us!" said Mum, triumphantly

"We're glad you had a good time at the Heywood Wood Wine and Roses Festival."

"It was embarrassing...I have to admit that Mum and Dad finally got me back."

"That coiled rubber snake scared the heck out of me!" I exclaimed

"Next stop on our trip was Bridgewater Lakes where we met up with Zoe and her family for a ride on the rubber tube!"

"Cassie helped George tie the rope ends to the tube and she volunteered to go first."

"We could hear her laughing and squealing with delight as she bounced up and down on top of the water... she had a lovely and thrilling ride... whilst holding on tight to that tube!"

"Zoe and Peter showed her the boat controls, she might need a boat driver's licence before she can drive one though!"

"Cassie played a prank on Nina... Ivy... and George... by switching their iPhones around and placing them in each other's bags."

"Cassie hid in the bushes and muffled her giggles but they heard her and used feathers to tickle her."

"We could hear her laughing hysterically like a kid...it made us laugh as well."

"Then, we visited 'Tarragal Limestone Caves'... with a great view of Discovery Bay... after climbing up fifty steep metres to the caves."

"Cassie made us laugh with one of her fantasy daydreams... that involved cruising around Europe... being served ice cream by white-suited... black panted... butlers... and winking at the local boys...it was so funny!"

"We eventually arrived in Portland where we embraced the fresh, clean and crispy air."

"One sunny Thursday, we invited everyone over for a fish and chip lunch near the Maritime Museum... Jessica and Jason's parents... as well as Oliver... Felicity... Jacinta... and Joseph."

"We had a fun time catching up and socialising... during that time Zara taught me how to paddleboard with an oar... while standing up on the surfboard."

"It wasn't easy at first but I picked it up fairly quickly and became very good at it."

"When Mum and Dad were coming near me in the kayak, it was another opportunity for a prank."

"As they got closer, I used my oar to tip them out!"

"Most of us thought it was hilarious...except Mum and Dad!"

"They tried to get me back by sneaking up to the paddle board and tipping me over...but I was in the kayak by the time Mum and Dad tipped the paddle board over."

"They were very surprised when it happened, as they weren't ready for the counter move at all!"

"It was so funny seeing them soaking wet and dripping seawater everywhere... it made me laugh out loud!" I giggled, as I told everybody

"We did not expect that move from Cassie we shall be wary in future!" Mum growled

"We were just enjoying the sea breezes on our way back from a beach walk when a local man named Jonathan needed our help."

"His cat named Jared was stuck up a tree... Mikayla and I couldn't reach Jared because he backed away when I climbed up... and hissed at Mikayla... when she tried to rescue him."

"Cassie volunteered to rescue Jared... we were so worried that she might fall and injure herself... or she might be too frightened to climb down when she reached Jared...thankfully, neither terrifying scenario happened and she made it... tucking him inside her jumper and climbing down gingerly but safely."

"Jonathan was so grateful and praised Cassie for her brave act."

"On the Monday we went to 'Portland TAFE Campus' to give a group of upcoming 'Life on Life' students... a lesson on how to wash a vehicle."

"We demonstrated on the TAFE car... before we got a couple of students to help out for the next vehicle."

Everyone was very interested to hear how the students went with their car washing!

"On the Thursday Rebecca and I celebrated our forty-second birthday... to kick things off Daniel and Cassie gave me a gift each... a novel... and a brooch... which was lovely of them."

"They cooked a delicious birthday breakfast...consisting of bacon and eggs."

"My birthday surprise was... a ride on the Portland cable trams!"

"It was my first time on a tram, as well as Daniel and Cassie's, so we enjoyed ourselves."

"Rebecca, you rang me while we were eating lunch at Harbour Lights... and in the evening we got ourselves ready for dinner...which was at the Gordon Hotel...Tom...Sally...and Mia... were also there."

"Tom, Sally and Mia talked to Cassie about her radio interview." Mum added

"Then the cake came out and everyone sang Happy Birthday... Cassie sang as well and enjoyed singing with us."

"It was a lovely forty-second birthday... I skyped Mum and Dad to finish off our beautiful day." Mum said happily

"We couldn't miss out on Portland Strawberries... so we went and bought a few things there... including Glenelg chocolates... and a punnet of strawberries.

"Mikayla and Cassie loved the chocolates... I admit I did too!" Dad grinned

Everyone chuckled. Who doesn't love chocolate?

"We went to Portland RSL for some bowling lessons... had a swim at the YMCA pool...and performed at the RSL...later that evening."

"It was all great fun!" I told everyone and they laughed

"Next adventure was to the 'Viewpoint'... looking for whales but we were unsuccessful... then we explored 'Cape Nelson Lighthouse'... including the' Maritime Room... which had some fascinating items in it."

"Portland Botanical Gardens' was a good place to visit and it brought back Valentine's Day memories, for Mikayla and I." Dad said, amid cheers from the men in the room 'stirring'

"We went on to stay at Victoria House... the garden was lovely... the food delicious... then we finished off the evening by watching an old classic movie in our robes... in front of an open fire."

"It was a lovely evening...but later that night Cassie felt a weird chill in her room... and then she saw the ghost of a young woman... which totally freaked her out!"

"She ran to our room... hurled herself on the bed and wrapped her arms around Mikayla's head!"

"Mikayla was reassuring Cassie that she was safe... when she saw the young ghost woman... and I did too!!!"

"The apparition then disappeared...as a result of that experience...we got very little sleep for the rest of the night!!"

After breakfast...we packed in a flash... loaded the car... and sped off...to the next destination...which was thankfully ghost-free!" said Dad, shuddering

I noticed nobody was laughing at that particular story!

"Port Fairy was next, where we saw pictures of Cassie's solo performance in Adelaide in the newspaper... that excited look on her face was delightful to see as she read the article... we kept it as a souvenir so she can look at it and read it anytime she wants to." Mum grinned at me, as she explained to all our family and friends

"I plan to do more solo performances and you can all come."

"I would love to see you there!" I said

"We will be there Cassie." Ivy replied

"At 'Railway Place' we saw the 'Mums' 'manning' a community market stall... selling produce like... slices... pies... and...pastries."

"When the Mums were on their coffee break... we crept in... pinched some wares... and put them in our bags."

"We drove to 'Oscars Waterfront Boutique Hotel' to eat as many as we could in our rooms!"

"The Mums found us eventually... we tried to blame each other...for our punishment we had to help them sell the rest of the wares...as payment for the goods we had eaten!"

"It was very humiliating for us...but for the customers... and the 'Mums'... it was very funny."

"We won't forget that...we don't want to experience that again." said Mum, pulling a face

Everyone laughed, they found our level of discomfort amusing and 'just desserts' for our bad behaviour

"What a pity there wasn't any footage of you getting into trouble... you know we would never let you live it down!" said Jason, gleefully

"We got away with similar pranks when we were young!" moaned Mum

"Yes, but you have grown up responsibilities now... it was a fitting punishment for you three...you managed to do a good job... in the end!" said Maria, in a serious voice

Then everyone at the party laughed hard to see Mum, Dad and I, getting 'ticked off' by Maria, we were all red faced with embarrassment... until we saw Maria give a 'wink' to the party goers and they all gave a big cheer! I guess Maria got her own back... big time!

"Carry on with your stories." said Maria, with a big grin

"Well we learnt lots about our Maritime History at Flagstaff Hill and looked at all the collections."

"Cassie loved that place and learnt loads about history there."

"We decided to try Ten-Pin Bowling together in Warrnambool."

"We got our bowling shoes...I overcame another challenge... tying my shoelaces for the first time!"

"I noticed that Mum... Dad...Kate... and... Adam... were previous champions in Lane Five...the lane we were bowling in... also that Mum and Dad bowled perfect scores of three hundred...winning a trophy for their efforts!"

"It was a fun game, it was close at halfway with fifteen and twenty points difference between us, in the end I was just too good for Mum and Dad!"

"During the game I set a new record... scoring a perfect three hundred... beating Kate in the girls' section!"

"I became champion, earning a trophy for my achievement, which read... 'Cassie Bontel Girls Champion 2012." I proudly told everyone

Then I took out my trophy and handed it round for everyone to see.

"Amazing effort Cassie... we're very proud of you!" Mia beamed

"Cassie, you might be able to participate in a family tournament here...or an international tournament overseas...with other family bowlers." said Jenna

"Thank you for the compliments."

"I might compete in a family tournament... maybe while I'm overseas."

"We'll see how I progress from here." I replied

# Chapter Sixty-Six
## Family Gathering

"We were invited to participate in an International Mini-Golf Tournament... at 'Mini-Golf by the Sea'... near Lake Pertobe in Warrnambool." I continued

"We competed against fifteen other autistic celebrity families from overseas... who were golfing... and mini-golfing champions."

"We progressed to the semi-finals against Team USA... where we had some sledging going on...before we defeated them and progressed to the Grand Final... against Team Sweden who won several titles between them."

"At the eighteenth hole, the scores were level and Cassie volunteered to putt the ball into the hole."

"It was nerve-wracking she stepped up and hit the ball hard."

"It raced up the first of the two steep hills... went through the middle and hit the wall of the second steep hill... then rolled...very...very...slowly... towards the hole."

"We all gasped when the ball stopped on the edge of the hole...then an amazing thing happened!"

"The ball rolled over the edge and into the hole... giving 'Team Australia' the victory...and the five thousand dollars prize!"

"What a magnificent moment that was for us!"

"The adults chatted in groups...whilst the girls played in the maze...and on the playground equipment."

"Cassie bought fifteen ice-creams for her new friends... which everyone enjoyed." said Dad, smiling

"That sounds like great mini golf fun!" said Darren

"It sure was!"

"When Mum, Dad and I, get to travel the world I might visit some of my new friends and have fun socialising with them... I'd love that opportunity." I grinned

"In Castlemaine, we visited 'Buda' historical home and gardens... we learnt about the history of the Leviny family... who came from Hungary in Budapest."

"We viewed their collections of furniture... art works... and significant belongings."

"We viewed the rose-gardens, which had lovely roses and the smell was similar to my 'Red Rose' perfume." Mum added

"There was one moment that I took a wrong turn though." I told the gathering

"I did a bit of modelling in the wrong place."

"I was... err... how shall I put this... I modelled in front of some local boys in my lingerie at the local pool."

"Mum and Dad were shocked when they saw me...I got into big trouble!"

"They taught me a couple of lessons...including...that my body belongs to me... and modelling in my lingerie is to be kept to my bedroom only!"

"I apologise if I shocked anyone with that information." I said sincerely

Everyone accepted my apology.

"Anyway, moving right along." I said quickly

"In the afternoon, we went on the Victorian Goldfields railway train to Maldon…we embraced the Edwardian elegance of the first-class compartment carriage…it gave us the impression of stepping back in time as we entered the carriage."

"After we arrived in Maldon, we visited the old 'Maldon Lolly Shop'… we were like the proverbial 'kids in a candy store'… just mesmerised by all the different lollies!"

"There were so many to choose from we didn't know which ones to pick!"

"There were also Murray Brewery Cordials…we eventually chose a few each… it was one lolly shop we will never forget!" said Mum

"Cassie thank you for sending me some pictures of the Victorian Goldfields Railway Train."

"I love looking at them, I'll add them to my train photos collection, which belongs with my train collection!"

"I'm glad you three had an awesome time there." said Mia, happily

"I've seen a few photos of you three wearing your bling and you looked stunning!"

"You can wear them with your popstar clothes Cassie, you will look very beautiful, you might even attract the boys' attention!" said Jenna, with a mischievous smile

"What girl doesn't love her 'bling'… showing her friends… and of course the boys too!" I said giggling

"We caught up with Ken and Wanda in Bendigo, we were happy to see them again, especially Mum."

"We had lunch with them at a place called 'Rocks on Rosalind'."

"We planned some activities to do together… the Golden Dragon Museum… and Chancery Lane… were on top of our list."

"The Chinese history in Bendigo is fascinating… it opened our minds to the multiculturalism in the places we have visited."

"Chancery Lane was unique we have never visited a lane quite like that before!"

"'Foodies Haven' was first, featuring global wines and exotic foods."

"Lunch was very tasty at the European style-hub!"

"Fashion… cosmetics… salons… and… boutiques, were next."

"There were a few things for the ladies…or should I say… several hundred to try on…while Ken and I talked!"

"It was a fun afternoon… Ken and Wanda had a fun time too." Dad smiled

"We could tell you all had a good time together…you have been lucky to catch up with quite a few relatives during your road trip… that must have been great fun along the way?" Jim nodded

"Catch ups with family ARE fun!"

"Even when I used to be shy and family would visit…before I overcame my shyness." I smiled at Jim

"During my spa bath that evening… I poured in too much bubble mixture which made a huge frothy mess over the bathroom floor …as I laughed and frolicked in the water."

"Unfortunately, Mum came in and saw the mess…which I denied making… I always blame it on the fairies when mess happens…Mum handed me the cleaning gear… it was not looking good for me!"

"I argued and whinged a bit but it was no good… I had to clean up the mess that I had made."

"I was initially in a bit of a grumpy mood as I cleaned, giving Mum a 'dirty' look at one point and mumbling and grumbling under my breath, but then I realised the job wasn't as bad as I thought."

"Mum checked the floor to see if I did it properly and thank goodness, she was happy that I did the job well!"

"The next day we went on the Central Deborah Gold Mine Tour."

"We had to dress up in miner's clothes and climb six sets of four metre ladders to two levels where we learnt about life underground in historical times."

"We also explored the surface...saw the vintage mining machinery...the interpretive museums...and learnt about Bendigo's 'gold' history."

"We had such fun doing that gold mine tour."

"I didn't let the depths and dark frighten me, the whole tour was enjoyable...Ken and Wanda had fun with us too."

"We've got a couple of photos to show you all." I said, passing the photos to everyone

"We travelled back to the coast for a couple of days before our trip to Tasmania." I said

"We stayed at Lorne overnight and had some beach fun...swimming...splashing...and throwing the Frisbee about."

"You know, whilst we were relaxing on a Geelong beach a tourist ad camera crew spotted me and asked if I would appear in a tourism advertisement promoting Geelong."

"Mum and Dad checked it out with the camera crew and gave their permission."

"The director and his crew explained the basics of how to shoot a tourism advertisement… they gave me suggestions… like play and swim in the water… relax on my towel… listening to my boom box… playing pop music."

"I did several takes… it was a good advertisement…I put in lots of effort to get it right." I grinned

"You did an excellent job...you will be a 'beach star girl'!" said Rebecca

"Well done."

"Thanks."

"It's gone viral on YouTube...what a blast!"

"Mum made a similar ad in 1981... as I'm sure you all remember."

"I hope Geelong gets lots of visitors from the promotion!"

"Later that night I had a weird and funny dream!"

"I was in Bridgetown Barbados walking along a beach... I winked at a couple of local boys who were catching a cricket ball... then I was swimming in the Bridgetown ocean... and next being massaged by a man named Richard!"

"What a weird dream...it's my favourite so far!" I said in great appreciation... to which everyone laughed uproariously which made me blush bright pink

"I'm not going to comment on that dream... or I might be the next one blushing!"

"Moving right along…" said Mum quickly, everyone giggled to see her discomfit

"Also, in Geelong, I staged my third solo concert and three girls were picked from the audience for a 'meet n greet' session with me, after the show."

"We had fun talking and laughing together… I pretended to be a magician like Dad used to do… during the 'Playground Kids' years."

Just then I received a message from the OZ Music Awards… a big grin spread all over my face as I read the message out… I felt the bright and happy vibes spread within me.

*'Congratulations Cassie Bontel. We have a surprise for you as well as your family, winning five OZ Music Awards…you have also personally won the award for 'Best Children's Album' for 'Cassie and Friends'! Well done! You can collect this award at the same time as the family OZ awards! Congratulations all round.*

"Yippee!"

"That is awesome!"

"An OZ Music Award for Best Children's Album!"
"I seem to be as big a hit with the kids... as Dad is with the ladies!" I said playfully, as Dad glowered at me
"You know that 'Playground Kids' inspired me...I thank them for that!"
"Wow!"
"I never expected this to happen to me!" I said, excitedly
Everyone clapped.
"You have done so well to earn that award Cassie."
"We have seen you becoming confident and brave around children since your road trip started... to hear you perform live to an audience of children with all abilities... is the best thing you have done as a musician!"
"We all listened to the album, your voice shines on all of the tracks."
"The special schools in Australia, loved it too." said Olivia
"It is the best performance I have given as a solo artist... even though it was my first time as a children's musician."
"When our world tour comes up in the future, I can see myself performing in different countries...like USA...Canada...Germany...Taiwan...Netherlands...Denmark...Norway... and even Sweden."
"Children are the same everywhere...they love music...they love to sing and dance...and to have fun!"
"We drove back to Melbourne the next day, but the road trip wasn't over!"
"We still had Tasmania to explore."
"We booked a cabin on the 'Spirit of Tasmania'... I told Mum and Dad that I was feeling a bit nervous as I had never been on a boat before...they reassured me they would help...so that I could enjoy the journey onboard."
"When we drove towards the terminal, I saw the size of the ship and my face turned pale."
"We pulled over into a vacant spot and I told Mum and Dad all about my fears... like I might fall overboard and drown...or get lost onboard...or I can't find our cabin."
"They were glad that I let them know how I was feeling... even though I was anxious and upset."
"Mum reassured me in a soothing voice and Dad promised me progress awards when we got onboard."
"I was enjoying the excitement, but still feeling nervous at the same time, as I struggled to adjust to the new environment."
"I looked out the window at the ocean...tears were streaming down my face...the ocean is usually a therapeutic place for me...somewhere where I could go to for solace and relaxation."
"Mum held my hand and stroked it...I told her what was making me sad...that I needed a bit more help before I would be confident enough to feel safe on the ship."
"They contacted the 'Spirit of Tasmania' guided tour section onboard who sent a nice man named Tony, to meet us."
"He showed me around the rooms and all the facilities... Mum and Dad came along too in case I got upset again...I didn't... afterwards I felt much braver and far less anxious."
"As we walked out on deck we could hear 'Ice World' being performed."
"We turned around and who did we see?"
"There was 'Quirky Service' performing all their songs from 'Blizzard Blast'!"
"I don't know how they got onboard before we did...they sure tricked us."
"Mum thought up a counterplan in our cabin... we dressed as Italian waiters... Chiara... Ricardo... and Aurora... serving 'Quirky Service' their dinner orders."
"When we served their desserts...we poured cream all over them... instead of on the desserts!"

"Kate stood up and told 'the waiters' that they would be replacing the cost of everyone's' evening clothes… she never got to finish her sentence as she stepped in a puddle of cream… and slid across the floor in a tangle."

"From that moment on chaos reigned!"

"Adam slid past Nicole… trying to stop himself as he clutched at thin air… still on his feet as he skidded by!"

"Amelia tried to steady herself by grabbing Nicole's arm…. which made them both fall in a heap under the table."

"We tried to take a photo but we were laughing too hard… we ran back to our cabin elated about the outcome to our waiter prank…however, there were repercussions to come."

"Most of the dining room was covered in cream… Mum and Dad had to settle the bill for the mess we made."

"The prank became much more involved than we had originally envisioned… it didn't turn out quite as we had expected!"

"After docking in Devonport and settling in to our hotel, we caught up Quirky Service later that afternoon at the beach at Mersey Bluff Reserve…where we confessed that we were the 'fake' waiters!"

"They were very cranky with us… we apologised to them…we also settled the bills for their clothes and cleaning."

"They were our best clothes… what a mess you caused with that prank of yours!" said Kate, who I suspect is still steaming

"At least you settled the bill!" said Adam, through gritted teeth

"Our friends Eve and John thought it was hilarious…we didn't find it very funny at all!"

"It went viral with the public… who thought it was hilarious!" said Nicole, screwing up her face

"We were all such a mess by the end of it all…it took us so long to clean up!"

"That prank of yours went way too far… we didn't see it coming at all!" said Amelia, crossly

"I think it might be time for another coffee break." said Mum, diplomatically

Looking round at a sea of grumpy faces… someone at the back of the room laughed… which broke the tension. After we all stopped for refreshments, people were looking happier again… and ready to continue the journey around Tasmania with us.

Dad continued the next recollection.

"We were discussing the future 'Bontel Family' tour bus and Cassie made a couple of cheeky remarks… including that we would need to get a booster seat for Kate…Nicole…Adam…and Amelia."

"This theme was carried on before our Devonport concert…where Cassie made a couple of funny jokes about Kates' height… making her blush."

"With each height joke Kate became even redder… until Kate stopped Cassie…by agreeing that she was indeed short…but not unkind!"

"The audience became silent and it was Cassie who now had the red face."

"Cassie realised that she had got a bit carried away with herself and shamefacedly apologised to Kate."

"Kate forgave her…she knew Cassie meant no harm…it taught her a valuable lesson."

"Cassie, you were unkind to Kate… it was right for you to apologise to her when you went too far…you have been learning about life… valuable lessons along the way." said Belinda, nodding

Kate gave me a quick hug… I was feeling mortified that Dad had bought up my bad behaviour in front of all the family…I know it's a good lesson to remember…it's not one I am likely to forget in a hurry…that's for sure!

"It was a good lesson for me to learn…from now on I'll consider what I say and the effect it might have… on how someone feels."

"Thanks Kate… for teaching me a valuable lesson." I said, sincerely

Kate smiled at me and gave me a big hug, then everyone clapped in appreciation.

"Mum, Dad and I, looked for a suitable location for my first autism talk… before we eventually chose Devonport High School."

"My audience consisted of six autistic teenagers and some parents…it was a bit nerve-wracking…I tried my best to talk openly and honestly about my autism."

"The topics I spoke about…included my early years…sensory issues…school life…fears and routines…and also…the positive gifts that my Autism, and Hyperthymesia…have given me." "Towards the conclusion of my talk I gave some advice on how to live a happy and beautiful life…also how your autistic children love you in their own 'particular' way."

"I spoke about having bad days and good days…I covered a little about our 'Bontel Family' band…then I answered a few questions from the audience…one question was what 'stimming' behaviours did I have, if any."

"I played the audience a couple of 'Autism News' videos…which included one of Mum, Dad and I."

"Two of the autistic teenagers…sibling twins, Sarah and Sean aged fifteen…thanked me for talking to them and giving them more confidence."

"They had found out they were different when they were thirteen, which initially upset them…their parents comforted them and talked about autism with them…which gave them confidence too."

"I am glad I helped them to realise that they are not alone…that they can be brave and try new things… step out of their comfort zones…and gain confidence."

"That was excellent Cassie…we all watched and thought you did well…we are so proud of you… hopefully you can inspire autistic people and their families wherever you go… even overseas!" said Peter, with a grin

"Thanks, it is the beginning of my autism talks… when Mum, Dad and I eventually go overseas I plan to give more talks on autism in Europe…Scandinavia…Asia…Oceania… North America…South America…and maybe even Africa!" I said, happily

"We saw so many great places when we were in Tasmania…we visited the Turner Berry Patch…the Vietnam Veterans War Memorial…the House of Anvers Chocolate…Mersey Bluff Lighthouse…and then we visited Tasmania's largest emporium… the Antique Emporium." I said reeling them all off

"There were lots of treasures old and new…antiques…collectables…old style books…even French furniture."

"We started at level one…treasures of yesteryear…model cars…records…dolls…teddies… and Coca-Cola memorabilia."

"The toys reminded us of our childhood." Dad smiled

"Nearby was Butterball's Lolly shop…that certainly reminded me of childhood too!" smiled Mum

"Level two had French wrought iron…giftware…and 'Captain Jack Sparrow'…from 'Pirates of the Caribbean', memorabilia."

"There was 'the shed'…containing everything a bloke needed to decorate his man cave!" Dad said, with a big grin on his face.

All the men laughed at that they knew just what he meant!

"Old tools…garage fittings…and 'prime' junk…among them."

"It was man cave heaven for me!"

"I was thinking of buying tools...garage pieces...anything that might look good on my walls...Mikayla was hoping I wouldn't buy any taxidermy!" Dad grimaced, and all the men in the room threw back their heads and laughed, whilst the women looked unimpressed

"We checked out 'Shelia's Kitchen' next...this time Mikayla was in 'heaven' with the contents."

"It had retro kitchen items...vintage magazines...and cookbooks...from years ago!"

"Level three had antiques...collectables...quirky items like...postcards...medals...and old toys."

"The last level was four...there were books of every possible genre...from sport to comics... fiction...and Australian and Tasmanian books."

"I own the Jo Nesbo books...you all know that I enjoy English literature...I read them for hours on tour... especially on trains."

"Mikayla loves comics...Wonder Woman comic books...classic novels...passed on to her from Belinda... and Grandma Macdonald."

"Cassie used to love children's books... then maths...geography...sports...and...travel."

"A lot of her knowledge came from those books...encyclopaedias too."

"It was a place well worth visiting." said Dad

"I enjoyed looking at the postcards, gaining knowledge, and I loved learning about coin history too."

We had dinner that evening at Danneborg Café, I saw a group of teenagers doing normal teen things without their parents help, I knew I had to speak to Mum and Dad about my independence, when we got back to the hotel."

"I explained to Mum and Dad, how I felt embarrassed when they told me not to go too far ahead, so they can see where I am in case of hidden paparazzi that might try to photograph me."

"That I want to make my own way in life, whilst maintaining our music careers, both family and solo."

"I may still need a little more assistance with some issues...but I need to gain my independence as I get older...maybe one day find a boyfriend...marry and have children of my own."

"I could make the move to the Bontel-Macdonald mansion...where I can practice my music...attend the University of Melbourne...eventually have my own family to raise."

"Mum and Dad were sympathetic...they listened to what I had to say...they told me it is their loving duty as parents to ensure my safety and well-being...until I reach adulthood and can fend for myself."

"They told me they are keeping me safe from the paparazzi for privacy reasons...also to protect me...and avoid tarnishing my personal reputation...and our professional image."

"They understand that I get embarrassed when they tell me things...they also told me...as I am still under eighteen they need to protect me and do what is best for me until I am an adult...they don't want me to be humiliated...or depressed...by all the unwanted attention."

"They will let me have a bit more independence where they can and help me when I need it, or ask for assistance."

"I listened to all they were saying... I wasn't sure about everything they said... so I will need to show them that I am capable of much more than they can see!"

"Everybody makes mistakes...that's how we learn things... I'm keen to see so much more of this big wide world."

"I also told them that although it is difficult for them to let go of me...they need to take a closer look... because I am nearly grown up."

"Mum and Dad were shocked to hear what I had to say."

"I had given them so much to think about."

"I thanked them for talking with me about my independence."

"They were still stunned and quiet... I went and rested for an hour... they had a lot of information to digest." I grinned ruefully, at my listening family

"That was a brave talk to have Cassie, you amaze us all with your will to be independent... to choose your own way in the next stages of your life."

"Tom and I are about to go through the same process with Mia... as she is growing up fast." Sally said

"Andrew and I will be at having the 'big talk' with Jenna soon!" said Caroline, with a not very enthusiastic look on her face

Mia and Jenna nodded eagerly they were keen like me to experience independence in their futures. All the parents in the room with teenage children looked nervously at each other, too pre-occupied with their own thoughts, to notice their offspring's enthusiastic response to the situation, as they high-fived each other!

Dad bought the subject back to the Tasmanian trip, I think he was glad of the distraction from his mind racing about thoughts of me loose, travelling the world!

The weather was good, so we decided to have a picnic lunch by the Tamar River."

"We took in the lovely views by the river for a couple of hours, before returning to our accommodation."

"Later back at our accommodation, Maria rang Daniel to see how the road trip was going."

"He told her about the prank we played on Quirky Service."

"He admitted to Maria that we had gone too far and that he had paid for replacement clothes and settled the bill for the dining room mess."

"Maria told him that he had done a disgraceful thing and to behave himself!"

"It was funny to hear Dad being told off by his Mum on the phone... he sounded just like a naughty little school boy when he answered Maria!" I said, laughing

"You're never too old to be told off by your Mum." said Andrew wisely, as his Mum appeared in the background

"We went to City Park Radio Museum in Launceston...which was a 'gem'!"

"There were radios from the 1930s...it reminded us of the radio shows our families used to listen to."

"Mikayla and I use classical music in our massage therapy work, it has always soothed Cassie when she gets anxious or upset as well."

"I made a Dad joke about our hit... 'Pop Radio'...Cassie groaned about that one!"

"Anyway, she got me back with a 'golden oldies crack!"

"I let her know I'm in my prime...only problem with that...was Mikayla laughing behind my back!"

"I turned the tables on her by bringing up her famous radio 'blooper' from 1988!"

"It was my most embarrassing 'gaff' on live radio...I can laugh about it now." said Mum, with a smile

"Did you know we saw the oldest wisteria tree in Australia?"

"It was one hundred and sixty-five years old!"

"I took some photos of it...so did Cassie."

"Cassie told Maria about the Tamar River." said Mum

"She then went on to tell Maria that she was a 'hot and sexy' singer...when she singing in the shower...that made Maria chuckle a lot!"

"Daniel says that phone call took ten years off his life...for multiple reasons!"

Everyone laughed at Dad who was looking distinctly uncomfortable.

"When Cassie said that 'hot, sexy, shower singer' comment, the smiles were wiped off the faces of Daniel and I, quicker than lightning!" said Mum, mopping her brow in mock perspiration

Everyone in the room laughed heartily and I blushed quick smart!

"I think Cassie is an excellent shower singer!" said Jessica, stirring the pot

Mum intervened with the next stage of the journey.

"Next, we visited Swirlz milkshake and lolly shop...trying a few unusual flavours!"

"They all had very strange names like...Chuck Norris...Tiger's Blood...and...Monkey Mayhem!"

"They may have had unusual names but they got our taste buds going and opened up our choices of new milkshake flavours!" said Mum, with a smile

"We never heard of that place or those flavours of milkshake, but they seem...interesting."

"Where can we find it?" asked Jim.

"It is located in Launceston at fifty-nine Brisbane St."

"We recommend it to all of you." I said

"We might go there." said Nina

"The date of April the twenty-first 2012 arrived!"

"My seventeenth birthday!"

"I woke up very excited, Mum and Dad pretended they didn't know anything special about that date."

"I gave them the 'glare stare', before they wished me a happy birthday."

"I thought they were getting 'old-timers' brain!"

Everyone laughed at that comment, Mum and Dad looked highly offended.

"We started off at the Grand Hotel Chancellor for my birthday, with a breakfast buffet that the staff kindly made for me."

"After breakfast, came present opening time!"

"I received a Jennifer Lopez album and a 2011 AFL Almanac."

"The weather was a little cool but still fine enough to spend some time at Sandy Bay, where I received birthday text messages from the Williams...Jones...Smith...and...Wilson... families."

"Later we changed into party clothes and we went to Cascade Gardens for my birthday lunch."

"The cake was a Cadbury white chocolate...there were also cupcakes...party pies...and lollies...followed by presents from Kate...Nicole...Adam...and...Amelia!"

"My gifts included...a pop music CD...story joke book...puzzle books...and a bangle!"

"Then Mum decided to cut the cake!"

"When she did...it deflated like a tyre going flat... which made a nearby couple get the giggles, plus Dad and I."

"Mum wasn't laughing!"

"She had a thunderous look on her face as she asked who swapped the cakes around!" whilst wildly gesticulating at the flat blob on the plate

"Mum got much angrier though... when I threw a cupcake... which unfortunately, landed in her hair!"

"I knew I was up that proverbial 'creek' without a paddle...as Mum chased me around Cascade Gardens... with Dad laughing uncontrollably at the funniest sight he has ever seen!"

"No matter how hard Mum ran... I was too fast for her."

"Mum really wanted to have words with me...glaring was about all she could manage...her cheeks were flaming...and she had no air left in her lungs to talk with!"

"Dad was no help to Mum at all... he had stomach ache from laughing so much at the sight of Mum charging around Cascade Gardens after me... like an angry bull!"

"They both had to recover for a while... by which time I was getting restless for cake!"

Mum eventually managed to gasp out...

"Let's have the birthday cake." whilst giving Dad a 'well you were no help at all' look

Everyone in the room was in 'stitches' as they imagined that scenario! They all needed to calm down and have a cup of tea before I continued with the next part of my story.

# Chapter Sixty-Seven
## Party, Party, Party!

I continued on with the rest of my tale.

"That afternoon was my solo performance on my seventeenth birthday...I thanked the fans who wished me 'Happy Birthday'...and performed twelve songs...plus four cover versions for them...it all went down well!"

"Later at teatime a limo came to pick me up and take me to the Astor Grill restaurant...where my family were meeting me for my birthday dinner."

The driver wished me a 'Happy Birthday'...there was a beautiful sunset...which I used my eyes and memory to capture."

"When I stepped out of the limousine there were a couple of fans with autograph requests which I signed... giggling when one of them wished me a 'Happy Birthday'."

"As I walked inside, I pretended to blow kisses to my left and right...whilst chuckling to myself...just like walking the red carpet to a music premiere!"

"I made my way confidently if cheekily, to the table...where Mum and Dad...plus Aunt Betty...Uncle Glen...and cousin Jacinta, who had come from Sydney to celebrate with me...were waiting to celebrate my birthday."

"I was dressed up in my favourite colour blue...a shiny blue dress...blue shoes...and blue headband."

"Mum and Dad handed me their card which had coloured butterflies... and a heart-warming message inside."

"Glenn...Betty...and Jacinta...gave me presents...a Kevin Wilson CD...a Carlton mug...and a newly released maths book."

"Mum told a story about the time she and Dad hid a Kevin Wilson CD in her old room when she was sixteen...so that Belinda wouldn't find it."

"It wasn't until Mum was twenty-one that Belinda came across it whilst she was cleaning out her old room!"

Everybody at the party laughed when I retold the story of Mum and Dad and Belinda with the Kevin Wilson CD!"

"Soon it was cake time again!"

"Chocolate mud cake...it looked so rich and tempting!"

"Everyone sang 'Happy Birthday'...I put on my headphones just in case!"

The room giggled when I said that.

"After thanking everyone for the lovely dinner we made our way to our Hobart family concert."

"The audience wished me a 'Happy Birthday' as we walked on stage…Glenn…Betty…and Jacinta…were in the audience for our concert."

"There was lots of joke telling going on between Mum, Dad and I to warm up the audience, before we started playing."

"Mum embarrassed me with a joke and I went red in the face!"

"There was worse to come…when Dad decided to tell a lovey-dovey story about the time he and Mum met!"

"I was thinking, '*Get me a bucket… I'm going to vomit*'!"

"I told him he was a bad boy which made the audience laugh and to make it even more embarrassing… Dad told a funny story about me!"

"I asked Mum whether she was hiding any mischievous or naughty secrets… hoping she would tell them to me… she went red in the face." I relayed to eager listeners at the family party

"I then reminded Mum about her and Dad kissing when they sixteen years old in the Melbourne Botanical Gardens!"

I said.

'What's redder than this fan's shirt over here?'

"Mum said through compressed lips… 'It's pink Cassie'… to which I replied… it was more like 'electro fairy floss'!"

"The audience screamed with laughter and Mum's outraged expression was priceless."

"Then the stage guy dropped a load of streamers on me from the roof and I freaked out a bit…it was a birthday surprise!"

"Mum commented that I looked more like a 'Christmas tree' than a girl… which I didn't find funny to begin with…I had to smile in the end."

"It was a brilliant…wicked…concert…the best I've ever performed in Australia!"

"I'll never forget it and the fans enjoyed themselves too!" I laughed at the memory

"That was the best birthday you have ever had Cassie!" said Jason

"I know!"

"I loved my presents…my first limo ride…my mud chocolate cake…I have some photos of my Hobart concert that you may want to see."

I passed the photos around to everyone and they all loved looking at them.

"Wow Cassie!"

"You look like a popstar angel in that pretty blue dress and headband"

"The day after that we were having lunch at Caldew Park… watching some children having fun."

"Cassie got an idea for modelling with a tutu!"

"She wanted to dress up as a ballerina in a tutu…sit on a bench in the park…where we would take some photos of her… Mikayla and I weren't too sure at first."

"We weren't too sure about how we could pull this idea off in a playground, fortunately Cassie had an idea."

"Once she was in her blue ballerina's costume, we went back to Caldew Park…Cassie sat on the bench… Mikayla and I, took photographs of Cassie's ring…her butterfly bangle… ballerina wand… and favourite Cadbury chocolate bars!"

"Cassie had a fun time doing the model photos, which Mikayla uploaded later on." said Dad, smiling

"We loved your 'model ballerina' photos Cassie."

"You look cute and pretty in them…I enjoyed dressing up as a ballerina when I was younger just like you." said Ivy

"Perhaps, my photos will inspire young girls not to be afraid of being themselves…I would be proud if that happened."

"We went back to our hotel to escape the cold… Cassie was sitting on the balcony in a patch of sun when a butterfly came to visit her."

"I could hear a soft voice talking on the balcony and went to take a look, Cassie asked me quietly to take a photo of the beautiful butterfly." said Mum

"We saw the butterfly photos…they were adorable."

"Nature's creatures can brighten up everyone's day when they visit…that smile on her face tells a story… like the sun shining through a dark cloud." said Belinda

"Fifteen minutes later Cassie had another visitor drop by…in the shape of a brown-coloured bird with a red chest."

"She offered him a few crumbs of her white chocolate cookie that she was eating at the time…he seemed to agree with that idea…ate a few crumbs…then flew away."

"That also brightened Cassie's day even more!"

"However, another visit from the natural world a bit later in the evening when she was about to take her shower… was not so warmly received!" said Mum, grinning

"Cassie noticed something moving…she peered around the shower curtain…and spied a daddy-long-legs, which freaked her out!"

"She shrieked for help and Daniel and I ran to the bathroom!"

"Daniel tried to reassure us that daddy-long-legs are quite harmless, but Cassie told him to get rid of it!"

"He did what Cassie asked and put it in the bin…she thanked him and told him he was a hero and a guardian angel all rolled into one!" said Mum laughing, I was looking a little sheepish as everyone laughed at what Mum had just said

I decided it was time to change the subject at this point and carried on with another part of our holiday journeys.

"In Hobart we decided to form a one-off rock band to experiment with rock music!"

"We tossed around several names before finally settling on 'Rockstar Family'."

"An old rock musician turned recording studio manager named Daryl, overhead our conversation."

"We told him we wanted to record some rock songs to challenge ourselves and make a one-off rock album… he agreed to help us record a rock album…so we went to the Red Planet Recording Studio the next day."

"We had chosen fourteen rock songs which took two weeks to record… our stage names were Rock Star Cassie… Rock Star Dan… and Rock Star Kayla…there were no tattoos involved!"

"That was a 'rocking' good time you had…when I heard that you had formed a one-off rock band…I thought you had better not get any tattoos!" Maria said, wagging her finger at Dad

Everyone laughed when Maria said that!

"At seven on the night of June fifth 2012 we went on stage… lots of people had turned up WOW!"

"We introduced ourselves and then, we really… really… really… 'rocked the house down'… we had a wicked…brilliant…time!"

"We were 'buzzing' from the electric atmosphere created by that fabulous concert…we needed time to wind down…it was such fun experimenting with rock music!" Dad beamed at everybody like a little kid at Christmas time, and everyone smiled back

"The next day we viewed Battery Point... looked at the weatherboard houses at Arthur Circus... saw the remains of the Governor's Cottage on the hill nearby... spent a few hours at Sandy Bay... then had dinner at the Hope and Anchor Tavern, where we played a couple of games of pool."

"The Spiky Bridge is unique to Swansea and its locals...we learnt about its history...and walked along it too."

"We went on to Kate's Berry Farm...there were berries...jams...and...country produce."

"We ate freshly baked scones topped with jam and thick cream...on the way out we bought a bag of handcrafted chocolate each!" said Mum, gleefully

Everyone chuckled at that...most of us do love our chocolate...don't we?

"We have never heard of that place before...after hearing your experiences there...we would love to go and sample some of their wares." said George, licking his lips at the thought

"On the thirteenth of May it was a special occasion for Mum and all Mothers!"

"It was Mother's Day!"

"Dad and I, cooked a Mother's Day breakfast...we gave her our gifts after breakfast...Dad's a Collingwood beanie and 'MDNA' Madonna's recent album from me!"

"I also gave Mum a picture that I drew of us all...singing on stage in our coloured popstar party clothes."

"She really enjoyed her gifts."

"When it was nearly time to go to lunch...Mum had an unfortunate accident...she spilt milk on her best yellow dress."

"She was not happy!"

"I suggested that she look through her suitcase...none were suitable...and her other dresses needed washing."

"At this point Mother's Day was starting to go down the proverbial drain...Dad had a flustered look on his face as he checked on his iPhone...to see if there were any clothing stores nearby!"

"The children's clothing store wouldn't do...thank goodness there was... 'The Lair'...which had clothes galore!"

"Mother's Day was saved!"

"The assistant led us to the dress section...Mum was in dress heaven as she looked through the dresses... trying to choose which one to buy!"

"Eventually...she chose a yellow satin dress...I chose a blue satin dress...and Dad chose a green silk suit." *'That will turn the ladies' heads when he walks by.'* I thought with a snigger, when I saw him in it

"We revealed the surprise restaurant destination to Mum...called 'The Saltshaker'."

"Mum had trouble deciding which dish to order...so Dad and I surprised her with an order of 'Salt and Pepper Calamari'...with...Vietnamese Rocket Salad!"

"Mum loved it...I thought about all the nice things Mum has done for me over seventeen years...I told her that I feel happy and safe to have a supportive...positive...and... understanding Mum...one who is always there to help me when I need her." Everyone nodded in agreement

"Dad recalled when he was eighteen and gave Mum chicken soup when she was sick with the flu...and how he sang Lionel Richie's... 'Hello'...to cheer her up."

"He told Mum that she is his beautiful 'Mikayla'...and Mother to his pretty daughter...that he will never leave her side...and that we will make memories and share joy and laughter together... always."

"It was a lovely sight to see Mum's eyes brimming with happy tears as she hugged and kissed us both."

"I could hear a lot of sniffling at this point in the room... then one of the men called out in a gruff voice."

"Must be time to put the kettle on... I'm sure the ladies could do with a cuppa!"

To which all the men agreed…coughing and clearing their throats as they shuffled out quickly behind him…to 'assist' with the afternoon tea… leaving the wives…partners…and girlfriends…to chat about their 'Mother's Day' experiences.

"We skyped Maria and Belinda…before we went to Swansea Waterloo Restaurant…for Mother's Day dinner."

"We enjoyed Mother's Day too…Jenna and Andrew took me to a Melbourne pub for dinner for a nice meal…earlier in the day we spent time at the beach." said Caroline

"Nina…Ivy…and…George…made me a nice chocolate cake…Peter gave me a romantic DVD…and we went to a pizza parlour for Aussie pizza!" Zoe smiled

"Zara and Melinda took me to the salon for a make-over…Jason cooked me a lovely roast lunch…then in the afternoon we all surfed and paddle-boarded…in the evening we went to a posh restaurant…where I was spoilt rotten!" said Jessica, grinning

"For our Mothers' Day…Tom and Mia cooked me breakfast in bed…we had a lovely afternoon drive to the cliffs and looked at the spectacular views…before we went to an Indian restaurant to dine…which topped off a lovely Mothers' Day!" said Sally, enthusiastically

Just as Sally finished talking the men arrived back in the room carrying trays of mugs… cups…and saucers…coffee…tea…sugar…and milk. They carried the trays to the large table…next to the hot water urn…and set them down.

Everyone broke for refreshments and went to help themselves to a plate of food and a 'cuppa'…they were all ready for something to eat and drink after all those stories!

Later, when everyone had filled themselves up…with sandwiches and sausage rolls…slices and cream cake…washed down with mugs of tea and coffee…everyone moved back to hear more tales of the great Australian trip!

"At Geeveston I decided that the Tahune Airwalk would be a great activity for Mum, Dad and I, to undertake."

"Luxuriant forest and tranquil scenery everywhere…as we walked up the one hundred and twelve concrete steps…it relaxed all parts of us…mind…body…and…soul."

"At different spots along the way we stopped to sit and rest…taking photos…it was well worth the effort when we reached the top…the view was spectacular!"

"We loved your scenery photos, it makes me think of the holiday destinations that I have been to, I felt relaxed and soothed by them."

"Thanks for sending me that special photo Cassie." said Jenna, smiling at me

"You are welcome Jenna I knew you would love that one."

"I wanted to try a couple of brave activities… so a few days later I chose to explore Tasmania's wild rivers and stunning scenery… via the Huon jet boat at Huonville!"

"It sounded adventurous…I pulled Mum and Dad along to hurry them up!"

"We put our life-jackets on…boarded the jet boat and started going along the river…we were weaving in and out of the forest canopy…through the landscape…experiencing three-hundred and sixty-degree spins!"

"All my senses were buzzing…it was awesome!" I grinned, remembering

"That's fantastic Cassie!"

"You were very keen to give it a go…I'm so glad you enjoyed it so much!" Olivia, grinned too

"Thanks, I wouldn't even try an activity like that before… because I would meltdown… but now I'm more open to trying new activities."

"Whilst we were having a picnic…I opened up about my fears of doctors… dentists… needles…and hospital…I recalled fleeing an ambulance into the centre of Melbourne…when I was fifteen!"

"Mum and Dad are going to help me when I have to go to the doctor or dentist again."

"We will research my best options…visit the doctor several times…learn all about the things that go into a visit…like making appointments…meeting staff…and procedures."

"Hopefully we will go on our world trip without any drama or fuss…or me freaking out… but… there's my fear of flying to get over…before we can attempt that trip!" I said

"We will contribute in any way we can, Cassie."

"We will support you when you go on that world trip…and hopefully you can make many more memories… like Daniel and Mikayla have made over the years."

"You can send us some photos…that would be great!" said Olivia

"Your help will be much appreciated, Aunt Olivia."

"Perhaps I could start a blog… 'Princess Globetrotter'…gain followers and fans as I go!" I mused

Dad took up the narration as he told of our next destination and 'Tassie' story!

"Strahan was next on our list…we decided to give the 'Bonnet Island' experience a try…as it sounded like a great activity."

"We boarded the 'MV Sophia'…the twilight sky was beautiful to look up and see."

"I took a photo of Cassie looking at the twilight sky." Mum added

"When we arrived, we explored this remote and isolated island where families once worked."

"The most adorable sight were the penguins waddling back to their burrows… how cute they were… instead of camera flashes we used infra-red torches… to take pictures in the dark night sky."

"Those penguins must've been cute to look at under a beautiful twilight sky, what a great backdrop for the experience."

"We loved the penguin photos you sent us." said Melinda

"Would you like to take the Bonnet Island experience with us…Zara… Melinda… Jason and Jessica…if we did it again?" I asked

"We sure would Cassie."

"Zara and Melinda have never been to Tasmania before, so this would be a great activity for them!" said Jason, enthusiastically

"When it was evening, we were offered cheeses…soft drinks…and hot chocolate, as the evening was cold…we decided that hot chocolate was the best way to go!" Dad remembered

"We made our way back to Devonport for our last day or two…before re-boarding the Spirit of Tasmania… to cross the Bass Strait…back to Victoria."

"Yes, I was enjoying the view of the bright blue ocean…before, I felt a bad feeling in my stomach…I was feeling seasick!"

"I felt guilty…I told Mum and Dad through tears…that I was sorry for ruining the overnight journey…they told me it happens to lots of people when they travel on a ship."

"They also told me I was a brave girl for telling them that I was going to be sick… so that they could help me quickly."

"After we had plenty of rest…we docked the next day and drove home… on arrival we collected our mail where we got soaked by Rebecca…driving her car through a large pool of water by the mailbox!"

Everyone giggled when they heard that… fancy taking a sea voyage without getting wet… then getting drenched when you get back to your front door!

Rebecca and Olivia helped us to unpack…then today we got dressed up in our fancy clothes… 'blinged' ourselves up… for our arrival at our Bontel-Macdonald mansion welcome home party…and here we are!" I crowed, triumphantly

"Your Tasmanian journey was a fun time for the three of you… except for the seasick bit Cassie… we loved the photos of Tasmania and the stories as well." said Nicole

"Well…that's all the stories of our family road trip around Australia now!" I said happily

"Thank you all, for being our support crew and spending time with us… we hope you loved our Facebook posts…photos…and videos… and we hope we may have inspired you all… to start a road trip of your own!" I said, cheerily

"You certainly did!"

"We want to make some memories of our own!" said Andrew, enthusiastically

"Now, before the cakes come out… we've got late presents to give!" said Mum, excitedly

"Father's Day gifts first!"

Mum and Dad gave Darren and Jim their gifts…an Australian pop CD…and a 'Richmond' beanie. They loved them and gave Mum and Dad a big bear hug each. Mother's Day gifts were next. Mum and Dad gave Maria and Belinda…a cook book…and a moisturiser set… and a bear hug each. There were my gifts to Aunt Kate…Jenna…and…Mia. Dad…Olivia… Mum…and…Rebecca…gave each other birthday gifts too. After all the presents were given out…it was time for the cakes!

I'm getting hungry and excited! Rebecca brings four cakes out…one each for Mum…Dad… and I…and one for my late birthday…with white chocolate…whipped cream…and… strawberries.

"Daniel…remember that prank you played on Mikayla and I…in Bunbury?" asked Rebecca

"Do I ever… it was priceless…the looks on your faces!" said Dad laughing

"Well…I have a cake for you… here it is." said Rebecca, smiling sweetly

The cake went 'Splat' in Dad's face! We all laughed…except Dad…who looked stunned for a minute. Then he licked the cream and said…

"Mmm, delicious!"

"Thanks for that cake Rebecca."

"Here's one of my own… I prepared earlier." he said, handing Rebecca a cake on a plate

"It looks temping." said Rebecca

Cutting a piece, she tasted it.

"Yuck… Blurgh… Erk…Ugh!…" Rebecca spat it out violently, whilst everyone laughed

"What did you put in that cake Daniel?"

"It tastes disgusting!" fumed Rebecca

Dad held up a tin of sardines with a big smirk on his face.

"It's a sardine-flavoured cake…Rebecca."

"Do you like it?" asked Dad cheekily, as he winked to everyone

Rebecca said nothing… she just glared at Dad! For good measure…Dad pushed the cake into her face.

"Daniel Fred Bontel…I'll get you back for that!" said Rebecca, with cake dripping down her face and on to her dress

"Aunt Rebecca."

"You look delicious…but you don't smell so good."

"Phwoar!"

"You need a wash and a change of clothes!" I said… holding my nose

"Fortunately, I have a spare set with me!" said Rebecca, crossly

Rebecca went to her old bedroom to get changed into another dress…after first showering thoroughly…to get rid of the sardine 'pong'!

"Before we eat the proper cakes…I would like to thank you all for supporting us during this road trip…and recall one or two highlights…with you all."

"Maria, you were the first to check up on us…and to encourage us to have fun together."

"At the Port Fairy markets with Belinda and the other Mums…we crept in and pinched your wares to eat…Mum's loud burp gave the game away…then we had a lesson to learn from you…as we were put to work for the rest of the day to sell the remaining produce…and make restitution for the stock we had stolen and eaten!"

"I'll never forget when you busted me eating your stock…I tried to blame others…but you knew I ate them."

"We won't do that again in a hurry Maria!" I said sincerely, and everyone cheered

"Belinda, I love the banter between you and Mum whenever you get on skype."

"You cringe when Mum tells a dirty joke or two…and I love it when you call her incorrigible!"

"When we saw you in Brisbane after playing the prank using disguises…you questioned Mum about who gave the Dad's month holiday location away…she tried not to grin but she did."

"Jenna, we've been best friends since we met last year at the MSC… and you are doing well with your horse-riding championships."

"You gave me reassurance that the autism talk didn't have to be scary…and I sent you the photo of the Goldfields Railway train…because I knew you would enjoy it."

"Caroline and Andrew…you two were helpful to me when I met Jenna…and along with Jeanette…helped me to get on a horse and learn some of the basics of how to ride."

"I love horses now…I no longer fear them since that time."

"Zoe…Peter…Nina…Ivy…and George…we have had lots of fun together over the years… you all encouraged me to eat the pineapple pizza that I chose…even when I was too afraid to try it!"

"Bridgewater Lakes was fun…riding the round rubber tube attached to the boat…I *really* enjoyed it."

"Nina…Ivy…and…George…the prank I played on you was hilarious…but you got me back with the feathers…and the tickling!"

"I then tried out the feathers under your noses…do you remember?"

"ACHOO!

"ACHOO!"

"ACHOO!"

"Very funny Cassie." muttered Nina

"Funny…funny." muttered George, not looking like it was funny at all

"Good laugh…good laugh." muttered Ivy, through clenched teeth

Everyone else in the room laughed to see them 'squirm'

"Jessica…Jason…Melinda…and…Zara…we had fun and laughs together…the first time was at Blackall Caravan Park…where we played a prank on you using a fishing rod with a hand attachment…to pinch your cake!"

"You got us back by placing whoopee cushions on the chairs…so that when we sat on them…they went off!"

"We had a lovely picnic afterwards…then later we broke down with a flat tyre…Dad forgot the spare…and you came to our rescue with a new one!"

"The second time we met up was in Portland."

"We had fun kayaking...Zara you taught me how to use an oar and paddle with the paddleboard...thank you for teaching me."

"Mia...Tom...and...Sally...we had an awesome time in Sydney...the Harbour Bridge climb was a bit scary at first...but fun in the end!"

"You gave me support and encouragement when I got dizzy at the half-way point...and when I did reach the summit...I felt like I was on top of the world...conquering another fear!"

"Grandma Georgina and Grandad Lucas...it was great fun seeing you again."

"We chatted to each other and shared ginger crunch...we love you always...I will want to visit your house again...and have a good old cup of tea and a classic movie...and maybe some more of that ginger crunch!" I said, laughing

"Nan Diane, I loved chatting with you on the phone at Longreach...when you told me that I am your special and unique granddaughter...no matter how different I am...after I questioned you about being weird!"

"At Perth, we had a good time with you and Uncle Mitchell...on Christmas Day."

"I had fun doing the Christmas Day dinner...and playing that prank on Uncle Mitchell...oh ho... it was funny."

"Kate...Adam...Nicole...and Amelia...our debut album knocked you off the charts in some countries and you tried to prank us for that...we pranked you back via the maze at Mount Gambier...then later onboard the Spirit of Tasmania."

"We have chatted to you on the phone...and caught up with you in Devonport."

"You four contributed to my seventeenth birthday...I plan to do a solo album featuring you all...I hope we can do that in the future!"

"I love all four of you to bits...I always will!"

"I want to make a special mention to Abby and Tina who sadly can't be here with us today... they looked after our house while we were taking our road trip...I thank them for doing a great job!"

"Last but not least as they say... to Mum and Dad... you have helped and encouraged me ever since this road trip started."

"Before our trip began... I was very shy... I had never travelled outside of Victoria... I feared the unknown... but I broke through each barrier...overcame my fears and in spite of a few teary, anxiety laden moments... I have made giant progress...it has changed my life forever!"

"When we go overseas...I plan to overcome many more of my fears...make lots of new friends...and inspire others."

I gave Mum and Dad a big hug and kiss and they did the same to me.

"This road trip was a huge success... 'you guys' are the best support crew we could ever have!"

"I would like to toast to the success of our Aussie road trip and to all our future travels!"

"Let's get this party jumping...time to crank up the music!"

"Cheers!" I said.

"Cheers!" yelled everyone

Well there it is dear readers...the story of my road trip around Australia! I made big progress...broke through barriers...learnt a few new skills...and many new lessons.

I took you on an Australian journey... I hope you enjoyed reading about it... as much as I enjoyed writing it for you.

I have so many plans buzzing round my head...I want to do a world tour with the Bontel Family...a solo album...a 'Bubblegum Dance' album as my alter ego Miss-Tique...maybe a Eurodance...and...a Eurobeat album too! To accomplish all those dreams...I must first overcome my fear of flying!

Since I took this trip around Australia...I know now that I am capable of so much more than I ever imagined before. I can do this...I can really do this!

Well right now I've got a party to celebrate... I'll catch up with you after my next trip!

See you later!

## THE (END) BEGINNING

# BIBLIOGRAPHY

## Victoria
Adventure Fun Park, Gippsland. 459 Princes Highway, Lucknow
Bairnsdale Bazaar. 5/2 Macleod Street, Bairnsdale
Bairnsdale Colonial Motor Inn. 335 Main Street Bairnsdale
Beechworth Honey Experience. Corner of Ford & Church Streets, Beechworth
Bonegilla Migrant Experience. 132 Bonegilla Road, Bonegilla
Border Gateway Motel. 6 Moorefield Park Drive, West Wodonga
Buda Historic Home & Garden. 42 Hunter Street, Castlemaine
Budj Bim Tours. 12 Lindsay Street, Heywood
Cape Nelson Lighthouse. Cape Nelson Road, Portland West
Cardinier Reservoir Park. Cardinier Reservoir Access Road, Emerald
Casterton Railway Station. Casterton Railway Line, Casterton
Central Deborah Gold Mine Tour. 76 Violet Street, Bendigo
Central Hotel Port Fairy. 56 Sackville Street, Port Fairy
Collins Booksellers Shepparton. 262 Maude Street, Shepparton
Concordia Cottage. Comyn Street, Murtoa
Discovery Bay. Bridgewater Bay, Portland
Echuca Holiday Park. 8 Crofton Street, Echuca
Emerald Lake Park. Emerald Lake Road, Emerald
Emerald Lake Model Railway. Emerald Lake Wading Pool, Emerald
Eureka Tower. Eureka Skydeck, 7 Riverside Quay, Southbank, Melbourne
Falls Creek Alpine Resort. Alpine National Park, Australian Alps
Family Vet Centre Wodonga. 75A Thomas Mitchell Dr, Wodonga
Flagstaff Hill Maritime Village. 89 Merri Street, Warrnambool
Foodies Haven. Chancery Lane, Bendigo
GIGS Art Gallery & Studios. Lincoln Causeway, Wodonga
Glenelg Chocolates. 99 Whyte Street, Coleraine
Golden Dragon Museum. 1/11 Bridge Street, Bendigo
Gordon Hotel. 63 Bentinck Street, Portland
Grampians National Park. Halls Gap
Great Ocean Road Ten Pin Bowl. 153 Timor Street, Warrnambool
Gundjitmara Aboriginal Cooperative. 135 Kepler Street, Warrnambool
Harbour Lights Portland. 53 Bentinck Street, Portland

Heywood Wood, Wine and Roses Festival. Edgar Street, Heywood
Hume Dam. 3 Little Mitta Street, Lake Hume Village
JB Hi Fi. 413-451 Wyndham Street, Shepparton
King City Chinese Restaurant. 167 Corio Street, Shepparton
Kurrajong Gap Lookout. Kurrajong Gap Road, Bethanga
Kurrajong Heights Hotel. 1349 Bells Line of Road, Kurrajong
Last Hoot Café Bar and Pizzeria. 9 Slalom Street, Falls Creek
Lower Glenelg National Park. Winnap
MacKenzie Falls. Northern Grampians Road, Zumsteins
Maldon Lolly Shop. 20 High Street, Maldon
Melbourne Town Hall. 90 – 130 Swanston Street, Melbourne
Melbourne Zoo. Elliot Avenue, Parkville
Mickle Lookout. 1 Moodie Street, Casterton
Motel Traralgon. Princes Highway & Lodge Drive, Traralgon
Murray Brewery Cordials. 29 Last Street, Beechworth
Old Gippstown. Gippsland Heritage Park. 211 Lloyd Street, Moe
Old Melbourne Gaol. 377 Russell Street, Melbourne
Oscars Waterfront Boutique Hotel. 41B Gipps Street, Port Fairy
Port Fairy Community Market. Railway Place, Port Fairy
Portland Botanical Gardens. 1 Glenelg Street, Portland
Portland Cable Tram. 2A Bentinck Street, Portland
Portland Maritime Discovery Centre. Lee Breakwater Road, Portland
Portland RSL. 10 Wolgan Street, Portland
Portland South West TAFE. 154 Hurd Street, Portland
Portland Strawberries. 87 Princes Highway, Bolwarra
Portland YMCA. 22 Bentinck Street, Portland
Puffing Billy Railway. 1 Old Monbulk Road, Belgrave
Rocks on Rosalind. 10/12 View Street, Bendigo
Royal Botanic Gardens Melbourne. Birdwood Avenue, South Yarra
Shepparton Veterinary Clinic. 2 Wanganui Road, Shepparton
Sir Reginald Ansett Transport Museum. Ballarat Rd & Riley St, Hamilton
Solo One. Crawford Productions. 1976
SWTAFE Hamilton Campus. 200 Ballarat Road, Hamilton
Tarragal Caves. 611 Bridgewater Lakes Rd, Cape Bridgewater
Traralgon Train Reserve. Hiscox Street, Traralgon
The Beechworth Sweet Company. 7 Camp Street, Beechworth
The Pet and Hobby Shop Wangaratta. 43A Ovens Street, Wangaratta
University of Melbourne. Royal Parade, Parkville
Victorian Goldfields Railway Train. 3 Kennedy Street, Castlemaine
Victorian Goldfields Railway Train. Hornsby Street, Maldon
Victoria House. 5-7 Tyers Street, Portland
Wangaratta Veterinary Clinic. 3 Baker Street, Wangaratta

Water Tower Museum. 1 Comyn Street, Murtoa
Wodonga Beauty Room. 171 Lawrence Street Wodonga
Wodonga Pizza. 3/2-6 Roadshow Drive, West Wodonga
Wodonga Family Vet Centre. 75a Thomas Mitchell Drive, Wodonga

## Australian Capital Territory

Australian National Botanical Gardens. Clunies Ross Street, Acton ACT
Canberra Symphony Orchestra. 11 London Circuit, Canberra ACT
Captain Cook Memorial Jet
City Car Care. 19 Lonsdale Street, Braddon ACT
Gelato Messina. 4/21 Lonsdale Street, Braddon ACT
Hotel Realm. 18 National Circuit, Canberra
Lake Burley Griffin
Llewellyn Hall. The Australian National University. Building 100, William Herbert Place, Canberra ACT
Parliament House. Parliament Drive, Canberra ACT

**New South Wales**
Aussie Bush Leather. Peel Street, Tamworth NSW
Barraba Visitor Information Centre. 114 Queen Street, Barraba
Big Chook. 3, Park Avenue, Moonbi
Bridge Climb Sydney. 3 Cumberland Street, The Rocks NSW
Domino's Pizza Newcastle City. 13 Steel Street, Newcastle
Morree Cemetery. Greenbah Road, Morree
Morree Thai Cuisine. 52, Ann Street, Morree
Peel Inn Hotel. 89 Jenkins Street, Nundle
Pylon Lookout. Sydney Harbour Bridge, Sydney NSW
Queen Victoria Building. 455 George Street, Sydney
Sydney Cricket Ground. Driver Avenue, Sydney
Sydney Harbour Bridge Climb. 3, Cumberland Street, The Rocks
The Big Golden Guitar. 2 Ringers Road, Tamworth
The Metro Theatre. 624 George Street, Sydney NSW
The Pig & Tinder Box. 429 Peel Street, Tamworth
The Powerhouse Motorcycle Museum. 250 Armidale Road, East Tamworth
The Sydney Opera House. Bennelong Point, Sydney
Toyota Park Tamworth. 2 Ringers Road, Tamworth
Winchester Motel. 54 Ann Street, Morree
World Tower. 95 Liverpool Street, Sydney

## Queensland

Arcadia Village Motel. 1/4 Marine Parade, Arcadia Magnetic Island
Australian Age of Dinosaurs Museum. Lot 1 Dinosaur Drive, Winton
Balamara Bakery. Lot 4 Vindex Street, Winton
Blackall Caravan Park. 53 Garden Street, Blackall

Brisbane Family Pub. 8 MacLachlan Street, Fortitude Valley, Queensland
Brisbane Holiday Village. 10 Holmead Road, Eight Mile Plains, Queensland
Brisbane YMCA. 107 Brunswick Street, Fortitude Valley
Burleigh Heads Beach. 1833 Gold Coast Highway, Burleigh Heads
Charleville Historic House & Museum. 87 Alfred Street, Charleville
Dangi Pub. Margaret Street, Piturie
HMAS Gladstone II (decommissioned). 25-47 Flinders Parade, Gladstone
Heinemann's Bakery. 84 Alfred Street, Charleville
Isa Hotel. 13 Miles Street, Mount Isa
Jumbuck Motel. 45 Ilfracombe Road, Longreach
Magnetic Island Ferries. Ross Street, South Townsville
Mario's Italian Restaurant. Shop G48-52 Oasis Shopping Centre, Victoria Avenue, Broadbeach QLD
Massage on Magnetic. 42 Warboys Street, Nelly Bay, Magnetic Island
Miles Historical Village Museum. 141 Murilla Street, Miles
Mount Isa Village. 22 Simpson Street, Mount Isa
PJ O'Brien's. 87 Lake Street, Cairns Qld
Planet Chill Ice Skating Rink. 122 Ferny Avenue, Surfers Paradise
Pro Dive Magnetic Island. Nelly Bay
Redearth Restaurant. 16-20 West Street, Mt Isa
Riversleigh Fossil Centre. The Gap, Mount Isa
Royal Hotel. 21/23 Moran Street, Hughenden, QLD
Sealink Magnetic Island Ferry. Breakwater Terminal, Sir Leslie Thiess Drive, Townsville
Sea World. Seaworld Drive, Main Beach QLD
Sheraton Grand Mirage Resort. 71 Seaworld Drive, Main Beach QLD
Stanthorpe Heritage Museum. 12 High Street, Stanthorpe QLD
Starline Motor Inn. 97 Murilla Street, Miles QLD
The Old Windmill. Spring Hill, QA
The Musical Fence. Winton QA
Tyreplus. 733 Sturt Street, Townsville
Walkabout Creek Hotel. 27 Middleton Street, Mc Kinlay
YMCA Brisbane. 107 Brunswick Street, Fortitude Valley QLD

## Northern Territory
Alice Springs Reptile Centre. 9 Stuart Terrace, The Gap
Daly Waters Hi-Way Inn. Corner of Stuart and Carpentaria Highways, Daly Waters
Darwin Entertainment Centre. 93 Mitchell Street, Darwin City
Larapinta Trail
Mercure Kakadu Crocodile Hotel. 1 Flinders Street, Jabiru NT
Museum and Art Gallery of the Northern Territory. 19 Conacher Street, Darwin City
Northern Territory Library. Parliament House. 4 Bennett Street, Darwin City
Pine Creek Hotel Restaurant. 40 Moule Street, Pine Creek NT
Redbank Gorge. West MacDonnell Ranges, West MacDonnell National Park

Simpsons Gap. West MacDonnell Ranges, Alice Springs
Stuart Tree Historic Site. Daly Waters NT
Timber Creek Hotel. Victoria Highway, Timber Creek NT
West MacDonnell National Park. Alice Springs

## South Australia

Adelaide Aquatic Centre. Jeffcott Road, North Adelaide
Adelaide Botanic Gardens. North Terrace, Adelaide
Adelaide Central Market. 44-60 Gouger St, Adelaide SA
Adelaide Skate Park. Park 15 Wakefield Road, Adelaide
Café Brunelli. 187 Rundle Street, Adelaide
Ceduna Foreshore Caravan Park. 25 Poynton St, Ceduna SA
Chicken Boss. 98 Commercial St E, Mt Gambier
Cliche Exhibition Restaurant. 26 O'Connell St, North Adelaide SA
Gambier City Bowl. Cnr Commercial West & Elizabeth St, Mt Gambier
Goog's Track. Yumbarra Conservation Park, SA
Hahndorf Village. Main Street, Adelaide Hills
Heysen, Hans - The Cedars. Heysen Rd, Hahndorf SA
Heysen, Nora
Hotel Ibis Adelaide. 122 Grenfell St, Adelaide SA
Mintaro Maze. Jacka Rd, Mintaro SA
Norwood Concert Hall. 175 The Parade, Norwood SA
Playford Restaurant. 120 North Terrace, Adelaide SA
Quest Port Adelaide. 36 N Parade, Port Adelaide SA
South Australian Maritime Museum. 126 Lipson St, Port Adelaide SA
Stamford Plaza Adelaide. 150 North Terrace, Adelaide
Sunset Food and Wine. 4564 Hog Bay Rd, Kangaroo Head SA
The Cedars. Heyson Road, Hahndorf SA
The Gov. 59 Port Road, Hindmarsh SA
The PaintBox. 100A Mount Barker Rd, Hahndorf SA
The Playford Restaurant. 120 North Terrace, Adelaide

## Western Australia

Active Gymnastics. Unit 5&6/30 Hines Rd, Perth O'Connor
Bunbury Farmers Market. 2 Vittoria Rd, Glen Iris WA
Bunbury Wildlife Park. Prince Philip Drive, South Bunbury WA
Busselton Jetty. 3L Queen St, Busselton WA
Cape Naturaliste Lighthouse. 1267 Cape Naturaliste Rd, Leeuwin-Naturaliste National Park,
Esperance Stonehenge. RMB 4323, Merivale Rd, Esperance WA
Fibre Active West Perth. 305 Fitzgerald St, West Perth WA
Galleria Shopping Centre. Collier Rd & Walter Rd, Morley WA
Geographe Maritime Whale Watching Busselton. Foreshore Parade, Busselton WA

Halls Creek Motel. 198 Great Northern Highway, Halls Creek WA
Heritage Walk and Tourist Trail. Mt Magnet
HMAS Sydney II Memorial. Gummer Avenue, Geraldton WA
Holiday Massage & Spa in Perth. U2 45 Central Walk, Joondalup WA
Hotel Lord Forrest. 20 Symmons St, Bunbury WA
Mojo's Restaurant. Victoria St, Bunbury WA
Monkey Mia. 1 Monkey Mia Place, Monkey Mia WA
Mount Magnet Airport. Mount Magnet WA
Mount Magnet Grand Hotel. 65 Hepburn St, Mount Magnet WA
Mt Magnet Post & Lotteries. 82 Hepburn St, Mount Magnet WA
Mount Magnet Visitors Centre. 22 Hepburn St, Mount Magnet WA
Nicola's Ristorante. 62 Victoria St, Bunbury WA
Ningaloo Beach Resort. Lot 900 Madaffari Drive, Exmouth
Ocean Centre Hotel. Catherine Avenue & Foreshore Drive, Geraldton WA
Parmelia Hilton Perth. 14 Mill St, Perth WA
Perth Entertainment Centre. Wellington Street city centre.
Perth Zoo. 20 Labouchere Rd, South Perth WA
Pink Lake Tourist Park. 113 Pink Lake Rd, Nulsen WA
Port Headland Market
Rambla On Swan. South Shore Shopping Centre, 39/85 South Perth Esplanade WA
Seashells Broome. 4/6 Challenor Drive, Cable Beach
South Headland Aquatic Centre. Leake Street, South Headland
South Headland Courthouse. 812 Hawke Street Place, South Headland
Spinifex Hotel. 6 Clarendon Street, Derby
Subiaco Oval. Subiaco Rd, Subiaco WA
Swagman Roadhouse. LOT 599 Hepburn St, Mount Magnet WA
Swan Valley. Guildford and Bells Rapids, Western Australia
Tanker Jetty Playground Park. The Esplanade, Esperance WA
The Silver Star Café. 12A Edgar Street, Port Hedland
Tuart Forest National Park. Higgins Rd, Capel WA
Valencia Vineyard Restaurant. 55 Benara Rd, Caversham WA
Western Australian Cricket Association. WACA Ground, Nelson Cres, East Perth WA

## Tasmania
Antique Emporium. 51 Formby Road, Devonport
Arthur Circus. Runnymede Street, Battery Point
Astor Grill Restaurant. 157 Macquarie Street, Hobart
Caldew Park. Hill St & Warwick St, West Hobart
Cambridge House B&B. 2 School Road, Geeveston
Cascade Gardens. 2 Mcrobies Road, South Hobart
City Park Radio Museum. 45 Tamar Street, Launceston
Danneborg Café. 161 Rooke Street, Devonport

Devonport Art Gallery. 145/151 Rook Street, Devonport
Devonport City Council. 137 Rooke Street, Devonport
Devonport High School. 91 Best Street, Devonport
Freycinet National Park. Freycinet Field Centre. Private Bag 5, Bicheno TAS
Gordon River Cruises. 24 The Esplanade, Strahan TAS
Grand Hotel Chancellor. 1 Davey Street, Hobart
Great Oyster Bay. Coles Bay Road, Freycinet National Park
Hobart City Council. 16 Elizabeth Street, Hobart
Hobart Limo Service. Hobart
Hope and Anchor Tavern. 65 Macquarie Street, Hobart
House of Anvers Chocolate. 9025 Bass Highway, Latrobe TAS
Huon Jet. 44 The Esplanade, Huonville
Mersey Bluff Lighthouse. 39 Bluff Access Road, Devonport
Red Planet Recording Studio. 248 Elizabeth Street, Hobart
Private Secretary's Cottage. Tasmanian Museum & Art Gallery. Dunn Place, Hobart
Quest Savoy. 38 Elizabeth Street, Hobart
Saltshaker Restaurant. 11A Franklin Street, Swansea
Sandy Bay. Sandy Bay Road, Hobart
Sir George Cumine Strahan. Governor of Tasmania 1881 to 1886
Spiky Bridge. Tasman Highway, Swansea TAS
Strait off the Boat. 17 Forbes Street, Devonport
Swansea Waterloo Inn. 1A Franklin Street, Swansea
Swirlz. 59e Brisbane Street, Launceston
Tahune Airwalk Centre. Arve Road, Geeveston
Tasmanian Arboretum. 46 Old Tramway Road, Eugenana
The Lair. 11889 Tasman Highway, Rocky Hills
Turners Beach Berry Patch. 4 Blackburn Drive, Turners Beach
Vietnam Veterans Memorial Avenue. Bluff Road &Victoria Parade, Devonport
Wrest Point Entertainment Centre. 410 Sandy Bay Road, Hobart

# Internet & World Wide Web

## Victoria
www.alburywodongaaustralia.com.au > the-army-musuem-bandiana
www.bbc.co.uk > programs
www.bairnsdalefunpark.com.au
www.beechworthhoney.com.au
https://bonegilla.org.au
www.brequet.com
www.bridgewaterbay.com.au/bridgewater-lakes/
www.bushheritage.org.au > species > Murray cod
www.centralgippsland.com.au
www.chelbec.com.au
www.citizenwatches.com.au
www.cricket.com.au
www.echucaboatcanoehire.com
www.echucamoama.com > billabong-ranch-adventure-park-trail-rides
enquiries@gippslandheritagepark.com.au
www.eurekasskydeck.com.au
www.emeraldlakemodelrailway.com.au
www.espncriaro.com
www.explorebeechworth.com.au
www.exploreyackandandah.com.au
www.fallscreek.com.au
www.flemington.com.au > Melbourne-cup
www.flyingscotsman.org.uk
www.gippslandheritagepark.com.au
www.hotelrealm.com.au
www.maldon.org.au
www.mealsonwheels.org.au
www.melbourne.vic.gov.au
www.visitmelbourne > regions
www.vpa.gov.au > types-of-fish
https://parkweb.vic.gov.au
www.polycraft.com.au

puffingbilly.com.au
rslvic.com.au
www.seikowatches.com
www.taste.com.au > recipes
www.travelvictoria.com.au
www.versace.com
www.vgr.com.au
www.visitgeelongbellarine.com.au
www.vhd.heritagecouncil.vic.gov.au
www.wodongaplaza.com.au
www.zoo.org.au

## Australian Capital Territory
www.abc.net.au > antiques-roadshow
www.anbg.gov.au
www.aph.gov.au
www.citycarcarebraddon.repcoservice.net
cso.org.au
www.hotelrealm.com.au
nca.gov.au/attractions- and- memorials/captain-cook-memorial-jet
visitcanberra.com.au > attractions >lake burley-griffin

## New South Wales
barraba.com.au
barraba.com.au > bird-watching
www.bridge climb.com
www.fossickersway.com > barraba
www.goldenguitarmotorinn.com.au
www.goldmineguesthouse.com > café-and-museum
www.morreetourism.com.au > about-morree-plains > kamilaroi-culture
www.nationalparks.nsw.gov.au > visit-a-park > terry-hie-hie
oxfordartfactory.com
powerhousemotorcyclemuseum.com.au
www.meriton.com.au
www.qvb.com.au
www.scgt.nsw.gov.au
www.sydneyoperahouse.com > Our Story
www.visitnewcastle.com.au
www.thewiggles.com.au

## Queensland

www.arcadiavillagemotel.com.au
www.artspacemackay.com.au
www.australianageofdinosaurs.com
www.australiasdinosaurtrail.com > winton-local-attractions
www.autismawareness.com.au
blackallcaravanpark.com.au
www.blackalltambotourism.com.au
blueheelerhotel.com.au
www.bounceinc.com.au
www.brisparks.com.au
www.dreamworld.com.au
www.fitzroyislandcairns.com
www.fitzroyisland.com
kidspacegoldcoast.com.au
www.mackay.qld.gov.au
mamutropicalskywalk.com.au
mariosrestaurant.com.au
www.matildacountrytouristpark.com
www.metrohotels.com.au
www.miamimarkette.com
www.navy.gov.au
www.outbackqueensland.com.au
www.pacificfair.com.au
parks.des.qld.gov.au > parks > combo-waterhole
www.peoplewithpotential.org > hyperthymesia
www.queensland.com/coolangatta
www.questapartments.com.au
www.ripleys.com
www.royallifesaving.com.au
seaworld.com.au
www.starlinemotorinn.com.au
www.surfersparadise.com > Things To Do > Attractions
https://theculturetrip.com > Australia > Music
www.townsvillenorthqueensland.com.au > destinations > magnetic-island
www.triplem.com.au > Brisbane
www.visitbrisbane.com
www.ymcabrisbane.org

## Northern Territory
www.aussietowns.com.au > town > pine-creek-nt
www.dalywaterspub.com
https://www.jabirusportsandsocialclub.com.au
https://northernterritory .com >Alice Springs & Surrounds >
ntl.nt.gov.au
https://nt.gov.au > parks-reserves
https://parksaustralia.gov.au > kakadu
www.pinecreekrailwayresort.com.au
timbercreekhotel.com.au
www.treklarapinta.com.au
https://www.visitkatherine.com.au

## South Australia
https://adelaideaquaticcentre.com.au
https://www.botanicgardens.sa.gov.au
cafebrunelli.com.au
https://journeybeyondrail.com.au > journeys > the-ghan

## Western Australia
www.activegym.com.au
https://www.austadiums.com
www.broomecycles.com.au
https://bunburyfarmersmarket.com.au
www.cgg.wa.gov.au
www.derbytourism.com.au
https://www.discoveryholidayparks.com.au > pilbara-porthedland
https://www.geographemaritime.com.au › geographe-bay-whale-watching
www.hallscreekmotel.com.au
https://www.hmassydneymemorialgeraldton.com.au
https://holidaymassage.com.au
https://www.margaretriver.com › members › cape-naturaliste-lighthouse
www.mtmagnet.wa.gov.au
museum.wa.gov.au
www.porthedland.wa.gov.au
www.sharkbayvisit.com.au'> sharkbaycamels
www.tackleworldexmouth.com.au
www.theesplanadehotel.com.au
www.visitbroome.com.au
https://www.visitgeraldton.com.au
https://www.westernaustralia.com > business > attractions > cable-beach

## Tasmania

artgallery@devonport.tas.gov.au
cityparkradio@cityparkradio.com.au.au
coh@hobartcity.com.au
enquiries@anvers-chocolate.com.au
grc@gordonrivercruises.com.au
gardens.rgb.tas.gov.au > huon pine
guestservices@wrestpoint.com.au
info@astorgrill.com.au
info@centrewayarcade.com
info@hobartlimousineservice.com.au
info@swanseawaterlooinn.com.au
info@huonjet.com
mapcarta.com. Mersey Bluff State Reserve
parks@hobartcity.com.au
peopleaustralia.anu.edu.au
tasard@tasmanianarboretum.org.au
tasmania.com > eat-and-drink > cheese
www.antiqueemporium.com.au
www.homestolove.com.au > plantguide > wisteria
www.tmag.tas.gov.au
www.railtrails.org.au > trailsearch

# Extra Sources

ARIA Music Awards
Facebook
Vintage Crop 1993
Let's Elope 1991
Shocking 2009
Google Maps map data
Instagram
Internet
shop.nationalgeographic.com > products > dolphin-plush-toy
Skype
thehatstore.com.au
The 10 best things to do in...
tripadvisor Australia
Twitter
YouTube
www.autocorrectfails.com
www.afl.com.au
www.american-rails.com
www.calmingmoments.com.au > Weighted Lap Blankets
www.citizenwatches.com.au
www.gentlemensgazette.co > panama-hat
www.michelherbelin.com.au
www.seiko.com.au
www.monashsds.vic.edu.au > autism_id_talk
https://www.ariacharts.com.au
www.country.com.au
www.dancenikkiwebster.com.au
www.katyperry.com
www.llewellynhall.com.au
www.madonna.com
www.metrotheatre.com.au
www.playbillvenues.com.au
www.rickastley.co.uk
thewiggles.com.au

stephaniemeyer.com > the-twilight-saga
www.tcmf.com.au

## Authors and Books
Gunn, Jeannie. We of the Never Never. 1908
Meyer, Stephanie. Twilight. 2005 New Moon. 2006 Eclipse. 2007 Breaking Dawn. 2008
Nesbo, Jo. The Leopard. 2009 Norway. English version 2011
The Book of Australian Trivia. Five Mile Press. 1985

## Films
Australia. 2008
Bridget Jones's Diary. 2001
Goldeneye. 1995
Pirates of the Carribean. 2003
The Nutty Professor. 1996
We of the Never Never. 1982

### Actors
Ales, John
Brosnan, Pierce.
Depp, Johnny.
Jackman, Hugh.
Kidman, Nicole
Murphy, Eddie.
Punch McGregor, Angela.
Zellwegger, Renee.

## Musicians and Music
A-ha. Hunting High and Low 1985
Amorosi, Vanessa. This is Who I Am 2009
Aqua. Aquarium. Barbie Girl. 1997
Asia. Heat of the Moment. 1982
Astley, Rick. Never Gonna' Give You Up. 1987
Australian Crawl. Boys Light Up. 1980
Autrey, Gene & The Country Boys. Here Comes Santa Claus. 1947 Frosty the Snowman. 1950 Santa Claus is Coming to Town. 1953
Barnes, Jimmy. Working Class Man. 1985
Befour. We Stand United. Live Your Dream. Germany 2008
Brand, Adam. Little Sisters. 1993
Bubblegum Land. I Love Jingle Bells. 2006
Ceberano, Kate. Brave. Bedroom Eyes. 1989
Chambers, Kasey. The Captain. 1999 Not Pretty Enough. 2001 Rattlin' Bones. 2008
Cherona. Sound of Cherona. Dragonfly. Germany 2009

Clark, Justine. I Like to Sing. 2005 Gumtree Family. 2005 Dinosaur Roar. 2008 Painting a Picture. 2008 Doin' it- Making the Garden Grow. 2008 Imagination. 2008

Cochrane, Tom. Life is a Highway. 1991

Combe, Peter. Spaghetti Bolognaise. 1985 Newspaper Mama. 1987

Connors, Graeme. The Road less Travelled. 1996

Conway, Deborah. It's only the Beginning. 1991

Crosby, Bing. White Christmas. 1942 Jingle Bells. 1945 Let it Snow, Let it Snow, Let it Snow. 1988

Crow, Sheryl. Real Gone. 2006

Cyrus, Billy Ray. Achy Breaky Heart. 1992

Daddy Cool. Eagle Rock. 1971

Divinyls. Boys in Town. 1981

Farnham, John. Age of Reason. Two Strong Hearts. 1988

Fleetwood Mac. Tango in the Night 1987

Helms, Bobby. Jingle Bell Rock. 1957

Henri, Franciscus. White Pyjamas. 1990 Dancing in the Kitchen. 1991 Mr Whiskas. 1997

Hi-5. Move Your Body. 1999 Robot Number One. 2000 So Many Animals. 2000 North, South, East and West. 2000 You're My Number One. 2001 Rain, Rain. 2001 E-N-E-R-G-Y. 2002 Come on and Party. 2003 Snakes and Ladders. 2003 Making Music. 2005 T-E-A-M. 2005 Wow! 2007 Party Street. 2007 Happy Monster Dance. 2009

Houston, Whitney. Whitney Houston. Saving All My Love For You. 1985

Huey Lewis & The News. Hip to be Square. 1986

Jamelia. Superstar. 2003

John, Elton. Goodbye Yellow Brick Road. Tiny Dancer. 1971 Candle in the Wind. 1973

Kernaghan, Lee. The Outback Club. 1993 She's My Ute. 1993

Ke$ha. Tik Tok. 2009

Lauper, Cyndi. True Colours. 1986

Little River Band. Help is on its Way. 1977

Lopez, Jennifer. Love. 2011 Let's get Loud. 2000

Madonna. Like a Virgin. 1984 Holiday 1983

Marks, Johnny. Rudolph the Red-Nosed Reindeer. 1949

Melanie. You're My Best Friend. 2010

Men at Work. Who can it be Now? 1981

Mental as Anything. Live it Up. 1985

Midnight Oil. Blue Sky Mine. 1990

Minogue, Kylie. Kylie-The Album. Locomotion 1987 Aphrodite. 2010

Mondo Rock. Cool World. 1981

Noll, Shannon. What About Me. 2004 Lift. 2005

Orbison, Roy. Mystery Girl. 1989

Perry, Katy. Teenage Dream. Teenage Dream. 2010

Pitbull. On the Floor. 2011 collaboration with J-LO

Pseudo Echo. Living in a Dream. 1986

RAGGS Kids Club Band. Raggs Kids Club Band Theme. 2006 Colors. 2007 You Gotta Move. 2007 Star Baby. 2010 Wag & Wiggle. 2010

Savage Garden. To the Moon and Back. 1996
Schneider, Melinda. Courageous. 2008 Be Yourself. 2008
Shakira. Whenever, Wherever. 2001
Sherbet. Howzat! 1976
Short Stack. Planets. 2010
Skyhooks. Living in the Seventies. Horror Movie. 1974
Smile.dk. Party Around the World. Sweden. Koko Soko. 2008 Europe 2010 Japan
Spears, Britney. Hit Me Baby One More Time.
Split Enz. I Got You. 1980
Survivor. Eye of the Tiger. 1982
The Cockroaches. The Cockroaches. She's the One. 1987
The Go Go's. Beauty and the Beat. 1981
The Fairies. Fairy Dancing. 2006 Fairy Bootscooting. 2006 Fairy Friends Forever. 2007 The Fairy Twist. 2007
The Hooley Dooleys. Yumbo Jive. 1996 Fire Truck Song. 1996 Chicken Talk. 1997 Pizza. 1998 Ooga Chuga (in the jungle). 1998 Aeroplane. 1998 Hello. 1999
The Wiggles. Get Ready to Wiggle. 1991 Dorothy the Dinosaur. 1991 Rock-a-Bye-your Bear. 1991 Here Comes a Bear. 1992 I Love it When it Rains. 1992 Dancing Ride. 1992 Dorothy's Birthday Party. 1992 Henry the Octopus. 1993 The Monkey Dance. 1994 Fruit Salad. 1994 D-O-R-O-T-H-Y. 1994 Joannie Works with One Hammer. 1995 Can You? 1995 Dorothy's Dance Party. 1995 Wake up Jeff! 1996 Wave to Wags. 1996 Dorothy would You Like to Dance? 1996 Henry's Underwater Big Band. 1996 Romp Bomp a Stomp. 1996 Ooh, It's Captain Feathersword. 1997 Toot Toot Chugga Chugga Big Red Car. 1998 Look Both Ways. 1998 Move Your Arms Like Henry. 1998 We're Dancing with Wags the Dog. 1998 Go Captain Feathersword Ahoy! 1998 Wiggly Party. 2001 Captain's Magic Buttons. 2001 Play Your Guitar with Milly. 2001 Luna's Workshop. 2003 Lights, Camera, Action, Wiggles! 2003
The Wolverines. Gonna' Ride all night Long. 1996 Certain Circles. 2006 Good ol' Boys. 2011
Thirsty Merc. In the Summertime. 2005
Three. Lucky Number. Sweden 2010
Tiffany. Feelings of Forever. 1988
Uncle Kracker. Follow Me. 2000
Urban, Keith. Days Go By. 2004
Webster, Nikki. Strawberry Kisses. 2001
Williams, Warren H. So much Trouble. 2005
Williamson, John. True Blue. 1986 Chandelier of Stars. 2005 Better than a Picture. 2008

www.ingramcontent.com/pod-product-compliance
Lightning Source LLC
Chambersburg PA
CBHW081341080526
44588CB00016B/2347